THE TREASURE DIVER'S GUIDE

BY JOHN S. POTTER, JR.

The Treasure Diver's Guide—Revised 1971
The Treasure Diver's Guide
The Treasure Divers of Vigo Bay

BY R. I. NESMITH AND JOHN S. POTTER, JR.

Treasure Hunters
Treasure . . . How and Where To Find It

The Treasure Diver's Guide

REVISED EDITION

—

John S. Potter, Jr.

—

Florida Classics Library
Port Salerno, Florida
1988

*Published by arrangement with
Doubleday, a division of Bantam,
Doubleday, Dell Publishing Group Inc.*

Library of Congress Catalog Card Number 72-97681
Copyright © 1960, 1972 by John S. Potter, Jr.
All Rights Reserved
Printed in the United States of America
Revised Edition
ISBN0-912451-22-X

TO MY DARLING JOANIE
AND OUR SONS
JOHN III
WILLIAM
ROBERT

Foreword

*I*N THE EARLY DAYS when I first became interested in treasure hunting, there were several books out on the market allegedly giving the precise locations of hundreds of ships—*all naturally carrying millions in gold, silver and precious stones.* While they made interesting reading, providing you like fiction, I soon found that they contained virtually no authentic information on the locations of shipwrecks and were more of a nuisance than a help, because most of the shipwrecks were the inventions of the imaginative minds of the authors. To me, this made treasure hunting an even greater challenge and I started off on my own, without the aid of these phony books, and subsequently my quest resulted in the greatest treasure recovery in modern times.

By 1960 my associates and I were just getting started on some of the wrecks of the 1715 fleet. Although a leading expert on shipwrecks and naval history assured us that the 1715 fleet had sunk in the Florida Keys, the artifacts we began finding indicated that this fleet had sunk in the area between present-day Fort Pierce and Sebastian Inlet. Research undertaken by one of my associates, Dr. Kip Kelso, and myself soon confirmed this fact.

When John Potter's Book—*The Treasure Diver's Guide*—was first published, I was reluctant to buy it, believing that it was as useless as the others I had read. I remember thinking to myself when someone mentioned I should read it: "Hell, who would be crazy enough to give real locations of treasure wrecks? If someone has this type of information he would use it himself and not give it away in a book." Somehow I got around to getting the book and was as surprised at what it contained as I was when I found my first piece of eight on a beach.

This book should not have been named *The Treasure Diver's Guide*, it should have been named *The Treasure Diver's Bible*, as it is one of the most essential tools a treasure hunter needs if he wants to be successful. My associates and I found it especially useful in properly identifying and dating artifacts and the shipwreck themselves. In the area where the 1715 fleet was lost, there are also many other shipwrecks of other periods and we would have lost a great deal of time and money if we had not been able to weed out the right wrecks that we knew were of the 1715 fleet and carrying great amounts of treasure.

After news leaked out of our first big finds, the local libraries had to take Potter's book out of circulation, because of the great reader demand for the book. Someone even offered me $45 for my copy of the book.

I receive hundreds of letters from persons around the world every year requesting information on shipwrecks in their areas or hoping that I can identify artifacts they have recovered. Here again, I find Potter's book indispensable; otherwise I would have to spend great amounts of time trying to find the myriad of answers these people want.

Everyone in the treasure-hunting business owes John Potter a great deal of gratitude for producing the first edition of his book, and now even more so for coming out with this new revised edition.

Kip Wagner, Chairman
Real Eight Company, Inc.

Satellite Beach, Florida

Foreword
Original Edition

Author's Note: Dan Stack's Foreword to the original edition of the Guide has become a classic definition of treasure hunters. The author is proud to include it in this revised edition.

*T*HERE ARE four types of treasure hunters. The first, and nearly all of us do and should belong to this group, is that of the armchair adventurer who thrills to vicarious participation in the treasure-hunting exploits of others. He draws his excitement and pleasure from the spoken or written word. His interest need be whetted only by a mere hint; his active imagination will take over from there. He dreams of digging up pirate loot while on vacation. Being generous, as are all genuine adventurers, he rejoices when someone else first reports a find, and he becomes positively ecstatic if the find actually turns out to be other than just another hoax.

The second type is the scientist, the historical researcher, the man who doesn't care a farthing about finding doubloons, the man who derives his joy from proving or disproving, from identifying and cataloguing. It is to this breed of men that the next two categories of treasure hunters often turn for help.

The third group is composed of the active adventurers, the present-day soldiers of fortune. They actually go out and search for treasure, although often they seek will-o'-the-wisps. What they really seek is adventure. If it were the actual hard cash which they really sought, most of their searches would die aborning and never mature out of the cocoon of mental imagery into full-blown argosies, for these men do not take the trouble to do the research necessary to insure that the sought-for treasure ever really existed, or if it existed, what the real circumstances of its loss were.

The fourth group has the fewest members—but we are the hardened professionals. We bring to bear upon the glamorous world of treasure the vital resources of the mundane world of business. We commit major amounts of capital; we assemble adequate equipment and supplies; we gather together professional crews; we do careful research; we utilize the latest scientific know-how; we are able to protect ourselves legally—in short, we are generally the permanent corporate groups devoted to salvage and the related fields. We are the only ones geared to make a living in this field.

However, regardless of the category in which the reader places himself, this book is perfect for him! It literally has something for everyone.

For the past year and a half Treasure Hunters, Inc., has been financing John Potter's Vigo treasure operation. Thus we know from firsthand experience just how authoritative his words are. We are familiar with, and often awed by, the amount and quality of his research. His diligence in pursuing elusive bits of historical evidence among the long-forgotten archives of a never-to-be-repeated era of treasure shipment, and his resourcefulness in fitting the uncovered fragments of evidence into the mosaic of historical fact, will satisfy even the most scholarly. The armchair man will be set to dreaming. The adventurer will be off diving. Those of us who pursue this business for profit will be set to computing possible return on investment.

The technical aspects of modern treasure hunting are carefully summarized and explained in a manner that will give even the uninitiated a working (or perhaps, dreaming) grasp of the field. John Potter's divers, equipped with Aqua Lungs and using a magnetometer, are a far cry from the primitive salvors of yesteryear who dived with buckets over their heads so as to prolong bottom time.

But most important of all—and this for all four groups—John Potter is a treasure hunter who has lived an incredibly romantic and inspiring adventure—and he knows how to write!

If you are interested enough to have picked up this volume, you will enjoy it. In fact, when you find yourself hopelessly caught up in it, and the fever hits you, you may come to curse it. But I guarantee that you will not put it down—unless it be to look up ship departures!

Surely this is a book destined to be a classic in the field.

Daniel Stack,
President,
Treasure Hunters, Inc.

Washington, D.C.
July 1960

ACKNOWLEDGMENTS—*Original Edition*

The information compiled for this book required tens of thousands of man-hours of patient digging through old and new volumes and documents in several languages by researchers who knew where to look and what to look for. Some extracts were taken from logs and reports written centuries ago in pen and ink, undecipherable to anyone but a specialist. Other accounts are the fruits of long research on a particular wreck by one man who was interested in it, and permitted me to use the results of his work. Descriptions of many of the treasure sites given in this book include the contributions of as many as four distinct investigations apiece, carried out by naval historians in archives, on-the-spot treasure *aficionados*, and SCUBA divers. To the many, many people all over the world who have generously and enthusiastically co-operated in this production, I give my sincere thanks.

To Vera Baker, who worked with me throughout the preparation of this book, I am more grateful than words can express. Without her help and constant encouragement this *Guide* would never have been written. Thanks, Vi!

To two friends, recognized authorities on old ships and marine history, goes the credit for the bulk of the research which made up the backbone of this book and produced dozens of previously unknown treasure wrecks. A lieutenant at the Naval Museum in Madrid covered the Spanish armadas, whole-heartedly aided by other naval officers and historians, and specialists on early maps at the Cartography Section of the Biblioteca Nacional. Gregory Robinson, with the full co-operation of E. K. Timings at the Public Records Office and Mrs. M. W. Hesketh-Williams at the British Museum, provided detailed accounts of British treasure wrecks as well as valuable data on Spanish and Portuguese losses caused by British naval actions. To the Spanish naval lieutenant and Mr. Robinson, and those who co-operated with them, my deepest appreciation for their help.

Bob Nesmith, "Curator" of the Foul Anchor Archives at Rye, New York, is quoted and referred to throughout this book. Besides numismatic facts and data on Spanish and Portuguese treasure losses, he supplied numerous leads which guided our research, particularly on the Manila galleons and Florida wrecks, as well as photographs from his vast collection. During the past year Bob has repeatedly substantiated his reputation as the American "treasure hunter's clearing house." Thanks, "old pirate!"

Jim Auxier, editor of *Skin Diver* magazine, put me in contact with many on-the-spot treasure-diving enthusiasts through his kindness in publishing my letter asking *Skin Diver* readers for information. In addition he provided the names of correspondents who have sent local data on wrecks and recent salvage work in their areas of interest. His help is much appreciated.

I wish to extend my gratitude to a number of friends who have generously supplied the results of many-year personal researches into sunken treasures, and permitted me to quote historical accounts which they found—often only after lengthy digging—in local archives. My fellow treasure diver at Vigo,

Robert Sténuit, has contributed heavily to sections on European treasure wrecks and submarine archaeology in the Mediterranean. Bob Marx detailed his own activities around Yucatán and eastern America, in both treasure and archaeology fields, in many letters postmarked Quintana Roo. Expert diver and lecturer Owen Lee, of the *Calypso,* has supplied data on eastern Caribbean wrecks. Walter Deas of Dundee, and more recently Australia, turned over the products of a thorough personal research into Spanish treasure wrecks around Great Britain and Dutch carracks, and in addition supplied the locations of many Invincible Armada losses which maps do not show. Roberto Díaz, a champion SCUBA diver from Barcelona, supplied pages of news on the praiseworthy accomplishments of the C.R.I.S. in the field of submarine archaeology off the Costa Brava. Antonio Ribera, dean and chronicler of the Spanish Mediterranean diving group, and author of three books about their activities, supplied additional facts as well as several photos and his map of archaeological discoveries. Michael H. Buckmaster, historian, diver, and author, provided coverage and photographs on the Bermudas. Dr. J. J. Markey and Dr. Eileen Herbster of the San Luis Rey Historical Society, California, sent me detailed accounts of their quest for the *Trinidad* and the research that preceded it, as well as photographs of recovered treasure. John M. Erving, Jr., of Gulfport, Florida, made many contributions to the Florida Keys picture. Treasure-finder Art McKee brought the coverage of his own accomplishments up to date and helped me with the geography of his "back yard," the Florida Keys. Jim Thorne, SCUBA diver, actor and Athlete of the Year, has drawn on his knowledge of Florida and Bahamas wrecks to provide material for this book. "Down under" correspondents Dr. T. E. Canning, Ron Reid, T. E. Davis, and others of the Tasmanian group described in many letters their interesting work off those shores while marine authority Harry O'May supplied the story of the *General Grant* and more treasure wrecks. E. A. Robinson, Lyle Davis, and David Fordham of Australia gave good accounts of the sunken treasure picture off their continent. I have had the pleasure of knowning Ed Link and Mendel Peterson, whose names appear frequently in this book, since the early part of our own treasure hunt. Both gentlemen have co-operated generously in supplying news of their own accomplishments and data on wreck identification.

Among the many contributors to this book, I particularly want to thank: Ian Douglas Campbell, Duke of Argyll, and Ian C. MacLennan, Chamberlain of Argyll, for their photograph of and details about the "Glede Gun" from the "Tobermory Galleon"; Ian Fraser, V.C., of Universal Divers, Liverpool, England, for his description of the Tobermory wreck; Leslie Cooper, of Haverford, Pennsylvania, for his information about the Lake Guatavitá treasure and submarine electronic developments; Peter Throckmorton of New York and Turkey, for his news of Mediterranean submarine archaeological finds; Jean Jacques Flori, champion French diver, for his contributions to submarine archaeology; Manuel Santaella and Rafael Arnal of Caracas, Venezuela, for their firsthand descriptions of the *San Pedro Alcántara* and Venezuelan SCUBA activities; Bill Hixon of Coral Gables, Florida, for data on detecting devices; Galeazzo Manzi-Fe, president of CITOM-SORIMA, Genoa, Italy, for his information about SORIMA's work over the *Elizabethville* and other wrecks; Ed Ciesinski of Key West, E. Lewis Maxwell of Miami, and Van H. Ferguson and Lester D. Plumb of the Department of Agriculture for helping round out the Florida picture; Patrick Kelly of San Francisco, who applied his considerable abilities developed through Paris research on our

"Monmouth's Galleon" to getting facts about the *Yankee Blade* and other California wrecks; ex-Vigo frogmen John Nathan (Caribbean), Owen Lee (Virgin Islands), Florent Ramaugé (Mallorca) and Howard Williams (Canary Islands and Tangier) for their reporting from their new areas of activity; Otto Bochow and Fred Foyn for treasure-diving news from Japan; Louis E. Dauer, Jr., of Honolulu, for mid-Pacific coverage; James A. Gibbs, Jr., (author of *Shipwrecks of the Pacific Coast*), John Huston, secretary of the Council of Underwater Archeology, Mel Fisher of Redondo Beach and Gary Keffler of Seattle for their contributions to news from the West Coast; Gosta Fahlman of the Royal Swedish Naval Administration, for his data on Swedish wrecks; Ed Downing of Somerset (discoverer of the *Sea Venture*) for Bermuda news; John E. Johnstone, New Guinea, for his interesting letter; Jack Gilbert and Luis González for information from Acapulco, Mexico.

News of accomplishments in the field of submarine archaeology supplied by Dr. Stephen F. Borhegyi, director of the Stoval Museum, University of Oklahoma, and Dr. E. Wyllys Andrews, director of the Middle American Research Institute, Tulane University, is very much appreciated. I wish to also express my thanks to Ledyard Smith of the Peabody Museum, Harvard University, the officers of the Archives Office, British Government, Malta, and of the Molas Museum, Terragona, for their contributions to the same subject, and to the personnel at the Service Historique de la Marine and Musée des Invalides, Paris, and Royal Institute for the Tropics, Amsterdam, for their co-operation in obtaining historical facts. I am indebted to the offices of X. and F. Calicó, Barcelona, and to Carl B. Livingston, the Development Board, Nassau, for their pamphlets on old Spanish coins and ingots whose contents I have quoted.

Veteran submarine archaeologist Elgin Ciampi—underwater photographer for *Life*, shark psychiatrist and author of *The Skin Diver*—has contributed substantially to the Caribbean and Bahamas chapters.

To my old friend F. Herrick Herrick—world adventurer, movie producer, shark fighter and treasure finder—a hearty thanks for those many hours of treasure tales. As I promised, I have not given away your secret of the location of that hoard of Spanish silver and gold coins you found on an island in Panama Bay . . . but some day we'll go back to that galleon wreck there and get the rest!

Technical information about electronic detecting equipment has been supplied by W. C. Blaisdell of Bludworth Marine, by officers of the Institut Dr. Fürster, Reutlingen, West Germany, of Pye, Ltd., Cambridge, England, and numerous other manufacturers. Facts about the new "Diving Saucer" were provided by officers of La Spirotechnique, Paris.

Miss Nora B. Stirling of New York has kindly permitted me to draw from the comprehensive accounts of the Corregidor Treasure, the La Plata Island silver, and other treasures described in her excellent book, *Treasure under the Sea*. I have also quoted from the manual *Deep Diving and Submarine Operations*, by Sir Robert H. Davis, and referred to sunken treasures listed in Lieutenant H. E. Rieseberg's *I Dive for Treasure*, and Ferris L. Coffman's *1001 Lost, Buried or Sunken Treasures*. I wish to thank Lieutenant Rieseberg and Mr. Coffman for the information and photographs which they kindly sent me.

ACKNOWLEDGMENTS—*Revised Edition*

Possibly the greatest reward an author can receive is the satisfaction that his work has contributed toward making possible the attainment of his readers' goals. In this respect, I have been richly compensated through letters from numerous treasure divers and underwater archaeologists telling me that information presented in the original edition of the *Guide* was helpful to them through identifying promising sites, supplying leads to locations, assisting with wreck identifications, and providing hope—through true accounts of the achievements of others—that "it can be done." Firsthand reports of recent successes which so often accompanied these letters have permitted me to add to this revised edition accurate and detailed reports of many new accomplishments. These, in turn, may supply useful and practical information to the treasure finders of the future. For your letters and generous contributions, I wish to sincerely thank all of you who have collaborated with me in updating the *Guide*. To a considerable degree, this is your book.

Kip Wagner, Chairman of the Real Eight Company, Inc., has written the Foreword. I am very honored, and deeply appreciate his kind words. I wish to express my gratitude to Harry Cannon and Dan Thompson, as well as Kip Wagner, for their information and patient replies to my questions, and especially to Bob Marx for his pages of news and his proofreading of my account of today's greatest treasure salvage.

Once again I gratefully say to Bob Nesmith, my close friend of many years, that without his wholehearted assistance this book might well never have been finished. His experienced suggestions guided me throughout the two years of preparation.

My particular appreciation goes to Carl J. Clausen, Florida State Archaeologist, for permission to quote from his knowledgeable texts on archaeology and salvage techniques, and for the information he provided on Florida wrecks and measures being taken to protect them. I also thank Robert Williams, Executive Director of the Florida Board of Archives and History, for his generous assistance.

A number of contributors to the first edition of the *Guide* have once again collaborated with me in preparing this revision. I am very grateful to Art McKee and Teddy Tucker for their kind assistance with wreck locations and news of their recent achievements; to my Vigo Bay associate Robert Sténuit for the account of his salvage of the *Girona*; to Mel Fisher, instigator of the breakthrough in search and salvage technology, for his letters of news; to Walter Deas of Seasports, Sydney, for his contributions from Australia; to Pablo Bush Romero, the driving force of C.E.D.A.M., and Dr. J. J. Markey of the San Luis Rey Historical Society; and to my old diving companion Howard Williams. Also, a special word of thanks is once again in order to Mendel L. Peterson and Edwin A. Link, who have contributed so effectively to the field of underwater archaeology.

A number of new detailed salvage accounts appear in this book, including several major treasure recoveries. I am indebted to the men directly responsible: for the *San José* off Florida, my sincere appreciation to Captain Tom

Gurr, President of the Marine-Tech Salvage Company; for *Le Chameau* off Canada, I am grateful to Alex Storm, who located and salvaged the ship; for H.M.S. *Association* off England, "Chippy" Pearce was kind enough to send news and photos, and check my manuscript; for the *Santa María de la Rosa* off Ireland, I wish to thank Sidney Wignall; for the Lucayan silver wreck, I am indebted to Jack Slack; for the details and photos of work undertaken by Expeditions Unlimited, Inc., at Chichén Itzá and other sites, I am grateful to President Norman Scott and Donald Ediger; for the intriguing account of Ceylon's Great Basses silver wreck, Arthur C. Clarke, Mike Wilson, and Rodney Jonklaas have my sincere thanks; I very much appreciate the assistance I received from Harry Cox of Bermuda, who briefed me on his treasure find and moreover sent information on salvage laws pertaining to the island; and finally, for the account of the *Elingamite*'s salvage—and those samples of recovered treasure—I heartily thank Kelvin Tarlton and Wade Doak of New Zealand.

The strong response to an ad placed in *Skin Diver* magazine provided introductions to many active underwater archaeologists and wreck explorers whose stories are in this book. I wish to thank editor Paul J. Tzimoulis for his assistance in locating old copies of *Skin Diver* for my reference, and to Hong Kong's SCUBA enthusiast John Fortune for making them available.

A number of Florida's successful researcher-salvors have made available for this book the results of their considerable studies in Seville's archives, details of their up-to-the-minute search and salvage techniques, and accounts of their work. I am especially grateful to Burt D. Webber, Jr., President of the Continental Exploration Corporation, and to Goin E. Haskins, Jr., President of the Southern Research & Salvage Co., Inc., for their major contributions covering wrecks off Florida, the Bahamas, and Padre Island. Colonel Frank F. Tenney, Jr., has been kind enough to provide descriptions of several new wrecks which he located. Dennis Standefer, President of Fathom Expeditions, Inc., brought my accounts of H.M.S. *Leviathan* and H.M.S. *Oxford* up to date. Harold Holden, President of El Dorado Salvage Company, described his work on a wreck believed to have carried treasure in 1715. Chuck Mitchell sent photos and accounts of his salvages off the Keys and in the Bahamas. My sincere appreciation to these gentlemen, and to so many others working the Florida waters, for their assistance.

The contribution of research to successful salvage is becoming more and more appreciated. For their generous sharing of information gathered over many years, I am grateful to Dave Horner, SCUBA diver, author, and authority on East Coast wrecks; to Walter and Teddy Remick, who so importantly contributed to the Great Lakes section; to Walter and Richard Krotee, whose information on the East Coast produced new treasure wreck candidates; to Russel Parks for his information and map of Florida sites; to Ray Eaton for his comments on the *Defence* and other lost ships; and to many others who were kind enough to provide information on specific locations and areas.

Dr. Colin Jack-Hinton, formerly of the Western Australian Museum, kindly supplied data on the W.A. wrecks and permission to quote from his published articles. I am especially indebted to Mr. Hugh Edwards, author-diver and authority on all the Western Australian wrecks—some of which he located and surveyed himself—for his generosity in spending time to correct and update this section of the book, and even pen a few lines in the manuscript.

Mr. James E. MacDowell, President of MacDowell Associates, was kind enough to send me several pages of useful facts about magnetometers from which anyone planning a mag search would benefit. I thank him most sincerely for his letters.

To my old Madrid *compadre* Mr. F. Herrick Herrick I say again thanks for the news of the *San José*. And to Mr. K. Tsujino of Okinawa, and Mr. Serafín Barcelona of Manila, my appreciation for information on wrecks which they supplied.

Finally, to the many, many other correspondents whose names could not be included here and who contributed in modest but important measures with facts on specific wrecks and areas, *Gracias, amigos!*

Contents

Introduction

*T*HE WORLD'S WATERWAYS can be compared to an enormous treasure bank. Each ship that sinks makes a deposit; every successful salvage is a withdrawal. Unlike other banks where deposits are returned, however, the ocean holds on tenaciously to hers and permits withdrawals only with the greatest reluctance. And for tens of centuries, from the time of the first lost shipments of gold from King Solomon's Ophir mines and Cambodian rubies for the Chinese emperors, submarine vaults have been amassing a share of man's material wealth. The value of gold, silver, precious stones and pearls lost under the seas is so large that it cannot even be guessed at.

Most of this underwater wealth lies under the main ocean trade routes along which treasure was shipped in large quantities before 1900, when the steamship and radio made navigation comparatively safe. The most important routes:

(a) The Spanish armadas, from the Caribbean to Spain, 1500–1820. Some $12,000,000,000 in treasure crossed the Atlantic; about 5 per cent was lost; about 2 per cent, or $240,000,000, never salvaged.

(b) The South Seas armadas, from Peru to Panama, 1534–1810. Nearly $2,000,000,000 in silver and gold moved up the South American west coast; over $50,000,000 was lost; of this, probably $30,000,000 remains unsalvaged.

(c) The Peru transports, from Peru to Spain via Cape Horn, 1651–1820. About $2,000,000,000 went via this route; perhaps $30,-000,000 was lost; at least $5,000,000 remains under the sea.

(d) The Manila galleons, crossing the Pacific back and forth between Acapulco and the Philippines, 1570–1815. Over $1,500,000,000 was transported aboard these big ships; at least $50,000,000 was sunk; $30,000,000 has never been recovered.

(e) The "Spice Route" traversed by the Portuguese and Dutch carracks and British East Indiamen, joining Europe and the Middle and Far East, 1502–1870. About $2,000,000,000 moved across the Indian Ocean; at least $50,000,000 was lost; scarcely any has been salvaged.

(f) The Australian gold shipments, from Melbourne to England via the Straits of Magellan, 1852–1900. Over $500,000,000 was shipped; several million were lost and never recovered.

(g) The California gold route, to New York via Panama or the Straits. Nearly $300,000,000 was shipped from 1849 to 1869 alone.

(h) The Yukon gold route, to California. Over $100,000,000 went south during the decade after 1897.

Certain points along these treasure movement routes, where reefs, chronic bad weather, etc., presented exceptional hazards to ships, hold proportionately high percentages of sunken wealth. A glance through the treasure maps in the second section of this book will locate these very rich zones. Some are well known: the Florida Keys, the western Caribbean, and the Gulf of Mexico, the Bahamas, and Bermuda. Others just as interesting—described in the following chapters for the first time—are practically unknown to treasure divers: the Azores (with $15,000,000 sunk around their shores); southeast Africa ($15,000,000); the Philippines ($13,000,000); and one of the most attractive of all, the Marianas, with at least $6,000,000 in silver from the Manila galleons lying on their reefs.

To collectors of "sunken treasure" maps, the above figures may seem insignificant alongside such "authenticated" hoards as $30,000,000[1] sunk with a single "galleon of the Spanish Dons." They have an advantage, however, in that their gold and silver actually exists today (see chapter entitled "Ghost Galleons"). In describing values in sunken wrecks throughout the treasure chapters of this book I have given actual figures taken from reliable documentary sources whenever they could be found. When no specific notation was made other than the usual commentary like "the people and treasure were all lost," I have made a conservative estimate based on the normal lading which the referred-to type of ship would carry on that run during that period. In the case of Spanish wrecks—which were by far the most numerous—a general breakdown of treasure cargoes is listed in Chapter 1 (B). Values given are only for "treasure" in its classic concept: that is, gold, silver, gems, and pearls. Unless specifically stated otherwise, precious metal is assessed intrinsically, as bullion, at 1970 world market quotations: gold, about $35/oz., and silver, about $1.65/oz. Taking into consideration numismatic values, these figures could in many cases be doubled or tripled.

The treasure chapters in the second section describe nearly 1000 underwater sites where between $200,000,000 and $300,000,000 lies today. Some have been signaled out as recommended. Those with one star are noted because they contain important amounts of confirmed treasures that should be accessible to the SCUBA diver. The two star wrecks are especially interesting, while the ones with three stars rep-

[1] Rarely was more than $3,000,000 carried on a galleon; never more than $10,000,000.

resent to our researchers and me the cream of the underwater treasure targets awaiting salvage.

A number of wrecks have been described in the treasure chapters which contain only small amounts of treasure—in some cases no more than ship's funds and passengers' money. I have qualified them with comments that they are uninteresting treasurewise, and included them (and many other wrecks of archaeological interest only in the submarine archaeology sections) to aid the diver in wreck identification in case he should come across one of them.

Many descriptions of Spanish wrecks in the treasure chapters include quotations (i.e., "some of the treasure was recovered") without further comments. Nearly all these quotes are taken from reliable "first level" reference volumes listed below. I have usually omitted footnotes explaining the sources since they would be repetitious.

The research that went into the preparation of this book drew from just about every information source that exists. Hundreds of old and recent volumes were examined; naval battles studied; original documents tracked down; historians and geographers consulted; armadas' manifests copied. The sources of much of this information are named in the Acknowledgments and Bibliography. The research covered not only general and specific treasure cargoes, but also their backgrounds—where the treasure came from, how it was shipped, what conditions brought about its loss, whether salvage techniques at the time of loss could have permitted its recovery, more recent salvage efforts, etc.—all aimed at two targets: pinpointing the treasure's location and determining how great a value is *really* still there.

The information in this book is the result of several years of work by a dozen or so main contributors and the co-operation of literally hundreds of other naval historians, SCUBA divers and treasure hunters. The data was assembled by European researchers in London, Dundee, Amsterdam, Stockholm, Brussels, Paris, Nice, Madrid, Barcelona, Seville, Lisbon, Tangier, and Italy; by Americans in New York, Washington, Rye, Miami, the Florida Keys, San Francisco, Los Angeles, Oceanside, and Seattle; by correspondents and friends in Havana, Jamaica, Caracas, Cozumel, Acapulco, Honolulu, the Marshalls, Australia and Tasmania, Tokyo, Hong Kong and Manila; by divers and historians in the Bahamas, Bermuda and Canary Islands. On-the-spot treasure-hunting *aficionados* from nearly every part of the world contributed toward making this book as complete and accurate as possible.

As treasure sites turned up they were evaluated. Those with promise were referred to researchers and on-the-spot correspondents for further study, and a number of starred wrecks in the treasure chapters have been subjected to fairly intensive research. Many fell by the wayside as more was learned about them. Some, even, ended up in the "Ghost

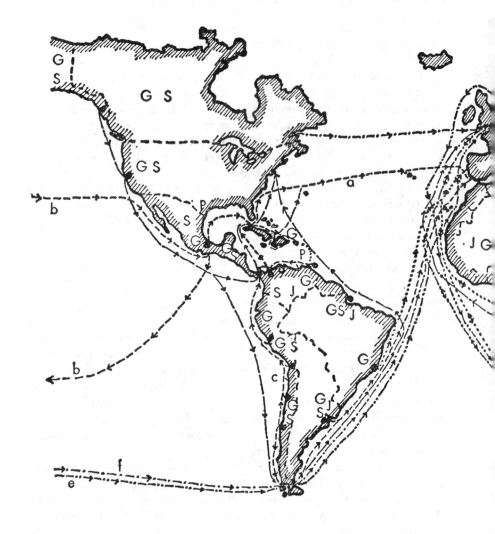

PRODUCTION
G   Gold
S   Silver
J   Jewels
P   Pearls

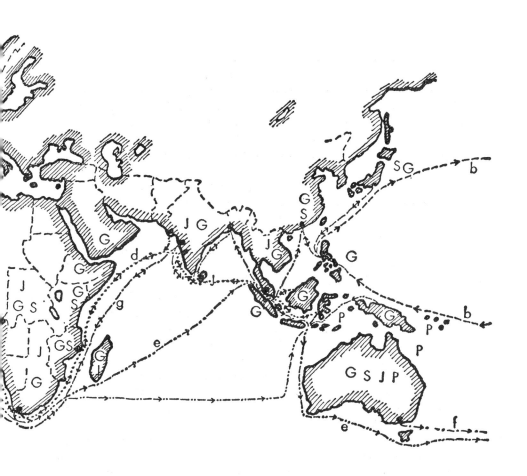

OVERSEAS TREASURE MOVEMENTS

------ Spanish   **a** New Spain & Tierra Firme Armadas

········· Portuguese   **b** Manila Galleons

-·-·-· English   **c** South Seas Armadas

------ Dutch   **d** Portuguese Carracks (East Indies)

– – – American   **e** Dutch Carracks (East Indies)

-··-··- Belgian   **f** Wool and Gold Clippers

                    g East Indiamen

Galleons" section. These include a number of the most famous "treasures" —which we learned probably do not exist at all.

Documentary research on most wrecks can go on nearly indefinitely. With few exceptions, all of the major treasure finds of the past decade have been due in some measure to historical research. Examples of important finds toward which research made a large contribution are Kip Wagner's 1715 galleons, Robert Sténuit's *Girona*, and Alex Storm's *Le Chameau*.

Research can be said to run through three levels. The first, covering data available fairly easily in old newspapers, naval histories, maritime histories, published accounts of witnesses, etc., has been applied to nearly all the treasure sites in this book, augmented by any facts that general research or world-wide correspondents have provided. The real digging begins at the "second level," where references to other harder-to-find documents are followed up, logbooks tracked down, captains' letters and courts-martial studied, out-of-print biographies located and examined for clues, monastery records translated, etc. On several of the more interesting wrecks we have carried research into this phase. From there on comes "third level" research, where unclassified archive documents are painstakingly tracked down, families or descendants of survivors located and interviewed, old commercial and bank records obtained and examined, etc. Link's research on the *Santa María*, Markey's on the *Trinidad*, Korganoff's into "Phips's Galleon" and ours at Vigo have continued to this level.

In the case of Spanish treasure ships, our "first level" research drew from the basic nine-volume work by Fernández Duro, *Armada Española*, from the tremendous study of armadas contained in the many-volumed *Seville et l'Atlantique*, from the *Historia de la Marina Real Española*, *La Marina de Castilla Desde su Origin*, *Naufragios de la Armada Española*, *Las Naos Españolas en la Carrera de las Indias*, *Naufragios en las Costas Chilenas*, *Salvamento de Naufragios*, *Les Flottes de l'Or*, etc., from other volumes referring to wrecks in specific areas, and salvages, from invaluable details in Navarrete's numerous folios, handwritten, of which only one set exists, and so on. The total information culled from these sources, augmented by other data turned up in Madrid Naval Museum research and facts provided by on-the-spot correspondents, has given a pretty good coverage to even the average unstarred Spanish wreck in the treasure chapters.

When we ran into conflicting accounts, which was not unusual, I have usually given them all. In cases where long-forgotten geographical references could not be located on the many, many old charts examined, I have indicated the general area. The material included in this book is only a small part of the many thousands of pages of notes taken and letters received, selected for its usefulness to the treasure hunter.

What might seem unnecessary details on history and general products of countries are included to substantiate the values of their exports carried on lost ships.

With few exceptions, usually at out-of-the-way parts of the world such as the Marianas, there are few "perfect" treasure wrecks to salvage. Nearly all fall into the following categories: (a) those broken up in shallow water (to about 65 feet depth) against reefs and coasts: most were located and salvaged soon after their loss in intensive and surprisingly thorough jobs. Many Florida Keys wrecks fall into this group. What remains on their ballast mounds today is only a small part of their original lading. There are exceptions, however, where difficult conditions or early wreck dates prohibited large recoveries; (b) the middle depth wrecks, from 65 to 180 feet: the most interesting to the SCUBA diver, as a large proportion have never been located nor salvaged, while their approximate sites are known; (c) the deep wrecks, down to 500 feet: only strongly financed companies would be interested; (d) the very deep wrecks, which cannot be worked with equipment available today. Salvage of nearly all the above groups of shipwrecks is complicated by other factors such as poor visibility, coral, and mud.

But difficulties and complications only whet the appetites of treasure divers. The treasure-hunting breed—though often considered crazy by his less adventurous fellow man—has a rare combination of qualities that equip him to tackle hardships and obstacles. The history of salvage is rich with examples of his success.

During the updating of this revised edition of the *Guide*, the author was impressed by the great advances made in the field of treasure diving since 1960, when the original edition was published. In the past decade alone probably as much has been accomplished as in the previous three hundred years. Many treasure wrecks—some not even included in the original *Guide*—have been located and salvaged. The existence of countless more has been disclosed following massive research programs carried out throughout the world. Bob Marx alone, in his thoroughly documented lists of lost Spanish ships, has brought to light information on literally hundreds of new wrecks. Similar contributions have been made by Burt Webber, Jack Haskins, the Remicks, Dave Horner, the Krotees, Hugh Edwards, and other specialists in certain regions and types of vessels. In addition, tremendous advances have been made in search techniques incorporating advanced electronic devices; in salvage methods such as the revolutionary "blaster" for uncovering shallow wrecks; in the knowledge of wreck identification, the science of preserving recovered artifacts, and legislative interest in the protection of historically valuable sites.

Because of this massive infusion of new information, what started as a routine revision of a ten-year-old volume turned into the production of what is effectively an entirely new book. Scores of treasure sites have been added; new maps prepared and inserted; and detailed accounts of the major recent treasure finds have been included, with the facts supplied by the people directly involved. The estimated values of treasures are probably very conservative because of the increased price of silver and the higher numismatic prices for old coins. So rapid are advances in the field of treasure salvage and underwater archaeology that, by the time this volume goes to press, several important new achievements will no doubt have already been made.

THE TREASURE DIVER'S GUIDE

Section One

CHAPTER 1

The Golden Galleons

Only a few years earlier most of them thought that the Atlantic fell off the edge of the Earth into a bottomless void. Yet here they were, safely across, in the midst of the most beautiful, serene new world that could be imagined. Under their bows the emerald Caribbean, tepid and crystal-clear, bubbled soothingly as balmy winds swelled the overhead latine-rigged sails. Coral reefs of every hue lay off to the sides, dotted with golden sand cays shaded under palm fronds and mangrove. The climate was warm and peaceful, the skies blue, the environment lulling . . .

Then they learned. The beauty and tranquillity were an insidious camouflage. Dangers, subtle and violent—for which Mediterranean schooling had given them no preparation—lurked everywhere. The warm Caribbean waters seethed with hungry little teredo worms that made sieves of stout hulls and sent their wooden ships under. Clear blue skies could suddenly darken and unleash hurricanes of incredible fierceness that wiped out flotillas without a survivor. Coral reefs, jutting up without warning from mile-deep ocean, lay waiting for their keels. The green and gold islands were the homes of cannibal Carib tribes with a fondness for white meat.

One after the other their exploratory caravels disappeared, often without a trace, sometimes with tales of shipwreck and bitter survival struggles told by a few who stayed alive. The fate of the *Maestro Juan* was a mystery for a full year after her loss. Then the story of her last voyage came from the mouths of a band of half-dead seamen picked up from a cay. On a short passage from Santo Domingo they had put into a cove to take aboard fresh water. As the boat was being lowered a hoard of shouting Caribs swarmed out from shore in war canoes. Poisoned arrows showered among them while they hacked at anchor rope and loosed sail. An offshore breeze carried the ship to safety. But their luck didn't hold. Only a few weeks later the breeze swelled into a storm and dashed their caravel onto the reefs of Serrana Island—a barren, arid cay off Honduras named after another wreck. Here the survivors grubbed out a bare existence, drinking tortoise blood to stave off thirst, until they were rescued.

Another sailor, the only survivor, spent ten lonely years on the banks of La Plata River in South America until the exploratory flotilla of Rodrigo de Acuna found him in 1521. Even Columbus, on his fourth and last voyage, was marooned. With a fleet of four ships he visited Panama in 1503 and founded Nombre de Dios. Two of his four caravels

were found unseaworthy, their hulls eaten by shipworms, and had to
be abandoned there. The other two made it back as far as Jamaica where
they had to be run aground to prevent them from sinking. With four
crews stranded on the unpopulated coast, Columbus sent an officer,
Diego Mendez, in a canoe to bring back transportation from Santo
Domingo. It was seven months before help arrived.

The explorer's life was dangerous, yet they kept coming—the soldiers
of fortune, the jailbirds, the debt-plagued aristocrats and the dreamers—
some seeking escape, others their fortunes, all adventure. From the first
base established in 1494 at Santo Domingo they fanned out across the
Caribbean and down South America. By 1500 the Antilles islands had
been discovered and explored. Then the navigators Solis and Pinzón, who
returned to the Indies after taking the *Pinta* back with news of Columbus' discovery, charted Cozumel and Tabago islands, and the coast of
Yucatán which some still believed to be China. Panama and the tip of
Florida, Trinidad, the mouths of the Amazon were found, and Lake
Maracaibo. As news of rich lands was carried back, the Catholic Kings
set up an organization to supervise its development. This was the *Casa
para la Contratación y Negociación de los Indias,* or Bureau of Trade,
established at Seville on February 14, 1503. During its long life this
office was praised for its contributions toward the conquest of the
Americas and damned for the stupidity and corruption of its officers.
Its authority was sweeping. The Bureau controlled nearly every aspect
of navigation and commerce. Its officials were given civil and criminal
jurisdiction over ships, officers, crews, and freight. Without a permit
from the Bureau's representatives no vessel could leave port, no cargo
could be loaded or discharged and no appointments, except those of the
king himself, could be made. During its latter years the Bureau's functionaries were notoriously corrupt—incompetent, court-appointed favorites whose only interest seemed to be in squeezing larger bribes for
allowing the armadas to carry contraband. Yet at the onset it was
staffed with competent men—many themselves navigators—who were an
aggressive motivating force.

Under their orders every ship's captain took careful notes of his observations wherever he went, paying especial attention to tides, currents,
winds, depths, land formations, and reefs. These reports went to Seville
where they were examined and their new data recorded. More information was brought back by navigators on exploratory flotillas of
one 60-ton and two or three smaller ships sent by the Bureau to probe
the eastern American coasts, then the west coasts and finally the Pacific.
Charts began to take form with rough outlines of shores inked onto
previously blank paper, numbers for sounded depths, and arrows marking
currents and prevailing winds. By 1550 most of the New World's head-
lands and bays and many Pacific islands had been roughly mapped

and given their latitude positions. The longitudes were usually in error, for to take them a chronometer was necessary and none existed. Finding an accurate timepiece became a major preoccupation of the Bureau's navigators. Despite continual efforts they still had not developed one in 1650. Since Cádiz was Spain's main Atlantic port, longitudes were computed from there, resulting in a difference of 6° 20' from those shown on modern charts.[1] Celestial fixes were taken with astrolabes, quadrants and octants, some of which were remarkably accurate. After 1731 the sextant came into general use.

While the Spanish explored the American continents the Portuguese were pushing east from Africa. Their caravels had crept down the Atlantic coast in the late 1400s and Bartholomeu Dias entered the Indian Ocean in 1488. Under the terms of the 1494 Treaty of Tordesillas which replaced the earlier Papal bull dividing the "heathen world" between these two countries, all land east of the meridian "370 leagues west of the Cape Verde Islands" belonged to Portugal. This included the tip of Brazil—visited by ten of their ships in 1500—and as far as they knew might encompass entire continents in the South Atlantic. Magellan sailed his caravel *Conceição* under South America trying to find out. Although he was killed in the Philippines, some of his men completed the voyage home in the 90-ton ship and proved that the globe was very much larger than had been believed.

From 1520 to 1540 was the heyday of the conquistadors. In 1519 Hernán Cortés landed on the Mexican coast and began the conquest of the Aztec Empire. By convincing Montezuma that he was the god Quetzalcoatl he made the Indian ruler his servant and through this relationship opened the doors to a treasury of silver, gold, and precious stones such as Europeans had never seen. Heady with his new power, Cortés broke with Diego de Velasquez, the governor of Cuba, who had originally sent him, and beat a Spanish force sent to bring him back in chains. Then he struck west across Mexico, retaking the rebelling Aztec capital Tenochtitlán in 1521. His former subordinate Montezuma, who had become disillusioned in the white god, was killed in battle. In 1526 he completed the destruction of the Aztec Empire by crushing its last leaders in Honduras. This accomplished, Cortés established a second Spanish gateway to the Pacific at Acapulco a few years after Balboa had looked out over that ocean from Darien, and sent his lieutenant Francisco de Ulloa north by sea to find the mythical Seven Cities of Cibola. The result was the discovery of California.

Two thousand miles down the Pacific coast another conquistador, Francisco Pizarro, was then gaping in greedy awe at the mountain of gold for the Inca's ransom being piled before him. Ten years after Cortés

[1] Until the Conference of 1884, when the Greenwich Meridian was internationally adopted, most nations took their own capitals or principal observatories as their standard meridians from which longitude was measured.

took Mexico, Pizarro had solidified control over Peru and sections of Bolivia and Chile. Francisco de Montejo was beaten back in Yucatán, but his son took the area in 1546. Colombia was invaded by Quesada and other leaders whose mounted bands of armored soldiers of fortune fought their way into the Andes mountains, killing and torturing the Chibcha natives for information about the legendary Golden One—*El Dorado*. By 1550 Spanish colonies were planted throughout the American continents: at Veracruz, Mexico City, and Acapulco in Mexico, Panama and Nombre de Dios in Panama, Cartagena, Buenaventura and Santa Fe de Bogotá in Colombia, Gibraltar on Lake Maracaibo and Margarita Island off Venezuela, Lima and Cuzco in Peru, and Arica, Antofagasta, Coquimbra, Valparaíso and Concepción along the Chile coast. During the rest of the century ports were added in Brazil and the Argentine, at the estuary of La Plata River and on the Cape Verde, Azores, and other Atlantic islands. San Francisco and San Diego were settled in the early 1600s, and then San Augustine, Florida.

By 1650 the conquest of the Indies had been completed.

(B) THE TREASURE

It began with a trickle at the end of the 1490s—gold and silver from Cuba, Hispaniola, and Puerto Rico, and pearls from the Lesser Antilles. The first caravels carried a hundred pounds, then a thousand, then several tons. From the south sprang another rivulet: gold, pearls, and emeralds from Panama and the Columbia coast. The two streams joined at Santa Domingo and flowed across the Atlantic to Spain, growing in volume until by 1520 a million dollars was coming out of the Indies per year. With Cortés' conquest of the Aztec Empire, a cascade of silver and jewels poured from Mexico, swallowing up the lesser streams in its $20,000,000 torrent. It subsided, and the flow dropped off to $4,000,000 yearly when down in Peru a dam broke and a tidal wave surged up— $20,000,000 in gold from the Inca king's ransom. Two hundred million dollars of silver, gold, pearls and emeralds crossed the Atlantic between 1530 and 1560.

Then the treasure storehouses of native empires were empty, and the mining began. Ruthless Spanish administrators converted entire Indian communities into slave laborers, driving them by the hundreds of thousands into rivers to pan dust and under mountains to extract ore. Throughout Mexico, Honduras, Colombia, Peru, Chile, and Bolivia existing mines were developed and new sources discovered. It mattered little that droves of laborers died of exhaustion under the brutal pressure— that the entire Cuban Arawak Indian tribe was killed off. What counted was gold and silver: new rivulets, and larger flows from the hundreds of mines already producing, to swell the torrents pouring from mines to mints to embarkation ports onto the armadas.

By 1600, $35,000,000 in treasure was flooding out of the Americas each year and by 1700 this figure had nearly doubled. It came in more or less equally rich outpouring from the three main viceroyalties into which the continents had been partitioned: New Spain, or Montezuma, which included Mexico, Honduras, and until about 1700 eastern Venezuela and Margarita Islands; New Granada, also called Tierra Firme, or the Mainland, comprised of Colombia, most of Venezuela, Central America, and Panama after 1740; and Peru, which included its neighbors Bolivia, Chile, and Ecuador, and Panama until 1740. Each was delivering about $15,000,000 annually in 1650, and by 1810–20, when the colonies revolted, the output had grown to near $35,000,000. The Antilles were all taken away from Spain by English, French, and Dutch forces by 1655 except Cuba and Puerto Rico, whose mines were nearly depleted by then.

The New Spain Viceroyalty was the silver producer. High grade ore was found in the Central Mexico mines at Endehe, San Ivan, and Santa Barbara in New Biscay Province, in San Martín and Aume in Zacatecas, and in the Trinidad, Navarro, Santacruz, Santa Eulalia and Real del Monte mines. This was usually cast into bars for shipment until 1536, when the first mint in America was opened at Mexico City. Here some of the silver was coined.

Mexico led the world in silver production during the seventeenth and eighteenth centuries just as it does today. In 1956, 43,000,000 ounces worth $70,000,000 were refined there; under the viceroys, after 1550, the New Spain annual yield averaged 20,000,000 ounces of silver, with which about 150,000 ounces of gold was extracted. Much of this went to the mints. In the forty-year period, 1732–72, Mexico City alone turned out 478,305,907 silver "Dos Mundos" dollars—the first round milled peso—for an average of nearly 12,000,000 per year. In one exceptional season after the minting of gold was authorized it delivered 25,807,078 silver pesos and 1,359,814 of gold. On the whole, some 22,000,000 silver pesos were produced yearly in New Spain. Of these, two to five million were shipped out of Acapulco on the Manila galleons as "silk money." Another five million were absorbed into the local economy and the remainder—about 14,000,000 pesos together with 100,000 ounces of gold, opals, and amethysts, worth $27,000,000 in all —went on muleback to Veracruz where it joined the gold and gems from the Far East and the pearls from Margarita Island aboard the New Spain armada.

The New Granada (Tierra Firme) Viceroyalty, or Mainland, yielded gold and silver, nearly all the world's emeralds, and platinum—which the Spanish called "false" silver and valued less. The Chocó region of the north Andes range, between Santa Fe de Bogotá and the Pacific, became by itself a gold producer that equaled the whole Viceroy of Peru. In

1956, 438,000 ounces worth $15,500,000 were refined there; under Spanish administration between 200,000 and 400,000 were extracted each year, as well as large amounts of silver. Most of this was sent by mule to Santa Fe de Bogotá where a Royal Mint went into operation about 1627. Silver cobs were struck there and gold coins, as well, from 1630 onward. The finished money came down from the mountain city by boat and pack train to Cartagena on the coast. Here were also brought the diamonds, silver, and gold from Venezuela, and pearls from the offshore islands. In the average year about 4,000,000 silver pesos, 300,000 ounces of gold and $700,000 in emeralds, diamonds, pearls, amethysts, turquoise, and other semiprecious stones, with a value of $19,000,000, were shipped out on the Tierra Firme armada.

The third and richest division of Spanish America was the Viceroyalty of Peru, encompassing nearly the entire western coast of South America. Long before Pizarro set foot here the Incas were mining silver, gold, tin, copper, and mercury. The Spaniards enlarged producing ore sources and discovered new ones: a silver field was accidentally revealed when an Indian tripped and landed on a gray ingot. Much of the gold was extracted from the hills of the Carabaya, east of Lake Titicaca, but other ore concentrations were worked throughout the viceroyalty. The principal silver mines were at Potosí, Oruro, Caucca del Negro and Carangas in the Los Charcas district near Lake Poopo, around Chucuito, Cuzco and La Paz near Lake Titicaca, and inland from Trujillo. From 1572 to 1664 Potosí alone produced 641,250,000 silver pesos. Mines at Cerro del Pasco led the world in silver production during 1661–80. Conveniently located nearby at Huancavelica was a major source of mercury for refining the ore. In the second half of the sixteenth century, Royal Mints at Potosí and Lima were striking silver cobs and Potosí was minting gold. Other mints were started later at Trujillo, Cuzco, and Cayllona to absorb the output from widely separated areas along the coast.

Both gold and silver, in immense quantities, came out of the Peru Viceroyalty. Today Bolivia and Peru alone account for 30,000,000 ounces of silver per year. During the seventeenth and eighteenth centuries, with metal from Chile and Ecuador added to these countries' output, well over 300,000 ounces of gold and 15,000,000 silver pesos were produced annually. Most of this came down to the coast from the interior on the backs of llamas and accumulated at the main ports where transports of the South Sea armada picked it up. Until about 1720 nearly all of the Peruvian treasure was sent north in single galleons or convoys to Panama for transportation across the Isthmus onto the Tierra Firme armadas. After this date it was usually loaded onto warships and frigates for direct shipment to Spain via the Strait of Magellan, although there were still occasional convoys to Panama.

Once production got going, the annual treasure export of the Peru Viceroyalty was about 250,000 ounces of gold and 12,000,000 pesos in silver, worth about $39,000,000.

The total value of precious metal, pearls, and gems (excluding perishable merchandise) which the Spanish took from the American continents during the three hundred and over years of their colonies has been variously estimated at from six to nearly fifteen billion dollars. Possibly the most accurate figure—$10,000,000,000—was arrived at by Dr. William Robertson in his *History of America*. Since this estimate was made, however, the price of silver has increased in terms of dollars, and a realistic value today would be close to $16,000,000,000.

The estimates, by period, given below were made on the base of this total, and recorded data on many armadas' registered treasures, Spanish trade statistics, and individual treasure shipments on vessels when they were recorded. They concern only nonperishable silver, gold, precious stones, and pearls, registered and contraband. Precious metal is assessed at its intrinsic value, with no attempt being made to compensate for the greatly increased worth of coins, as collector's items. Figures are in yearly averages, and in units of $1000.

Period	From Panama & Hispaniola	From New Spain	From Tierra Firme (with Peru Trans- shipments)	From Peru Via Panama	Direct to Spain	Total
1501–1520	800	—	—	—	—	800
1521–1523	1500	5000(a)	—	—	—	6500
1524–1533	1500	2000	—	—	—	3500
1534–1538	2500	3000	7000	6000(b)	—	18500
1539–1555	2500	5000	7000	3500	—	18000
1556–1572(c)	1500	10000	10000	7000	—	28500
1573–1620	1500	12000	15000	10000	—	38500
1621–1650	800(d)	13000	20000	12000	—	45800
1651–1710	little	15000	28000	12000	3500	58500
1711–1740(e)	—	20000	35000	10000	10000	75000
1741–1775	—	22000	30000	8000	16000	76000
1776–1810	—	25000	30000	5000	25000	85000
1811–1820(f)	—	25000	15000	—	30000	70000

(a) Aztec loot; (b) Inca loot; (c) beginning of the armadas; (d) loss of the Antilles; (e) discontinuation of the armadas; (f) revolt and independence of the colonies.

(c) THE SHIPS

The word "treasure" immediately brings to mind the connotation "Spanish galleon." The galleons often carried treasure—although this was not the main function for which they were designed—but so did the other classes of ships which crossed the Atlantic: the caravels, galleys, *urcas*, carracks, *naos*, *galleoncetes*, and *pataches*, and in much larger quantities the later frigates and warships. Each of these had its function, special characteristics and era of popularity, replacing one another in the evolution of sailing ships which ended with the clipper.

The GALLEY was used in the Mediterranean and along the Spanish and African Atlantic coasts from about 1300. It ranged in size from 200 to 800 tons and was propelled by both sail and oars, useful in waters where winds were light. The larger galleys carried 220 slaves, chained six to the oar. They were usually lightly armed transports for cargo and soldiers. From about 1500 galleys were tried in the Indies but were found too flimsy to navigate under conditions there so much rougher than the quiet Mediterranean. Of a group of ten sister ships built for Caribbean service in the 1550s, every one was wrecked within five years. Construction was stopped after 1660.

The CARAVEL was the favorite of the explorers. It was used by Columbus, by Magellan to cross the Pacific, and by Bartholomeu Dias to round the Cape of Good Hope and enter the Indian Ocean. During the fifteenth century the caravel was considered the best-sailing of all types of ship because of its sturdy construction, maneuverability, shallow draft which permitted it to enter rivers and bays, and ability to sail close to the wind. It was usually latine-rigged with one or two decks and housing at the poop and prow.

The caravel was small, usually between 35 and 90 tons, although some of the later Portuguese ships grew to twice this size. Its crew was roughly one man to the ton, or from 30 to 120. As trade developed and larger volumes of cargo crossed the Atlantic the caravel lost out to the heavier *naos* as a transport and to the faster *pataches* as a dispatch carrier. By 1575 it had nearly disappeared.

The CARRACK was the early freighter, used by the Portuguese and Dutch for the long cargo and passenger hauls between Europe and the East Indies on voyages that took from six to eighteen months. It was a floating warehouse-fortress, massive, bulky, with the enormous cargo capacity of 1500 or more tons plus accommodations of a sort for crew and passengers totaling 1000. Strong wooden castles at the prow and poop towered fifty feet over the water and were fortified with swivel guns. From their protection soldiers could pour down a deadly cross-fire on boarding parties that attained the ship's waist.

As a sailer the carrack was a disaster. It lumbered along slowly, always needing a following wind, and had no maneuverability. This made it vulnerable to contrary winds and gunfire from smaller, faster ships. Between 1550 and 1650, when they were replaced by *naos*, a hundred carracks were lost without a trace by the Portuguese alone, plus many more by the Dutch.

The GALLEON and NAO[2] were identical in construction and differed

---

[2] *Nao*, and more recently *nave*, were generic terms meaning "ship."

only in name and armament. The designation "galleon" was given to ships of this class used for fighting and convoy, heavily armed and usually prohibited from carrying cargo except registry treasure. The "*nao*" was the transport and freighter carrying few guns or gunners to serve them. In the armada convoy system a *flota* of *naos* was escorted by two to four larger galleons.

This class evolved as the fittest survivor in early efforts to develop a ship with a combination of qualities that neither the galleys, carracks nor caravels had: construction strong enough to weather all but the worst storms; large cargo capacity; shallow draft; maneuverability. As to the latter it was an improvement on the earlier designs but never really satisfactory since it could not sail close to the wind and "needs a hurricane to make it move." But it was sturdy, especially after improvements in design, and its broad beam permitted 300-ton ships of this class to "anchor in a bit over nine *codos* [fifteen feet] fully loaded."

By 1450 the galleon prototype was developing and in 1510 the first of these ships were in service. Their main characteristics were a tall poop, broad beam, and during several periods a very shallow draft—limited by orders of the Bureau of Trade despite the fact that this curtailed mast height and sail capacity and reduced stability. The reason was the shallow draft of the Sanlúcar Bar, over which these ships had to pass to get up the Guadalquivir River to Seville where they were often required to load and unload. Later, when common sense prevailed over entrenched Seville interests and the armadas could end their voyages at the far more suitable port of Cádiz, drafts were deepened to maximum limits permitted by the entrances to Lisbon and Veracruz.

From 1550 to 1600 the typical galleon or *nao* ranged in size from 300 to 600 tons (a ship's tonnage was its cargo capacity) with occasional exceptions that reached 1000 tons. The 400-tonner of 1590 was 103 feet long, had a 32-foot beam and a 20-foot draft. Its armament was 8 bronze and 4 iron cannons and 24 bronze or iron *versos*. A ship of 600 tons had two main decks and four decks at the poop, carried a complement of about 600 sailors, soldiers, and passengers, was 135 feet long and 36 broad, and mounted 66 guns plus 8 chase guns at the prow. By 1650 the average tonnage was greater while the draft decreased due to more length and breadth. A 700-tonner was 140 feet long, 38 wide and only 17½ deep. The largest *naos* of this period exceeded 1200 tons, while armada-escorting *Capitanas* and *Almirantas* varied from 700 to 2000 tons, carrying as many as 90 bronze cannons in three tiers and having poops that rose 45 feet over the water. By 1700 the size of *naos* was generally reduced to between 450 and 900 tons, with a typical 894-tonner having a length of 145 feet, breadth of 44 and draft of 17½. A 1500-ton *Capitana* or *Almiranta* was 165 feet long, 46 in beam and carried a mainmast 130 feet tall.

Galleons and *naos* continued in service until well past 1750, when frigates and other ships of more recent design replaced them.

The GALLEONCETE was a scout and light freighter used from 1550 to 1650. It varied from 100 to 200 tons, had a low poop and was faster than the galleon. Its usual armament was four double-*versos* and two chase guns at the prow.

The FELIPOT was another small dual-purpose ship with cargo capacity of 120 to 300 tons and 8–12 cannons, carrying 24 musketeers and 6 arquebusers for defense against pirates. It was named after King Philip and used in the early 1600s.

The URCA was a freighter fairly similar to a *nao*, popular from 1575 to 1700. It varied in cargo capacity from 80 to 800 tons.

The FRIGATE began its development in 1580 and was in action with all European fleets by 1640. This popular class of ship was fast and maneuverable with a sweeping maindeck rising slightly at the poop. It varied in size from 900 to 1700 tons and carried between 36 and 72 cannons and carronades. A large Spanish frigate of 1755 was of 1500 tons, 125 feet long and 26 broad, and carried 68 guns in two tiers. From 1700 onward frigates were used more and more frequently to carry treasure shipments, some bringing back cargoes worth nearly $10,000,000 from Peru.

The SHIP OF THE LINE or NAVIO was the seventeenth and eighteenth century battleship. Its prototype was the 1861-ton *Royal Sovereign*, launched in England in 1637. By 1700 these ships passed 2000 tons and carried 100 cannons. The average *navio* ran between 1200 and 1800 tons, mounting from 60 to 112 guns in three or four tiers. The Spanish often used them to transport treasure. Spain discontinued their construction in 1797, when her naval power was at its peak.

The PACKET BOAT OR PATACHE was the scout and general-utility ship used throughout the period 1500–1770. It grew gradually in size from 50 to 300 tons in 1730. Treasure consignments of $1,000,000 and even $2,000,000 were sometimes carried by ships of this class.

The PIROQUE was developed by the Spanish navy in 1670 to fight pirates. It was long and narrow, fast, and propelled by sail and oars. A typical 90-foot piroque was only 18 feet wide, mounting at its prow a 9-foot 6-pounder chase gun and 4 stern *pedreros*. On several occasions squadrons of piroques destroyed pirate ships by superior maneuvering.

The CORVETTE came into use about 1800 as a light warship and scout. It was built on the lines of a frigate but was much smaller, carrying about 20 10-caliber guns. Sometimes Spanish corvettes carried treasure.

(D) THE ARMADAS

There was little order in ship schedules to and from the Indies at first. Caravels came and went much as tramps do today, although impromptu fleets, such as Bobadilla's of 1502, often assembled to return together. As news of rich cargoes spread, appetites were whetted and envy aroused. The Barbary Coast pirates, with long experience in the business, were the first to act. Their large fleets of dhows hovered off the Spanish and Portuguese coasts and intercepted ship after ship. Then French freebooters joined in, followed by English and Dutch. Some operated under the farce of letters of marque issued by greedy governors and monarchs, giving their captains pseudo-legal authority to steal and kill at sea. Others claimed to be nothing but plain honest pirates. Their depredations soon roused near-panic in Spain and officials of the Bureau of Trade scurried to do something to check the menace. The counter was the armada system and the coast-guard squadron.

In 1522 the Bureau issued an order that no caravels of less than 80 tons were to cross the Atlantic alone, and that all ships must carry guns. At the same time the first guard squadron of galleons was formed to patrol the Portuguese coast and escort transports through the offshore pirate-infested waters. Three years later the Council of the Indies, another recently formed bureau to supervise the New World trade, worked out a plan for convoys. Cargo ships were to cross the Atlantic in fleets of six to ten, each escorted by four 250–300-ton galleons and two 80-ton *pataches*. In 1537 a new order stipulated that all returning ships must meet in Santo Domingo and cross in an *armada*.

In Spain there was already bickering between power groups for the right to send ships to the Indies. From 1504 to 1509 officials of the Bureau required that all vessels load and discharge at their head-quarters in Seville, up the Guadalquivir River—a nuisance and danger to ship crews and merchants alike. Other ports like Cádiz and La Coruña wanted to join in on the lucrative trade as well. Bitter in-fighting broke out with opposing groups striving to win the king's favor. In 1509 Cádiz merchants broke the Seville monopoly and enjoyed the right to trade until 1536 when a shipwreck there gave the Bureau's functionaries at Court the weapon with which to cut that port off. Throughout the 1500s this tug of war went on, with some periods when Seville had a monopoly and others when as many as seven ports were open to trade. By 1600 things had settled down with trading rights limited to Seville and Cádiz. It was not until 1717 that this status quo was relaxed.

The convoy system was further developed in 1543. New orders from the Bureau stipulated that all Indies trading ships must be of at least 100 tons, leaving Seville in groups of ten or more twice yearly, on March 1 and September 1. Departure dates were changed to a month earlier in 1554 as the result of better information on hurricanes. Then in 1565, with the establishment of viceroyalties in the New World, the Bureau issued its first comprehensive armada plan.

Two Indies armadas were formed: the New Spain (called "The Flota") and the Tierra Firme (called "The Galleons"). These left Seville together before the first half of May every year following a course calculated to take advantage of the elements. They sailed down the coast of Africa to the Canary Islands where water and supplies were loaded, then westward with the equatorial current and trade winds to the Antilles. Here they separated. The New Spain armada went to Puerto Rico, then south of Hispaniola and Cuba, across the Gulf of Mexico to Veracruz where it discharged its mercury and European export cargoes. Along the way it dropped off *pataches* and 300-ton *naos* at the islands to load their products. The Tierra Firme armada sailed across the coast of Venezuela and Colombia to Cartagena, with small ships separating to put in at coastal settlements. A dispatch was sent to Lima, Peru, that the armada had arrived, and its transports were unloaded.

About two weeks before the Tierra Firme armada reached Cartagena a third fleet, called the South Seas Armada, had assembled at Callao, Peru. Its galleons and *naos* carried crude products from Concepción, Valparaíso, Coquimbo, Antofagasta, and Arica in Chile and the Peru ports. When word arrived that the Tierra Firme ships were in, the South Seas Armada sailed north picking up other transports at Guayaquil and Buenaventura, where Colombia silver was often sent. The South Pacific cargoes were discharged at Panama. From here they were freighted across the Isthmus on mules and in Chagas River boats to Portobelo—which replaced Nombre de Dios—where Tierra Firme ships which had unloaded at Cartagena were waiting. These took aboard the cargo and carried it back to Cartagena while their sister ships were loading Colombian and Venezuelan products there. Smaller transports which had been dropped off along the north coast came in. Then the Tierra Firme armada sailed north, skirting the Serranilla shoals, up the Yucatán Channel to Havana.

Here it usually joined forces with the New Spain armada, which had meanwhile loaded silver and other Mexican and Honduras products and sailed from Veracruz. *Naos* and *pataches* came in from the Antilles. The combined armadas set out on the return voyage. This could take them into the Atlantic through one of two routes: the Old Bahamas Channel, which ran eastward between the north Cuban coast and the Bahamas reefs past Columbus Banks then northeast through Mayaguana, Caicoa, Mouchoir or Silver Bank passages; or up the New Bahamas Channel off the east Florida coast as far as Cape Hatteras, then eastward toward Bermuda. Both routes were hazardous, with the armada spending many days in coral reef-strewn channels, vulnerable to even a strong breeze in the wrong direction—let alone a hurricane.

If they survived the Bahamas crossing the armadas sailed past Bermuda across the Atlantic, pushed by fitful westerlies and the Gulf Stream, often becalmed for weeks in the Sargasso Sea while thirst and disease took a heavy toll of lives. Near the Azores they made a secret pre-arranged rendezvous with galleons of the coast guard armada of the Indies route which escorted them back to Cádiz or Seville. The round trip took from seven to nine months.

The 1565 order was specific. Two fighting galleons—normally the largest and strongest available—accompanied each armada. One was designated the *Capitana* and carried the commanding officer, called the general, who was responsible for safety and welfare, for the guns, charts, soldiers, and adequate provisions. He was watched by spies of the Council of the Indies and severely accountable if a ship was lost through his fault.[3] The *Capitana* sailed at the head of the armada. Bringing up the stern was the other galleon, called the *Almiranta* and carrying the admiral, second in authority. He took command when there was fighting. Other high posts were held by the commander of infantry, inspector of artillery, comptroller general, ship's captains, and other officers. All were political appointments, often sold by the king. The holders, by allowing contraband cargo to be shipped, by permitting private trading ships to sail with the armada, and in numerous other ways, made enough profit above the cost of their appointments to retire after a few years if they were still alive.

After several disastrous experiences when ships were lost in battle through incompetence, regulations were further tightened in 1572. The *Capitana* and *Almiranta* were prohibited from carrying any cargo except the king's treasure and were required to be maintained ready for combat at all times. In the past these galleons had often been so cluttered with cargo piled in hatches and on gun decks that the cannons could not be properly served. A third war galleon of 300 tons, sometimes called the *Gobierno*, was added to each armada, also forbidden to take on freight. Besides fighting, its function was to rescue treasure and passengers from any *nao* in distress. Generals were advised, at their discretion, to favor the New Bahamas Channel on return crossings. Too many ships were going down against shoals north of Hispaniola.

In 1580 the schedules were again changed. The New Spain armada set out in early April accompanied by a separate fleet for Honduras, and returned from Veracruz the following February. The Tierra Firme armada left Spain in August and returned in January. An East Indies flota, trading with the Antilles, was maintained for a few years but was never important.

The number of ships in the armadas was surprisingly large. In 1520 some 30 vessels returned from the Indies. By 1548 the total

---

[3] In 1634 a general was beheaded for cowardice.

had jumped to 73. Until 1700 between 50 and 80 galleons, *naos* and *pataches* crossed the Atlantic yearly. During the 1700s, due to larger merchantmen, the quantity fell off to around 40. The armadas were gradually discontinued in the early 1700s although convoys continued during times of war or exceptional danger from pirates.

Throughout the period of Spain's colonies, with the exception of two or three groups of years when kings were unusually aggressive or concerned, the navy and transport fleets were treated like stepchildren despite their obvious essential role as the treasure lifeline. There were seldom enough funds appropriated for ship construction, never sufficient numbers of warships and *naos*, always bickering among the top-heavy bureaucracies which grew up around the Indies trade and smothered any chance for efficiency with ineptitude. Graft and corruption were normal and accepted: an official paid the king for his job and was expected to milk it for what he could get, even at the king's expense. The result was the needless loss of countless vessels, half a billion dollars in captured treasure, and finally the loss of the Indies cornucopia.

(E) THE TREASURE CARGOES

The discovered wreck of an unsalvaged Spanish galleon or *nao* could hold anywhere from millions of dollars worth of treasure to barely a few thousand. This would depend on many factors, most important being the direction of the ship's voyage. Probably one third of the galleons lost in the Caribbean and Bahamas were on their westward crossings. These were richly laden, but unfortunately largely with perishable exports from Europe. During an average year some $12,000,000 in wines and cognacs, expensive hats and gowns, ironware, mining equipment, cheeses, paper, cloth, glassware, and even Italian silk stockings were shipped across. Whatever part of this has survived the centuries under the sea would have only archaeological value today. With these finished products came 200–500 tons of mercury yearly, carried aboard one, two or three specially prepared freighters of the New Spain armadas called *azogues*. Its sale to mine owners in Mexico was an enormously profitable Royal monopoly. How the miners used it is explained by Robert I. Nesmith: "The early method of refining by the mercury process used in Spanish-Colonial America was very efficient. Silver bars of the period (McKee's) assayed 999.0 and 999.1 thousandths pure silver."

Several mercury shipments were lost in the Caribbean and Gulf of Mexico, each worth $1,000,000 or more. This quicksilver is the only westbound general cargo that would have conserved its value to the present. But how about salvaging it from the bottom of crevices and sand pockets?

Aside from freighted cargoes the Spanish transports, both coming and going, had valuables aboard. This included the money and jewelry of officers and passengers, silver dining services for officers, and the ship's money stored in a chest bolted to the floor of the captain's cabin. Nearly any westbound wreck, depending on its size and the wealth of the passengers aboard, can be counted on for between $2000 and $25,000. Their ballast mounds lie off the Canary Islands, the Antilles, Puerto Rico, south Dominica and Cuba, Venezuela, northwest Yucatán and the southern coast of the Mexican Gulf. With the exception of Cuba any wreck found in these waters was most likely sailing *from* Spain.

Between 1500 and 1820 about 17,000 eastward crossings from the Americas brought back nearly twenty billion dollars in treasure. In the average year fifty ships transported $50,000,000 between them. If this silver, gold, and precious stones had been equally distributed each of them would have carried $1,000,000 and every unsalvaged wreck of a returning ship would be piled with loot.

But that was not the way things worked out. Treasure values on homeward-bound freighters varied from nothing to nearly $10,000,000. What a ship had aboard depended on the year, the voyage, and its function. If it were part of an armada its treasure value can be roughly estimated. If it returned after 1740, alone or in convoy, there is no way to even guess at it without documentary help. During 1753, for instance, 22 ships from the Indies delivered to Spain 21,426,101 pesos in registered treasure. To this must be added another unregistered 50 per cent to reach the actual value carried—about $45,000,000. The names, arrival dates, and cargoes unloaded from these ships have been recorded. Values varied from 15,597 pesos on the *San Joaquin* to 7,187,381 on the *navio Dragón*. Eight carried a million or more in registered gold and silver, five between 500,000 and 1,000,000 and nine less than 500,000.

The "registered treasure" was that part which was recorded on the ship's manifest and taxed by the king. Under the Bureau of Trade's laws all gold and silver had to be registered. But the officials responsible for enforcing this law were the Bureau's corrupt functionaries. They waxed fat and wealthy by allowing merchants to send back unregistered, or contraband, cargo on the armadas, thus avoiding its taxation. The bribes paid to the Bureau officials and armadas' officers who co-operated in permitting contraband shipments were high, but nevertheless not so much as the king's tax—usually a "Royal Fifth," or 20 per cent of the value—so at every opportunity shippers paid bribes and either undervalued their cargoes or simply arranged to have them omitted from manifests. An example of how this worked came to light in 1555 when 350,000 pesos in precious metal were salvaged from a small armada off Tarifa, Spain. The manifests showed only 150,000 pesos loaded. This was an extreme case. Usually only about one third of the total treasure aboard was unregistered, or contraband.

From the time of Cortés and Pizarro the king was allotted a share of the Indies booty, called the Royal Fifth. It was not always the fifth part. In the early days he demanded one fourth of the value of everything looted, mined or raised, from jewels to tobacco. About 1550 this was lessened to one fifth and in the middle 1700s was again reduced to one tenth.[4] It was assessed on the manifested values of cargo sent back and paid normally in silver pesos. In addition the king received the entire produce of many mines in the New World which he owned. This Royal treasure was given preferential treatment and after 1572 was sent whenever possible on the *Capitana* and *Almiranta* of each armada. Depending on the current total production and the degree of dishonesty of law-enforcing officials the king's share varied from $3,000,000 to over $10,000,000 per year.

A rough estimate of registered plus contraband values of nonperishable treasure aboard Spanish ships, by dates, is given below. Figures are in yearly averages, in units of $1000.

Period	Caravels	Early Naos	Armada Capitanas & Almirantas	Armada Naos & Convoy Ships Later	Later Frigates, Warships	Pataches
1501–1520	20	—	—	—	—	—
1521–1523	20–500	—	—	—	—	—
1524–1533	20–100	20–300	—	—	—	20
1534–1538	20–250	100–1,000	—	—	—	20–100
1539–1572	20–500	50–500	—	—	—	20–100
1573–1650	—	—	1,500–2,000	200–400	—	20–500
1651–1740	—	—	2,000–3,000	500–1,500	500–1,000	20–1,000
1740–1820	—	—	—	500–2,000	500–9,000	20–1,000

The wrecks of the treasure ships are distributed off:

The South American west coast south of Callao, Straits of Magellan, Portuguese and southwest Spanish coasts: Peru frigates and warships, some with huge values aboard; the South American west coast north of Callao: galleons and *naos* of the South Seas armadas, carrying from $200,000 to $6,000,000; the western Caribbean, western half of Cuba, the Bahamas channels, Florida Keys and east coast, Bermuda, Azores, Portuguese and west Spanish coasts: galleons and *naos* of the Tierra Firme armadas, with $200,000 to $3,000,000; the northern half of the Gulf of Mexio, north Cuba, the Bahamas channels, Bermuda, Azores, Portuguese and west Spain coasts: galleons and *naos* of the New Spain armadas with $200,000 to $3,000,000.

[4] For a detailed breakdown see *Les Epaves de l'or* by Robert Sténuit.

The treasure was carried either in or close to the captain's cabin at the poop if it were in gold and jewels, or silver in small quantities. Coins were packed in small wooden barrels or chests. Where heavy shipments were made—and frequently 200 tons or more went on a single *Capitana, Almiranta,* or frigate—their stacks of ingots and chests of coins were stored on the ballast at the bottom of the hold. In the case of the Vigo Bay armada of 1702 from New Spain an enormous quantity of silver—12,000,000 pesos—was sent on the two command galleons. The *Almiranta* and *Capitana* each carried over 200 tons packed in 4580 wooden chests, about 2620 pesos weighing 160 pounds to the chest. Nearly all of the armadas' *navos* carried privately owned treasure. Some was in casks and chests while smaller consignments were concealed in bales and boxes of merchandise. An example of this is the 1600 gold doubloons which Art McKee found in a barrel of pitch.

The unsalvaged wreck of any ship returning from the Indies will hold treasure, worth possibly only a few thousand dollars in the case of an early caravel from Hispaniola, or millions if the finder is lucky enough to have hit on a *Capitana, Almiranta,* or treasure frigate or *navio* from Peru. About 85 per cent of all wrecks were those of armada *naos,* and these usually had about $750,000 aboard.

(F) THE "CAT OF OUR SILVER"

Shortly after becoming King of Spain, Charles V received a bitter letter from one of his Indies viceroys commenting that "the French pirates are the masters of the Antilles seas while we control the Guadalquivir River." The writer was exaggerating, but not much. Although Spain was richer than all the rest of Europe combined, her profligate kings never seemed to grasp the importance of a strong navy—or, if they did, were too busy spending money on themselves to divert funds for ship construction and naval disbursements. The result was a fleet that was pitifully small and shabbily maintained, seldom able adequately to convoy treasure armadas or meet enemy squadrons on even terms, low in morale. This classic example of a "penny wise, pound foolish" policy cost in captured treasure ten times the price of maintaining a strong and adequate naval force.

The Barbary pirates practically ruled the Mediterranean and Straits of Gibraltar in the 1400s and early 1500s, and fired the starting gun for raids on the returning treasure ships in 1521 when they intercepted two of three caravels, taking "much gold and an emerald as big as the palm of a hand." Several more similar losses in quick succession provoked King Charles into building the coast guard squadron of galleons. While the Barbary Moors were held at bay, new attacks came from the north. In 1523 French pirates operating from Dieppe under Jean Fleury seized six caravels sent by Cortés with Aztec treasures, off Cape St. Vincent. Their cargo included "62,000 ducats of gold, 600 marks of pearls [a mark is roughly ½ lb.] and 2000 quarters of sugar." Other French corsairs joined in, taking a caravel with "100,000 gold pesos" in 1536 and four more carrying "20,000 gold and silver pesos" in 1542, all off Cape St. Vincent, at Seville's front door.

Then the English jumped in. In 1554 their raiders attacked a convoy of 5 *naos* and 9 caravels all the way from Santo Domingo to the Azores, sinking a caravel and capturing another with $30,000 in gold, pearls, and cochineal. Drake appeared off the Peruvian coast and took $2,000,000 from *Nuestra Señora de la Concepción* and other South Seas transports in 1579. The aftermath of the Invincible Armada left King Philip with enough warships from his immense construction program to suppress piracy fairly well for several years, although the Earl of Cumberland's privateers were able, in 1594, to capture the *Madre de Dios* and to sink the *Cinque Chagas*—both with huge treasure consignments—off the Azores. A few years later Barbary pirates snatched a *patache* carrying 200,000 gold ducats from the mouth of the Guadalquivir River. This led to orders for treasure to be transferred onto warships at the Azores and landed at Lisbon. Undaunted, the pirates moved north and captured several ships off Lisbon.

King Philip was stung into taking counteraction. Every year from 1615 to 1621 he sent an anti-pirate fleet to Africa to "sweep up" the Moors. In 1630 General Tomás de Larraspuru topped off this house-cleaning by successfully attacking the pirates at their bases in Salé and Mámora. From then on the Barbary bandits pretty well kept their place.

Spain built up a strong navy during the Thirty Years' War, as did France, England, and Holland. This period from 1618 to 1648 was a time of continual attack and counterattack at sea and in the colonies. A Dutch squadron under Admiral van Noort raided Peru and the Philippines in 1600. He was followed by other hostile fleets, causing Spain to maintain a strong Far East naval force throughout the seventeenth century. In the Caribbean a New Spain galleon carrying 300,000 gold ducats was captured in 1609. Four *naos* of Luis de Almeida's armada were taken in 1629. Two Tierra Firme ships carrying 2,000,000 pesos were seized in 1656 and two more sunk off Cádiz. The Dutch attacked Portuguese and Spanish colonies in Brazil and established a naval base at Baía. From here their admiral, Piet Heyn, captured a Portuguese armada loaded with sugar and tobacco in 1627 in Todos Santos Bay and raided Arrecife and Santa Marta. The next year he captured or destroyed most of the Tierra Firme armada in Matanzas Bay, Cuba. Other Dutch forces ambushed a plate fleet off Cádiz in 1640 and the following year entered Lake Maracaibo, seizing a huge loot from Gibraltar. So successful were the voracious Dutch that they received a backward compliment from the illustrious Spanish poet Lope de Vega:

> *The Dutch pirate,*
> *Cat of our silver,*
> *Who infests the seas* . . .

The loss of the Antilles to English, French, Dutch, and pirate forces during 1635–55 was a blow to the armadas, which passed through this island chain on their way to the Caribbean. To avoid ambush there the westward route was changed each year, following secret instructions opened at sea. Other sealed orders gave the generals a rendezvous point with the Spanish coast guard armada off the Azores on their return voyages. Often generals sent ahead false information of their routes to be captured by and mislead the enemy.

During the reign of Charles II, from 1665 to 1700, Spain was more or less at peace with her European neighbors. This was the heyday of the Caribbean buccaneers, however, and losses to pirates ran high. A Spanish historian estimated that during these 35 years the "filibusters" captured 60,000,000 pesos in treasure. In 1673 pirates seized several *naos* off Hispaniola. Bartholomew Sharp and his band crossed the Isthmus on foot in 1680 and stole the galleon *Santísima Trinidad* from Panama harbor. Using this as his pirate ship he seized the *Rosario* and several other prizes. François "the Fierce" L'Olonnois, Mansvelt, Lorenzo, Corneli, and a host of others took two dozen *naos* and *pataches* in the Caribbean. Between 1668 and 1671 Henry Morgan attacked Cuba, sacked and demolished Gibraltar on Lake Maracaibo, seized New Providence Island and finally marched across the Isthmus and plundered Panama. Mérida—and even Veracruz—were raided in 1683 and rich loot taken. Striking back weakly with newly designed piroques, Spanish forces killed or captured several hundred pirates off the Isle of Pines, Cuba, in 1684 and destroyed a Pacific pirate fleet off Panama the next year.

French, English, and Dutch attacks on Cartagena, Vigo, and San Augustine ushered in the next century. Cartagena surrendered to French naval forces after a long bombardment and yielded 6,000,000 pesos in loot. Admiral Sir George Rooke's assault in 1702 on the New Spain armada holed up in Vigo Bay netted England and Holland $50,000,000 in silver and other Mexican produce. The Tierra Firme *Capitana* and an *urca* were captured by a British squadron, and another two ships sunk off Cartagena in 1708 with 15,000,000 pesos in treasure lost to Spain. Two ships were seized off Paita, Peru, with 400,000 aboard in 1720 and the *Príncipe Federico* at Veracruz with 304,000 pesos in 1726.

From 1728 to 1744 British vessels captured 850 Spanish ships of all classes and well over $20,000,000 in treasure. During the same period the Dutch took $1,500,000. The Peru treasure frigate *Hermiona*, her captain unaware that Spain and England were at war, was taken by surprise in 1762 with 2,600,000 pesos in gold and silver and $5,000,000 in other cargo. The same year other British forces captured Havana and a $6,000,000 booty, and a year later drove the Spanish from Florida.

The close of the eighteenth century, although Spain's naval power was at an all-time peak, was the beginning of the end. A French corsair captured the galleon *Santiago*, carrying 1,000,000 gold pesos from Callao, off west Spain in 1793. Another Peru treasure shipment of $5,000,000 aboard four frigates was sunk or captured off Cádiz in 1804. The next year brought Lord Nelson's victory at Trafalgar, from which the Spanish Navy never recovered. The loss of the American colonies, and the end of the fantastic treasure flow from the Indies, followed soon afterward.

CHAPTER 2

Research, Search, and Salvage

Finds of sunken treasure are made either by accident or as the result of a systematic search following clues tracked down in research. In the former case the lucky finder—usually with no idea of becoming a treasure hunter—is dumfounded with surprise at what he has stumbled upon. He is the spear fisherman or submarine sightseer who suddenly finds himself looking down on a ballast pile cluttered with ship's cargo and cannons. He is also the sponge diver, or the abalone gatherer, or the sunken outboard motor searcher with other thoughts in mind when he hits pay dirt.

The real treasure diver begins with information that a ship was lost in a certain area, and that it held silver or gold in its cargo. From first indications, it seems possible that the treasure can be recovered. He sets about trying to do so. Before him lies a three-stage task: first, to obtain and evaluate all possible *true* information about the cargo and the ship's location; second, to find the wreck; finally, to salvage its precious cargo. The following pages, while by no means a complete treatment of the three subjects, provide a guide to the prospective treasure hunter.

RESEARCH (see Index: Research Methods)

The first rule in this category is: don't take as the gospel everything that appears in books, magazines, and particularly "treasure trove" maps. Do your own research. Get information from firsthand sources whenever possible. Starting with data given in this book (which covers practically every known important sunken treasure), or from whatever other source you have, make a thorough study of the wreck in which you are interested, tackling the research from every possible angle. Here are a few suggestions:

(1) Insurance company records: If the loss is comparatively modern and the underwriters can be located chances are good that they will have in their files accurate descriptions and values of the treasure cargo. Lloyd's of London has been interested—either directly or through reinsurance—in a high percentage of maritime losses since it was founded in 1688. Unfortunately its records were destroyed during a fire in 1838 and the syndicate's information would date only from then. Lloyd's has no list of "treasure ships," and is best approached for data through the good offices of one of its 300 brokers.

(2) Ships' manifests: If the loss is comparatively recent, it is possible that a copy of the ship's manifest can be found in the files of the company or its agent at the port where the treasure was put aboard.

(3) Ships' log books: These can be useful in determining the position of the sinking. Although the log of the lost ship is rarely salvaged—and when it is, contains little of value except the last recorded position and course—quite often other vessels were in the vicinity at the time of the disaster and comments on position, weather, time, etc., in their logs are useful. If the treasure ship was sunk in a naval engagement by all means check the logs of all the participants.

(4) Official reports: Detailed descriptions are often contained in officers' reports of battles. Most countries' naval archives hold volumes of original letters written by officers after naval engagements. These—if pertinent ones can be found—are extremely valuable.

(5) Letters by, and reports of interviews with, survivors: Usually these are hard to track down and may be inaccurate, but a thorough research should include an attempt to locate them. Survivors (if still living), or their families or descendants, should be interviewed if possible.

(6) Contemporary newspapers, magazines, pamphlets: Disasters at sea have been front-page news since the first days of reporting. Every wreck of any importance is described in print, and bound volumes of old newspapers of most nations are relatively easy to locate and examine. Comments on a wreck are likely to be spread over several weeks—or months—as information comes in. First reports are sometimes wildly distorted; later ones usually fairly accurate. If the disaster is especially sensational or gory, pamphlets sometimes appeared a few months later (frequent in cases of Portuguese and English wrecks). These are not likely to be useful except for general information.

(7) Court-martial records: It was routine procedure in the British Navy for courts-martial to be held on captains who lost their ships. Many of these records—containing detailed and complete data—are stored in the Public Records Office in London. Court-martial records in other nations' navies are usually preserved and available. If the treasure ship was a naval vessel, one of the first points of attack should be to check for a court-martial and read through the notes.

(8) State papers: Where more than one nation was interested in a cargo loss there was frequently an exchange of letters commenting on it. These are usually stored in the archives of government museums and libraries, classified under "Foreign Affairs" or such, and can be counted upon for reliable information as to cargo values, etc.

(9) Museums, libraries: The following have data on treasure wrecks: SPAIN: Archivo General de Indias (see below); Museo Naval, Madrid; Archivos General, Simancas; Museo Marítimo, Barcelona; PORTUGAL: Arquivo Nacional, Museu de Marinha, Lisbon; FRANCE: Musée de la Marine, Bibliothèque Nationale, Service Historique de la Marine, Paris; HOLLAND: Netherlands Royal Archives, The Hague; Nederlandisch

Historisch Scheepvart, Amsterdam; ENGLAND: The British Museum (Reading Room, etc.), The Public Records Office, The Admiralty, London; The National Maritime Museum, Greenwich; AUSTRALIA: The Western Australian Museum, Perth; CEYLON: The Colombo Museum; MEXICO: Archivos Generales de la Nación, the C.E.D.A.M. Museum; JAMAICA: Institute of Jamaica, Kingston.

(10) Interviews with local fishermen: Wrecks are the homes of congers and other sedentary fish, and coastal fishermen have a surprisingly complete knowledge of where they lie. Learning of wrecks from fishermen is usually an exasperating and lengthy phase of research, and may lead to nothing, but should not be overlooked.

(11) Reports of earlier salvage attempts: If these can be found they can supply a wealth of data. Not a few "treasure ships" were completely salvaged decades and centuries ago. By studying the accounts of the salvors, the modern treasure hunter might be spared useless expense and disappointment when he finds his ship empty.

(12) Serious maritime histories: The Bibliography of this book contains the names and authors of the principal maritime histories of nations whose ships carried treasure cargoes. These are excellent reference sources and nearly always accurate.

(13) Other books: In cases of important losses or where well-known personages were involved detailed studies can sometimes be found in contemporary books. Dozens of volumes have been published on the Invincible Armada. Many biographies of admirals and sea captains are in print (for this reason I have included the names of officers wherever possible in the treasure chapters).

(14) The Archives of the Indies at Seville: correctly entitled Archivo General de Indias, this massive storehouse of original documents dealing with the Spanish colonies was set up in 1784 when the king ordered the transfer of literally countless bundles of yellowed papers, wrapped in bundles called *legajos*, from the Simancas Archives to Seville in the old Bureau of Trade building. Although most of the Simancas *legajos* were moved, some were left behind at the former repository. During his tremendous researches throughout Spain, Bob Marx discovered nearly a thousand bundles still at Simancas, many with erroneous titles. Commenting on the Archivo General de Indias, Seville, in his book *Shipwrecks in Florida Waters*, Marx observes that "If a team of 100 researchers spent their whole lives searching through the more than 250,000 large *legajos* in the Archives of the Indies, I doubt that they could locate all the important documents . . . The majority of the *legajos* are not catalogued, and about twenty percent of those shipped from Simancas in 1784 have never been opened."

Bob Marx, Kip Wagner (see Real Eight section in chapter 12) and others have obtained valuable information from the Archives at Seville, but any search project there is a major undertaking. Although any desired information is probably penned in archaic Spanish somewhere in those millions of pages, even the best professional researchers could spend years and find nothing. There are a number of good researchers, but Marx advises that he knows of only one who corresponds in English, and she charges a high fee. The present director is Señorita Rosaria Parra, who replaced Dr. de la Peña recently. A personal visit to Seville would probably be the surest way to have any serious research program started there.

SEARCH (see Index: Search Methods)

The combination of developments in the electronic field, the "Man-under-Sea" programs and the Deep Submergence Vehicles technology has so improved undersea search capability that probably any existing wreck could be found today with sufficient resources. As far back as 1963, the wreckage of U.S.S. *Thresher* was located at a depth of 8400 feet despite the facts that the search area was a full ten square miles and the shattered remains of the sub were widely scattered over a rough ocean bed, which precluded the possibility of obtaining a silhouette of the hull with superaccurate depth-recording devices.[1] This, of course, is an extreme example where the full resources of the U. S. Navy were mobilized. The suggested search methods that follow are more in line with modestly financed civilian groups.

(1) Visual search: This is efficient and inexpensive where (a) the water is reasonably clear, (b) the depth is not excessive, and (c) the object of the search is not completely buried under the sea bed or coral overgrowth. Many recent treasure finds have been made visually (*Le Chameau*, the Lucayan silver, the Great Basses wreck, most of the Florida ballast mounds, etc.). A search pattern can be laid out with either anchored buoys or a grid on the sea bed (chains, weighted ropes) and each sector examined. In shallow clear water the search can be carried out from the surface through a viewing plate (water glass, face mask, glass-bottomed boat). In deeper water where the search area is small, it can be systematically covered by one diver working outward from a center point such as an anchor or rod driven into the ocean floor. A line is attached to this "hub" with knots tied on it at distances predetermined by the visibility (i.e., if visibility is 10 feet, the knots could be about 18 feet apart). The diver swims in concentric circles around the hub, moving outward one knot after each circle has been completed. Another straight line running out from the hub and firmly anchored can be used to alert the searcher that he has completed a circle whenever he passes it.

Where a large area is to be searched, and many divers are on hand,

[1] See June 1964 *National Geographic Magazine.*

the "swim line" or "running jackstay" method is recommended. There are several variations, depending on the number of boats and equipment. In essence, the swim line consists of a number of divers in a more or less straight line moving forward together side by side in a direction perpendicular to the direction of the search sweep. To control the relative position of each diver, a light nylon line, along which the searchers are "strung" at fixed intervals, is kept straight and taut. The distance separating each diver depends on the visibility, but each participant must be within sight of the men on either side of him. This helps keep the line straight and permits good visual coverage of the zone allocated to each searcher. If ten divers are available and the visibility is 20 feet, the men are spaced about 18 feet apart and the total length of the line is 160–165 feet, permitting a track of bottom about 190 feet wide to be swept as the line moves forward. Directional control is usually kept by the man at the extreme right end who takes his bearings from a wrist compass, or better, from a weighted base line, along which he swims, which has been laid down straight across the bottom in a direction parallel to that of the sweep. This base line can be marked with surface buoys for accurate charting of each path as it is searched. If a base line is not used, the two end divers can pull lines to light surface buoys permitting observers on top to chart the area of each sweep. At the start of each sweep, two boats are usually used to position and unreel the swim line. Fixed buoys or very accurate shore bearings are necessary to mark the boundaries of each day's coverage.

(2) Powered visual search: A great variety of underwater "scooters" are available, offering obvious advantages to those who can afford them and have facilities to recharge and maintain them. A scooter can triple a diver's search efficiency.

(3) Submarine metal detectors: Compact, hand-operated metal detectors are available from several manufacturers. The best-known "work horse" model is probably the Bludworth UML-20, which has been used with good results in the location of too many treasures to list here. It offers the advantage of showing a visual signal on a meter, rather than an audible signal through earphones which can be confused with other sounds. A metal detector is basically a simple electronic instrument that uses a radio frequency signal. There are two common types: the transmitter-receiver, or "TR," and the beat frequency, or "BF." The former transmits a radio signal at a given frequency and amplitude through an antenna which is called the "search coil." This is picked up by the receiver element as a steady tone, or hum. The presence of any conductor such as metal in the radio frequency field of the transmitter will affect the feedback and is reproduced either through earphones or on a meter. The "BF" type has two oscillators

operating on the same frequency. One of these is variable and its inductance coil is known as the search coil. When the two oscillators operate at the same frequency there is no difference in the two feedbacks, or signal. The presence of a conductor in the field affects the variable search coil feedback, causing a hum or beat because of the two different frequencies, which is again reproduced through earphones or on a meter. This second type is slightly harder to adjust, but can be more effective. A complete explanation of how metal detectors work is given on pages 55–61 of the book *Treasure . . . How and Where to Find It* by Nesmith and Potter.

A finely "tuned" metal detector working under good conditions will locate a piece of conductive metal (gold, silver, copper) with a square surface area of half a foot at distances up to 5 feet. Salt water diminishes efficiency, but despite this metal detectors are invaluable for detecting metallic parts of wrecks (even some forms of ballast stones) buried under sand, mud, or coral. A single coin can be found at a depth of 6–12 inches.

(4) Finding oil slicks: Oil-burning ships can be located in deep water months after their sinking by oil seepage from their fuel tanks. Aerial search is recommended. Although oil slicks from the *Andrea Doria* were seen over a wide area of ocean, it was not until Ken Mac-Leish flew over the site that he was able to distinguish a huge spiral oil slick. Tracking it to the center, he was able to buoy the ship's near-exact position.

(5) The sweep: Where large tracks of *flat* bottom are to be covered for a wreck, the time-honored method has been to trawl a heavy cable, or chain, between two ships as much as half a mile apart. If wreckage is believed to be in dispersed, small pieces, a rope with grapples tied to it at intervals is effective.

(6) Submarine television: In relatively clear water, underwater TV with artificial illumination can be effective to great depths. Wreckage from an English Comet jet plane was located in this way off Italy in the 1950s, and since then much more sophisticated units have been developed. High cost and difficulty of maintenance limit the use of this excellent tool.

(7) Echo sounders: Underwater sonic probing has developed into a very complex and sophisticated field in which a wide variety of applications has been found ranging from anti-submarine warfare devices to sub-bottom profiling for oil prospecting. In the location of wrecks two basic types of echo sounders are used. This section will consider the common depth recorder. Like all instruments of this type, it sends out sound waves and records their echoes when they bounce back from the bottom or some other object (like a school of fish). As the speed of sound through water is, for such purposes, constant,

the time interval between transmission and receipt of each sound impulse can be readily converted into the number of feet which it traveled going out and returning, and electronically recorded on a moving graph paper at the rate of several "ticks" per second, forming a silhouette line giving the depth and contour of the sea bed over which the boat is passing. An experienced operator can tell a lot about the type of bottom from the form of this line. A good depth recorder mounted on a stable boat platform in calm sea is accurate to within 1–2 feet. For wreck location purposes, MacDowell Associates, Inc., is developing a high resolution sonar with a resolution of under 2 inches at 1000-foot depths.

Ideal conditions for searching with depth recorders would be over a flat sea floor, where an intact ship's hull is outlined like a church steeple. Even on a rough bottom, a fairly intact hull can easily be distinguished. A ballast mound can often be spotted on a flat bottom as a higher table formation, but scattered wreckage is nearly indistinguishable even on a flat sea bed.

(8) Seismic sub-bottom profiling equipment: The impetus of the search for oil has caused the development of superpowerful echo sounders capable of penetrating 100 feet or more of soft ocean bottom and outlining harder formations like salt domes buried there. Dr. Harold E. Edgerton of MIT pioneered the production of these "thumper" or "mud-pinger" devices. Units made by his E.G.&G. International have produced excellent results in certain applications. Although a recent attempt by Burt Webber, Jr., to locate buried ballast mounds with this equipment was frustrated by the presence of too many other hard natural objects like buried coral, sub-bottom profiling offers definite promise.

(9) Aerial search: Many wrecks and ballast mounds have been spotted from the air. Kip Wagner, Captain Don Gurgiolo of Islamorada, and others have used low-flying planes off Florida; Teddy Tucker tried a balloon towed behind a boat off Bermuda and spotted several wrecks from altitudes of about 200 feet. Even helicopters have been tried—since small planes are usually too fast—but their downward air current churned up the water surface underneath, making them unsuitable, as a fairly calm surface is necessary. In aerial searching, unnatural formations on the sea bottom—particularly straight lines—are signs of wrecks.

(10) Place names: One of the best, and least appreciated, clues to nearby wrecks are names and nicknames given to landmarks such as points of land, reefs, rocks, etc. Chameau Rock put Alex Storm on the track of *Le Chameau;* Spanish names along the Irish coast led Robert Sténuit to the *Girona;* Looe Reef marks the site of this wreck; H.M.S. *Thetis* gave her name to Thetis Cove.

(11) The magnetometer: The original 1960 issue of the *Guide* described this electronic search instrument as "the answer to the treasure

hunter's dream." This statement has been echoed countless times since by the growing number of underwater searchers who have located sunken iron surrounding treasure lodes with this "magic wand." Magnetometers of one type or another have been instrumental in making possible probably one half of all the important recoveries during the past decade accounting for no less than 75 per cent of the value of salvaged treasure.

Originally developed as the MAD (Magnetic Anomaly Detector) during World War II in anti-submarine warfare, the standard prototype models were large and extremely complicated, requiring constant expert attention by specialists. Some war surplus U. S. Navy models such as the AN/ASQ-3 are still available at prices of $1000 or less. Their sensing heads—or probes—are about 4 feet long and must be moved above the surface of the water, preferably from blimps. For practical purposes these are obsolete today.

During the Vigo Bay treasure hunt, the author, on advice from Ed Link (who pioneered the new application of the U. S. Navy instrument in his search for the *Santa María*), tracked down and successfully used a battery-powered portable model manufactured by the Institute Dr. Fürster, Reutlingen, West Germany. It was light enough to be carried in a suitcase, rugged, and detected iron at considerable distances. It was divided into two components: a metal box the size of a table radio which contained the circuits and tubes, controls and meter; and the submarine "probe"—a yard-long aluminum cylinder, only 3 inches in diameter, containing two "magnetism-feeler" coils and designed to withstand the pressure at great depth. Both elements were joined by a long submarine cable. The box was kept on board; the "probe" lowered to where it hovered a few yards over the ocean bottom. (We later rigged it so that it could be trawled from our boat over even very jagged rock bottom.) When the "probe" passed within 23 feet of an old iron cannon this was clearly shown on the meter. It signaled the proximity of a 50-ton iron wreck from nearly 100 feet away. It even marked the ticking of a watch nearby.

The magnetometer works because any piece of magnetizable metal causes deviations in the uniform lines of the earth's magnetic flux nearby. The larger the piece of metal, and the longer it has remained in its position, the more widespread is the effect of this distortion. Before being put to use the Fürster magnetometer is adjusted to zero for the earth's normal magnetic field in the area where it is to be used. Then, when its "probe" passes through a zone where magnetic lines of force are distorted by nearby iron, this is plainly indicated by characteristic movements of the meter needle. A compass swings around when brought near iron. The magnetometer can be roughly compared to a supersensitive compass.

During the past fourteen years the magnetometer concept has been so improved that today's instruments, compared with ours, would correspond to the Boeing 747 versus the DC-3. Throughout the treasure chapters of this book references are made to specific types of magnetometers and how they are used (see Index: Magnetometers). There are proton mags, flux gate mags, rubidium and cesium mags, and even hydrogen proton precession mags. All are excellent, and range in price from a few hundred dollars to $25,000 or more. No attempt will be made here to define the different types—to which improvements are continually being added—since a comprehensive explanation would fill a highly technical book. The following suggestions may be of service to wreck searchers interested in purchasing, or renting the use of, a magnetometer.

MacDowell Associates, Inc. (a subsidiary of the Real Eight Company, Inc.), 900 Pine Tree Drive, Indian Harbor Beach, Florida 32935, has been developing a range of portable magnetometers specifically tailored to wreck location, for use both from the surface and submerged. Their "Snooper" model, tested to 200-foot depth, is reliable and manageable by the average SCUBA diver. Aside from this, MacDowell has—or can design and produce—models to nearly any specification. President James E. MacDowell and his staff have both scientific know-how and practical experience.

AZA Scientific, Inc., 105 South Ann Arbor Street, Saline, Michigan, offers the "Discoverer" series of magnetometers, which are simple to operate but nevertheless effective for wreck search, and depth-tested to 200 feet.

Together with the Fürster instrument, both of these models are priced for the average SCUBA diver's pocketbook.

The two companies most closely identified with the more sophisticated types of magnetometers are Varian Associates and Mel Fisher's Ocean Search, Inc. (a subsidiary of Treasure Salvors, Inc.). Their instruments are generally more complicated and often used with recording devices which permit the preparation of a map covering the search area on which the location of each magnetic reading, and its intensity, is plotted to within a few yards. Thus a completely buried wreck, invisible to the diver's eye, can be outlined through the positions of its dispersed cannons, anchors and other iron (or steel) artifacts (see map).

A reference to the Index under Varian Associates will give the reader examples in this book where the various instruments manufactured by this company have been successfully employed—notably in the Padre Island wrecks and the salvage of Captain Cook's cannons off Australia.

The "sea mag," marketed by Ocean Search, Inc., 3544 Ocean Drive, Vero Beach, Florida 32960, has contributed directly to the salvage of something like $4,000,000 in treasure by locating and outlining the forms of probably a hundred old wrecks off Florida, the Bahamas, Bermuda, and other sites. This proton magnetometer, developed by Fay Field, can be purchased for $14,500 or leased for $1000 per month on a lease-purchase basis. It can be used on a surface tow, from a helicopter, from small submarines, or on a deep tow at great depths. The sea mag played a major role in the treasure recoveries by Treasure Salvors and Real Eight off Florida. Its use here, and the results, are described by Carl J. Clausen in a monograph entitled "The Proton Magnetometer: Its Use in Plotting the Distribution of the Ferrous Components of a Shipwreck Site as an Aid to Archaeological Interpretation."[2]

The application of the magnetometer is not new in the search of sunken ships by persons interested in the recovery of valuables (Potter 1960: 52–54), or by those with a genuine but untrained interest in the recovery of historical objects from underseas wrecks (Link 1959:71–75). Until recently, however, utilization of this instrument, a device for measuring total magnetic field intensity in a given area, has been more or less limited to attempts simply to locate wrecked vessels. There apparently have been no successful attempts to further utilize the instrument in plotting the distribution of the ferrous elements of an individual wreck as an interpretive aid. This restricted usage has arisen not because of any lack of ingenuity or experimentation on the part of the salvagers, who readily developed quite adequate systems for searching large areas (Harnett 1962), but primarily because of certain limiting factors in most currently available units, designed principally for various geophysical applications where read-out frequency is less critical, have response rates ranging from once every two seconds to about twice a second. This rate is not sufficiently rapid to be used in the efficiency-dictated survey method; i.e., manually navigating a motor vessel trailing the sensing element through a predetermined pattern, to produce useful measurements.

The survey was carried out from a small fiberglass inboard-outbard vessel which was equipped with an engine revolution counter and a compensated marine compass, and was stocked with a quantity of buoys made with empty bleach bottles for floats and concrete blocks for anchors. An accurate stop watch was carried.

The subject wreck lies in shallow water close to shore some 4,200 yards south of the Sebastian Inlet on the Florida East Coast below Cape Kennedy. Archeological and documentary evidence supports this site as the location of the wreck of the flagship or *Capitana* of General Don Juan de Ubilla, commander of the *Flota* portion of the Spanish fleet wrecked in this area in 1715 (Fernandez Duro 1900: Vol. 6, 121–27). Ashore, opposite the wreck on a narrow island, is the site BR-139, the 1715–16 camp of the survivors and salvagers of the fleet (Smith 1956:88–94).

The salvagers had worked at this site for several seasons and made significant recoveries; but due to the strong surge, limited visibility, shifting sands and scattered condition to the wreckage, there was little factual knowledge concerning the extent or orientation of the wreck.

The survey required the systematic exposure of the wreck site to the magnetometer. This was accomplished by towing the sensing element of the instrument behind the survey vessel at a constant speed back and forth

[2] *The Florida Anthropologist*, Volume XIX, Nos. 2–3.

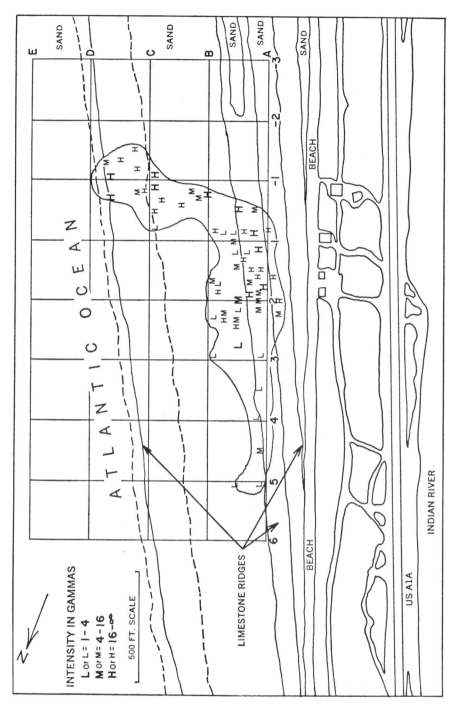

Ferrous distribution of the shipwreck as determined by the magnetic survey. (*Courtesy of Carl J. Clausen*)

over the wreck site and surrounding area on a series of equidistant parallel courses. The spacing of the courses was dictated by the desired overlap in readings, the depth of the water and the sensitivity of the instrument. Runs too closely spaced were inefficient, as the intense magnetic disturbances or anomalies created by massive iron objects such as cannons or anchors cancelled out the smaller anomalies, while wide spacing naturally resulted in incomplete data. For the purpose of this survey, a spacing was chosen which insured, it was felt, that large anomalies would appear only on adjacent courses. This compromise appeared to assure that a representative sample of the smaller ferrous components would be included in the survey. To visually guide the helmsman in the surveying process, a grid system of buoys was installed over the area. The grid, oriented on a base buoy surveyed in from ashore, was laid in the following manner: The X and Y axes were established by the survey vessel closely passing the base buoy while proceeding at a set speed (tachometer) on a magnetic heading and setting a predetermined number of buoys at timed intervals (stopwatch). This process was repeated on a course at 90 degrees to the first. The balance of the grid was set using the same technique; timed runs parallel to the first axis at intervals of the second.

Data on magnetic distortions encountered by the instrument in surveying the area were permanently recorded on a continually moving graph. The operator of the magnetometer noted on the moving tape the coordinates and direction of the particular course through the grid and the point at which the sensing element entered and left the pattern and crossed grid lines perpendicular to the direction of travel. In this manner a record was produced of the anomalies, their intensity and location, from which it was a simple matter to construct a magnetic chart for the area in which the major ferrous components of the wrecked ship, i.e., the cannons, anchors, main structural fastenings and concentrations of smaller fittings and ship's gear were located . . .

By associating to scale the data from the magnetic survey with a map drawn from both black and white and color aerial photos of the underwater terrain and features ashore, a graphic portrayal of the ferrous element of this wreck's distribution in relationship to its physical surroundings emerges. (See accompanying figure.)

AN ANALYSIS

An examination of the results of the survey as plotted clearly indicates that the remains of the ferrous components of the vessel, its gear and cargo, lie dispersed in a crescent-shaped area of more than eight acres. This scattering which appears in other 1715 wrecks (Clausen 1965:1–5, 27), can be attributed to the circumstances of the loss of the fleet. The testimony of the survivors of the disaster relates that most of the vessels were driven aground during the height of a severe hurricane during the night of Wednesday, July 31, and the early morning hours of August 1, 1715. Further statements place the wind which drove them ashore as coming from "just north of the east" with an intensity which caused the sea at first light to appear as "shooting arrows" to those huddled ashore (Menendez, Captain Sebastian and Barriga, Captain Don Fernando Ignazio. Testimony in A.G.I. 58–1–30).

Under the above conditions, most of the vessels probably suffered massive structural damage on or shortly following contact with the submerged ribbons of lime and coquina rock paralleling the coast. The intense action of the sea apparently dashed the vessels to pieces, scattering wreckage over acres of offshore bottoms.

The documents previously cited also contain statements which seem to indicate that the *Capitana*, probably a frigate 40–50 guns, may have sectioned horizontally, possibly along the turn of the bilge, upon impact with the offshore rocks and that the superstructure broke up closer to shore.

The nature of the demise of the *Capitana* alluded to in these documents may account for the general "crescent shape" of the wreck's distribution. With the east winds working seas against the coast, which in this area trends generally northwest, a powerful northward current would be generated along the shore. The disintegrating superstructure lightened by the loss of the ballast and possibly most of the heavy, registered cargo of silver, would be forced to the west by the action of the seas and wind; and, as it approached the shore, would come increasingly under the effect of the powerful northward current paralleling the beach. Under the resultant of these two forces, the wreck would be expected to follow a more or less elliptical path as it broke up.

Evidence amassed from different areas of the wreck during several seasons of salvage supports the above explanation . . .

The systematic survey of an underwater historical period shipwreck site using an advanced proton-type magnetometer has permitted us to plot the distribution of the major ferrous components of the wrecked vessel *in situ.*

SALVAGE (see Index: Salvage Methods)

This is the pay-off phase of a treasure hunt for the lucky few who reach it. The technology of salvage is very complicated, the subject of many entire volumes, and can be only lightly touched upon here. For more detailed information such books as Davis' *Deep Diving* can be studied.

Once the submerged treasure has been located, its condition will pretty well decide the salvage method most suitable for its recovery. These range from the prosaic suspended bucket to the bizarre. Nearly all are discussed in connection with accomplished salvages in the treasure chapters of this book (see Index under Salvage Accomplishments). A few lend themselves particularly well to the treasure diver working on wrecks as deep as 140 feet:

(1) The air lift: Where mud, sand, or stones are to be cleared away —or small objects raised to the surface—this is the best instrument to use. An air lift (or *suceuse* in French) is simple and inexpensive to build, easy to use, nearly impossible to damage, and very effective at depths over 15 feet (its force increases with depth). It is essentially a tube made of iron pipe, reinforced rubber hose, etc., with one end held on the bottom over the stuff to be lifted and the other end protruding above water overhead where the discharge can be poured

onto a filter if desired. It is powered by compressed air, sent down
to its lower end in a plastic or rubber hose, and injected into the
tube there. The air bubbles rise within the tube and make an emulsion
with the water. This mixture of water and air is of a lower specific
gravity than pure water outside, causing an inrush of water into the
lower end as nature tries to neutralize the pressure difference. This
sucking force can tear a glove from a diver's hand. (For a complete
account of the air lift, how it works and practical hints, see the author's
book *The Treasure Divers of Vigo Bay*.)

The air compressor should be selected depending on the depth and
diameter of the tube. Its pressure must be at least two atmospheres
more than that at the bottom, and in general the greater the volume
of air the stronger the suction. At depths of 40 feet a 6-inch-diameter
tube fed 1000 liters of air per minute will suck up small cannon balls.
During the salvage of cargo from the *Diamond Knot* in 1947 8-inch
air lifts each raised about 1000 gallons of water per minute—together
with some 800 tins of salmon. Link, McKee, Cousteau, and a host of
other modern salvors use the air lift as a basic tool. A convenient
table correlating the diameter, working depth, air volume and air
pressure for air lift construction is given on page 72 of Mendel Peterson's *History Under the Sea*.

(2) The short air lift: Where powerful suction and/or a surface
screen are not desired, the top of the air lift need not protrude to
the surface. A vertical distance of 6–10 feet between the intake and
the discharge points will cause enough pressure difference gently to
clear off overburden. When using the short version, a current to carry
off the discharge is desirable to keep it from coming down on the
diver.

(3) The injection dredge, or gold dredge: Because of its relative
simplicity of operation and power, this type of suction excavator has
found wide acceptance. It can be built to handle differing volumes
of overburden and sizes of stones. An average injection dredge has a
chamber, which is a tube, from 3 to 6 feet long with a series of
riffles arranged in a riffle box at its back end where heavy material
like gold is caught while lighter sand and mud is swept on out the
open back. Two handles are fixed on top of this tube. A strong head
of water is injected into the front end of the chamber, rushing through
it and creating a suction that draws in material from the intake opening.
This is the front end of the tube, which is turned downward at an
angle of about 70° and may be 2 feet long. The intake can measure
from an inch to a foot in diameter. In theory, each doubling of diameter
means the processing of four times the volume of overburden. Water
is injected in a stream parallel to the body of the chamber through

a hose connected to a pump and motor overhead. This can be a gasoline motor/pump combination on a raft. A 7½ hp motor is adequate for a dredge with a 6-inch intake.

(4) Lifts: There are many types, ranging from large steel pontoons to simple Port-A-Lifts found in dive shops. They are sunk either full of water or collapsed, and filled with air from hoses or air tanks after being secured to the object to be raised. A simple lift of this type can be made with old 55-gallon drums. Five drums will raise about a ton.

(5) Tide lifts: Here the rise and fall of tidal water is used, with the object to be lifted secured tightly by strong cables to an overhead float (boat, barge, pontoon) at low tide. As the rising tide raises the float, the object is lifted off the sea floor. At high tide the float is moved into shallower water until the object grounds. At the next low tide the process is repeated.

(6) The "blower" or "blaster": This recent invention has revolutionized excavation techniques to a depth of 25–50 feet. It was invented by Mel Fisher's dynamic Treasure Salvors in 1964 (see Real Eight chapter), ironically not as an excavating tool, but simply as an attempt to send down a column of clear water to divers working in poor visibility. The results were beyond anyone's wildest expectations. In his "A New Underwater Excavating System for the Archaeologist,"[3] Carl J. Clausen comments:

> The first unit was an ugly, square, boxlike affair constructed of sheet metal, which captured the thrust of the vessel's single propeller and directed it against the bottom. In action, the powerful column of water forced the sediment into suspension and simply blew it away . . . The versatility of the blower for excavation purposes is astounding . . . One medium-sized unit can move an estimated 100 to 200 cubic feet of sediment per minute . . . The same unit, running at greatly reduced speed . . . can gently remove the sand from around artifacts in an area 10 feet in diameter, exposing them as carefully as a diver fanning with his hand.

Mel Fisher's "mailbox" was the first stage. This was soon followed by a second-generation blower consisting basically of a propeller in a cylinder, connected to a motor on deck via a differential, and firmly suspended underwater from the ship. Attempts made to extend the working depth by lengthening the cylinder with extensions have not been very successful, and Clausen predicts that the third-generation blower will be a nearly independent unit that can operate near the sea bed, deep under the surface, using a 60-inch propeller.

(7) Flotation through injection of buoyant plastic substance into the wreck: One of the newest and most technically advanced contribu-

[3] From *The Conference on Historic Site Archaeology Papers*, 1967, Volume 2, Part 1, Stanley South, ed., Sept. 1968.

tions to salvage was made by Olin Mathieson. In this process chemical
ingredients are pumped under pressure into a sunken ship, where they
combine *inside the hull* in a chemical reaction which produces buoyant
urethane foam. This spreads through the passageways and cabins, then
solidifies, displacing thirty times its weight in water! While doing this,
the foam also seals openings in the hull. This method is being used
by the Murphy Pacific Marine Salvage Company and others. Successful
salvages include a 2400-ton ship from 60-foot depth off Vietnam.

There are countless other salvage devices, ranging from simple hand
hoists to complicated and expensive devices like the grab on the
bottom of the bathyscaphe *Trieste* which picked up a piece of the
Thresher's wreckage 8400 feet deep. Possibly the most efficient was
used by Captain Cousteau's divers to recover amphorae. They simply
filled them with air and let them float to the surface to be collected.

PRESERVATION OF ARTIFACTS

This is a comparatively new science that has developed hand in
hand with underwater archaeology. It is more exacting than it seems.
There are no simple halfway steps; either the artifact is thoroughly
treated with the correct procedures—which can last through a period
of several months—or it is inadequately protected against eventual
deterioration. Every classification of artifact has its own method, and
sometimes alternate methods, for preservation. The more complicated
processes should be undertaken by experienced people, but anyone
with a little knowledge of chemistry can correctly treat most of the
artifacts likely to be raised from an old wreck with readily available
chemicals in his own home "laboratory"—the kitchen or bathroom.

There is one Golden Rule: Do not allow any artifact vulnerable
to deterioration (this includes objects ranging from cannon balls to
wood) to remain out of sea water for longer than absolutely necessary
until preparations for its treatment have been completed. A description
of the various treatments for different items in this book would be
redundant, since this subject is covered thoroughly in pages 29–53
and 81–105 of Mendel Peterson's *History Under the Sea* (1969 edition).
Mr. Peterson not only explains how to preserve artifacts; he also details
the chemical and other processes by which each classification of material
is attacked by its enemies, ranging from electrolytic action of salt
water to coral polyps. Pages 200 and 201 of *History Under the Sea*
list a bibliography of some twenty books and articles on this subject
for reference by those who are especially interested.

UNUSUAL SUNKEN TREASURES

Recent explorations of the ocean floor, both at the mouths of rivers
and at greater depths, have resulted in the discovery that the sea bed

offers a variety of treasures that are not necessarily cargoes of sunken ships. Among these are:

DIAMONDS

Offshore mining has now become a big business. Along the southwest coast of Africa several companies operate barges from which dredges suck up alluvial soil carried out to sea by rivers running through diamond-rich earth. From depths as great as 100 feet this sediment is filtered for precious stones. One company has recorded yields of 700 carats of diamonds per day—mostly of industrial quality, but also including some gem stones—worth about $25,000. Groups of SCUBA divers with lighter water-jet and air-lift equipment are also making profitable recoveries.

GOLD

Off the coasts of Alaska and California undersea placer mining is also growing. Core samples have revealed strata of gold-rich sediment all the way down from the surface of the sea bed to depths of 100 feet or more.

OTHER PRECIOUS STONES

Emeralds are being found in rivers of South America by daredevil groups working under difficult and dangerous conditions. Other gem-producing areas of the world offer interesting prospects for river and offshore mining which have not yet been exploited. A suggestion of what might become a commercially viable new enterprise is contained on pages 209–10 of Arthur Clarke's *The Treasure of the Great Reef*, where he describes the high content of "ruby sand" on a reef a full hundred miles away from Ceylon's famous jewel mines at Ratnapura. In alluvial deposits closer to this region, and to other gem-producing areas in Burma, Thailand, etc., there should be larger precious stones of marketable size.

UNDERSEA JADE

Not long ago a 5-ton mass of jade was recovered from the Pacific Ocean south of Big Sur, joining another two jade rocks weighing 2300 and 750 pounds which had been previously salvaged from off the California coast. The finders of the 5-tonner were Donald Wobber, James Norton, Gary Carmignani, and Sonny Phillips. They estimated its value at $180,000.

MANGANESE AND PHOSPHORITE NODULES

An industry of the future will nearly certainly be the large-scale mining of nodules, which vary in size from golf balls to footballs or larger, found on the ocean bed at depths from 200 feet to many miles. As they are far richer than the highest-grade ore, and contain metals and chemicals with high market values, several companies involved in oceanography are studying this previously untapped source of wealth from the sea to develop methods of profitably recovering these metallic deposits.

SEA SHELLS

An increasing demand by a growing number of shell collectors has been steadily boosting the value of many types of sea shells. Some are very valuable today. The market value of hundreds of kinds of popular shells, descriptions, and locations where they can be found are given in the *Standard Catalogue of Sea Shells*, edited by R. J. L. Wagner and R. T. Abbott and published by D. Van Nostrand Company.

"WORTHLESS" ARTIFACTS FROM OLD WRECKS

Old bottles, clay pipes, and other artifacts once considered not worth the bother of raising from ballast piles have recently become sought after by divers. Reference to Mendel Peterson's *History Under the Sea*, pages 125–27, 182–89, and 204–6, will provide a good introduction to this subject. Even Teddy Tucker, with his many treasure wrecks to work, does not hesitate to collect bottles whenever he has the opportunity. The subject of old bottles is a complete field in itself—and an interesting one to SCUBA divers when the market for these can range from $10 to over $100 for a single old porter or melon flask.

CHAPTER 3

"Ghost Galleons" and Treasures Already Salvaged

One morning while we were digging through documents on Spanish armadas at the Navy Museum in Madrid, an officer who had been helping us with research there brought me a letter. It was from Florida, written in excellent Spanish. "Look," he smiled. "Another of you treasure hunters wants information."

I read the typed pages with interest. The writer asked about the *Santa Rosa*, a widely reported "treasure galleon" sunk off Key West in 1520 with $30,000,000 in Aztec loot aboard, and right up on top of our check-off list of sunken ships. I asked our friend what information he had about this galleon.

He shrugged. "The *Santa Rosa*, the *Santa Paula* . . . we receive so many letters for facts about lost galleons. We do the best we can to help supply them. But so often there is no data to send back; in fact, there is nothing in the records to show that the ship ever existed." He shook his head in resignation, adding, "I don't know where people get these so-called treasure ships from—these ghost galleons."

The *Santa Rosa* was one baby on which I intended to dig up all the available facts for the Florida chapter, and dig we did. For three weeks, on and off, our researchers combed every available information source for references to this ship and her vast treasure. In the end we had to give up. As far as Spanish records went, the *Santa Rosa* simply didn't exist. But news came in from America. Sure, the *Santa Rosa* sank off Key West with $30,000,000. An American Navy diver had found her in 1939, 200 feet deep, and had even described the hull's condition: well-preserved, coral-crusted, etc. Someone said that the diver had removed a chest of gold from the captain's cabin. "Where did you get that information?" I wrote back. "What's the diver's name?" No one knew.

Then gradually another picture formed. The *Santa Rosa* had been born not in 1520, but in the 1930s, at the time that a movie about sunken treasure came out. The ship was built not of wood in a shipyard, but of paper and ink in a press agent's typewriter. The whole tale was fiction, created as a publicity stunt for the movie. The *Santa Rosa*, her treasure, the diver who "found" her and his chest of gold were all pure imagination, spread across newspapers twenty years ago and since then absorbed in treasure-hunting media as straight fact.

One of the most widely accepted sunken treasures in the world— a phony! It was enough to shake one's faith in movie press agents. I began wondering about other sure-fire treasure wrecks. What about the vaunted *Santa Margarita,* sunk in 1595 with $4,000,000, $6,000,000 or $7,000,000 off East Palm Beach, off Cutler, under the Hillsboro Rocks, off Sebastian Inlet, and even off the Florida west coast, depending on which source of information is believed? Well, we finally did find the source of this report. Unfortunately, recorded data (in the Florida chapter) and the above accounts have very little in common.

Before we finished our Spanish research several other letters had arrived, at least two of which wanted copies of the log and manifest of the *Santa Paula,* reported sunk off southwest Cuba in 1679 with her log saved and sent to Spain. Our researchers—who are among the best in the business—searched high and low for that log and ended up in a blind alley. They not only couldn't find the log, but also were unable to track down any record of the *Santa Paula.* As far as they were concerned, she and her treasures belonged to the armada of "ghost galleons" which had never sailed beyond the printed page.

We began our work on lost treasures with a long list reported in magazine stories, books, newspapers, and maps. Spanish wrecks were investigated by researchers in Madrid and Seville, English ones by our friends at the Public Records Office in London, and so on. By the time their task had been completed a large part of the popularly accepted undersea hoards of silver, gold and gems seemed to be nothing more than chimerical illusions, and had to be considered "ghosts." The mountains of documents sorted through in the preparation of this book covered the subject pretty thoroughly. In some cases they referred to the "treasure ship" and showed conclusively that no treasure had been aboard. In others, sunken ships never sank. Again, treasures went down but were later salvaged. And finally, a number of "treasure ships" were confirmed as having gone down as reported with no substantiating evidence that they held gold or silver.

I have included ships in the last category in the treasure chapters of this book, often with comments that their cargoes should be checked out before expensive salvage operations are undertaken. Some of them probably do contain treasure. Most of the other very doubtful wrecks have been left out entirely, while a handful—the most widely accepted of the lost treasures on which our research failed to turn up one piece of substantiating evidence—are listed below.

FLORIDA "GHOSTS"

The *SANTA ROSA,* the *SANTA MARGARITA,* and the *VINE-YARD.*

NORTH AMERICAN EAST COAST "GHOSTS"

H.M.S. *HUSSAR:* has been the subject of several intensive research programs, and both the British Public Records Office in London and

American records sources in Washington have been receiving letters of inquiry on this vessel for over a century. Her history is described by Bob Nesmith in his book *Dig for Pirate Treasure,* and in several other books and articles.

The *Hussar* was a British 28-gunned frigate which sank in 1780 off Pot Rock in Hell Gate, New York harbor. She has been widely reported to have had $5,000,000 in gold and silver aboard. After the loss her Captain Sir Charles M. Pole and his officers were given a court-martial—routine Admiralty procedure—during which the following testimony was made by the Master: ". . . finding her swing off we let go the best bower anchor, sent a kedge ashore to steady her, but finding there was no possibility of saving the ship, we ordered a sloop alongside in order to save the men and what stores were possible. Soon after she went down." Throughout the court-martial there was not one mention of gold or silver. "What stores were possible" is the only reference to cargo. It is inconceivable that if $4,800,000 in treasure had been on the ship there would not have been long pages of testimony covering efforts to transfer it to the sloop, if this could have been done, and why not otherwise. For his negligence in losing such a valuable shipment, unless he was completely innocent of blame, the captain would have been roundly condemned. As it was he was acquitted.

Neither the U. S. Treasury nor the British Public Records Office contain any reference to treasure on the *Hussar,* and in a letter written in 1812 and published in the Boston *Evening Gazette* in 1823, Captain Pole stated: "I am not aware that there was any treasure on board her or anything but stores belonging to her as a 28-gun ship . . . This may perhaps serve to prevent disappointment for future seekers of treasure trove." It didn't. Simon Lake and several other salvage men have spent fortunes trying to recover the *Hussar's* legendary gold.

Other British "treasure ships" which belong in the same "ghost" category are the *LEXINGTON,* sunk in 1781 under the East River, and the *MERLIN* and *AUGUSTA* sunk in 1777 in the Delaware Channel off New Jersey.

NORTH AMERICAN WEST COAST "GHOSTS"

The *CITY OF RIO DE JANEIRO* sank on February 22, 1901, near Mile Rock off Fort Point Rocks near San Francisco. Captain William Ward and 129 others died. Within a week after the disaster a rumor spread through San Francisco that she had carried $500,000. The sum grew with passing time until it has reached $2,000,000 or more today. In fact, the *City of Rio de Janeiro* was loaded with tin, tea, and silk when she sank on that foggy morning. Diver Bill Wood said that he had found her wreck in 1937, but having seen the manifest, was not interested in trying to salvage her.

There are a number of other California coast "treasure wrecks" whose gold cargoes first appeared after their loss, in popular imagination.

THE CARIBBEAN AND GULF "GHOSTS"

These are so numerous that only two will be described here and the dozens of others left out entirely.

There are several accounts that Sir John Hawkins's *JESUS OF LU-BECK* sank off San Juan de Ulúa, Veracruz harbor, in 1568, carrying treasure to the bottom. This ship did not sink; she was captured by the Spanish and there was some money aboard which was taken ashore. Describing the incident, the Spanish vice-admiral reported to King Philip II that a certain creole had stolen a "coffer" containing gold and silver from the English ship. He took steps to have this man arrested, but received countermanding orders from the Viceroy of Mexico that the creole was not to be touched. The inference is that the viceroy and the thief were working together.

The *VILLE DE PARIS* has been reported to have sunk in Mona Passage, east of Hispaniola in 1782 with $5,000,000 in gold and silver. She was the flagship of the Count de Grasse, captured on April 12 of that year off Dominica by the English Admiral George Rodney. She did not sink there. About September 17, 1782, as she was being taken to England by a prize crew, the *Ville de Paris* went down in mid-Atlantic during a hurricane. There was only one survivor, James Wilson, picked up afterward lying on some floating wreckage, nearly delirious. He remembered nothing of the sinking of his ship but did recall that another French prize, the *Glorieux*, had been in tow and cut adrift as she was floundering. British records confirm positively that there was no treasure on either of these vessels when they sank.

PHILIPPINE "GHOSTS"

Several years ago, after the end of the Pacific war, newspapers were full of accounts that a Japanese hospital ship, sunk by American planes, had aboard $50,000,000 in gold bullion. This steamer was reported to lie off Bongao Island between North Borneo and Sulu. An American professor was quoted in news dispatches as having said that he found her while diving for rare shells. Latest reports from Honolulu, where the principals of the shell-gathering expedition live, indicate that no treasure was discovered while other information from the Philippines seems to contradict the story of the hospital ship having carried gold.

WEST EUROPEAN "GHOSTS"

H.M.S. *HAMPSHIRE* is a real mystery ship, about which dozens of conflicting stories have been circulated. What is certain is that she was a British cruiser, en route to Archangel, Russia, carrying Lord Kitchener on a mission to confer with the Tsar. On the night of June 4, 1916, while escorted by a destroyer, the *Hampshire* struck a mine west of the Orkneys and sank, stern-first, within a few minutes. Lord Kitchener and most of the crew were drowned.

Her hull was discovered accidentally about two months later by an anti-submarine flotilla of small boats, called drifters, from which steel nets were hung under the sea. Describing the incident, Naval Authority Gregory Robinson ways: "I happened to be based in the Orkneys in the summer of '16 trying to catch submarines in a steel indicator net. One of my drifters thought she had a submarine in her net one day. When I suggested she had hold of the bottom, the old Scotch skipper snorted, 'Catching the bottom with my twenty fathom net in forty fathoms o' water!' However we had caught something, and it wasn't a submarine." It was not until later, when the *Hampshire*'s loss was revealed, that the crews of the drifters knew what the obstacle had been.

The treasure legend that has grown up around the ship: the Tsar, sensing the revolution approaching, had asked for English money to strengthen his position. Lord Kitchener was supposedly bringing £10,000,000 in gold bars which were in the *Hampshire*'s strong room. This would be 47 tons, worth over $50,000,000. Mr. Robinson's comment on this is: "I remember that before the war was done there were yarns about the *Hampshire*—that she was sunk by treachery, and others. It would be interesting to learn of the first time the story of gold was told. If it were true the Admiralty would certainly have tried to salvage it like they did the *Laurentic*, and of course, no attempt was ever made."

There is a tale of non-Admiralty salvage efforts, though, which has circulated in Europe. It tells of a disguised salvage boat, the "*K.S.R.*," which visited the *Hampshire*'s site in 1933. Aboard were three expert divers, an Australian named Costello and two Americans, Courtney and Mansfield. Assisting them were two German demolition specialists, Brandt and Weissfeldt. They dynamited the cruiser's hull (the story goes), opening a passage to the strong room, and had raised several hundred ingots when one day, while the Germans were below, a storm sank the salvage craft. Brandt and Weissfeldt died, their air cut off. The others escaped but their "*K.S.R.*" and its gleaming ingots went down to join the *Hampshire*.

Commenting on a number of British frigates sunk in fairly shallow water around the Great Britain coast, Mr. Robinson cautions that whatever treasures they might have contained when they sank would normally have been salvaged long ago. Citing the *GUERNSEY LILY*, he says: "She went down in Yarmouth Roads, off the Isle of Wight, in sheltered waters. H.M.S. *Gladiator* after collision with the *St. Louis* sank there and was salvaged by the Liverpool Salvage Company within my memory. I am sure the company would have picked up anything else worth having."

The *GENERAL BARKER*, reported sunk off Holland about 1781 with several millions in gold, is another "ghost" according to our England researchers—despite accounts of $1,000,000 or so having been salvaged from her hull.

MEDITERRANEAN AND BLACK SEA "GHOSTS"

One of the most-celebrated of all "treasure ships" is *L'ORIENT*, flagship of the French Admiral de Brueys which was sunk on August 1, 1798, in Abukir Bay, Egypt, by Admiral Horatio Lord Nelson. Aboard was reputed to be three separate treasures: the payroll for the French fleet, worth millions; a similar sum with which to bribe Egyptian officials into favoring the French cause; and the Treasure of the Knights of Malta, taken aboard there a month before. Estimates of the total value run as high as $10,000,000.

As to the first two, there was scarcely any money at all when *L'Orient* arrived at Egypt. The financial situation aboard the French fleet was desperate, with barely enough cash at hand to keep the crews fed. What money was carried on the flagship was sent ashore during the first half of July and stored in Alexandria under the protection of Jean Kléber, who commanded Napoleon's forces in Egypt. And the "Treasure of the Cathedral"—enormous silver statues, candelabra, etc.—and other loot from the Knights of Malta's hoard? Half was left at Malta (later captured by the English) while the remainder was landed and sent to Alexandria before the Battle of the Nile.

Unaware of this, salvors working in conjunction with King Farouk tackled the 45-foot-deep wreck in 1950. They recovered iron, lead, brass, and bronze artifacts, but not a single louis d'or.

The *BLACK PRINCE*, sunk in the Black Sea, is another vaunted "ghost." This British warship was rumored to carry a large shipment of gold belonging to the Bank of England when she was lost about 1850. Since then Russian, English, and Japanese expeditions have worked on her hull. Salvage attempts stopped in 1914 when it was revealed that her gold cargo had been disembarked at her last port of call, Constantinople.

The NAVARINO BAY WRECKS, specifically the Turko-Egyptian command ships *CAPITAN BEY* and *GUERIENNE*, hold up to

$100,000,000 in fictional loot from Greece. Nearly ninety ships were destroyed in the Bay of Pilos (then called Navarino) on October 20, 1827, by twenty-four warships commanded by Admiral Sir Edward Codrington in a crippling blow to the Egyptian pasha Mohammed Ali, whose ships had been up to then supporting Turkey in her efforts to crush the seven-year-old Greek struggle for freedom.

In fact, there was little—if any—precious metal aboard the Turko-Egyptian fleet. When it arrived Greece was a desperately poor nation, already stripped by a succession of invading armies. To win rich booty you have to find it, and the Hellenic state had none. Any venture to dredge up intrinsic wealth from the shallow, mud-buried *Capitan Bey* and *Guerienne* would nearly surely be a waste of time and money.

Somewhere between Rome and Carthage, deep under the Mediterranean, lie the remains of a "treasure ship" sent by Genseric, King of the Vandals. It is popularly believed to contain the "loot of Rome" —the richest treasures of the entire Roman Empire—which Genseric's hoards captured in 455 A.D. Featured in this amassment are the massive gold seven-branched candelabrum of the Temple of Solomon and the fabulous jewel collection of the Roman emperor Heliogabalus.

Recently the Belgian treasure diver and submarine archaeologist Robert Sténuit has completed the first attempt ever made to learn the facts about this treasure. He says: "I finally found and translated a firsthand account of the fate of the loot, written in Greek by a chronicler who accompanied the Roman army which reconquered Carthage and destroyed the Vandal Empire. With his own eyes he saw the candelabrum and jewels, as well as most of the other loot, when the Romans recaptured it and brought it back to Rome. So it did not sink in the Mediterranean. The same writer says in an earlier chronicle, when describing the sack of Rome, that only one of three ships full of booty was lost, and this carried only the marble statues, carvings, and columns from the Capitol and possibly—we don't know—the golden sheets which had covered the Capitol's roof. There was no description telling where the ship sank."

AUSTRALIAN "GHOSTS"

Aussie skin divers and marine historians have turned up their share of treasures-that-aren't. Recently the Underwater Research Group of Brisbane tracked down a rumored "galleon" and discovered it to be the bark *Wistaris*, sunk in 1887 off Heron Island with neither gold nor silver.

The Underwater Skin Diving & Fishing Society of Tasmania, teamed up with Mr. Harry O'May, have found enough "ghosts" around their little down-under island to fill a haunted house. Of these, the *CATHER-*

INE SHARER (not *Shearer*) is perhaps the most interesting. She was a 400-ton bark which blew up and sank in 1855 while lying at anchor off Port Esperance. Her hull lies 50 feet deep on a clean sandy bottom, the bow about 100 feet away from the rest of the ship. A million-dollar treasure is supposed to be aboard. Tasmanian SCUBA divers T. E. Canning, Col. Reid, Terry Lobban, Merv Morley, Don Reid, T. E. Davis, and others began tracking down the position of the *Sharer* late in 1955 and after several false leads made the first dive on her wreckage in November 1957. From earlier studies they knew that a "treasure" of about $15,000 in copper coin tokens, packed in eight cases, lay in the ship, but their interest in finding her was largely archaeological.

Describing their accomplishments, Dr. Canning says: "We have recovered small metal objects, pottery, a few bottles of olive oil and numerous tins of white lead. The iron tins have long ago corroded away and the white lead lies about as solidified cylinders . . . we raised the anchor in March 1958, using an LST with a 10-ton winch. It now graces the Van Diemen's Land Museum. We have not yet located the coinage which she was reputed to carry. Amongst the pottery salvaged are some jars with scenes of the Crimean War . . . we also brought a barrel of gunpowder to the surface, well past the explosive stage."

Another Tasmanian wreck, the *BRITOMART*, is called a "mystery ship." "She was lost in Bass Strait near Preservation Island," says Don Reid, "but no definite spot was ever found. The only inhabitants of that place in those days were the Sealers, a rare bunch of ruffians from all accounts. It is recorded that they thought it a great night's work to light signal fires, lure an unsuspecting ship to her doom on some reef, dispose of the crew and passengers, and then having got what they could of the cargo, clear out post haste! The *Britomart* was reported lost and a ship sent to search for her. This vessel made some interesting discoveries, including deck timbers, dead sheep, cargo and some very flush Sealers." Harry O'May, on the same subject, says: "If the *Britomart* did have a considerable sum of money on board, the Sealers got it."

The "treasure ships" *NEVA* and *CATARAQUI* seem destined never to yield a single sovereign, while the better publicized *WATER WITCH*, reported sunk in Bass Strait in 1855 with millions in gold, "ran into fairly shallow water and was quickly salvaged."

The trouble with "ghost galleons" is that once they have appeared on a treasure map or in a pulp magazine article they are picked up by later writers and chart makers as the real McCoy, usually embellished, and carried on as an integral part of treasure fact—as was the

Santa Rosa. People will spend money to get information on wrecks with treasure, but not to eliminate "ghosts" except as a by-product following disappointing experiences in trying to recover their treasures. In this book I have tried to eliminate valueless wrecks, but am sure that despite the large number we sifted out, a small percentage of the ships listed in the treasure chapters as genuine, interesting treasure ships are themselves "ghosts." Even careful research will allow some to slip through.

It would be interesting to sum up the total value of all treasure ever salvaged from under the sea. Such a figure should reach well into the hundreds of millions of dollars. The treasure chapters of this book describe in detail several dozen salvage operations which were not fully completed. Some others, where no further treasure remains, are covered in the next pages.

WESTERN HEMISPHERE

About 1640 the *nao LA ANUNCIADA*, loaded for departure with the rest of the ships in General Antonio de Oquendo's Tierra Firme flota, sank in Cartagena harbor. Divers raised two barrels of silver from her hull the same day and within a month had brought up the rest of the treasure and a large part of the cargo. Sixteen years later another Spanish treasure ship, the *MARAVILLAS*, was wrecked in the Bahamas with a cargo of silver. In 1657 an expedition to salvage her was fitted out at Cartagena by Governor Pedro Capata. Its ships went to Havana, then to the wreck, from which nearly everything valuable was retrieved. Laden with the silver, the fleet was en route to Cádiz when English vessels attacked them and captured the treasure.

A Spanish *nao*, wrecked in Samaná Bay, Hispaniola, about 1675, was salvaged so thoroughly that when William Phips's divers scoured the hulk in 1686 they could find nothing but bits of broken pottery.

In 1815 the Spanish schooner *EMPECINADA* sank off Amelia Island, east Florida. Her treasure cargo was entirely recovered soon afterward.

The iron steamer *PRINCE ALFRED* went down against Duxbury Reef off San Francisco on June 14, 1874. The $25,623 in Wells Fargo gold which she carried was salvaged.

EUROPE AND AFRICA

A galleon of Bernardino de Mendoza sank in the Azores islands in 1549. Her cargo of $250,000 or so in gold and silver was raised within two months.

In 1557 two Spanish ships, carrying between them 22 cases of gold money, were wrecked in the English Channel. All of their gold was recovered "with great efforts" by skin divers, under orders of the King of Spain.

The galleon *SANTIAGO* and one *patache* of the armada of Fadrique de Toledo sank in the Bay of Morbihan near Belle Island, France, in 1627. Their cargoes and money were brought up soon after.

The *SORPRESA*, a Spanish brigantine, was wrecked off the beach at Rota, Spain, in 1822. Thorough salvage work recovered, among other cargo, 109,520 silver pesos and 3416 gold coins that she had brought back from the Indies.

The *ALFONSO XII*, a Spanish iron steamer, sank off Point Gando, Gran Canaria Island in 1885 with ten boxes of gold coins worth $500,000 in her strong room. This treasure was stored on the lowermost deck, just over the propeller shaft, and lay at a depth of 160 feet. The master diver Alexander Lambert and his partner Tester blasted their way through three overhead decks and sent up nine boxes worth $450,000. The tenth box was officially never recovered. In 1957 the *Alfonso XII* was worked over by a group of three SCUBA divers, the American Howard Williams, the Dutch demolition specialist Bill Goezinnen, and the Austrian engineer Clement Brandt. They were interested in recovering several hundred tons of copper coils stored in one of her holds, but also kept an eye out for the missing gold. After a careful search of the strong room—now a jumble of flattened wreckage and sheet iron—Williams commented cryptically: "The box isn't there, and if you ask me, hasn't been there since those first divers got through. After all, the *Alfonso* is a damn dangerous place to work, with those horrible currents, and I think those guys deserved a bonus for getting the treasure out . . ."

The S.S. *SKYRO*, sunk off Mexiddo Reef, Cape Finisterre, Spain, in 1891, seemed too deep (175 feet) for her cargo of silver ingots to be salvaged. Several attempts were made, nevertheless, but failed. Then a Spanish diver, Erostarbe, began the assault. With characteristic Basque stubbornness he returned to the wreck again and again, fought against storms and currents, and finally blasted enough of the wreck open to reach the treasure. Every ingot was recovered by the end of two years' heroic work.

The P & O liner *OCEANA* sank 80 feet deep in the English Channel in 1912 after a collision, taking down over $3,000,000 in gold sovereigns and silver ingots. During a long and aggressive salvage program the capable divers Lambert, Anderson, Fabian, and Eriksen meticulously stripped her strong room, recovering nearly every bit of this treasure.

The *EMPRESS OF IRELAND* sank off England in 1914, settling to 170 feet. Her consignment of $250,000 in silver was salvaged some time later.

ASIA

Chinese pirates and a depth of over 160 feet did not prevent two determined divers, Ridyard and Penk, from recovering $250,000 in silver dollars in the hull of the *HAMILLA MITCHELL*. The ship had sunk near Leuconna Reef, off Shanghai. Despite general opinion that her silver could not be saved, Captain Lodge, supplied with divers and equipment by Siebe, Gorman & Co., decided to make the attempt. They raised $200,000 in 1869. The balance was brought up later.

Obviously, it would be well for any prospective treasure hunter to check this list of "ghosts" and already salvaged ships before embarking on any actual search.

CHAPTER 4

Wreck Identification—I

(also see General Index: Wreck Identification)

A recent wreck like the *Andrea Doria* can be recognized without any special preparatory training. Her name is there, painted black on white on the lifeboats and in yard-high letters at the bow, stern, and bridge. An older iron or steel hull may no longer carry a legible name, but can be identified by comparison of her dimensions, number of decks, and so forth against the builder's or owner's plans. The finding of the *Egypt* was nearly positively confirmed when one of her davits, broken loose and raised, matched the dimensions of one shown on the ship's blueprints.

These identification chapters are not concerned with such recent losses. Their subject is the old wooden ship, sunk a century or more ago, whose wreckage seems on first investigation to be nothing more than a junk pile. Yet the same junk pile holds numerous clues which can be ferreted out and placed in a pattern which will usually reveal the ship's nationality and approximate date of loss, often the class of vessel, and sometimes, even, details right down to the name.

You've found an old wreck: ballast mound, cannons and cannon balls, bits of copper, lead and oxidized iron artifacts and a huge anchor nearby. At a glance you realize it will take months and cost quite a bit of money to clear off the coral or mud or sand and get down into where the pay dirt might lie. But will there be treasure to make it worth while putting your time and money into the work? Is this a Spanish galleon? You want to keep the find a secret so that every diver in the vicinity won't be plundering it, but there is no reliable archaeologist at hand to look it over. What can you do?

You can make a pretty fair appraisal of the wreck yourself, knowing what to search for—the artifacts that carry messages from the past— and knowing how to read these messages. Nearly every part of an ancient ship holds significance to the archaeologist, and through use of the facts given on the following pages you can become a pretty fair artifact identifier yourself, competent enough to give the wreck a semi-expert appraisal as to the possibility of treasure being there. In this connection it would be a good idea to check her location and period against treasure wrecks and others of only archaeological interest described in the later chapters. You may find your ship's name and history, and details of what salvage has already been carried out over her. And whether treasure remains in the ballast.

You will have a detective puzzle on your hands, but armed with knowledge can approach it with the confidence of a trained investigator.

There is one thing to keep in mind always: until the ingots and coins begin to appear, don't take anything as final. An English cannon *can* turn up on a Spanish galleon and vice versa. Copper sheathing, characteristically non-Spanish, *did* cover some Spanish frigates' and warships' bottoms after 1800. Your identification job will be essentially cross-checking the wreck's date of loss, as you narrow this down, against the type of artifacts carried on ships of various nationalities at that period. Once the ship has been identified as Spanish or Portuguese or Dutch or whatever nationality she turns out to be, consult the wreck chapter covering the region in which you found her for background information as to what chances there are of treasure being on board.

GENERAL BACKGROUND

Old wrecks are nearly always protected from treasure hunters by one of nature's submarine barriers: coral, sand, and mud, poor undersea visibility because of silt or plankton in the water, or turbulent seas overhead and chronic bad weather. Scarcely any treasure ship lies uncovered in calm, clear water offering herself to the diver. Nearly all are broken up and decomposed. The rate of disintegration of a submerged wooden ship varies with the depth, the temperature of the sea and the water motion. The warmer the water, the shallower the depth and the rougher the ocean, the less of the ship remains. A galleon sunk in 40 feet on the weather side of a Caribbean reef will have been battered and eaten to ballast pile and very badly oxidized iron within a century. Forty-six years after the 1641 *Almiranta* sank in 40 feet in the Bahamas, William Phips found her hull split open, the decks caved in, much of her broken away by waves and eaten by teredos. What remained was disappearing under coral. On the other hand the *Wasa*, although nearly 350 years under the sea, still remains nearly intact and whole, her wood strong, because she lies fairly deep under cold, protected Swedish waters.

Sand and mud are excellent preservatives. Solid wood beams, undamaged by borers and as strong as new, were brought up last year from mud-covered wrecks where they had lain for two and a half centuries. Copper is an anti-borer preventative because it becomes coated with poisonous copper sulfate in the sea. The wood planks on the bottom of a copper-sheathed vessel are usually intact. Iron rusts from contact with air bubbles and dissolved oxygen in the water. If it lies under breaking waves oxidation will proceed very fast and an entire cannon can be rusted through within fifty years. On the other hand half-inch plates usually receive no more damage than a thin veneer of rust in the same submerged period if they are at 100 feet or more down. Iron buried under mud in plankton-rich water becomes badly sulfided and calcified through the dolomitic process: a gray-white chunk of metal raised from the Vigo galleons—which looked like silver—turned out to have been converted iron, containing 10 per cent magnesium, 10 per cent calcium, 1 per cent potassium and 1 per cent sodium.

Gold is never changed by chemical action under salt water. Silver undergoes a chemical reaction, turning into black silver sulfide. Pieces of eight alter in appearance to slightly larger "cookies" after a century submerged, so if you come across black "cookies" don't throw them away. The silver content is still there, and can be recovered nearly one hundred per cent by melting them down. If silver lies in contact with iron, though, or another element with a higher valence, it will remain pure silver since electrolytic chemical action will pass it by to attack the more active iron. Thus silver coins found touching a cannon ball will be in excellent condition. Ingots become coated with a thin cape of black sulfide but are seldom badly damaged.

AN AVERAGE WRECK

Unless sunk suddenly in a storm or through severe rupture in the hull the damaged wooden ship was usually the scene of a desperate struggle between her crew and the sea. If she was leaking, heavy objects would be jettisoned: first the cannons and sometimes the cannon balls, then the anchors unless they were considered essential for holding the ship off reefs, then the cargo. For this reason there will often be a trail leading to the wreck itself. In case the hull was holed, a sail was passed under the keel in hopes that the canvas would plug the leak.

Once settled on her submarine grave, the ship went through a steady disintegration. If wave motions or currents extended their effect to where she lay (nearly always the case), the wooden beams would be worked back and forth by water pressure, gradually coming loose to be dragged away or fall, waterlogged, alongside. As iron spikes and nails were rusted away this breaking up increased in tempo. After fifty years the wreck would be reduced to the wood of her sides and lower deck, already porous from the attacks of borers. By the end of a century there would be nothing left except what was preserved underneath the ballast, or sand or mud, if she was buried, with porous stumps of the lower ribs rising up outlining her form. After the first 150 years little further change took place, for by then all that remained was the ballast mound with keel and lower ribs and planks underneath the ballast and heavy, indestructible cargo on top. This is the usual wreck encountered.

HULLS AND CONSTRUCTION (see Index: Ship Construction)

The surviving wood of an old ship can give pointers as to its nationality. This wood can be identified by any carpenter after it has been soaked and washed in fresh water. If it is:

(a) oak, the ship could be of any nationality. The keels and ribs of Spanish *naos* were usually of oak.

(b) cedar, there is an excellent chance that it is from a ship built in Spain. The galleons often had planking of cedar.

(c) mahogany, again there is an excellent chance that it is either cargo or fittings on a Spanish ship in the Atlantic, or from the hull itself, if found in the Pacific where Philippine mahogany was used for keels, ribs, and planks.

(d) fir, it could be a part of the masts and spars on Spanish Pacific ships, cut from Oregon forests.

(e) pine, if found in the Atlantic or off Africa or India it could be from a Portuguese caravel or carrack constructed from wood of the Leiera forests.

(f) teak, there is a good chance that it is either a Portuguese or Dutch carrack built of Indian teakwood. The Manila galleons were also often decked with teak.

Throughout this book are given full descriptions of the wood found in various types of vessels.

Details of construction of the hull will be limited to that part which could be buried and consequently have survived: the lower ribs and planks, keel and keelson. The early Spanish caravels and *naos* were weakly constructed, having few reinforcing longitudinal beams and no keelson. During the period 1620–60 ships were strengthened: ribs were fortified, the keelson—a huge wood beam, more or less 1½ by 2 feet in size—was added, firmly bolted on top of the keel and running the length of the ship. Also four thick wooden beams were added to the lower inside of the hull, extending from bow to stern, bolted or nailed to the lower ribs. These were two to the side, running along the bilge. Inner planking or strakes, nailed to the ribs, was added to make a double bottom. A ship having a keelson and four wood beams running down the sides, particularly if there is also double planking on her bottom and bilge, can be dated as after 1630.

The keel is a good indicator of size. Its length was increased during the 1620–60 period of Spanish ship construction improvement. In 1587 a 400-ton *nao* had a keel 68 feet long; by 1611 it had been extended to 92 feet. The following table gives some indication of ship's sizes based on the keel's length:

Date	Nao's Tonnage	Length of Keel	Ship's Length	Ship's Breadth	Draft
1587	400	68 feet	104 feet	32 feet	21 feet
1611	400	92 "	119 "	36 "	18 "
1666	500	100 "	124 "	35 "	16½ "
"	700	106 "	130 "	37 "	17½ "
1691	500	110 "	127 "	37 "	14½ "
"	900	134 "	148 "	45 "	17½ "

The use of iron and brass spikes and bolts in holding the hull together varied so much that they are not good indicators. In general the galleons' planks were attached to the ribs with iron spikes, while those on the later warships were fixed with brass bolts. Iron was replaced by brass as the result of experiences where it rusted in salt water.

Some final identification aids, applicable only in rare cases: galleons and *naos* were gilded on their poops up to 1633, and from then on only in the captain's cabin; after 1781 all Spanish ships were painted yellow.

THE BALLAST

If there is an old ship, there will be ballast. Unfortunately this is not very useful in identification, except to give a rough indication as to whether the wreck dates before or after 1800. Before this date the ballast was usually of small stones varying in size from golf balls to footballs. Many of the Spanish *naos* and galleons were ballasted with a smooth round granite known as "egg rock" which has a clean look and a soft light brown shade.

Sometimes chalk was used on English ships. Teddy Tucker's 1595 *nao* was ballasted with flint, as were some of the Vigo galleons of 1702. Silver and gold ore were occasionally piled on the bottom—so if the stones have shiny specks, don't overlook this possibility. Two cannons attached side to side, muzzles to breeches, are a good indication of a Spanish cargo *nao*. (They were placed on the stone ballast to lower the center of gravity and tied in pairs to keep them from rolling.) After 1800 iron ingots often replaced stone for ballast.

SHEATHING ON THE BOTTOM

Here is a very useful aid in wreck identification, and worth tearing up bottom planks to reach. The old wooden ships were of three types: those with paint or pitch teredo preventatives on their bottoms; those with lead sheathing, in sheets or strips; and those with copper sheathing. Nearly always, the following will be true:

(a) If you find nothing but wood on the bottom of the ship's hull, it could be either Spanish before 1520, Portuguese before 1580, English before 1760, or French or Dutch before 1780. These were the approximate dates that these countries' vessels began to be sheathed.

(b) If you find ⅛ to ¼ inch lead sheeting on the wreck's bottom, nailed to the outside of the lower planks, the ship is probably Spanish, between 1520 and 1810. The Spanish were the first to realize the extent of teredo damage in the Indies' warm water and after unsuccessful experimentation with paints and tars, tried lead sheet on the caravel *Santa Catalina* in 1514. The results were so good that other ships were given lead sheathing and by 1520 nearly all Spain's vessels were thus protected. The English, French, and Dutch, whose ships were normally not obliged to spend many months at a time in tepid Caribbean seas, did not use lead much. Some English vessels were sheathed after 1640. They did, however, carry lead sheets for hull patches which were nailed in place with copper boat nails.

(c) If you find very thin copper sheeting underneath, the wreck is possibly English after 1770, or Spanish after 1810. The English were the first to try copper on their Pacific frigates in 1767, with favorable results both as a protection and as a detriment to barnacles and other sea growths (alienated by the poisonous copper) which kept the bottoms clean and added knots to the ships' speed. By 1783 all English vessels were copper sheathed; by 1778 the French, who had preferred paint or pitch, began sheathing their ships with copper; and in the early 1800s the Spanish followed suit. The only drawback in sheathing was that it concealed the position of leaks.

ANCHORS, CHAINS, AND CABLES

The importance of the anchor in ship identification was manifested recently when Mendel Peterson of the Smithsonian Institution dated one found by Ed Link off Haiti as of the epoch of the *Santa María*. The whole science of identifying anchors is complicated, involving cross-comparisons in size and shape with others of known ages, and is best left to experts. In general, however, the following hold true: If the anchor is hand-forged, it was made before 1510. If cast in one piece it can be dated after 1510. If it has an iron stock, or crossbar, it was made after 1820. If a rectangular hole penetrates the shank near the top, at right angles to the arms and flukes, the anchor dates before 1820, and had a wooden crossbar. Flukes with heart or cloverleaf shape were usually before 1700.

The size is not a good indication of the ship's tonnage, because often as many as six anchors were carried on a *nao* or caravel. In general, if the shank is no longer than 9 feet, the ship was small— a caravel or *patache*. The larger galleons, *naos*, frigates, and warships all had anchors about 15 feet long and 12 feet from fluke to fluke, which varied so little in construction between 1600 and 1800 that an expert often cannot identify their period. An English order in 1684 decreed that the Broad Arrow and the anchor smith's mark must be "cut deep" on English anchors. As an idea of the ship's tonnage—provided all of her anchors are found—in 1611 Thomé Cano published a book on Spanish shipbuilding in which he stated that 4 per cent of the vessel's total weight should be in her anchors and the heavy rope cables that hold them. This was not necessarily the case, though, and sometimes the proportion was as low as 2 per cent.

Anchors were suspended from rope cables, often 20 inches in circumference, until the early 1800s. If an anchor chain is found, it dates the wreck as after 1815.

Aside from money and cannon, which are the most important artifacts for identification, the following are valuable:

(a) Navigation instruments: astrolables, quadrants, and octants were used until the middle 1700s. The sextant was invented by John Hadley in 1731 and was originally an octant with arc of ⅛ of a circle. The arc was enlarged to ⅙ to meet needs of navigators by a Captain Campbell in 1757.

(b) Equipment: copper pumps and salt water distillers appeared on Spanish vessels after 1550. Uniforms were introduced in the Spanish Navy in 1744 and copper buttons would date after this. The copper powder bucket, called a *perulera*, appeared in 1769 for holding black powder. It is recognized by its distinctive appearance: about 18 inches tall, a foot in diameter at the bottom and narrowing toward the 6-inch-diameter opening in the top. Lead sheeting with nail holes inside the hull, or on top of the ballast, would probably date the wreck after 1783, when storerooms began to be lined with lead. In 1788 steam pumps replaced hand pumps for bailing out the hold. Electrical lighting was introduced in 1880 on the S.S. *Columbia* and spread quickly to most ships by 1900.

(c) Cargo: breakdowns of nontreasure cargoes in The Golden Galleons and the wreck chapters of this book, by area, have been included partly as an aid in ship identification. A batch of glassware, for instance, would indicate the carrier was from Europe bound for one of the colonies, without treasure on board. Stacks of copper ingots would signal a transport from Peru, very likely carrying silver and gold. Cochineal, which can often be recognized by its scarlet color, if found underneath sand or mud, shows the voyage to have originated in the Caribbean, with good possibility of treasure. Precious woods sometimes survive: rosewood indicates a likely voyage origin in Honduras or Brazil. Pottery is found in every wreck and is a clue as to both the ship's nationality and its port of loading. Pieces of thick clay jars, reddish in color, would have come from Mexico or other parts of the

New World. A green or gray glaze on pottery points to Mexico. Porcelain dishes and cups often carry dates and the names of European manufacturers. The dates are valuable, but the country of origin can be deceptive, since Spanish ships often carried French and English services. Chinese porcelains in the Pacific mean a Manila galleon. The field of pottery identification is highly involved, and an expert will be needed for appraisal. Barrels of tar or pitch found in a wreck place it after 1550, when this was discovered to be a good preservative for foodstuffs and began to be carried on ships.

MONEY AND INGOTS (see Index: Money and Ingots)

It should be unnecessary to warn divers not to overlook any round or variously shaped blackened and corroded objects, for they may be encrusted coins, ingots, or bars of gold or silver. These (plus jewels, of course) are the real treasure generally worth many times their weight in bullion. Moreover, it is also possible sometimes to date the wreck from coins or bars recovered and so get help in identification.

The Florida galleon wrecks lost in the hurricane of 1715 would not be carrying pieces of eight of a later date and the wrecks from the 1733 hurricane, such as those found by Art McKee, were identified because the two thousand coins recovered were all struck before that date. In fact, many of them were the first so-called "Pillar or *Dos Mundos*" coins first struck in Mexico in 1732 with the screw press, and hence very valuable. Large quantities (say, five hundred or more) of coins of approximately the same date found in one spot would indicate a chest of registered treasure from a *Capitana* or *Almiranta*. The mints from which these coins originated will provide a good lead as to whether the wreck was part of a New Spain or Tierra Firme armada. Metal ingots provide the same information. The gold bars from Teddy Tucker's big find were all from Colombia (Nuevo Reino de Granada) and one was stamped with the name of the mining region PINTO, indicating that the ship most likely sailed from Cartagena.

Mints operated during Spanish colonial days at Mexico City, which first struck silver in coins of 4, 3, 2, 1, ½ and ¼ reales beginning in 1536 under Charles and Johanna; in Peru at Lima mint which first struck silver coins of 8, 4, 2, 1, ½ and ¼ reales in 1568, under Philip II; at Potosí (then Peru) about 1572; at Santa Fe de Bogotá (Colombia) as early as 1627, under Philip IV; in silver at Santiago de Chile in 1751 (Pillar design) under Philip V; in Guatemala about 1733. There are known silver coins supposed to have been struck in Santo Domingo, but it has never been proved that a mint operated there, although one was authorized in 1573.

Gold coins were struck at Santiago de Chile in 1744 as trial pieces only and were first issued in 1749. Gold escudo pieces have been found from the Nueva Reino de Granada mint at Santa Fe de Bogotá dated 1635 (El Mesuno Hoard). Gold was first coined in Mexico City in 1679. Before that date it was shipped from Mexico only in bars. Peru coined gold from 1697 on.

A Spanish ounce contains 28.6875 grams and the old Spanish-American gold piece of eight escudos was also called onza (ounce) and doubloon. It seldom weighed a full ounce. In fine condition it generally weighs 27 grams.

Documentary references to cargo values on old ships are given in all kinds of obsolete units of weight and currencies. For example, the 1590 plate fleet landed treasure in the port of Viana in Portugal amounting to "13,243 arrobas and 20 pounds, in bars weighing 25 to 30 pounds each. 1125 pack animals were used to transport it to Seville. . . . In the 1591 fleet they took to Spain safely over 5 to 6 million in gold and silver and 800,000 ducats worth of cochineal."[1] The *New York Gazette* of December 17, 1733, records: "On the 25 and 26th past, the Fleet from Pernambuco arrived [at Lisbon in September] bringing about 6000 chests of sugar, 1000 hides, some wood, tobacco, diamonds and about one million crusados in gold."

Converting old weights and values into present-day equivalents is very difficult and frequently almost impossible since currencies changed frequently in value over the years. In the seventeenth century gold was 16 times more valuable than silver; today it is worth some 20–21 times more.

A frequent question that comes up when old coins are recovered is "How much is this worth?" There is no pat answer. With the help of world-recognized numismatists such as Bob Nesmith, the author has tried to make a table of values for the most common Spanish, Portuguese, French, English, Dutch, and Italian moneys found in wrecks, but has given up the attempt. Each coin varies widely in market value depending upon its condition, the current numismatic interest in its type, and above all, the supply and demand situation. As will be apparent in the treasure recovery accounts in Section Two of this book, one of the main preoccupations of those who salvage large quantities of similar coins is to prevent them from flooding the market and depressing the value for that type, mint, and date. One example of the difficulty in attempting generalizations would be the Spanish maravedi. Between 1157 and 1642 this coin was minted in gold, silver, and vellon, and had twenty different values ranging from half a cent to over $7.

Examples of prices paid at auction for some of the coins and ingots salvaged by the Real Eight Company from the 1715 armada are given

[1] From *Further English Voyages to Spanish America*, by Irene Wright, Hakluyt, London, 1949.

in that chapter, and accounts of many other treasure recoveries in this book name values at which coins were sold *at the time they were sold*. For illustrations of moneys often found in wrecks, the reader is referred to Mendel Peterson's *History Under the Sea*, pages 134–51, and pages 46–51 of *Treasure . . . How and Where to Find It* by Nesmith and Potter.

There is one rule followed by every treasure finder with experience: If you find coins or bars, do not melt them for their metallic value. Unless they are in very poor condition, with no legible markings, they are worth much, much more to collectors.

CLAY PIPES

Nearly every wreck site dating from the early 1600s will have some of these, and clay pipes are becoming a valuable type of artifact from which to derive both dates and nationalities of ships. Examples of pipe forms and corresponding dates are given on pages 186–89 of Peterson's *History Under the Sea*.

BOTTLES AND GLASS FRAGMENTS

Like clay pipes and ceramics, bottles are developing into a very useful aid in identifying wrecks by their approximate dates. There has been a definite evolution in the shapes of bottles and the composition of glass used over the past centuries, and experts can identify the period of nearly any bottle to within a few decades. This is particularly true of the "onion bottle" found on so many wreck sites.

CHAPTER 5

Wreck Identification—II

(also see General Index: Wreck Identification)

(a) MEDIEVAL WEAPONS: from the 1400s to the end of the 1500s, *naos* and caravels to the Indies as well as Mediterranean galleys carried shields, breastplates and helmets, long pikes, medium pikes or spears and light lances. The harquebus, a long-barreled, heavy, matchlock rifle supported near the end of the barrel on a swivel, was common aboard ships until the early 1600s. It fired lead or iron balls of about a quarter pound. The *ballesta*, a large crossbow shooting iron darts or arrows, would indicate the 1400s or 1500s.

A 1520–70 *nao* of under 200 tons carried about 12 harquebuses, 12 *ballestas*, 24 long pikes, 144 medium pikes or spears, 180 light lances, 12 shields, 12 breastplates and 20 helmets. A 200-ton *nao* of the same period would have aboard 20 harquebuses, 20 *ballestas*, and proportionately more of the other weapons. A *nao* of 250 tons or more carried 30 harquebuses, 30 *ballestas*, and so on.

(b) MUSKETS: the *matchlock* musket, which came into use on shipboard about 1544 and was common on all ships, would date a wreck 1540–1700. The *flintlock* musket was introduced in 1685 and soon replaced the matchlock. If muskets are salvaged from a wreck in fair condition their nationality can probably be recognized by an old-weapons expert.

(c) PISTOLS: were first referred to in Spanish documents in 1665, and they probably came into use aboard ship at about that date.

(d) CARBINES: were introduced about 1660, and if found in a wreck would place it as of or after this date.

(e) HAND GRENADES: these were used from the 1400s onward in many different forms, the ball being usually of iron but also of bronze (Spanish) and even clay (Swedish, 1600s) or glass (Spanish, 1600s). It had a fuse hole and was filled with gunpowder. Unfortunately hand grenades were so widely used in similar forms that they are nearly impossible to identify by date and nationality.

SHIPBOARD GUNS

We learned the identification value of cannons from a submarine archaeologist. After half a year of searching at sea for the *Monmouth's* galleon, our team found a mass of cannon balls, and two encrusted cannons, at the foot of a reef. This, we were sure, was it—part of the wreckage of our treasure ship! The cannons seemed just like the others we had been raising for a year from Spanish *naos*. Then Ed

Link visited us and took a dive on our "galleon wreckage," during which he carefully looked over one of the guns, still on the bottom. After coming up he gave us a sharply differing opinion. "I wouldn't be too sure about that gun," Ed said. "It has an English look to me and besides seems to be of a much later date than your galleon. The trunnions are centered . . ."

We didn't know the difference between a trunnion and a cascabel, let alone what a centered trunnion was. Yet Ed, after a glance, could read a historical message in the gun which to us was just another cannon. Like a trained detective, he knew how to recognize clues and what they meant. Of course he was right. The gun turned out to be English, of about 1840, instead of a Spanish cannon of 1695.

Following this object lesson I began to dig up information on guns, realizing, as I became more acquainted with them, that they are the most valuable class of artifacts for identifying old wrecks. They offer the diver one incomparable advantage—their universality. If a wreck yields one single artifact, chances are it will be a cannon, big as day, unmistakable, nearly impossible to overlook, and even if badly oxidized still preserving its general form. For this reason I am going into some detail on guns in this identification chapter. To cover the subject thoroughly would require a lifetime of preparation and many volumes, and the following pages are necessarily only an introduction. Yet in them is included enough data directly related to recognition and identification— all superfluous information being eliminated—to permit a cannon-finder to make a positive identification of nearly every type of gun carried on treasure ships and to reach a close estimate of its period and nationality.

The subject is presented in stages: first an introduction and certain necessary definitions; then a breakdown of guns into easily identifiable classes, in turn subdivided into specific guns with a comment on each; and finally physical traits applicable to guns as a whole, valuable for narrowing down the period and nationality. It must be noted that Spanish ships often carried French, Dutch, and Italian guns, purchased from those nations.

INTRODUCTION, NOMENCLATURE AND DEFINITIONS

Shipboard guns fall into a number of groupings, each recognizable either at a glance or after taking a few measurements. The first step in identifying a cannon will be to fit it into one of these general classes which are described in the next section. To help with this some definitions should be made clear. The parts of a gun are diagramed and described below.

LENGTH: distance from front end of the muzzle to back of the breech (but not including the cascabel).

MUZZLE: the very front of the gun barrel.

BREECH: the build-up at the very back of the gun, usually being the back half-foot of the barrel.

VENT: the touch hole, or fuse hole, passing from the top of the barrel (just forward of the breech) into the bore or chamber where the gunpowder was placed.

VENT FIELD DIAMETER: the outer diameter of the gun barrel at the vent.

CHASE: the forward third or half of the gun barrel, from the muzzle to just in front of the trunnions.

CHASE DIAMETER: the outer diameter of the gun barrel at the chase, taken a few inches back of the muzzle.

BORE: the hollow tube inside of the barrel, along which the cannon ball was shot.

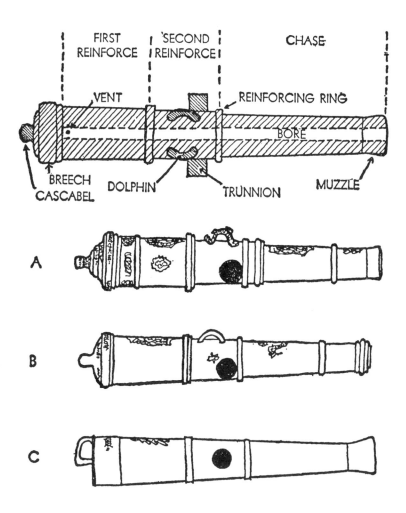

BORE LENGTH: the length of the bore (this can be calculated from the outside, by measuring the distance from the front of the muzzle to one inch back of the vent).

BORE DIAMETER: the diameter of the bore (this can be taken at the muzzle), usually equal to diameter of trunnion.

CALIBER: for our purposes this will be used only in one of its meanings: the ratio between the bore length and the bore diameter. A 20-caliber gun has a bore length 20 times the bore diameter, i.e., the World War II Navy "5-inch 38" has a bore diameter of 5 inches and a caliber of 38, therefore a bore length of 5×38 or 190 inches.

CASCABEL: the knob sticking out from the back of the breech, sometimes pierced with a hole or having a handle joining its end to the top of the breech (through which ran ropes to check the recoil).

DOLPHINS: usually two (rarely one) handles on the top of the barrel over the trunnions, at the balance point, to keep lifting cables from slipping when the barrel was lifted.

TRUNNIONS: two tin-can-shaped solid cylinders cast with the barrel protruding from its opposite sides near the center, which supported it on its gun carriage.

REINFORCING RINGS: rings circling the barrel, either fitted over the barrel (in the earliest lombards) or cast with the barrel (most guns). They are about 1 inch high and 1–2 inches wide, often ornamented with astragals and fillets.

The measurements of importance for identifying a gun are: (a) *caliber* (already defined). (b) the ratio between the vent field diameter and the bore diameter, which we will call the *vent-bore ratio*. If the diameter at the vent field is 18 inches and the bore diameter is 6 inches, the vent-bore ratio is 3:1. (c) the ratio between the chase diameter and the bore diameter, which we will call the *chase-bore ratio*. If the chase diameter is 8 inches and the bore diameter is 3 inches, the chase-bore ratio is 8:3. In the following references I will use these three terms: caliber, vent-bore ratio and chase-bore ratio, since they are important for recognizing certain classes of guns.

Guns are often referred to as "3-pounders" or "24-pounders." This means the weight of the projectiles—cannon balls, or shot—that they fired. The following table relates different weights of *solid iron* shot (cannon balls) to the bore diameter which fired them, and is useful both for estimating the size of a cannon from salvaged shot, and vice versa. Not all shots were solid iron balls (see section on projectiles). Some types of guns fired round stone balls, which weighed about ⅓ as much as iron balls of the same diameter, and the carronades fired hollow iron balls, which weighed about ½ as much as solid shot.

Shot Weight	Bore Diam.	Shot Weight	Bore Diam.
½ pounds	1.5 inches	11 pounds	4.5 inches
1 "	2.0 "	12 "	4.7 "
2 "	2.5 "	18 "	5.2 "
3 "	2.8 "	24 "	5.8 "
4 "	3.0 "	26 "	6.0 "
5.2 "	3.5 "	36 "	6.6 "
6 "	3.7 "	42 "	7.0 "
8 "	4.0 "	48 "	7.3 "
9 "	4.2 "	60 "	8.0 "

CLASSES OF GUNS

Nine general classes of guns, grouped both by dates and certain physical features which permit recognition, are described below. To fit a cannon into one of them, read over the outstanding features of each, then compare them with the salvaged gun. It may be necessary to take measurements of the gun: the bore diameter, the vent field diameter and the chase diameter. The gun's weight and the weight of its shot might also be necessary in some cases for close identification. The weight of the shot can be ascertained from the bore diameter through a glance at the above table.

(1) THE "HOOPED BARREL" GUNS. Recognition feature: the outside of the barrel is wrapped with a series of thick iron rings (be careful not to confuse this class with early cannon, some of which were cast with reinforcing rings along their barrels).

(a) The LOMBARD. Characteristics: open at both ends; breech-loading: usually a chambered breech block was loaded with powder and shot, fitted into the open-ended breech and wedged in place; constructed like a barrel, with *forged* iron strakes, like barrel staves, running lengthwise to form the barrel cylinder, held in place and reinforced by 12 to 20 tough iron bands or hoops spaced every 4 inches or so along the entire barrel length; very large and heavy, weighing from 1500 to 4500 pounds, between 8 and 12 feet long. Vent field diameter 2 feet or more, bore diameter 10 or more inches; shot round *stone* balls, usually from 70 to 90 pounds in weight. Very low caliber of about 12 (see A in photograph opposite page 97).

Significance: this was the first shipboard cannon, used in the Mediterrean in 1400 and aboard the first caravels and *naos* and carracks. The *Pinta* carried one, and there were usually two or more on the vessels of the Spanish and Portuguese exploratory fleets of 1450–1550, and as many as 8 on a 1530 200-ton *nao*. Period: 1380–1575, occasionally as late as 1590. Nationality: any European country, but if found in the Caribbean, likely Spanish.

(b) The PASAVOLANTE (aslo called CERBATANA and DRAGÓN in Spanish and DRAGON and DRAKE in English). Characteristics: no cascabel; muzzle-loading; usually very high caliber of 40–44, infrequently as low as 32; very heavy, very thick barrel with vent-bore ratio of 3½:1 or 4:1 and chase-bore ratio of 2:1 or slightly more. High muzzle velocity earned the name *Pasavolante* which means "hasty action." In appearance long and slender with forged or cast barrel reinforced at about 4-inch intervals by 10 to 30 iron hoops; length varied from 4 to 20 feet, the usual shipboard size being about 11 feet long, with vent field diameter of 1 foot, chase diameter of 7 inches, bore diameter of 3 inches; usually fired a *lead* ball of 6–7 pounds, sometimes an iron ball of 4 pounds (see illustration B of cannons).

Significance: these guns were standard armament on the first *naos* to the Indies. A 1522 ordnance stipulated that 16 *pasavolantes* of various sizes be carried on a 300-ton *nao*. Period: 1500–1630. Nationality: any European country, but very likely Spanish.

(2) THE SWIVEL GUNS. Recognition feature: small, under 6 feet in length, mounted on a swivel joint whose hinges are probably still attached to the gun's sides. Instead of a knoblike cascabel, an 8-inch prong or solid tube.

(a) The VERSO.[1] Characteristics: bronze or iron construction, breech-loading: the top half of the barrel to about one foot forward of the breech is cut away and the gun was loaded by pushing forward the shot and powder into the barrel through this opening, then wedging in place a cork-shaped removable iron breechblock. The swivel mounting was either on trunnions or bearings fitting into holes on the barrel's sides in place of trunnions. Length 4–6 feet, vent field diameter about 6 inches (measured forward of the cut-away breech section), chase diameter about 4 inches, bore diameter 1½–2 inches; fired an iron ball of ½ to 1 pound (see illustration C of cannons).

Significance: these guns were carried on all early caravels and *naos*. An early ordnance stipulated that a 200-ton *nao* carry 18 *versos* and a larger ship at least 24. Period: 1480–1600. Nationality: very likely Spanish.

(b) The SWIVEL. Characteristics: usually cast bronze, sometimes cast iron; muzzle-loading; caliber about 24. Length from 4 to 6 feet, vent field diameter about 6 inches, chase diameter about 4 inches, bore diameter 1½–2 inches; has trunnions; fired an iron ball of ½ to 1 pound; often flared and decorated at muzzle. Distinguished from *verso* by being muzzle-loaded (see photo D of cannons).

Significance: later date than the *verso*. Period: 1525 to after 1800. Nationality: all countries.

(3) THE EARLY LIGHT CARRIAGE GUNS. Recognition feature: under 1400 pounds in weight.

---

[1] The Perrier, similar in form and period of use, usually shot stone balls.

(a) The FALCONETE. Characteristics: about 20 caliber; muzzle-loading; cast bronze or iron, trunnions; cascabel. The French, English, and Spanish models varied so much in weight and size as to make this a distinguishing feature. French: about 400 pounds, 3½ feet in length, 1.5 inches bore diameter, weight of shot ½ pound. English: about 500 pounds, 3 feet 9 inches in length, 2 inches bore diameter, weight of shot 1 pound. Spanish: weight from 600 to 1200 pounds, 5–7 feet long, 2 to 2½ inches bore diameter, weight of shot from 1 to 2 pounds. The above sizes were usual, but had exceptions.

Significance: this gun was common aboard ships of all European countries, one 1200-pounder being standard armament of the 200–400-ton Spanish *naos* of the 1500s. Period: 1510–1675, especially around 1550. Nationality: the above breakdown by size and weight helps permit identification.

(b) The FALCON. Characteristics: caliber from 24 to 28; cast iron or bronze; muzzle-loading; cascabel; trunnions. French, English and Spanish models again differ characteristically. French: weight about 550 pounds, length about 5 feet, bore diameter 2 inches, weight of shot 1 pound. English: weight 650–700 pounds, length 6 feet, bore diameter 2½ inches, weight of shot 2 pounds. Spanish: weight from 1000 to 1400 pounds, length about 8 feet, bore diameter 3 inches, weight of shot 3 to 4 pounds. Again, there were exceptions.

Significance: this gun was primary armament on some smaller ships and secondary armament on larger ones. Period: 1520–1600, and rarely to 1650. Nationality: broken down by weight and size above.

(c) The MINION. Characteristics: thinner barrel, with vent-bore ratio of 2¼:1 and chase-bore ratio of 1¾:1; caliber about 21; cast bronze or iron; cascabel; muzzle-loading. Weight about 1050 pounds, length 6 feet 6 inches, bore diameter 3.5 inches, weight of shot 5.2 pounds.

Significance: this gun was usually English, sometimes French of the 1520–1620 period.

(4) THE SAKERS. Distinguishing features: long, slender barrel, weight up to 2100 pounds, caliber of about 24. Named after the saker hawk, this was a long-range, relatively accurate early gun. Cast bronze or iron; trunnions; cascabel; muzzle-loading. Vent-bore ratio of 2½:1 and chase-bore ratio of 2:1 (see illustration A).

(a) The SAKER (Spanish: SACRE). Characteristics: the common English saker was smaller than the Spanish model, being about 1400 pounds in weight, nearly 7 feet long, with a bore diameter of 3.65 inches, firing a 6-pound shot. The Spanish *sacre* weighed from 1400 to 2000 pounds (1515–50) and from 1700 to 2100 pounds (after 1535). The usual Spanish gun was 8–9 feet long, weighed about 1700 pounds, had a bore diameter of 3.8 to 4.3 inches, and fired a ball from 7 to 10 pounds in weight, usually about 8 pounds.

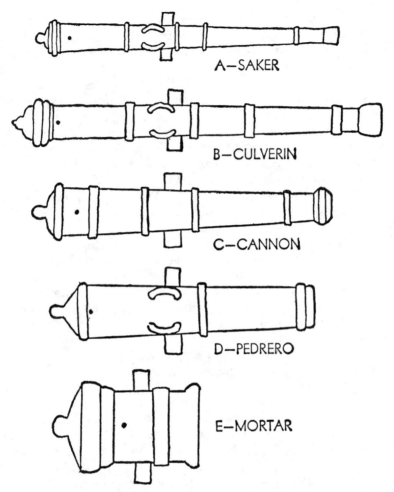

A—SAKER

B—CULVERIN

C—CANNON

D—PEDRERO

E—MORTAR

Significance: the saker was used from 1515 to after 1800 by Spanish and English, as well as other nationalities, being secondary armament on frigates and top deck guns on warships. An idea of the difference between English and Spanish models, and general dates, is given above.

(b) The LIGHT SAKER (Spanish: MEDIA SACRE). Characteristics: about ⅔ the general measurements and weight of the saker (*note:* some Spanish *sacres* were built practically in miniature, down to the size of swivel guns. These are distinguishable from swivels by their more slender barrel and cleaner lines. See photo E of cannons).

Significance: these were usually Spanish, the English using them rarely in later years. Period: 1515–1750.

(5) THE CULVERINS. (Spanish: *CULEBRINA*, French: *COU-LEUVRINE*). Distinguishing features: exceptionally great length, heavy

weight, very thick barrel. Caliber of 30–32, vent-bore ratio of 3:1 and chase-bore ratio of 2:1. Length of 11 feet or more, weight from 2400 to over 7000 pounds. Muzzle-loading; trunnions and cascabel; cast bronze or iron (illustration B).

(a) The CULVERIN. Characteristics: French, English, and Spanish models differed in size and weight. French: about 4200 pounds in weight, 9½ feet long, bore diameter of 5 inches, firing a 15-pound ball. English: 3800 to 4500 pounds in weight, about 12 feet long, vent field diameter of 1 foot 4 inches, chase diameter of 11 inches, bore diameter of 5.2 inches, fired an 18-pound ball. Spanish: ranged in weight from 4000 to 6500 pounds, being usually from 4000 to 5500 in the 1515–50 period and larger after that. In length they varied from 11 to 17 feet and had bore diameter of 5.4, 5.8, 6.2, 6.9, and 7.7 inches. They fired shot weighing 20, 24, 25, 30, 40, and 50 pounds. The most common Spanish *culebrina* was about 14½ feet long, 1½ feet in vent field diameter, 1 foot in chase diameter, 5.8 inches in bore diameter. It fired a 24-pound ball.

Significance: the culverin was used from the early 1500s until the 1800s, going through several changes of decoration during this long time of employment (see section on general identifying characteristics). All nations used this type of gun for long-range, accurate shooting. Because of its size the barrel was nearly always elaborately marked.

(b) The DEMICULVERIN. (Spanish: *MEDIA CULEBRINA*, French: *DEMICOULEUVRINE*). Characteristics: about ⅔ of the weight and dimensions of the culverin, with a caliber of about 28 instead of 30–32. Again French, English, and Spanish models differed. French: weight about 2400 pounds, length about 8 feet, bore diameter 3.9 inches, fired a 7½-pound ball. English: weight about 3400 pounds, length about 9 feet, bore 4 inches, 8-pound shot. Spanish varied greatly, the most common size being 3200 pounds, 11 feet in length, with a bore diameter of 4.7 inches and shooting a 12-pound ball.

Significance: one or two bronze demiculverins of 3000–3200 pounds were standard primary armament on the 1550 Spanish *nao*. Demiculverins were used from 1520 to late in the 1700s, being secondary armament on many classes of warships and frigates, of all nationalities. If bronze they are likely Spanish, if iron, English. Each of these guns is usually well marked for identification.

(c) The CULVERIN BASTARD. Characteristics: about ¾ the weight and general dimensions of the English culverin, except much shorter, as though two feet of the chase had been sawed off. Caliber only about 20. Usually about 3000 pounds, 8½ feet long, bore diameter of 4.56 inches.

Significance: probably English, of 1530–1650 period.

(d) The THIRD-CULVERIN (Spanish: *TERCIO DE CULEBRINA*).

Characteristics: about ⅔ the weight and general dimensions of the Spanish *culebrina*, except that again it is much shorter.

Significance: very rare on shipboard, probably Spanish of 1540–1620 period.

(e) The SMALL CULVERIN. Characteristics: about 700 pounds, 6½ feet long, 2.5 inch bore diameter, 2-pound ball. Caliber about 25.

Significance: French, of 1540–1650.

(f) The GREAT CULVERINS (Spanish: *CULEBRINA REAL, DOBLE CULEBRINA*). Characteristics: enormous weight and length, conforming to the 30 culverin caliber.

Significance: very rare, Spanish of 1540–1650.

(6) THE PEDREROS. Very short; only half as heavy as a culverin of the same bore diameter; fat appearance. Cast iron and bronze, with cascabel, trunnions; muzzle-loading. Fired only *stone* balls. Caliber very low, about 7; vent-bore ratio 2:1 or less and chase-bore ratio 1⅓:1 or 1½:1. This gun usually had a chambered barrel like most mortars—the actual bore ended about 2 feet forward of the vent, instead of just behind it, and a smaller bore ran back to the vent. This smaller bore, or chamber, was filled with gunpowder while the stone ball was rolled back to the end of the bore itself. (To measure the caliber of a pedrero, take the distance from the muzzle to 2 bore diameters forward of the vent.) (Illustration D.)

(a) The PEDRERO. Characteristics: varied through a range of sizes, all easily recognized from the above. An average pedrero was of 3800 pounds, 9 feet long, 1 foot 10 inches vent diameter, 1 foot 5 inches chase diameter, 1 foot bore diameter, and fired a 40–50-pound round stone.

Significance: used on all European ships infrequently. Period: 1540–1700, and in some cases as late as 1850.

(b) The DEMIPEDRERO. Characteristics: about ⅔ of the above.

Significance: same as pedrero.

(7) THE CARRONADE. A cross between the pedrero and the cannon. Recognizable by its large bore diameter, clean lines, thin barrel, short length, and particularly by its big, *hollow* iron projectiles. The carronade was first built in 1778 in Scotland following a design by the English military engineer, Benjamin Robins. By 1781, they were carried by 429 English ships. The weights of shot were 9, 12, 24, 32, 42, and 68 pounds with the bore diameter of the gun for each being about one third more than for corresponding weights of solid shot. Iron carronades were in common use on British ships from 1780 to 1870, on French ships from 1795, and from 1800 onward were standard armament on vessels of all nationalities, including those flying the Jolly Roger. Nearly all had markings on their upper barrels designating their nationality and often their casting date. Hollow iron shot, *with no gunpowder inside*, are

peculiar to carronades and permit positive identification. Two odd weights of carronade shot are probable signals of certain nationalities: a 16-pounder is Spanish and 18-pounder Spanish or Portuguese.

Very low trunnions would date the gun as probably 1780–1800, centered trunnions: 1800–20. Carronades after 1820 often had no trunnions, but instead lugs through which a bar was passed to secure the barrel to the carriage. Early models had a little depressed channel or groove on the top of the vent field, running from the vent to the base ring, to protect the train from wind.

Significance: most ships of nearly all classes included carronades in their armament from 1800–50, making them important for identification of vessels of this period. The above-described characteristics, and markings on the barrel, place the gun by period and nationality.

(8) THE MORTARS. These guns were usually limited to mortar bombs and certain other classes of bombardment ships that would not carry treasure. They were used from the late 1500s to well in the 1800s. Although sometimes warships carried as many as 12 mortars, they were not popular afloat. Mortars are easily recognized by their large diameter bore, big circumference and short, stubby appearance like two kitchen pots, one on top of the other. They weighed up to several tons (illustration E).

(9) THE CANNON. The chances are that most guns found in wrecks dating after 1600 are cannons. The distinguishing features of this class are great weight for its length, a "normal" appearance—neither long and slender nor (with some exceptions) short and stubby. The cannon 5–8 feet long, 1¼–2½ tons and shooting a 4–8-pound ball from a 3–4-inch diameter bore is the usual gun found in old wrecks. During its evolution from 1500 to 1850 the cannon went through many modifications as one nation, then another, improved the design. It ranged in size from one-pounders weighing 400 pounds to monsters of four tons and more, shooting 74-pound shot (see illustration C).

Cannons all had trunnions and cascabels. They were muzzle-loading. Their usual caliber was from 14 to 22, vent-bore ratio between 3:1 and 4:1, and chase-bore ratio from 2:1 to 3:1. They were cast iron and bronze. Nearly all had markings and other identification features discussed later. They made their appearance as cast bronze and iron muzzleloaders with low trunnions about 1520. Until the 1700s they were all sizes and shapes, having little uniformity in design. During the 1700s cannons became standardized. The most logical way to cover their evolution would be by nationality.

English: from 1520 to about 1760 cannons were very heavy—more so than any other nation's—weighing up to 310 pounds per one pound of the projectile's weight. They ranged in caliber from 18 to 22, and had a vent-bore ratio of 3½:1 or 4:1 and a chase-bore ratio of 2½:1

or more. They were decorated, but less so than the Spanish and French guns, had thick first and second reinforces and four or five heavy reinforcing rings. Their shot weights could be nearly anything during the 1500s, but by 1625 had become fairly standardized to 3, 6, 9, 12, 18, 24, 32, and 42 pounders. From 1630 to 1760 the caliber was about 20, the first reinforce was ²⁄₇ of the barrel's length, the second reinforce about ³⁄₁₄, and the chase about ½, with the trunnions very far forward, about ⁴⁄₇ of the way to the muzzle, and low. From 1760 to 1850, following John Müller's reforms, the length was shortened by a quarter and the barrel was lightened by nearly a half. The 1760–1850 cannon is characterized by the following: weight of barrel per one pound of shot: about 150 pounds; reinforcing stages practically eliminated, resulting in a smooth, tapered barrel with only two low reinforcing rings; trunnions brought back to the halfway point and raised to center; caliber greatly reduced to only 15, resulting in a much shorter barrel. Shot weights were of 3, 6, 9, 12, 18, 24, 32, 36, 42, and 48 pounds. The table below shows the gun lengths and shot weights before and after Müller's reforms:

Shot Weight	Before 1760	After 1760
3 pounds	4 ft. 6 in.	3 ft. 6 in.
4 "	6 "	—
6 "	7–8 "	4 " 4 "
9 "	7–8 "	5 "
12 "	9 "	5 " 6 "
18 "	9 "	6 " 4 "
24 "	9 " 6 "	7 "
32 "	9 " 6 "	7 " 6 "
36 "	—	7 " 10 "
42 "	9½–10 ft.	8 " 4 "
48 "	—	8 " 6 "

Spanish: guns of the 1520–1700 period are characterized by elaborate decorations and heavy reinforcements. A 4800-pound cannon of 1540 often had the sculptured figure of an eagle, or an indian with a club, or a crown with the corresponding name LA AGUILA or EL SALVAJE or LA CORONA on the top of the barrel. There were sizes and shot weights varying through the whole scale. From 1700 to 1812 Spain was dominated by France, and employed the French armament standard (see below). Guns had cleaner lines, but were often decorated with names of ships, kings, animals, saints, and hoped-for results: EL ASIANO (warship *Asia*), EL TORO (The Bull), EL DESTRUZO (The Destroyer), etc., characterize this epoch, but if sculpture is excessively elaborate might pertain to the 1550–1700 period. Weights of shot were 4, 8, 12, 16, 24, 32, and 48 used by France, but also 6, 10, 18, 36, and other non-French sizes. These Spanish guns were of 20–25 caliber and weighed about 250 pounds to the pound of shot until after 1780, when they were reduced following Müller's suggestions. In general characteristics they were fairly close to English models of the same periods. Smaller iron cannons of 1 or 2 tons had been simplified by 1680, having little decoration and clean lines (see photograph of Vigo cannons).

French: from 1550 to 1700 guns again varied greatly, the French being even more unstandardized than the Spanish. A 33-pound cannon would be French of this period, or Dutch. After 1700 French models were fixed at 4, 8, 12, 16, 24, 32, and 48 pounders. After 1765 the barrel's weight was reduced from around 250 to 150 pounds per pound of shot. Elaborate decorations were usual before this time, and cut down after.

Swedish: cannons were lighter per pound of shot, but followed the general trend.

Dutch: tended to follow the Spanish, French, and English at different periods.

Portuguese: same as Spanish from 1580 to 1640, and followed the same general trends afterwards.

Other classes of cannon: the cannon family ranged through a wide variety of models, among them: the QUARTER-CANNON, the THIRD-CANNON, the DEMICANNON, the BASTARD CANNON, the CHAMBERED CANNON, the DOUBLE FORTIFIED or REINFORCED CANNON and the LIGHT CANNON. These all conform more or less to the 15–22 caliber, 3:1 and 4:1 vent-bore ratio and 2:1 and 3:1 chase-bore ratio. The quarter and third cannons are exceptions, being stubby and having calibers as low as 10. The demicannon was very common on third-rate ships from 1600–1750. An average gun of this type was 11 feet long, weighed 5500 pounds, had a 5.8 bore diameter and fired 24-pound shot. The bastard cannon was about one third thinner in its vent and chase diameters, but with the same length and bore. The double fortified model had vent and chase diameters about one fourth more than normal, and was very popular during 1550–1600. The light cannon was small, as light as 300 pounds with a 2-inch bore diameter. The chambered cannon had a chambered bore like a pedrero. They were all used by various nationalities throughout the 1520–1850 period and adhered to general distinguishing features already discussed.

DISTINGUISHING FEATURES

(a) DECORATIONS and MARKINGS: on the barrel of nearly every gun will be found marks and reliefs. These fall into categories of (1) pure art, (2) founder's signature and date, (3) facts about the gun and owner, (4) ordnance marks.

(1) Some guns were so highly decorated that they classify as art

treasures. Fancy scrolls, curlicues, statues of animals, fish, Indian savages, mermaids, etc., in high and low relief, denote them as Spanish or French of the period 1530–1650. Samples of this type, nearly always bronze, were the 4700-pound cannons called "coronas" because they carried a royal crown sculptured in high relief forward of the vent, the 5500-pound "pelicano" (sculptured pelican), the "salvage" (sculptured savage carrying a club), etc. Fancy coats of arms and many inscriptions in Latin were also on the top and breech. The "Glede Gun" from the Tobermory galleon, cast in the 1540s by Benvenuto Cellini, is typical, but with cleaner lines than most. It is bronze, about 3 tons in weight, 10'3" long, 9'1" bore length, 5½" bore diameter. This gun was cast for King Francis I of France. The Salamander, which was that king's emblem, is on the breech; his royal escutcheon is on top of the barrel forward of the vent; along the chase are the marks of the Fleur-de-Lis alternating with the letter "F" for François.

Barrels of the period 1650–1760 were also elaborately decorated, but only in low relief except where such natural protrusions as the cascabel were sculptured in the form of a lion's head, etc. These 1650–1760 guns usually had their breeches and upper surface of the barrel engraved with two or three inscriptions encased in elaborate scrolls, a big escutcheon forward of the breech, and low relief designs on other parts. Such a gun would be probably Spanish or French.

After 1760 barrels were much cleaner, with usually only scattered engraved names, escutcheons, ogees, and symbolic figures, like a spread-winged eagle over the trunnions, to break their smooth surfaces. English barrels were fairly plain at all times.

(2) On French, Spanish, and Dutch bronze pieces the founder's name in Latin, and the casting date, were often carved around the back of the breech. Typical of this is the marking on "El Asiano," a gun cast by one of the Solano family in Spain. It reads: SOLANO FECIT. HISPAÑA. ANNO. 1762. (made by Solano. Spain. Year 1762). Other famous Spanish gunsmiths were Francisco Mir—FRANCISCUS MIR FECIT—(1720-40), Pedro Ribot—RIBOT FECIT—(1696-1733), and José Barnola—JOSEPHUS BARNOLA FECIT—(1738-44). A Dutch gun might carry LAMBERTO BORGERINCK ME FECIT.

(3) Valuable bronze guns were often decorated with beautifully engraved escutcheons of reigning families, and even iron cannons frequently carried simpler marks of kings. These run through dozens of patterns—too many to detail here. Some of the more frequently encountered: the arms of Castile and León appeared on Spanish cannons at all times, incorporating many variations and additions (i.e., the chain square and diagonals of Navarre, appearing about 1790); the Rose and Crown of the Tudors were frequently on English cannons up to 1714.

From 1714 onward the flowery initials GR (George Rex) were cast on the barrels of most English guns; the Fleur-de-Lis on a cannon identifies it as French (it was also, however, incorporated into the shield of Spain from 1700 to 1808); a big N with or without a spread-winged eagle, the mark of Napoleon, would indicate a French gun of the 1808–15 period. (The eagle can be misleading, for it was also used later in France and by the Germans, Romans, etc.)

Latin names of kings, such as CAROLUS II.D.G.HISPAN.ET.IND.REX (Carlos II, King of Spain and the Indies), were often cast around the back of the breech, telling the nationality and period. The name of the carrying warship was sometimes cast on the barrel, as in the case where guns for the Spanish *navio Asia* bore EL ASIANO. Other inscriptions such as EL TORO, EL ESPANTO, VIOLATI.FULMINA.REGIS (thunderbolts of an outraged king) can be useful for recognizing nationality and often dates.

(4) Ordnance marks appeared on barrels of many nations at different periods. English guns nearly always carried the Broad Arrow cut on top, forward of the breech. This is a mark in the form ⌁ or ↑ with each indent only 1 or 2 inches long and consequently easily overlooked. The closed form was generally used later, from about 1700 (but not always). English guns were also marked B.O. (for British Ordnance) at some periods.

For illustrations of representative markings on gun barrels, the reader is referred to pages 152–69 of Mendel Peterson's *History Under the Sea*. The names of more detailed books are listed in the Bibliography under WRECK IDENTIFICATION.

(b) METALS and REINFORCES: both iron and bronze were used simultaneously by all countries, and the construction metal offers by itself little of identification value. (Exception: extensive analysis of bronze might determine nationality and epoch.) In general, most English guns were of cast iron while Spain and France always favored bronze for fighting ships. One very important aid for identification can be drawn from the gun's metal. In a wreck identified as Spanish, if all or most of the guns are (a) bronze, it is nearly certainly a *Capitana*, *Almiranta*, or war galleon. Such a find in the northwest Caribbean or along the return route would denote registry treasure. The *Capitanas* and *Almirantas* carried from 24 to 90 guns, depending on their size, usually all bronze; (b) iron, the ship is a cargo *nao*.

Guns of the time before 1510 were forged (although casting was tried as early as 1470). A mixed group of forged and cast guns in a wreck would place it in the 1510–30 period (the Spanish *nao Angela*, in 1518, carried 31 forged and 10 cast guns). After 1530 guns were cast, with trunnions, although earlier forged pieces were still in use years later.

Reinforcing of cannons went through stages. From 1500 to about 1700 the typical barrel looked like three cylinders, each of smaller diameter, fitted end to end with a large hoop at each joining point and several more in between on the cylinders. This reinforcement in stages, progressively larger toward the breech, was smoothed out somewhat during the 1700–60 period (see example "B"). Müller's reforms eliminated it entirely after 1760, and guns of this later period slope in a straight line (see example "C"). Reinforcing rings, adorned with fillets, astragals, and moldings, numbered as many as six along the barrel of the 1500–1700 gun (example "A"). They were much simpler in form and usually limited to three or four during 1700–60 (example "B"). After 1760 only two rings, small and clean in form (example "C"), were standard.

(c) The CASCABEL: this was usually a simple knob, like a doorknob, and is of little value for identification purposes, except that a hole running sideways through it or a handle joining its end to the top of the breech (see example "C") would tend to place the gun as after 1700. French cascabels were sometimes elaborately decorated.

(d) The BREECH. Breech-loading guns were of the earlier period, from 1350 to 1520. Guns from 1520 onward were muzzle-loading until recent times. Early breeches were rounded or even pointed (examples "A" and "B"). After 1750 they were usually flat ("C").

(e) The VENT. IF two vents, side by side, are found on a barrel the gun is of the 1700–1850 period. One of the vents will be plugged, the other open.

(f) The DOLPHINS. Some barrels had them, others did not, with apparently no particular reason. In general the barrels of guns up to 1770 would be more likely to have dolphins than those made after this date. Their name stems from the popular design in which they were cast in the 1500s and 1600s—two dolphins arched in the air with their heads and tails joining the barrel ("A" and photograph D of cannons). After 1770 simple handles tended to replace the more elaborate fish and other sculptured designs ("B").

(g) The TRUNNIONS. These are important for dating. From 1476 (the earliest known) to about 1520 they were centered on the horizontal level with the gun's axis, sticking out the sides halfway up the barrel. Early in the 1500s they were lowered to the bottom of the barrel ("A" and "B") and remained down until about 1760, when Müller raised them to the center again. From 1760 onward they were centered ("C").

(h) The MUZZLE. Muzzles on the first guns were likely to open outward like the end of a trumpet. After 1540 the enlargement was less pronounced, but still there. From about 1670 to 1730 the banded muzzle ("B") was in vogue for bronze guns. A flared, or bell-shaped muzzle, was characteristic of the period 1730–80 (example "C") and from then onward the simple clean muzzle (see example "A"). Spanish iron guns from 1600 onward were much cleaner in design than bronze ones.

The identifying of a gun barrel is a big help in wreck identification, but these points must be considered: first, as said before, the ship's nationality is not always that of the gun. Cannons were valuable prizes and when captured were used by the victors; second, the casting date on a gun provides only the earliest possible date of the wreck. The normal life of an iron barrel was 20 to 40 years; a bronze one could still be in use 100 years after casting and they frequently were.

To round out the subject of marine guns, here is a sampling of the type of armament found on representative ships of different periods:

1338: English ships *Mary, Bernard* and *Christopher of the Tower* carried forged bronze and iron guns.

1500: the Spanish royal galley *San Juan Bautista*, on Mediterranean service, carried:

  1 "fat" lombard of 4300 pounds with ten stone projectiles
 12 smaller lombards
 12 pasavolantes

1515: a *nao* of under 200 tons carried:

  1 bronze saker of 2000 pounds and 30 balls
  1 falconete
  6 "fat iron guns"
 12 versos

1515: a *nao* of 200 tons carried:

  1 3000 pound demiculverin
  1 bronze saker of 1400 pounds
  1 falconete of 1200 pounds
  8 lombards
 18 versos

1515: a *nao* of 250 tons carried:

  1 demiculverin of 3200 pounds or 1 cannon of 4200 pounds
  2 sakers, one of 2000 pounds, the other of 1400
  1 falconete of 1200 pounds
 10 lombards
 24 versos

1522: the smallest ship to the Indies carried at least:

  4 cannons
 16 pasavolantes
 26 long muskets

1538: a fleet for the Indies carried:
4800-pound cannons called "Coronas"
5500-pound cannons called "Pelicans," "Eagles," "Savages"
pedreros
culverins
demiculverins
sakers
falconetes
pasavolantes
demipedreros

1572: a 750-ton *Capitana* carried:
  5 large culverins
  3 medium culverins
  2 sakers
14 cannons
12 double versos

1628: Swedish warship *Wasa* carried:
48 24-pounder cannons
  8 3-pounder cannons
  2 1-pounder guns
  6 mortars

1656: the Tierra Firme armada ships carried:
Capitana: 26 bronze guns
Almiranta: 24 bronze guns
Naos and *Urcas:* 26–30 mostly iron, some bronze, guns

1702: the New Spain armada carried:
Capitana: 44 bronze guns
Almiranta: 54 bronze guns
Buffona (extra war galleon): 54 bronze guns
Naos: 24 to 40 iron guns apiece
Pataches: 8 to 12 iron guns each

1702: H.M.S. *Pembroke* (two-decker warship):
20 24-pounder cannons (or demicannons)
  2 12-pounder cannons
  2 3-pounder cannons
20 demiculverins
10 sakers

1720: Spanish 776-ton warship *Conquistador* carried:
26 18-pounder cannons
28 12-pounder cannons
10 8-pounder cannons

1758: Spanish 990-ton warship *Astuto* carried:
24   18-pounder cannons
26   12-pounder cannons
8   6-pounder cannons

1787: Spanish 1360-ton warship *Fulgencio* carried:
26   24-pounder cannons
28   12-pounder cannons
10   8-pounder cannons

1801: Spanish brigantine *San Francisco Javier* carried:
4   carronades of 16 pounds
10   6-pounder cannons
4   4-pounder cannons

1804: H.M.S. *Indefatigable* carried:
26   24-pounder cannons
16   carronades of 42 pounds
12   mortars of 12-inch bore diameter

Descriptions of the armament of other ships are given throughout the treasure chapters.

PROJECTILES

Cannon balls and shot are valuable in identification. The kinds likely to be encountered in old wrecks are described below.

(1) STONE BALLS: until the early 1400s all projectiles were stone, sometimes given a coat of lead. After 1420 iron shot replaced stone except for use in pedreros, perriers, and lombards (see previous section). Any stone projectiles found in the Atlantic or Caribbean would likely be for these kinds of early guns.

(2) LEAD BALLS: if very small, up to one inch in diameter, would be shot for the arquebuses and early muskets. Lead balls of 4 pounds or over would be shot for the pasavolante.

(3) CAST IRON BALLS: these were introduced for all classes of guns except those mentioned in (1) and (2) in the early 1400s. By 1500 iron shot were in general use and continued to be used late in the 1800s. Their weight can be useful in determining the size of gun which fired them but otherwise they have little identification value. Often a mark will appear on the iron shot—we found several with circular imprints in which was a relief of what seemed like a spread-winged eagle—but these are probably sprue marks from the mold when they were cast.

(4) BAR SHOT or DOUBLEHEAD: these are valuable for dating. They appeared in the 1600s in the form of two cannon balls joined

by a 5- or 6-inch-square iron bar. These, of forged iron, denote the period 1640–1760. Later bar shots were milled (a blacksmith can tell the difference) and the bar joining the balls was usually round. Bar shot found with disks at the ends instead of cannon balls would probably be of the later date, from 1760 onward. Round cannon ball and half-ball ends continued to be used, however, until the 1800s.

(5) CHAIN SHOT: appeared in the 1700s and was used through the middle 1800s. It consists of two cannon balls joined by about 6 inches of chain.

(6) EXPLOSIVE PROJECTILES: these were hollow iron balls, filled with gunpowder, with a fuse hole. They were used from the late 1300s until the 1800s nearly exclusively in mortars, and after 1800 in guns. From 1700 to 1800 there was usually a little round neck projecting from the ball with the fuse hole in its center. After 1800 this neck was replaced by a little groove on each side of the fuse hole where tongs could grab the ball. After 1850 the inside of the projectile was often channeled like the outside of a modern hand grenade.

(7) The CARCASS: this was an incendiary projectile, hollow and filled with combustible chemicals or pitch. Penetrating the sides were 3 to 6 little holes through which flames streamed out. It was used from the middle 1600s to after 1800.

(8) CANISTER or CASE SHOT: consisted of a light can filled with odds and ends like musket balls, scraps of iron, etc., which broke on being fired and unleashed its contents to kill and wound crews of enemy ships. It was used throughout the 1460–1800 period.

(9) GRAPE SHOT: from 1550 to about 1800 grape or cored shot was made by wrapping a canvas covering around 20–40 small iron balls, about an inch in diameter, against a wooden rod with wood disks the size of the gun bore at each end. The canvas was tied in place, holding the balls inside, by cords (hence the term "cored shot" sometimes used). The wood broke upon being fired, releasing the balls. After 1800 the wood frame was replaced by an iron rod with three or more tiers of iron disks. The space between each two disks was filled with twelve or more iron balls, and the whole shot was wrapped and tied up.

(10) CARRONADE SHOT: is distinguished by a hollow iron ball containing no gunpowder nor pitch. Its dates of use were 1780–1870 (see previous section).

(11) HOT SHOT: were rarely used after the experience of the French in the 1700s, who set more of their own ships afire than those of the enemy. A furnace was necessary between decks, on which iron balls were heated red hot then dropped in the barrel.

(12) FLAMING SHOT: were used in the 1800s. They can be distinguished by their small solid iron balls in which a slight hole was made. The end of a piece of cloth, impregnated with saltpeter, was

wedged into this hole. It was shot, flaming, into the sails of enemy ships, where the cloth was pulled loose and stuck as the ball went on through.

(13) UNUSUAL BAR SHOT: new varieties have been recently found in wrecks. One, which seems unique, was discovered by Colonel Frank F. Tenney, Jr., in his "Minnie Ball Wreck" off Key Vaca. Its two halves are hinged together. Another unusual design is a sliding bar shot where the two end disks are held together by interlocked bars, permitting them to slide apart after firing.

(14) MORTAR PROJECTILES: are readily identified by their large size—usually a foot or more in diameter—and were filled with gunpowder. They were used rarely except from specialized mortar-firing ships.

By tabulating the variety and size of shot, a great deal can be learned about the ship that carried them. For example, if three distinct sizes of shot are found on a wreck site, the ship in all probability carried three classes of guns and was a two- or three-decker. Large 48-pound cannon balls would indicate a warship carrying heavy guns, small shot only would signify a smaller vessel, and so on. Interesting examples of the identification of wrecks from the types and sizes of the projectiles found are the *Girona* and *Santa María de la Rosa*.

CHAPTER 6

Submarine Archaeology—I

During recent years a new kind of treasure diving has been growing in popularity. Its rewards are not dripping ingots and coral-crusted doubloons; they are Greek amphorae, bronze Spanish sakers, Stone Age tools, Roman marble carvings, and American historical relics. These, the artifacts of our ancestors, are the treasures of the submarine archaeologist. Money can be gained from their sale to museums, yet this is not their appeal to divers. It is rather the satisfaction of contributing to the knowledge of mankind. For the worthless-appearing bits of junk scattered over the ballast of lost ships, or lying buried in the mud of once-sacred lakes, or piled amid animal bones in sunken caves, are historical links with the past, rich with information about our forerunners and their ways of life.

Treasure divers take naturally to submarine archaeology. Nearly everyone with a normal amount of curiosity will become an enthusiast after he has made a find or two of old artifacts. The conversion follows a set pattern: a diver goes down on sunken ships drawn by his hope of finding a million dollars. When he discovers that the sea bed is not paved with gold he begins to wonder about the other stuff that is there, on the mounds of ballast stones, and raises some of it and asks questions. Then he tries to learn about the wreck itself— and has already become an enthusiast. Nearly all the old pros in the world of underwater exploration—McKee, Link, Marx, Tucker, Cousteau, Dumas, Sténuit, Throckmorton, Díaz, to name a few—have taken this route.

To find coffers of money on the ocean floor you have to be either exceptionally lucky or well prepared, yet nearly anyone with access to a navigable ocean, river, or lake can find a sunken ship with interesting artifacts.

Archaeological knowledge can be very useful to a "straight" treasure hunter. It will help him in the identification of old wrecks and often set him on the track to a real intrinsic treasure. By recognizing its cannons, for instance, he can usually distinguish a galleon from a warship. Or he might, while searching for a lost ship, come across and identify some of its drifted wreckage and know that he was getting close. This happened off Vigo Bay, Spain, in the search for the *Monmouth*'s galleon, when one of the divers found a wooden pulley on the ocean floor—and recognized it as being identical to others raised thirty years earlier from another galleon and recorded in photographs. It happened to Thompson when his hope was failing during the early part of the excavation from Chichén Itzá. Perfume balls, which he knew from his study of the Mayan rites were used in their sacrifices, turned up in the dredged mud. He knew then that he was getting warm.

There is another advantage to being an amateur submarine archaeologist. This hobby can turn an otherwise fruitless hunt into an outstanding success. Instead of returning empty-handed, without a single piece of eight, the diver can have the satisfaction that he has found and identified a much-sought-after sixteenth-century *verso* or a worm-eaten quadrant, and, having recognized their value, can see that they end up in a museum instead of a junk yard. Teddy Tucker's famous "Bishop's Cross" could probably be duplicated today for a few thousand dollars, which would be its intrinsic value. Historical interest has caused it to be appraised at $25,000–$75,000. Thompson's artifacts from Chichén Itzá, merely valuable for their gold, are considered priceless by the Peabody Museum because of their ancient Mayan origin. The "Glede Gun" from the *Tobermory* galleon is worth perhaps a thousand dollars in bronze, but as an archaeological work of art could bring a high price. Even a clay amphora from a Greek galley, which has no intrinsic value at all, sells for $50 to $100 because of its historical interest.

The "Bishop's Cross" and Mayan artifacts, made of precious metal and stones, fall under the popular "treasure" classification. But the gun and amphora can be sold for money, as well, which is more or less the definition of treasure. All can be considered "treasures" because they are valuable, and also "archaeological treasures" because their historical interest gives them a great part of this value. Most of the older sunken treasures described in this book, from pieces of eight in Spanish galleons to Roman bronzes in one way or another fall into the "archaeological treasure" category. Excluded today would be such modern losses as the coins and ingots in the *Egypt;* yet five centuries from now these, too, will command a far higher price than their intrinsic worth, because they will have acquired historical value with passing years.

These chapters on submarine archaeology will cover losses and recoveries of ancient artifacts with limited intrinsic worth which would not generally be considered "treasure," but which, because of their value to museums and collectors, are treasures in some respect far more valuable than silver or gold.

There was little known of the rich archaeological hunting ground under the seas until Captain Cousteau's salvage of Marcos Sestios' Greek galley off Grand Congloue near Marseilles. The publicity given this work in the *National Geographic Magazine* and other publications alerted divers all over the world to this new field. In America, Ed Link and Mendel Peterson, Art McKee, and several others joined the search for relics of the past. When treasure-hunting fever spread they worked hard to bring order to the secrecy and suspicion that sprang up with the discovery of wrecks, and to stop their senseless destruction by hit-and-run dynamiters looking for a fast buck—and leaving in their wake destroyed museums.[1] The Smithsonian Institution's pamphlet on the finding and identification of H.M.S. *Looe* was one of the first serious studies into this subject and makes very instructive reading. Peterson has subsequently published other guides for those who come across old ships and has helped identify countless artifacts salvaged by divers in various parts of the world. Bob Nesmith has made valuable contributions through his expert identification of money recovered from the sea.

A paragraph in a letter written ten years ago by John Huston, Secretary, Council of Underwater Archaeology, San Francisco, sums up neatly the situation as it still remains today in areas where measures have not been taken to protect old sites:

> Underwater archeology today is in about the same position that land archeology was in the eighteenth century. Divers are making chance discoveries and are taking the objects from the secret sites in the hope of finding articles of monetary value. The tragedy is that treasure is one in a million, but the looting of the site disperses objects so that the clues to the history of the wreck are lost. More important, we lose the wreck itself since the removal of the deck cargo obliterates the site and prevents future discovery. . . .

Fortunately for historians and treasure divers alike, steps *have* been taken in many states and countries to control historical wreck salvage. In the chapters of Section Two of this book, I have made frequent references to archaeological bodies interested in old wrecks, and the steps being taken to prevent their wanton destruction. Mr. Carl J. Clausen, Florida State Archaeologist who has been closely involved with the salvage of artifacts and treasure from dozens of Spanish galleon and *nao* wrecks off the coast and Keys of Florida, explains the benefit accruing from scientific wreck salvage in *Some Comments on Pre-1800 Sites—Maritime*, published in *Historical Archaeology 1967:*

> There is a growing interest among an increasing number of disciplines in the world underwater. Following the development of relatively inexpensive and safe systems for exploring shallow water areas, the archaeologist has been offered the opportunity to extend his domain. The new underwater environment offers a source of information of interest to the archaeologist specializing in historic sites work. This source is the considerable number of wrecks of vessels of various types and nationalities and their cargos which were lost along the coasts and in the navigable water-

[1] An extreme example: Recently an entire early seventeenth-century wreck, perhaps the only one of that nationality and year, was destroyed for *two copper coins.*

ways of the Americas during the periods of exploration, colonization and
early development in this hemisphere.

Many of these wrecks, because of their association with significant events
or phases of our past, are important historical sites in their own right,
comparable in many ways to those on land. Examples which come to
mind range from the wreck of the flagship of Columbus on a reef off the
north coast of Haiti, through those wrecks of ships of the ill-fated French
expedition to Florida in the mid-1500's, and the loss to storms of ships of
homeward bound Spanish fleets laden with the produce of the Americas,
to wrecks of vessels of the fledgling Navy of the United States.

Shipwrecks in general have one advantage over the majority of historical
period sites on land which bears comment. This advantage might be referred to as the "time capsule factor." It stems first from the fact that the
generally violent circumstances surrounding the demise of most vessels
insures that a cross-sectional sample of at least the sea-borne material culture of the period will be isolated at the wreck site; and secondly, that
these wrecks and their associated materials can often be placed temporally
through historical research occasionally to the day, even the exact hour,
that the sample entered the water.

This "capsule" feature, in conjunction with the fact that through the
entire period under consideration in this paper, i.e., late 15th century to
the end of the 18th century, an ever-increasing number of vessels of many
nationalities were lost, creates in effect almost continuous series of tightly
dated sites covering approximately three centuries through which the
development of many aspects of culture could be traced. The potential
for comparative data alone in such a series is, I think, readily apparent.

While the survival of materials in underwater wreck sites is admittedly
selective in favor of inorganic, relatively dense substances, surprising in-
stances of preservation have occurred. For example, pages of a book with
legible print have survived more than three centuries in a wreck lying off
present-day Cape Kennedy in Florida (Harnett 1965: 39–45). Items which
do survive are often in a condition unequalled in coeval archaeological
sites on land, wrested from men's hands unbroken or before their useful
life had ended. Occasionally, materials are present which, because of their
mundane character, were passed over entirely in the literature of the
period. As examples of all the above, we have hafted tools—hammers and
hatchets—with large portions of their handles remaining, intact spirit bottles, and wooden packing chests for lead shot and silver coins recovered
recently from a 250-year-old Spanish flagship off the Florida coast.

The potential of this wreck population as a prime source of information
for the historic sites archaeologist is perhaps best exemplified by the
recovery of the early 17th century Swedish warship *Wasa*, raised largely
intact from the muddy bottom of Stockholm Harbor. Although an example from Europe and perhaps unique, this vessel contained, in addition
to the basic data on marine design and construction (information which,
I might add, was generally considered unavailable until much later in that
century), intact sea chests full of personal belongings, complete sets of
apparel, trousers, hats, sweaters, shoes, boxes of tools, sails and even foodstuffs (Franzén 1966).

Recovered materials, particularly those from a salt water environment,
do present special problems in handling and preservation, but continued

research is providing answers. Albright[2] at the Smithsonian has recently achieved great success in preserving organic materials, particularly wood, recovered from wrecks.

Techniques for the controlled recovery of information from archeological sites underwater are also developing both abroad[3] and to a limited extent in this country. Recently, a magnetometer has been used to plot the distribution of the ferrous components of an individual historic period wreck as a guide for further recoveries.

Since Goggin[4] first spelled out the nature and limitations of underwater archaeology, very little serious research has been accomplished in this country. What we are considering here is virtually an untouched resource. In these brief comments on pre-1800 wrecks, only a few points have been brought out. I feel that as research in the area of wreck archaeology grows, as it most certainly will, and new techniques are developed to counter the hostile environment offered by the sea, the interest of the historic sites archaeologist will be increasingly drawn to information gained from the wreck population. Certainly it holds the answers to many of the questions that will be posed from work on land.

An idea of the growing popularity of submarine archaeology can be gained by the great number and variety of finds being reported. Nearly every day, in some part of the world, divers come across the artifacts of some old civilization which have lain, undisturbed, on the ocean floor for centuries or millenniums. Some of the more interesting are described in the following pages.

THE MEDITERRANEAN

In the field of submarine archaeology, the logical place to start is the Mediterranean, for this is the birthplace of western civilization as well as the site of many of the earliest recoveries. Nearly every part of its offshore perimeter covers sunken ships and cities dating back as much as 4000 years. The eastern flank, off the coasts of Egypt and Israel, holds hundreds of vessels of the Assyrian, Persian, and Macedonian empires. Off Alexandria lie galleys of Caesar and Ptolemy, while nearby, in Abukir Bay, are the hulls of thirteen of Napoleon's warships sent to the bottom by Lord Nelson in 1798.

In Palestine's Dead Sea archaeologists hope to find traces of ships from the period of Christ, while just off its west coast lies the historic

[2] ALBRIGHT, ALAN B.
   1966 "The preservation of Small Waterlogged Wood Specimens with Polyethylene Glycol." *Curator*, Publication of the American Museum of Natural History, Vol. IX, No. 3.
[3] BASS, GEORGE F.
   1964 "Excavating a Byzantine Shipwreck." In *Diving Into The Past* (J. D. Holmquist and A. H. Wheeler, Eds.), Proceedings of the 1963 Conference on Underwater Archaeology. St. Paul, Minn.
[4] GOGGIN, JOHN M.
   1960 "Underwater Archaeology, Its Nature and Limitations." *American Antiquity*, Vol. 25, No. 3.

Roman-Jewish port of Caesarea, which has settled into the sea. Two thousand years ago Caesarea was described by a Roman author as enormous, with a long mole reaching out from shore on which stood a temple and three tall columns on stone block pedestals. In recent centuries fishermen have dragged up from its silt Roman sarcophagi, vases, and sculptures. A French skin-diving expedition visited the site in 1954, followed two years later by Ed Link in conjunction with the Smithsonian. He discovered the partly silted-over sea wall of the mole when he dived there, as well as shaped stone pedestals of columns and other relics.

Fascinated by his findings, Link returned a few years later aboard his *Sea Diver* with a group of diver-archaeologists including *Life* Senior Editor Ken MacLeish, Professor John Bullitt of Harvard, Marion Link, and their son Clayton. From under the harbor of the ancient port—built by Herod, King of the Jews, ten years before Christ was born, and residence of Pontius Pilate—the divers airlifted sediment and recovered fragments of Roman jars and vases, a complete amphora, a unique scalloped lamp, ivory hairpins, bronze nails and coins, together with carvings and building material believed to have been used in the construction of two colossi at the entrance of the harbor. The most significant find was a small commemorative medal, or *tessera*. On one side appeared the Greek letters KA (Caesarea) and a miniature picture of the port showing the colossi and Roman ships in the harbor. Ken MacLeish wrote a beautifully illustrated account of the expedition for the May 5, 1961, issue of *Life* magazine.

A few miles north, off Lebanon, is a sunken museum of Phoenician and Persian ships in the vicinity of Sidon and Tyre. In their long histories these Phoenician ports were visited by countless trading ships and ancient men-of-war. It was at Tyre that Alexander the Great constructed a mole joining the island fortress to the shore so that his armies could bypass its naval defenses, and, according to Aristotle, sent down a diving bell whose occupant cut away submarine defenses— 2275 years before our frogmen did the same at Normandy! Tyre must be ringed with ancient vessels.

Just off western Turkey are at least three submerged archaeological hunting grounds. The American Peter Throckmorton, diving with members of the Izmir Divers' Club, has spent months exploring the area. He reports: "There are some sunken waterfronts in places like Cyme and other classical towns that have lost part of their sea frontage because of gradual land subsidence. We did locate many wrecks." Among them is a gem that sent archaeologists into ecstasies: an intact galley off the Bodrum peninsula, 90 feet deep, laden with a treasury of tools and artifacts used by our Bronze Age ancestors—3300 years ago. The "Gelidonya wreck" has been scientifically and systematically excavated by Throckmorton and Dr. George Bass, with a team from the University of Pennsylvania. The work is described in two *National Geographic Magazine* articles (May 1960 and May 1962 issues) and several monograms by Dr. Bass and Throckmorton. It was the subject of a presentation by Dr. Bass at the Third Conference of Underwater Archaeology held in Miami during March 1967, during which Dr. Bass described the tremendous effort to clear off overburden, largely by fanning the surface. The Bodrum Archaeological Museum, Bodrum, Turkey, displays a full collection of the artifacts salvaged from this wreck, as well as several other ancient ships off the coast.

Several galleys full of amphoras have been located near the biblical port of Halicarnassus, once a trading center. And at the south entrance to the Dardanelles is Troy. Who can tell what vestiges of Homer's Trojan War might lie, sunken and undiscovered, beneath its cliffs and beaches?

The Aegean itself covers a cemetery of Persian, Greek, Roman, and Turkish ships. Just off Salamis Island lie the bones of hundreds of triremes and biremes destroyed in the decisive naval battle of 480 B.C. carrying little-known war implements of the Persian Empire. Piraeus, Samos, Mytilene, Rhodes—all these ports must hold Greek relics.

Take Melos Island, for instance. It was here, in 1820, that a Greek farmer is said to have found one of the world's great art treasures—the Venus de Milo. Most people assume this statue was discovered without arms, but Venus was plowed up complete. After passing through the hands of several owners, she was loaded aboard a vessel bound for Constantinople. A French warship was then in the harbor and its officers decided Venus would make a nice gift for the king. When they came alongside to confiscate her—the story goes—the Greek sailors, hoping that the French would not take a mutilated statue, broke off the arms and threw them into the harbor. They were wrong, and Venus ended up in the Louvre. About 1960 a Melos-born American businessman, Mathon Kyritsis, created considerable interest when he announced plans to lead an expedition to recover the missing arms from the bottom of the Melos harbor.

The waters off Crete, to the south, around the ruins of ancient Cnossus and Cydonia, hide secrets of the legendary Minoan civilization, as well as artifacts of the later Byzantine Empire. In Greece itself, off Navpaktos (Lepanto) in the Gulf of Corinth, is a Turkish fleet destroyed in 1571 by Spanish and Italian warships of the Holy League. Farther south, close to Pilos, are the remnants of the Turko-Egyptian navy sunk during the Battle of Navarino in 1827. Their silted-over hulls probably contain interesting old artifacts looted from the shore. Greek fishermen have been responsible for the discovery of some valuable museum pieces. From "the *Anticythère* Wreck," some 225 feet deep off Cnossus, they raised in their nets some of the most beautiful bronzes of the Athens Museum's collection. Captain Cousteau dived on the spot and found the wreck to be completely buried in sand. Its salvage will be difficult. Near Cap Artemision, some thirty-three years ago, fishermen hauled up a bronze statue of Zeus, and off the beach of nearby Marathon a statue of Ephèbe was recovered. As interest in diving spreads through Greek waters many archaeological treasures will come to light.

Under the Tyrrhenian Sea, west of Italy, is a museum of ancient Roman commerce. This area has been invaded by a growing group of enthusiastic Italian divers who are making discoveries of amphorae-laden galleys off the coasts of Tuscany, Corsica, and Sardinia. Farther to the south is lost a rich collection of marble carvings and columns which Genseric looted from Rome in 455 A.D. Near the toe of Italy, off Crotone, divers found relics of the ancient temple of Hera Lacinia, barely covered by shallow water into which its foundation had settled. Columns, steps, and other artifacts such as vases have been seen below the surface here.

Possibly the first venture ever made into submarine archaeology was commissioned in the fifteenth century at Lake Nemi, twenty miles southeast of Rome, by Pompeo Cardinal Colonna. It was on this little lake, nearly 2000 years ago, that Caligula used to visit his two pleasure barges—floating palaces with temples, gardens, pavilions, and luxurious bedrooms decorated with the magnificence that only a Roman emperor could muster. They sank and lay on the shallow bottom for fifteen centuries. Then, under the cardinal's orders, one Leon Battista Alherti was set to work and presently managed to raise a galley's prow. Several other attempts took place in succeeding years, and in 1895 Elizo Borghe made a major recovery of splendid bronzes—a statue of Diana, a lion's head, and a decorated helmet—as well as beautiful designs in glass and marble-and-copper columns. Many of these pieces are now in the Vatican Museum, the British Museum, and the Louvre. The level of Lake Nemi was lowered in 1929 when it was partly drained and the two galleys came into view. One had the shape of a turtle and measured 220 by 64 feet. Surprisingly, the wooden construction was still intact—an interesting commentary on the preservation capacity of still, fresh water. The deck was surmounted by an elegant parapet with gilt bronze columns and mosaics and an ingeniously constructed rotating platform. Below was an entire hydraulic installation. The second barge was even larger, measuring 225 by 75 feet, looking from above like the deck of an aircraft carrier. Among its decorations recovered was a balustrade 3½ feet high and several dozen pieces of cloth of gold. These galleys are being salvaged and reconstructed.

The Malta islands are ringed with sunken Phoenician, Greek, Carthaginian, Roman, and Saracen transports as well as shipborne mementos of the campaigns of the Knights Hospitalers—better known as the Knights of Malta—who successfully fought the Barbary pirates. When General Mustafa laid siege to their fortress in 1565 the Knights, under their grand master Jean Parisot de La Valette, held off the Turkish armies and finally forced them to retreat. The Turks had brought with them two of the most magnificent siege guns ever constructed—bronze basilisks weighing over ten tons apiece, capable of shooting 200-pound projectiles. The larger of these broke loose as it was being loaded into a galley and fell into Valletta harbor where it lies today, buried in the mud under relatively shallow water—an archaeological gem that would be hard to equal.

SCUBA divers are reporting new discoveries of *champs d'amphoras* ("fields of amphorae") off the shores of south France. These old wrecks have been spotted the length of the coast, with eighteen separate ones found off Marseilles along. There must be dozens more, because this port has been the outlet for French wines and grain since its days as the Greek colony of Massalia in 600 B.C. As each wreck is plotted new information about the commercial centers and trade routes of dead civilizations is gained, as well as fresh knowledge of ancient ships and their cargo. In the following pages Robert Sténuit, well-known submarine archaeologist and author, and the former president of the Commission d'Archéologie Sous-Marine de la Fédération Belge de Recherches et d'Activités Sous-Marines, who has visited many of these wrecks, summarizes the French scene:

It is on the wrecks off the French coast that for the first time the recognized methods of land archeologists have been applied undersea. These include, specifically, a surface grid under which a three-dimensional recording of the position of every recovered artifact, in relation to the grid, is made either by photographs or drawn plan. In land excavation the purpose of this procedure is for the dating of recovered objects through their relative positions in layers of earth as compared with other discovered objects of recognizable age. For instance, if an unknown artifact is found buried at the same depth as a recognizable one, it can be concluded that both were contemporary; if in a deeper strata, older; if nearer the surface, more recent.

A similar procedure is used in the excavation of an old wreck, especially if it is buried. This time the purpose is not to determine the unknown artifact's age, but its use. Rather than raise each uncovered artifact pell mell, the modern submarine archeologist carefully records its relative position on the ship, *in situ*, before sending it up. If it were found on deck, it was probably part of the ship's navigating equipment such as fittings, rigging, etc.; if found near the stove (which was constructed of brick or fired clay on the galleys) it was probably a kitchen utensil, and so on. This is the only way by which archeologists can learn of the stowage plan of old vessels. This recording of the position of wooden pieces of a ship's hull permits naval architects to make a reconstruction.

This truly scientific method was tried by Captain Cousteau's team on the famous buried galley at Grand Congloue islet, in front of Marseilles. Here, for the first time, scholars were able to observe on a TV screen different aspects of the work going on below, thanks to the underwater camera guided over the bottom by a diver. Commander Tailliez, a little later, applied aerial photography techniques under the sea on another wreck near the Balise du Titan (Ile du Levant). As systematic excavation progressed, the buried ship was uncovered in stages. At each stage the exposed surface was photographed in many different pictures which were assembled into a composite mosaic showing that whole level of the ship, complete with construction plan and cargo stowage.

Divers working with the British archeological group of Athens laid down over their wreck a pattern of white plastic wires in squares, with each intersection identified by number. This was further refined by Italian divers clearing a wreck near Sicily: every uncovered artifact was photographed *in situ*, showing its relation to the wire pattern, by a submarine photographer.

It is only in this manner that it is possible to extract from the remains of an ancient wreck—which is in fact a "slice of history," a microcosm which summarizes the condition of civilization at a certain instant—all the messages which it contains for us. And these messages tell of naval architecture, of the history of commercial and cultural exchanges between nations, of trade routes, of art, warfare, industry and technique. They also tell of scientific progress and discoveries: for instance, we have learned that the ancient Greeks understood the phenomenon of metallic destruction by electrolysis—and even how to prevent it—through the ingenious manner in which they mounted their metallic fittings below hulls.

The First International Congress of Submarine Archeology, uniting French, Spanish, English and Italian scholars, was held in 1955 at Cannes under the presidency of Professor Fernand Benoit, Conservateur of the Musée Borley at Marseilles (where the most interesting artifacts salvaged from the Mediterranean are on display) and Director of France's Twelfth Archeological Division. Professor Benoit, in his address to the congress, strongly endorsed the new method of systematic wreck excavation and stressed the moral responsibility of those salvaging archeologically interesting wrecks. He condemned wreck robbers and called for more realistic laws governing the field, and their enforcement. These regulations have since been promulgated. The International Congress has been meeting regularly since, and submarine archeology is now a recognized branch of scientific study.

New methods and techniques are being developed regularly. For example: color underwater stereophotography (3-D) with electronic flash to record artifacts in their relative positions; new treatments to preserve wood and iron artifacts raised from salt water[5]; application of X rays to spectrographic analysis of artifacts—study of their diffraction pattern

[5] In the Smithsonian Institution's pamphlets, Mr. Mendel Peterson describes some of these methods of artifact preservation. The July 1950 issue of *Skin Diver* magazine carries an excellent article covering the subject.

permits their structure to be determined without the necessity of damaging them in chemical analysis.

A joint collaboration by French, North African French, Spanish, Italian, and Greek specialists is bringing up to date the classification of amphorae made some fifty years ago by the German Dressel. His book is a working tool of major importance, permitting the standardization of numerous types of amphorae known then, but has been made obsolete by the great number of recent submarine discoveries.

The amphora was the container of antiquity. It was simultaneously the case, the bag, the barrel and the tin can. It transported grain (the Romans called their huge grain amphorae with rounded bottoms, enormous bellies, narrow collars and little handles: "dorias"), as well as wine, olive oil, preserved fish or "garum" (a fermented condiment with a fish base), and so on.

The big freighters used to carry several thousand amphorae, but every one of the old ships—even warships—had some aboard in which were kept provisions, wine, etc. Amphorae can often be identified as to their owner by his mark, usually cut on the rim or in the plug (which was made of cork, clay or a compressed volcanic powder called *pouzzolane*). Some amphorae from the Grand Congloue wreck carried the seal of a famous Greek exporter called Marcos Sestios whose seal, reported to have been found on amphorae as far distant as Germany, can still be seen in the mosaics of his garden's ruins at Délos.

Amphoras most usually found along the French coast are of two main families, each of which ranged through a whole series of modifications in their evolutions. In general the Roman amphora had a long, stretched-out, narrow body, pointed base, and long, slender throat on each side of which was a gracefully-curved handle running down one-third of its length. The Greek amphora was shorter, with a pear-shaped body bulging over a teat-shaped point, very short neck and small, rounded handles. Much rarer along the French and Spanish coasts are the Phoenician (cylindrical body and little round handles) and Cretian and eastern Mediterranean amphorae. These are found off Greece and Italy in increasing numbers.

Interesting finds of amphorae include a galley near the Isle of Veste, between Marseilles and Toulon, full of Greco-Roman jars of the first century B.C., 65 feet deep. Just above the Spanish border, off Agde, the Béziers Archeological Society found three galleys packed with them. Amphorae of a very ancient type, possibly Phoenician, were found in 1955 off Cap d'Antibes. One unique specimen dating to the first century A.D. was spotted off Fos-sur-Mer. Its color, according to the French finders, was "lively red culminated with the tones of technicolor." Two divers found a "field of amphorae" under the Château d'If where the Count of Monte Cristo went for a dive. Every few weeks a new site is reported along this coast.

Off the shores of Costa Brava Barcelona skin-diving groups have been carrying out outstanding work in the field of submarine archeology. With no financial aid other than what they have been able to provide themselves, these capable young Spanish divers have made significant

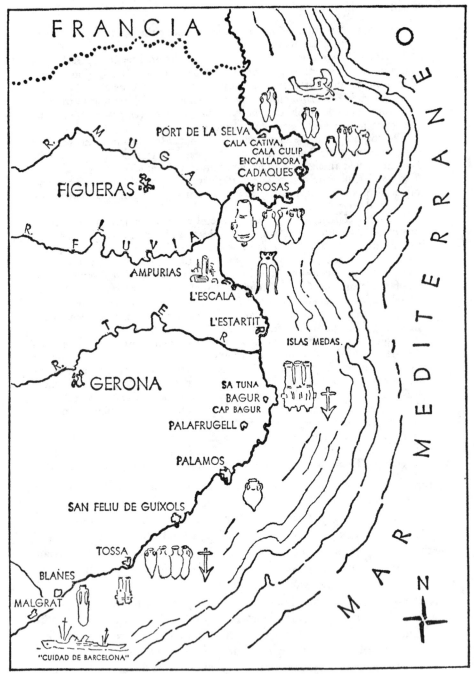

FRANCIA

MAR MEDITERRANEO

R. MUGA

FIGUERAS

R. FLUVIA

PÓRT DE LA SELVA
CALA CATIVA
CALA CULIP
ENCALLADORA
CADAQUES
ROSAS

AMPURIAS

L'ESCALA

L'ESTARTIT

ISLAS MEDAS

R. TER

GERONA

SA TUNA
BAGUR
CAP BAGUR

PALAFRUGELL

PALAMOS

SAN FELIU DE GUÍXOLS

TOSSA

BLAÑES

MALGRAT

"CUIDAD DE BARCELONA"

Courtesy of Antonio Ribera

contributions to the knowledge of Greek and Roman shipping in the Mediterranean.

Antonio Ribera and his fellow divers Roberto Díaz, Eduardo Admetlla, Climent Vidal and others located numerous archaeological treasures off the Costa Brava. In a creek called Cala Culip on Cape de Creus they raised artifacts from a Roman galley of the second or first century B.C. which lay partly buried in mud fifty feet deep. Among these were 48 amphorae, a ceramic plate, pieces of a ceramic crucible for melting metals and earthenware jars and plates. The galley itself, they learned, was about ninety feet long. Nearby, on the sandy bottom 65 feet deep between the cape and the islet of Encalladora, the explorers located another "field of amphorae" but strong currents there made salvage difficult. It was from this wrecked ship that the first recorded archaeological salvage in the Mediterranean was made in 1894 when helmeted divers brought up 62 amphorae.

Just to the south is the Bay of Rosas—one of the richest of all archaeological hunting grounds, containing mud-covered hulls of Greek, Roman, French, Spanish, and probably Phoenician and English ships dating across a span of over 2000 years. Roberto Díaz, in describing these wrecks, says: "We've seen on the bottom there much evidence of sunken hulls, some with ribs visible over the mud, others just mounds. It's difficult to identify any of them because since the Greeks founded their colonies of Rhode and Emporion on the bay it has been the site of an infinite number of shipwrecks and naval battles. These took place regularly, every time the French invaded our territory or were driven away. In just one of these battles the Catalan Navy, commanded by Roger de Lauria, totally destroyed a fleet of seventeen French galleys which were chained together in the center of the bay. That place is a veritable submerged museum and it's impossible to calculate the number of wrecks that have gone down in its waters since remote times."

Of all the recoveries from the Bay of Rosas the most interesting is a bronze mortar weighing 2700 pounds, nearly five feet in circumference. Attempts to identify this magnificent piece were stymied when it was seen that the only marking on it was "N° 1" engraved on the breech, just back of the vent. Some opinions are that this gun is French, while others guess that it was part of the armament of the Spanish warship *Triunfante* which sank there in 1795. Whatever its origin, this mortar created more havoc after its salvage than it ever managed to do lobbing projectiles. No sooner had it been placed on the pier than the customs appeared, ordering that the C.R.I.S. pay an import tax on its bronze metal. Then the navy stepped in. The cannon was an archaeological treasure and must be delivered to their museum. At this point the government metal control bureau

demanded a percentage of the bronze for the national industry. Things
were coming to a boil when the local priest suggested a solution:
that the entire gun be donated to the church for melting down and
casting into bells.

During 1958 the divers located the remains of a ship in front of
the port of Palamós. Two huge anchors nearby and 14 cannons,
each ten feet long and nearly two tons in weight lying on the rotted
wood and ballast, indicate that this was a large man-of-war. Not far
off, near the Palamós lighthouse, they found 6 iron culverins which
they identified as being of the 1650 period. In Blanes the Spanish
divers found two more cannons, one of especial interest as it had
eight reinforce rings along its length. North, off the Cape of Creus,
they added two more "fields of amphorae" to their submarine museum. One was of a type recognized by archaeologists as pre-Hellenic
and hitherto uncatalogued. During summer exploration Díaz and Admetlla found in 70 feet off Blanes four lead anchor stocks with a
new feature: they had carvings on their sides. Nearby they noted
signs of stone construction on the ocean floor. They raised the stocks,
which weighed about 300 pounds each and were nearly six feet long.
The carvings were identified as mythological dolphins and columns
complete with capitals and bases. These unusual finds are the first decorated stocks ever seen, probably Roman.

All the way down the Spanish coast skin divers have been reporting
discoveries of amphorae and cannons. Five miles from Tarragona in
Cala de la Mora, one of them stumbled on a real archaeological
treasure. It was spotted in 1946 by a spear fisherman, Manuel Alvarez,
who first thought he had found a car which had rolled down into the
sea. He returned to the spot two years later and realized that the
crusted, weed-coated rectangular object was marble. He told some
friends about it. A girl passed on the news to the Molas Museum
in Tarragona and a few months later the prize was salvaged. It
turned out to be a magnificent Roman sarcophagus, carved of white
marble with tints of green, blue, and gray identified as coming from the
quarry of Luna, in Italy. Its inner surfaces are smooth while the
outside, measuring 7 by 3⅓ by 3½ feet, is beautifully decorated
with the finest Roman sculpture of the time of Adrian, depicting the
Greek mythological legend of Hippolytus and Phaedra. Archaeologists
believe that this coffin was dug up by the Moors and stripped, then
left near the shore. Erosion by the sea caused the land to cave in and it
fell, several hundred years ago, into the water. A pamphlet describing
this art treasure has been issued by the Molas Museum, where it is
now on display.

Around the Balearic Islands lie the wrecks of many Roman galleys.
One was buried until recently under two yards of sand off the

beach of Porto Cristo, Majorca. A storm uncovered it and today its cargo is being salvaged by local archaeologists who believe it to be an exceptionally large ship of the second century. Other galleys are being discovered farther off shore. From these wrecks members of the "Majorca Sharks" have brought up a number of Carthaginian and Greek amphorae.

An intriguing salvage was made off Majorca without a single diver in the picture, from the yawl *Red Rover*. As her owner prepared to set sail from an anchorage in the lee of a sheltered cove he found that the anchor was fouled on the bottom—strange, because the sea bed was sand. Straining by all hands finally pulled the hook free. When it broke water the crew saw an encrusted mass stuck between the shank and a fluke. They got the anchor aboard and were about to dump the mass overboard when someone noticed the glint of metal. Captain Arthur Watkin scratched at it with a knife. "Looks like silver!" the veteran treasure hunter exclaimed.

Realizing that he might have pulled up a valuable artifact, the owner took the mass to a museum in Rome to be cleaned chemically. He soon learned that his suspicion was correct. The salvaged object was a silver-inlaid bronze mask of a satyr dating from the Imperial Roman period. Research revealed that it was one of two such masks attached to the handles of a *situla* (bucket) which had been sent to Majorca on a galley, but never arrived. This valuable artifact was donated to the Metropolitan Museum of Art in New York City. And on the bottom of the cove where the anchor fouled, the location known only to those aboard the yawl, lies its twin still attached to the *situla*—and probably the wreckage of a Roman galley as well.

This roundup of the Mediterranean concludes with the Barbary Coast of North Africa, off whose shores are the relics of Carthaginian ships, Roman galleys, French, English, and Spanish warships, and the pinnaces and dhows of the Barbary pirates themselves. The Gulf of Tunis holds 2500-year-old trading and merchant ships which once bustled to and fro from the port of Carthage; Tripoli harbor covers the burned hull of the American ship *Philadelphia*, set afire there by Stephen Decatur in 1804. The ancient Phoenician colony of Sabratha, on Tripoli's coast, was the scene of an underwater exploration in 1967. A concrete-topped 150-yard underwater quay was surveyed, and other harbor construction that has subsided under the Mediterranean. Columns, pottery, and other relics of an ancient civilization were salvaged.

Most famous of the wrecks along this coast is the *Mahdia* galley, which Captain Cousteau describes in his book *The Silent World*. Despite salvages of beautiful marble columns and carvings from the ship, there are probably many tons of them lying on the bottom today. They have been studied carefully and identified as Greek, of various epochs, the latest being about the first century B.C. Their number and variety point to the looting of a city. Archaeologists trying to track down their origin believe that they were part of the booty which Sulla took from Athens in 86 B.C. and shipped back toward Rome. The galley was apparently caught in the deadly northeast *borée* blowing down from Greece (the same wind which wrecked Ulysses) and sunk off Tunisia. Many other wrecks lie near this coast, victims of the same wind.

EUROPE AND THE BRITISH ISLES

Evidence of Greek civilization on the Black Sea came to light when a Hellenic city was discovered there under shallow water, just offshore. The Australian journalist and marine photographer, James Aldridge, visited the site with special permission from the Soviet government. He found that accumulations of silt had covered the whole community except for one building, whose walls remained visible. Aldridge believes that his exploratory dives have interested Russian archaeologists who will follow up his pioneering with dredging to uncover what might turn out to be a fascinating window across twenty centuries.

Off the southwest corner of Spain, near Cádiz, a Roman settlement has been sighted on the rock and sand sea floor in a narrow strait between the island of Sancti Petri and a coastal town of the same name. Stone walls running down into the sea from the leeward side of the island and submerged outlines of partly buried undersea buildings, twenty to forty feet deep, indicate that the coastal shelf of south Spain is steadily dropping. This theory is subtantiated by the discovery of a 120-foot-deep petrified forest, with some of its trees reported to be still standing erect, near Gibraltar. Both the Roman city and the petrified forest lend support to geologists' opinions that a land bridge joined Africa and Europe across the present Straits of Gibraltar in relatively recent geological times.

The cold, muddy waters of Scottish lochs are being penetrated frequently by doughty members of the Dundee Undersea Research Group formerly headed by Walter Deas. With his companions Alan Doyle, Roger Bruce, and Geoff Wilson, Walt made numerous attempts to locate recorded wrecks off the coast and in the summer of 1958 took part in a large-scale search for the Loch Ness Monster. The two dozen participating divers did not find "Nessie"—as they call it—but did come across chunks of Urquhart Castle which had fallen into Loch Ness. While still living in Scotland, Walt Deas stimulated interest in numerous wrecks which his researches into old records identified. Among these are the *Santa Catarine*, off Collieston, probably a Flemish ship of the Spanish Netherlands, from whose wreckage sixteenth-century cannons and artifacts have been raised, and another wreck dating back to 1588 which has yielded brass cannons one of which carries the markings: "Richard and John Philips, brethren, made this piece, anno 1584" together with the ER and Rose and Crown.

R. H. Davis, in his book *Deep Diving*, describes some of England's ancient cities sunk under the sea:

> Poets have written much about the lost Lyonesse, the submerged land lying between Land's End and the Scilly Isles. Beneath passing of ships, lie once verdant hills and valleys; and not only the wrecks of ships, but also the remains of towers and castles and dense forests.
>
> > In the crystal depths the curious eye
> > On days of calm unruffled, could discern
> > . . . her streets and towers,
> > Low-buried 'neath the waves.
>
> A thousand years before Christ, the Phoenicians traded with the natives of Lyonesse, exchanging gold and silver and fine linen and other commodities for tin.
>
> Of the more important places which the sea has stolen from England may be mentioned Ravenspur, Yorkshire—originally the Praetorium of the Romans—and 12 other towns and villages.

The Roman port of Mablethorpe sank under the North Sea, and the remains of a Roman fort, nearly two thousand years old, lie about one mile off Selsey Bill, Sussex. From here, Major Hume Wallace salvaged an 80-pound round stone believed to be a catapult projectile. Old towns of Dunwich, Goseford, Orwell, and many others have all been lost to the sea.

Danish frogmen with constitutions of polar bears have been busy adding to knowledge of Stone Age life in Scandinavia. They have discovered more than a dozen settlements sunken under the sea off their coasts. From depths of ten to more than fifty feet off the west shore of Feyn Island and other areas the diving Danes have raised over 700 prehistoric implements, including axes and crude harpoons, from the period 4000–3000 B.C.

Divers of the Royal Swedish Navy in conjunction with their National Maritime Museum are continuing explorations and salvage of centuries-old warships sunk near Stockholm. Despite very poor visibility and frigid water they have been making recoveries of numerous wooden statues and figureheads of these wooden vessels, as well as pottery, dining services, cannon balls and grenades, and even tar barrels. Nearly all are in a remarkably good state of preservation thanks to the icy water which is evidently inhospitable to marine borers. Their most interesting finds have been in three warships: the *Riksapplet*—which they call "The Apple"—a 185-foot, 90-gun man-of-war which sank

in 1676 in fairly shallow water during a storm; the *Grone Jagaren,*
a 90-footer with about 25 cannon, lying 95 feet deep under the main
shipping route into the harbor; and the *Wasa,* of about 1200 tons
and 64 bronze guns, discovered 100 feet deep three years ago by a
diving amateur archaeologist. Most of the *Wasa's* cannon were salvaged
soon after her loss in 1628 by men working in diving bells at the
cost of several lives in one of the earliest recorded recoveries from
such a depth. The recent salvage of the *Wasa* and her reconstruction
as a museum was a milestone in the history of undersea archaeology.
As stated by Carl Clausen earlier in this chapter, the achievement
has been of great value to historians.

In the Mediterranean and off the shores of Europe lie many wrecks
interesting to submarine archaeologists. Among Spanish vessels are:

THE MEDITERRANEAN

The *Real Carlos* and *Hermenegildo,* then Spain's largest warships,
carrying 112 cannons each, blew up in front of Tanger in 1801. Nearly
all their crews perished, and the ships sank immediately.

Off the Barbary Coast port of Mámora, during Spain's naval battles
with the pirates, several more ships were lost: in 1625 the galleys
San Martín and *Santiago* grounded and were wrecked on the bar; in
1628 two more galleys sank close to the coast while attempting to
bring reinforcements to defenders of Mámora. Their crews were
captured by the Moors and sold as slaves; in 1639 a caravel, bringing
supplies to the port, was wrecked there.

Off the Spanish coast: in 1648 the galley *Santo Domingo* sank off
Malaga; in 1784 the 64-gun warship *Septentrión,* commanded by Diego
Quevedo, stranded and broke up eight miles from Malaga. Some of
her cargo was saved; in 1639 three galleons of the Duke of Maqueda
sank in Almeria port; the following year five ships of the Duke of
Najera were wrecked on Almeria beach; in 1799 the 34-gunned frigate
Guadalupe sank off the Cape San Antonio, on the Denía coast, with
loss of 147 including the captain José de la Encino; in 1793 the 34-
gunned frigate *Rosario* sank at the mouth of the Llobregat River,
with all saved; in 1698 the galleon *San Carlos* was lost off the
Cataluna coast; in 1658 the galleys *Patrona de Sicilia* and *La Sandovala*
were sunk during a storm in Barcelona harbor with great loss of life;
in 1684 the galley *Capitana de España* and two other ships were sunk
in Barcelona with three hundred drowned; in 1715 eight merchant
ships and fourteen caravels were sunk in Barcelona during a storm;
in 1794 the 68-gunned warship *San Isidora* sank off Palamós. She may
have been the wreck recently discovered by the C.R.I.S. divers.

The *Patrona de Sicilia,* a galley, sank during a storm off Majorca in 1697 with fifty-nine of her crew drowned; another galley, the *San José*, sank in the same storm off Ibiza with only fifty-two saved.

Off the south of France: in 1635 nine galleys and two warships under the Marquis de Santa Cruz sank in the St. Tropez-St. Raphael area, with great loss of life, during a violent squall.

Off Italy: in 1632 twenty-three galleys of the Naples squadron sank there at their moorings in a tempest; in 1646 the galley *Santa Barbara* went down off the Tuscany coast with forty-six galley slaves drowned; in 1675 the warship of Melchor de la Cueva sank against the Mesina lighthouse, two galleys floundered in the Gulf of Salerno and the *Capitana de Sicilia* was struck by lightning, burned and sank in Melazo harbor.

Spain: the galley *San Francisco* sank off Gibraltar in 1660; in 1783 the 74-gunned warship *San Miguel*, built ten years earlier at Havana, was wrecked against La Tunara.

In 1805, following the Battle of Trafalgar, a storm gave the coup de grace to: *Rayo*, 94 guns, wrecked on Sanlúcar; *Neptuno*, 74 guns, wrecked off Cádiz; *San Francisco de Asís*, 74 guns, wrecked off Cádiz; *Monarca*, 74 guns, wrecked on Arenas Gordas, near Cádiz. Hundreds were drowned.

The Bay of Cádiz was the scene of many other disasters. Among them: in 1563 fifteen galleons, loading cargo for America, sank in a storm; in 1633 another storm destroyed eleven ships under the Marquis de Caldereita as they were preparing to sail; in 1658 the 64-gunned *Capitana de Nápoles* and fourteen other ships were wrecked, again by storm; in 1660 rough weather sank the warship *Dragón*; in 1663 seven ships under the Duke of Albuquerque were wrecked at Rota; in 1760 the war frigate *Bizarra* burned and sank off Puntales; in 1809 eleven ships, including the cannon boat *Tigre*, sank in a storm.

At the mouth of the Guadalquivir River, on Sanlúcar bar, are the sand-covered remains of countless galleons and warships. Among these are the *Capitana* and *San Francisco de Padua* of the armada of Tomás de Larraspuru, which grounded there in 1622 with loss of all outgoing cargo. Records dated 1670 show that no less than nine *Capitanas* and five other ships had sunk on this treacherous bar by that early date.

Along the western Iberian coast: on October 28, 1596, thirty-two warships and nearly fifty caravels and pataches of the armada of Martin de Padilla were sunk and wrecked along the coast of Corcubion and Finisterre during one of the worst storms to have ever struck this dangerous area. More than two thousand drowned; in 1630 the *Almirante* and seven ships of a flota sailing from Cádiz to Lisbon were lost; in 1635 two ships of the Masibradi squadron were sunk off Galicia; in 1815 the 114-gunned three-decker *Fernando VII*, under Captain de la Lama, was wrecked on Bugio Island, Portugal.

Western France: in 1615 the galleon *San Luis, Capitana* of an armada under Diego Brochero, sank in Dunkirk; in 1652 the little galleon *San Antonio* was wrecked and lost at the foot of the Castle of Blaye at the mouth of the Gironde River; in 1786 the *patache San Cristóbal* sank off Bayonne.

CHAPTER 7

Submarine Archaeology—II

Christopher Columbus' flagship *Santa María*[1] grounded on a coral reef off Haiti on Christmas Night, 1492. After futile attempts to free the caravel, the crew stripped her of what they could remove and left the hull to break up where it lay. Aside from possible Viking relics, the coral-entombed remnants of the ship should contain the oldest European artifacts in the Western Hemisphere. It follows that one of the oldest-established American underwater archaeologists should lead the hunt to find them.

It was exactly 462 years later when Edwin A. Link began his search, after a long research program to which Samuel Eliot Morison and other historians contributed. Armed with a magnetometer and Bludworth metal detectors, Link and his diving associates examined the most promising reefs off Cap Haitien, and were rewarded with the salvage of an iron anchor, hand-forged in several sections, and identified as being of the Columbus era. The anchor was donated to the government of Haiti and later transferred to the Smithsonian Institution.

A second attempt in the spring of 1960 to locate the caravel's wreckage ran smack into "treasure hunters' luck." As the Link group, aboard his new *Sea Diver II*, prepared a magnetometer search of the most promising section of the reefs a passing iron freighter went off her course and struck a shoal. The sinking ship drifted down on the *Sea Diver II* and sank nearby. "Of course," Link explains, "the proximity of that huge iron hull right next to our reef made searching with the magnetometer out of the question since it distorted the magnetic field there. That freighter might even have settled right on top of the *Santa María*." Smiling wryly, Ed adds, "We figured the chances of such a thing happening just as we were starting our search at something like a million to one!"

The remains of two more of Columbus' caravels have been located in St. Ann's Bay, on the north coast of Jamaica near Ocho Rios. Returning from his final exploratory voyage in the Caribbean, the navigator found two of his ships—the *Capitana* and *Santiago de Palos* —leaking so badly that he grounded the hulls in the cove. Robert F. Marx, veteran diver and underwater archaeologist, began searching for

---

[1] The wreck of a very old ship which might be the *Santa María* was located in 1968 by members of the Santa Maria Foundation. A brass spike, a brass shackle, wood, and pottery recovered from the site have been dated at 1475 plus or minus a hundred years.

the wrecks in 1967 while in Jamaica salvaging Port Royal. He found them in a few hours with the aid of Dr. Harold Edgerton of MIT, from the following description given in Columbus' diary: "We grounded the caravels in a small harbor enclosed with reefs near an Indian village, a crossbow shot from land, and near two fresh water creeks." They are buried under sand in a 10-foot depth of water. Using an airlift, Marx recovered wood, ballast stones, iron nails, Venetian glass, shards of pottery, flint, charcoal, animal bones, and black beans. Mauricio Obregón, a Colombian businessman associate, has stated that during sonar soundings on the site two large objects were revealed under the sand, side by side. Frédéric Dumas and other top divers and historians are interested in the project to salvage the ships, under the auspices of the Jamaican government.

On the opposite side of Jamaica is an underwater archaeologist's hunting ground which has repeatedly attracted both Link and Marx, as well as others. It is Port Royal, the pirate "Hellhole of the Caribbean." During a cataclysmic earthquake on June 7, 1692, the waterfront of the port at the tip of a long spit of land sank under the sea. Forts, churches, buildings, and even the H.M.S. *Swan*—anchored at her berth—disappeared. During Link's first visit, he "dredged through the six to eight feet of debris and mud with an air lift and reached down to its actual site. There is a recorded account in the Institute of Jamaica of a Canadian diver who dove on Port Royal a hundred years ago and recovered a cannon. Also, about six months before I dove there, one of the Du Pont boys of Wilmington discovered and reported its present condition authentically. I am probably the first one to definitely establish the site of the sunken Fort James and the related parts of Port Royal. I recovered a cannon and brought up artifacts for establishing its authenticity. The Institute of Jamaica is fully documented with a map I prepared orientating my finds with past information already on hand." Link gave some stones from the fort wall to Art McKee for his Fortress of Sunken Treasure and a number of other recoveries such as clay pipes, bones, and bottles to the Smithsonian.

Encouraged by the first visit, Ed returned to his sunken city during the spring of 1959 with his specially constructed *Sea Diver II*. For two months the Link party, strengthened by six U. S. Navy divers on loan, dredged the area mapped out earlier. "We have had a very rewarding time," said Ed on his return. The beautifully illustrated account of this project which appears in the February 1960 issue of the *National Geographic Magazine* certainly confirms his opinion.

Robert F. Marx made his mark on Port Royal along the road of a career that would bewilder most archaeologists. Majoring in history and archaeology at UCLA, he frequently journeyed south of the border to take part in diving expeditions off the shores of Mexico, Guatemala, and Yucatán. His interest in the Mayan civilization made him an authority on it, and drew him into the cenotes he explored. After three years in the Marine Corps as a diver, he announced, in 1955, the discovery of the Civil War ironclad *Monitor*. "That old ship was the roughtest baby I ever worked on," he says. "I first located her from a plane after searching two years on and off. Then I dived on her with a buddy and verified her. She lies about one mile from the Hatteras Light in about 35–50 feet of water. She was covered with sand up to the turret the day that we dived on her, but when I spotted her from the plane she wasn't. I can't say about the hull, but I know the turret is in good condition. I believe that the sands covering and uncovering her keep her in great shape."

From his base at the Cozumel Beach Hotel on Cozumel Island, Marx ranged far and wide across the western Caribbean and Yucatán, turning up a surprising number of discoveries. He dived into lagoons searching for ancient sunken temples, then advanced a thousand years in history when he decided to trace the landing of Francisco de Montejo, who tried to conquer Yucatán and failed. "In 1527 Montejo left Cozumel and went to the mainland with three ships and 400 men. They landed near the Mayan ruins of Tulum and made camp. To quell a mutiny among his troops, Montejo set fire to two of his ships and they sank. I first located on land the ruins of the old fort that he built, then later found the wrecks. From the age of the cannons and several other artifacts that I found I am positive these are his vessels. They lie off a place called Punta Soliman which is about 8 miles north of Tulum. The wreckage is scattered all over a reef about 30 feet deep."

A huge anchor and six cannons which he spotted off Matanceros Point, Acumal, led to Marx's find of what Peterson has called "the most important merchant-ship site ever discovered in this hemisphere." During 1958–59, with his diving buddy Clay Blair, Jr., and members of a big flotilla of assembled salvage craft, Bob chipped loose from the coral-crusted wreckage enough trading artifacts to give it the nickname "The Five and Dime Wreck." Among recoveries: corroded pewter plates, brass and pewter buckles, silver-plated kitchen spoons, religious medals, and costume beads. A commendable research program took Blair to the Archives of the Indies where he learned the wreck's history. She was the 270-ton merchant *nao Nuestra Señora de los Milagros* (nicknamed *"El Matancero"*—hence Matanceros Point), wrecked in 1741 en route to America. Blair tells the whole fascinating story in his book *Diving for Pleasure and Treasure*.

In the fall of 1962, Marx followed Columbus' footsteps as co-organizer and navigator on the voyage of *Niña II*—a replica of the *Niña* which traced the discoverer's passage to the New World. Then he took up an appointment as marine archaeologist for the Institute of Jamaica. He organized and trained several divers, including his man Friday, Caynute Kelly, set up a base on shore, and during many months of study and dredging the harbor floor made important discoveries about Port Royal and recovered a museum-full of artifacts used there nearly three hundred years ago. Early in his work he learned to look for artifacts under collapsed walls that were uncovered by his dredging. Since the depth is only 30 feet, most of the "treasures" in the sunken city that were not concealed under the remnants of structures were salvaged shortly after the earthquake.

Well over 10,000 individual artifacts were brought up. Among these: thousands of clay pipes bearing at least 140 different makers' marks; more than 500 onion bottles of various forms; dozens of pewter plates and platters, spoons, tankards, and other utensils; silver cups and tableware; a complete copper rum still; brass dividers; a complete medicine chest of vials; pieces of swords, halberds, pikes, and knives; building bricks and other construction materials; bits of shoes; a human jawbone; one opal; and several coins. The recoveries included no treasure. "However," said Marx, "what we have represents a treasure in valuable archaeological information—information that will give us a more detailed picture than has ever been revealed before of the life in Port Royal at the time of the disaster." Anyone who reads Bob's thoroughly researched and exciting book, *Pirate Port*, will agree.

The tough, capable members of the Venezuelan Society for Submarine Activities have been making forays into the Caribbean off that country's coast, around Margarita Island, since 1955. Manuel and Eduardo Santaella, Domingo Manini, Rafael Arnal, and other Caracas businessmen with a yen for adventure have raised ship's artifacts from the *San Pedro Alcántara* (see next chapter) and supplied historic organizations with massive anchors and a cannon found on the nearby shoals of El Cuspe southeast of Coche Island. They believe these to have been jettisoned from a Spanish warship about 1750. The anchors—15 feet long and 10 feet across the flukes—were donated to the New Cádiz Museum of La Asunción.

The cenotes of Yucatán Peninsula in east Mexico are submarine storehouses of ancient Mayan artifacts. They were created naturally as the result of Yucatán's unusual geological formation. The peninsula is porous limestone, into which rain water seeps downward until it reaches stratae of harder rock underneath. Here, for millenniums, water has been accumulating in subterranean pockets or flowing across the hard rock in underground rivers. The limestone dissolved, and vaults were formed. Sometimes their roofs caved in, and the resulting holes, resembling huge wells, are the cenotes. Since Yucatán has no surface lakes or streams these cenotes were the only source of water for the Mayans who built their cities near them. They vary in size and depth and clarity of water. The most famous of the cenotes is that of Chichén Itzá (see Chapter 10). Many of the others, while perhaps not containing gold ornaments, hold archaeologically interesting artifacts and several museums have sent expeditions to dive for them.

One very successful program was carried out by the Middle American Research Institute of Tulane University, headed by Dr. E. Wyllys Andrews, at the cenote of Dzibilchaltun. Bob Marx, the first to enter the cenote, found two intact water vases dated at 300 B.C., bones of both humans and animals, and many broken bits of pottery. From this and other cenotes Marx has recovered weapons such as hatchet heads, spear points, and flint knives and countless artifacts, including a ceramic life-size ceremonial face mask, pottery, offering dishes, and jade beads. Comments Dr. Andrews: "The cenote collections have been a valuable addition to the stratigraphic collections from our excavations above . . . They have offered a wealth of intact pottery vessels, and undamaged artifacts, which often assist us greatly in the reconstruction of broken fragments found in the trenches." An illustrated account of Dr. Andrews' work, by Luis Marden, is in the January 1959 issue of *National Geographic Magazine*.

Near Guatemala City, beautiful Lake Amatitlán has been the site of "Aqua Lung archaeology" work by the Stovall Museum of the University of Oklahoma, directed by Dr. Stephen F. de Borhegyi. For about 3000 years the borders of this lake have been inhabited by tribes who, in many periods, regarded it as the seat of gods and made sacrifices to its waters. Dr. de Borhegyi believes the reason to stem from hot geysers at its perimeter and an active volcano overhead. During 1957 and 1958 groups of diving archaeology students brought up from Lake Amatitlán a rich haul of artifacts. Some were found in clusters near shore; others lay at random on the bottom which reaches 131 feet in depth.

Thousands of objects have been recovered. Among them: incense burners with realistic representations of jaguars, spider monkeys, bats, birds, iguanas, papaya fruits, flowers, etc.; grotesque seated figurines holding bowls in their laps; a bowl made from a human skull; a sacrificial jar containing mercury, cinnamon, graphite, and many ceremonially smashed jade ear spools; numbers of offering vessels, their sides carved with human heads and skulls. The size of these artifacts varied from a few inches to over four feet. An illustrated article on Dr. de Borhegyi's work during 1957 appeared in the July 12, 1958, issue of *The Illustrated London News*, and a report on the 1958 results can be obtained from the Stovall Museum by those interested in getting the details of this fascinating project.

Lake Titicaca in Peru holds the ruins of at least two ancient cities: the Inca Chiopata, discovered several years ago; and a pre-Inca city reported to be 95 feet deep by William Mardorf who took submarine photos of the remains.

Paul J. Tzimoulis, editor of *Skin Diver* magazine (to which references are made throughout this book), describes a number of historical wrecks around St. Thomas Island in the June 1968 issue of his magazine. One of these, in Hull Bay on the north of the island, has yielded a half-ton cannon and many artifacts. In the harbor of St. Thomas alone there are estimated to be some hundred wrecks, of which sixty were lost in the 1867 hurricane. Northeast of St. Thomas is a rock named after H.M.S. *Mercurius,* which vanished nearby.

The experienced divers forming Pablo Bush Romero's C.E.D.A.M. (*Club de Exploraciones y Deportes Acuáticos,* but also transposed into English to read "Conservation-Exploration-Diving-Archaeology-Museums") have earned considerable respect in the world of archaeology through their numerous contributions. Just about every historically significant wreck off Mexico, or submerged depository of Mayan artifacts, has been visited by members of the group, and probably photographed and systematically salvaged. The C.E.D.A.M. Underwater Archaeological Museum in Mexico City holds relics from expeditions ranging from gold and terra-cotta Mayan sculptures from Chichén Itzá to cannons, jewelry, silverware, and trading beads cracked loose from the coral on "*El Matancero.*" From this wreck alone, over twelve thousand items have been salvaged so far—even an eighteenth-century watch, thimbles, and eyeglasses.

A site frequently visited by C.E.D.A.M. is a semicircular coral atoll nearly forty miles long called Alacrán Reef. Over 250 wrecks lie on its shoals, some 65 miles north of Yucatán, from which divers have retrieved artifacts going back to the early 1500s. The whole reef is strewn with cannons covering practically every type made for three centuries. Although gold and silver coins are found here (Chapter 10), this site is pre-eminent for its archaeological treasure. Culverins, lombards, and 12-foot cannons, Wedgwood china, silver-framed mirrors, medicine jars, brass candlesticks, and dinner bells are just a light sampling of this reef's yield to date. From one wreck, a 300-foot sidewheeler sunk about 1850, such diverse items as a gold pocket watch and a 40-pound lead flask containing mercury were found. C.E.D.A.M.'s American associate, C.E.D.A.M. International, participates in joint ventures with the Mexican group, as do other organizations dedicated to underwater archaeology

THE U.S.A.

At a meeting of the Florida Board of Archives and History in Tallahassee on January 16, 1968, Executive Director Robert Williams presented a "Proposal for Reserve Areas" which had been prepared by the Board's Advisory Commission and State Marine Archaeologist Carl J. Clausen. With the unanimous passing of the historic motion, Florida's four preserves came into being. Three are shown on Florida map ❊1. The fourth runs between Cape San Blas and St. Marks Lighthouse along the north coast of the Gulf. The proposal for these preserves, in which Carl Clausen was very interested, read as follows:

> From shortly after the discovery of the New World to the present, the waters surrounding the peninsula of Florida have accrued a significant number of ship wrecks through storms, errors in navigation, and military actions. It is estimated that this shipwreck population probably numbers between 1200–1800.
>
> The majority of the wrecks (more than 70%) are currently for various reasons of limited archaeological and historical significance. The remainder, broadly speaking, those wrecks of vessels of the various Maritime Nations, including the United States, which sank during the 16th, 17th, and 18th centuries, *are of primary archaeological and historical importance.* They sank during the periods of exploration, colonization, and development of overseas commerce–all vitally important phases in the history and progress of the Americas. These wrecks and the scientific information they contain constitute an *extremely valuable but numerically limited resource.*
>
> Unfortunately, it is the same small percentage of wrecks which contain scientific data nowhere else available which are under attack by the commercial treasure salvager and curio hunter.
>
> During the past several years it has been the policy of the State to grant leases and contracts to these companies for the purpose of salvaging treasure and artifacts from the wrecks. Although these leases and contracts contain provisions which help in preserving the information which might be found on the wrecks, a great deal of data is still lost due to the essential commercial nature of the salvagers' operations.
>
> In many cases the retention by the State of a 25% share in the artifacts recovered commercially by a salvage company does not adequately compensate us for the destruction of the wreck in terms of its historical worth to the public. Also, contrary to popular thought, the long-term net worth of the wrecks is not the commercial value, but in their scientific and historical meaning to the public. The laws enabling us to administer the wrecks also demand that they and the articles recovered from them be handled in the best public interest. It would be difficult to justify, for example, the marketing of any portion of the State's share of the recently recovered treasure as serving the best public interest. We would be selling a collection of coins which are not only rare collector's items, but part of the historical heritage of the people of Florida.
>
> With this in mind, it might prove difficult at some future date to justify the continually accelerating depletion of a valuable and limited reserve by commercial interests at the expense of the public.
>
> In our opinion proper administration of the salvage program requires that measures be taken to conserve this resource.
>
> Another reason in support of the recommendation for Reserves Areas is the fact that the old Board of Antiquities, and now the Florida Board

of Archives and History,[2] has not been appropriated funds for the proper cleaning and preserving of artifacts. The State presently has in its possession considerable quantities of artifacts in barrels of water in storage at the space provided by the State Road Department at Fort Pierce. In addition to these artifacts, there are quite a few more in possession of the salvors pending our ability to receive and clean them in order that a proper division may be made. To grant additional contracts for salvage without setting aside these Reserve Areas could conceivably cause the State to lose valuable artifacts after they were recovered.

This proposal was submitted to the Advisory Commission to the Florida Board of Archives and History at a meeting held in Tampa, Florida, on December 14, 1967, for their consideration and recommendation. After discussion among the Commission members and with Mr. Carl Clausen, State Marine Archaeologist, and the Executive Director a motion was made, seconded, and unanimously adopted that the Advisory Commission endorse the proposal for Reserve Areas and request the Executive Director to recommend the adoption of such a proposal by the Florida Board of Archives and History.

One method to assure that a broad sample of our historically significant wrecks will be preserved for the future would be the setting aside of several Reserve Areas in which treasure hunters would not, at present, be permitted to secure salvage contracts. With this object in mind the . . . areas selected are recommended on the basis of their potential and known wreck population . . .

Four hundred or more historically valuable wrecks lie around the coast of Florida, of which by now probably 250 have been found by divers. They lie everywhere, some in deep water and some right up on keys and beaches. About 70 of these are mentioned in the Florida treasure chapter. Archaeological interest in these wrecks began during the early 1950s when Art McKee and other pioneers began displaying their salvaged artifacts. Inventor-businessman-diver Edwin A. Link did much to promote their archaeological value,[3] and his endowments to the Smithsonian Institution made possible a large part of the first historical work carried out along the Keys. With his wife Marion, the Smithsonian's Mendel L. Peterson, Captain Weems of the U. S. Navy, Dr. and Mrs. George Crile, Jr., and other associates, Link joined McKee on the wrecks of H.M.S. *Winchester*, H.M.S. *Looe*, and an unidentified slave trader carrying a cargo of ivory tusks. These ships had all been discovered earlier by skin divers, but it was the Link-endowed Undersea Hall of History of the Smithsonian, managed by diver-historian Curator Mendel L. Peterson, that made careful studies of their histories and identified and classified recovered relics. A few years later Ed Link sold his first boat, the *Blue Heron*, and acquired the *Sea Diver* with which he gained the reputation of a first-rate underwater

[2] Changed July 1, 1969, to the Division of Archives, History and Records Management.
[3] Described by Marion Link in her book *Sea Diver*, Rinehart & Co., 1959.

archaeologist following explorations for the *Santa Maria*'s remains, into Caesarea's sunken harbor, and at Port Royal.

Many other underwater archaeologists have made important contributions in Florida. Their names and achievements are described in the treasure chapters that follow. One, who typifies the modern breed, is General Exploration Company's Colonel Frank F. Tenney, Jr., USAF (Ret.). From his 62-foot twin diesel yacht *Saucy Q*, rebuilt into a dive boat, he has explored many wrecks off the coast and Keys. Fellow divers on his team are Phil Pepperdine (chief engineer), John Acteson (chief electrician), Richard Abate, Dave Criner, and Gene Kulla. Equipment includes compressors for the air lift, hookah system, and SCUBA tanks, as well as an uncommon X-ray unit carried aboard for studying the contents of encrusted masses raised from wrecks.

Although the *Saucy Q* has anchored over many exciting sites, the most interesting wreck encountered lies near Delta Shoals off Key Vaca. From the distribution of the artifacts Tenney has concluded that this ship bilged herself on an outer reef and—leaving a trail of ballast stones—was pushed in a NNE direction to the point where she sank with her bow toward the east. Excavations into the ballast mound, about 4 feet high at its center, show that it spreads for 25 feet to the right of the keel and only 15 feet to the left, indicating that the ship settled with a starboard list. While most of the stones are the common beach stone type, small pieces of rectangular granite and slabs of red building brick, 1 foot by ½ foot and 2 inches thick, are unusual. Some 70 feet of keel remain today, measuring 22½ by 19 inches near the center and tapering toward the ends. The planking is fastened to the ribs, 10½ by 6½ inches in size, with wood pins about 1 inch in diameter. Besides a wide sampling of artifacts, the wreck site holds hundreds of musket balls $2^{7}\!/_{32}$ inches in diameter, leading to its designation as "the Minnie Ball wreck."

Probably every state in the union has ocean front, rivers, or lakes under which historically interesting artifacts lie. Florida diving speleologists discovered, in a cave under a lake, mastodon bones and teeth and bone spearheads together with charcoal. It is accepted that mastodons were extinct long before cavemen learned to use fire, but this coincidence has raised questions. Throughout the eastern U.S.A. Revolutionary War and Civil War relics are being retrieved in ever growing numbers. One of the first divers interested in these artifacts was Jackson Jenks, who found wreckage in a river near Richmond that Mendel Peterson dated at the Civil War period. The remains of a ship believed to be a Union gunboat have been located in the Appomattox River; a search is reported to have recently found the historic *Savannah*, the first steamship to cross the Atlantic, off Fire Island; the U.S.S. *Tecumseh*—sunk by a mine in the Battle of Mobile Bay in 1864—was located in 1965 by

Sonny Wintzell, and then became the subject of a Smithsonian project
to raise her and bring her to Washington, D.C.; Dr. Harold Edgerton
and Brad Luther, Jr., found the historic Vineyard Sound lightship in
1963 off Cuttyhunk. On the West Coast the divers of C.H.A.O.S.
(Cannon Hunters' Association of Seattle), headed by Don Clark, have
been working since 1967 on the salvage of the 182-foot Yankee clipper
War Hawk under Port Discovery Bay, using a grid system; some years
ago Neil Tobin found several undersea collections of Indian ceremonial
metates—or bowls—off the California coast, and from their depth, and
geologists' opinions of the rate the land is sinking, they have been
dated at about 6000 B.C. Hundreds of other historically valuable underwater operations are going on today throughout America.

THE ATLANTIC

The famous *Lusitania*, torpedoed in 1915 off the southern Irish coast,
was in the news a few years ago when John Light bought the wreck
for £1000 on behalf of two Boston businessmen who intended to salvage
her. The 40,000-ton Cunard liner was resold, as she lies, for scrap.
The Aquaknights of Atlantis, an Azores U.S.A.F. diving club, have
raised an anchor dated at about 1859 from wreckage of an old ship
they located. In the Bahamas the salvage of galleons and frigates
continues, as well as just as interesting pottery and statuettes of the
extinct Taino Indian tribe—probably the first Americans to meet Columbus—from the sea floor around Isla Verde.

Off Bermuda Teddy Tucker, Robert Canton, Ed Downing, Harry
Cox, and other reef searchers have brought up enough historical artifacts
to fill a warehouse. Some 550 wrecks of many nationalities and covering
a span of over four hundred years are known to lie among reefs off
Somerset, Ireland, St. George's and Bermuda islands. This area makes a
real museum for archaeologists. From the French sixty-gun ship *Her-
moine*, sunk in 1838, Tucker and Canton recovered an entire armory
of early nineteenth-century naval weapons. Among these were 3½-ton
cannons made by the important armorers Ruelle in 1828—identified by
the name and date on their breeches—swords and cutlasses, and flintlock
muskets. From the sunken hulls of other ships pottery, navigation instruments, and a wealth of artifacts are being raised under strict supervision of the Colonial Government authorities, who make it clear that
they do not wish visits from hit-and-run treasure hunters. One of the
most interesting of these historical recoveries was made by Tucker from
the wreck where he found his famous treasure. As quoted in Bob
Nesmith's authoritative book, *Dig for Pirate Treasure*, Tucker describes
these artifacts:

> We uncovered some breech-loading culverins or swivel guns; hand
> grenades; a steel breastplate; sounding leads . . . a terracotta inkwell in

the form of a lion's head; brass hour glasses and a pair of navigator's brass dividers . . . we also recovered some interesting pottery of native Carib make. One cruet . . . is red clay with green glaze. A small six-inch pitcher with a spout is set on a ten-degree angle so that its center of gravity makes it less likely to tip over when used on shipboard . . . nothing like it in style has ever been seen before.

A collection of Carib Indian weapons was being carried by some passenger to show the folks in Spain. One ceremonial spear five feet long is carved in an intricate design for about two feet along the handle. We also found bows and arrows. These weapons were fire-treated to harden them, and the water and worms that attack ordinary wood have had no effect on them.

Bermuda historians are particularly exuberant over the discovery of the wreck of the *Sea Venture* which carried the first colonists to that island in 1609. This vessel was the flagship of Sir George Somers, bound for Virginia with 150 emigrants from England, when she became separated from eight companion ships during a terrible storm. Badly damaged, with 10 feet of water in her hold, the *Sea Venture* was on the point of sinking when lookouts saw land. Somers managed to ground the hull between two rocks three-quarters of a mile from Bermuda's beaches. All aboard reached safety.

During the following months most of the wreck's lading which had not already been jettisoned was taken off. Some of the beams were used in the construction of a pinnace aboard which most of the colonists continued their interrupted voyage to America. A few years later skin divers recovered two guns, and in 1622 another saker, an anchor, and some barrels of iron and lead ingots. Then the wreck's skeleton vanished.

In June 1958, SCUBA diving enthusiast Edmund Downing, a Virginian who had settled in Bermuda seven years before, decided to try to find the *Sea Venture*'s remains. Research through early histories told him that it lay off the southeast shore, appropriately enough near Sea Venture Shoal. In October his search was climaxed when he saw the outline of a ship's hull on the sand bottom 30 feet deep. He reported his discovery to authorities, who showed surprising interest. An intensive effort was made to learn if Downing's wreck was, in fact, the *Sea Venture*. Among experts called over to look at it was the Smithsonian's Mendel Peterson. Bit by bit clues were unearthed as a salvage team headed by Teddy Tucker cleared away covering sand. They all tallied with recorded data: the wreck lay in the right place at the right depth; measurements of timbers raised from the hull conformed with those of the *Sea Venture*'s class; the scarcity of cargo indicated that much had been jettisoned or salvaged earlier; the few artifacts recovered—a vase, a stone jug, a clay pipe, an harquebus—were of the correct period. Near-certain confirmation was provided by the marking on a cannon which had been buried.

The Bermuda government announced that the *Sea Venture* had been found. The island's 1959 Somers Day celebration, commemorating the 350th anniversary of its first colonists' arrival, was made especially significant by Ed Downing's venture into submarine archaeology.

THE PACIFIC

Many references to the National Geographic Society in this book reflect the important role in submarine archaeology played by this organization. Usually the name of Luis Marden appears in the text. A few years after giving world-wide publicity to Cousteau's salvage from the Grand Gongloue galley this organization sent its famous undersea photographer, Luis Marden, to track down the resting place of Captain William Bligh's *Bounty* off Pitcairn Island. Marden's six-week diving search and crowning success are described in the December 1957 issue of the *National Geographic Magazine*. The charred remains of the *Bounty*, stripped, burned, and sunk in 1790 by Fletcher Christian and his mutinous crew, still contained some of the old ship's copper sheathing and fittings.

The World War I German raider *See Adler*, carrying historically interesting records and objects from captured ships, was scuttled off Papeete, Tahiti. Expeditions Unlimited has announced plans to send divers to probe the wreck and recover its contents.

THE INDIAN OCEAN

No roundup of undersea archaeology would be complete without the names of Arthur C. Clarke and Mike Wilson, the Ceylon-based team of divers, writers, and submarine photographers whose many books, illustrated articles, and color movies about wrecks distributed from the Barrier Reef to the Great Basses (see Chapter 22) have initiated many SCUBA divers to archaeology. They have visited numerous underwater sites ranging from sunken temples to wrecked East Indiamen.

AUSTRALIA

Captain James Cook's journal describing the historic exploration voyage of H.M.S. *Endeavour* through the South Pacific contains many amusing anecdotes. One of these is how the kangaroo got its name. While the English crew was ashore in Australia one of these strange animals hopped by, causing a sailor to ask an aborigine what it was called. "Kangaroo," was the reply. Later it was found that in the aborigine language this meant "I don't know." In his account Captain Cook also tells of the nearly impossible task he had rounding up his exhausted crew after they discovered the swinging girls of Tahiti, and of his encounter with the cannibals of New Zealand where he decided not to go ashore.

An incident which was not so amusing to Captain Cook took place after the discovery of Botany Bay, near Sydney Harbor. The *Endeavour* sailed northward as Cook meticulously charted the unknown east Australia coastline. The Great Barrier Reef came into view far to the east. As the 370-ton rebuilt collier continued north the coral barrier closed toward shore, narrowing the safe passageway. The leadsmen were on twenty-four-hour duty calling out soundings. Several times the course was changed to avoid the deadly banks. Then on the night of June 11, 1770, the coral shoaled too suddenly. In the darkness the ship bilged herself on a ledge.

Before sailing from England, Cook had doubly reinforced the *Endeavour's* hull, anticipating the possibility of running aground in uncharted waters. This farsighted move saved the ship from destruction. Despite the strengthened hull, coral had broken through and the pumps were inadequate to cope with the water level, which rose steadily in the bilge. The tide fell, and the ship heeled over with her bottom cradled in the contour of the reef top.

After studying the damage, Cook decided that the leaks could be checked long enough for the *Endeavour* to reach the coast—if she could be freed from the coral. As he wrote in his Journal, to lighten the hull "we throw'd overboard our guns, iron and stone ballast, casks, hoops, staves, oyle jars" and other cargo. Anchors were taken out by the boats and dropped into deeper water. At high tide every man threw himself at the capstan bars. The anchor cables grew taut, and slowly, as chunks of coral crunched loose, the *Endeavour* was kedged off the reef. A waterproofed sail patch was hauled down the side with ropes, covering the breach, while stuffing was wedged against the holes from within. With shifts straining at the pumps, Cook sailed thirty-seven miles across to Australia and beached the *Endeavour* at the mouth of a river, where the damage was repaired. The site later became Cooktown and the waterway was named Endeavour River.

From descriptions in the Journal and other data, the location of Endeavour Reef was well known to several groups of divers who searched for the jettisoned cargo, and particularly the cannons. None were successful. Then in late 1968 two American scientific groups camped on nearby Hope Island. One was a seven-man team from Philadelphia's Academy of Natural Sciences, headed by Dr. James C. Tyler. The other included several members of New York's Explorers Club. Their leader, Mr. Virgil Kauffman, had become interested in the cannons during a visit to the Barrier Reef in 1961. The most important piece of equipment brought to the site was the Varian Associates' new V-4938-G cesium gradiometer magnetometer, operated by Kenneth Myers, President of Sea Borne Electronics Company.

On January 11, 1969, the magnetometer's sensor was towed over

Endeavour Reef from a chartered boat in a systematic search pattern. Contact was made with such precision that SCUBA divers were put right onto the first cannon. About 20 feet deep, it was invisible to the naked eye because of the coral growth that covered it. The magnetometer located the other five cannons. Four of the 6-foot guns were carefully freed from under 4 feet of coral with small gelignite charges and winched aboard the trawler *Tropic Seas*. After undersea storage at Hope Island they were turned over to Mr. W. G. Douglas, the Queensland Receiver of Wrecks. The other two cannons were recovered later by Commonwealth Department of Shipping divers. All six were sent to Melbourne, where the Defence Standards Laboratory undertook their restoration. Describing the process, the scientist in charge, Dr. Colin Pearson, was quoted as saying: "Our first step was to tap off the casing of coral with a hammer. To treat the corrosion in the metal, we are using electrolysis. Each gun will be kept in a dilute caustic soda bath through which a low-voltage electric current is passed for about six weeks. The electrolytic bath extracts the corrosion compounds which have formed on the top layers of the cast-iron body of the cannon." After treatment, the guns were washed in distilled water for several weeks.

The first of the restored cannons weighs just over 1300 pounds, corresponding with the markings 11 2 15 chiseled on the barrel,[4] and bears on its breech a crowned GR 2, dating it during the reign of King George II (1727-60). Inside the barrel when it was recovered were a cannon ball, a charge of powder, and a piece of hemp wadding.

Walter Deas, the Sydney-based member of the Underwater Research Group of New South Wales and author of *Beneath Australian Seas*, brought with him a keen enthusiasm for underwater archaeology when he moved there from Dublin in 1969. He has dived on many of the better-known wrecks off the east Australian coast and has plans to organize the salvage of the *Porpoise* and *Cato*, among others. Deas is researching for the preparation of a new book, which will be welcomed by Australian divers, in which he intends to list and describe nine hundred of the most interesting wrecks lying on the Great Barrier Reef and other shoals.

While the recovery of the *Endeavour*'s cannons made the headlines, Australia's competent SCUBA divers have located and worked innumerable other historic wrecks on the Great Barrier Reef. Among the ships from which cannons, anchors, old pewter and silver tableware, and other nineteenth-century artifacts have been recovered are the *Cato* and *Porpoise*, wrecked together in 1803 on Cairns Reef, which was aptly renamed Wreck Reef after the *Echo*, *Jennylind*, *Mahiaco*, *Lone Star*, *Guichen*, and other ships went down along its twenty miles of coral.

[4] See the Great Basses Reef Silver Wreck, Chapter 22.

On nearby reefs lie the remains of the *Oliver van Noort, Rodney, Bona Vista, Doelwyck,* and several more old ships which have been recently discovered.

At least forty-five wrecks under Sydney Harbor have been yielding artifacts to SCUBA divers. Among the better known are the *Edward Lombe,* a 370-ton brig sunk in 1834 at Middle Head, with three hundred gold sovereigns aboard; and the *Catherine Adamson,* whose cargo was fought over by rival divers in the late 1800s and from whose wreckage a 400-pound cannon, salvaged in 1968 by John Strano, caused something of a tempest in a teapot when it was confiscated by the New South Wales Receiver of Wrecks.

Off the coast of Victoria, recent salvage from the ninety-year-old wreck of the *Loch Ard* also caused intervention by the Receiver of Wrecks for Victoria, when ownership of her lead and copper cargo was disputed. The wreck of *Eric the Red,* which sank in 1880 with a cargo of American trade exhibit goods, has yielded ornaments, silver plate, toys, and other merchandise since its survey by SCUBA divers in 1965. Artifacts have been raised from the *Cheviot,* and from such other famous wrecks as the *Schromberg, Fiji,* and *Marie Gabrielle.*

Some of the archaeologically interesting Spanish shipwrecks in the Pacific and other parts of the world are:

The Canary Islands: in 1780 five trading ships sank in the harbor of Santa Cruz de Tenerife in a storm.

The Caribbean and Gulf of Mexico: CUBA: in 1762 the 64-gunned warships *Europa* and *Asia II* and the 68-gunned *Neptuno II* were hastily scuttled against the Castillo de la Punta in Havana harbor in a desperate attempt to block the entrance against English attackers. There are conflicting reports as to whether these ships were stripped before they sank; in 1784 the sloop *Carlota* was wrecked off Matanzas Bay on a voyage from Cádiz; in 1786 the 34-gunned frigate *Santa Tecla* burned and sank in Havana; in 1807 the 8-gunned schooner *Piedad* was wrecked at Bani, Cuba. CARTAGENA: in 1780 the 6-gunned schooner *San Miguel II* sank off the port; in 1795 the 10-gunned schooner *Victoria* was wrecked on Negrillo Reef, near the entrance; on April 15, 1741, six major warships were scuttled at the Boca Chica entrance in an effort to blockade the harbor against an English attack. These were: the *Dragón,* 64 guns; the *Galicia,* 70 guns; the *Conquistador II,* 62 guns; the *África,* 64 guns; the *San Carlos II,* 66 guns; the *San Felipe II,* 70 guns. PUERTO RICO: in 1623 the *Almiranta* of the Biscay armada was sunk at the entrance to San Juan, with most of the cargo saved; in 1818 the schooner *Eugenia* was lost off Aquadilla. VERACRUZ: in 1738 the 50-gunned *Victoria* was wrecked in a hurricane; in 1739 the 62-gunned *San Francisco II* was sunk in a storm; in 1808 the schooner *Felicidad,* of 8 guns, was struck by lightning and exploded, killing her captain and many of the crew. Somewhere between Havana and New Orleans the brigantine *Galgo* was lost in 1783, carrying naval supplies.

Florida: in 1630 two galleons were wrecked near Cape Kennedy, carrying supplies; in 1814 the 3-gunned felucca *Intrépido* was wrecked on the beach of Pensacola; in 1815 the 6-gun schooner *Empecinado* sank off nearby Amalia Island; in 1820 the 18-gun brigantine *Ligero* and the merchant galleon *Pájaro,* with a valuable general cargo, were sunk off east Florida in the New Bahamas Channel.

Bahamas: in 1812 the brigantine *Almiranta* of Ignacio Checón, carrying 20 guns, sank off North Cuba with 25 drowned.

South America: RIO DE LA PLATA: in 1718 the 60-gun warship *Pembra* was lost off Montevideo; in 1792 the 40-gunned frigate *Loreto* and several other ships sank off Montevideo during a storm, with 23 drowned; in 1806 the cutter *San Ignacio* disappeared with all hands at the mouth of the river. CAPE HORN: in 1716 the 60-gun *San Francisco* was wrecked on Patagonia; in 1741 the warship *Hermíone* sank off the Cape with 500 drowned; on January 9, 1765, the warship *Concepción* ran aground on Tierra del Fuego, fifteen miles from the Straits of Le Maire. The crew dismantled part of the ship and built a schooner, in which 189 survivors sailed two months later to Buenos Aires; in 1819 the 74-gun *San Telmo* was wrecked, a total loss, at the tip of Cape Horn. WEST COAST: in 1788 the frigate *Fama* sank in Valparaíso harbor; in 1789 the frigate *San Pablo,* on a reconnoitering voyage, sank off Valdivia; in 1794 the 34-gunned frigate *Santa Barbara* broke up on Juan Fernández Islands.

California: in 1511 a caravel of General Diego Garcia's armada sank in Bahia de Todos los Santos, at the tip of Lower California; in 1769 the caravel *San José* was lost en route from La Paz to San Diego where it was carrying supplies; in 1797 the patache *San Carlos,* sailed up the coast of California, struck a rock off Yerba Buena and was battered to pieces.

The Pacific: in 1552 the caravel *Santa Margarita,* making an exploration of the Marianas, sank among these islands; in 1569 another caravel was wrecked on Guam, with the crew saved; in 1585 the *Santa Elena, Capitana* of an expedition to Molucca Island, was lost there with all her cargo.

The wrecks described above are, of course, only a tiny sampling of the hundreds of thousands of archaeologically attractive ships sunk in the oceans of the world, selected at random from among known Spanish wrecks.

Section Two

IT WILL BE NOTED that the maps showing locations of sunken treasures described in the following chapters are accurate, but small. This might be disappointing to the treasure enthusiast who has seen large, detailed, many-colored sunken treasure charts with arrows pointing to the "exact spot" where his galleon lies, and a word of explanation is due.

In the first place, a prospective treasure hunter, before embarking on his quest, should procure an up-to-date hydrographic chart of the region in which he is interested—and it would be manifestly impossible to include hundreds of these wall-sized maps in this book. Secondly, it would serve no useful purpose toward pinpointing the treasure's location to do so, since in all but a few cases only the approximate site is known. Were the exact points where treasure ships went down common knowledge, their gold and silver would have already, obviously, been cleaned out. In the text describing each treasure I have narrowed down locations with relation to geographic names as far as our research has permitted, and have included any speculative ideas as to likely reefs, etc., that came to mind. Further research, and the search itself, are the only ways in which positions could be determined more accurately. So for the purposes of this book the maps are adequate.

As stated in the Introduction, I have placed one, two, or three stars next to the treasure locations that have checked out as the most promising for the modern treasure diver. For quick reference to these "hot" sites I would refer the reader to the Index of Sunken Treasures by Year where the stars can easily be spotted.

CHAPTER 8

The Eastern Caribbean
(Hispaniola, the Antilles, and Venezuela)

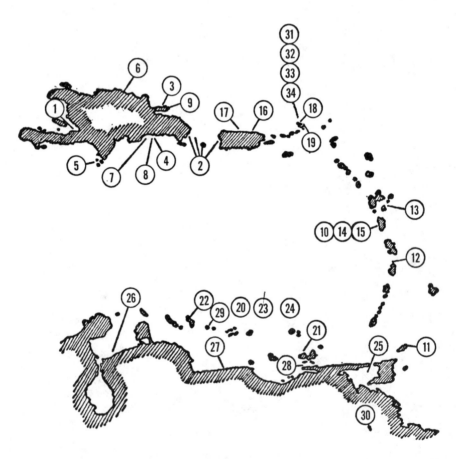

MAP A

A CORAL REEF was responsible for Columbus' selection of Hispaniola as the springboard from which he and his successors went out to conquer the New World. On Christmas Night 1492, six weeks after making landfall in the Bahamas, the *Santa María* approached the north coast of Haiti after threading her way down the islets and cays. Just off Cap Haitien the little caravel jammed her bottom onto a reef. There was no way to get her off, and she was dismantled and taken ashore, bit by bit. Her wood and guns became part of the fort which Columbus built at the site of the first Spanish colony in the Indies, Navidad. He named the new land *Isla Española*—Spanish Island.

Upon his return from a triumphant reception in Spain, Columbus found that the little colony at Navidad was gone, wiped out. He founded a second colony on the south coast which he named Santo Domingo (Trujillo). This prospered and became, for several decades, the most important base in the New World and the assembly port for returning flotillas. Columbus was its governor until 1500 when complaints of his harsh rule, and politics, caused his replacement by Francisco de Bobadilla who promptly sent the great navigator back to Spain in chains. Columbus returned, however, to carry out further explorations in Honduras and Panama and founded Puerto Plata in 1503 on north Hispaniola. This later became a staging port for the armadas.

The Spanish were puzzled and disappointed in "The Indies." They had expected to bring back from here Indian gold and Chinese silks, but instead of the splendors of which Marco Polo had written they found only tropical islands inhabited by barbarian tribes. It was not until later voyages disclosed that this was not Asia after all, that they realized that an entirely new continent had been reached. Their early chagrin over the scant mineral wealth of the islands was offset by thousands of pounds of pearls collected from oyster beds off Margarita and the Antilles. Gold, too, was found in Cuba and Hispaniola. The new masters drove subjugated native Indians into mines and onto sugar-cane plantations, compensating from slave labor what they had lost in oriental treasure. A large agricultural output was achieved, with tobacco, coffee, cocoa, and other crops being added.

Caravels began returning to Spain laden with these products and citrus fruits, bananas, pineapples, coconuts, cassava and sisal, hides and skins as well as growing quantities of gold and pearls.

The Hispaniola Coast

The TWO CARAVELS (1)

The first of hundreds of treasure cargoes recorded lost in the seas of the New World was in 1501, when a hurricane sank two caravels of a flotilla commanded by Rodrigo de Bástidas in the Gonave Channel near present-day Port-au-Prince. Aboard these little ships was 200 tons of "gold, and jewels, clothes and arms with a value of 5,000,000 maravedis" (worth at that time about one cent apiece). Nearly all of this consisted of uninteresting general cargo while something like $15,000 was in pearls and gold.

These two wrecks would be difficult, if possible at all, to find now. Deeply crusted over with coral, they could lie at the edge of a shallow reef or on the wide channel's bottom, which drops to below 200 feet. Except for their historical value as the first New World treasure wrecks, they would have little appeal to the treasure hunter.

DE TORRES' FLEET (2)

Poetic justice in a tragic form took place on July 4, 1502. A fleet of 32 caravels had assembled at Santo Domingo four day before, making ready to sail for Spain. Among the passengers on Antonio de Torres' flagship, *El Dorado*, was the scheming Bobadilla who had imprisoned Columbus two years before. By coincidence, their paths crossed again when Columbus put in at Santo Domingo on his return from a voyage. He didn't like the feel of the heavy, still atmosphere, recognizing the familiar forewarning of hurricane. He told Bobadilla as much, but his advice was scorned.

Perhaps Bobadilla remembered the navigator's warning four days later as he struggled for his life in the watery fury of the worst hurricane ever recorded to that time. During twelve hours of July 4 its cyclonic winds and massive waves tore the flota to shreds, swamping a dozen of the ships in the Mona Passage and breaking most of the rest against the shores of Puerto Rico, Santo Domingo, and Mona islands. Only five lived through that day. Twenty-seven caravels, among them *El Dorado*, were lost with over 500 lives, including Bobadilla's.

There was treasure, in quantity, on the destroyed ships. Perhaps half of its gold nuggets and dust, and pearls, had been stowed aboard *El Dorado*. The single richest item was a solid gold table, reputed to weigh 1½ tons, through which Bobadilla intended to express his gratitude to the Catholic Kings for his appointment as governor. The flagship was believed to have gone down in the Mona Passage, where depths of 1000 feet are encountered. No trace of its wreckage was discovered during the salvage work along the coasts after the seas had subsided. Much was recovered from wrecks which had been thrown up onto reefs and beaches, but at least $3,000,000 in gold and pearls was gone. If accounts of Bobadilla's 3310-pound golden table are true, about $2,000,000 in treasure lie in the remnants of *El Dorado*, way down under Mona Passage. Some of the other wrecks against the coasts, partly salvaged or beyond reach of 1500 Indian skin divers, might make worthwhile targets for modern SCUBA-diving treasure hunters, but *El Dorado* and her treasures will probably never be found.

The *SAN MIGUEL* (3)

By the mid-1500s Puerto Plata was being used as a final staging port for departing fleets. In August, 1551, the 200-ton *nao San Miguel* set sail from here bound for Spain. "Thirty leagues" out she struck a reef and sank. Her hull settled onto a shallow sea bed, permitting extensive salvage work which recovered a large part of the cargo, including silver and gold from Mexico. There might be a little left still on the *San Miguel's* ballast heap, but not much.

The ARMADA of COLUMBUS (4)*

Following the death of Christopher Columbus, neglected and discredited by the nation which his pathfinding had made the richest in Europe, belated recognition was given to his descendants. Today a young naval officer, Cristóbal Colón, Duke of Veragua, holds the honorary title of Admiral of the Spanish fleet and receives the salutes of officers at official functions. In 1553 another officer of the same name, Columbus' nephew, was placed in command of an armada of sixteen galleons, *naos* and *pataches* aboard which was "up to 30,000,000 pesos" in New World treasure when it assembled at Santo Domingo late in the year.

There a hurricane caught it just as the ships were preparing to get under way on their return voyage. Three *naos*, which had left port, were dashed against the reefs of Andres Point a few miles to the east. Another eleven vessels were wrecked in port. One small *patache*, coming up from the south, sank at sea about a mile off Santo Domingo. "Much gold and silver" from Veracruz and Cartagena, as well as Antilles pearls, were lost with these sixteen ships. About half of this was recovered from wreckage in Santo Domingo harbor. No salvage was even attempted on the cargoes of the four ships lost outside.

There should be good hunting among the shoals off Andres, where three coral-caked ballast mounds hold about $100,000 in gold and silver. The harbor floor, as well, might yield treasure from under its sand and mud.

DE CARVAJAL'S TWO *NAOS* (5)

In 1556 two vessels en route to Santo Domingo from Tortuga Island to join the forming armada of General Gonzalo de Carvajal were wrecked against the south Hispaniola coast during a storm. They grounded in fairly shallow water, permitting native divers to recover much of their cargoes. Some pearls, worth perhaps $10,000, were hidden in the wreckage and could not be found.

The *SANTIAGO* (6)

This galley was wrecked against the reefs of Puerto Plata in 1584. Salvage carried out over the broken *Santiago* brought up all but a few thousand dollars' worth of her silver and gold.

The *NAO* (7)

An unidentified ship, returning from Veracruz in 1603, sank off Santo Domingo. She was too deep to salvage then, and probably still is.

The *ALMIRANTA* (8)

There was about $200,000 in gold and silver aboard the *Almiranta* of the Honduras flota attached to the 1605 New Spain armada as she approached Santo Domingo in a thunderstorm at night. Lightning struck the mainmast, setting her afire. She burned and sank "not far from the coast" with only 11 survivors of the 101 people that she carried. Because of the depth no effort was made afterward to salvage the *Almiranta*'s treasure. She lies probably in 1000-foot-deep water, but may have settled on the shallower ledge reaching out a short distance from the coast.

The *GUADALUPE* and *TOLOSA* (9)

General Baltasar de Guevara's New Spain armada was approaching the Samamá coast of Hispaniola after crossing the Atlantic when, on August 25, 1724, a hurricane struck. Two *azogues*—mercury transports —the 50-gun galleon *Guadalupe* and the 58-gunned *Tolosa*, were hurled against the point of the peninsula where they grounded on the bottom 20 feet deep and broke up. Some of their stout casks of quicksilver survived the pounding of the waves and were recovered intact. Others were broken and their silvery contents plummeted in heavy streams onto the rocks below.

These were big ships, of 1000 or more tons. Their mounds would make interesting hunting grounds for SCUBA divers. Besides the lost mercury probably $20,000 in silver dining services and ornaments, ship's money and passengers' jewelry lies scattered there.

The Antilles Islands

The TIERRA FIRME ARMADA WRECKS (10)*

A hurricane piled several galleons and *naos* of the 1567 Tierra Firme armada, returning via an unusual route through the Antilles chain, onto reefs surrounding Dominica Island. The wrecked ships carried "over 3,000,000 pesos in gold, silver, and pearls." The survivors who straggled ashore, congratulating themselves on their narrow escape, soon changed their minds. Carib natives caught and ate most of them. Some got away to safety, though, and from their reports Spanish authorities learned what happened to the ships' treasure.

When the seas calmed the Indians went out in canoes to the broken ships, still awash on the reefs. They stripped them of everything they could get, especially the iron spikes for spearheads. Some of the treasure was also recovered, and, according to the survivors, was placed in a cave on the beach. There the recorded accounts end. The mystery of what happened to the treasure in the cave seems to have never been solved. There were some recoveries from the wrecks later, but it is a good bet that the Dominica reefs there still hold $1,000,000 in treasure.

The FIVE SHIPS of ERASO (11)

A hurricane in 1572 wrecked five ships of General Cristóbal de Eraso's New Spain armada, bound for Veracruz, on Tobago Island. There were no metallic valuables aboard except ship's funds and passengers' jewelry.

The *SAN FERNANDO* (12)

Ferris L. Coffman, in his book *1001 Lost, Buried or Sunken Treasures*, reports that this galleon with a large treasure lies 300 feet deep off Point Ducap in Santa Lucia Island.

The *CAPITANA* and TWO *NAOS* (13)

The 1603 New Spain armada sailed from Cádiz in June. As its ships were approaching the Antilles chain two months later a hurricane moved in and smashed the *Capitana* and two other ships against the shoals and islets of Desirade and Petite Terre just east off Guadalupe. Some money and personal valuables, and merchandise worth 1,000,000 pesos, were lost.

The *NAO* (14)

A ship of the 1605 Tierra Firme armada became separated from the protection of the convoy and was attacked and sunk by pirates off

Dominica. She was westward-bound and carried no more than a little money and jewelry.

The PIRATE SHIP (15)
There have been several accounts that a privateer, usually described as French, struck a reef off Dominica and sank with an enormous amount of loot.

Puerto Rico and The Virgin Islands

The BIG GALLEON (16)*
Less than an hour after setting sail for Spain on July 24, 1550, a galleon, described as being the largest ever to have visited the Indies up to that time, sank about three miles out of San Juan de Puerto Rico. She carried a cargo of five hundred tons of sugar and other agricultural products, and gold and pearls with a value of at least $75,000.

Although her position is narrowed down no closer than "one league from the port" in the account of her loss, it is possible to guess at the spot. Three miles east from the tip of San Juan peninsula a land promontory pushes north into the ocean. Off its point are several islets and shoals. Passing eastward across this site on a course previously considered safe for shallower-draft vessels, the galleon could have struck an unknown pinnacle and sunk several hundred yards offshore.

The *CARLOS V* (17)
There is certainly money and possibly a treasure consignment in the wreckage of the *Carlos V*, a 50-gun warship wrecked against the north Puerto Rico coast in a hurricane of 1720. Over 500 men died in the disaster.

LA VICTORIA (18)*
Within six years the treacherous shoals outlying Anegada Island, a hundred miles east of Puerto Rico, claimed two treasure ships sailing for Spain. *La Victoria* was a warship bringing back a consignment of between $1,000,000 and $1,750,000 in silver and gold. She sank off Anegada in 1738 with the loss of all her cargo. As far as is recorded no salvage was attempted over her hull. This would be a very interesting wreck to consider.

The *SAN IGNACIO* (19)
This cargo *nao* belonged to the Company of Caracas, one of the privately owned corporations authorized to do business with the Indies in the 1700s. She had aboard several hundred tons of Venezuelan products including gold and crude diamonds when she went down against

the Anegada reefs in 1742. The hull lies southeast of the island, probably not very deep.

The "GREAT SPANISH GALLEON" (31)

Robert Marx' *Shipwrecks of the Virgin Islands,* published by the Caribbean Research Institute, College of the Virgin Islands, under Dr. E. L. Towle, includes information about 134 shipwrecks compiled from many sources. In this treatise several references are made to "a great Spanish galleon laden with treasure" lost against Anegada Island in the late 1600s. Some or all of the gold and silver was said to have been buried on the shore by a few survivors, and never retrieved. The wreck may lie off what was referred to as "Ye Treasure Point" on a 1775 chart.

NUESTRA SEÑORA DE LORENTO Y SAN FRANCISCO XAVIER (32)

This 212-ton galleon, commanded by Juan de Arizón, sank off Anegada Island in 1730 en route from Spain. There was probably some money aboard.

The SPANISH SLOOP (33)

Reportedly carrying some treasure salvaged from *Nuestra Señora de la Soledad* (see the North Carolina Coast section), this Spanish ship was wrecked off Anegada in 1750.

The UNIDENTIFIED SPANISH GALLEON (34)

A large and valuable mercury cargo was lost with this ship, en route from Spain to Mexico, when she was wrecked near Anegada in 1731.

The Venezuela Coast

The CARAVEL (20)

In 1561 a small caravel was reported lost off the Costa Firme (Venezuela).

The FOUR NAOS of CÓRDOBA (21)

General Luis de Córdoba's Tierra Firme armada, arriving in 1605, dropped off several *naos* along the top of Venezuela as it crossed westward to Cartagena. Four of these had been assigned to pick up pearls from Margarita, and tobacco, sugar, gold, and diamonds from the Nueva Asparta district at Cumaná.

They had loaded their cargoes and assembled off Margarita Island when a hurricane struck. All four ships were swamped or capsized and went down with their crews. Fourteen hundred people drowned and a quantity of gold, pearls, and rough diamonds estimated at $150,000 was lost.

The *CAPITANA* and *PATACHE* (22)

Another storm wrecked the *Capitana* and a *patache* of a westward-bound flota from Spain against the steep north shore of Bonaire Island in 1610. These ships sank deep and contained, in the way of recoverable treasure, only ship's funds and personal money and jewels of passengers.

The *NAO* of ECHEVERAI (23)

An unidentified *nao* of the 1632 Tierra Firme armada of General Juan de Echeverri sank "off the Costa Firme" carrying only jewelry of passengers and the ship's money.

The *SANTIAGO* and *SAN MARTIN* (24)

These two *naos* were reported sunk during a storm of 1658 "off the Costa Firme." They may have carried only cargo from Europe, or might have been en route to Cartagena with pearls and other treasure from Cumaná and Margarita Island.

The GULF of PARIA WRECK (25)

A report of many years ago indicated that cannons and Spanish coins had been brought up during channel dredging in the Gulf of Paria west of Trinidad Island. If this is true, there is apparently either a Spanish or English wreck in the area with more of the same.

The *CAPITANA* (26)

Two important cities lay in the Lake Maracaibo basin: Maracaibo at the narrow throat connecting with the Caribbean, the "outside city"; and Gibraltar, far back in the lake and a trading center with the interior, or "inside city." The wealth was at Maracaibo, and in such great quantities that during the hundred years from 1600 to 1700 pirates and enemy fleets attacked it five times for loot.

In 1668 Henry Morgan assembled a force of twelve ships ranging in size from sloops to his frigate *Oxford*. With a small army of 700 buccaneers from Jamaica he stormed and captured Maracaibo then went deep into the lake and razed Gibraltar so thoroughly that it never recovered. Couriers had been sent to Cartagena as soon as the pirate fleet was seen off the lake, and the New Granada viceroy, seriously worried over the incursions that the Caribbean "Brotherhood" was making against Spanish interests, decided to put an end to their nuisance. Three strongly armed war galleons were dispatched to accomplish this.

They arrived after Morgan and his men had completed their withdrawal in shallow-draft boats to their larger ships, which could not enter the 5–15-foot-deep Lake Maracaibo basin and had been left anchored off the entrance. As the Spanish closed to attack, one of the pirate sloops separated from the others, drawing close to the *Capitana.* Grapples flew and tangled in the galleon's rigging, then flames ran up the ship's side. Too late the Spaniards realized that a fire ship had caught them. The *Capitana* blazed. Explosions tore off her decks, and she settled on the 40-foot bottom of the Gulf of Venezuela. The other two galleons were lost soon afterward, one captured and the other grounded and burned.

Morgan learned from tortured prisoners that there was money aboard the *Capitana,* whose charred wreckage was visible below the surface. Good swimmers were collected from the pirate crews and sent down into the hull, recovering a reported 15,000 silver pesos. When the pirate fleet departed Spanish salvage boats went out to the site and their divers went down, bringing up cannons and more silver. There are reports that private groups have visited the site with helmet divers since, but probably some of the *Capitana's* silver remains there on the ballast under several yards of mud. Although this wreck's site would be easy to find there is no reason to believe that it holds more than a small quantity of money. A ship loaded with treasure would hardly be sent to fight pirates.

The SAN FRANCISCO DE PAULA (27)

Silver dining services and a little money were lost with this 74-gun warship when she burned and sank in Caracas harbor in 1784. Some of this was recovered together with the cannons and equipment. What remains would be worth little.

The SAN PEDRO DE ALCÁNTARA (28)**

On February 17, 1815, the largest and strongest naval task force ever assembled for the Indies put out from Cádiz. Under General Pablo Morillo's command were 18 warships, 42 transport vessels and 15,000 soldiers. Sealed orders from the king were opened at sea. The armada's task: suppress the revolution in Venezuela. Early in April the fleet reached Tobago Island. After watering, its ships dispersed along the Venezuelan coast on their missions and eventually, by the 24th, had reassembled at the anchorage southwest of Coche Island between Cumaná and Margarita Island. One of the last to arrive was the warship *San Pedro Alcántara,* 64-gunned *Almiranta* of the force. She had been built at Havana in 1788 and had put in long service in the Caribbean. On this mission she was assigned the combined jobs of storeship, ammunition ship and payship. Until the 23rd, when General Morillo transferred his quarters from the *San Pedro* to the *Ifigenia,* she had also been acting command ship.

On the afternoon of the 24th the attention of the other vessels anchored in the vicinity was focused on the *San Pedro*. An officer aboard one of them, Captain Seville, describes the reason in his *Memorias de un oficial del Ejército Español*:

> At 4 P.M. we noticed much confusion aboard. They seemed to be calling us with speaking trumpets. We heard what sounded like a mutiny and saw many people jumping overboard and swimming to the gunboats [near the *San Pedro*'s bow] . . . We immediately sent over a launch carrying an officer and a picket of armed soldiers to suppress the mutiny. But when we got there Pereira appeared at the poop and told us to go back, that it was not a mutiny but a fire on board.
>
> [The fire got out of control and had spread when, at 6 P.M.] we saw over the warship an immense, indescribable flash like lightning; then a colossal black and red mass rose like a volcano's eruption to the clouds, followed by an unbelievable, awful noise, prolonged. The sea trembled, concentric waves foaming outward. A gigantic globular cloud tore asunder the air, seeming to menace the sky and crush the Earth. Where the warship had been the ocean was hidden by black smoke. When the noises subsided one of our officers said: "Gentlemen, God help those who have died . . . and now let's beg God to save us from that cloud."
>
> "What about that cloud?" asked a captain.
>
> "That cloud that's coming down on us—that cloud of cannons, cannon balls, guns, wood, bodies and a thousand other heavy things."

When the smoke finally cleared there was no sign of the *San Pedro*. Fifty brave men who had remained aboard, fighting the fire until the explosion, were gone. So were 8000 guns, an equal number of pistols and swords and tons of military supplies. And so was the treasury of the entire task force.

The quantity of money on the *San Pedro* has been the object of long and careful investigations by several people. Captain Seville's *Memorias* stated that it consisted of 600,000 pesos in the army funds and another 500,000 pesos of navy money. Other Spanish officers believed it to be only 300,000. Captain Conway, an American from Boston who salvaged part of it, concluded that at least 3,000,000 pesos had been aboard, half in silver, half in gold *onzas*. The Venezuelan historian Arístides Rojas went along with Captain Conway's opinion up to a point, but from there on . . .

"What caused the explosion?" asked Rojas. Officially the start of the fire was blamed on spontaneous combustion in the liquor storeroom where a hogshead of *aguardiente* was thought to have burst into flame. Anyone who has swilled this liquid fire will cheerfully go along with this explanation, but Rojas—and several others familiar with the state of morale in Spain's Navy—reached clear back to the time when the fleet left Cádiz for the reason. The *San Pedro*'s treasure coffers had been looted before she left that port, they believed, either by General Morillo or by a group of the ship's officers. To support his views

Rojas, in 1850, called attention to the result of salvage efforts over the warship's remains.

"It is clearly proven," he wrote to Captain Conway who had asked him for information, "that up to June 1850, no less than 300,000 pesos have been recovered from the *San Pedro*'s hull and the ocean bottom surrounding it . . . all of this in silver, in royal pesos, not even one ounce of gold having been found. This confirms that half of the treasure was stolen in Cádiz and that only the silver portion of it, that is to say 1,500,000 pesos, reached Venezuela."

Why did General Morillo pick the eve of the explosion to transfer his headquarters to another ship? wondered others. Was the explosion set off deliberately—arson to cover the theft? Many believed so. Whether arson or *aguardiente* was the cause, it became increasingly apparent that the *San Pedro* had carried no gold money. A single golden object was raised by native skin divers in 1847—a crucifix, encrusted with jewels, which was sold in New York for $13,000. After 1850 several more expeditions made recoveries: Captain Conway's divers brought up 70,000 pesos; another group salvaged 30,000 in 1855; 40,000 more were recovered during two years' work from 1857; and finally Captain Escandella, despite enormous efforts, could find only 1286 in 1871. As far as is known with certainty in Venezuela, the *San Pedro* has yielded nothing since. These recoveries reach a total of something over 440,000 pesos—all in silver.

It seems likely that the treasure value on the payship lay between Sevilla's figure of 1,100,000 pesos and the Rojas-amended Conway estimate of 1,500,000. Such a large expeditionary force would have taken at least a million. The reasonable assumption that Seville's 1,100,000 had been aboard and that 500,000 have been recovered leaves 600,000 silver pesos still lying in and around the hull of *San Pedro Alcántara*.

In the summer of 1956 a group of Venezuelan businessmen-turned-SCUBA-diving-aficionados became interested in her. Since then they have been visiting the sunken ship regularly, sometimes in a group of eight divers, other times only the hard core of Manuel and Eduardo Santaella and Domingo Manini taking part. Their historical researches discovered that the big ship sank in an upright position and originally was more than half intact. In 1833 the bowsprit was still there, rising high over the bottom. The rudder and some wood were salvaged in 1842. Describing her condition today, Manuel Santaella says:

> "The *San Pedro* lies on a mud bottom, pretty well buried under the mud. We found that she was broken into many parts as the result of the explosion. There is scarcely any visibility on the bottom there, even in the three best summer months. Because of this we've been able to find only the one section that our guide knows.
> "The upper decks must have been destroyed in the explosion because

nothing is left now except the lower deck and bilge planking and the ribs, covered with shellfish, rising majestically over the bottom. From their huge size we can estimate the enormous proportions of the warship. We raised some planks and found they were made of pine. Still anchored in the ribs we saw bronze bolts that held the longitudinal timbers of the ship's side. We tried to loosen some but couldn't since we had no tools. There was an iron ring anchored in the wood, big enough to swim through. We fastened it with a strong cable which we had taken down and afterwards hauled it up on our ship. It was a huge dead-eye used to anchor the cables which braced the masts.

"On later visits we brought tools and were able to cut loose various bronze bolts and spikes and some more wood. There was cedar, oak, mango, and birch, besides pine, in the ship's construction. We found two cannons in the wreckage, made of bronze and having inscriptions which we couldn't read in the darkness. There was also a small anchor. When we have a chance we're going to salvage those cannons."

Another of the group, Rafael Arnal, comments: "Some of the wood we found was mahogany—so rotted that we could break it with our fingers. The wreck is full of fish including the biggest groupers I've ever seen. We're hoping to return and salvage as much as we can one of these days."

The *San Pedro Alcántara* lies five miles due south of the western tip of Coche Island, at a depth of 70 feet. Señor Santaella is hoping to organize a full-scale salvage project on her soon and it might easily be successful. Besides the tons of bronze metal in the unrecovered cannons there is always that silver—about $500,000 worth.

The SAN CARLOS II (29)

In the early 1800s a Spanish schooner, the *San Carlos II*, was wrecked in the Islas Aves, east of Bonaire Island. Some treasure may have been aboard.

RIVER DIAMONDS (30)

Prospectors have long known that gold nuggets, carried downstream by the force of the current, tend to accumulate in the deeper pockets where they fall. Recently prospectors for precious stones have applied the same theory to emeralds and diamonds.

At the easternmost part of Venezuela, near the borders of Brazil and British Guiana, is a wild mountain and jungle area called La Gran Sabana. Millenniums ago it was the site of violent volcanic upheavals, during which the pressure of cooling lava turned carbon into its diamond form. Numerous rivers crossing this region picked up gems and carried them north toward the coast, where natives recovered them for trade with the Spaniards. Some years ago a group of American and British prospectors, led by Victor Norwood, camped at their base in La Gran Sabana where several tributary streams, cutting through diamond-rich peridotite soil, meet to form a 170-foot-deep pool. From the mud bottom of their pool Norwood and his associates, formed into the Vixen Exploration & Development Corporation, brought up treasure: rough diamonds, some as large as six carats. They recovered nearly a thousand carats of precious stones with a value of $50,000.

They used SCUBA gear and a gravel pump which was flown in through the jungle. Mud and gravel sucked up from the bottom through its hose are sprayed against a filter system from which the gems are picked out. The sucking mouth of the tube is guided over the pool's bottom by SCUBA divers working in relays.

CHAPTER 9

Cuba

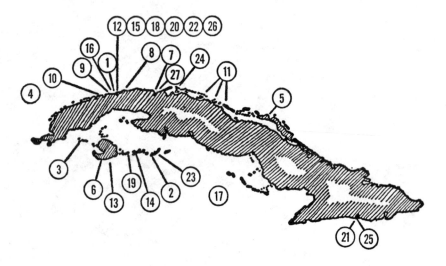

MAP B

WITH THE FORMATION of the New Spain and Terra Firme armadas Cuba usurped the position formerly held by Hispaniola as the sending-off point for returning ships. Columbus had discovered the island in 1492 en route to Haiti and colonies were started here in 1511. The main port, Havana, was founded in 1519 and became the capital thirty years later. It was developed into one of the strongest-fortified cities of the Indies, situated on a peninsula with limited land approaches and the massive fort of Morro Castle guarding the narrow entrance to its harbor. Its beauty and prosperity gained for Havana fame as "The Pearl of the Antilles."

The armadas from Veracruz approached Havana from the northwest, entering the Straits of Florida between the Dry Tortugas and the west Cuba. The Tierra Firme ships, coming up from Cartagena, rounded the long and narrow west peninsula terminating at Cape San Antonio then turned east. Through this gap between Cuba and the Florida Keys at least 13,000 treasure-laden ships passed between 1550 and 1800. The law of averages came into play with the result that many dozens were wrecked along Cuba's western tip.

The *SANTA MARÍA DE LA ISLA* (1)

Coming in to Havana in 1544, the caravel *Santa María de la Isla*, commanded by Captain Vincente Martín, sank a few miles offshore with the loss of all her cargo. About $50,000 in Mexican silver went down with this ship. It lies far beyond SCUBA range, 1500 feet deep.

ROELES' FIVE SHIPS (2)**

Four galleons, *naos* and galleys and one *patache* of the Tierra Firme armada of General Pedro de las Roeles were wrecked on the Jardines while approaching Cuba in 1563. A survivor wrote:

> . . . We sailed on July 8, navigating with good weather until the 15th after which were two days of calm. The pilots thought that the currents were taking them so far from land [Honduras] that they were afraid we would strike against the Caiman Islands. The opposite was true. Because of fog we were unable to take bearings until Sunday, July 18 at 2 or 3 in the morning and while we were taking them we struck against the reefs which are called the Jardines; first the *nao* of Pedro Rebolo then the *Capitana* of Pedro de Corro and the galley of Pedro Menendez and the others. Those from the galley went in a small boat to

an islet which was at less than a league distant from them. From that islet
to the island of Cuba there are eight leagues. . . .

Three-quarters of a league separated the ship of Pedro de Corro which
was the formost and the *patache* which was at the rear, and in between
were the others. They call this place where we were lost "The Jardines
of Canarreo." They are reefs 4, 3, 2 and 1½ fathoms deep and two
leagues from some cays which the ocean does not cover; all the others
are covered with water and become visible when the waves recede. From
the highest of the dry cays to the nearest shore, which is Cuba, there
are 8 or 10 leagues and to the Island of Pines which is unpopulated
there are 12.

As soon as news of this disaster reached Havana the Governor of
Cuba sent people by land and sea to aid the survivors and begin
salvaging the sunken treasure. Much cargo was raised from four of the
wrecks, although "some silver" could not be recovered. The fifth of
the lost ships carried Archbishop Salcedo and his aides, and their
immense personal riches, as well as registry silver and gold. The archbishop drowned with most of his shipmates. This wreck was too deep
to salvage, lying at about 100 feet between two shoals. There is about
$1,000,000 in treasure, including richly jeweled personal ornaments,
under the coral cape which covers her ballast today.

Guided by directions in the reports quoted above, and by closer
details which can certainly be unearthed in Havana, it should be possible
to obtain a close fix on the position of the archbishop's wreck. A
magnetometer survey in the deeper valleys of this area could well
signal the spot where her untouched treasures lie.

The *SANTA CLARA* and *SANTA MARÍA DE BEGOÑA* (3)*

Two more Tierra Firme *naos* with treasure were lost in 1564 on the
reefs under western Cuba. The armada of General Esteban de las Alas
was caught in the tail end of a hurricane as it entered the Yucatán
Channel. The 300-ton *Santa Clara* struck a rock and started to fill. Other
ships closed in when the seas grew calmer and removed her people
and gold and silver cargo, which were transferred to the *San Pelayo*,
before she went under.

The *Santa María de Begoña* broke her bottom and went down quickly.
Thirteen of her crew and passengers were drowned and most of her
treasure lost. Both she and the *Santa Clara* had struck shoals outlying
San Felipe Cay, halfway between the west coast of the Isle of Pines
and Cape Frances on the mainland. They lie at depths of about 75
feet. On the ballast of the *Santa María* should be $200,000 in silver
and gold.

The *SANTA LUCÍA* and TWO OTHER *NAOS* (4)

Three ships were sunk off the Cuban coast by a hurricane in 1565.

Two went down with all their cargo and no survivors. The third, the *Santa Lucía*, was kept afloat long enough for her people and part of the gold and silver to be transferred to other ships. All three vessels lie in deep water.

The *URCA OF PEÑALOSA* (5)

During a storm in 1567 a 300-ton *urca* under the command of Gonzales de Peñalosa capsized and sank just off Cayo Romano, probably settling on a sea bed 75 feet deep. No salvage was attempted for the $50,000 or so in silver aboard. With a better fix through research this *urca* could probably be located.

The SUPPLY SHIP (6)

There was a small quantity of money in the captain's chest of a supply ship from Spain which sank off the Isle of Pines in 1612.

The MATANZAS BAY DISASTER (7)

On July 21, 1628, the New Spain armada of General Juan de Benavides Bazan set sail from Veracruz on a pitifully snafu voyage. The winds died and the becalmed *Capitana* drifted aground just off San Juan de Ulúa, damaging her hull. The thirty tons of silver on her was transferred to other ships, during which operation a frigate, *Larga*, was sunk (see Chapter 10). It was not until August 8 that the repaired *Capitana*, the three other war galleons and the eleven merchant *naos* got under way again. Off Havana two Dutch fleets commanded by Admiral Piet Heyn were waiting, cutting them off from the shelter of Morro Castle's guns. General Benavides made a run past the port and took shelter in Matanzas Bay sixty miles beyond.

The Dutch fleets blockaded the bay while their admiral planned his next move. His twenty-eight ships mounted 600 cannons against the 175 bronze and 48 iron guns on the Spanish galleons. And within Matanzas Bay, General Benavides was in a state of nervous indecision. Underlining worries of his personal safety was the knowledge that he was responsible—with his life at stake—for the armada under his command. This was a situation he had not bargained for two years earlier at court in Madrid. He called a council of his officers during which it was decided to take the treasure ashore and bury it. His ships were ordered to penetrate the bay as close to shore as their drafts would permit, to reduce the distance across which the boats would have to ferry ashore coffers of silver and gold. The four galleons promptly ran aground.

Admiral Heyn launched his attack. His warships could not get in as far as the shallow-drafted Spanish vessels, so he sent in launches packed with soldiers and his lightest-draft frigates. A welter of confusion swept through the Spanish ships, whose officers lacked an effective leader to coordinate the defense. The *Almiranta* and other two galleons, experienced captains taking over, fought long and hard. Then the *Almiranta* was set afire and the Spaniards' determination to resist collapsed. The Dutch boarded stranded and floating ships, meeting scattered resistance from die-hards aboard some, but soon taking control. Only three of the Spanish merchantmen escaped to Havana under cover of nightfall.

It was a major triumph for Admiral Heyn. Four galleons and eight *naos*, with most of their cargo, had fallen to his forces. The Dutch had suffered only a few casualties while 300 Spaniards had been killed in battle or drowned. In the final stage of the assault some of the Spanish crews had jettisoned treasure. Others had broken holes in their grounded ships, allowing water to fill them. For a full week Heyn's salvage crews stripped these wrecks. When they sailed the Dutch took with them a booty of 11,499,176 pesos in gold, silver, and valuable cargo and four of the Spanish *naos* which had been found seaworthy. The loot's total value was $14,000,000.

Left behind on the shallow mud floor of Matanzas Bay were the smoldering hulks of another four *naos* and the four galleons, ransacked of guns and fittings. With the Dutch "Cat of our silver" safely away, Spanish salvage groups arrived to dredge up what could be found. Some jettisoned gold and silver was recovered from the mud and the bottom of charred wrecks, but it was a slim picking considering what had been there two weeks before. General Benavides received a certain distinction for his efforts during the battle. He was sentenced to death for cowardice.

The ballast-covered wooden keels and ribs of the burned and scuttled ships remain in Matanzas Bay, sunk into its shallow bed. Scattered on them and lost in the surrounding mud amid cannon balls and waterlogged stumps of wood whose silt covering has protected it from teredos, is perhaps $50,000 in jettisoned silver and gold. As a submarine archaeologist's hunting ground Matanzas Bay might turn out to be rich; for treasure hunters it would be a poor bet. Admiral Piet Heyn lost much of his booty soon afterward (see The Bahamas).

The *SANTIAGO* (8)

Piet Heyn's forces had a final farewell lick at the Spanish before they departed. Early in 1629 some of his ships pounced on the *nao* *Santiago* from Honduras as she was approaching Havana. They drove all her cargo in water too deep for Indian skin divers to reach. Probably $50,000 in gold and silver that went with her lies just off the Havana shore at something over 75 feet depth.

The *NAO* (9)

On October 5, 1634, an unidentified *nao* carrying Chief Engineer Francisco Roaño y Gamboa and a treasure of about $250,000 was lost off Mariel, probably in deep water.

IBARRA'S SHIPS (10)

The 1638 Tierra Firme armada commanded by General Carlos de Ibarra had reached the entrance to the Straits of Florida when it ran into headwinds off Pan de Cabañas on August 26, just forty miles from Havana. In four days of tacking Ibarra's galleons and *naos* advanced only twenty miles along the coast, and were offshore from Mariel on the thirtieth when "the Dutch pirate, Wooden Leg" attacked with 17 ships. The Spanish fought well and valiantly, refusing to surrender a single vessel to the superior enemy fleet. Several of their ships were holed and sank off Pan de Cabañas as the engaging forces drifted westward with the wind. Nightfall allowed the remaining Tierra Firme ships to slip away. They ran for Veracruz, arriving there safely several days later.

One of the lost ships was a galleon commanded by Sancho de Urdanivia. She grounded on the coast and her silver was removed to safety ashore. Two or three others went down with all their cargo nearby, but in the melee of the battle their locations were not noted. They may lie just offshore in shallow water, or a mile out in 1500-foot depths. About $1,000,000 in gold and silver is in their hulls.

The *GALLEON* and FOUR *NAOS* (11)

The hurricane of September 1641 smashed the ships of Juan de Campos' New Spain armada against reefs from Cuba to Silver Bank (see chapter 14). Five of these, a galleon and four *naos*, were driven south by the quirks of the howling wind against the coast of Cuba, where they sank with the loss of nearly everyone aboard and over $1,000,000 in silver among the cays between Cruz del Padre and Romano. Most of these wrecks lie in shallow water. It would take a lot of luck to find one of silver-laden wrecks along that 100-mile wilderness of reefs and cays.

The *CAPITANA* and *PATACHE* (12)

The *Capitana* of General Pedro de Ursúa and an accompanying *patache* were wrecked in 1647 at the entrance of Havana, under Morro Castle. Most of their cargo and perhaps all the treasure was salvaged by the Spanish. There is a chance that some remained, lost in the wreckage.

The *CAPITANA* and *SAN GABRIEL* (13)
The squadron commanded by General Juan Roca de Castilla was crippled on the night of February 1, 1677, when two of the strongest war galleons were wrecked and sunk south of the Isle of Pines. Everything on them—and 600 lives—were lost in this major disaster for Spain. There might have been treasure aboard the *Capitana* and *San Gabriel*, although no mention is made of this in contemporary reports. There was certainly money and officers' personal jewelry with a value of at least $30,000. These ships probably sank in very deep water.

The *NAO* (14)
An unidentified Spanish ship has been reported to have sunk in 1680 south of Cayo del Rosario, off the east shore of the Isle of Pines, with some treasure.

The GALLEON OF BLANCO (15)
Another of the hulks lying on the ocean floor off Havana is that of a galleon commanded by Captain Francisco Blanco. Coming in to the harbor in 1689 she struck a rock and went down. The people were taken off in time but some of the cargo could not be salvaged. There is no recorded indication whether treasure was being carried on this ship.

The *ALMIRANTA* and THREE *NAOS* (16)
Somewhere against the coast "leeward of Havana"—probably near Mariel—lie the bones of the *Almiranta* and the three *naos* of the 1711 New Spain armada. These ships were driven south onto reefs by a sharp storm which caught them coming in from Veracruz. Nearly all their crews and passengers reached safety ashore before the ships were battered to pieces and most of the treasure which they carried was recovered afterward by native divers. The comment "nearly all the silver was saved" indicates that some could not be located in their tangled wreckage. The positions of these ships could be pinpointed with a little research. Their crusted ballast should hold ten to twenty thousand dollars in ingots and coins.

The *RUBÍ PRIMERO* (17)
Twenty-seven years after she was built this 50-gun war galleon finally ended her career on the ocean bottom near the south coast of Cuba in 1727. Details of her location and depth, and what cargo she carried on her last voyage, were not recorded in general accounts of the loss. Since this class of ship often carried treasure back during the years after 1715 there is a chance that some was aboard *Rubí Primero*.

The *INVENCIBLE* (18)

On the night of June 30, 1741, all but a few unfortunate residents of Havana were indoors while a violent thunderstorm raged outside. A flash of lightning lit the harbor, followed by a sharp peal of thunder. As its echoes faded away another flash, brighter and yellower than lightning, glared over the city. The roar that followed shook buildings and shattered windowpanes for hundreds of yards from the port. Curiosity dominated over caution and comfort as hundreds rushed to the seafront to see what had happened. They stared in awe at the sight of the proud, 70-gun *Invencible*, a roaring inferno of powder fire and smoke, slipping under the harbor. A pall of hissing steam drifted up. When winds carried it off there was no galleon to be seen —only tall masts, crossed with flapping smoldering sails.

Lightning—together with reefs, hurricanes, and enemy action—was a major cause of losses among ships of the Spanish flotas. At least a dozen sank as the result of fire and explosion during thunderstorms. From the first years of its existence the officials of the Bureau of Trade racked their brains trying to find a satisfactory lightning deflector, but had still not succeeded in the early 1800s, long after Ben Franklin's invention of the lightning rod.

One of the greatest of all lightning-induced losses was that of the *Invencible*, *Capitana* of Rodrigo de Torres' armada which was in Havana loading supplies before departing for Spain. The harbor was strewn with pieces of the ship. Salvage for her silver was surprisingly successful despite the explosion's blast, and not more than $15,000 remained when work was discontinued. The remnants of this 1300-ton galleon are lost among the hundreds of other wrecks sunk into the harbor's floor.

The SMALL *URCA* (19)

A twenty-gunned *urca*, captured by pirates in 1745, was reported wrecked against the Jardines soon afterward with a cargo believed to include silver. She should lie within SCUBA range off the south side of the bank of reefs.

The 1768 HAVANA WRECKS (20)

Seventy ships of all sizes and classes were wrecked in Havana harbor and more than 100 men died during a hurricane in 1768. Although there was no treasure armada in port at that time, several of these vessels had money aboard, not all of which could be salvaged.

The "PARLIAMENTARY SHIP" (21)

A full load of VIPs were passengers aboard a Spanish frigate which was carrying them to Fort San Juan de Nicaragua in 1780, when on

October 3 a hurricane sank their transport near the coast of Santiago. Ninety-five people died and a $150,000 cargo of personal valuables and money was lost. The "Parliamentary Ship" went down several miles off Santiago in very deep water, where she will probably never be found.

The 1794 HAVANA WRECKS (22)

A hurricane on August 28, 1794, destroyed 79 ships in Havana, many of which had come in for shelter. The galley *Flor*, with silver and pearls aboard, was swamped in the center of the harbor. Twelve warships were thrown up onto the shore. Sixty-four merchant vessels of all types were swamped or wrecked. For months afterwards salvage boats dotted the harbor's surface, their diving bell dangling below while tons of cargo were recovered. Much more, including money, was lost in the jumble of wreckage strewn across the port's bottom.

The FIVE *NAOS* (23)*

Five other ships were casualties in the August 28, 1794, hurricane. En route to Havana from the south, they were dashed against the Jardines and broken to pieces against its cays and shoals. Most of their crews reached safety in boats or on the shore, but valuable cargoes— including some gold from Cartagena—was never recovered from their wreckage. The ballast mounds of these ships lie in relatively shallow water along the outer ridges of the Jardine bank, bringing to over a dozen the number of treasure wrecks in this area.

The *PALAS* (24)

This 34-gun Spanish frigate, Captain Pedro Saenz commanding, stranded in 2½ fathoms on a reef called Colorados de la Cruz del Padre just north of Cruz del Padre Cay in 1797. A rich cargo from Veracruz was nearly totally destroyed when fire broke out and consumed the 1000-ton ship to the waterline. When the flames had died out the interior of the smoldering hull was a black pool with charcoal and pieces of charred wood floating on the surface. Tides and waves cleaned out the dirty water and presently divers could go under to search. Silver coins began coming up, some still in their waterlogged blackened cases, others in fused lumps, still more singly. Tens of thousands of pesos were salvaged and when work was discontinued there were still thousands remaining, scattered in the crevices of the hull, hidden under tons of junk.

The *Palas'* ballast heap would make a good summer vacation treasure-diving spot. It could be located fairly easily at its depth of only 12 feet and a little scrounging around might turn up pocketfuls of sulfide-blackened Mexican pieces of eight.

The *LIGERA* (25)

In 1822 the 40-gun frigate *Ligera* sank off Santiago during a storm. There was possibly a consignment of treasure on this ship.

The 1846 HAVANA WRECKS (26)

The greatest of all the hurricane disasters in Havana took place in 1846, when over 200 ships were sunk and wrecked in its harbor. Most of their cargoes were salvaged later, but at least $50,000 in money could not be found. The totals of losses in 1846, 1794, 1768, and other years in Havana harbor runs to nearly 400 vessels. At least $200,000 in precious metal, pearls, and gems must lie buried under its silt- and dirt-covered floor.

The *SAN PEDRO* and *ROSARIO* (27)

Two of the *naos* wrecked in the 1733 disaster (see chapter 13) were swept south in the hurricane's blast and piled up against the Matanzas shoals. The *Rosario*'s people and cargo were saved when she grounded in three fathoms; the crew and passengers from the *San Pedro* reached shore safely, but her cargo was lost. Later some was salvaged.

CHAPTER 10

The Gulf of Mexico
and Yucatán

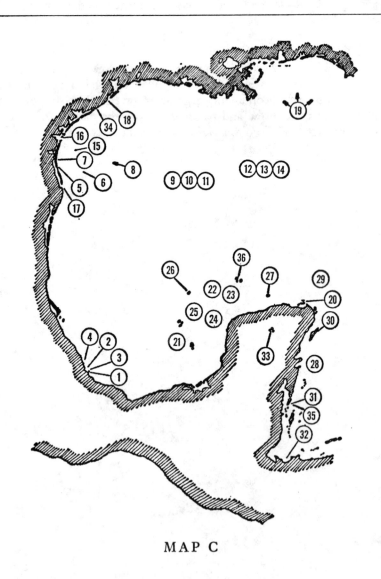

MAP C

*F*OR MORE THAN 300 years after Hernán Cortés and his band of conquistadors landed nearby and pried open the Mexican treasure cornucopia, Veracruz was the funnel though which its bottomless torrent of wealth was pumped out. At first it was gold, silver, and precious stones looted from the Aztec Empire that passed through this Spanish beachhead onto caravels anchored offshore; these yearly shipments averaged $1,000,000 or more during the 1520s. After the Aztec booty was exhausted came a period of less valuable exports while Cortés, de Soto, and Coronado searched for the Seven Cities of Cibola, rumored Mayan gold temples and other chimerical treasure worlds to conquer. Meanwhile the production of native wealth was being developed, and from about 1550 until 1821, when they were driven out, the Spanish extracted steadily increasing tonnages of products from their Viceroyalty of Montezuma. Accumulations of cargo crammed onto the armada at Veracruz reached values of $35,000,000 in some years of the latter two centuries.

During the early period an average New Spain armada of ten to twenty 120–300-ton caravels and galleys could carry only 2000 to 3000 tons. With the development of larger *naos*, galleons and frigates yearly shipments grew until by the middle 1600s the usual flota transported 6000 to 10,000 tons. By volume and weight more than 90 per cent of this was commercial cargo owned by merchants in Seville, Cádiz, Havana, and Mexico. It consisted of products from all territories of the Viceroy of Montezuma. From Mexico itself came sacks of cochineal and indigo, bales of leather and skins, parcels of opals and amethysts, pearls from the Nueces River beds, sugar cane, cotton, wheat, bananas, and other fruits. To this were added shipments from the south carried to Veracruz on coastal transports: sugar, citronella, vanilla, lignum vitae, coconuts and tobacco from Honduras; campeachy wood, rosewood, cocoa, and cassava from Nicaragua; and often pearls from Margarita Island. Another $2,500,000 or so of Far Eastern treasures—ornamental gold and precious stones, silks, porcelains, and spices—carried across the Pacific on the Manila galleons and overland from Acapulco, was sent out every year. Sometimes, even, when conditions off Panama and Colombia were dangerous, Peruvian gold and silver joined the hoard.

Whereas the weight was in this merchandise, more than two-thirds of the value lay in silver and gold. Depending on factors prevailing at the time, anywhere from $5,000,000 to $20,000,000 in precious metal, about 75 per cent of its value in silver, left Veracruz every year on the armada. In weight this varied from 150 to as much as 500 tons. It is no wonder that a single ship of the armada, the *Fulgencia*, could load 7,000,000 pesos—over 200 tons—of silver at Veracruz in 1799.

Considering the key role that it played in the New Spain empire, Veracruz was a disappointment as a city. Small, dirty, notoriously unhealthy, it came to life only for a few months each year while the armada was in port. The harbor was somewhat better, but still surprisingly undeveloped for such an important port. An inadequate breakwater was started sometime in the 1550s but was never extended to the point where it was effective in storms until 1880. On the south side of the port a reef called "Los Hornos" was a constant threat to ships and the fortress island of San Juan de Ulúa to the northeast, while protecting Veracruz from naval attacks, also claimed a large number of Spanish vessels on its rocks.

No less than a hundred caravels, *pataches*, *naos*, galleons, frigates, and warships were wrecked in Veracruz harbor during the reigns of the Viceroys of New Spain. Probably a quarter of these had treasure aboard. The greater part of this precious metal was salvaged from the shallow depths soon after each loss, but there are many coins and ingots that have never been recovered.

The VERACRUZ HARBOR WRECKS (1) *

In 1545 a caravel arriving from Seville broke her bottom on "Los Hornos" and sank immediately. Cargo with a value of 100,000 pesos was lost as well as personal treasures of important officials among the passengers. Not all of this could be raised by skin divers.

A hurricane in the summer of 1590 dashed to pieces fifteen ships of General Antonio Navarro's New Spain armada then loading in port. More than 200 people were drowned. Although the registry silver had not yet been taken aboard these *naos*, a large part of the commercial freight—well packed with contraband silver and gold—was scattered with the armada's wreckage among submarine rocks bordering the harbor. Probably $50,000 in cobs and ingots could not then be salvaged.

Eleven years later, in 1601, another hurricane caught the armada of General Pedro Escobar Melgarejo as it arrived from Spain. Fourteen ships were swamped and wrecked off the Veracruz entrance. A contemporary account stated that 2,000,000 pesos in merchandise and over 1000 crewmen and passengers were lost. Although the cargo consisted of only finished products from Europe there was also money and personal jeweled ornaments on these *naos*.

The *San Bartolomé* (nicknamed "*El Cambio*"), *Capitana* of the 1726

New Spain armada, caught fire and sank soon after dropping anchor in the port. Again some money and private valuables were lost.

A storm smashed the Spanish frigate *Concepción* against the teeth of "Los Hornos" in 1732, and 500 people were drowned. This 30-gun frigate also served as the mercury ship of General Gabriel Pérez de Alderete's armada. There is no mention in fragmentary data examined whether the *Concepción* was entering with barrels of quicksilver or leaving with coffers of silver. In either case a fortune went down with her hull. The loss of so many people indicates that she probably sank in fairly deep water off the port, so there is a good chance that she could not be salvaged. This would be an interesting wreck to look into further.

On February 18, 1736, the 56-gun *La Rosa* sank in Veracruz bay. She was a galleon of the squadron commanded by General Manuel Lopez Pintado. Often these warships were used to transport silver and there might have been a consignment aboard. Most of it would certainly have been salvaged.

Two more galleons were sunk in the harbor during a storm in February 1739. These were the 58-gun *Incendio* and the 62-gun *Lanfranco*. Again, there might have been silver lost.

Five ships were smashed into pieces against the Veracruz harbor reefs during the hurricane of November 30, 1771. No record has been found of the cargo aboard four—the *nao San Nicolás*, the *urcas San Carlos* and *San Juan* and the sloop *Begoña*—nor of what was recovered from them. The fifth vessel, the 74-gun *Castilla II*, sank adjacent to San Juan de Ulúa. Her cargo was nearly entirely salvaged afterward at the cost of a diver's life. Recoveries included 885 bags of grain, 100 bags of cocoa, 5 cases of vanilla, and 5860 slabs of copper.

The *Volador*, an 18-gun barkentine, sank during a storm on August 17, 1810, in nearly the same spot—"against the castle of San Juan de Ulúa." Divers recovered 143,000 silver pesos from the wreckage but were unable to bring up her entire consignment of treasure. Some 30,000 pesos, worth nearly that number of dollars, still remain with her ballast stones under the western shadow of the fort.

The registry treasure had already been loaded on the 14-gun barkentine *Tigre III* when her captain sensed the approach of bad weather. He returned the silver ashore. His judgment proved sound, for the hurricane of 1811 was on its way. Two days later the *Tigre III* existed only as a splintered mass on the bottom of Veracruz harbor. Some personal valuables and an unknown quantity of money concealed in the general cargo were lost.

The unsalvaged precious metal from these 42 ships—and probably others as well—has accumulated over the centuries in Veracruz harbor.

In all, there must be a value of at least $250,000 scattered among its shallow rocks and sand.

The Veracruz Coast

THE SPANISH *NAO* (2)

A 200-ton merchantman whose name has not been recorded capsized and sank during a sudden storm in 1555 soon after passing San Juan de Ulúa on a course to Havana. Aboard was a consignment of registry silver estimated at 350,000 pesos. The disaster came so quickly that the entire cargo was lost and every person aboard drowned. There probably was no attempt at salvage.

This ship's remains, with about ten tons of silver ingots and cobs, lie approximately five miles north of Veracruz. The depth could be anywhere from 150 to 3000 feet, depending on whether she crossed the edge of the continental shelf, which falls off sharply here, before sinking.

The *LARGA* (3)*

The Spanish frigate *Larga*, carrying about 400,000 pesos in registry silver, sank just after leaving Veracruz in 1628. Nearly 100 feet of water overhead prevented salvors from recovering more than a part of her treasure and cannons. Some money remains on the ballast a short distance to the northeast of San Juan de Ulúa. Its value could run over $100,000.

The *CAPITANA* (4)

A registry shipment of about 2,000,000 pesos went down with the *Capitana* of General Miguel de Chazarreta's New Spain armada of 1631 soon after she set sail from Veracruz. The remains of this galleon lie ten or twenty miles up the coast, probably over 1000 feet deep.

The Gulf and Padre Island

On their passage from Veracruz to Havana the New Spain armadas used to advantage the Gulf Stream current, following its flow north along the Mexican coast then eastward across the Gulf at about the 25th parallel. Right at their turning point, running in a curve a few miles off the lower Texas shore, is a narrow, 110-mile-long strip of beach and sand dunes called Padre Island. As it passes Padre the Gulf Stream becomes eccentric, sending westward an offshot of its main current which flows in a wide, blue marine river toward the center of the long island at a place called "The Devil's Elbow." Toward this spot seems to drift a large part of the flotsam in the Mexican

Gulf. Cedar and mahogany logs, coconuts, bits of ships' wreckage and even Florida oranges are carried there by current and the summer east winds. More valuable objects also accumulate on the shifting sand of Padre's beaches and dunes. Coins of every imaginable type have been picked up there, causing at least two of the dunes to be named "Money Hill."

The beach off Padre Island slips lazily into the Gulf with a gentle slope that reaches a depth of only 90 feet two miles from shore and does not drop off to 150 feet for another three miles. The sea bed here is hard clay, and on it, partly buried, are the rotting hulls and ballast mounds of untold numbers of lost ships. This is the graveyard of the Gulf. Amid the ghosts of rumored pirate wrecks are the metallic remains of several Spanish galleons definitely known to have sunk in this area. Others listed only as "Lost in the Mexican Gulf" probably came to rest on this same clay floor. The waters off Padre Island are a first-rate treasure-hunting site.

The MYSTERY WRECK (5)

There have been reports of everything from Spanish bronze cannons to Jean Lafitte's brass spikes buried under the Padre Island dunes. And time and again comes the persistent story of an old wooden ship interred in its sand. It has many variations: the ship was one of Lafitte's pirate fleet, laden with gold; it was a Spanish galleon lost in 1811, the Spanish frigate *Santa Rosa* wrecked in 1816, a "Spanish treasure ship" which grounded in 1818. What seems to be a fact is that the bones of an old sailing ship are hidden in Padre Island above the water mark, where they were pushed up during convulsions of the sand caused by hurricane winds and waves. This ship was probably a Spanish galleon: an amateur archaeologist who saw its wood recognized it as cedar from which galleons were constructed. He found several brass bolts in the protruding ribs and noticed that their heads had unusual shapes of stars and half-moons. Sketches which he made of these bolt heads found their way to Rye, New York, where Bob Nesmith, avid collector of pirate souvenirs, filed them in his Foul Anchor Archives.

As to treasure? Thousands of Mexican pieces of eight have been found in the same general area. Some of these could have been washed from the "mystery wreck's" hull while it was still submerged centuries ago. There may be more on its buried ballast today, although this is unlikely.

The *CAPITANA* (6)*

A few days out of Veracruz the 1552 New Spain armada was attacked by pirates. Carrying out his duty, the general ordered his

Capitana to close with the enemy and occupy his attention in a
running rear-guard action while the rest of the caravels and *naos*
scurried to safety. For nearly half a day the men on the galleon
battled against odds, and they were still fighting when their ship,
badly holed at the water line, carried them down under the waters
of the Gulf. Three hundred of them were killed or drowned and
a large part of the registry treasure was lost. The *Capitana* carried
probably thirty tons of silver and gold, worth well over $1,000,000.
From recorded descriptions of the battle it seems likely that it took
place not far from Padre Island, and that this treasure ship sank
somewhere off its shore.

The SAN ESTEBAN, SANTA MARÍA DE YSASI, and ESPÍRITU SANTO (7)**

A rich New Spain armada of twenty ships carrying two thousand
people ran into a hurricane soon after leaving Veracruz in 1553. The
vessels in the rim of the winds were battered, but sailed to safety.
Three reached Seville half a year later. Another limped back to Veracruz bringing the bad news that three[1] heavily laden treasure ships
had been wrecked against the bars of Isla Blanca, now known as Padre
Island. Only three hundred of the passengers and crew made it safely
to shore. The sailors salvaged what they could from the nearer wrecks
and gathered the casks and boxes of food that washed ashore from
the broken ships.

For six days the survivors rested on the beach but saw no one.
Then, on the seventh day, they awoke to find themselves surrounded
by painted savages. These were the fiercest cannibals north of Mexico,
the Karankawas (or Kronks). The savages approached the survivors in
peace with bows unstrung. They even brought fish and showed them
how to make fire with sticks. The Spaniards received the fish with
delight and soon were roasting food over the fires.

Suddenly the savages let fly a salvo of arrows, and with screams
of terror the Spaniards fled for the protection of the dunes. They
hoped to get to Panuco, the northernmost settlement (now Tampico),
but with no food and water, the blazing sun and the cannibals always
pursuing, they were gradually slaughtered. Dona Juana Ponce de Léon,
whose beauty had caused men to search for the Fountain of Youth,
was among those who died and lay unburied on the sands of White
Island.

Fray Marcos de Mena with five arrows in his flesh, one through
his right eye, was left behind by a handful of the strongest who

---

[1] The number of wrecked ships may have been higher, although research carried
out by both the author and Mr. Goin E. Haskins agree at three. The names of the
wrecks were kindly made available to the author by Mr. Haskins, who located
them a few years ago during his researches in the Seville Archives.

covered him with sand but left his head exposed so that he might breathe. When dawn came, he awoke and stumbled forward. He passed his former companions, all dead, and for four days of torture kept going until he met with two men by a stream. They carried him to their village where he was nursed back to life. He finally reached Panuco and then Mexico where he told the story of the flight of the three hundred.

One other survivor, Francisco Vasquez, escaped and stayed on the beach, hidden among the dunes, living on water dug through the sand and on food salvaged from the wrecks. Summer passed, fall came, and Vasquez built a hut, snared fish, and waited. At the coming of cold weather, the Kronks had gone north to the shelter of woodland regions.

It was early in April 1554 that salvage ships dropped anchor off Isla Blanca. Vasquez was saved. The Viceroy of New Spain, Don Luis de Velasco I, had sent out ships equipped with crude diving bells, the best native divers from Yucatán, and with knowledge of the location from captains who escaped the storm and from the testimony of Fray Marcos. The site was located, and the rescued Vasquez became one of the most important men in the salvage fleet.

Divers found that the silver and gold bars had sunk to the clay bottom, and some were recovered. Casks and unbroken chests were taken from waterlogged hulls. In all, probably more than half of the treasure was salvaged. It is told that Vasquez was awarded a share of the salvage equal to that paid to the salvage commander, Villafana. As rumors of rich recoveries went around a flood of claims was launched "to recover what each had sent out" and many people in Mexico became rich off the property of others who had died aboard the ships.[2]

For years coins along Padre Island have attracted treasure hunters. One was a Gary, Indiana, businessman named Paul Znika who became interested after finding coins south of the Causeway in 1964. With several associates he formed the company Platoro, Inc., and recruited a salvage team. Meanwhile a second venture headed by ex-U.D.T. diver Jeff T. Burke and Gois E. (Jack) Haskins, Jr., was at work. "The salvage reports made by the Spanish," notes Haskins, "state that the ships were located near Rio de las Palmas in 260½ degrees of latitude which would put them right near Port Mansfield. In the spring of 1968 Jeff Burke of Rio Hondo and I were able to locate all three of these ships using an ASQ-3 magnetometer. There can be no doubt from the evidence that we gathered that these ships are all sixteenth-century vessels and most probably the ones which carried

[2] Sources: *Historia de la Fundación y discurso de la provincia de Santiago de México* and *Padre Island*, by Writer's Round Table, The Naylor Co., 1950.

the unfortunate three hundred lost on Padre." In an affidavit published
later Haskins stated that during a magnetometer search they had made
contacts at points three and a half and eight miles north of Port Isabel,
about two and three miles south of Bob Hall Pier, and at several sites
north of Port Mansfield. Joining the Platoro group, Burke participated
in the salvage of a wreck about 4000 feet offshore, two miles north
of Port Mansfield Channel. In 1967 their boat anchored over the site
and scoured the 25-foot-deep bottom with a "blaster" which directed
the prop wash downward. Recoveries described in later testimony included big swivel guns and lombards, a crossbow, a valuable gold
crucifix, a gold bar and several gold coins, clumps of silver coins and
silver disks with Spanish mint marks.

The treasure find, and ensuing publicity, created a furor. Burke
left the Platoro group, and he and Haskins took the position that the
salvage was made possible by their magnetometer search results. Znika
countered stating that Platoro made its own magnetometer search.
Texas Land Commissioner Jerry Sadler asked the attorney general to
take action against Platoro and an injunction was issued on January
15, 1968. Texas House Bill ⅀734 was introduced to protect wreck
sites, but was still pending in March 1969 when the Znika group,
registered in Texas as Galleons, Ltd., obtained authorization to operate.
The wide-open question of jurisdiction rights over sunken treasure in
tidelands was raised following the disclosure that Sadler had made a
contract—apparently unsigned—with the Znika group under whose
terms 50 per cent of recoveries would be turned over to his department
for the use of the Permanent Free School Fund of the state. Meanwhile State Archaeologist Curtis Tunnell entered the picture in strong
support of Bill ⅀734, designated the Antiquities Code of Texas, to
protect historically valuable wrecks from exploitation.

Legal sparring over the rights to the wreck sites, and the treasure
and artifacts already recovered, continued. A press release in August
1969 quoted Commissioner Sadler as saying that "pilfering, plundering
and pillaging" pirates have looted the treasures of the lost ships. "But
we will catch them," he vowed. "We will find these pirates and
bring them and their booty into a court of justice if we have to trail
them around the world."

In January 1970 the attorney for Platoro, which was suing the state
of Texas for the treasure, was quoted as saying that the state was
interested in reaching a settlement. He was promptly contradicted by
Assistant Attorney General Nola White, who was quoted as stating:
"We want the whole hog. We think we're entitled to it. We think
these people [Platoro] violated the law."

In Texas, as in other areas where finds of sunken treasure are first
given publicity, the birth pangs that usually lead to protective legisla-

tion were just beginning. From all indications to date the various claimants are set for a long battle for the custody of the salvaged artifacts, and the salvage rights. Are they worth it? Comments Jack Haskins: "I believe this area will yield riches parallel to Kip Wagner's 1715 find."

The *SANTA MARÍA DE GUADALUPE* (8)

This *nao* sank in the Gulf of Mexico in 1564 after several days of hard pumping by all hands to keep up with leaks. Before she floundered all her registry silver was transferred to other ships of her New Spain armada. What remains is only contraband. The *Santa María* may lie off Padre Island.

The *CAPITANA* (9)

Somewhere on the floor of the Gulf are the remains of General Diego de Rivera's *Capitana* of the 1591 New Spain armada. This galleon disappeared at night with all hands lost—as well as a large part of that year's registry treasure. About $2,000,000 in precious metal went down with her.

The *SAN CRUCIFIJO DE BURGOS* (10)

She was an exceptionally large galleon for her time, carrying 600 tons of lading. The *San Crucifijo*, under Captain Pedro de Medatiaga, became separated from the other ships of the 1595 New Spain armada bound from Veracruz to Havana and sank somewhere in the Gulf. Her consignment of that year's registry shipment was well over two million dollars in gold and silver.

The *SAN JORGE* (11)

During a storm in 1625 the *San Jorge*, a *patache*, floundered in the Gulf within sight of her accompanying vessels whose crews were too busy trying to keep their own craft afloat to come to her assistance. Descriptions of this disaster conclude with: "Treasure and people lost."

The *CONSTANTE* (also called *SAN ANTONIO*) (12)

This 60-gun warship had a short life. Built at Havana in 1727 she sailed across to Veracruz, loaded, and eight days out on her return voyage sank with all hands in the Gulf, probably close to its center. About 20 tons of silver were lost with her.

The *CAZADOR* (13)

Commander Gabriel Campos sailed this 64-gun warship out of Veracruz in 1784, set a course for Havana, and disappeared without a trace. The *Cazador* carried treasure.

The *ARDILLA* (14)

The entire crew and cargo of the *Ardilla*, a Spanish barkentine of 18 guns, was lost in 1808 when she sank in the Gulf of Mexico. There was probably silver aboard.

The S.S. *PAISANO* (15)

She was an American passenger-freighter on the Gulf run. One afternoon in 1873 the *Paisano* steamed out from Brazos Santiago at the lower end of Padre Island, bound for Galveston 400 miles to the north. She never reached her destination.

As weeks passed without any sign of the ship people began to speculate about her fate. It was revealed that on this last voyage the *Paisano* had carried 200,000 silver dollars in canvas bags. There was talk that some of her crew might have pirated this treasure and scuttled the ship with everyone but themselves. More likely is that the *Paisano* encountered one of those unpredictable maritime accidents that happen to ships and sank suddenly off Padre Island.

MAXIMILIAN'S TREASURE (16)

In her book *Blaze of Gold*, Dee Woods tells an intriguing version of what might have happened to part of Maximilian's $2,500,000 treasure.

She reports that in 1940, during the Humble Oil Company's drilling operations in the shallow Laguna Madre between Padre Island and the coast, some seventy Maximilian dollars were pumped up from the sea bed by a dredge. This find dovetailed with a story that following the death of Emperor Maximilian a group of loyal Austrians arranged for his treasure to be smuggled out of Mexico for shipment to Empress Carlota in Europe. It was said to have been packed in flour barrels piled up on wagons, to conceal its true nature from fifty soldiers who escorted fourteen loyal Austrians and Mexicans aware of the secret. Rolling along toward Galveston, this procession encountered ex-Confederate soldiers and hid from Comanches on the warpath. It was the fifty convoying soldiers who did the dirty work, however, murdering all but two of the faithful fourteen after discovering the treasure. The soldiers buried the loot and dead bodies. A little later the rampaging Comanches caught up with them and they received their just desserts.

The two Austrian survivors later rounded up help, returned to the site of the buried treasure, found it and transported it secretly to Corpus Christi Bay. Here it was rumored loaded into a boat for storage pending the arrival of an ocean-going vessel. And here, presumably, it was sent to the bottom in a storm.

The MATAMORAS WRECKS (17)

There have been published reports that two American steamers, the

Jessie and the *Lea*, sank off the Matamoras coast with silver money aboard.

The GALVESTON WRECKS (18)

Several American steamships were reported to have gone down between Galveston and the Brazon River mouth during the 1875 flood, carrying various amounts of money. They were all probably salvaged.

The AMERICAN GULF COAST WRECKS (19)

At least a dozen "treasure laden vessels" have been reported and rumored sunk along the American Gulf coast.

The Yucatán Gulf Coast

LA NICOLASA (20)

The Mujeres Island fishermen know the ancient curse protecting this wreck, warning that its looted cargo of "Mayan gold, money and temple stones are guarded by the bells of La Asunción Church which were placed aboard by women and can never be disturbed." The curse held for 432 years, until the fall of 1959. Then a scientific-minded diving exorcist came along and shattered its spell.

Returning from Port Royal, Ed Link stopped off at Mujeres Island where he was told of a brass cannon, recently salvaged by a local resident. He went to see it, accompanied by an expedition member, Elgin Ciampi. "There were two other guns there as well," recalls Ciampi. "Iron lombards. Ed Link studied them, then told the owner, 'You have an important find here. These guns are of the Cortés period.' The next day we anchored the *Sea Diver* over the wreck where those guns came from. It's about eighteen feet deep, thickly overgrown with coral. There are several pockets of ballast stones visible, but no mound. Right away I saw two breech-loading swivel guns.[3] We all chipped away the coral with the boat's pneumatic hammers and raised them, then I went over the reef with a metal detector. There was metal everywhere under the coral!"

The wreck was historically important, Link knew, after a glance at the cannons. Unable to remain longer, he contacted Pablo Bush Romero, head of the Mexican Water Sports Explorers Club, setting into motion a major archaeological treasure hunt. The Caribbean Archaeological and Exploring Society of Dallas joined in. Research by marine historian Jesus Bracamontes of the National Institute of Archaeology indicated that the wreck is *La Nicolasa*—one of four caravels from which Francisco de Montejo raided Yucatán in 1527. The others re-

[3] Photo in *The Skin Diver*, by Elgin Ciampi, Ronald Press, 1960.

turned to Havana with Mayan treasure aboard. *La Nicolasa* was lost
with her loot.

The *SANTIAGO* (21)

This galleon was built in Havana in 1647 and proceeded to Veracruz
to load cargo for Spain. On her maiden return voyage she was caught
in violent winds and driven southeast toward the Yucatán coast. Four
days out from San Juan de Ulúa, the *Santiago* was dashed against
an unnamed reef in Campeche Bay where she quickly broke up. Most
of the crew managed to reach safety on a nearby sand cay where
276 of them survived to be picked up by a passing ship. Skin divers
later recovered some of the cannon and silver from the registry shipment that had been aboard, but not all. About $25,000 in cobs and
ingots are still there for anyone who can find the right reef.

The *SAN GRONI* (22)

Bound from Veracruz to Cartagena, this merchant *nao* was swamped
while approaching the Yucatán coast. There was probably money aboard.
Her cargo and crew were all lost.

The THREE MERCURY TRANSPORTS (23)

General Francisco Cornejo's New Spain armada of 1718 ran into
bad weather as it entered the Gulf from Cádiz. Just after crossing
the top of Yucatán the three largest galleons, the *Capitana San Juan
Bautista*, *Almiranta* and *Santo Cristo de Maracaibo* piled into a submarine shoal and broke up. They were the mercury transports of
the flota, carrying hundreds of tons of this precious metal in small
barrels. Much of it was lost on the rocks and coral together with
money and valuable belongings of the officers and important passengers
aboard.

The *CAMBI* (24)

The *Capitana* of the 1725 New Spain armada, commanded by General Antonio Serrana, caught fire in Campeche Bay as she was approaching Veracruz. Despite frantic efforts by the crew to put out
the blaze, it spread down into the powder magazine. The *Cambi* exploded and sank like a plummet. Four hundred people were killed.
One of the few survivors was General Serrana, who found himself
in the water and unhurt after the blast. Nearby was a floating table.
The general climbed upon it and stayed there until wind and current
carried him to safety ashore. Probably $25,000 in money and personal
effects went down with the blazing *Capitana*.

The *SANTA MARTA* (25)

This 38-gun frigate sank in Campeche Bay in 1780. Captain Andrés Valderrama and his crew were rescued by other ships but the guns and cargo, which included some money, could not be taken off in time.

The *DRAGÓN II* (nicknamed *"GALGO"*) (26)

For nearly forty years the 60-gun *Dragón*, built in Havana in 1744, put in good service for the Spanish kings escorting treasure *naos* and patrolling the Caribbean with other warships of the coast guard squadron. Then in May 1783 she reached the end of her career on the rocks of Bajo Nuevo while sailing from Havana to Veracruz under the command of Captain Miguel de Sousa. Waves soon tore apart the old timbers of this venerable *"Galgo"* and her remains disappeared into the reef. Sixty of her crew were drowned and several chests of money were believed lost.

The *IFIGENIA* (27)

Just north of Yucatán is a group of submerged rocks whose uppermost points just break the water's surface. It is named Iphigenia after the 38-gun Spanish frigate *Ifigenia* which broke up there. Shortly after leaving Veracruz in 1818 the ship's captain, Alejo Gutiérrez de Rubalcava, was informed that rotten planks along the bilge had given way and water was flooding into the hold. The *Ifigenia* would not remain afloat until they reached Havana. Captain de Rubalcava ordered her run aground on the nearest shallow bajo. The shock snapped off the foremast, but placed the half-submerged hull safely on a ledge. Here the frigate was stripped as quickly as possible: most of the guns, some cargo and a registry consignment of 2,000,000 pesos were transferred onto other ships. The remainder of the cargo could not be removed before rising waves destroyed the hull. Probably $15,000 in contraband silver is still scattered around her ballast.

The Yucatán East Coast

The *ALMIRANTA* (28)

Coming up the Yucatán coast from San Fernando de Omoa, bound for Veracruz with a valuable cargo of Honduras products, the *Almiranta* of the 1579 coastal flota was struck by lightning during a storm. She caught fire and sank within two hours. Her charred timbers lie somewhere off the coast, well over 1000 feet deep. Some gold and silver, and probably pearls, went down with this ship.

The TWO 1581 TIERRA FIRME *NAOS* (29)

General Antonio Manrique's 1581 Tierra Firme armada lost two of its *naos* off the northeast tip of Yucatán. These vessels, sailing from Nombre de Dios to Havana, were sunk in a storm with all their cargo. A large shipment of "gold and treasure"—worth at least $1,500,000— went down with them to a depth of half a mile.

LA CANDELARIA (30)

This 250-ton *nao*, commanded by Juan de Paternina, was wrecked off Cozumel Island in 1623 on a voyage from Santo Domingo to Veracruz. Money and personal valuables were lost.

The OXFORD (31)

In 1957 skin divers reported having discovered a wreck off Ambergris Cay near Belize which they hoped was a frigate of Henry Morgan's carrying six chests of treasure. A 13-foot anchor, cannon balls and pottery were reported sighted, as well as several old chests partly buried in the sand. As yet, no report of recovered treasure has been heard.

The frigate in question was the 22-gun *Oxford*, given by the British Admiralty to Sir Thomas Modyford, Governor of Jamaica, who in turn presented her to Morgan in 1668, together with a commission as a privateer. The *Oxford* and her buccaneer crew plied their trade in Caribbean waters, then in 1669, during a drunken brawl on board, she caught fire and blew up. Before the explosion her captain had been run through with a sword by one of the pirates, Collyer, who survived to become Morgan's second in command. There was probably looted treasure on the *Oxford* when she went down.

H.M.S. LEVIATHAN (32)

A British squadron attacked the Spanish port of San Fernando de Omoa in 1799 and took booty estimated at a million pesos from this Honduras trading center. A part of this loot was put aboard H.M.S. *Leviathan*. As she was leaving the port a violent storm swept in and caused her to capsize and sink a short distance off the coast. Some $200,000 in precious metal and gems was on board.

Her wreck was recently found by Dennis Standefer's enterprising Fathom Expeditions. "We located the *Leviathan* with a magnetometer and worked it from May 1968 to January 1969," Standefer advises. "We used 6- and 8-inch gold dredges, which are more powerful than air lifts for bringing everything to the surface. There were eight to ten divers in the operation. We used our 50-foot boat, *Fathom 1*. The *Leviathan* is 54 feet deep, covered with silt, about four miles south of the Omoa fort. In almost zero visibility, with many sharks, we went over the whole site twice. The ballast is stone and there is a lot left of the copper-sheathed hull. Besides pottery, spikes, cannon balls up to 24-pounders, and rum bottles, we raised an unusual pair of dice made from shot. We also salvaged almost a thousand coins, the latest dated 1778. There were pieces of 8-, 4-, 2-, and 1-reales. Two 1-reales dated 1749 from Potosí were in mint condition. One brought $500. We found two badly corroded iron cannons far from the wreck, which we are sure was salvaged earlier. They missed some; we didn't."

CHICHÉN ITZÁ (33)

At the turn of the century a twenty-five-year-old American attached to our consulate at Mérida, Edward Thompson, became interested in Mayan history and began studying the subject. One of the books through which he dug his way was the *Relaciónes de las Cosas de Yucatán*, written in 1566 by the Spanish Archbishop of Yucatán, Diego de Landa; and one of the passages which fascinated Thompson the most was the archbishop's description of a sacred well—or cenote—into which the Mayan priests threw gold and virgins in yearly sacrifices to their god of water, Chac. Weeks of research and careful checking with maps made Thompson conclude that the referred-to well was at the ruins of Chichén Itzá, deep in central Yucatán, nearly fifty miles away.

At his first opportunity the young American hired a guide and visited the site. The cenote was nearly round, about 175 feet across, and dropped 70 feet down into the water below. Thompson's soundings showed this to be 60 to 70 feet deep, with a mud bottom. On one side were the remains of a stone platform which he reasoned must have been the place from which sacrifices were made. Thompson returned to the United States and visited the archaeological directors of the Peabody Museum at Harvard University. His enthusiasm—and hard facts which he produced—convinced them that his project to dive for the Mayan artifacts at the well's bottom was sound. With a grant from Peabody, Thompson took diving lessons and bought diving dresses and other equipment which he would need. In 1904 he was back in Yucatán, where he rounded up guides, bearers, a Greek diver named Nicholas and supplies.

The procession penetrated the Yucatán jungles and eventually made camp at Chichén Itzá. Huts were thrown up, lookouts posted to give warning of hostile Indians, and a derrick was mounted on the edge of the stone platform. Thompson began his exploration of the cenote's bottom with a heavy bucket, lowered and raised from the winch. After a first fruitless day when only mud came up, several small ovate balls appeared in the bucket. Thompson studied them, wondering if they could be copal incense balls of which he had read, used in Mayan ceremonies. He heated one over a fire and the sweet perfume confirmed his hopes. There *had* been sacrifices made here. This knowledge sustained his hopes over the many days which followed during which mud was the only recovery. Then one day bones and skulls, together with bits of cloth, appeared. The small size of the human remains indicated young people, obviously the sacrificed girls. Thompson knew then that he was on the right track. But where were the golden artifacts, he wondered. Could the archbishop's account have been wrong?

On a hunch he made a raft and lowered himself to the water's surface. Probing with a long pole, he found that under the mud floor was a stone foundation, pock-marked with holes and crevices into which the bucket would not fit. If heavy gold was thrown in, he reasoned, it might have sunk through the mud into these crevices. The only way to find out was to dive. A larger raft was constructed and lowered from the winch, air pumps and other equipment mounted on it, and Thompson and Nicholas began their work.

From the first, diving was dangerous, exciting, and successful. After several close shaves with collapsing mud walls the divers—groping blindly in black mud with their hands—began raising treasure. A 10-inch gold disk was followed by hundreds of other objects: rings, earrings, pendants; pieces of shields, and masks; bells, knives and candlesticks; figurines of snakes, frogs, monkeys; a beautiful tiara of entwined snakes. All were of beaten gold. Every day for nearly a month Thompson and Nicholas struggled through the cenote's mud bottom, often completely buried, their hands feeling the sides and bottoms of crevices for loose objects. When they gave up their task the overhead warehouse was crammed with yellow artifacts. Shares were taken by Thompson, Nicholas and the guides, and the bulk of the gleaming treasure was shipped back to Cambridge, Massachusetts, where it is to this day on display in the Peabody Museum—probably the richest archaeological find ever made. The gold's intrinsic value is impressive; but the real worth—as archaeological treasure—is beyond estimate. The Peabody Museum has published a full account, beautifully illustrated, of the Mayan treasure in Volumes XI and XII of its *Memories: Chichén-Itzá and Its Cenote of Sacrifice* by Alfred M. Tozzer, and *Metals from the Cenote of Sacrifice* by Samuel L. Lothrop.

A venture in 1960–61 by Norman Scott's Explorations Unlimited, in association with the National Geographic Society, enjoyed modest success. Scott had been recommended by Pablo Bush Romero, of C.E.D.A.M. Benefiting from this experience, Scott and Bush planned a combined operation by their organizations, supported by Mexico's National Institute of Anthropology and History. An attempt would be made to drain the cenote, permitting stratified excavation, and failing this, to clarify the water. Substantial financial and material assistance would be needed. In a tour de force, Scott interested some twenty-five American companies, who contributed equipment, technology, and skilled personnel. The late F. K. Johnson, Jr., provided working capital.

On September 19, 1967, twenty-one vehicles carrying equipment and personnel arrived at Chichén Itzá. While the base camp was built on top a large raft was assembled and lowered by crane onto the water. It carried engines, air lift compressors and filter screens, drainage pumps, and other gear. An "umbilical cord" of electric wires, and four long hoses, connected the raft with the upper world. As pumps worked in conjunction, below and above, the draining began. In six days the water level had dropped 7 feet. A mud bank which Thompson's bucket dredging had formed over sixty years earlier was uncovered. Dry excavations on this site produced artifacts that Thompson had missed: skulls, gold and copper bells, beads, and ceramic fragments. The rate of drainage now slowed considerably, indicating seepage into the cenote through underwater feeding streams. Despite extension of the pumps' drainage point to a distant sump the inflow continued. Moreover the water was turning acid, threatening corrosion to the pumping equipment. The first plan was abandoned.

Filtration and chlorination was stepped up to clarify the water. After a near tragic incident caused by chlorine gas escaping as it was injected from the raft, this gas was fed into the water from an automatic chlorinator at the top of the cenote. In four days the water had cleared slightly, but the rate was unsatisfactory. Scott and the technicians decided to halt all work below while an unprecedented attempt was made to clear all the particles floating in the water in one massive effort. Experts from Purex and other companies, working around the clock, introduced six hundred pounds of flocculants to coagulate suspended particles and precipitate them on the bottom. Simultaneously 200 pounds of chlorine were injected daily, with muriatic acid to neutralize alkaline deposits. Three days later the incredible had happened: The cenote sparkled clear and blue.

With 30-foot visibility conditions dredging was carefully resumed. From below the sacrificial platform, the mud yielded remnants of the ancient temple. There were carved stone pillars, sculptured serpents' heads, and the temple's foundation stones. Traces of blue dye corroborated accounts that the victims were stripped and painted this color before their slaughter. Hundreds of recovered bones and skulls were identified as mostly those of children and old men—destroying the legend that only virgins had been sacrificed here. As weeks of air-lift dredging continued a vast assortment of rare Mayan artifacts was collected. These included jade beads and carvings, many lumps of copal incense, bone figurines, flint points probably used in the human sacrifices, dolls of carved wood, wax, and even rubber, fragments of Tepehua ceramic ware dating to A.D. 1000 when Mayan culture was at its peak, copper, silver, and gold rings, and hammered gold masks. Beaten gold soles from sandals that showed no signs of wear were also found. These had probably been on the feet of the victims. In all, more than 1100 artifacts were catalogued by April 1968.

The joint Mexican-American archaeological venture had been an immense success. Pablo Bush Romero's C.E.D.A.M. group and Norman Scott's Expeditions Unlimited team—assisted so strongly by American industry—had added new pages to our knowledge of the Mayan civilization. Many of the recovered artifacts, including beaten gold artifacts, jewelry, and terra-cotta fragments, are now on display in the C.E.D.A.M. Underwater Archaeological Museum in Mexico City.

The full account of the expedition's achievements is told in *Well of Sacrifice* by Donald Ediger, assistant to the president of Expeditions Unlimited, Inc. Norman Scott's enterprising company had its roots back in the 1950s when Scott, a diving enthusiast, explored wrecks in the Caribbean. He salvaged enough artifacts to catch the treasure bug and moreover to become interested in archaeology. He was recommended to lead the National Geographic Society expedition at Chichén Itzá. With financial backing from F. K. Johnson, Jr., he incorporated Expeditions Unlimited in 1963. The following year his group worked the *"Genovés"* and in 1966 salvaged five wrecks in the Bahamas under contract to the government.

In 1968 Mr. Robert C. Tyo took over the position of chairman of the board. Norman Scott remained president, and other offices were held by Captain Sam Scott, F. Mike Freeman, Dori A. Dowd, and Donald Ediger. The Florida-based company further expanded in 1968–69 and is in the process of going public with a stock issue. Says Donald Ediger: "We have become one of the largest treasure-hunting organizations in the world."

On Expedition Unlimited's agenda are salvage plans for the *Andrea Doria*, at Lake Guatavitá, on the wreck of the World War I German raider *See Adler* off Tahiti, and at several other promising sites. In addition, the company is interested in the recovery of artifacts from what may be a 1715 wreck off Florida with Miami's Sea Labs Exploration, Inc., who were awarded license number E-19 by the Florida board. The deep diving field is also of interest to Norman Scott, who expects to enter it with Hannes Keller, the Swiss mathematician who astounded the world with his 1000-foot-deep "bounce" dive in 1962.

The ST. BERNARD BAY NEW SPAIN GALLEONS (34)

During a hurricane in October 1766, between three and five galleons en route from Veracruz to Havana were wrecked in a bay at the mouth of the San Bernard River. It is recorded that one or more carried consignments of silver. Although no information has turned up about salvage, it seems certain that the Spanish must have made strong efforts to recover their lost treasure.

H.M.S. *YEALDHAM* (35)

Dennis Standefer's Fathom Expeditions, tracking the *Oxford*, did find a 27-foot-deep wreck on Ambergris Cay north of San Pedro. In 1957 and 1965–68 his team salvaged a 13-foot anchor, cannon balls, rum bottles, Chinese porcelain and fine pottery, silver spoons, forks and melted candlesticks, and eight brass candlesticks. The guns had been salvaged earlier. Iron ballast was found 100 yards out on the reef. UCLA experts dated the artifacts at about 1800, and Standefer thinks the wreck is the *Yealdham*, lost that year.

The ALACRÁN REEF WRECKS (36)

The C.E.D.A.M. divers of Mexico have located dozens of the estimated 250 wrecks, spanning nearly three centuries, lost on this dangerous coral atoll sixty-five miles north of the Yucatán coast near Mérida (see Submarine Archaeology–II). Quite likely some of the lost ships described earlier in this chapter lie along its thirty-seven miles of shoals. Although not on the route of the silver-laden New Spain armadas sailing from Veracruz, the Alacrán Arrecife has collected treasure aboard the vessels wrecked there. A side-wheeler, dated at about 1850, has yielded both gold and silver coins, and old money is being brought up with artifacts from other sites whose age goes back to 1511, when the first caravels broke up on the coral. Mercury, from New Spain vessels en route from Spain to Veracruz, has also been salvaged.

CHAPTER 11

Central America and the Western Caribbean

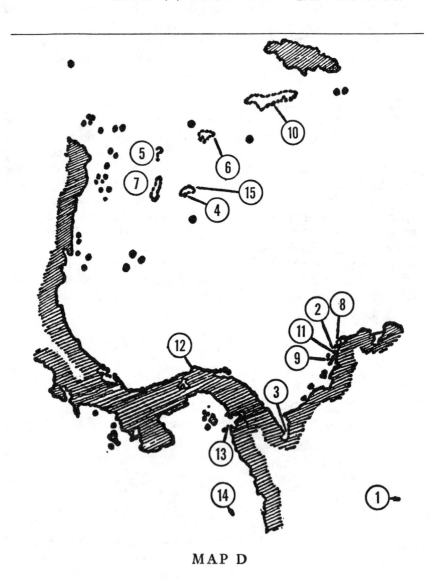

MAP D

The LAKE GUATAVITÁ TREASURE (1)**

> *"Shadow," said he,*
> *"Where can it be—*
> *This land of Eldorado?"*
>
> *"Over the Mountains*
> *Of the Moon,*
> *Down the Valley of the Shadow,*
> *Ride, boldly ride,"*
> *The shade replied,—*
> *"If you seek for Eldorado!"*
>
> E. A. Poe

And boldly ride they did, by the thousands, in their quest for Eldorado. Columbus had heard the faintest whispers of its existence. Balboa and his explorers, striking inland from Nombre de Dios in 1513, met Indians who seemed amused at their excitement over gold and emeralds. "Why, in the mountains to the south," they laughed, "is a place where these things you seek are common as dirt . . . in the land of the Golden One."

Thus was born the legend of El Dorado. It spread through the ranks of the conquistadors, growing with repetition into a glittering Emerald City of Oz secreted high in the vastness of the Andes, over whose treasures presided a high priest—the Golden One. Expedition after expedition of Spaniards and German mercenaries penetrated south into Colombia and even Venezuela, questioning, looting, torturing and killing, in their search for this treasure land. In 1529 four hundred mounted and foot adventurers led by the Germans Dalfinger and Seyler reached the Magdalena River. The next year Federmann, with another band, probed deep into New Granada. A force led by Antonio Sedeño went up the Orinoco River, followed in 1534 by Dortal and his party. All of them were unsuccessful and more than half of the men who set out were killed in constant skirmishes with the aroused Indians.

Then, in 1537, a group commanded by Gonzalo Jiménez de Quesada reached the dwelling place of the Muysca tribes, in the Chocó region of Colombia, and after a furious fight conquered the natives. They captured a huge loot: gold valued at 246,976 *pesos de oro*—nearly $1,000,000—and 1815 emeralds, some of great size and value. They had discovered the source of Colombia's enormous gold and emerald wealth, but the treasure city of El Dorado still eluded them—for it existed only in legend.

Yet there was a Golden One and a treasure trove of incalculable riches. High in Colombia, inhabiting the uplands between the Cauca and Magdalena rivers, were the Indians of the Chibcha tribes. Their chief and head priest was El Dorado. In this region

> . . . the numerous lakes of the plateau were holy places. Each of them was regarded as the seat of a special divinity, to which gold and emeralds were offered by throwing them into the water . . . Among the many lakes of the tableland of Bogota known as such places of offering, the lake Guatavitá became eminently famous as the spot where the myth of *el dorado*, or the gilded man, originated . . . A legend was current among them [the Chibcha tribes] that the wife of one of their earlier chiefs had thrown herself into the water in order to avoid a punishment, and that she survived there as the goddess of the lake. Besides the Indians of the tribe of Guatavitá, pilgrims came from the communes around to cast their offerings of gold and emeralds into the water. At every new choice of a *uzaque* of Guatavitá, an imposing ceremony was observed. The male population marched out in a long procession to the *paramo*. In front walked wailing men, nude, their bodies painted with red ochre, the sign of deep mourning among the Muysca. Groups followed, of men richly decorated with gold and emeralds, their heads adorned with feathers, braves clothed in jaguars' skins. The greater number of them went uttering joyful shouts, others blew on horns, pipes, and conchs. *Xeques*, or priests, were in the company, too, in long black robes adorned with white crosses, and tall black caps. The rear of the procession was composed of the nobles of the tribes and the chief priests, bearing the newly elected chieftain, or *uzaque*, upon a barrow hung with discs of gold. His naked body was anointed with resinous gums, and covered all over with gold-dust. This was the gilded man, *el hombre dorado*, whose fame had reached to the seacoast. Arrived at the shore, the gilded man and his companions stepped on a balsa [raft] and proceeded upon it to the middle of the lake. There the chief plunged into the water and washed off his metallic coverings, while the assembled company, with shouts and the sounds of instruments, threw in the gold and jewels they had brought with them.[1]

This incredible offering of treasure to the lake took place two or three times yearly over a period of several hundred years, ending about 1497 when the Guatavitás were wiped out by another tribe. During each festival hundreds of gold and emerald objects—necklaces, nose rings, earrings, beaten gold breastplates and helmets, statues and figurines of monkeys, crocodiles, snakes and turtles—were tossed from the shore and the raft[2] into Lake Guatavitá. What the total value of the accumulated tons of gold and bushels of emeralds would be worth

[1] *The Gilded Man, El Dorado,* by Adolph F. Bandelier.
[2] The November 24, 1969, issue of *Life* magazine carries a photograph of a 6½-by-4½-inch gold model of such a raft, found in a cave near Bogotá.

today can only be guessed at. One estimate, by a Monsieur de la Kier of the Royal Institute of Paris, was $5,000,000,000. This seems impossibly high, for even at the present rate of production Colombia could not supply such a value in treasure in five centuries, and surely the entire supply of gold and emeralds mined by the Chibchas would not have been sacrificed to the goddess of the lake. There is an immense treasure there, however, and some of it has already been recovered.

In 1540 Hernán Pérez de Quesada, brother of the conquistador Jiménez, reached Lake Guatavitá after bird-dogging the *El Dorado* legend and learned from natives that this was the sacred place of the rites. He tried unsuccessfully to drain the lake but was able to recover only 4000 pesos' worth of gold lying just off its shores. Forty years later, in 1580, a Spanish merchant Antonio de Sepulveda obtained a concession from King Philip II. His efforts to wrest treasure from the lake changed its landscape. Guatavitá lies in a high mountain bowl, surrounded by earth and stone bluffs. De Sepulveda decided to cut a channel through the mountain walls and let the water flow out. An immense army of native slaves toiled for years digging and carting away earth until a gap, over a hundred feet deep, had been cut through one face. The water flowed out in a torrent, and Lake Guatavitá's surface dropped fifteen feet. From its muddy banks about $200,000 in sacrificed objects were collected, including a magnificent emerald which sold in Spain for the equivalent of $80,000. But the efforts gained no profit for de Sepulveda, for King Philip took most of the gains.

A new attempt was begun in the 1820s by José Ignacio Paris and Captain Charles Cochrane, but was soon abandoned. Then in 1893 a Colombian syndicate spent $8000 trying to drill a drain hole under de Sepulveda's gap, without success. An English company, Contractors, Ltd., appeared in the early 1900s and in 1913 Lake Guatavitá was once again partly drained. Sticky mud, which soon hardened to cement consistency, was uncovered. On its surface were found golden snakes, bowls and a warrior's helmet, and several emeralds. Apparently at some time earlier in the century a collection of these salvaged artifacts was on display in Bogotá, but recent investigations have failed to locate any sign of them.

After World War II an American diver-engineer, Leslie "Buzz" Cooper of Haverford, Pennsylvania, undertook a study of the historical background and reported having carried out a survey to determine technical and financial requirements. "We are convinced the gold is there," he said. His venture never got started. Recently Norman Scott's Expeditions Unlimited, Inc., entered the picture and is giving the lake priority on its list of new ventures. Donald Ediger of the company states, "on our recent reconnaissance dives in the lake divers encountered visibility of 2 to 4 feet down to the 30-foot level, and virtually nothing beyond that point. Depth was measured at 65 feet. The altitude of the area is more than 10,000 feet." The company projects a serious archaeological undertaking with the authority of the Colombian government during which the mud from the bottom will be airlifted into filter screens.

In spite of historical evidence pointing to the existence of the treasures, a shadow of doubt has appeared during the past ten years. Lake Guatavitá has been surveyed by several competent teams of SCUBA divers. Although their searches have been only cursory, they did not produce one single artifact as far as has been reported to the author. There is another cold fact to be considered: Just where are those fabulous gold artifacts and emeralds salvaged by Pérez de Quesada, de Sepulveda, and Contractors, Ltd.? A prerequisite to a salvage expedition would be the confirmation that these treasures do really exist somewhere. Because of the weight of supporting historical data Lake Guatavitá will remain a two-star site in this issue of the *Guide*.

Despite poor visibility, the lake floor should be relatively easy to excavate. A search grid would not be disturbed by wave motion, and metal detectors would work perfectly in fresh water.

The *CAPITANA* (2)

Except for the caravels lost off Hispaniola in 1501 and 1502, the oldest treasure wrecks in the Americas lie off the shore of Colombia. In 1504, three years after Panama was discovered by Rodrigo de Bastidas, another flotilla of three ships, commanded by Cristóbal Gracía, visited Nombre de Dios then cruised eastward along the Colombia coast putting in at likely bays where the crew traded with natives for gold and emeralds or simply took what they could seize. Approaching Punta de Canoas, just north of the site of the future Cartagena, the *Capitana* of these caravels struck a reef and sank. An accompanying vessel was able to rescue nearly all the crew. When the ship went down most of the fruits of a successful voyage were lost. Gold nuggets and dust as well as several rough emeralds were aboard. No attempt could be then made to recover this treasure.

The FOUR CARAVELS OF LA COSA (3)

Another flotilla visiting the same region later that year was deep in the Gulf of Urabá when a tropical storm struck. The four caravels of Juan de la Cosa were unable to escape from the narrow waterway and were dashed against the rocky coast. Of their combined crews of 200, only 25 remained alive. Once ashore, it was all they could do to return to Nombre de Dios from that then-unknown land, let alone try to salvage the Panama gold lost with the wrecks, worth some $50,000. As far as is known, it was never recovered.

During the next thirty years other flotillas arrived and the Colombia coast was explored. Indications of great mineral wealth inland were discovered. Cartagena was founded in 1533, the first colony in South America and the gateway to the treasures of the interior. It grew rapidly into a city, usurping the position of Nombre de Dios as the major port of the southwest Caribbean. As the western anchorage of the Tierra Firme armadas and the headquarters of the New Granada Viceroyalty, Cartagena had become, by 1650, probably the most important city in all the Indies.

It had a permanent population of 2000 prosperous Spaniards and was defended by massive forts. The principal one was at the mouth of the harbor, heavily garrisoned and mounting 33 cannons. A second fort, Santa Cruz, with fewer guns and men, was set off by a moat. Two others, Manzanillo and San Luis de Barajas, were gunless façades. Cartagena itself was protected by heavy walls on which 84 bronze cannon were mounted. Once every year during the two months that the armada was in port the city grew in size to 10,000 as merchants from all over the continent gathered here to trade with agents from Europe, buying the armada's cargo and replacing it with South American exports. In some years the business turnover approached $100,000,000 during these trade fairs.

When they had been concluded, the ships in port were laden with the products of Colombia and Venezuela: hides and skins, mahogany and rosewood, sugar, tobacco, cocoa, sisal and abaca fibers, and yams, coconuts, bananas and other fruits; balsam of Tolú and tamarind. In addition there was the treasure: gold in huge quantities, silver, emeralds, diamonds, amethysts, pearls and semiprecious stones. Peru treasure came in on ships from Nombre de Dios or Portobelo. The registering of declared cargo was closed, the king's "royal fifth" stowed aboard the *Capitana* and *Almiranta,* and the Tierra Firme armada set sail for Havana.

The preferred route was north through the deep channel between Serranilla shoals and the *Placer de la Vivora,* or Pedro Bank. But not every armada was favored by weather during this passage and the coral banks off Honduras bear the names of several unfortunate ships lost on them as well as such picturesque designations as Quita Sueño—Stop Dreaming—Shoals.

The *PEDRO SERRANO* (4)

The *Pedro Serrano* was one of these hard-luck *naos.* It would have been little consolation to her survivors to know that not only an island,

Serrana, but the hundred-mile-distant Serranilla Bank as well, was named after their ship. They were too busy trying to keep from dying of thirst on the treeless, waterless cay where they were marooned. Captain Jorge Osorio and many of his shipmates were dead, drowned in the storm waves which had driven their vessel onto reefs south of Serrana.

When the seas calmed they were able to recover much of the treasure and enough wood for rafts from the wreckage before other storms demolished it completely. They found the secret of keeping alive in the giant tortoises that inhabited Serrana with them. They ate the flesh of these animals and, during rainless periods, they drank the blood. The *Pedro Serrano*'s survivors were finally picked up by another ship, as well as the treasure which they had salvaged from the captain's cabin. The rest of the silver, stored in the ship's hold, had been too deep under water to reach and is most likely still there.

WEBBER'S SEVENTEENTH-CENTURY WRECK (15)

Burt D. Webber, Jr., made several visits to San Pedro Bank, Serranilla, and Serrana during the 1960s with Art McKee and others. After founding his own Marine Archaeological Research Corporation in 1963 he located a badly scattered seventeenth-century wreck on the northeast side of Serrana Bank. Working here during 1964, Webber's group raised two iron swivel guns and an iron cannon. From the same site Caymanians salvaged two large bronze cannons acquired by McKee.

The SAN FELIPE (5)

In 1572 the *nao San Felipe* of General Esteban de las Alas' Tierra Firme armada caught fire and sank in a waterway which the old records named the "Golfo de las Yeguas," or Gulf of the Mares. Careful research through charts of this period could locate no such geographic name on the route between Cartagena and Havana, so it must be assumed that the writer was using a local term.

Wherever she was lost, the *San Felipe* would make a valuable salvage prize, for in her hold and cabin was about $500,000 in gold and jewels. None of this was saved before the ship went down, taking 120 of her crew with her.

The FOUR NAOS OF CÓRDOBA (6)*

Serranilla Bank, lying just west of the route of the Havana-bound fleets from Cartagena, claimed a heavy toll during the 260 years that the armadas passed by. The worst of these disasters took place in January 1605, when four ships of the Tierra Firme armada commanded by General Luis Hernández de Córdoba were torn to bits on its shallow teeth during a violent storm. They were the 600-ton galleon *San Roque* under Captain Ruy Lopez, the 750-ton galleon *San Domingo* with Captain Diego Ramirez, *Nuestra Señora de Begoña*, a 500-ton *nao* under Captain Pedro Munoz, and Martín de Ormachea's 450-ton *nao San Ambrosio*. Thirteen hundred lives, and by two accounts, "two millions" and "many millions in treasure," were lost with these ships.

A large-scale salvage attempt was able to recover a part of this gold, silver, and precious stones. Very probably half could not be found and raised, and it is a good bet that on the coral-hidden ballast of these four, and other Tierra Firme ships lost on Serranilla Bank in 1677 and later, a million dollars' worth of treasure has accumulated. The ridge of reefs running in a northeast line on the extreme east of the bank, called *La Valira* by the Spanish, was signaled out as dangerous. A magnetometer search along the outer border here would likely make contact with some of the coral-hidden wreckage of these destroyed galleons and *naos*.

The *SANTIAGO* (7)

In 1660 one of the merchantmen in General Juan de Echeverri's Tierra Firme armada was separated from the others in a storm and wrecked "on a deserted isle near Honduras." She was the *Santiago*, carrying gold and silver worth half a million dollars. For 52 days the survivors worked, building a schooner from driftwood, nails, and canvas salvaged from their ship. The product was found seaworthy and the 276 men squeezed in and sailed across to the mainland.

There is no recorded information that the *Santiago* was salvaged although it is probable that an attempt was made. The deserted island referred to could be any of the numerous cays off the eastern Honduras coast.

The FOUR SHIPS OF BRENES (8)

The 1683 Tierra Firme armada of the Marquis de Brenes was caught in a hurricane shortly after setting sail from Cartagena, as its ships were heading northward about twenty miles off the Barranquilla shore. Within an hour after the winds struck the galleon *Santa Teresa* was swamped at sea, with only four survivors. A *noa* and a *patache* lasted only a little longer, their crews fighting to get back to Cartagena, then went down far off the coast. All three lie in depths of over 500 feet.

The galleon *Santiago* was wrecked near the shore and most of her people reached safety. Her treasure cargo was never salvaged, as far as is recorded.

The *SAN JOSÉ* (9)***

Possibly the most valuable treasure shipment ever to leave Cartagena was aboard the seventeen galleons and *naos* of the combined Tierra Firme and Honduras armadas which set sail for Havana on June 8, 1708. The War of the Spanish Succession, which had been going on for seven years, had already cost Spain most of the silver on the 1702 New Spain armada destroyed at Vigo, and crossings were few and treasure-packed. At least $35,000,000 in Colombian gold and Peru silver was distributed among the vessels of this fleet.

Scarcely had the armada left port when lookouts spotted English sails bearing down with the north breeze. Warning shots were fired and signals run up ordering all ships to run back to Cartagena. The English warships were faster and it was soon apparent that the armada would be intercepted. Assuming command, the admiral ordered the four armed ships of the flota to confront the enemy in a rear-guard line of battle. The 64-gunned *Capitana San José*, the 64-gunned *Almiranta*, a third galleon called the *Gobierno* mounting 44 guns, and the *urca* of Francisco Nieto dropped back to shield the merchantmen.

At sundown the English squadron closed with the rear guard. Commodore Wager had his pennant on the 70-gunned *Expedition*. With him were the 60-gun *Kingston*, the *Portland* with 50 guns and the *Vulture*, a fire ship. The battle raged into the night. After an hour and a half the *San José* blew up in the darkness. Only eleven of her 600 men were picked up by the *Expedition*'s boats. Commodore Wager then engaged the *Gobierno*, which fought gallantly for four hours before surrendering. Nieto's *urca* ran aground on the tip of Barú peninsula and was set afire by her crew, who escaped ashore. Alone of the four Spaniards to survive, the *Almiranta* limped under the shelter of Cartagena's guns, bringing back her treasure of 6,000,000 pesos.

A pilot offered to take the *Kingston* into Cartagena to capture the *Almiranta* but her Captain Bridges decided not to make the attempt. For this decision he and the captain of the *Portland* were later court-martialed and found guilty of bad judgment, while exonorated of cowardice. Aboard the prize *Gobierno* the English found thirteen chests of pieces of eight, fourteen bars of silver and some personal riches. The ship's main cargo was cocoa. Most of the *urca*'s lading was destroyed by fire, but the Spanish later recovered her treasure.

The loss of the *San José* stunned the Bureau of Trade's and king's agents at Cartagena. Stacked in chests and piled in barrels aboard this big galleon was the largest consignment of treasure ever to have left the port on a single ship. Some said that it was 7,000,000 pesos; others put the value at 12,000,000; still other estimates ran as high as 30,000,-000 in gold!

By an eyewitness report she went down "off Barú Island," between the Isla del Tesoro (Treasure Island) and Barú peninsula. The sea floor in this area is jagged and irregular, varying greatly in depth, but nearly all within SCUBA range. A closer fix on the *San José's* position has already been determined through researches in England and can probably be further narrowed down with patient and well-guided digging in Cartagena and Seville. The wreckage of this *Capitana* can be counted on for at least $5,000,000—mostly in gold. It is one of the most attractive treasure salvage prospects in the world.

The "*GENOVÉS*" (10)

Nuestra Señora del Carmen gained her nickname from her origin in Genoa, Italy, where this 54-gun frigate was launched early in 1730 and sold to Spain. In August of the same year she was loaded with "3,000,000 pesos" in silver and gold at Cartagena and Portobelo. Then her captain, Francisco Guiral, headed her north for Havana. Among the passengers returning to Spain was Field Marshal Manuel de Alderete, former president of Panama and governor of New Granada.

As the "*Genovés*" neared the channel between Serranilla and Pedro shoals a hurricane swept up. The frigate was driven east of her course and, on September 4 (August 23 by the English calendar), broke her bottom against the Banner Reef section of San Pedro Bank. Powerful waves swept in across the stern, killing Field Marshal Alderete and many others as the housing and upper deck were demolished.

When wind and waves subsided the strong, new ship was still visible, planted on the reef, her housing and upper deck demolished. Survivors who had reached the nearby cay returned and scrambled over beams and spars that were awash, stripping and salvaging what they could. A part of the gold from the captain's cabin, estimated at 100,000 pesos, was floated ashore. An English frigate, H.M.S. *Experiment*, arrived on the scene. Her crew assisted in the salvage of treasure and took off the shipwrecked men. Other ships appeared with native divers and more salvage was carried out, recovering the anchors, half the cannons and another 1,000,000 or so pesos. Storms further demolished the battered ship. By the end of the year she had been reduced to bilge and ballast, over which sand was piling up. With diminishing returns, efforts to recover the remaining treasure fell off.

The one-and-a-half-mile-long Banner Reef has five indentations of blue water along its edge. One of these "blue holes," a half mile from the southwest end, holds the remains of a wreck which could be "*La Genovés*." Cayman Islanders were reported to have recovered $6000 in gold here in the early 1900s. Art McKee visited the site in 1955, 1963, and again in 1963 when he raised five cannons in an expedition aboard the *Rosalie* with Burt Webber. These were sold to

Jamaica's Reef Club Hotel. Hundreds of divers have dredged probably 500 tons of sand and coral from the blue hole. Their recoveries include seventeen cannons, countless cannon balls, canister shot, timbers, planks and bits of rigging, spikes, rusty swords, flintlock muskets and pistols, bones, knives, combs, and religious medals. Some of these are on view at the Smithsonian, Art McKee's Sunken Treasure Fortress, and the C.E.D.A.M. Museum. Possibly the most significant find was made by Expeditions Unlimited, Inc., in 1964. It is a religious medal depicting a saint canonized in 1671 (dating the wreck after that time).

For all this work, the reported treasure salvage has been only a few gold ornaments and a few hundred corroded silver coins. Whether the wreck is "*La Genovés*" or not, the blue hole has been so thoroughly plundered that further efforts would seem unjustified.

The BRILLANTE (11)

This 74-gun warship caught fire and sank at Cartagena in 1790. There was money and probably some treasure on the ship, most of which would have been salvaged.

Panama Coast Wrecks

The SEVEN NAOS OF AGUAYO (12)

A storm in 1563 wrecked the *Capitana* and six other ships of Antonio de Aguayo's Tierra Firme armada which were loading Peru treasure at Nombre de Dios. Five of the *Capitana*'s crew were killed and $500,000 in silver and gold was lost. Nearly all of this was recovered afterward.

The Almiranta (13)**

Just before arriving at Panama after coming up the Peru and Ecuador coasts, the 600-ton *Almiranta* of the South Seas armada of 1631 capsized and sank in the Bay of Garachine off Cape Escarpado. There was about $2,000,000 in treasure from Callao aboard.

The depth where she lies could vary from 70 to 150 feet and further research might produce a closer fix on her position. If the site of this galleon could be determined more exactly, she would be a first-rate salvage target since no attempt has ever been made to locate her wreckage.

The SAN ROSARIO'S SILVER (14)

Captain Bartholomew Sharp and a band of buccaneers crossed the Isthmus of Panama in 1680 and after a bloody battle seized the Spanish ship *La Santísima Trinidad* (The Blessed Trinity) and four smaller ships in the Armadilla at Panama. Taking three of the ships and 51,000 pieces of eight, they sailed south along the coast, capturing prizes and raiding towns.

One of the most valuable ships captured was the *San Rosario*. Besides 6500 Spanish dollars, they found 700 pigs of plate, "which we supposed to be tin." They took only one bar to cast into bullets, leaving the rest in the Spanish ship. "Worthless chunks of tin!" they growled in disgust. One-third of the bar was later sold in England for 75 pounds sterling. "Thus we parted with the richest booty we got in the whole voyage, through our own ignorance and laziness." They had left behind them 42,000 pounds of silver bars. Somewhere off the Panama or Ecuador coast the treasure lies on the ocean floor, probably lost forever.

The buccaneers did not, however, overlook "a great book of sea charts and maps, containing an accurate and exact description of all the ports, soundings, rivers, capes, and coasts of the *South Sea*, and all the navigation usually performed by the Spaniards in that ocean. This book for its novelty and curiosity was presented unto His Majesty, King Charles II, on the return of some of the buccaneers to England, and was translated into English by His Majesty's order."[8] There are four known copies in English of this atlas, one of which is in the Henry E. Huntington Library, in San Marino, California. On some of the charts added information tells of treasure wrecks, and valuable information such as "Jama shoals. . . . on this shoal Domingo Antonio was cast away in the ship *Gonzalo Beltran* going too near the shore in the year 1612. In this ship was aboundance of plate and other treasure."

The atlases were transcribed into English by William Hack but were never so printed and most of the original charts in Spanish are preserved in the libraries of the Admiralty and the British Museum.

[8] The *Buccaneers of America*, London, 1684.

CHAPTER 12

South America—West Coast

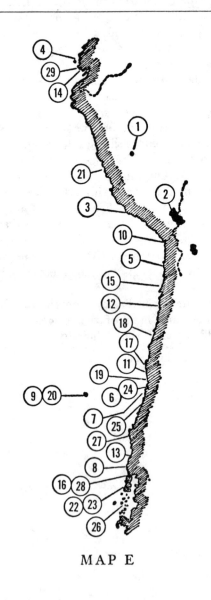

MAP E

THE INCA EMPIRE stretched for 3000 miles along the western border of South America, encompassing all the land from Colombia to the middle of Chile. It was an absolute dictatorship where seven million Indians lived and worked for only one purpose—to serve their living symbol of God, the Inca King. These subjects were superbly organized: every man and woman had his assigned function in the unit. Some were farmers, some running couriers, others were priests; two hundred thousand were soldiers. And every year, during the four warmest months, a great horde of men and their women went up into the ranges of the Andes east of Lake Titicaca to extract mineral treasure from the sacred *huacas* in the Carabaya. Here they panned rivers and collected high-grade ore for smelting in mountaintop furnaces, and the resulting pure metal was carried down on the backs of llamas to the capital city, Cuzco. The yearly influx has been estimated at as much as 7,000,000 ounces of gold and an even greater weight in silver—over $250,000,000 in bullion value. So plentiful was the precious metal that it had no monetary significance; instead it was used to symbolize the beauty of the sun and moon in religious and ornamental decorations. A sampling of these are described by Victor W. von Hagen in his study, *Realm of the Incas:*

> The most fabulous edifice in Cuzco was *Curi-Cancha*, the "Golden Enclosure" . . . most stupefying, ancient and sacred of Incan shrines . . . The Temple of the Sun enjoined the Golden Enclosure . . . This complex structure had six major buildings [surrounding] the *Inti Pampa*—the Field of the Sun. A fountain in its vast center was encased in gold on which was etched the image of the Sun, the same which fell to the conquistador who gambled it away one night. The outside of the building . . . was covered with gold plate so massive that each sheet weighed 4–10 pounds.
>
> To the utter amazement of the first Europeans to see it, *Curi-Cancha* had in its fields a golden mimicry of plants: maize, actual size, was "planted" and its stalks cunningly wrought in gold, and Cieza tells of the "garden where the clods [of earth] were pieces of fine gold, and it was artificially sown with cornfields which were of gold, as well as the stems of the leaves and the cobs.
>
> "Besides all this they had more than twenty llamas of gold with their young, and the shepherds life-size, with their slings and crooks to watch them . . . all made of gold."

This was the Inca Empire which Francisco Pizarro was determined to conquer when he landed on the Peruvian coast in 1532 with 177 mounted and foot soldiers and one small cannon. Only a man of his

insane courage and treachery and luck could have succeeded. His
meeting with King Atahuallpa at the hot baths of Cajamarca, the
subsequent attack on the unarmed Inca, his imprisonment and ransom
are common history, as is the story of the ransom payment of gold
sufficient in quantity to fill a 25 by 15 foot room to the height of
seven feet, and twice as much silver. In today's values this quantity of
precious metal has been calculated by Dr. S. K. Lothrop and Mr. von
Hagen at $19,851,642, being "1,326,539 pesos of gold and 51,610 silver
marks." This mountain of glittering treasure left the Spanish conquistadors goggle-eyed; to the Inca it signified no more than a fraction
of his wealth.

Pizarro's brutal murder of Atahuallpa was a financial mistake which
he could not have realized. Even in his wildest imagination he did
not anticipate that the gold and silver already delivered was but an
hors d'oeuvre of the vast hoard that was then winding its way over
the Royal Roads from all parts of the empire toward Cajamarca in
response to the Inca's orders. News of Atahuallpa's death caused a
stunned, enraged reaction throughout the land. In their bitterness the
priests and laborers determined to dispose of the transported treasure
where the Spaniards would never find it. Overnight it disappeared into
hiding places deep in jungle caves and under lakes. Tales of these
lost treasures have been frequently told and retold during the centuries
since then, but at best they are unreliable. Nearly every lake has
its legend of gold, carried down from the dim past.

LAKE ORCUS' GOLDEN CHAIN (1)

One of the most often repeated stories concerns an incredible chain
of gold which was known to have encircled the market square of
Cuzco. In length it was reliably described to reach 700 feet; the
links were said to be a foot in diameter. Hundreds of men were
required to lift it. At the time of the Inca's call for gold it was picked
up by a long file of struggling men and marched northwest from
Cuzco toward Cajamarca. Somewhere along the 450-mile track it vanished. Many small lakes have been suggested as its hiding place, including Lake Orcus, into which the chronicler Solorzano, in his accounts, reported that it was thrown. If this is true some tens of
tons of gold, worth as many million dollars, lie under the mud bottom—enough to compensate amply a lucky finder for the costs of
overland transportation of the floating crane needed to haul it back
up!

LAKE TITICACA'S GOLDEN SUN MIRROR (2)

After the Inca's murder Pizarro and his plunderers struck inland,
looting and raping, until in 1533 they occupied the capital city of

Cuzco. Here the conquistadors swept up and tore loose another torrent of gold. As before this was divided among them, after the Spanish king's share had been set aside. Richer than they could imagine themselves, the Spaniards began to gamble for some of the highest stakes the world has ever known. Amid the Cuzco treasures was the golden mirror from the *Inti Pampa* which had been mounted to catch and reflect the first rays of the sun every morning. On its immense surface was etched the sun's image. Considered too large and beautiful to melt down into ingots—the fate of nearly all the other artistic treasure— it was awarded as his share to a noble, Mancho Serra de Leguicamo.

The Spaniards were acquiring another form of loot as well. After their first wholesale rapings of the Virgins of the Sun whom they found in holy temples some of them began settling down with one or more favorites, and even falling in love, as did Pedro de Barca with Princess Toyllor-Tica. She was a chosen woman of the Sun Temple of Cuzco and—as dedicated women will—beguiled him to gamble with de Leguicamo for the fabulous sun mirror. All night long Pedro and Mancho went at it, with the result that by dawn a substantial share of the glittering prize belonged to Pedro. The gamblers parted after agreeing to resume the game the next night. With the soft voice of his princess in his ear, Pedro broke the promise. At the first opportunity, he and his woman, and the mirror, carried by fifty accompanying sun priests, sneaked away toward a hiding place to the south presumably to live happily evermore.

They didn't quite make it. A troop of twelve horsemen was sent by Pizarro to recapture them. After a full week of chasing along false trails while the fugitives staggered along their route, Pizarro's men caught up with them at the shore of Lake Titicaca where the mirror had already been loaded onto two big balsa boats for transport to a sun temple on one of the lake's islands. The priests sacrificed their lives in a rear-guard action while the boats carrying Pedro, his princess, and the mirror were rowed away from shore. Then a volley of harquebus bullets struck them down. The boats overturned and the golden disk, like a giant gleaming manta, plunged to the bottom.

This story is told by de la Vega in his *Historia General de Perú*. If it is to be believed—and considering the other just as incredible factual occurrences in Pizarro's conquest, there seems no reason to doubt it—the many-ton sheet of gold lies today within harquebus shot of Lake Titicaca's shore facing an island where once stood a temple to the sun. The water is deep and cold, and the mirror is certainly buried in mud. Careful historical research followed by a systematic examination of the right area of the lake's bottom with submarine metal detectors—which would function at maximum capability in this fresh water—might produce this priceless treasure.

An offshoot of this incident of so many centuries ago is a proverb which is still heard in Spanish-speaking countries: "Don't gamble with the sun before it has arisen"—meaning "Don't spend what is not yet yours."

CHULI SILVER (3)

The first torrent of treasure captured by Pizarro was carried down to the sea, loaded on caravels and shipped up to Panama for overland transportation to Portobelo and reshipment to Spain. The flood of gold subsided, then resumed as Spanish-directed slave laborers by the millions wrested precious metal from the old fields, and new ones, not only in Peru but in Chile and Ecuador as well. Ports were developed along 4000 miles of coastline: Buenaventura and Tumaco in Colombia; Guayaquil in Ecuador; Chiclayo and Callao in Peru; Arica, Antofagasta, Coquimbo, Valparaíso, Talcahuano, Valdivia, and Osorno down the Chile shores. To each came a trickle, then a heavy stream of gold, silver, copper, and general cargoes of native produce.

To handle this wealth a new flota of ships was built and called the South Seas Armada. Its caravels and *pataches,* and later its *naos* and galleons cruised up the coast on schedules, loading cargo from port after port on their way north to discharge their wealth at Panama. These ships were leisurely maintained under the command of the new Viceroy of Peru and unarmed, for the South Seas was Spanish, unmolested by foreign "pirates" who did not possess even the most rudimentary charts of its waters.

Then, in the first month of 1578, a tide of consternation swept up the coast; just a day or two ahead of it was a ferocious sea-going hornet called Sir Francis Drake. His *Golden Hind* had rounded Cape Horn during the winter. Slipping into Valparaíso where his ship was welcomed as a Spaniard by the unsuspecting authorities, Drake initiated the most successful pirating operation in history by "relieving" the *Capitana* of a fortune in treasure as well as kidnaping the ship itself. For a fantastic four months he cruised up the coast capturing unarmed, unsuspecting ships and raiding port after port while sweating couriers pounded up the roads with news that "El Drago" was at large. Nearly invariably their warnings were met with the rueful answer: "We know." Drake had already come and gone.

A courier from Arica did beat the *Golden Hind* to its next port, however. When Drake slid into Chuli he saw anchored in its harbor a caravel whose sides were still wet for several feet above the water line. A heavy cargo had obviously just been discharged. This was 300,000 pesos in silver bars. There are differing testimonies as to what happened to it. According to one Benito Díaz Bravo: "Because he was a day late, he missed taking the bars, and he saw many llamas loaded with bars going on a hill further on, and many men on horse-back to guard them." However, in another authoritative account obtained by the Hakluyt Society: ". . . the silver bars were put overboard in six fathoms."

Common sense indicates that in such a tiny port on such short notice (one day at most) unloading facilities and transport for all ten tons of silver could not be arranged—particularly since long, heated discussions would precede any orders for action whatsoever. What most likely happened is that at the last minute some of the silver was carried ashore in boats and loaded on hastily commandeered animals, while the remainder was jettisoned. Drake did not stop to try to salvage it. The Spanish no doubt recovered some. There should remain today, buried in the bottom under thirty feet of water in Chuli port, some-where around $75,000 in blackened but still intact silver ingots.

LA PLATA ISLAND SILVER (4)

Early in March 1578, after a long chase, the *Golden Hind* caught up with the largest and most beautiful galleon of the South Seas Armada, *Nuestra Señora de la Concepción*, on the last lap of her trip to Panama. Because of her armament of two guns, this ship was affectionately nicknamed by the Spanish *Cacafuego*—for which a euphemistic translation would be "Spitfire." Not many weeks later "Spitfire" had been changed to "Spitsilver," and Drake's vessel was so heavily laden with her treasure of 1,350,000 pesos that he regretfully decided that she must be lightened before setting out across the Pacific. In a little cove on the north side of Cano Island off Ecuador he and his men jettisoned 45 tons of silver ingots and coins onto the sandy bottom some 50 feet below. Then, after a final tweak or two at the Spanish king's nose, Drake sailed west-ward to complete his circumnavigation of the globe.

Spanish and English alike had been witnesses to the dumping of Drake's treasure, and Cano Island was from then on called La Plata, or Silver Island, to commemorate it. And, of course, men came to try their luck at salvage. One of the first was the English pirate, Bar-tholomew Sharp, who anchored over the right place. He and his crew fished up several hundred pieces of eight, using weighted tallow on lines. This same method was repeated in 1584 by the men of Captain John Cooke's ship *Bachelor's Delight*, who raised another 1500 or so pesos. Other intermittent attempts by fishermen brought up more small quantities. Then, in 1930, a wheezing ancient dredge called the *Goole* sneaked into the cove and clattered into life. When it departed some weeks later there were over ten tons of ingots and blackened cobs aboard. The full story of this nearly unbelievable but successful salvage venture is told by Nora Stirling in her book *Treasure under the Sea*.

Since there is no secret as to the dumping site of Drake's silver, there have doubtless been more ships that clandestinely visited this spot, and some that left might have been floating deeper in the water. Just the same, some of the jettisoned silver should still remain there buried under sand in the shallow cove.

CHIPANA BANK *NAO* (5)

In 1596 a Spanish *nao*, reportedly northbound with gold and silver in her cargo, broke her bottom on a reef several hundred yards off Chipana, Chile. She sank quickly. There is no record that the hull was even located after the disaster. Her treasure is probably still there.

SAN JUAN BAUTISTA (6)

There was over 300 tons of cargo including several chests of gold and a number of silver ingots aboard this warship when she dropped anchor at Valparaíso, Chile, in 1600. A sudden storm came up. The *San Juan Bautista* capsized and sank. Salvage was carried out for months afterward and much that was aboard was saved, but some of the precious metal was never found.

THE *BUEN JESÚS'* GOLD (7)

The 60-ton caravel *Buen Jesús* was sailing up the Chile coast toward Valparaíso on May 15, 1600, when her owner Francisco de Ibarra spotted a group of ships closing in. Soon he recognized them. They were Dutch frigates, commanded by the notorious Oliver van Noort who had been lately raiding the coast. Aboard the *Buen Jesús* was a cargo that would send the Hollanders away with happy grins, but de Ibarra was determined that they would capture none of it.

There was a hurried conference. As the enemy closed from seaward the water under the *Buen Jesús'* starboard side began to boil with the splashes of jettisoned bags and barrels. When the Dutch flagship *Hope* drew alongside, her boarding crew found nothing aboard but a general cargo of skins and wheat. There had been no need to swear the Spanish crew to secrecy; each man knew what would happen to him if van Noort learned of what they had just done. The *Buen Jesús* was partly stripped, and later burned after all the crew except the pilot and one slave were released. Then van Noort sailed on.

It was weeks later, from a captured port official, that he learned about the *Buen Jesús'* jettisoned cargo. Under torture the pilot and slave confessed the truth. During the fifteen minutes before their ship was taken 10,300 pounds of pure gold—five hundred ingots and 100 pounds of coins—had been dropped into the sea!

In the depths of the ocean, somewhere southwest of Valparaíso, this $5,000,000 in ingots and coins trace a golden path across the rocks and sand, lost forever.

BUEN BARCO (8)

This light *patache* was constructed on the bank of the Rio Bueno, which runs westward to enter the sea near Osorno, Chile, for use as a local transport. She was riding at anchor off the same port one night in 1601 when a sudden storm capsized and smashed her to pieces. Not a single member of her crew escaped and nearly all the cargo aboard, including perhaps a few barrels of gold, was lost. It lies scattered on the bottom off the Osorno waterfront.

VIGIA (9)

There was probably treasure aboard when this 200-ton *nao* broke up on a reef on the Juan Fernández Islands in 1632. Everybody aboard reached shore safely and most of the treasure was salvaged, except possibly a small quantity.

SAN NICOLÁS (10)

On May 13, 1647, a cataclysmic earthquake completely destroyed Concepción and a number of other cities along the Chile coast. It was followed by a series of tidal waves which swamped nearly everything afloat. Among the victims was a merchant *nao*, the *San Nicolás*, anchored off Arica in the Penco River preparing to discharge cargo from Papudo. Her fear-crazed crew saw a mountain of roaring green water crush down on them—and it was all over. The ship disappeared; there were no survivors. Some of the lighter cargo was found deposited hundreds of yards inland with other rubble when the ocean receded, but of the hull there was no trace. It must have been dragged out to deeper water by the undertow, perhaps smashed to pieces.

There had been 200,000 pesos of gold—nearly 30,000 ounces—aboard when the sea struck. If any part of the hull remained whole this $1,000,000 treasure could well be lying over it. Otherwise the golden coins and ingots were spread for miles up the river and along the coast.

TWO GALLEONS (11)

In the aftermath of the May 13 earthquake was an unusual tidal phenomenon: long-established currents off the Chile coast suddenly changed direction. Two ships, unaware of this, were cruising at night north of Talcahuano several weeks later when they smashed into reefs. Their pilots had assumed their positions to be ten miles seaward when this happened. A great deal was recovered from both hulls, with tallow, goatskins, tackle and cordage, as well as some gold, removed. Then storms destroyed the wrecks. In view of the uncompleted salvage there is a chance that some gold still remains around the bones of these ships.

SANTO TOMÁS DE VILLANUEVA (12)

When this important *nao* set sail from Concepción in 1650 she carried aboard $1,500,000 worth of Chile gold, silver, and copper. Her next port of call was Callao. She never arrived, nor was any of her crew ever heard of again, or any trace of wreckage found. For this reason the *Santo Tomás* probably floundered in deep water somewhere off the coast between these ports.

SAN JOSÉ (13)*

March 26, 1651, was a day of happy celebration for the fierce Araucanian Indians of the Valdivia coast of Chile, who for so many years had suffered under the brutal treatment of the Spanish. For a few joyous hours their cups flowed over while they noisily hacked to pieces the survivors of the *San José*, a warship which had the misfortune to become wrecked on the beach of Dotolauquen the previous night. She had sailed from Concepción a week before with reinforcements, supplies and 70,000 gold pesos of pay money for garrisons to the south. When a relief ship arrived at the scene some time later there was nothing to be found. The Indians and the pounding waves had done a thorough job. No salvage could be attempted without bringing in strong forces to hold the shore, and eventually the wreck was forgotten.

Its remains lie buried in the sand at a shallow depth. Somewhere in their vicinity is $250,000 in gold. The Araucanian Indians—at least those in the neighborhood of Dotolauquen Beach—are quite friendly today.

CAPITANA (14)***

The wreck of this great galleon is everything that a treasure hunter could desire. It contains a tremendous and authenticated quantity of gold and silver: worth between $2,000,000 and $5,000,000. Its approximate location and conditions of loss are known. It is not too deep to locate and salvage. It has never been worked on.

The *Capitana* was the registry ship of Francisco de Sota's armada which was carrying the 1654 accumulation of South America treasure northward. She had taken on barrels and cases of registry gold and silver at Concepción, Valparaíso, Arica, Callao, and Guayaquil, and was on the last lap of her voyage to deliver this immense treasure to Panama, when in the darkness of night her hull broke open on the sharp teeth of the Chanduy Reef, off Punta Santa Elena, Ecuador. The huge ship filled and sank within minutes with nearly everybody aboard killed. The wreck settled near the base of the reef. Over succeeding years wave motions and animals eroded its planks and timbers, while coral deposits formed and grew.

Today the multi-million-dollar *Capitana* no longer exists in the recognizable form of a ship. She may even have become part of Chanduy Reef. The area within which she should lie is not too large to sweep with a magnetometer. The finder would have to contend with coral or sand before he could break through to her treasure—but the prize would be worth it, in spades!

SAN BERNARDO (15)

This Spanish warship, carrying supplies and an undetermined amount of precious metal, disappeared without a trace during 1673 somewhere between Valparaíso and Callao. She probably lies in deep water.

ROSARIO (16)

The entryway to Chacao, in southern Chile, is a narrow channel separating Chiloé Island from the mainland to the north, well known for its treacherous shoals. In 1675 the warship *Rosario* was entering and struck, sinking in shallow water before her cargo could be taken off. In later salvage operations some of her cannon and heavy cargo were recovered, but a number of chests of gold coins—pay for the troops— were not recorded as recovered.

SAN JUAN DE DIOS (17)*

The most important passenger aboard this *nao* was Antonio de Morales, Bishop-elect of Concepción, en route south from Callao to his new post. With him were his personal as well as church treasures. Only a few days before reaching port, in 1684, the ship was dashed ashore in a tempest and broken up against the beach of Tanque. The Bishop-elect and nearly everyone else aboard perished. A valuable cargo shipment, including considerable precious ornaments, was lost and to this day there has been no recorded attempt to salvage any of it, although the shipwreck site can be pinpointed.

SAN NICOLAS (18)

This was a pirate ship about which little is known. She sank off Atacama, Chile, in 1685. No doubt there was plundered cargo aboard.

BEGOÑA (19)

Only a few hours after setting sail from Valparaíso in 1695, en route north to Callao with a valuable consignment of Chile gold and silver on board, the frigate *Begoña* floundered in heavy seas. Her hull lies today about two miles off the point of El Concon, some 300 feet deep. Her cargo of precious metal is worth approximately $250,000.

SPEEDWELL (20)

The English pirate George Shevelocke carried out a nice piece of business during his visit to Chile in 1721. He would put into a little seaport with his ship *Speedwell* and offer to leave its buildings standing provided that a satisfactory sum in pesos were promptly delivered aboard. Usually his price was right, and the buildings remained. Consequently when he decided to retire from the scene owing to rumors that several Spanish frigates were looking for him, he had aboard a nice profit—in hard cash.

He picked out a quiet island of the nearer Juan Fernández group where he intended to patch up the *Speedwell* and clean her bottom until things cooled off on the mainland. Before he could find a suitable bay for his purpose, however, the ship struck a submarine rock and filled. Everyone got off safely with a part of the wealth. A longboat was fitted out and set off with some of the crew. Shevelocke and the remainder built a schooner from the wreckage of their ship, named it the *Recovery*, and set sail themselves a few months later.

At the scene of the *Speedwell's* wreckage there should still be some Chile gold.

SANTO CRISTO DE LEÓN (21)

A violent earthquake and tidal wave struck the Peru coastal region in 1746, severely damaging shore installations and ships alike. The *Santo Cristo de León*, loading in the harbor of Callao, was swamped in the disaster. This galleon was on the coastal run and carried treasure when she went down. Some of this was salvaged.

ENCARNACIÓN (22)

This Spanish frigate was en route from Callao to the southern outposts with supplies, munitions and money when she ran aground on the coast of Chiloé in 1762. The rough seas drowned five of her crew and soon battered the ship so thoroughly that salvage was impossible. Her cannons and cargo were never recovered. There was about $75,000 in gold coins aboard.

SAN JUAN EVANGELISTA and SAN JUDAS TADEO (23)

These trading frigates were caught in a tempest while passing through the islands of the Chiloé archipelago in 1762. Before they could be taken into safe water the fierce gales had driven them against rocks. They broke up so thoroughly that no salvage was attempted. Although no record was found of their cargo, it is likely that they carried money aboard.

NUESTRA SEÑORA DE LA ERMITA (24)

She was another merchant frigate, picking up cargo along the Chile coast. In 1769, off Punta de Reyes, this ship was swamped during a terrible storm. Nearly all her crew drowned. Reports that there was "very valuable cargo" aboard could be misleading, but might mean that *Nuestra Señora* had taken on bullion at her last port of call, Valparaíso.

ORIFLAMA (25)

This registry galleon was returning to Callao with a cargo from Cádiz in 1770 when a storm drove her against the Huenchulami coast of central Chile. There was not one survivor and all her cargo was lost. The *Oriflama* carried no treasure, but did have aboard a small quantity of money.

TRÁNSITO (26)

The southern archipelagoes of Chile were a death trap for sailing ships. In 1786 the *Tránsito*, a merchant frigate, was caught in the Chonos Islands group and wrecked. She probably had aboard a parcel of precious metal. There was no recorded salvage.

SAN RAFAEL (27)

This 700-ton Spanish warship sailed from the port of Talcahuano in May, 1786, and was never heard of again. She was bound north with a cargo which included silver and copper from inland mines, and doubtless sank off the coast in deep water.

NUESTRA SEÑORA DE LA BALBANERA (28)*

The same waterway that claimed the *Rosario* in 1675 captured another sunken hull in 1788 when the pilot on the payship *Nuestra Señora de la Balbanera* tried to creep through Chiloé channel into the Gulf of Ancud during a rough night. At 1:00 A.M. on December 23 the 1000-ton frigate struck the reefs of Guapacho off San Carlos. By dawn all but 57 of the crew were dead and the ship's hull had vanished from sight.

There was a shipment of gold valued at about $200,000 on this ship. Neither it nor the cannons were ever salvaged. With the location so closely known, and being in shallow water, the wreck of *Nuestra Señora de la Balbanera* has the appearance of a likely salvage prospect. A magnetometer should be able to pick up her anchors and iron cannon.

SANTA LEOCADIA (29)**

This was one of the most famous shipwrecks of the South American coast, and its interest to treasure hunters has by no means yet ended. The *Santa Leocadia* was a 34-gun frigate built in the late eighteenth century and assigned to the South Seas region. On November 7, 1800, she sailed from Paita, Peru, to convoy an armada of merchant vessels north to Panama. Her captain was Antonio Barreda. She carried aboard 34 English prisoners and 2,100,000 pesos in registry gold and silver, packed securely in chests.

At 8:30 on the evening of November 16, as she led her convoy up the Ecuador coast, the *Santa Leocadia* smashed hard onto a shoal 100 yards from the beach at Punta Saint Elena. All night she hung, breaking slowly to pieces under the battering of waves. By morning her hull had been sheared off and nothing remained above the water. Over 140 of her crew were lost and another 48 were injured. The rest had reached the beach.

Within a few weeks salvage ships were anchored offshore and a base had been set up on the deserted beach. Stormy weather prevented work from beginning for two months, until February 1801. On the first day divers recovered 80,000 pesos. During the next eight months, whenever weather permitted, boats and skin divers worked in a co-ordinated effort. When the salvage was discontinued in October, 90 per cent of the *Santa Leocadia*'s cargo had been saved, including 1,800,000 pesos and 28 cannon.

The keel and ballast of this frigate lie in a depth of only fifteen feet, under the south face of a reef 100 yards off the beach at Punta Saint Elena. Coral and sea crustaceans have worked hard to hide these remnants, but a short search should discover them. And the results would be worth while. Six bronze cannon and more than 200,000 pesos in gold and silver—worth at least $250,000—are waiting for skin divers with the patience to track them down.

Its shallow depth, exact location, and the valuable treasure still remaining make the *Santa Leocadia* an interesting salvage prospect.

CHAPTER 13

Florida

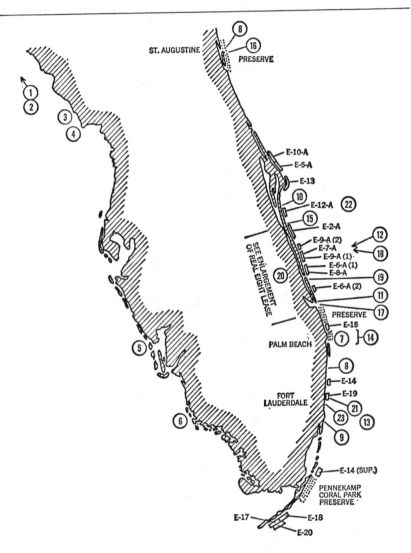

MAP 1   Florida. Leases and preserves.

Exploration:

E – 2 – A: Doubloon Salvage, Inc., Melbourne, Florida
        Jim Rathmann, President
E – 5 – A: New Channel Historical Survey Group, Edgewater, Florida
        William H. Andrews
E – 6 – A: Ocean Salvage, Inc., Fort Pierce, Florida
        Robert M. Jernigan, President
E – 7 – A: The Pioneer Company, Wabasso, Florida
        Fred J. Prestin
E – 8 – A: Pirate Village, Inc., St. Petersburg, Florida
        Mrs. Jeanne H. DuRand, President
E – 9 – A: Salvage Research Corporation, Vero Beach, Florida
        J. Earmann, Business Manager
E – 10 – A: William C. Saurwalt, Ltd., Allendale, Florida
        William C. Saurwalt
E – 12 – A: Tech Enterprises, Inc., Eau Gallie, Florida
        DeForest Tackett, President
E – 13: Alan J. Fischer, New Smyrna Beach, Florida
E – 14: Armada Research Corporation, Vero Beach, Florida
        Mel A. Fisher, President
E – 15: DuBois, Dugan & Nipp, North Miami Beach, Florida
E – 17: Oceanic Research & Salvage Company, Miami Beach, Florida
E – 18: Southern Research & Salvage Corporation, Miami, Florida
E – 19: Sea Labs Exploration, Inc., Miami, Florida
E – 20: Continental Exploration Corporation, Bedford Hills, N.Y.
S – 5: St. John's Salvage, Inc., St. Augustine, Florida
(Note: "A" following a contract indicates a renewal)

Salvage Leases:

Lease ⌗1329: Real Eight Company, Inc., Satellite Beach, Florida
        Colonel Harry E. Cannon, President
Lease ⌗1687: Martin County Historical Society

During the 1950s, as SCUBA diving grew in popularity, an increasing number of wrecks located off the Florida coast and Keys were raided by innocent amateurs unaware of their historic and archaeological value, as well as hit-and-run groups after a fast buck. Gradually responsible conservation officers and historians became aware of the irreparable damage being done by these scavengers and agitated for legislation to halt the destruction. The first effective step was taken when a law governing salvage operations went into effect on January 1, 1958. This proclaimed the state's authority over coastal waters extending three miles into the Atlantic Ocean and nine miles into the Gulf of Mexico, and appointed the Trustees of the Internal Improvement Fund as the body responsible for the allocation of exploration and salvage leases. Applicants for either type of lease were required to submit forms detailing their backgrounds, their salvage objectives, and other information. In addition, surety bonds of $500 or more were required, plus yearly rental fees of $100 which were renewable on a year-to-year basis. Quarterly reports were required describing the work accomplished and complete details of any recoveries made. Salvaged treasure and artifacts could not be sold until their value had been assessed and a royalty of 25 per cent (usually a quarter of the recoveries) taken by the Trustees.

This was fine in theory, but had flaws because insufficient provision was made for effective enforcement. While responsible men complied, the scavengers operating from hundreds of charter boats continued their dynamiting and looting of unprotected sites. The system of leases itself came under attack in courts, with accusations of bias in the awards. In one case a plaintiff challenged the state of Florida's jurisdiction over sunken wrecks. Exaggerated stories in the newspapers stirred up further discord and the situation became so aggravated that in January 1965 Governor Haydon Burns issued a moratorium on new treasure leases. The whole system was thoroughly reviewed.

Some fourteen months later the ban was lifted, and in 1967 the Florida Archives and History Act was passed. Under this, authority to issue and supervise leases was placed in the hands of the executive director of the Florida Board of Archives and History. While the earlier rules remained substantially unchanged, control was generally tightened and provision for enforcement was made through the organization of a marine salvage patrol staffed by conservation officers with training in diving and underwater archaeology. Annual fees were $600 for exploration contracts and $1200 for salvage contracts. Legitimate salvors thus had the benefit of not only protection for their property, but also guidance by trained board experts. Exploration and salvage contracts in force in 1969 are shown on Florida map 1.

On July 1, 1969, the Florida government was reorganized, and the functions of the former Board of Archives and History were transferred to the Department of State under the Division of Archives, History and Records Management. The former Division of Historic Sites and Properties was renamed the Bureau of Historic Sites and Properties. It is this bureau that retains the state's 25 per cent share of recovered treasure and artifacts and makes them available to properly qualified researchers in a variety of fields and for display with interpretation to the public.

The legal boundary between state and international waters on the Atlantic side of the Florida Keys remained set at three miles from the Keys until recently, when Monroe County Circuit Court Judge Aquilino Lopez made a decision extending the area under state jurisdiction to three miles beyond the outer reefs (Sombrero, Alligator, Molasses, etc.). This was challenged unsuccessfully in court. Judge Lopez' action was crucial to salvors operating off the Keys, since many of the wrecks such as "McKee's Galleon" and the *San José*—previously "open territory" in international waters—were transferred to state control by his decision.

The West Coast

SIX SHIPS OF DE LUNA (1)
One galleon and "five ships with topsails" of an armada commanded by General Tristan de Luna were wrecked during a 1559 hurricane in Pensacola Bay (then called Philippine Bay). They were sailing eastward on a coast exploration voyage. That at least one—probably the galleon—carried Mexican silver is indicated by the contemporary comment "the treasure was lost, but mostly recovered." The wrecks of these ships, sunk in shallow water, have been buried and do not make attractive salvage prospects.

The *VOLADOR II* (2)
This 10-gun Spanish schooner, under Captain Joaquin Viál, sank off Pensacola on May 25, 1815, during a storm with the loss of two lives. There was a small quantity of money aboard which may have been saved.

The AMERICAN SCHOONER (3)
There have been several reports that a United States schooner carrying a part of the purchase price for the territory of Florida, bought

from Spain the year before, was sunk in a hurricane of 1820 off the
mouth of the Suwannee River. The money was said to be in gold. In
view of the depth of only 30 feet and comparatively recent date it seems
likely that efforts to recover the money—estimated at several million
dollars—would have been at least partly successful.

Despite rumors that gold coins have been found over the past ten
years in this vicinity it would be a good idea to check government
records concerning the Florida indemnity payment before investing
money on any salvage attempt here.

The CEDAR KEY WRECK (4)

Fairly reliable reports of Spanish money being found on the western
shore of Cedar Key lead to the possibility that a New Spain armada *nao*
lost without a trace was dashed to pieces here.

The GASPARILLA ISLAND COINS (5)

There have been unsubstantiated stories of coins being discovered
around the Boca Grande Channel off Gasparilla Island, scene of the
pirate José Gaspar's last attacks. These tie in with the myriad legends
of his never-recovered treasure, said to be buried nearby or lost in the
sea.

The NAPLES WRECK (6)

Repeated accounts of money being found washed up on the Naples
beach have led to many treasure hunts and surveys with metal detectors. There is a chance that one of the lost Spanish ships from
Veracruz sank off this shore.

The East Coast

The THREE *NAOS* (7)

A hurricane in November 1554 drove three *naos* of the New Spain
armada, commanded by Angel de Villafañe and Garcia de Escalante,
against the coast—near present-day Palm Beach, from one description.
Nearly all their crewmen were drowned. Later salvage recuperated
"most of the gold and silver." What remains has been overgrown with
coral and could be as costly to salvage as it is worth.

The TWO *PATACHES* (8)

Over 200 lives were lost and some ship's money was dashed to the
bottom in 1572 when a hurricane caused two coastal *pataches* to break
up on reefs off San Augustine. The value of coin in their wreckages
did not exceed $10,000.

The FIVE NEW SPAIN *NAOS* (9)

During the hurricane of September 1641 five *naos* of the decimated New Spain armada (see Chapter 14) were wrecked with great loss of life against the Florida coast, probably just north of Miami. About $2,000,000 in silver went down with these ships. Some of this was reported salvaged later. Silver coins found by skin divers off Hillsboro Inlet during recent years, and a coral-crusted anchor raised in 1957 off Pompano Beach, might be from these wrecks.

The *SAN NICOLÁS* (10)

This 220-ton *nao*, captain Juan Christoval, was wrecked in 1551 on the coast of Aix south of Cape Kennedy. There was some treasure aboard which was largely salvaged by the Aix Indians.

The 1554 TIERRA FIRME *NAOS* (11)

Several treasure ships were separated from the 1554 armada in a storm and wrecked along the coast. Three probably broke up between Delray Beach and Boynton Beach, while at least another was wrecked north of St. Lucie Inlet. Robert Marx has identified among them[1] the 220-ton *San Esteban*, captain Francisco del Merceno, from which much gold and silver was taken by the Aix Indians; the *Santa María del Carmen*, captain Diego Diaz, completely salvaged by the Spanish; the *Santa María de Yciar*, captain Alonso Ozosi, 220 tons, which may have been partly salvaged.

The *NAO VIZCAYO* and the *URCA "EL MULATO"* (12)

Both ships were wrecked about 1568 off Indian River. They carried considerable treasure, much of which was taken by the Aix Indians.

The 1589 NEW SPAIN *ALMIRANTA* (13)

With a large registered treasure, this galleon sank in deep water during a hurricane, possibly off Miami. No salvage was attempted.

The 1591 SHIPWRECKS (14)

Several *naos* of this year's New Spain and Tierra Firme armadas were broken up along the coast during storms in August 1591. Very little treasure was aboard, and there may have been salvage.

The HONDURAS *ALMIRANTA* (15)

This large ship was wrecked in 1618 near Malabar and much of her cargo washed ashore. Although there was probably some silver aboard, the main lading was hides, indigo, and cochineal.

[1] *Shipwrecks in Florida Waters* by Robert F. Marx.

The 1626 SPANISH FRIGATE (16)

Carrying supplies and a payroll from Havana, this ship was wrecked on a bar while entering St. Augustine. From available data, only some wine, washed ashore, was recovered. If this wreck could be identified from the scores of others in the area, some $20,000 or more in silver coins should be scattered on her ballast.

The *REFORMATION* (17)

Captain Joseph Kirle's English barkentine sank near shore four miles south of St. Lucie Inlet in 1696, with Spanish silver coins.

MAJOR DASHIELL'S $23,000 PAYROLL (18)

U. S. Army Paymaster Major Jeremiah Dashiell was aboard the schooner *William and Mary* when she anchored off the mouth of the old Indian River Inlet on May 1, 1857. This waterway, now filled in, was too shallow for the ship to enter and the major and five others disembarked into a small boat to complete their trip to Fort Capron on the shore side of Indian River. As they approached the inlet's mouth a sudden cycloidal wave swamped the boat. The men were saved by the crew of another schooner, but $23,000 of payroll money which Dashiell carried in a leather pouch vanished under the sea.

In March 1963 Albert Ashley and James Gordy of Fort Pierce were diving for crayfish off Pepper Park when they found gold coins scattered on the top of a limestone reef a few hundred yards offshore. With Gordy's father, they formed the Gordy-Ashley Salvage Co., Inc., and on July 2, 1964, were awarded lease №2025 by the Trustees of the Internal Improvement Fund. On July 13, 1964, 105 gold coins were declared recovered and turned over to the state of Florida. Mr. Carl J. Clausen, representing the fund, dived on the site several times that summer as work was continued from a small boat. Coins were found scattered in an area of some 80 by 50 feet. Most were located by fanning away sand in shallow depressions; others were uncovered from deeper pockets with an injection dredge.

In September 582 gold coins including the 105 declared salvaged in 1963, and another 225 silver coins, were divided with the state of Florida, which received 146 gold pieces as its 25 per cent share. The gold coins were from five different American mints, dated between 1834 and 1856. Denominations were $1, $2.50, $5, $10, and $20. All were in excellent condition. The silver coins, mostly quarters, were badly corroded. Controversy about the actual value arose in 1968 when Ashley filed suit against the Gordys. Testimony given indicated that 3264 gold coins had actually been recovered during 1963 and 1964, with a face value of $23,025.50—practically the exact amount lost by the paymaster. There are today probably a few coins scattered around the bottom off Pepper Park, but not worth another search.

The EL DORADO SALVAGE COMPANY WRECK (19)

Under a former contract from the Board of Archives and History, Harold Holden's El Dorado Salvage Company team worked a wreck half a mile south of Fort Pierce Inlet for several summers after 1966. The 108-by-40-foot ballast pile, 4–5 feet high, indicates a large ship. The wreck was apparently salvaged long ago, as it lies only 12 feet deep. Numerous coins of the 1715 period found along the adjacent beach tell of treasure having been aboard, although despite an immense salvage effort none has yet been found. After examination of recovered artifacts—a small iron howitzer, a shattered ship's bell, a large anchor, a silver shoe buckle, many cannon balls, and two hollow 5½-inch-diameter iron grenades—Mendel Peterson has estimated that the ship was Spanish of the 1680–1720 period.

Holden's group uses a specially built 32-by-16-foot barge with a blower-type dredge mounted in an opening in its center. "This dredge has a 5-foot-diameter, four-blade impeller wheel 4 feet below the surface," explains Holden. "It has proved effective in removing sand and mud over a wide area up to 8 feet deep."

THE 1715 COMBINED ARMADAS** (20)

Eleven ships of the combined New Spain armada of General Juan Estéban de Ubilla and Tierra Firme armada under General Antonio de Echeverz y Zubiza left Havana on July 27, 1715, and sailed up the New Bahama Channel. Between them, the four *Capitanas* and *Almirantas* carried 14,000,000 pesos in registered treasure. Since the armadas' departure from the New World had been delayed a full year, contraband cargo was crammed onto its ships. An estimate published in 1868 by Jacobo de Pezuela valued the total cargo at 65,000,000 pesos. A figure of $30,000,000 in gold, silver, and jewels in today's values would be conservative.

Three days out of Havana, a hurricane caught the Spanish fleet in the narrows off Florida. Throughout the night of July 30 winds on its north front drove the line of helpless ships westward toward a forty-mile stretch of coast between Sebastian and St. Lucie inlets. As they approached shore, the vessels were swamped under breakers or hurled onto reef barriers running parallel to the beach. Only one ship, the French *nao Grifón*, survived.

Of the ships in Ubilla's New Spain armada:

The *CAPITANA*, a 50-gun frigate at the head of the line, struck the coast about two and a half miles south of Sebastian Inlet where three reefs parallel to the beach extend 800 feet into the sea. She broke her bottom on the seaward edge of the outermost reef, spilling ballast and heavy cargo onto the coral and the sand floor 30 feet below. The lightened hull was carried in over the reef by surging mountains of water, then across the middle coral barrier into a sand trough less than 100 feet wide separating the two innermost reefs. Here it disintegrated. Most of the cannons and lading spilled out onto the sand, only 15 feet deep and 300 feet from shore. A trail of gold, silver, and jewelry stretched inshore for 700 feet across coral and sand from the ballast. General Ubilla and 225 of his crew were killed.

The *ALMIRANTA* was wrecked in shallow water "a stone's throw from shore." Her hull was battered to splinters and 123 men killed.

The storeship *NUESTRA SEÑORA DE LA REGLA*, nicknamed *URCA DE LIMA*, grounded "at the mouth of a river" which may be Fort Pierce Inlet. Thirty-five of her crew drowned.

Two *pataches*, *NUESTRA SEÑORA DE LAS NIEVES* and *SANTO CRISTO DEL VALLE*, were wrecked in shallow water, probably between Sebastian and Fort Pierce. Part of the deck floated ashore from one, carrying a hundred survivors, while twenty-five others drowned. The second *patache* lost twelve of her crew.

Of the ships in de Echeverz' Tierra Firme armada:

The *CAPITANA*, a captured British ship *Hampton Court* renamed *NUESTRA SEÑORA DEL CARMEN Y SAN ANTONIO*, broke up "off a point of land" which is almost certainly Sandy Point, off Oslo. The general and 113 others were killed.

The *ALMIRANTA, NUESTRA SEÑORA DEL ROSARIO Y SAN FRANCISCO XAVIER*, was battered by waves across a quarter-mile-wide barrier of reefs at a spot about four miles south of Fort Pierce. Her ballast and some cargo dumped out at the innermost edge of the coral, about 900 feet off the beach. The wooden hull, breaking up along the way, was carried inshore across several smaller reefs. Remnants settled a few feet deep just off the beach. Sunken wreckage covered an area the size of seven football fields.

A Dutch *nao* nicknamed *LA HOLANDESA* grounded and broke up near the beach of "False Cape" with her entire crew saved.

The *nao SAN MIGUEL* and the *urca* nicknamed *LA FRANCESCA* disappeared without a trace.

Nearly a thousand survivors lay stunned under torrential rains on the barren coast the next morning. Many soon died from injuries. Then the searing sun came out and turned the beach into hell. A grounded longboat was found seaworthy and taken north by a crew to seek help at the Spanish post of St. Augustine. Rescue operations gradually got under way there, and at Havana, where the *Grifón* had returned with news of the disaster. Seven small ships carrying soldiers and supplies arrived in September, but during the six-week interval many of the survivors had died of exposure, hunger, and thirst. Others, trekking north to St. Augustine with pockets full of looted treasure, were caught by Spanish soldiers stationed to intercept them at Matanzas Inlet and executed.

Full-scale salvage work started in March 1716, with the arrival of a fleet of sloops from Havana. They carried soldiers, Indian divers, supplies, and guns. The commander, Juan del Hoyo Solórzano, established a main base near the wreck of Ubilla's *Capitana* where survivors had found a fresh-water spring. To protect the site, he built a small fort mounting four cannons. While soldiers dug through jungles of wreckage spread for miles down the beaches, the boats went out between the reefs and 280 Indian divers began work. By this time the grounded hulks, except for bilges and keels protected by ballast, had disintegrated into pieces of broken wood. Shifting sand had hidden much of the submerged cargo. The Indians, without masks for underwater vision, groped blindly over ballast heaps. In the deeper areas, some drew breaths from crude diving bells suspended under boats, but most had to surface for breath after two minutes below. Their number dwindled as accidents and swarming sharks took their toll. Nearly a hundred died.

The Spanish were not the only ones interested in the armadas' gold and silver. From the Caribbean islands and English settlements on the American coast, boats full of pirates and "gentlemen adventurers" set out for Florida. The Spaniards were unable to cope with the raiders that swarmed on them. While defenders chased away ten sloops "fishing" over one site, a dozen more would attack a beach camp or a ship carrying salvaged cargo to Havana. A gold cargo worth $100,000 was captured with a Spanish *patache*. Many times this amount was stolen from the wreckage. Up north the English governor at Williamsburg gave tacit encouragement to the freebooters. The most daring of these was Captain Henry Jennings, who dropped in with two brigantines and two luggers. In July 1716 he landed several hundred men and captured the main Spanish base and 350,000 silver pesos stored there for shipment.

During 1716 most of the salvage was completed and sent back to Spain from Havana aboard the *Príncipe de Asturias* and *Nuestra Señora del Carmen.* Two years later "diving contractor" Manuel Miralles arrived with a small squadron, and in a novel twist surprised eight sloops and luggers" "fishing" offshore. He captured 180,000 pesos they had recovered and two hundred English and ninety-eight Negro prisoners.

When salvage was discontinued in 1719, $6,000,000 in treasure had been retrieved by the Spanish, and probably another $1,000,000 by the pirates. About 4,000,000 pesos were taken from four wrecks: *La Holandesa* and *Nuestra Señora de la Regla*, both nearly completely salvaged; Ubilla's *Capitana*, from which 940 treasure chests were saved from her registered cargo of 1300; and Ubilla's *Almiranta*, yielding 136 of her registered 990 chests. Within another few years the story of the disaster disappeared into history. It was not until a feature article in the *National Geographic Magazine* broke the account of Kip Wagner and his Real Eight Company in January 1965 that the armadas' vast treasure returned to the headlines (see The 1715 ARMADA and REAL EIGHT).

THE 1714 SILVER DISKS SITE (21)

Donald Ediger of Expeditions Unlimited, Inc., has raised the possibility that another of the 1715 wrecks lies down the coast just north of Fort Lauderdale. "Permit ⚡E-19 was taken out in the name of Sea Labs Exploration, Inc.," he advises, "part of which corporation is owned by Expeditions Unlimited. Sea Labs personnel have recovered several silver disks that are dated from 1714. This and other information leads us to suspect that the vessel might have been among the 1715 ships."

The *SANTO CAYETANO* (22)

This 24-gun Spanish frigate was wrecked off the Florida coast in 1738 during a storm. Some money may have been lost.

The FORT LAUDERDALE WRECK (23)

While surveying wreck sites along the coast, Colonel Frank F. Tenney's team located a wreck off Fort Lauderdale that yielded many interesting artifacts and a number of Spanish coins dating from 1772 to 1816. The January 1965 moratorium on leases prevented Colonel Tenney from obtaining rights to the site, which lies in Florida waters, and the recoveries were turned over to the state.

The Florida Keys

Per square mile of sea bed accessible to SCUBA divers there is probably no richer treasure-hunting field in the world than the ridges of reefs outlying the 200-mile string of limestone and coral islets called the Florida Keys. From Triumph Reef off Biscayne Bay, down through Pacific, Turtle, Carysfort, Molasses, Conch, Crocker, Alligator, Tennessee, Coffin's Patch, Sombrero, Looe Reef, and the Tortuga Bank on the southwest end, they formed a solid barrier of teeth to smash in

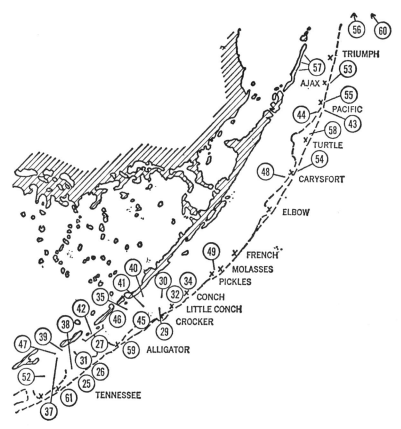

MAP 2 Florida. Upper Keys.

the hulls of the Spanish treasure ships winding their way from Havana into the New Bahamas Channel. From 1550 to 1800 probably 12,000 vessels passed along the flank of this submarine death trap. And every fifty or sixty years the law of averages would come into play and westward-rushing winds on the front of hurricanes would hurl a flota against their coral points.

Sometimes the doomed *naos* and galleons hung on the outer edges of reefs to be battered to kindling there. Often ships were carried right over these five to fifteen foot deep upcroppings and dropped into depressions under the sheltered sides, or even swept in and hurled against the keys themselves before finally going under. At least 25,

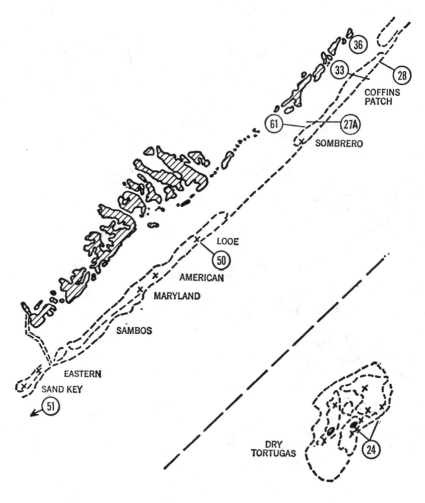

MAP 3 Florida. Lower Keys.

and probably closer to 50 ships of the Spanish armadas, sank along the Florida Keys.

As far down as Alligator Reef the water on the Atlantic side is clear, and visibility excellent. Below this point the keys and reefs are so broken by channels that sediment-laden water from the inner bay flows across, greatly reducing visibility. The SCUBA diver, with practice, can learn to recognize the most common indications of a wreck. If it lies on sand, the ballast mound will frequently be visible; if it has been overgrown with coral, unusual geometric formations—particularly straight lines—should be investigated.

The *VISITACIÓN* (61)

One of the first hurricane-wrecked vessels was the *Visitación*. In 1550, en route from Havana to Spain with $200,000 worth of treasure aboard, Captain Pedro de la Torre's 200-ton *nao* was dashed to pieces somewhere among Los Mártires—the Spanish name for the stretch from Lower Matecumbe to Elliott Keys. Some of the crewmen were rescued but the silver and gold could not be recovered. It remains in the coral-blanketed ballast of the *Visitación*, probably off Key Largo.

THE 1622 TIERRA FIRME FLOTA LOSS

The earliest major disaster involving a large part of an armada took place in 1622. On September 4 of that year the Tierra Firme "galleons," commanded by the Marquis de Caldereita (also spelled Cadereyta) sailed from Havana. The captain general of the fleet was Juan de Lara Moran, and other officers included Admiral Larraspuru and Pedro Pasquier. Eight registry galleons, seventeen cargo *naos* and three *pataches* were strung along the Straits of Florida two days later when a hurricane struck. The following account of the destruction of several of the treasure ships is quoted from the Royal Letter of the Marquis de Cadereyta which was found in *Legajo* 1145, *Indifferente*, at the Archivo General de Indias, Seville. I am indebted to Goin E. (Jack) Haskins, Jr., Southern Research & Salvage Corporation, Islamorada, for a summary of his and Burt Webber's findings on the 1622 loss during a tremendous research project, and permission to quote from this translation:

> When I arrived Monday, September the 12th, to Havana harbor [wrote the Marquis] I found 10 ships of the ones that carried the provisions, and the three galleons of silver: *Nuestra Señora del Rosario, Capitana* of the fleet *Santa Anna la Real,* and *Nuestra Señora de la Candelaria,* all of them without rigging or sails and making much water, and seven ships of the fleet, five of them unrigged, and all in very poor condition.
> And I saw Don Bernardino de Lugo, sea and war Captain of the galleon *Santa Margarita* of the silver ones, and having been injured about it and about the missing others, he said that on the day of the storm the Captain headed in the southwest direction until night; that the wind took away the sail of the foremast, and the galleon's remaining main mast broke, and also the rudder . . . on September 6th at dawn he threw the sounding line and took a depth of 40 *brazas* . . . the force of the wind and the currents pushed the galleon forward up to 10 *brazas* where it grounded and was lost in the sand bank which is located on the west side of the last of the Matacumbe Keys, next to the head of the Mártires off the Florida coast. At 7 A.M. of that day he saw one *legua* to the East the galleon named *Nuestra Señora de Atocha, Almiranta* of the fleet, without rigging or sails . . . and as he watched he saw it go down and sink to the bottom. At 10 A.M. the *Santa Margarita* was wrecked and most of his men drowned. He was thrown out of the ship by the force of the water, and was later picked up by the small boat of a Jamaican vessel. He then obtained ma-

terial to make a buoy and placed the signal close to the place where the two galleons sank.

On Tuesday, the 13th of September, the *Juan Bautista* . . . entered the port of Havana . . . and with it eight ships of the ones that carried provisions. He was asked about the rest of the ships and answered that he saw the *Nuestra Señora del Rosario* stranded on one of the Tortuga Keys. Fifty-four persons were saved. These people said that Gaspar Gonzales de los Reyes' ship capsized without leaving any survivors, and that he saw another ship, commanded by Juan de la Torre Agala, which also sank.

In all, ten ships were lost during the hurricane. Of these, the three treasure galleons—*Santa Margarita, Nuestra Señora de Atocha,* and *Nuestra Señora del Rosario*—were the subjects of immediate salvage attempts.

On the 15th of the same month the Governor, ministers and pilots of the army and fleet met to reach an agreement to prepare the ships in order to search . . . It was decided that Captain Gaspar de Vargas would go to make the recovery from the two lost galleons, and to search for the lost one around the Tortuga Keys, which he went out to do on the 16th of September with three *pataches* and two *chalupas* [smaller ships]. Having reached the right place, he discovered the small mast of the *Almiranta* . . . The galleon was in a depth of 10 *brazas* of water. The divers went down to enter the silver compartment, which could not be accomplished because the portholes and hatches were locked and the decks were in one piece . . . He then left to search for the *Santa Margarita*. The buoy was not found, neither was the ship. A storm kept them from working further.

He headed for the Tortuga Keys in search for the *Nuestra Señora del Rosario* which he found stranded in one of the keys, on the 24th of September, and found on the land its people and on a nearby key a *patache* of the fleet . . . They took out all the silver and twenty pieces of artillery.

NUESTRA SEÑORA DEL ROSARIO and a PATACHE (24)

As stated above, Captain Miguel de Chazarreta's galleon *Rosario*, and a nearby *patache*, were salvaged of their valuables. The galleon's upper decks were burned to facilitate reaching the silver. The remnants of both vessels are believed to have been located off the Dry Tortugas by Ray Eaton, of Hamden, Connecticut, and several others.

The attempts at salvage continued:

On October 13th I sent from [Havana] Captain Don Pedro de Ursua with three *pataches* and two *chalupas* and instruments to search for the galleon *Santa Margarita* . . . After a delay caused by a storm it was decided that Captain Gaspar de Vargas should go to the Matacumbe Keys . . . Vargas took saws, drills, and other new instruments to blow up or break the deck of the *Almiranta Atocha* and to take out the treasure and artillery, also from the *Margarita*. Divers were also taken.

[After more delays] . . . reaching the place where the *Almiranta* was lost he did not see the *mesana* [small mast], nor any other signs, and figuring that the October's storm had destroyed it, he went to look around all the Matacumbe Keys to find some signs. In one of them he saw half the side of the *Almiranta* . . . you can figure that the two decks were gone and that only the plan and ballast remained and in it the silver, artillery and other heavy items, and to collect them was sent Captain Gaspar de Vargas who was delayed by weather until November 18th . . . and the same day he departed he was caught by a storm that sent him to the port of Mariel . . . he returned to Havana to get supplies . . . [and so on].

The *SANTA MARGARITA* (25)*

Another account of this galleon's loss reads: "The first of the ship-wrecked galleons was the *Santa Margarita*, smashed against one of the keys of Los Mártires, where it broke into pieces and was destroyed. Few people could be saved and this is the interesting galleon." To-gether with the *Atocha* (see below), it remains very interesting indeed to Burt D. Webber, Jr., whose Continental Exploration Corporation was awarded Exploration Contract ※20 on July 18, 1969. The boundaries of this lease cover the region in which Webber is nearly certain both galleons lie. He writes:

Most people think that the *Santa Margarita* was a large and heavily armed galleon, which was not the case. Her dimensions, which were given on November 28, 1621, when she was approved for a silver galleon, were:
54 codes and 5/12 in length
17 short codes of extreme breadth by the first beam
8 large codes in depth of hold . . . and it seems to be
sufficient for a silver galleon.
The *Santa Margarita* carried approximately 25 pieces of artillery, some of bronze which were later recovered. Although sought by both Gaspar de Vargas and Pedro de Ursua, she was not found until 1626 by Francisco Nuñez Melian. In order to create an incentive among the slave divers, he agreed to grant freedom to the first diver to locate and recover a bar of silver from the site. A slave diver named Juan Banon did this, and salvage continued through 1630. I have a letter which indicates that the Indians also worked on this site, recovering gold and many reales, before the Spaniards ever located the wreck. I cross-referenced the registered bullion listings on the *Margarita* against the Nuñez Melian salvage records. As I recall, nearly 144 bars of silver and thousands of pieces of eight were un-accounted for. Although some 30 bars and cakes of gold were in the register, none were listed as salvaged. Did the Indians recover the unac-counted-for treasure? I don't know. The total registered treasure aboard the *Santa Margarita* was 420,000 pesos in gold, silver, copper and tobacco.

NUESTRA SEÑORA DE ATOCHA (26)**

The *Almiranta* took down with her Admiral Pedro Pasquier and nearly her entire crew when she sank. The 600-ton Tierra Firme galleon carried over 1,000,000 pesos in registered silver and other treas-ure, worth at least $2,000,000 today. She was found by the Spanish, as described earlier, and partially salvaged in 1623. Before work could be concluded the marker buoy on the wreck was carried away in a storm, and the site was never relocated. Shifting sand blanketed the ballast mound, which has probably disappeared from view. There should be at least $1,000,000 in gold and silver today in the ballast of the *Atocha*, buried under the sand in a wide stretch between two reefs, 30–60 feet deep, within the boundaries of Exploration Contract ⚹20.

Burt Webber's Continental Exploration Corporation is a dynamic, technically advanced organization. Still young, Webber started his salvage training in 1961 as chief diver on an expedition directed by Art McKee aboard the *Amigo* on which an eighteenth-century wreck on Banner Reef was excavated. During the next years he explored wrecks in the Caribbean, the Bahamas, and off the Florida Keys on expeditions managed by Gordon S. Patton and Fred Dickson, Jr., of Ocean City, Maryland, Captain Leo Barker of Miami, and others. On another McKee expedition in 1963 he helped raise five old cannons which were sold to an Ocho Rios hotel in Jamaica. He then formed a Jamaica company, Marine Archaeological Research Corporation, Ltd., and charted wrecks along Serrana and San Pedro banks. Webber spent much of 1965 and 1966 in Spain directing a program of research at the Archivo General de Indias and Museo Naval, during which over a thousand documents pertaining to the armadas were located, photocopied, and catalogued by his staff of translators and researchers. Then, fully equipped with information and experience, he formed Continental Exploration Corporation.

The preparations for the assault on the two Spanish galleons have cost already some $200,000. Much of this was spent procuring and testing such sophisticated electronic search devices as Dr. Edgerton's seismic profiling equipment and the Varian Associates' V-4937 proton magnetometer. In a search for more sensitive and reliable detection units, a whole new generation of rubidium and cesium magnetometers was checked out.

Webber's 136-foot research motor vessel *Revenge* is one of the most modern and fully equipped afloat. After purchasing her for $100,000, he spent another $85,000 on specialized search and salvage equipment, including a two-man dry submarine, recompression chamber, deep and shallow diving rigs, air lifts, pave-breakers, and a full range of navigation equipment. His associates include Art McKee, George MacDonald, Jack Haskins, and Kenneth Myers, the president of Sea Borne Electronics Company, whose Varian 4938-G magnetometer located the *Endeavour*'s cannons.

With such a competent management and team, researched information, and advanced equipment, it seems likely that the Continental

Exploration Corporation may well have located the *Atocha*—and possibly the *Margarita* as well—by the time this book goes to press.

SIX MERCHANT *NAOS* (27) (27A)

Four of the 1622 flota's *naos* were wrecked along Upper and Lower Matecumbe, while another two were swamped in deep water. The Spanish are believed to have partially salvaged the shallow wrecks, and at least one of them has been found recently. They probably all contain numismatically valuable coins, while the two swamped *naos* could hold considerable contraband silver and gold. One of these ships may be the wreck located northeast of Delta Shoal, about twenty-five feet deep. This has yielded iron and stone cannon shot, lead musket shot and 200-pound lead ingots, an early hooped barrel gun and some 1621 copper maravedi.

NUESTRA SEÑORA DE LOS MARAVILLAS (28)***

In the original *Guide* this three-star wreck was included in the Florida Keys section, and although Jack Haskins has raised some very pertinent doubts (see below) about this location, *Nuestra Señora de los Maravillas* will remain—hesitantly—in Florida waters in this revised edition as well.

In 1656 the *Almiranta* of General the Marquis de Montealegre's Tierra Firme armada, bound from Cartagena to Havana, was swept off course by a storm and wrecked "on the shoals of Los Mimbres, with a big treasure, more than four millions of pesos. The highest part of her hull was at six fathoms below the water." Of the 650 people aboard, 605, including Captain Matías de Orellana, were killed. Salvage operations got under way within six months, in early 1657, headed by Captain Tomás Somovilla. After three days of searching with grapples the ship was located near the outer edge of a reef where "the bottom was twelve fathoms deep." Scores of native divers were put to work and gold and silver bars and coins began coming up from the wreck. Salvage was difficult due to the depth—some 70 feet. Nevertheless when Captain Somovilla ended his efforts late in the summer, the recovery was 400,000 pesos. A second salvage attempt brought up another 900,000 pesos, and a third and final effort netted about 50,000. The Spanish then discontinued recovery attempts, and noted that "much more" treasure still remained. From these accounts, this should have a value of $2,500,000 to possibly $3,500,000 today.

During a "second stage" research project the author tried to pinpoint the location of the name Los Mimbres. It was not shown on modern charts, nor on earlier Spanish maps of Florida which were examined then. A Madrid naval historian finally found the following descriptions used by eighteenth-century geographers: "From Duck Key, which is the easternmost of the islands which form the Vacas, to Viboras [Long Key], there are five leagues and between them are three small mangrove islands . . ." and "Los Mimbres, which are three cays with reddish ravines almost north from one to the other, placed in a line, like the hops of a cannon ball, half a league apart, and have on them some very low shrubs." This spells out Conch Key and the two others between it and Duck Key.

Or does it? Jack Haskins believes otherwise. Starting with the description given above, he personally undertook a major "third stage" research in the Seville Archives during 1968 and moved the wreck clear across the Florida Straits to Matanilla Shoal. And for good reason:

> The term *Los Mimbres* is not really the most significant one used by the Spanish, as I found maps showing this site at Coffin's Patch, Roques, Orange Cay, Bimini, and Matanilla Shoal. The really important term was *Tumbado*. Manuel Martin Melgar said they went in search of the *Tumbado* at the *"desembocar"*—or "flowing out" of the canal of the Bahamas. Several maps will be found that show the *Tumbado* up at Matanilla Shoal. The name *Nuestra Señora de los Maravillas* I found mentioned only once in Somovilla's papers. Using this and applying it to the name Matanilla, and considering how names become bastardized and misspelled during the years, one can see how Matanilla Shoal got its name.
>
> The only disturbing thing about this theory is that Burt Webber came up with a sixteenth-century map which showed *Maravillas* and *Tumbado,* but from the information I have I can only conclude that either they are wrong about the map's date, or that it was upgraded at a later date. The salvage letters definitely mention diving at the point of the Isle of the Bahamas while awaiting good weather to go up to the *Tumbado* and the passage of the *Mimbres* wherein lies the *Almiranta* of Don Matías de Orellana.
>
> The Spanish were not the only salvors of the *Maravillas;* none other than that blasphemous braggart Capt. William Phips arrived on the scene in 1682. When he got there he found an enterprising captain from Boston on the wreck site with 80 divers and a lead diving bell. He drove them from the area. Upon parting, the Boston captain was heard to mutter he would not give one pound for any man's share of what was left on the wreck. Charles Salmon drew a map of the Bahama Bank as a result of the expedition with Phips. I know of several people who have tried unsuccessfully to find this wreck from Salmon's map, but the main reason they cannot find it is that the maps was purposely misdrawn to mislead any poachers.

And there it is—a $3,000,000 wreck by Coffin's Patch, or a site not worth a pound (but why draw the misleading map, then?) on Matanilla Shoal.

THE 1733 NEW SPAIN ARMADA DISASTER

One of the greatest losses ever suffered by an armada occurred on July 15, 1733, off the Florida Keys. General Rodrigo de Torres y Morales had sailed from Veracruz some two months earlier aboard his

Capitana, Rubí Segundo, with two other galleons and eighteen *naos* and smaller ships. At Havana a fourth galleon joined the New Spain armada. The twenty-two ships carried about 20,000,000 pesos, nearly all in Mexican silver. On July 14 General de Torres sensed the danger of a hurricane when the wind shifted abruptly to a freshening gale from the east. He ordered his captains to change course toward the southeast, heading up as close to the wind as possible in an attempt to return to Havana. The maneuver was carried out too late. During that night and the following day the hurricane tore through the long line of ships, driving them westward against the Florida Keys.

The General's *Capitana,* newly built at Havana and having a strong hull, grounded in 18 feet off Key Largo. The crew and passengers reached shore and walked to Upper Matecumbe, where water was to be found. They met survivors from other ships there. Later the *Rubí Segundo* was probably refloated (see "El Capitan") and returned to Havana. Fifteen 12-foot cannons dated 1732 and numerous cannon balls, which were recovered from the Key Largo Dry Rocks in 1957, may well have been jettisoned from this ship to lighten her. The sloop *Murgia* and two merchant *naos* were also refloated and saved. Two others, the *San Pedro* and *Rosario,* were swept all the way back to Cuba and wrecked there (see Cuba chapter). The other sixteen[2] ships —three galleons and thirteen *naos* and smaller vessels—were left in various stages of disintegration along the Keys, most of them between the outer reefs and the shore in depths of 8 to 40 feet.

The Spanish carried out a remarkably thorough job of salvaging the 1733 wrecks, considering the fact that only native skin divers were used. During the remainder of 1733 and 1734 12,000,000 pesos, nearly all in silver money and ingots, were recovered from the shallow wrecks. After that storms smashed them up so badly that skin divers could do no more. The project was abandoned with about $6,000,000 in cobs and ingots still scattered over the reefs and sand and buried in wreckage.

Arthur McKee, Jr., is a husky Florida-born ex-pay diver. Among treasure hunters his name is a household word, for Art McKee pioneered treasure diving and submarine archaeology off the Florida Keys and was responsible for putting the 1733 armada wrecks on the map. As a hard-hat professional diver working on the water pipeline to Key West during the 1950s, Art became interested in exploring for cannons and wrecks along the reefs. He was so successful at finding them that within a few years no less than twenty Spanish galleons and

[2] There are many conflicting accounts of this disaster. No two agree completely on the number, names, and fates of the armada's ships, and the salvage carried out by the Spanish. Frequent use of ships' nicknames complicates their identification. In reconstructing the following account, I have drawn information from the sources that seem the most authentic.

naos, English frigates, pirate vessels, and slavers had received his visits.

With a group of associates including Wes Bradley, Charles Brookfield, and Hugh Matheson, McKee began salvaging cannons and artifacts from his wrecks. Then, when he displayed his famous silver "sows" weighing 60, 70, and 75 pounds, ensuing publicity made him world-famous. One of the silver ingots was acquired by the Smithsonian Institution, where it lies in a place of honor surrounded by pieces of eight and other artifacts from Spanish wrecks. The Institution's Mendel L. Peterson became a frequent visitor to McKee's wrecks.

The state of Florida recognized his achievements as well. In 1952 McKee was awarded a salvage contract giving him exclusive rights to all wrecks in the huge area from: "Molasses Reef Light southwest direction along the edge of the Gulf Stream at the 10 fathom line to Alligator Reef Light, then northwesterly at 295° 15' from Alligator to a point at the upper tip of Lower Matecumbe Key, thence along the Atlantic shore line to Point Charles at Rock Harbor, thence along a line at 131° in a southeasterly direction to Molasses Reef Light." Under the contract's terms McKee was designated the state's agent to protect wrecks in his concession.

At just about this time, however, aqualungs were discovered by Americans. This plus publicity given to McKee's treasure finds, brought about a modern-day gold rush by professionals and amateurs alike from all over the continent. They swarmed out onto the reefs, digging every ballast mound they could find, even using dynamite, which destroyed priceless artifacts from which wrecks might have been identified. McKee was not given the tools to enforce his responsibility since he and a few others could not police dozens of sites miles apart.

His recoveries continued, however, and by 1959 he had brought up

A 3½-ton, 17-foot-long anchor
Twenty-one cannons, all iron
Hundreds of cannon balls, bar shot, grapeshot
Nautical instruments
Flintlock pistols, flintlock muskets, and lead bullets
Cutlasses, swords, and daggers
Pewter plates and drinking mugs, buckles and ornaments
Crockery, pottery, chinaware, glassware
Iron and copper spikes and nails, and pieces of wood from the
    hull under the stone ballast

and treasure:

Over a thousand silver coins, nearly all pesos dated before 1733
    including some rare and extremely valuable 1732 "Dos Mundos"
    milled dollars

Silver statues, candlesticks, silverware, knives, forks, and spoons, ornaments, a perfume flask, and buttons

Gold coins including a 1728 *pistole* minted at Lima, Peru

A gold earring mounting a 3-carat teardrop emerald

Gold rings, including one with three rubies of nine originally in
its setting.

On nearly every workable day McKee, accompanied by volunteer divers
from among his numerous friends, set out aboard the *Treasure Princess*
to spend eight or ten hours raising coral-encrusted chunks of ballast
and conglomerate. These were broken up later on shore and yielded
everything from copper nails to gems and coins.

As the accumulation of artifacts and treasure grew, McKee and some
interested financiers formed a corporation, McKee's Museum of Sunken
Treasure, Inc., and built the famous Fortress of Sunken Treasure at
Treasure Harbor, Plantation Key. In front of the fortress towers his
17-foot-tall anchor. Guns of every type and epoch are mounted around
the building. Inside, McKee's finest treasures, including two of the big
silver ingots and several top-condition 1732 pillar dollars, are displayed
for the many visitors. The fortress occupies much of McKee's time
and fully deserves the popularity it enjoys. Many of its treasures have
come from the best-known of the 1733 wrecks: "McKee's Galleon."

Today the 1733 armada wrecks have nearly all been located and
worked on by a procession of hundreds of SCUBA divers. Although
most of the known sites have been fairly thoroughly salvaged, artifacts
and money are still being recovered. It would be reasonable to say
that there is still "treasure" lying in the ballast of every one of these
ships, but only a few of the deeper and more recently located sites
still hold enough coins, jewelry, silver bars, and plate to offer prospects
of a major recovery. The chances of a big strike are probably better
in the deeper sand pockets around the ballast mounds, and along the
wreckage trails of the disintegrating hulls leading in from the outer
reefs.

Ballast mounds from which 1733-type artifacts and coins have been
recovered lie along the Keys all the way from Pacific Reef to Coffin's
Patch. Partly because of the early destruction and removal of so many
artifacts, positive identification of these sites is impossible. Yet there
are many valuable clues given in Spanish salvage records, including a
chart of the locations of nineteen vessels.[3] The "identifications" of
wreck sites that follow are those commonly accepted today. For much
of the material in the following pages I am indebted to Art McKee,
Carl J. Clausen, Tom Gurr, Russel Parks, and other wreck explorers
who have kindly contributed.

[3] Reproduced inside the jacket of Martin Meylach's book *Diving to a Flash of
Gold.*

EL CAPITÁN (29)

This is the famous "McKee's Galleon"—the source of many of the treasures, cannons, and artifacts in his fortress museum, and probably the most thoroughly photographed wreck in the world. It lies three and a half miles directly out from McKee's base at Treasure Harbor, between Crocker and Davis reefs, under 30 feet of clear water on a white sand sea bed. The huge ballast mound measures 100 by 40 feet in area, and rises 5 feet or more in height.

El Capitán is believed to have first been spotted by charter boat skipper Reggie Roberts, in 1948. Throughout the 1950s its mound was worked by Art McKee and his associates. It was the site of a famous confrontation between rival groups, and has since been dug by Tim Watkins and his Buccaneers, Martin Meylach, Don Thomas, Jim Conway, and just about every wreck explorer in the southeast U.S.A. It has yielded thousands of coins including pillar dollars and a rare 1733 gold escudo, gold rings, buckles and jewelry, artifacts of all kinds including pewter plates, silver utensils, clay pottery, a small armory of flintlock pistols and muskets and swords, hundreds upon hundreds of cannon balls, and several dozen heavy cannons. This salvaged material and the size of the wreck identifies it unmistakably as one of the 1733 armada galleons. The question is, which one is it?

The name El Capitán reflects the opinion of many divers and researchers who believe the wreck to be that of the Capitana, Rubí Segundo. According to this school, the Spanish were unable to refloat the command galleon after the hurricane. A reference to nearly 6,000,000 pesos having been salvaged from the Capitana, in a Spanish account, provides a strong argument in favor of this. The ballast mound could also be that of either the Infante or the San Joseph which are documented to have been lost in the vicinity. Regardless of the actual name, the widespread dissemination of photos and movies of "McKee's Galleon" and its artifacts recovered during the 1950s did much to dispel the public's illusions about old Spanish galleons lying on the bottom with creaking doors and intact stacks of treasure chests guarded by giant squids. It could well be said that Art McKee's salvage of El Capitán nearly twenty years ago ushered in the age of treasure diving and submarine archaeology in America. It can also be said that despite all the valuables recovered from the wreck to date, there are plenty more in that giant ballast mound and under the sand for hundreds of feet around it.

The SAN JOSÉ or SAN JOSEPH Y LOS ANIMAS (30)

Usually referred to as the San José, this galleon was also wrecked off Plantation Key and settled on a sandy bottom 30 feet deep between Davis and Little Conch reefs. Most of the people aboard reached shore safely, but by the time divers began their work her cargo was ruined and some of the registered treasure had been buried under wreckage where it could not be reached. After the Spanish departed, and with the passing of two and a half centuries, the heavy ballast mound settled deep into the bottom. Sand gradually built up and covered it, and patches of eel grass and weed spread over the sand. The last traces of the wreck disappeared from sight.

The *San José* came into the limelight in 1968 when Captain Tom Gurr, president of the Florida corporation Marine-Tech Salvage Company, Inc., announced the recovery of artifacts and money from the wreck. Captain Gurr had been researching the 1733 armada wrecks for ten years and had studied charts of their locations made by Spanish navigators after the hurricane. Of one, Tom Gurr says: "I found this location chart to be accurate within a mile or less, with the greatest error being in latitudes. With the help of this chart, and a proton magnetometer built by Fay Field of Treasure Salvors, Inc., made available to us under contractual agreement, we easily located these wrecks." At least twelve of the 1733 sites were surveyed by the Marine-Tech group.[4] "These wrecks were interesting to dive on, and most of them contain timbers and ballast, and skin divers still occasionally recover coins and artifacts. The *San José* and the 'Blunderbuss wreck' were the only virgins we worked."

In efforts to identify the *San José* correctly, Tom Gurr has carried out an in-depth research. One of many historical items discovered was a quotation from the journal of Edward McIver, chief mate of the brigantine *John*, who watched the armada sail from Havana in 1733. He referred to one of the vessels as a "New England built ship of three decks, had 36 guns, and mounted two teer or ports, no wast, 900 tuns." This description seems to fit the wreck, says Tom Gurr, which "was identified by an authority as the *San Joseph y los Animas*. The identification was based on the location, size, cargo, and construction. It was assumed that the ship was English and built probably in the year 1728 (the date on a salvaged lead water pipe) as her construction was white pine and oak. The fact that her name retained the English spelling of 'Joseph' rather than the Spanish 'José' also indicates possible purchase from England."

The site was located by Tom Gurr's group on May 27, 1968, when, after the magnetometer contact, Rudolph Palladino descended to the sea bed with a Bludworth detector. The bottom was flat sand covered with thick eel grass with roots in mats over 18 inches thick. A marine biologist later stated that the grass had not been disturbed in 150 years. There was no ballast mound or other indication of a wreck, yet

---

[4] Among locations identified by Tom Gurr is "*La Capitana El Rubí*," indicating, at least, that the *Capitana* was stranded when the chart was made.

the "needle on the dial went crazy." Digging with his hands below a
strong detector reading, Palladino encountered ballast buried under 1
to 2 feet of sand.

The salvage commenced in mid-July. Working from the M/V *L. R.
Parker*, a 90-foot diesel-powered Chesapeake lugger, and a 36-foot former
Navy captain's gig, Marine-Tech's ten-man team of contract divers
began a systematic excavation of the site. They used Desco rigs except
when the "mailbox" was working, at which time SCUBA gear was
substituted to avoid entangling air hoses. Dredging was done with
both the 30-inch "blaster" mounted on the gig and three 8-inch air
lifts which were found more effective because of the depth. Comments
ex-Vigo Bay treasure diver Howard Williams on the equipment: "We
use a simple lightweight aluminum tube for the old *supidor* air lift.
Works wonders! Turn on the air and it stands right up. The mailbox
is a 90° angle deflector on the stern of the gig. It hinges up out
of the water or down over the launch's screw. It really does blast
volcanoes in the bottom. In 20 feet of water, twenty minutes hovering
over a spot running the screw and the hole is really deep."

Describing the salvage, Tom Gurr says: "We removed over 3 feet of
sand overburden on the west end of the wreck and over 6 feet on the
east, after cutting through the growth of eel grass. On top of the
intact ballast pile were located four swords, two flintlock pistols, a
number of complete urns, bowls, and animal figurines of clay pottery.
The wreck area is approximately 150 feet in length and 80 in width.
There are twenty-three cannons scattered over the wreck, ranging from
6 feet to 9 feet in length. Two anchors were found under the ballast
at the east end, one 12 feet long and the other 18 feet through the
shank. Twenty-five gold wedding rings were found in the ballast
near the top. Silver coins were scattered all through. About 200 yards
to the south we located the rudder, which still had the 25-foot shaft,
pintels, and the lead-lined timbers intact. Also we found four cannons,
all 7 feet long, under the rudder. They were covered with coral. The
trunnions are all low and near the rear.

"We found 950 silver coins in all sizes, most in bad condition of
sulfide. Coins found in one cluster were in mint condition and we
found several rare pillar dollars and *recortados* dated 1733 with the
'F' assayer. One gold coin was found: a one escudo, Seville mint, no
date." Other salvaged material included eighteen silver plates all hall-
marked before 1700, small black glass figurines believed to be of Chinese
origin, a barber's kit with ivory comb, two compasses, a pewter plate
dated 1728, toys, carvings, and a human skull.

Like "McKee's Galleon," the site was believed outside the original
three-mile limit and Tom Gurr's work was carried out from a "doc-

umented vessel in international waters with a Federal salvage license to engage in this business." The situation was abruptly changed with Judge Aquilino Lopez' decision extending the coastline to the outer reefs. Considerable publicity was given to the subsequent four-month legal battle, which was terminated with an agreement under which recoveries to that date were turned over to the state. Marine-Tech resumed salvaging the *San José* under a state contract on a 50–50 basis, and is entitled to the usual 75-25 split on salvages from other sites; Tom Gurr's associate, and the author's old friend, F. Herrick Herrick, commented, "Tom's got a real humdinger. The good stuff's coming up and we think we'll be in on the bullion soon!"

The "*GALLO INDIANA*" (31)

Nicknamed "Cock of the Indies," this 58-gun galleon was the *Almiranta* of the armada. She had been constructed in Italy ten years earlier. During the hurricane, the galleon grounded on the Víboras —the section including Long Key and Lower Matecumbe. All her crew and passengers reached safety, and she was fairly thoroughly salvaged by the Spanish later. The *Almiranta* may lie just off the southern tip of Lower Matecumbe near a spot where armada coins have been washing ashore for many years. Some of these are 1731, 1732, and 1733 pillar dollars. One, dated 1732, was recently sold by the finder for $2900.

The *INFANTE* (32)

Another foreign-built galleon, this ship was purchased in Genoa in 1724. The 60-gun *Infante* was carried into shallow water, only 12 feet deep, and the people aboard reached safety ashore. Spanish salvors recovered her registered treasure of some 6,000,000 pesos and much of the other cargo, as well.

The ballast mound, lying just off Little Conch Reef, was one of the earliest found and has been repeatedly worked by dozens of SCUBA divers. During visits dating from 1955 Art McKee moved tons of the 7-foot-high coral-cemented ballast, and recovered many coins including at least a dozen Dos Mundos dollars, and truckloads of artifacts. Louis Ullian visited the wreck in 1946 while still a teen-ager. Craig Hamilton and Warren Conway, with other divers, made recoveries during 1955–63 including six 9-pounders, thousands of cannon balls, bar shot, grape canisters, iron grenades, pottery and glass fragments, a flintlock musket and pistol. They also salvaged treasure: money, gold, and silver rings, jeweled cuff links, Chinese porcelain, ivory fans, and a silver helmet. Tim Watkins and the Buccaneers worked the ballast. In the 1960s Russell Swanson, Dick Hall, Martin Meylach,

Don Thomas, and others raised silver cobs, all kinds of artifacts, and a sail needle (sold for $75). During 1965 the Royal Fifth Company group of Ray Manieri, Brad Pattern, Bob Weller, and Pat Patterson worked the ballast on weekends with an air lift from their dive boat *Big Fisherman*, and recovered another pillar dollar among their salvaged artifacts. *El Infante* is still being dug, and artifacts and occasional coins still turn up in the ballast and in masses of conglomerate in the sand bottom as far as 200 feet away.

The SAN FERNANDO (33)

This merchant *nao* settled off Coffin's Patch and most of the people were saved. After she broke up, Spanish divers recovered a large part of the cargo. A site believed to be either this ship or the *San Ignacio* is well known to Florida divers, who have raised from it silver plates, china, and silver cobs, and continue to salvage artifacts and money. One noteworthy find was reported by Chuck Mitchell of Key Largo, who has dived on many of the 1733 wrecks from the 65-foot boat *Quest* and spent time with the Treasure Salvors group. After becoming interested in the *San Fernando*, he writes, "We moved to Marathon where Captain Jack Steffaney, my son and I dove for five months before we hit it. We found only forty coins, but these included two 1732 pillar dollars plus many dated cobs and 4-, 2- and 1-reales, as well as a silver sword, a hand-carved Onyx sand shaker, shoe buckles, five beautiful pewter plates, dead eyes, door hasps, cannon balls, two 6-foot English minions and last but not least, two of the world's rarest artifacts: two miniature cannons 7¼ inches long. They weigh 2 pounds each and have a belled muzzle, reinforcing rings, low trunnions, and a pair of dolphins complete with eyes, mouth and tongue. Directly behind the dolphins is a touch hole and the crest and royal seal of King Philip V. I have not had them tested, but they appear to be silver."

"EL SUECO DE ARIZON" (34)

This *nao* grounded with her deck awash, and the people and much of the cargo were saved. Her site is believed to be marked by scattered ballast, only 7–9 feet deep, on the flats 1500 yards south of Conch Key. Located from a Spanish chart by Martin Meylach and Don Thomas, it has been worked by Dick Williams' Marathon Salvage Company, the Royal Fifth team, Treasure Salvors, and many other SCUBA divers. Using crowbars, hammers, and air lifts, modern salvors have broken up much of the main ballast mound and recovered artifacts of all kinds and numerous coins. Among material salvaged: olive jar sherds, porcelain and glass fragments, cannon balls, bar shot, fire bricks —and several hundred coins, mostly 4- and 8-real Mexico mint cobs dated 1720–33, and about a dozen pillar dollars, of which the state of Florida has received 25 per cent. Artifacts are scattered over an area of some 500 by 70 yards, amid scattered sponges, sea fans, turtle grass, and light coral growths. Crevices in the hardpan bottom around the wreck could hide other caches of coins.

LA FLORIDANA (35)
This sloop broke up near Windley Key, with only one survivor. Her cargo was well salvaged soon after the disaster, and treasure seekers would probably waste their time digging this wreck.

The SAN IGNACIO (36)
The passengers, crew, and most of the cargo were saved from this *nao* after she settled, deck awash, in about 12 feet of water off Duck Key. It is unlikely that many artifacts or coins remain in the ballast (see *San Fernando*).

The SAN FELIPE (37)
Another of the merchant *naos*, she grounded between Long Key and Lower Matecumbe. The people were saved and the cargo completely salvaged by the Spanish.

EL PODER DE DIOS (38)
This *nao* was battered to pieces, with several people lost, against a reef some three miles southeast of the southwest tip of Lower Matecumbe. Part of her cargo was salvaged, but there should be fair pickings in her 20-foot-deep ballast.

The SAN FRANCISCO (39)
A ballast mound 14 feet deep south of the southwest tip of Lower Matecumbe may be the remains of this *nao*. Spanish salvors recovered nearly all the cargo after the people aboard reached safety. The Buccaneers salvaged artifacts from a wreck which may be this one.

The ANGUSTIAS (also CHAVEZ) (40)
This merchant *nao* went aground near the southern tip of Plantation Key, just off Snake Creek, in very shallow water. The crew and passengers were saved, and most of the cargo was carried off the wreck by the Spanish. The small ballast mound is not interesting for treasure, but has occasionally yielded pewter and artifacts since the Roberts brothers discovered it from the air.

The "BLUNDERBUSS WRECK" (41)
Lying about two miles from the main ballast of the *Chavez* is

wreckage believed to be another portion of the same ship. It has yielded a number of small bronze cannons, which give the site its name.

The SAN PEDRO (42)

One of the wrecks was carried in across Alligator Reef and settled in Hawk Channel off Indian Key, southeast of the upper tip of Lower Matecumbe. The people and much of the cargo were saved. This site is usually referred to as the *San Pedro*, which was also documented as having been swept to Cuba. Despite having been thoroughly dug by everyone in the business, and having given up thousands of 1-real cobs dated 1731–33, the site still hides some treasure. Recently Captain Bob Klein found as unusual clump of ½- and ¼-real silver coins here, and there are doubtless more coins in sand pockets under the hardpan sea bed.

EL LINGUE POPULO (43)

This 14-gun corvette was swamped and sank with no survivors. The Spanish are not believed to have carried out any significant salvage. Her ballast mound may be that near the south end of Pacific Reef, near the reef ledge where seven cannons were found. Another seven guns in the wreckage add up to the right number. Martin Meylach, Bob Morgan, Carl Fredericks and Craig Hamilton have raised several cannons. There may be as much as $50,000 still buried in the ballast pile and widely scattered wreckage of this little ship.

"EL AVISO" (44)

Ten feet deep, on the south end of Pacific Reef, lies a ballast mound with some wood that is believed to be the remains of this consulate dispatch boat. The Spanish salvaged this wreck, and although several 9-pounders were recovered recently from 200 yards south of the ballast, any hope of treasure would be optimism in the extreme.

"LOS TRES PUENTES" (45)

Nicknamed "the Three-Decker" by the Spanish and more simply "the Tres" by the Florida diving fraternity, this *nao* was stranded, deck awash, in fairly shallow water. All of the people made shore safely, and during subsequent Spanish salvage work most of the valuable cargo was recovered. The ballast mound corresponding to recorded information about this ship was discovered by Martin Meylach, Don Thomas, Art Sapp, and Don Gurgiolo during an aerial search from Gurgiolo's plane. The ballast mound was covered over, but a grayish discoloration of the sand bottom protruding from a grassy area drew the experienced wreck hunters' attention to the site midway between Crocker and Alligator reefs, off Islamorada.

The long ballast mound was attacked by several salvage groups, who recovered cannon balls and bar shot, pottery shards, and generally uninteresting wreckage. Later Meylach and Thomas airlifted under the grass and struck a rich lode of conglomerate. They salvaged many coins, gold medallions, pewter ware, artifacts of every type, and several sand-cast silver ingots weighing 11 to 17 pounds. Meylach tells the story of his strike in his book *Diving to a Flash of Gold.*

Although "the Tres" itself is well salvaged, there could well be money and valuable artifacts under the surrounding sand.

LA CARMEN or HERRERA or HERRENA (46)

This merchant *nao* stranded less than a mile from the *Tres Puentes* on the inshore edge of Hawk Channel in three fathoms of water. The ballast was located from the air by the Roberts brothers and has been worked by Don Gurgiolo, Albert Welberry, the Buccaneers, Meylach, Thomas, and many others. No treasure to speak of was recovered, but amid the salvaged cannon balls and bar shot, pottery shards, barrel hoops, clay bowls, and animal hides appeared hundreds of small clay animals. These eventually caused the site to be given still another name: "the Figurine wreck."

"EL LERRI" (47)

A little ship, this pink was carried into water 15 feet deep one mile southeast of the middle of Lower Matecumbe. Many people drowned. She was well salvaged after the hurricane, as is attested to by the poor pickings she has offered to recent salvors.

H.M.S. WINCHESTER (48)[5]

In September 1695 this 60-gun English warship, carrying some loot taken in raids against the French in Haiti, sank during a hurricane off Key Largo with all 400 of her crew. Her wreckage was discovered in 1940 by Charles Brookfield and a friend. From the coral-buried ballast they raised cannons—by which the wreck was identified—money and silver plate, and a large collection of artifacts. The *Winchester* has since been visited by many divers and one was of McKee's favorite training grounds for apprentice divers. There is probably very little of value left on her.

The NAO (19)

There have been several reports that a Spanish ship, unidentified by name, was wrecked on the Bamboo Banks about 1720. These shoals

---

[5] The *Winchester* and *Looe*, while not treasure wrecks, have played an important role in the furthering of Florida Keys treasure hunting by the interest which their discoveries created.

are located south of Matecumbe and very likely hold the remains of other lost vessels as well.

H.M.S. *LOOE* (50)[6]

In 1950 Captain Bill Thompson, of Marathon, Florida, and Dr. and Mrs. George Crile, Jr., spotted a wreck 25 feet deep off Looe Reef. They were soon working on the site, bringing up among other things 6-pounder and 12-pounder cannons, bearing the Broad Arrow and Rose and Crown marks and a Swedish coin dated 1720. From these and other artifacts Mendel Peterson, who examined the site, placed the wreck as a small English warship of the 1720-50 period. Checking through the registry of lost British warships he came across the notation: "February 5, 1744, *Looe*, 44 guns . . . lost in America." The name of the reef, like so many others, had been taken from the ship which it sent to the bottom.

The ANCIENT CANNON (51)

In 1957 Captain Hugh Brown of Snake Creek Dock, Islamorada, recovered an ancient cannon from a wreck 60 miles west of Key West.

The ENGLISH MORTAR (52)

In 1958 the Miami "Glug Glugs" raised a 700-pound, 4½-foot English mortar which they spotted 50 feet deep between Long Key and Tennessee Reef.

The "RING WRECK" (53)

Craig Hamilton raised 18 Swedish cannons dated 1778 and 1779 from a ballast pile off Ajax Reef. A huge iron ring protruding from the mound—probably that of the ship's anchor which is buried—created the name. Nothing in the treasure category was reported located on the wreck, which is probably a schooner.

The CARYSFORT REEF CANNONS (54)

Craig Hamilton found another five cannons, of unknown date and nationality, off Carysfort Reef in 1957.

The PACIFIC REEF ENGLISH WRECK(55)

A ballast mound off Pacific Reef has yielded two carronades, cast in England in 1811, as well as two cutlass blades and other artifacts.

The SHIP CHANNEL WRECK (56)

Cannons and anchors have been reported raised from the bottom

6 See previous footnote.

of the channel into Biscayne Bay, leading to the likelihood that a wreck lies nearby.

BLACK CAESAR'S SPANISH PRIZES (57)
About 200 yards off the shore of Elliott Key lie three wreck sites believed to be those of Spanish ships captured and burned by the pirate "Black Caesar." They were no doubt thoroughly looted.

The "PILLAR DOLLAR WRECK" (58)
Named from the pillar dollars which have been recovered from this site, the wreck lies just northeast of Turtle Reef. It is believed to have sunk about 1772.

The "ALLIGATOR REEF SEVENTEENTH-CENTURY GALLEON" (59)
Captain Leo Barker of Miami and Burt Webber, Jr., searched the vicinity of Alligator Reef in 1962 for the wreck of a seventeenth-century galleon or *nao* which Captain Barker knew of. The crew dived from the 80-foot M/V *Norma*.

The FOWEY ROCKS TREASURE (60)
There have been a number of reports that silver ingots and coins were recovered from the ocean bottom off Fowey Rocks, but again proof seems to be lacking.

One of the most popular fishermen's tales is the old perennial about the man who fell asleep in his boat and awoke to find it grounded on a sand or coral bank (there are variations). He stepped out to push the craft off, noting that he was knee-deep in gray ingots which covered the reef. Thinking that they were worthless lead (or iron) he piled a dozen or so in his boat on a whim. Later he discovered that they were silver and has been dedicating his life ever since to trying to find that spot again. The usually given site of the fisherman's trove is off Pigeon Key, although other locations as distant as the Bahamas are heard.

Out of curiosity friends of Bob Nesmith made a serious attempt to track this tale down to its source but had no luck. It bears a definite similarity to an account of ingots piled on a reef told by a Spaniard many years before (see Chapter 14).

The GALLEON WRECKAGE TRAIL (61)
In his book *Diving to a Flash of Gold* Martin Meylach tells of a trail of wreckage indicative of a Spanish *nao* or galleon running inshore from the east end of Delta Shoal. Although no ballast mound as such

has been located, the trail has plenty of clumps of cannon balls, cannons, ship's fittings, pottery fragments, and other signs of a disintegrating vessel. Meylach reports that lumps of silver (but no coins) have been found amid this wreckage.

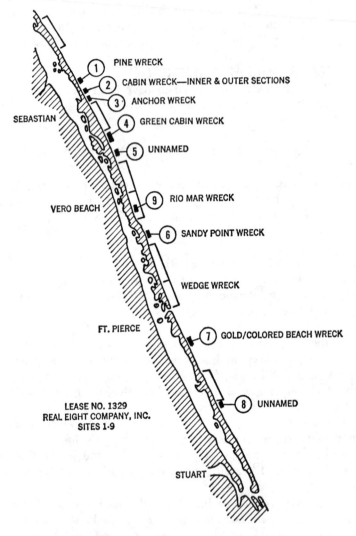

MAP 4   Florida—the big one.

THE 1715 ARMADA and REAL EIGHT

This is the big one. Never before has any treasure-recovery project approached Kip Wagner's Real Eight Company, Inc., in scope of operations, professional organization, depth of highly qualified personnel, volume of research, inventiveness and application of modern technology, contribution to undersea archaeology—and in value and variety of salvaged treasure. The intrinsic worth of bullion raised from the *Laurentic* and *Niagara* may still be greater; but how can comparisons be made when a 7-ounce gold ornament nets $50,000 at auction and one single coin—a gold 8-escudo "royal"—sells for $10,500? With recoveries exceeding $5,000,000 already in hand, Real Eight has only scratched the surface of the riches lying in its nine exclusive salvage zones off Florida and the growing number of contracted treasure wrecks off South America and the Bahamas.

In his book *Pieces of Eight* Kip Wagner presents a fascinating story of his gradual involvement with the 1715 armada and subsequent developments through 1966. Much of the following is enlarged upon in lively detail in this book. I am indebted to Kip (who wrote the Foreword to this edition of the *Guide*), and to his associates Bob Marx, Harry Cannon, and Dan Thompson, for supplying details of Real Eight's remarkable accomplishments to date.

Background

When Kip Wagner moved his family to Wabasso, Florida, after World War II to go into construction work, thoughts of treasure hunting had probably never crossed his mind. As his circle of friends grew he heard the usual tales of coins found on beaches off Vero and Sebastian, and of old Spanish galleon wrecks, but it was not until a friend took him beachcombing after a squall that he became mildly interested. During an hour's stroll the friend picked up seven irregular blackened coins. Some had strange markings.

Wagner became friendly with Steadman Parker, a retired ship's captain with doubloon fever. When Parker proposed forming a salvage team with three other men, he agreed to participate. In June 1949 they set up camp on a nearby beach. Eighty feet offshore, and only 4 feet deep, lay wreckage. They approached its salvage as engineers. One of the group with a dragline bulldozer shoved sand out into the shallow water until a causeway had been built to the half-buried wood. At low tide he ran the dozer out, scooped up sand from under water, and dumped this on the beach. The others sifted through the pile. They found ship's timbers honeycombed with teredo holes, metal spikes, and rusty iron. When the tide came in the waves washed away the sand pier. At next low tide the process was repeated with the same results. After two months of backbreaking labor the group disbanded. Their salvaged treasure was one 1649 copper maravedi.

Years later Wagner realized that the "wreck" was only superstructure that had washed in to shore. He had meanwhile bought a $15 war

surplus SCR-625 metal detector and used it during weekends along the
eight-mile beach between Sebastian and Wabasso. After breaking in
the instrument on an assortment of tin cans and rusty iron, he found
his first Spanish cob in 1951. Before long several dozen others, and a
few gold coins, had been collected. Other beachcombers told him that
the old money had been buried in the sand. Wagner wondered.

Gradually, prodded by discussions with his close friend Dr. Kip
Kelso, he developed theories about its origin. Since most of the money
was found on the tidal zone of the beach, and often on the sand after
storms, it must have washed in from the sea; since the coins were
concentrated in "lodes" at points along the shore, a source, probably
a wreck, must lie off each area; because the coins were all dated
1715 or earlier—if the first two premises were correct—a fleet of
treasure ships had been wrecked along here that year or slightly afterward.

Wagner sent a 1714 silver cob to a marine expert with a request
for information. The reply confirmed the loss of a Spanish plate fleet
in 1715—but two hundred miles away on the Florida Keys. Meanwhile
Mr. Henry Gruenthall, president of the American Numismatic Society,
saw the coin and remarked on its rarity. Numismatic expert Robert
Nesmith, who made a special visit to study Wagner's coin collection,
ventured a prophetic opinion: "These are the most important finds from
a Spanish plate fleet ever made in Florida, both historically and numismatically, as the future will prove . . ." From then on, Nesmith was
a close associate. He has contributed importantly to this account.

Research

"Doc" Kelso and Wagner began a massive research, which continues
today. The first information needed was the actual location of the 1715
shipwrecks. They dug into historical records in local libraries, at Miami,
Key West, and the University of Florida. When these failed to deliver,
Kelso visited the Library of Congress, where the helpful staff introduced him to Fernández Duro's *Armada Española*. This valuable work
acquainted him with general details of the armada's disaster and partial
salvage. Kelso then found a monograph on Spanish plate fleets by
Professor Irving Rouse which referred to *A Concise Natural History
of East and West Florida* published in 1775 by Bernard Romans. A
copy was located in the Rare Books Section. After months of patient
study, Kelso reaped rich rewards as he read: "Directly opposite the
mouth of the St. Sebastians River happened the shipwreck of the Spanish
Admiral, who was the northermost wreck . . . all laden with specie
and plate . . . drove ashore and lost on this coast, between this place
and the bleach-yard, in 1715 . . . repeatedly found pistareens and double

1. Hurricanes sank two galleon fleets in the Florida channel in 1715 and 1733. *Courtesy Robert I. Nesmith.*

2. Sir Henry Morgan's attack on Maracaibo. *Courtesy Robert I. Nesmith.*

3. The Submarine Search Magnetometer being adjusted by the author for its simplest manner of use from a rowboat.

4. Bob Marx holding tow head of Mac Dowell Mark 3 Magnetometer ready fo launch. *Courtesy James E. MacDowell.*

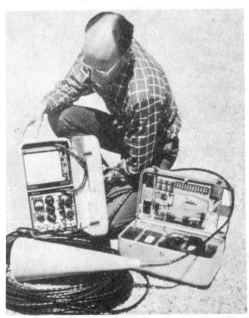

5. Fay Field with magnetometer he developed for searching for underwater wrecks. *Courtesy Treasure Salvors, Inc.*

6. Discoverer II is a true flux-gate magn tometer. Built by A.Z.A. Scientific, In this professional instrument directs its hig sensitivity toward the tasks of specific r covery, wreck debris mapping, and pipeli tracing. It is shown 140 feet down in t South Pacific. *Photo by* Dive *(New Ze land). Courtesy of A.Z.A. Scientific, Inc.*

7. Hand-held magnetometer in use to pinpoint metal in wreck. *Courtesy Treasure Salvors, Inc.*

. Varian cesium magnetometer with ower inverter, console readout, and anaogue recorder. This is the magnetometer et up as operated by Burt D. Webber, Jr., irector of Continental Exploration Corpoation. *Photo by Ken Matz, Marathon, lorida.*

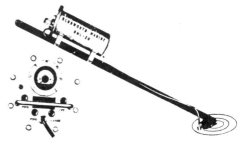

9. The Bludworth Marine Underwater Metal Locator.

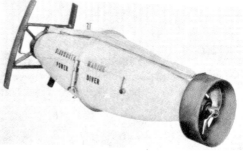

10. The Bludworth Marine "Power Diver."

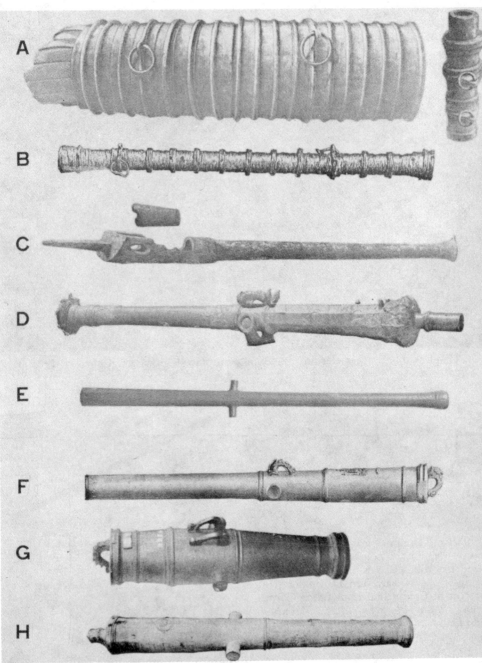

11. Representative cannons described in Chapter 5.

12. One of Captain Cook's cannons being unloaded at Cairns. *Photo by Wynne Law, 62 Abbott Street, Cairns.*

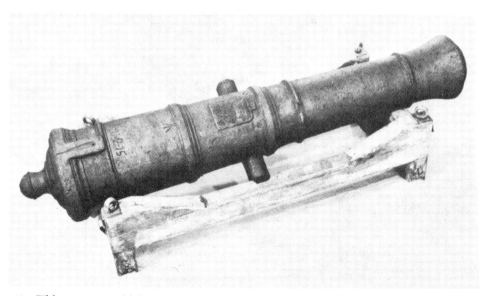

13. This cannon, which was preserved by the Defence Standard Laboratories, Melbourne, is seen to be in an excellent state of preservation after 199 years under the sea. The crowned monogram "G.R. 2," the chiseled weight of the cannon, 11-2-15, in hundredweights, quarterweights, and pounds, and the British Crown Property "broad arrow" are all clearly visible. *Courtesy Australian Government Department of Supply, Defence Standard Laboratories, Melbourne.*

14. C.R.I.S. divers recovering a two-thousand-year-old Roman amphora. *Courtesy A. Marin.*

15. Diver moving dredge pickup into position at seventeenth-century wreck site. *Photo by Anatole Szulga and Lee Mercer for Fathom Expeditions.*

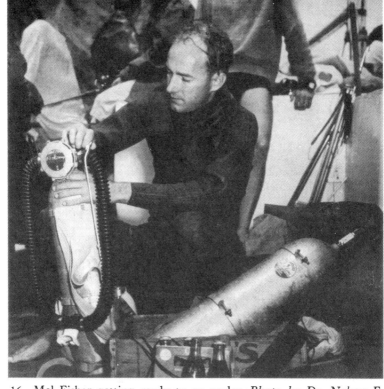

16. Mel Fisher getting ready to go under. *Photo by Dr. Nelson E. Mathison, Long Beach, California.*

17. Tim Alsop watches as Carl Ade hauls the exhaust end of the hydrolift as Expeditions Unlimited works the remains of the Spanish galleon *Genovesa*, located off the Pedro coast in the Caribbean. *Photo by Coles Phinizy*, Sports Illustrated.

18. Kip Wagner inspecting silver plate, brass pestle, and ceramic sherds *(17 wrecks). Courtesy Real Eight Company, Inc.*

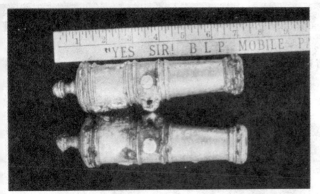

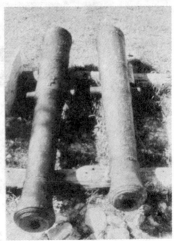

19. Charles E. Mitchell of Key Largo, Florida, found these 7¼-inch silver cannons on the scattered wreckage of the Spanish galleon *San Fernando*, after five months' work. The cannons weigh 2 pounds apiece and have twin arched dolphins centered over the trunnions. The dolphins are complete with eyes, mouth, tongue, and scales. Directly behind the dolphins is the touchhole and centered over the touchhole is the crest and royal seal of King Philip V of Spain. These cannons are identical and more than likely were a gift from the captain of the *San Fernando* to the King of Spain. *Photo by Robert Paulding.*

20. 1733 cannons, off *El Tyrri*, recovered by Ray Maneri. *Courtesy Jack Haskins.*

21. 1733 cannon, off the *Chavez*, recovered by Hugh Brown. *Courtesy Jack Haskins.*

22. 1733 cannon, off the *Herrera*, recovered by Hugh Brown. *Courtesy Jack Haskins.*

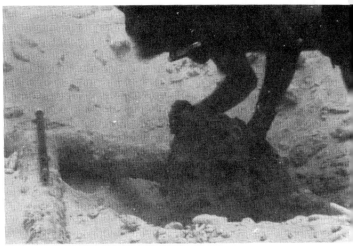

23. 1733 anchor, off *El Capi-tán*, recovered by Art Mc-Kee. *Courtesy Jack Haskins.*

24. Eleven-foot ancient woodstocked anchor found by Jack Haskins. *Courtesy Jack Haskins.*

25. Four lead Roman anchor stocks recovered by C.R.I.D. divers off the Costa Brava, Spain, in 1958. *Courtesy Roberto Diaz.*

26. Remains of one of McKee's Spanish galleons lost in the hurricane of July 15, 1733. All that remains of the wreck is a large pile of rock ballast, covering tons of coral-encrusted relics. Note cannon at top left and timbers uncovered from below sand while salvaging the wreck. *Courtesy Robert I. Nesmith.*

RESVMEN DE LO SALVADO EN TODOS

LOS NAVIOS DE LA FLOTA DE NVEVA ESPAñA, DEL GARGO DEL
feñor Theniente General Don Rodrigo de Torres y Morales, que naufragaron en los
Cayos antes de Boca de la Canàl de Bahama, el 15. de Julio de 1733. y regulacion del
valor de los frutos, para cargarles à fu refpecto el correfpondiente gafto de buzeo, condu-
cion, y beneficio, cuyo importe fe ha de reintegrar al Regiftro de Capitana, y Almiranta,
por averfe hecho de efte caudal el fuplemento en el Puerto de la Habana...............

GAPITANA.

En Plata acuñada, labrada, en pafta, y algun Oro de
    cuenta de particulares.................................... 5.258ɮ035.ps.

En 4145. arrobas, 23. libras de Grana, las 4078.
    arrobas 23. libras, 5. onzas, mojada avaluada à
    25. pefos la arroba, y las 67. arrobas feca à 60.
    pefos, que toda monta................................ 105ɮ981.ps.6.

En 995. arrobas 4. libras de Añil, mojado avaluado
    à 4. pefos, 4. reales arroba........................... 4ɮ478.ps.1.½.

727ɮ733 ps.1½.rs. En Plata acuñada, y barras de cuenta de fu Magef-
    tad.. ɮ

......ɮ......ps......... En 584. planchas de Cobre, con 290. quintales, 90.
    libras, idem... ɮ

                                 5.368ɮ494.ps.7.¾.

ALMIRANTA.

En Plata acuñada, labrada, y
    Oro, de cuenta de particu-
    lares...........................4.998ɮ397.ps.6.⅞

En 4820. arrobas de Grana,
    las 4065. arrobas mojada,
    242. arrobas mezclada con
    feca, y las 513. arrobas fin
    mojar avaluada, las dos pri-
    meras calidades à 25. pefos,
    y la vltima à 60. pefos....... 138ɮ455.ps.......⎰ 5.143ɮ245.ps.2⅓.

En 1420. arrobas 14. libras
    Añil mojado, avaluado à 4.
    pefos 4. reales arroba........ 6ɮ392.ps.4.....

729ɮ951.ps.5.rs. En Plata acuñada, labrada, y
    en pafta de cuenta de S.M. ....ɮ..........

......ɮ.......... En 439. planchas de Cobre
    con 232. quintales, 85. li-
    bras de cuenta, idem........... ɮ

1.457ɮ680.ps.6.½.

IN₂

27. A page from the actual salvage record of the 1733 fleet. *Courtesy Jack Haskins.*

28. The *Wasa* mounted on a concrete pontoon in the framework of the aluminum building that now houses her. In the background, left, old Stockholm. *Photo courtesy of the Maritime Museum and the Warship Wasa, Stockholm.*

29. The lower gun deck after completed excavation. View of the lower gun deck toward the bow of the *Wasa*. The mud that was in the ship is taken out and the decks are washed. Along the starboard side a gun carriage is lashed in front of each gun port. Through the square-shaped holes in the foreground light and air were let down to the lower decks. The huge horizontal beam in the background is the bitt around which the anchor cable was lashed. *Photo courtesy of the Maritime Museum and the Warship Wasa, Stockholm.*

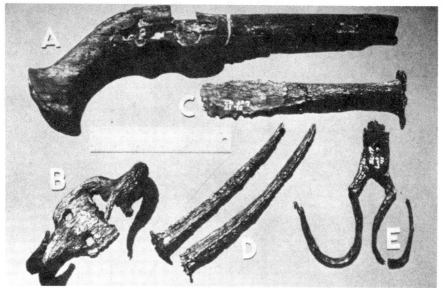

30. Artifacts cleaned and preserved in the new Research and Preservation Laboratory of the Florida Division of Archives and History. These items, which include the Miquelet pistol stock (A), and shears handles (E), were recovered from a wreck of the 1715 fleet (Florida UW 1). *Courtesy Florida Division of Archives and History.*

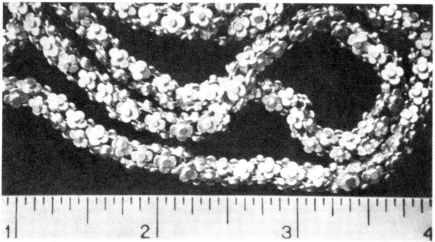

31. Complicated-pattern gold chain recovered from a 1715 fleet vessel (Florida UW 1). *Courtesy Florida Division of Archives and History.*

32. Obverse of Mexico-mint, 8-escudo gold coin of 1702 recovered from a wreck (Florida UW 1) of a ship of the flota portion of the 1715 fleet. *Courtesy Florida Division of Archives and History.*

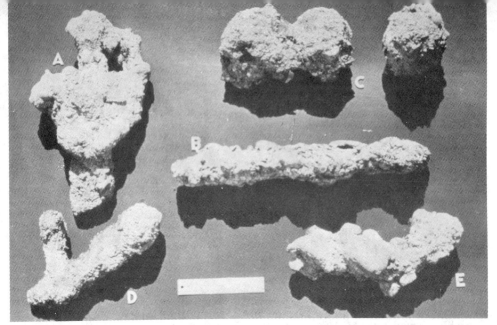

33. Uncleaned artifacts recovered from Florida site UW 1, first *patache* of the flota portion of the 1715 fleet, lost south of Cape Kennedy. Note the encrusted sword handle (A) and the silver coins adhering to the two cannon balls (C). *Courtesy Florida Division of Archives and History.*

34. Carl J. Clausen, Florida State Marine Archaeologist, examining wreck site UW 022, the remains of *El Infante*, one of the Spanish warships of the 1733 flota lost in the Florida Keys. *Courtesy Florida Division of Archives and History.*

35. Robert Sténuit, who discovered and salvaged the *Girona*, with a gold chain from the wreck. *Photo Sténuit.*

36. Mel Fisher and Moe Molinar with one of the gold disks found at a 1715 wreck site. *Courtesy Treasure Salvors, Inc.*

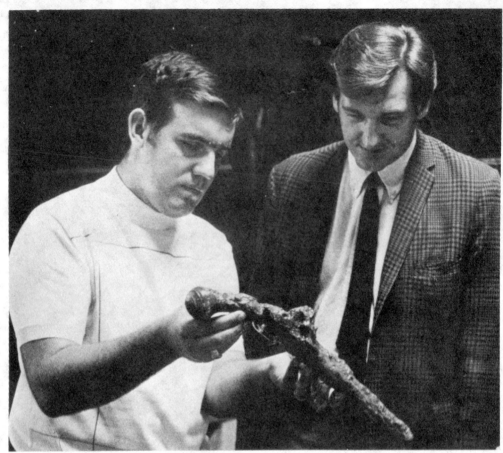

37. Carl J. Clausen (right) and Allen R. Saltus examining a flintlock pistol recovered from the site of the *San José* (Florida UW 36), wrecked in the Florida Keys in 1715. *Courtesy Florida Division of Archives and History.*

38. *Le Duc de Beaufort* being hoisted ashore. Photo by "Chippy" Pearce.

pistareens, which kinds of money probably yet remaining in the wrecks, are sometimes washed up by the surf." Inside the book's flap was a map that accurately detailed the coast and noted, at the site of Sebastian Creek: "Opposite this River, perished, the Admiral, commanding the Plate Fleet 1715, the rest of the fleet . . . between this & ye Bleech Yard." The "bleech yard" was at the mouth of the St. Lucie River.

Kelso later learned the story of the shipwrecked survivors' ordeal from documents at the Florida Historical Society at St. Augustine. Meanwhile Wagner, after unsuccessful attempts to obtain information from Havana and Mexico by mail, began a long and rewarding correspondence with Dr. José de la Peña, then curator of Seville's Archivo General de Indias. The first results were an incredible three thousand frames of microfilmed documents! When the pages were projected on the screen Wagner and Kelso looked at each other blankly. Although both were fluent in Spanish, not a word made sense. The writing was in archaic Spanish. They could not find anyone to translate and resigned themselves to deciphering the old script. Once they recognized the letters, words became legible, and after months of study they were able to read sentences. From those microfilmed pages unfolded the entire history of the 1715 armada, the disaster, the salvage work, and locations of many of the wrecks.

Preparation

For orientation purposes Wagner decided to find the Spanish base camp, which he had probably passed many times. Fortified with the new information, he combed the high ground in an area south of Sebastian Inlet. His detector's earphones whined frequently, and just as often he tossed aside metallic trash. Then one day, while walking with his dog, he noticed an unusual depression with a water hole surrounded by sharp-spiked palmetto groves. As salt-water springs were common here, and a cursory search produced nothing, he was about to move on when he saw the dog drinking. He scooped up a handful of water. It was potable, like the spring at the Spanish camp! The metal detector soon located a ship's spike and cannon ball. Wagner cleared the scrub with a bulldozer and over several months systematically excavated and charted the half-acre site. He accumulated a collection of Mexican and Chinese pottery fragments, musket balls, lead sheets, a bullet mold, and a pair of rusted cutlasses. Then, next to some kiln bricks, he found three blackened rectangles of silver. The following day yielded a 24-carat gold ring mounting a 2½-carat diamond and six smaller stones. Thirteen silver cobs were added over the next weeks as Wagner carefully reconstructed the outline of Hoyo Solórzano's fort. Clusters of cannon balls even showed him the positions of the guns.

Wagner had also been searching the sea bed through a homemade face mask for several years. Often he paddled out to the reefs on an inner tube, then aboard an advanced-design surfboard with a glass view plate. He knew that a wreck lay off the camp and concentrated his search in that area. Before long those months of studying archaic Spanish with Kelso paid off. On a shallow sandy bottom he spotted a cluster of cannons. Further skin diving searches located a large anchor. Part of the first wreck had been found. Wagner chartered a plane and scanned the reefs and shallow sand stretches for traces of the others. He knew now what to look for, and on his first flight recognized a ballast mound with cannons. Before long he had charted the locations of several other wrecks.

Kelso followed his progress enthusiastically, and even bought him his first SCUBA outfit. Wagner could now extend his underwater surveys. At the cannons-and-anchor site he found another cannon, artifacts, and his first sunken treasure—a fist-sized clump of tiny silver coins. He made several dives at another site off Fort Pierce, well known because of its huge ballast mound. While digging among the stones he retrieved several silver cobs of the 1715 period. A second armada wreck was found. Now he began mapping other prospects whose locations he learned through aerial observation and visual search, aided by information from friends who fished over ballast piles, and other divers. Kelso and he spent hours of detective work trying to correlate their sites with positions of 1715 wrecks learned through research. On March 11, 1960, in a farsighted move whose consequences would not be fully appreciated until later, Wagner obtained from the State of Florida Internal Improvement Fund exploratory search lease ⚓1329 encompassing the fifty-mile stretch of coast from Sebastian Inlet to a point between Stuart and Fort Pierce. He also obtained exclusive pinpoint salvage leases on the two wrecks where he had found coins. Wagner's careful attention to legal protocol and compliance with state regulations contrasted sharply with the hit-and-run tactics of many wreck scavengers in the area. The desire to co-operate with the authorities would be a distinguishing characteristic of the Real Eight Company throughout its growth.

While Wagner and Kelso were building a foundation for the future, a group of enthusiasts up the coast had been accumulating experience as a diving team. Louis J. Ullian was an ordnance engineer at the Cape Kennedy Air Force Missile Test Range. He had been diving since 1946, and in his teens had salvaged artifacts from the 1733 *El Infante* and other wrecks off the Keys. Delphine Long, a power equipment supervisor at nearby Patrick Air Force Base and president of a SCUBA club, had already found wreckage from a 1715 ship off Sebastian. He possessed a rare and happy quality for a treasure diver:

luck. Another club member, Ervin Taylor, introduced them to Wagner and Kelso in 1959. There was instant chemistry. Throughout that winter they gathered to discuss wrecks, treasure, and future plans. With them was Wagner's old friend of beachcombing days, Lisbon Futch. Two new enthusiasts from the Missile Test Range joined. Colonel Dan F. Thompson, Director of Operations, offered valuable assets as an experienced diver, organizer, and legal adviser. Lieutenant Colonel Harry E. Cannon, Chief of the Range Safety Office, contributed his 21-foot cruiser and under the group's tutelage soon added underwater proficiency to his other assets, which included a sharp business mind.

This was the original group: eight men with widely divergent backgrounds and talents, united by a common hunger for sea adventure and Spanish treasure.

The "WEDGE WRECK"

Remembering how the old Parker gang had fallen apart, Wagner resolved to test the mettle of the new team. His proving ground was the huge ballast mound off Fort Pierce where he had found a few coins. The stone pile measured 70 by 20 feet and lay 300 yards from shore at a depth of 18 feet. From visible evidence and historical research Wagner reasoned that one of the merchant *naos* had been dashed against the seaward edge of the narrow reef here, smashing in her bow, then tossed up and dropped across the reef top, where she broke in half. Ballast covered the small reef and the sand bottom on both sides. The surface was picked nearly clean, but the main ballast pile, 8 feet high in places, could guard treasures beyond the reach of Hoyo Solórzano's divers and modern scavengers. As a training ground this site offered advantages: The water was relatively clear, and wide sand channels on each side offered safe anchorages.

In January 1960 Wagner, Thompson, Long, Ullian, and Cannon anchored nearby. Reconnaissance dives pointed out the need for more equipment and a work boat. Wagner and Futch bought the boat, a battered 40-foot liberty launch ready for scrapping, for $1200 at Norfolk. In a navigational feat comparable to Magellan's, Futch brought the hulk down to Florida. It looked so much like junk that they named it *Sampan*. During months of weekend scraping, scrubbing, patching, painting, and structural modifications the *Sampan* was rebuilt into a serviceable work base. Taylor and Long mounted an engine and pump to provide water pressure for a small sand dredge they invented.

In April they attacked the ballast mound. Every weekend shifts of divers labored underwater moving by hand a thousand or so ballast stones weighing up to 50 pounds. The sand dredge began spitting out shards of Mexican pottery, which Mike Hrebec, an apprentice, collected for University of Florida archaeologists. By the middle of summer a 10-

foot-wide trench had been excavated across the center of the 100-ton mound. At the bottom were hundreds of cannon balls, porcelain shards, brass nails, corroded bits of copper, and ship's timbers. The wood was covered with a curious black substance that disintegrated on contact. This was identified later by Mendel Peterson as a previously unknown mixture of cowhair and tar used as a coating for protection against teredos.

A new trench was started across the stern, outside of the reef, on the theory that treasure had more likely been stored there. For weekend after weekend the unrewarding labor continued. There were shark scares, but lonesome wives at home were becoming more dangerous. The team lost enthusiasm and was on the verge of breaking up when Harry Cannon surfaced one morning with six 4-pound chunks of silver, 4 inches long, shaped like slices of pie. Pandemonium exploded as those on board grabbed diving gear and plunged over the side. On the ballast mound, as Wagner put it, "you practically had to dodge the raining storm of rocks" that were tossed around. Three more silver wedges were brought up. When assembled, eight of them formed a disk, or pie, 8 inches in diameter, weighing 33 pounds. Research disclosed that three such "pies," containing twenty-four wedges, filled a wooden keg weighing 100 pounds, considered a suitable load for an Indian slave.

By the end of August, when bad weather and clouded water stopped work, another half-dozen wedges and a few artifacts had been recovered. The team's *esprit de corps* was fully restored. Wagner bought a few more wedges from other divers who tried to poach on the wreck for $250 each. The Smithsonian purchased two of these at the same price. The "Wedge wreck," having served its purpose as a proving ground, was shelved as a regular work site, and dropped from the leases. It was probably the *Urca de Lima*.

The "CABIN WRECK"

On January 8, 1961, Wagner's experienced team began exploring the site that became known as the "Cabin wreck" because it lay offshore from a small cabin on the beach, two and a half miles south of Sebastian Inlet. The wreck where Wagner had found the clump of small coins was first located by Cannon, who caused chuckles when he surfaced and excitedly shouted his own name. The cluster of three cannons was some distance from the *Sampan*'s anchorage, in a sand channel barely 90 feet wide between two dangerous reefs. Although the sea that morning was not too rough to prevent the boat from entering, wave motion was strong enough to toss divers around on the 15-foot-deep bottom.

Thompson, who had also dived with Cannon, was swimming to join him when he came across a scattering of artifacts on the sand bottom.

His attention was caught by two rocklike masses, dark with greenish hues. Swimming toward them, he realized that the sand floor was littered with coins. He lifted the two big shimmering objects with the intention of carrying them across the sand to where the *Sampan* was anchored. They were too heavy. He surfaced, shouted to Wagner to bring in the boat, and returned to the bottom. After moments of panicky searching he relocated the clumps. Again he tried to move them toward the boat but had to drop one after a few steps. He deposited the other near a mast strap that would serve as a marker and returned to retrieve the first. It had vanished. He heard the boat approaching cautiously into the reef-walled channel, grabbed a handful of coins which he handed up to Ullian, and submerged with a line which he secured to the clump. After an exhausting struggle he brought the clump to the surface where the others helped him manhandle it on board. The mass weighed 77 pounds and consisted of over 1500 silver cobs! It measured 1½ feet across. The squarish shape and cloth markings on one side indicated that these coins had been in a wood treasure chest.

For the next few minutes the mature men aboard the *Sampan* behaved like children at Christmas. When Thompson managed to explain over the bedlam that another clump lay on the bottom the boat was instantly evacuated. One by one divers emerged, tossed aboard handfuls of coins, and plunged. The second clump was finally retrieved by Harry Acres, a friend who had come along for the ride. It weighed nearly as much as the first and had also been in a wood chest. While searching the bottom, Cannon was tumbled by a wave surge into a strange trench in the sand, some 4 yards long and 2 yards wide, with wood planking at the bottom. They guessed that this was a compartment from the wreck. On that particular day the waves had shifted sand, exposing it and the silver. One day earlier, or later, there might not have been a coin in sight. The trench was never found again. By early afternoon seas had built up so much that the tossing *Sampan* was drenched in spray from the reefs. The tricky passage out was made safely and the *Sampan* returned to base. That evening, after Kelso and Futch had joined the others, they estimated the recovery at nearly four thousand silver cobs worth something like $80,000. The figure multiplied as brandy started flowing.

The "Cabin wreck" was sealed off by heavy surf until mid-February, when the group took a chance and returned in risky weather. During those five weeks the configuration of the sand bottom had changed completely. Diving with Desco hookah air lines from the *Sampan*, the divers penetrated the sand with their dredge and exposed silver coins. Overhead a wave buffeted the *Sampan* so badly that an anchor fluke broke. She drifted rapidly toward a reef. Wagner started the

motor and took the boat into safer water after the divers returned
aboard. Despite surf breaking over their work site, Thompson and
Ullian insisted on returning there with SCUBA gear to examine a
strange coral formation. Fifteen anxious minutes later they swam back,
carrying another heavy clump. This one contained nearly two thousand
silver cobs.

Bad weather limited work until mid-June. In the meanwhile Long
and Taylor designed and tested a series of more powerful sand dredges,
finally settling on a 6-inch tube, 9 feet long, injection dredge. Ninety
pounds of water pressure carried down from a pump through a 2½-
inch fire hose jetted in near the base and swept upward, creating a
suction so strong that it pulled Long's wedding ring from his finger.
This "hungry beast," once the divers learned to handle it, gulped in
everything including cannon balls. The first day it was used on the
"Cabin wreck" several dozen coins were recovered. It was fortunate
that a stronger dredge had been built, because the sea bed often silted
up. On one day 6 feet of sand covered the wreckage, and marker
buoy lines attached to cannons disappeared into flat sand. To make
the excavation systematic, the divers attached lines to long iron rods
driven into the bottom and dredged outward in concentric circles,
marking the limit of each day's work with a knot. On some days
they salvaged hundreds of coins; on others as few as ten. Gradually,
the quantity increased. With the bonus of a small clump of cobs found
late that summer the group was confident and satisfied when they
closed operations in September. Besides the money, they had found
many artifacts and about twenty cannons. During early winter, more
artifacts were salvaged from shallow water near the cabin on the beach,
which became a convenient work base. The most interesting was a
3½-inch ornamental stopper for a brandy bottle with a silver figurine
of a moth.

The first sale of coins took place that fall. The selection offered was
carefully chosen to avoid disturbing the volatile numismatic market.
Prices ranged from $10 for an undated cob to $150 for a top-quality
dated piece. The proceeds were used to remodel the *Sampan* and
improve equipment. About this time Luis Marden of the *National
Geographic Magazine* became interested in the work and initiated discussions that led to a contract with that publication for exclusive
coverage of the salvage. As the water was clearer at the "Wedge
wreck," they returned to the ballast mound, where the skilled diver-
photographer took a series of photographs. The accompanying story,
which Wagner wrote, was not published until 1965.

Two new members had joined the group. Air Force Captain John
P. Jones, a West Point graduate assigned to Cannon's Range Safety

Office, was already an enthusiastic diver. Chief Warrant Officer Robert Johnson was a tug captain holding three master's licenses, and a salvage expert. Whenever weather permitted the *Sampan* returned to the "Cabin wreck." A big iron ring was located and created sufficient interest for its sand base to be dredged. It was fastened to wood which was probably the ship's buried rudder. Near the ring Wagner and Taylor found two flintlock muskets with 8-foot iron barrels and wooden stocks. Taylor brought up a bronze apothecary jar and a gold-plated pewter jewel box. Thompson, examining a new cannon, saw a silver plate and cup cemented to its barrel by coral. It was located right under breaking surf and he and Jones used up many tanks of air in the churning sea while carefully chipping it free. Several silver forks, and some good finds of cobs, were also brought up.

When heavy seas prohibited work at the "Cabin wreck," exploration continued for other lost 1715 ships. Wagner and Taylor constructed an underwater sled from aluminum tubes with a Plexiglas shield through which the rider could scan the bottom while being towed behind the *Sampan.* On other occasions divers wearing SCUBA gear hung onto ropes towed behind the boat—until a shark attack discouraged human trawling.

The major recovery that year was made neither under the sea nor by a regular diver. One day, right after a nor'easter, Wagner took his nephew Rex Stocker beachcombing. While Wagner was making a good haul of coins from the wet sand, Rex ran up to him, shouting. A shiny gold chain was wrapped around his arm. Examining it, Wagner knew instinctively that Rex had found something special. The gold chain turned out to be 11 feet 4½ inches long and constructed of 2176 delicately carved gold links. Attached to this was a golden dragon 2¾ inches long, of incredible beauty. Its open mouth was a whistle. A gold toothpick lifted out from a hinge on the serrated back. At the tip of the tail was a tiny ear spoon. Years later, after many appraisals and studies, it was determined that this unique piece was General Ubilla's badge of office: his emblem of naval command. It was nearly certainly made by Chinese craftsmen. The dragon was sold for $50,000 at the Parke-Bernet Galleries auction on February 4, 1967. The chain is the single most valuable item today in Real Eight's Museum of Sunken Treasure, worth probably another $50,000.

On a weekday early in June 1963, the bad weather suddenly abated. Underwater visibility at the "Cabin wreck," usually a few feet, spread out to over 50. For two years work had been concentrated in an area only 20 feet across. Now, finally, a wide visual survey was possible. Mike Hrebec was the first to score with a 70-pound clump of silver cobs, again shaped to indicate that it had been in a chest. At 20 coins to a pound, it contained about 1400 pieces. The following Tuesday Ullian and Hrebec, dredging near a ledge, uncovered five more clumps close together, each weighing between 50 and 75 pounds. Another 6000 or more silver coins! To top off that day's fantastic haul, Hrebec handed Wagner a classic silver crucifix encrusted with rainbow-hued shells. In a single day they had salvaged $100,000 in silver.

That weekend the whole team turned out. More silver cobs were brought up, then the dredge uncovered an alien grayish clay, sprinkled with chips of blue and white porcelain. Moments later Jones and Ullian found two matching halves of a cup. Working carefully, they un-covered two perfect cups and bowls. That afternoon twenty-eight pieces of porcelain, all in near-perfect condition, were gently lifted on board. The grayish substance turned out to be a special packing clay callel *petuntze* to protect the porcelain during shipment from China to Spain, via the Manila galleon and Mexico. Among the cups and bowls experts later identified three different designs of the K'ang Hsi period, all rare.

To permit some work to be done in bad weather a raft was built and kept in front of the cabin. Equipped with a light pump and compressor, and powered by a small motor, it could reach the "Cabin wreck" from the beach in minutes. Diving from it one day Johnson, Long, and Ullian had retrieved cobs, silver forks, and artifacts when Johnson sighted gold under a cannon. Ullian joined him in fanning away the sand. Inch by inch a 9-foot gold chain was reeled in. Attached to it was a gracefully designed oval gold and enamel devotional pendant with curved glass on each side under which miniature paintings had been eroded away by centuries under the sea. This was later sold at the Parke-Bernet auction for $4000.

REAL EIGHT COMPANY, INC.

Back in April 17, 1961, the original group had formalized their re-lationship with the incorporation of the Real Eight Company. The name was derived from the Spanish term for piece of eight, *ocho reales*. The officers were: President, Kip Wagner; Executive Vice-President and Treasurer, Dan Thompson; Secretary, Harry Cannon. One thousand shares were issued. Thompson, Cannon, Taylor, Long, and Ullian each received 120; Futch 110; and Wagner and Kelso the other 290. Later Rex Stocker transferred his general's badge of office and chain to the company for 40 shares, toward which each member contributed 5. Futch sold his shares to an interested banker, Robert Brown. Taylor later sold out to Brown and the group, while Johnson and Jones were each given a shareholding. In 1965 Real Eight shares were distributed: Wagner 175; Kelso, 100; Thompson and Cannon, 115 each; Long and Ullian, 100 each; Johnson, 85; Jones, 55; Stocker, 40; and Brown's estate (he had died), 115.

The "SANDY POINT WRECK"

On the California coast Mel Fisher was a celebrity in the diving and treasure-hunting world. When not running his popular dive shop in Los Angeles, Fisher, frequently with his diving champion wife Dolores, took expeditions out on their 65-foot *Golden Doubloon*. He had explored wrecks throughout the Caribbean, Florida, and California. Lou Ullian met him in California during the winter of 1962. The following year, between expeditions to Silver Shoals, Fisher visited Wagner at his home. In March 1963 he proposed bringing a self-sustaining salvage team to work in Real Eight territory on a 50–50 share basis of any recoveries his group made, after Florida's 25 per cent. Wagner's shareholders were favorably impressed, but no agreement had been finalized when Fisher's deputy, Rupert Gates, appeared with the news that Fisher had sold his business, home, and boat to raise funds and would soon arrive with his team. Gates made a very favorable impression, and at a meeting of the Real Eight Company, Fisher's offer was accepted.

Gates was invited along on the next visit to the "Cabin wreck." When Hrebec brought up several cobs on his first dive, Gates joined the others on the bottom and was soon participating in a salvage of coins and silver forks. That afternoon marked a new phase in Real Eight's history. Up to then, despite all the silver recovered, they had not one gold coin to show. Suddenly, Long, who was diving with Thompson near the inner reef, surfaced with a whoop. In his hand was a gold 8-escudo piece in mint condition. He and Thompson had uncovered a pocket of gold coins 9 feet deep. With everyone diving, twenty-three doubloons and smaller coins were found.

Fisher arrived that week with his Treasure Salvors team of four expert divers. The colorful Demostines Molinar had been diesel mechanic on the *Golden Doubloon*. Richard Williams was also a sportsman, radio operator, and engineer. Walt Holzworth, a construction man with a hobby of coin collecting, became a first-rate salvage diver at the age of fifty-two. Fay Field was an electronics expert, trained in radar, who took up diving to collect shells. Since these frequented wrecks, he developed a magnetometer to find iron. Over the years he had added improvements. The model he brought, affectionately called the "sea mag," was a highly advanced specially constructed proton type. In use the probe, or sensor, was trawled behind a boat in a search pattern.

The Fisher group bought a 50-foot boat, the *Dee-Gee*, whose state of deterioration reminded Wagner of his first encounter with the *Sampan*. September had come by the time the *Dee-Gee* had been rendered serviceable. Several magnetometer searches for new wrecks were made, then Wagner assigned the "Wedge wreck" to Fisher's team. Besides the magnetometer, the *Dee-Gee* was equipped with a 10-inch dredge so forceful that two men were needed to manage it. Before long Fisher's group had found another silver wedge and three clay toy animals.

Wagner had known about another wreck off Sandy Point for years and had helped to salvage cannons from its site for Art McKee's Fortress of Sunken Treasure. Because of the large number of cannons, and the location, Wagner believed this to be De Echeverz' *Capitana*, which was known to have been wrecked "off a point of land." Treasure Salvors moved here. The first coin, a cob in poor condition, was recovered from under a cannon by Ullian, who was working the dredge with Holzworth. During the next weeks, Fisher's group raised nearly two thousand cobs and three gold 2-escudo coins minted in Bogotá. The silver money was nearly all badly corroded. Other salvage included a ship's brass bell—unfortunately without an identifying name on it. Although it seemed that the "Sandy Point wreck" was unlikely to yield valuable treasure, the determined group kept working in rough seas until Fisher was thrown against a bulkhead, cracking several ribs.

During the bad weather they developed the prototype of a new form of dredge which would revolutionize salvage of objects buried under shallow sand or mud. They called it the "mailbox," or "the blaster." Fitted back of the *Dee-Gee*'s propeller, it deflected the water flow downward in a powerful jet stream so effective that a crater 6 feet deep and 10 feet across could be scoured in ten minutes. It offered a valuable bonus—while sand, shells, and light coral were swept out, heavy objects like coins tended to accumulate on the bottom of the hole. Divers needed considerable practice to be able to work under the waterfall and even experienced ones were often somersaulted away.

The "GOLD WRECK" or "COLORED BEACH WRECK"

In August 1963 three men visited Wagner with a proposal to deliver the location of a rich treasure site to Real Eight for a percentage of the salvage. As proof, they produced gold doubloons, dated 1714 and 1715. After a contract was signed, the men said that the site was a few miles south of Fort Pierce. Wagner recalled a wreck in that area in which he had not been interested since research indicated it was most likely *La Holandesa*, which the Spanish had salvaged. He asked Fisher to look it over. After Fisher's group wasted six hundred man-hours in futile attempts to locate it, the three men admitted that they had found the coins on the beach, and assumed there must be a wreck offshore. In face of this trickery, the contract was modified and Fisher's crew began a sea mag sweep. For three months the instrument, controlled by Field, signaled locations of one metallic object after another—even World War II mines. Finally, in April, a cannon with ballast was located far from the place indicated by the three men.

The blaster bored into the sea bed. Before long the Fisher group, aided by Ullian, Thompson, and Long, had raised a hundred cobs. Molinar was making a diving survey on May 8 when he spotted a gleam in the sand a few yards seaward. Moments later he climbed onto the *Dee-Gee* with two 7½-pound disks of 22½-carat gold. Their surfaces were stamped with assayer's marks and lot numbers in Roman numerals. After a well-earned celebration, and a frustrating delay due to bad weather, the *Dee-Gee* unleashed the blaster 50 feet seaward of the former site. Molinar presently retrieved a 1698 gold doubloon. Three more were found that day. Then on May 21 two hundred 4-escudo and 8-escudo gold pieces were recovered.

The big strike took place on May 24. The blaster excavated a hole 15 by 6 feet wide in a ridge between two rock formations. Molinar, Holzworth, and Ullian dived to see what lay on the bottom. They were momentarily blinded by the reflection from a "carpet of gold" the like of which had never before been seen underwater. All day long, as the blaster was left running to keep the hole clear, relays of divers struggled under the jet stream, picking up coins. By evening an unbelievable total of 1033 gold pieces had been brought up. Another 900 were added the following day. Before the week was out some 2700 gold coins were salvaged. Then the lode ran dry. Wagner and Kelso knew from research that a treasure chest would hold about this quantity of mixed large and small coins and calculated that the strike was the contents of one such chest—probably registered treasure. As only *Capitanas* and *Almirantas* would have carried such cargo they discarded their earlier theory that the "Gold wreck" (the "Colored Beach wreck") was a cargo ship. De Echeverz' *Almiranta* was a more likely candidate.

Work continued intermittently in bad weather. The wreckage area was mapped and systematically dredged. While the blaster was on, four anchors held the *Dee-Gee* in position. After each excavation was searched, the blaster was moved to an adjacent site. A steady salvage of treasure and artifacts went on. Fisher brought up a 35½-pound silver bar, the first such recovery. Long, during one exciting afternoon, found two more gold disks similar to Molinar's, and one silver disk weighing 27 pounds. Throughout the salvage, Gates worked overtime photographing and cataloguing every single coin and artifact brought up. In appreciation of Treasure Salvors' contribution, the Real Eight group amended the contract on June 19. From then on recoveries by either group were to be shared equally with the other.

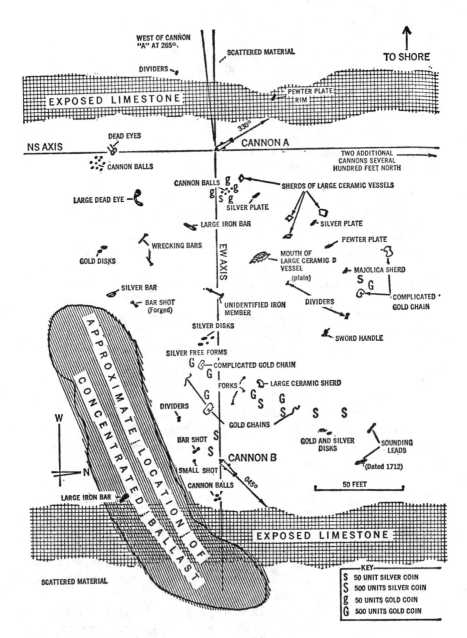

The "Colored Beach wreck" (*courtesy of Carl J. Clausen*)

Mr. Carl J. Clausen, the competent underwater archaeology authority who accompanied the salvors during that summer's work as representative of the Trustees of the Internal Improvement Fund of the State of Florida, analyzed the operations in *A 1715 Spanish Treasure Ship*, published in 1965 by the University of Florida. The following is condensed from Mr. Clausen's report.

The "Colored Beach Wreck" is located approximately three nautical miles south of the Fort Pierce Inlet, some 500 to 1,500 feet offshore in water varying from 8 to 20 feet in depth. Although the majority of artifacts and treasure were found in an area of just under two acres, the wreckage covered at least two additional acres. The vast majority of the material was deep beneath sand overburden in the broad hollows between [the limestone] ridges.

ANALYSIS OF ARTIFACTS: Five cannon were located. All were muzzle-loading smooth-bore. Bore diameter was estimated at 3¼ to 3½ inches. Cannon A: 7 feet 2 inches long . . . Cannon B: 7 feet 9 inches. Seventy-nine examples of cannon balls recovered, cast in two-piece molds, averaged 3 pounds 8 ounces [and] approximately 3⅙ inches in diameter. At least nine examples of bar shot were raised. Two types were found. A rather crude type, apparently formed by winding and forging strap iron around the ends of the square center bar until the desired diameter was reached, average weight was 9 pounds. The second variety consisted of iron spheres cast over the ends of a square forged iron bar, weighed about 6 pounds. Approximately 80 cast lead balls, projectiles for pistols or muskets, [were] approximately .59 caliber and weighed .78 ounce each. [They] displayed a raised casting ridge. Approximately 106 sherds of olive jars were collected . . . round-bottomed, more-or-less egg-shaped. Four pairs of navigational dividers [of which] three were of an interesting ring-topped design. When the points were moved apart the semi-circular portions, which formed the hinged ring at the top of the pair, moved through one another. Three sounding leads, two of these tapering, more-or-less eight-sided, weighing 18 and 18¾ pounds and measuring 41.8 and 44.3 cm. The bottom surface displayed a depression for tallow or pitch.

TREASURE: bulk precious metals: The prevalent form was a circular-shaped ingot with a round bottom. Six disks of silver or high silver content, six examples and fragments with high gold content . . . diameter from 241 mm. for the largest of the silver disks weighing approximately 27 pounds, to a gold disk 98 mm. in diameter and weighing 1 pound 15 ounces. Markings were found on the top surfaces of all the disks with a high gold content. Only the largest of the silver disks was so marked. The stamps on the largest gold disks consisted of Roman numerals which might or might not be followed by from one to three small circles. The Roman numeral stamp "XXII" probably indicates the gold content of the disk in carats. A single silver bar weighed 35 pounds 8½ ounces and averaged 397 mm. in length, 127 mm. in width, and 51 mm. in thickness.

TREASURE: specie: slightly more than 3,700 gold coins and over 200 pounds of silver coins were recovered. The salvaged specimens represent an extremely broad sample of Spanish Colonial coinage struck at all mints operating in the New World during the last years of the reign of Charles II and the first 15 years of Philip V. The gold coins included denominations and types previously unknown or for which only a few examples were known to exist. This was true in the case of all mints, but particularly for those at Bogotá and Cuzco.

Gold Coins: Minted in denominations of ½, 1, 2, 4 and 8 escudos. Approximately 88 per cent were struck in the mint at Mexico City. About 45 per cent were undated but fell into the 1700–1713 period. Seven per cent were dated between 1702 and 1713. Coins dated 1714 and 1715 made up slightly more than 45 per cent. The following examples of nearly round gold coins were recovered: a single 8 escudo piece dated 1695, ten 8 escudo pieces dated 1702, a single 4 escudo dated 1713, five 8 escudo coins dated 1714 [Note: these "royals" are particularly valuable]. Santa Fe de Bogotá: 1 and 2 escudo pieces. Cuzco: a 1 escudo and nine 2 escudo pieces.

Silver Coins: The vast majority are of Mexican origin from the 1700–1714 period. A small percentage are from the Lima mint, a smaller proportion from Potosí. The majority of these coins are of 4 and 8 reales.

In addition to the money and artifacts described above, sixteen gold rings, some decorated, eight pieces of gold chain, and three full chain circles were salvaged. Other artifacts were one gold and two silver buckles, badly deteriorated silver knives, forks, and spoons, two silver plates, two ornate silver candlestick tops, and a number of unidentified objects with high silver content. When hurricanes Cleo and Dora closed the 1964 diving season, $1,000,000 in treasure—mostly gold coins—had been salvaged.

To clean the thousands of encrusted cobs, Wagner and Long constructed a rotating box filled with steel shot and detergent. After two hours of burnishing inside, the silver coins were shining. On October 8, 1964, a small assortment of coins were auctioned by Henry Christensen. The best piece, a mint-condition doubloon dated 1711, went for $3600. A similar 8-escudo coin dated 1695 netted $3500. The total take from just over a hundred coins, mostly gold, was $29,000—an average of nearly $300 apiece!

That fall the Real Eight's salvage potential was strengthened with the addition of a new work boat, the *Derelict*. Like her predecessors, the 50-foot hulk with a 13-foot beam was in such battered condition when purchased that the name was bestowed spontaneously. She was rebuilt during bad weather periods and evenings. The most useful piece of new equipment was a modified version of Fisher's blaster, constructed by Johnson and Long. Its frame was a quarter-ton iron cylinder 8 feet long and 3½ feet in diameter. Inside this a four-bladed propeller was mounted with its shaft connected by universal joints to a Ford engine on the *Derelict*. The transmission was designed to permit power to be idled down for delicate work. During a test run in the harbor the 30-inch-diameter water jet sent mud swirling to the surface for 200 feet.

Early in 1965 salvage expert Bob Johnson resigned his job to become the *Derelict's* permanent skipper. Stocker, Hrebec, and Bob Conkey were signed aboard as salaried crew. Real Eight's weekend diving stage was over. The regular team still came out on weekends, and when possible joined the *Derelict's* crew during the week. Each day Johnson decided the most suitable site to work. The "Cabin wreck" required relative calm, while the "Gold wreck" could be reached in rougher weather. On May 19 he selected the "Gold wreck" and anchored about 200 yards north of Fisher's *Dee-Gee*. Nineteen doubloons were brought up that day. Two anchors and several cannons were soon found, along with pewter plates and more gold coins, emphasizing the size of the area over which wreckage could be strewn. Long, who was aboard the next weekend, had one of his phenomenal hunches. Pointing toward a spot some 300 yards away, he drawled, "I've got a feeling, fellows, that we're going to hit it big again soon—right over there." Anxious eyes followed Long's finger. A few days later Johnson anchored about 1000 feet offshore where he guessed that Long had pointed. From a sand bottom 24 feet deep 130 gold coins were salvaged.

On the next day, May 31, 1965, the all-time record in the history of treasure salvage was established. Nearly the entire Real Eight team went out. Underwater visibility was excellent. The *Derelict's* blaster scooped out an enormous crater measuring 30 feet across. When Wagner and the others saw the contents they could only stare, spellbound. A sheet of shimmering gold coins covered the crater's bottom right out to the limit of vision, where even more coins were stacked in little piles against the far reef. The salvage that day, in which Fisher's group participated, included 518 doubloons, 381 4-escudos, and 228 2-escudos for a grand total of 1127 gold coins! All but 183 from Lima had the Mexico mint marking. Since nearly half of the coins were big 8-escudo doubloons the recovery was practically the entire content of a treasure chest. Over $1,000,000 worth of coins, at prevailing numismatic values, were taken home that night, where the counting and recording went on until early morning.

Legal Developments

Because of careful attention to regulations and co-operation with Florida state authorities the Real Eight group enjoyed freedom of action until fall 1963. Each quarter they submitted to the Internal Improvement Fund representatives a detailed report of work done and an accounting for every coin and artifact recovered. An unorthodox, but mutually satisfactory, method was developed for determining the state's 25 per cent share. Wagner's group broke down the recoveries into separate classifications such as gold coins, silver cobs, and artifacts. Then each class was divided into four roughly equal piles. The state representative selected whichever pile he wanted. The first division was made public in September 1964, at a press conference during which officials displayed the state's 25 per cent of the treasure and artifacts with the announcement that they had insured it for $400,000. The news made headlines. For weeks Wagner was besieged by treasure hunters who swarmed into the Sebastian area. Another stampede began in February 1966, following press releases that the state's share of a second division had been insured for $460,000. Florida's share from a third division was only slightly less.

Until 1963, although Wagner's fifty-mile exploration lease was technically not exclusive, state officials discouraged others from intruding because of their confidence in Real Eight. Late that year a change of state personnel occurred. To his surprise, Wagner suddenly found his group on the defensive. An atmosphere of suspicion and jealousy replaced the easy working arrangement of the past. Sensational press stories appeared with innuendoes that not all the treasure was being properly accounted for.

To help clear the air, Real Eight's attorneys made a new arrangement with the fund's officers releasing the "exclusive" fifty-mile area. In return, the number of Real Eight's exclusive pinpoint salvage leases was increased to eight (a ninth was added in early 1969). Almost immediately another salvage company applied for leases adjacent to each of these. When their application was denied, they filed suit against the state of Florida but the case never reached court. Originally each pinpoint lease site was limited to about one acre. When Real Eight officers proved that wreckage from each ship was scattered over a larger area, the lease boundaries were increased to form a rough square with each side approximately 440 yards long. Eight of Real Eight's nine present leases have these dimensions, while lease #4 is considerably larger. Instead of the original one-year contract terms with year-to-year options for extensions, Real Eight obtained six-year leases. Their present contracts extend through 1975. The company has a cordial working arrangement with the Board of Archives and History, whose executive director is Robert Williams.

By late spring 1965, calmer weather permitted work to be carried on intermittently at the "Cabin wreck." Since neither ballast nor heavy timbers had been found here, it was apparent that this was only part of the ship. The heavier wreckage must have settled somewhere farther out. The *Dee-Gee* made several magnetometer runs and presently Field's "little black box" signaled the promixity of iron. The site was just past the outermost of the three parallel reefs, about 800 feet off the beach. A diving reconnaissance located a cannon. The *Derelict's* blaster uncovered nine silver wedges, three small clumps of cobs, and a new type of treasure—ten round disks about 1½ feet in diameter weighing from 44 to 105 pounds each. Analysis showed them to be an alloy of mostly copper with small quantities of gold, platinum, and silver. Onion-shaped bottles, still sealed, were also recovered. Several thousand more cobs were brought up the next day, and on June 24 the divers hauled in 665 pounds of silver—over ten thousand coins in one day! Twelve more wedges and eight silver disks, thousands of cobs, and two chunks of silver were added the next two days. In just one week, nearly a ton of silver had been recovered. Nine-foot-long cannons began to appear.

Obviously, they were on to something big. A grid pattern with chains at 25-foot intervals was laid out on the sand floor next to the reef. Ullian carefully charted every find on graph paper. The *Dee-Gee* was called over to allow Fisher's crew to participate. On July 7 part of the ship's wooden keel, with metal fasteners attached, was uncovered. Every day large numbers of cobs, some in clumps as heavy as 135 pounds, were raised, with more artifacts. Then, on July 25, Stocker found the first treasure chest recovered from a wreck in modern times. The cedar wood sides, measuring 3 by 1½ feet and 1 foot high, were intact except for one end and the top. A solid mass of about three thousand silver cobs inside cemented it together. Vast numbers of cobs continued to be recovered. The total for just one day, August 1, was four thousand. A find significant for identification purposes was a brass breechblock, 8 inches long and 9 inches in circumference, with the handle and locking screw intact. These would normally be carried only on war galleons.

Until the discovery of the deeper part, Wagner and Kelso believed the "Cabin wreck" to be Ubilla's *Almiranta*. The shallow part fitted the location, "a stone's throw from shore," and the cannons, measuring 9 feet as compared with the 7½-foot guns at the "Gold wreck," indicated one of Ubilla's fighting ships, which they knew from research mounted heavier guns than de Echeverz' galleons. Moreover, only a *Capitana* or *Almiranta* would have carried such quantities of silver money, ob-viously registered cargo. With the deep part found, the new wreckage distribution dovetailed precisely into the pattern of Ubilla's *Capitana*. Spanish salvage reports had described work over her wreckage at two depths—five fathoms and two and a half fathoms—corresponding with the depths of the deep and shallow sections. Romans' 1775 map and Seville documents placed this ship just south of Sebastian Inlet. Further confirmation was obtained through the patient efforts of Carl J. Clausen, Florida State Archaeologist, who continued to work closely with Real Eight. After many months of efforts he was able to provide Wagner with long-sought documents from Havana among which was a comment that Ubilla's *Capitana* had hit a reef in five fathoms where the bottom was ripped out, with ballast and heavy cargo, after which the lightened hull was swept inshore into shallow water. If further proof were neces-sary, the *Capitana*'s station at the head of Ubilla's armada should have placed her at the north of the wrecks—and Rex Stocker had found the general's badge of office nearby.

Of the 1300 treasure chests registered aboard, 940 were known to have been salvaged by the Spanish. Probably another few dozen were taken by pirates. The 50,000 or so cobs recovered by Real Eight accounted for the contents of another 20–30 chests. When storms halted work that September, contemplation of those remaining 300 chests, and their half-million silver pieces of eight, was in everybody's mind.

The Company Grows

In December 1964 the National Geographic Society sponsored a special exhibition of Real Eight's treasure and artifacts in its Explorers' Hall in Washington, D.C., to promote Wagner's article in the January 1965 issue of the magazine. For two months attendance records were broken. The exhibition was moved to the Florida State Museum, where again it attracted thousands of people. This interest, together with the group's desire to maintain most of the treasure intact, led Cannon to propose the establishment of a permanent museum. This was opened on April 30, 1965, under the direction of Lieutenant Colonel Joe Salvo, in a suite of rooms at Satellite Beach. A VIP gathering of several hundred people attended the celebration and enthusiastic comments made the wire services. In six months over twenty-five thousand visitors paid admission.

Kip and Alice Wagner visited Spain late that year on a grant from the National Geographic Society. His first stop was the Archivo General de Indias in Seville. Dr. Peña was sick and unable to meet him, but Wagner received a warm welcome by his staff, who guided him through the mountains of old documents. Wagner engaged the services of two researchers in Seville, and another at Barcelona's Maritime Museum later. Their task was twofold: to find the manifests of the 1715 ships among documents returned from Havana; and to track down facts about a collection of jewelry that King Philip V had ordered for the Duchess of Parma. Tantalizing references to this priceless assortment of pearl- and gem-encrusted golden treasures crafted in the Orient and the Americas had appeared in various documents. Wagner knew that it had been entrusted to General Ubilla and loaded aboard his *Capitana*, but had found no further information. The jewels were so important that the Spanish King had twice recalled Hoyo Solórzano to explain why they had not been recovered.

While in Spain, Wagner became better acquainted with diver-archae-ologist-historian Robert Marx, who was spending three years in Seville's archives compiling information for his definitive six-volume work on the armadas. A highly readable and beautifully illustrated summary of this, *The Treasure Fleets of the Spanish Main,* was published in 1968. Mutual interests and achievements led to an understanding between Wagner and Marx which brought him into Real Eight three years later.

The diving seasons of 1966 and 1967 were, as usual, interrupted by bad weather, but salvage work went on at an accelerated pace. Whenever possible, the *Derelict* and *Dee-Gee* teams worked the high-yield "Cabin wreck" and "Gold wreck." In poorer weather they reconnoitered other sites. The "Cabin wreck" disgorged additional thousands of gold and silver coins, including a second treasure chest filled with cobs with only the top and sides missing. Gold jewelry included twenty 24-carat rings, some elaborately carved, seven gold links, and a pair of earrings mounted with pearls. Among the silver artifacts were forks, many stamped with an eagle—the King's mark of purity—medallions, and a jewel box. A Chinese gold-plated teapot and a silver greatcoat with 2-inch buttons stirred up interest. One of the salvaged cannons had several silver plates cemented to it with coral. More muskets and brass dividers were found. From the "Gold wreck" the flow of doubloons, smaller gold coins, and silver cobs went on and included a rare 1714 "royal." Gold chains and rings, and a 6-inch pendant decorated with a sculptured woman and dogs, were among the salvaged jewelry. Other artifacts included silver knives, forks, and spoons, a silver sword handle, and navigational instruments. During the 1967 season alone more than $500,000 in precious metal was recovered.

The famous Parke-Bernet Galleries held a widely publicized auction of a selection of the Real Eight treasure salvage on February 4, 1967. Topping the list was the $50,000 general's badge of office. The shell-encrusted silver crucifix, only 3½ inches high, sold for $2000, and a 2-inch plain gold cross for $1900. A gold and diamond ring brought $2300 and a plain gold one $600. A 9-pound round gold ingot was bid up to $7500. Another $4000 was paid for a 43-pound silver bar. The K'ang Hsi porcelain cups and bowls went for between $400 and $750 each. Tableware was in demand: A silver plate brought $750 and pewter plates about $500 each, while silver forks and spoons netted up to $400. Topping the coins were a 1714 full round gold 8-escudo piece and a 1711 full round 4-escudo, which brought $9000 and $6500 respectively. Other gold coins averaged $1000 for 8-escudos, $800 for 4-escudos, and from $300 to $500 for 2-escudos. Prices paid for silver coins ranged from $10 for tiny 1-real cobs to over $300 for good-condition pieces of eight.

The "sleepers" of the auction were the iron artifacts that litter ballast mounds. The 12-foot iron anchor from the "Cabin wreck" brought $1000; bar shot, about $100 each; cannon balls 3 and 4 inches in diameter, about $20; and even iron nails sold for $6 apiece. During the auction 376 lots were sold. Their total sale price was $227,570!

Ever since the near-certain identification of Ubilla's *Capitana*, Wagner and the others had pondered the location of the wreck that could yield the richest treasure of them all: Ubilla's *Almiranta*. Only 136 of the 990 treasure chests registered aboard had been salvaged by the Spanish. The contents of those other chests—two million silver cobs and probably considerable gold—lay only "a stone's throw" off some point of that long stretch of beach. Where? Of Real Eight's salvage leases, the "Wedge wreck" had been given up. Another new wreck site, near Wabasso, replaced it on Real Eight's leases. The "Sandy Point wreck" and the "Gold wreck" seemed to account for de Echeverz' *Capitana* and *Almiranta*. Four other wrecks sites under salvage lease to Real Eight in 1968 were candidates.

The "Pine wreck" had been known to Wagner for years. He had fished over its relatively deep ballast off the south point of Sebastian Inlet, slightly north of the "Cabin wreck." Recent investigations have indicated that this may be a third part of Ubilla's *Capitana*. Since the *Almiranta*'s station in Ubilla's armada formation would normally have been at the stern, its wreckage should lie just north of de Echeverz' *Capitana*—the "Sandy Point wreck"—which led the second armada. Two wrecks, besides the new one, were in this zone. The survey of one, the "Anchor wreck," is beginning and not much is known of her. But the second, the "Green Cabin wreck" off Indian River Shores, has already yielded surprises. The unusually wide spread of wreckage here is indicated by the large size of Real Eight's salvage lease, which runs half a mile along the beach front. In the early 1960s four brass cannons were recovered from this area, one of which bore the date 1594. During 1968 exploratory probes were made into the bottom around other cannons and ballast. Several hundred Mexican cobs were recovered, dating back to Philip II and III in the late 1500s and early 1600s. As more artifacts were examined it became apparent that an intruder from an earlier century—and an unusually large ship at that—lay inside Real Eight's lease boundaries. Efforts to identify her are under way. Meanwhile, coins dated just before 1715 were also found, as well as artifacts of the same period. A ship, or part of one, from the 1715 armada had also broken up there. A thorough survey is being made of this area, as well as site #5 off Wabasso. The southernmost of Real Eight's leases (#8), a few miles north of St. Lucie Inlet, is also on the survey schedule.

A discovery was made in 1968 that led to a reappraisal of several areas considered thoroughly salvaged. On a hunch Johnson returned to a spot that had previously yielded gold and silver. Work had been discontinued upon encountering a layer of apparently old coquina. When the *Derelict*'s blaster was directed against this, the crust of solidified shells and coral crumbled, revealing a cache of gold and silver coins that nature had nearly succeeded in sealing off.

The "RIO MAR WRECK"

A major new strike was made in 1969 at a site for which Real Eight had obtained its ninth lease just a few weeks before. It is called the "Rio Mar wreck" and lies nearly three miles north of the "Sandy Point wreck"—assumed to be de Echeverz' *Capitana*—where Mel Fisher's group had been so disappointed in 1963. Under contract to Real Eight, Treasure Salvors began surveying the new site, off the Vero Beach golf course, on May 31, 1969. Says Mel Fisher, "The first day of work on this wreck we made a fabulous find which included two large gold crucifixes, one of which is pearl-studded. We also found sixty gold coins, Bogotá mint, a magnificent emerald, ivory dice, jewel-studded brooches, gold pendants, gold earrings, gold cuff links, gold hair pins, a beautiful well-marked gold bar [believed to be the largest ever found in a Florida wreck], several silver cobs, and two truckloads of artifacts. Previously Kip Wagner had found some coins on the beach and then we surveyed the area, placing fluorescent stakes 50 feet apart in double rows so as to grid out the ocean into 50-foot sectors. We then used the sea mag, making runs perpendicular to the beach, each one lined up on two of these stakes, for several thousand feet out to sea and back on the next parallel bearing 50 feet over. We had our magnetometer recorder chart paper for each run. We transferred all the readings to a large graph paper plotting the precise location of all metal objects located by the sea mag." Once again Fay Field's invention, in the capable and experienced hands of Fisher's professionals, produced results.

The 15-foot-deep wreck seems to be the lower hull of de Echeverz' *Capitana*. The South American origin of the first recovery of gold coins (worth $60,000) indicates a Tierra Firme ship, and examination of the surprisingly intact hull indicates that it is indeed *Nuestra Señora del Carmen y San Antonio*, ex-*Hampton Court*. And what about the "Sandy Point wreck," from which so many cannons and so little treasure were recovered? It could possibly be the upper decking of the same ship—broken loose and carried nearly three miles by the hurricane's force before grounding. A parallel exists in the "inner" and "outer" Cabin wrecks." The hull of de Echeverz' *Capitana* could contain the rich cargo of registered treasure known to have been aboard the ship, and probably not salvaged.

Other exciting developments can be expected. Real Eight had programmed surveys on a galleon in the Bahamas and possibly the gold-laden *San José*. Besides the contracted services of Treasure Salvors, Inc., Real Eight employs up to two dozen divers on its constantly increasing number of projects.

The Corporation

In 1967 Real Eight Company, Inc., entered a phase of accelerated growth. Operating funds had previously been generated largely through the sale of coins and artifacts, and loans from the First National Bank of Satellite Beach, in whose vaults the treasure was stored. In September 1967 the company went public with an offering of 250,000 shares through New York's Hancock Securities. Through a split, the group's original 1000 shares were converted into 1,000,000 of the new stock. By 1968 1,200,000 shares of Real Eight stock had been issued, and are quoted on the National Stock Exchange. Kip Wagner holds the position of Chairman of the Board. Harry Cannon is President; Dan Thompson Vice-President; and John Jones Secretary-Treasurer. Bob Marx, who joined Real Eight in 1968, is Director of Research and spends considerable time appraising the prospective worth of the numerous propositions offered to the company. The developing electronic search programs are headed by Mr. Robert Judd, of Columbia University, who controls the magnetometers and sonar and is also a competent diver.

On June 29, 1968, the new $1,000,000 Museum of Sunken Treasure on A1A, just north of Cocoa Beach, was formally dedicated. Managed by the respected authority on Spanish artifacts and coins Bob Page, this showplace of Real Eight's treasure is drawing large crowds. A second and third museum, for Washington, D.C., and Miami, are being planned.

Real Eight Company, Inc., has moved strongly into the sophisticated new world of undersea technology. In December 1967 it acquired control of Sigma, Inc., a service-oriented company in Melbourne, Florida, specializing in certain advanced areas of radar development. Its staff of experienced electronic technicians is headed by President Don Foreman. In the summer of 1968 Real Eight purchased MacDowell Associates of Indian Harbour Beach, an electronics firm involved in the defense program. Both companies have expertise and facilities that are already providing Real Eight's underwater exploration program with the latest developments in electronic search equipment such as sonar specially designed for shallow-water work and a range of magnetometers. Early in 1969 the highly respected Rebikoff Underwater Products, Inc., of Fort Lauderdale was acquired by Real Eight, contributing advanced systems for underwater photography and such search devices as the famous Pegasus diver propulsion unit with an underwater cruising range of six miles at three knots. A prototype has been fitted with a side scan sonar unit and a magnetometer permitting its SCUBA-equipped rider to carry out two kinds of electronic search simultaneously while cruising over the sea bottom. A further development is the unmanned Poodle, which can carry a sonar unit, a magnetometer, lights, and cameras to a depth of 1000 feet and will be used to locate deep wrecks.

A 72-foot, 83-ton ship was bought for oceanographic and salvage research in 1967. The *Grifon*, named after the survivor of the 1715 disaster, is equipped with the latest radar, sonar, and other electronic gear as well as salvage equipment, and can cruise for forty-two days with a complement of over twenty aboard. She had already completed several oceanographic research contracts for such organizations as the University of Florida and Johns Hopkins University's Applied Physics Laboratory, and has a full schedule ahead.

Looking over the operations of the dynamic company, Kip Wagner must smile as he recalls that day back in 1960 when President Harry Cannon surfaced with those six confidence-restoring silver wedges.

Treasure Salvors, Inc.

Never in the history of treasure diving has there been a team quite like Melvin A. Fisher's freewheeling, inventive, resourceful, exciting, and successful group. While continuing his rewarding relationship with Real Eight, Fisher has spread out into many new activities, ranging from salvage in his company's own two lease areas (license E-14 and E-14 supplementary) to displaying some of his hoard of salvaged treasure aboard a 500-ton replica of a galleon called the *Golden Doubloon* moored at Fort Lauderdale. Besides the mother company, Treasure Salvors, Inc., four more subsidiaries are active today: the Armada Research Corporation, licensee of the two Florida leased sites; Treasure Displays, Inc., which merchandises salvaged treasure and artifacts for promotions by other companies; Ocean Search, Inc., controlling sales and contract surveys of the sea mag; and Treasure Ship, Inc., the unique museum aboard the *Golden Doubloon* galleon replica.

Besides the original team of Rupert Gates, Walter Holzworth, Demostines Molinar, and Mel's wife Dolores Fisher (Fay Field is now with Varian Associates), an engineer, Richard Williams, has joined the fold and contributed by creating the treasure exhibit. A new salvage barge, the *Gold Digger*, was designed specifically for working shallow wrecks. Three huge propellers point straight down below it in a superpowerful blaster that "moves about one thousand times the volume of sand which can be moved by an air lift in the same amount of time." On deck are compressors for diving air and for the operation of underwater air tools, and four electric winches with which the barge can be positioned precisely on any site.

After the location of over fifty shipwrecks in the Vero Beach area and at least forty off the Keys, Treasure Salvors, Inc., is forging ahead as strongly as ever. Only Fisher knows what new projects are in the books for his dynamic team.

CHAPTER 14

The Bahamas and Bermuda

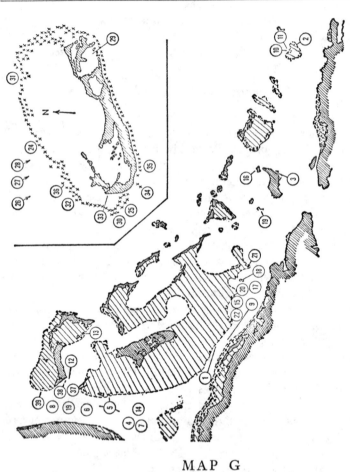

MAP G

The Bahamas and Straits of Florida

From an earth-circling satellite they would resemble pieces of a giant's jigsaw puzzle, brightly colored with the gold of sand and the emerald, garnet, sapphire, and rose hues of coral, strewn at random in the corner of the blue Atlantic between Cuba, Hispaniola and Florida. They spread for 750 miles from Silver Bank on the east to Grand Bahamas Island on the northwest—enormous, oddly shaped submarine cliffs from mile-deep serpentine canyons that separate them. The vast underseas sand flats that cover their tabletop surfaces vary in depth from a hundred to only a few feet, and are broken here and there by mounds that push up above the water in 700 dry islets and scrub cays that form the Bahamas. Other wrinkles, tens of thousands of them, jut up to scratch at the surface in treacherous rock and coral reefs.

These Bahama islands and shoals made a formidable labyrinth through which Spain's treasure fleets had to find passage to reach the Atlantic. At first they crept cautiously eastward through the twenty-five-mile-wide Old Bahamas Channel between Cuba's north coast and shoals of Guinchos, Lobos, Mucaras, and Santo Domingo on the southern edge of the Great Bahamas Bank, then passed west of the Inaguas up through Caicos or Maraguana passages. Later, when the wider New Bahamas Channel was explored, these ships sailed northeast from Havana, skirting the deadly points of Los Roques on Cay Sal Bank, then cruised north between Little Bahama Bank and the Florida coast as far as Cape Hatteras, where they turned east.

Throughout this Bahamas crossing the galleons and *naos* were vulnerable. The slightest miscalculation of course at night, a strong wind from the flanks—to say nothing of a hurricane—a still unknown and uncharted pinnacle of rock, laxity of the helmsman—any of these could cause wooden bilges to be crushed on coral or stone and send them to the bottom. Considering the many thousands of ships that navigated this passage the losses are surprisingly light; yet many dozens of treasure-laden merchantmen were lost in the Bahamas during the two and a half centuries that the armadas returned through their cays and reefs.

The *SANTA MARÍA DEL CAMINO* (1)

Captain Alonso Martín sailed from Havana in 1555, hugging the north coast of Cuba as his ship approached the narrows off Cayo Romano.

A gale sprang up from the south, driving the 200-ton *nao* off course against the reefs of the Grand Bahama Bank. The *Santa María del Camino* broke in her stem and sank at the edge of the canal. There is no record that her cargo, which included about $100,000 in silver, was salvaged.

The SAN CRISTÓBAL (2)

On the voyage home from Santo Domingo this 120-ton *urca* of General Tristan de Salvatierra's armada was wrecked in 1563. Thirty-five people were drowned and a consignment of about $50,000 in treasure lost. No salvage was attempted. The position of the reef is not given in accounts, but it was probably a part of the Silver Bank.

The INGOTS and THE PIRATE SHIP (3)

The tale was told by a two-time loser, Hernando del Castillo, who had two ships taken from under him in succession. The first was the *nao*, on which he was voyaging home, captured off Havana by English pirates in 1599. He wasn't forced to walk the plank but was taken prisoner. The second was the vessel of his pirate hosts which struck a reef and sank a few weeks later. He reached safety "on a large cay near Inagua Island," where he lived until he was picked up by a Spanish ship.

After returning to Havana he told the authorities of his adventures, then added some interesting news. Hernando said that he had seen "on a cay further from shore and smaller than" the one where he had been marooned "many gold and silver ingots, and many cannons, from an earlier wreck there." He had taken the bearings of the cay where this treasure reposed. Furthermore, in the hold of the pirate ship there was silver captured from his and other vessels. He knew where that lay, too.

Did an expedition set sail, with Hernando at the helm, to recover these riches? We don't know since the account ended there. There is a good chance that the tale was not believed—and possibly it shouldn't be—or that no ship was available to send out on what might have been a futile waste of tonnage and salaries. Hernando's story could make sense, for there was a report of an unidentified *nao* being lost with treasure near Inagua in 1563 (probably not the *San Cristóbal*) and a ship could hang on a coral ledge for months in the Bahamas wilderness, while its crew died of thirst, without being sighted by others.

There is a thin possibility that Hernando's treasure trove is still where he saw it—on a small cay farther out from a larger cay off Inagua. A visitor to the area might do worse than looking over charts to see whether he could spot such a location. This tale has overtones of that told by the Florida fisherman (see Chapter 13).

MENÉNDEZ' *NAO* (4)

In 1567 a 250-ton merchantman commanded by Pedro Menéndez sank at the entrance of the New Bahamas Channel, off Florida, with the loss of all the cargo and many lives. The ship went down in deep water.

The *SAN JUAN* and FOUR OTHERS (5)*

A violent storm slashed at the ships of General Juan de Guzman's New Spain armada of 1586 as they sailed north in a long column into the New Channel between Cape Florida and the Biminis. Five of the topheavy *naos*, including the 120-ton *San Juan* commanded by Captain Martín de Irigoyen, were swamped in the passage or wrecked on shoals from Castle Rock to Great Isaac. As far as the accounts of this loss describe, there was little salvage—indicating that most of these vessels sank to below 75 feet. Several of them, with about $1,000,000 in treasure aboard, probably settled under the west edges of the reefs where SCUBA divers could reach their coral-embedded remnants.

The *SANTA CATALINA* and *JESÚS MARÍA* (6)

The 1589 New Spain armada lost two *naos* in the New Channel: the 350-ton *Santa Catalina*, with Captain Domingo Ianez Ome, and the 400-ton *Jesús María* under Captain Francisco Salvago. Each carried about $250,000 in Mexican silver. They probably went down to the 2000-foot-deep channel bottom.

The FOUR *NAOS* (7)

The returning New Spain and Tierra Firme armadas combined at Havana in 1606 and set out up the New Channel for Spain. Only a day from port they were caught in a hurricane which sank four ships off the Florida Keys, all in deep water. Captain Domingo de Licona's *Trinidad*, a 350-ton *nao* of the New Spain armada under General Francisco de Corral, capsized in the howling wind and sank with all her crew and cargo. Three other ships attached to General Luis de Córdoba's Tierra Firme armada sank soon afterward. Several hundred lives and a treasure estimated at over a million pesos were lost in that storm.

The *ALMIRANTA, ESPÍRITU SANTO,* and *SANTÍSIMA TRINIDAD* (8)

General Antonio de Oquendo's New Spain armada had nearly reached safety at the upper end of the New Channel when a hurricane struck on April 20, 1623. The *Santísima Trinidad*, a 600-ton galleon commanded by Captain Ysidro de Cepeda, heeled over under the gale and capsized. She sank instantly, taking down $1,000,000 in gold and silver. A second 600-ton galleon, *El Espíritu Santo*, was swamped and floundered with her Captain Antonio de Sota and nearly everyone aboard. Another $1,000,000 in treasure was lost. The *Almiranta* of the armada was battered by heavy seas but remained afloat, deep in the water, until the wind had subsided. *Pataches* closed to her sides and lowered boats which took off the people and "1,000,000 pesos of treasure" before she went down with $1,000,000 still in her hold. More than 250 people lost their lives that April day.

The lost fortune of $3,000,000 in silver carried aboard the three sunken ships lies about 1000 feet deep some 25 miles off West Palm Beach near the center of the channel.

The THREE *NAOS* OF CAMPOS (9)

Thirty-one vessels of the 1641 New Spain armada, commanded by General Juan de Campos and Admiral Juan de Villavicencio, left Havana on September 13. Villavicencio's *Almiranta* was found to be taking water and the fleet returned to port. There the galleon was patched up and again, on September 28, the armada set sail, taking the Old Bahamas Channel. Off north Cuba it was battered by a hurricane and the ships were scattered. Ten *naos* were wrecked along Cayo Romano and the coral wall on the south of the Great Bahama Bank, and three more swamped in deep water with most of their crews and passengers drowned. Some of the shallow wrecks were partly salvaged by the Spanish and others (see following account), but considerable silver lies in the ballast of others.

It is quite possible that more than one of the wrecked 1641 *naos* settled into the veritable ship junkyard along Mucaras Reef, which is a popular hunting ground. Between fourteen and twenty ballast mounds have been identified along the eight-mile bank, some practically on top of one another. Nearly every serious visitor brings back artifacts and coins. Art McKee has surveyed the site, and on a recent expedition Chuck Mitchell found a cannon dated 1578 T L and a "little stack of eight pewter plates under one of the cannons."

NUESTRA SEÑORA DE LA CONCEPCIÓN (10)

This was the *Almiranta*, command galleon of veteran navigator Juan de Villavicencio. This respected mariner had protested in Havana that his ship was unseaworthy despite the jerry repairs made there, and had sailed reluctantly after a bitter argument with the general. Only Villavicencio's expert seamanship and jettisoning of cannons had kept the galleon afloat during the many days of battering by heavy waves and screaming wind, while the *Almiranta* was hurled first westward, then eastward along the channel, rolling and pitching wildly, often out of control on a helter-skelter voyage. When the storm abated five feet of water splashed in her hold, the sails were shredded and the mainmast broken. Constant pumping was necessary to keep her from going under. She was separated from the other vessels, alone on the sea.

For a month the treasure galleon drifted, at the mercy of wind and waves. Then, with makeshift repairs completed, a council was held to decide what to do. The ship's two young pilots wanted to head south; Villavicencio, with years of experience in those waters, warned that such a course would meet reefs. Under the Bureau of Trade's regulations the pilots' voice was decisive in such cases and again the admiral was overruled. Disgusted, Villavicencio publicly washed his hands in a basin of water, signifying that he relinquished responsibility for the pilots' actions. His warning was vindicated a week later when the lookout screamed of reefs ahead. It was 9 P.M. of November 1.

Anchors were dropped—nearly too late. The *Almiranta*'s hull scraped against coral teeth, then floated free. At dawn the boats were launched and took *Nuestra Señora* under tow. All day long sweating crews of oarsmen pulled the cumbersome galleon through gaps in the coral labyrinth while passengers and crew alike worked at the pumps. At nightfall anchors were dropped again, and when their lines severed spare anchors, and finally cannons, were used for mooring. Toward midnight a wind sprang up. At 2 A.M. the lines suddenly gave way and the *Almiranta*'s bow smashed on a reef. With water gushing in, she slid back, turned around, and settled. The poop grounded on the shallow shoal while the bow vanished under water. Many people were drowned. The survivors clambered onto the poop castle and filled the boats.

During the next days the wreck was abandoned. The pilots thought they were near Puerto Rico and led several boatloads of people to their deaths. Admiral Villavicencio knew the ship's position was north of Hispaniola, in the Abrojos. Those that followed him reached safety. Three dozen people remained on the reef, whose surface was awash at low tide, waiting for rescue. Meanwhile they stripped the settling poop of gold and silver from the captain's cabin, piling it on the reef top. Weeks later, with no help in sight, they sailed off in a boat toward the south. It was wrecked on north Hispaniola with only one survivor. Of the *Almiranta*'s 525 people, 200 remained alive.

Legends of the treasure piled on the reef top spread and gradually the Abrojos (meaning "keep your eyes open!") acquired another name: Banco de Plata, or Silver Shoal. But despite several salvage attempts by Villavicencio (who was acquitted for the loss of his galleon while the pilots were condemned) to return to the wreck, it remained, untouched, for nearly half a century. The value of its treasure was at least $2,000,000 (the *Capitana*, which survived the hurricane, brought back 2,840,000 registered pesos).

The story of William Phips and his fantastically successful salvage of a treasure galleon has been told in dozens of accounts. Possibly the most accurate and detailed is in *Trésors Engloutis*, by Latil and Rivoire, which draws its information from the comprehensive research carried out by Alexander Korganoff. Korganoff's conclusions vary distinctly from other accounts of "Phips' Galleon": he believes—and can produce documentary proof for support—that this ship was Villavicencio's *Almiranta* (see below for another version). After a fruitless first voyage, William Phips returned to the attack on his treasure ship in 1687 with two ships, the *James and Mary* and *Henry of London*, and began the most rewarding salvage ever made up to that time. During earlier questioning he had learned that the ship lay near a tall rock which rose like a fang over the reefs. This rock was not located until after the first ingots were raised—and for reason. Under the pounding of waves it had been eroded until its peak was barely awash. Near its base Phips' native divers found the wreck, already overgrown with coral and seaweed. Among the rotted and worm-eaten timbers of the collapsed hull were bronze cannons and sulfided silver ingots. The wood of treasure chests had disappeared, but their contents—over 2000 pieces of eight to the chest—were fused together in solid masses of silver. When these were broken open the coins in the center tumbled out in undamaged condition. From February 22 until April 19 relays of native divers, drawing air from weighted barrels suspended near the sea bed, sent up treasure. Phips' journal (examined by Korganoff) gives a day-by-day account of their activities. Sample:

> 4th. This morning the wind being at E.S.E. a small gale, our boats went to work on the wreck and in the evening brought on board: 2399 weight of pounds which we suppose to be on silver and which we putt into 32 baggs . . .[1]

When Phips' expedition returned to England its vessels carried 37,538 pounds of silver pesos, 27,556 pounds of silver ingots, 347 pounds of silver plate; 25 pounds, 7 ounces of gold ingots; several bags of gems and pearls. The value as bullion: about $700,000. There was twice as much still unsalvaged in the wreck. In London, Phips badgered his "Gentlemen Adventurers" associates to send a follow-up expedition, and several ships were fitted out. When they finally reached Silver Bank, after many delays, Phips saw to his dismay that the secret was out. More than two dozen vessels of all types were busily "fishing" over the wreck. The *Almiranta* was nearly stripped clean. Despite this disappointment Phips and his investing syndicate had made a fortune. The treasure hunter was knighted by King James II and returned to his native Massachusetts, where as Sir William Phips he became the Royal Governor of Massachusetts in 1692.

---

[1] From *Trésors Engloutis*, by Latil and Rivoire.

The Silver Bank galleon, though probably nearly cleaned out by Phips and scores of other groups, holds a continuing fascination for treasure hunters. In the late 1930s John D. Craig (author of *Danger Is My Business*) and Waldo Logan spent weeks searching for the once-again lost wreck. Korganoff has visited the site. And only a few years ago Ed Link anchored his *Sea Diver* next to the famous rock which marks the galleon's grave. A detailed account of his search and findings is contained in Marion Clayton Link's book *Sea Diver*, and makes fascinating and instructive reading. Armed with the assets of exhaustive research (by Korganoff and Link) and the latest in search equipment (metal detectors, magnetometer, etc.) the *Sea Diver*'s complement scoured the area. They examined pockets of ballast and two ancient, coral-crusted anchors on the bottom and raised part of a deteriorated cannon, pieces of hand-blown greenglass bottles, bits of coral-caked ship's rigging, a rusted spike—and fragments of silver coins so badly sulfided that they were little more than powder. Korganoff believes these traces are of the *Almiranta*. Link thinks not: the glass bottles were later identified by his friend Peterson as of the middle eighteenth century; the anchors, the larger of which measured 9 feet in length and 6 feet from fluke to fluke (although the flukes had the heart- or cloverleaf-shape characteristic of the seventeenth century), seemed too small for such a galleon; the gun barrel fragment was too oxidized to be of use in identification. Ed believes that these come from a smaller ship, perhaps one of those "fishing" over the wreck years later. The remains of the *Almiranta*, he thinks, lie under coral, an integral part of the reef of Silver Bank.

Is Phips' *Almiranta* a worthwhile target for modern treasure hunters? Probably not, from the experience of one of the strongest and best-equipped companies in existence. During three visits to the site, armed with a chart from Kip Wagner, Mel Fisher's Treasure Salvors, Inc., was able to recover olive jars, lead, cannon balls, and buttons in 1963—but no gold or silver.

The *CAPITANA* OF DE GUERRO (11)

This wreck nearly certainly belongs in the "Ghost" section, but is included here because of its long association with Phips, who believed himself that his treasure wreck was not the *Almiranta* of Villavicencio but de Guerro's *Capitana*, supposedly wrecked on Silver Bank in November 1643 with $2,500,000 in silver and gold. Research in Spain turned up only one ship wrecked in the Bahamas that year, making scarcely any mention of it. Had an entire armada been lost—as is stated in several accounts—there would certainly have been comments on the disaster.

The LUCAYAN SILVER WRECK (12)

Years of diving on unproductive wrecks strewn over the Grand Bahama reefs had given Jack Slack immunity to treasure fever when his snorkeling companion Gary Simmons returned to their boat with a report of an interesting old anchor nearby. To Slack, this indicated probably just another ballast heap with perhaps a few cannons. The hard cash from the clients they had taken out diving that day was more tangible. That was on August 26, 1964.

By the following afternoon Slack was smitten with the worst case of treasure fever to have struck the Bahamas since the time of William Phips. He and Dick Tindall, partners in a charter boat business, had returned with Simmons to survey the anchor, which might be interesting to show diving clients. It was only 10 feet deep on the shoreward side of a live coral reef colorfully decorated with sea fans and sponges, about one mile off the south Lucaya shore. Snorkeling down, Slack confirmed Simmons' opinion that the anchor was old. It measured 9 feet and had a round shank and spade flukes. The crossbar was gone, its wood long since devoured by teredos. Coral had formed on the iron.

Simmons called Slack's attention to a peculiar dark glittering formation on the reef top nearby. Visible through its coral encrustation were curious tiny parallel grooves like the edges of stacks of coins. Slack froze. They *were* the edges of coins—thousands of them! As he describes his reaction in his thoroughly entertaining book *Finders, Losers*, Slack "must have surfaced fifteen feet out of the water, yelling or shrieking or babbling in some incoherent but entirely comprehensible manner."

Within minutes he had put on SCUBA gear and returned from the boat. Using a pry bar, he broke loose the huge chunk of encrusted coins, which fell over on the sand. Staggering under the weight, Slack lugged it to beneath the boat, where all three men hoisted it on deck. For many moments they stared in awe at the stinking 200-pound conglomeration cemented together by black silver sulfide and coral. Then bedlam broke loose.

They worked the wreck until dark, bringing up several thousand more silver cobs. After docking at their base in nearby Freeport they loaded the loot, concealed in burlap rags, onto their station wagon and drove it home. Wives were sworn to secrecy and the excited discussion lasted late into the night. It was apparent that the wreck contained much more treasure, the bulk of it buried under sand. To retrieve this they would need equipment. Slack flew to Miami the next day for machinery while Tindall obtained a 10-foot plastic tube, 4 inches in diameter. Two days later they had an air lift operating.

As it sucked up sand one cluster of coins after another was uncovered, to a depth of 3 feet. Below this the silver ran out. The treasure pocket seemed to extend indefinitely across the reef surface. With an area 20 feet in circumference cleared, they were still recovering three hundred coins per hour. The salvage work was interrupted frequently by charter trips necessary to provide income. The accumulating hoard of silver could not be used to pay bills.

The third partner, who had put up most of the capital for the charter business, flew in from America. He was Bissell Shaver, a construction engineer. During visits to their attorney they finalized the incorporation of their company, Sosco Ltd. The first decision was that capital would be needed. On November 18 Sosco, Ltd., entered into a contract with a nonprofit foundation, The Bahamas Oceanographic Society, which in effect made available substantial funds in return for a 20 per cent share of the recoveries. At that time there were no regulations covering treasure troves since the Bahamas government had never been approached on the subject. It was agreed that the Oceanographic Society, with strong political ties, would sound out government opinion regarding the awarding of exclusive salvage rights to the sunken treasure and the terms under which such a concession could be obtained. As yet only a few people directly involved were aware of the magnitude of the treasure find, and what rumors had begun circulating were met with skepticism.

The Sosco team was strengthened with the addition of Richard Stanfield, an instructor in the charter boat business, who became an excellent diver. Before the end of the year the number of their salvaged coins approached ten thousand. One artifact, the most valuable of all, was left undisturbed on the bottom. It was a low-trunnion iron saker with a cluster of cobs encrusted to the breech. Being in direct contact with iron, the silver remained in excellent condition. Another cannon, this one a falconette, and two anchors marked the pile of ballast and pottery shards.

To obtain an estimate of the treasure's value, Shaver took a selection of the coins to New York, where several were appraised at values from a few dollars to $225 each. These cobs were rare and would realize high prices as long as they remained in short supply. If ten thousand pieces suddenly appeared on the numismatic market—or even if news of such a quantity got out! Inevitably, Shaver was recommended to Robert Nesmith, who studied the coins carefully. His expert opinion was that they included some of the oldest Spanish pieces in existence. Noting the letter P on one, he explained that it had been struck at the Potosí, Bolivia, mint. A large proportion of the coins bore Mexico mint marks. The latest recognizable date was 1641, while the majority were minted in 1628. The oldest coin was dated 1584!

While Shaver was still in America, trouble began. A boat with two men aboard appeared over the wreck one day while Slack, Simmons, and Tindall were ashore. They raced out in their boat and drove away the intruder after an eyeball-to-eyeball confrontation. The partners had by now given coins to friends, and even used them to pay for drinks at local bars. The final cover on secrecy was shattered just after New Year 1965 by a newspaper headline: $9 MILLION TREASURE FOUND IN FREEPORT. Inaccurate in other details, the text was chillingly correct in one: that ten thousand coins had been recovered. Wire services picked up the story, and in New York Shaver listened in despair as quotations for his coins plummeted.

While a full-time watch was kept on the wreck site to chase off intruders, the Sosco group realized that legally they had nothing to substantiate title to the treasure. The claim which they had presented to the Port Authority had yet to be approved. To make the wreck location less obvious to poachers, the coin-encrusted cannon, a second big gun, and one of the anchors were moved to safety, leaving only one anchor on the site.

A prominent businessman, according to Slack, was now publicly claiming the wreck. Before long his boat, carrying a formidable diving crew, appeared on the scene. The Sosco members appealed to the Port Authority to intercede with the Bahamas government for police protection, only to learn that law enforcement was beyond the Authority's jurisdiction. They succeeded, through personal representations, in arranging for a police boat to be on call. Just then three old friends arrived in Freeport and offered their assistance. Thus it was that diving champions Don Delmonico, Bruce Monier, and Jacques Mayol were aboard a small flotilla of boats alongside the Sosco cruiser, with a police launch standing nearby, on the morning of the famous clash that made newspaper headlines: ISLANDERS TO FIGHT MIAMIANS FOR THE SUNKEN TREASURE.

Anticipating the arrival of the challenging team, Slack had dived on the wreck while his "diver below" flag fluttered prominently on the surface. The "hostile" cruiser approached with eight men aboard, and passed by just as Slack came up—violating international law protecting divers. After protesting, Slack signed an official complaint aboard the police boat. The cruiser was then ordered away from the wreck site. It moved off about 100 yards and anchored. Four of the intruding divers swam toward the wreck and submerged. Diving quickly, Slack and Simmons tore the face masks off two who were picking up artifacts, forcing them to the surface. While Simmons confronted them, Slack seized a Hawaiian sling and rushed back in a thoroughly determined frame of mind. Shouts and whistles from the police boat finally broke up the melee. The police then ordered all the boats away from the area under penalty of arrest. Shortly afterward the wreck was put out of bounds to all divers and a police force aboard a small tug was instructed to put a twenty-four-hour guard on the site. The publicity jarred the Bahamas government into finally taking action, which it did by passing a law prohibiting the removal from the colony of gold or silver coins dating back fifty years or more. There was still no decision on Sosco's application.

Unable to continue working their treasure site, the Sosco group became involved in a series of new contracts with outsiders and wildgoose chases which are recounted with considerable wry humor in *Finders, Losers*. On April 1, 1965, they signed an agreement with an American whereby his organization was given 25 per cent to act as agent for the marketing of Sosco's coins. This was followed by a second contract which in effect put him in charge of their company. Under his instructions huge sums of money were committed, borrowed, and spent. One bill, for $14,000, covered the rental of a nuclear proton magnetometer through a Texas company, together with a technician to operate it. The instrument was used during an unsuccessful month-long search of Bahamas reefs for new wrecks. Quarrels broke out within the Sosco group. A number of valuable coins from the recovered treasure disappeared. Salvage pirates, operating from boats too fast for the police tug to apprehend, made hit-and-run raids on the site, causing the Sosco members to dash out in their new fast cruiser to chase them away. After a storm, when a spot check revealed a 100-pound clump of coins exposed by wave action, the Sosco team discreetly moved it into hiding to protect it from these raiders. The company was now heavily in debt.

It was not until late spring 1965—eight months after work was suspended—that the government's decision was issued. Sosco was awarded exclusive salvage rights to the sea bed in the vicinity of the Lucayan wreck for a period of five years. Simultaneously a retroactive law was passed under which the government would receive 25 per cent of salvage recoveries, either in material or in payment of its assessed value. The Sosco group was requested to agree to this and complied. There was some question about the validity of such a retroactive law, especially since legal experts who had been consulted in America, Great Britain, and the Bahamas had given opinions that during the time the salvage had been made no applicable law existed in the Bahamas.

As matters stand now, Bahamian regulations stipulate that a Government Search License is a legal prerequisite for wreck searching. To obtain this license the applicant must make a commitment to notify the government of any finds, and to accept the 25 per cent share condition. This license is difficult to obtain, but authorizes the holder not only to search but also to carry out salvage.

With the decision made in Sosco's favor, work on the treasure site resumed. This time equipment included new boats, underwater metal detectors, and powerful 8-inch air lifts. Huge quantities of sand were vacuumed from the reef top, then from its base. The flow of silver continued. When a Bludworth detector signaled metal deposits beneath the reef, divers dug under the shelf until it was too dangerous to proceed further. Then dynamite was used to blast away overhead coral. As recoveries were made, the silver was stored for safekeeping in a Freeport bank whose officers had granted most of the loans incurred by Sosco.

The American agent-manager returned from the U.S.A. with a group including numismatist Dr. Hans M. F. Shullman, who was reported to have valued the silver cobs at a high figure. The Bahamas government brought in an English expert for its own appraisal. Meanwhile the American manager continued drawing on Sosco's credit. His expenditures were such that the Oceanographic Society, disillusioned with his extravagance, finally withdrew all support from Sosco. The four partners then dismissed him in a rare moment of co-operation.

The damage, however, had been done. Despite the tremendous value of the treasure Slack, Simmons, Tindall, and Shaver had very little equity left for themselves. The government owned 25 per cent; the Bahamas Oceanographic Society, 20 per cent; another 25 per cent was committed to the American agent on any sale of coins. Outstanding bills amounting to hundreds of thousands of dollars had to be paid. Slack, who considered this carefully, sold his shares in Sosco, Ltd., for a nominal figure.

Eventually the flow of treasure dwindled, with about sixteen thousand coins raised, and salvage was discontinued. The Bahamas government received 25 per cent of the total, electing to use the Florida system, where their representative selected one of four equal piles of coins. Top-quality pieces from this share are occasionally presented to visiting VIPs. Early in 1969, four and a half years after the Lucayan discovery, the first fifty-two silver cobs were sold at auction in New York under the supervision of Dr. Shullman. The coins—mainly 4-real and 8-real cobs of the Philip III and IV period—will continue to be sold.

There are still cobs lying in crevices and buried under sand in the environment of the Lucayan wreck. A lucky SCUBA diver with an underwater detector might locate a few after a storm.

What about the treasure ship itself? Several marine historians have gone to considerable efforts in attempts to identify it. Some opinions are that it was a part of the Dutch admiral Piet Heyn's fleet—possibly the *Van Lynden,* or a prize. Jack Slack, who has been as closely involved as anyone, has his own views about the wreck:

> There was a previous salvage job. Indications are that the earlier salvors were unsophisticated—probably Bahamian fishermen. They no doubt raised a large quantity of gold ingots. As a rule Bahamians do not

skin-dive. Their salvaging was probably done by glass-bottom bucket. Gold is obvious even to the unsophisticated eye; not so sulfided silver conglomerates. The wreck had too much silver NOT to have contained gold. No other cannons were found because no others were carried aboard the ship. She was accompanied by a sister ship to protect her. She didn't break into parts; we've searched the surrounding waters thoroughly.

It is my opinion that she was either Dutch, or a Dutch prize of Spanish origin. Mendel Peterson gave an opinion that the saker was some fifty years older than the falconette, indicating that the saker was used as ballast. The Spanish admiralty was rather strict about surveying cannons over thirty years old and completely prohibited the use of cannons as ballast. Not so the Dutch.

I have no idea what ship she was and I seriously question this favorite hobby of salvors who "name" their particular finds. The identification of any old wreck, without the finding of some identifying artifact such as a specially constructed gudgeon with the builder's initials, etc., is nearly impossible. Every nation used each other's cannon, anchors, silverware, and even personal items captured from other vessels. It's great fun as speculation, but unfair to be presented as fact.

With this final word it appears that the name of the Lucayan treasure ship—one of the most important finds of the past decade—will remain another mystery of the sea.

The GORDA CAY TREASURE (13)

The history of this famous treasure site and its salvage is told below in detail, along with a possible lead that might still show the way to some of the ship's silver ingots lying under the sea in another area. Recently several final attempts have been made to recover more treasure, all unsuccessful. A survey made in 1966 produced the opinion that "the area has been worked to completion."

The story of this wreck goes back to many years ago, when a storm washed ashore some coins. Word spread, and an American diver arrived. He questioned the friendly local fishermen about ballast mounds and cannons and was told of a wreck off Gorda Cay, where the reef drops off into blue nothingness. Other fishermen had brought up lead ingots from it to ballast their smack boats. *Lead* ingots? asked the American. Yes, lead, replied the native. They went "clunk" when you hit them. Iron went "clank."

That did it. With the fisherman as a guide, the American dived to the reef surface, only twenty feet deep, and soon recognized the telltale signs of a wreck. It had obviously been salvaged—probably centuries ago—as only ballast and cannon balls remained on the coral. Is this where those "lead" ingots came from, the diver wondered. He soon had his answer: yes! There was one . . . and another . . . and another! Meticulously he worked over the wreckage, prying among the coral-encrusted ballast stones, until he reached the point where they ended at the reef's edge. Looking over, he wondered how much of the wreck's treasure lay below. Then he loaded on board his salvage of 70-pound silver bars and departed, convinced that the reef's ledge was stripped of treasure.

He was nearly right. Other treasure hunters searched, and left empty-handed. Then, in 1950, the *Yes Sir* anchored on the site. Aboard were two Nassau businessmen, Howard Lightbourn and Roscoe Thompson, and their friend John Storr, a university professor. They had also heard rumors of treasure and come to have a try. But they had one advantage over their predecessors: an underwater metal detector. Thompson took it down. There were several false alarms over cannon balls. And then—

"I used a pickax and a shovel to loosen some of the formation—and there it was. It was encrusted with coral but you could easily tell that it was extremely heavy for its bulk and was oblong. We hoisted the thing to the surface and in a few minutes chipping hammers revealed that it was what we had been looking for. Although we didn't know its origin then, it was apparent that it was a solid silver bar with plain markings.

"Excited, we worked the shoal for a little over an hour more. Several rare Spanish coins, sabers, and an assortment of cannon balls were brought up. Darkness was drawing near, though, so we marked the location with a floating drum and headed back, intending to return the next day. That night we sat around a campfire and talked over what we thought we'd do with the vast other part of the treasure. We sat around drinking gin and coconut water until after midnight. I guess that was our mistake, because we didn't make it back to the treasure area until late the next afternoon. There was no marker anywhere. We were never able to find the exact spot again, but eventually we'll find it, I'm sure."[2]

The near-perfect condition of the ingot and its markings permitted numismatologist Andrew J. S. McNickle to reconstruct its entire history until shipment. This is given in detail in a pamphlet entitled *The Lost Treasure of King Philip IV* published by The Development Board, Nassau. In brief, the "Thompson-Lightbourn ingot" has the following characteristics: weight 144 marks (72½ pounds); cast at the Royal Mint at Santa Fe de Bogotá, Colombia, in 1652; assayed twice, with the markings of the first assayer destroyed by the second, who struck his own "=9=178" meaning that the bar was worth 9178 reals; fineness of eleven *dineros* and four *granos* (standard at that time), meaning 93.3 per cent silver and 6.7 per cent copper (to stiffen it for coining). The Royal Seal, stamped all over the upper surface so that it would show on all the pieces if the bar were cut up, has the castles of Castile, the lions of León, and the

---

[2] This quotation is taken from a newsletter put out by the Bahamas News Bureau.

grenadine of New Granada (Colombia). Its legend reads PHILLIPVS.D.G.-ISPANI, indicating that the *quinto*—or "Royal Fifth"—had already been deducted for King Philip IV. The name of Miguel de Rojas, chief of all South American mints in 1652, is clearly visible.

This famous bar was purchased by Albert E. Worswick and presented to the Nassau Development Board in whose offices it can be seen today.

One of the coins, a peso, was only slightly damaged during its immersion and its legible marks reveal that it was also minted at Santa Fe de Bogotá. Besides a NR on its surface, meaning *Nuevo Reino* and used by this mint, it has the grenadine at the bottom of the shield with lions and castles—a peculiarity of the Santa Fe de Bogotá mint. Other mints stamped the grenadine in the center of this particular shield.

It is generally felt that this wreck is the *San Pedro*, a *nao* that was blown off course about 1660, and that her treasure-laden stern broke off the ledge and lies far below.

But not all the remaining silver ingots are down there. The fisherman's story of those "lead ingots" used as ballast rings true. They have been traced to two fishing "smack boats"—and both of them were wrecked and sunk not far from Abaco Island . . .

The *SAN LUIS* and *SAN ANDRÉS* (14)

Two warships, the 60-gun *San Luis* and the 30-gun frigate *San Andrés*, were crippled in a violent storm in the Bahamas area, probably in the New Channel, while escorting the Tierra Firme armada of 1720. The people were taken off before these ships sunk but most of the treasure that was aboard was lost with them.

The *ANDALUCÍA* (15)

In 1740, ten years after she was launched in nearby Havana, this 62-gun warship struck a rock and sank in the Old Bahamas Channel. She carried no treasure except ship's money and plate, and the jewelry of her officers.

The *INFANTA* (16)*

This 18-gun barkentine, under Captain Casimiro de La Madrid, was bound for Spain with about $200,000 in treasure in 1788 when she struck a reef off Inagua Chica. Her crew and passengers escaped in the boats before the ship went under, but the treasure could not be salvaged. It lies on the *Infanta*'s wreckage, at a depth of probably no more than one hundred feet.

The *DIANA* (17)

She was a mail frigate, en route to Cádiz with a small quantity of silver and gold in 1791. The *Diana* was caught in a storm in the Old

Channel and her planks so badly sprung that leaks overtook the pumps and she was abandoned, sinking soon afterward in deep water.

The POSTILLÓN (18)
On July 12, 1804, Commander Ramón Pardo de Lama's 14-gun brigantine struck a shoal and sank in the Old Channel. No lives were lost. It is quite possible that the *Postillón* carried treasure. Her remains lie against a reef on the south edge of the Great Bahamas Bank.

The ARAUCANA (19)
Somewhere off the Florida coast, in the New Channel, the 6-gunned schooner *Araucana* commanded by Benito de la Rigada was capsized and sunk by a sudden storm on October 26, 1811. She was probably returning to Spain with some silver and gold in her cargo.

The GALGA (20)
The only comments on the loss of the schooner *Galga* are that she "ran aground in the Bahamas and blew up." She was homeward bound in 1816 with a small quantity of treasure.

The ALMIRANTE (21)
About $300,000 in silver lie in the wreckage of this 20-gun barkentine. Under the command of Ignacio Checón, the *Almirante* struck a reef near the Cayo de Santo Domingo in 1821 and went down immediately, drowning 25 of her crew. The sunken ship was too deep to salvage then—probably over one hundred feet.

The MAGICA (22)
This barkentine sank in 1824 in the Old Channel with the loss of several lives and some treasure.

ADMIRAL PIET HEYN'S TREASURE FLEET (37)
Information from Nassau gives a good picture of the fate of the four Spanish *naos* and some of the treasure captured by Piet Heyn during his attack in Matanzas Bay. The Dutch fleet was sailing up the Florida Straits with the Spanish prizes when it was caught in a hurricane. The warships and *naos* were swept eastward into the Northwest Providence Channel and wrecked, one by one, along the north reefs of the Great Bahamas Bank between Great Isaac and Stirrup cays. Some may have been carried over the edge as far south as Mackie Bank. Nearly every ship was lost. Several ballast mounds that have been located recently in this general area could well be those of the admiral's ships. There should be Spanish treasure on more than one of these.

The "SILVER POINT WRECK" (38)

About half a mile west of Lucaya lies a ballast mound on a shallow reef which is referred to as the "Silver Point wreck." Recorded recoveries from this site have been limited to pottery and glass fragments, brass nails, and a few other artifacts, indicating that the wreck has been fairly thoroughly worked. The ship seems to have been ballasted with shale.

The MEMORY ROCKS WRECKS (39)

Under contract to the Bahamas government, divers of Expeditions Unlimited salvaged two of the wrecks lying around this reef in 1966. From one, Norman Scott's team recovered a quantity of silver Spanish coins in excellent condition, minted at Potosí and Lima, and dated from 1693 to 1697. Several old cannons and other artifacts were also salvaged. It has not been possible to identify these ships, but it is believed that they were Spanish.

The HOGSTY REEF WRECKS (40)

Donald Ediger of Expeditions Unlimited, Inc., describes his company's salvage operations along this reef: "Hogsty Reef is the site of many wrecks, but our personnel are still surprised at the great volume of wreck material. Because of this factor, difficulty was encountered in identifying the finds. Many French and British cannons were recovered, along with anchors, most of which date from the eighteenth century." Along the outer shorelines of this four-sided atoll, on every stretch, lie anchors, cannons, and wreckage. Hogsty has long been recognized as a promising treasure-hunting ground, and there are stories that a Miami treasure diver found many valuable coins here in the late 1950s.

The "PITCH BARREL WRECK" (??)**

One story of recovered treasure stars Art McKee and includes all the details except the answer to the 64 doubloon question: Where? Back in his early pay-diver days, when he chuckled at "crazy treasure hunters with that gleam in their eye," Art was approached by a man with a proposal. Unlike so many others, this involved cash on the barrelhead and Art accepted. After a voyage of unspecified duration the man pointed down and Art went over. They were at the edge of a shallow reef. Within a short time McKee had found two iron cannons embedded in coral. Then he looked over the precipice into 80-foot-deep water below and saw more cannons.

Three days later, after developing calluses from hacking at coral with his pick, Art spotted an odd round coral growth and gave it a tentative whack. There was a hollow space inside where barrel staves had rotted away. The coral wall hid the contents of a barrel. But not an ordinary barrel, Art was quick to note.

"I hit the coral a couple more whacks . . . and inside was hard black pitch or tar, with gold coins sticking out of it. I broke off a hunk of the pitch and sent it topside and they got eighteen gold doubloons out of it. I was sure excited. I had never seen gold on the ocean bottom before and this glistened like new. I broke up the mass and we found over sixteen hundred gold doubloons altogether."[3] With the exception of a handful donated to McKee and now in his museum, the owner melted down the entire numismatic treasure. From the gold bullion he received about $56,000. Had he sold the one-ounce coins to collectors he would have realized at least $250,000.

It is possible that this episode had something to do with McKee becoming a treasure diver . . .

And what about the rest of the wreckage of this established treasure ship wreck? Art has wondered about it frequently. "I'd honestly like to find that wreck again," he says. "But I don't know where it is. Probably it lies along the Bermuda Bank somewhere, since I remember that we passed an oil tanker on the way there."

Bermuda

BERMUDA LAW COVERING TREASURE SALVAGE[4]

Following Teddy Tucker's treasure finds, the Bermuda government became aware of the intrinsic and historical value of wrecks on the reefs, and in 1959 the legislature passed the Wreck and Salvage Act. This carried home one main message: that Bermuda has sovereignty over her reefs. Much of the act reiterates law which pertained to salvage in the past, but two fundamentally new features were introduced:

1. The term "Historic Wreck"—defined as a ship which is of historic interest or value and which is not less that fifty years old;
2. The creation of a new body, "The Bermuda Historical Wrecks Authority," whose function is "to tender advice to the Receiver of Wrecks on matters as he may refer to them on the exercise of his powers and the performance of his duties under Part II of this Act."

Thus the act defines historic wrecks and empowers the Receiver of Wrecks, on advice from the Authority, to protect them. It empowers the Receiver, at his discretion, to grant to "any person whom he is satisfied is a fit and proper person" a license to conduct research on, explore, and remove parts of a historic wreck. It makes it illegal for any person without a license to dive on historic wrecks. The period of

---

[3] From R. I. Nesmith's book *Dig for Pirate Treasure.*
[4] The information in this section was kindly provided by Mr. Harry Cox.

validity of a license—formerly three years—is now one year. There are about a dozen licenses issued at the present. The Receiver may attach any conditions he wishes to any license, such as permission to use air lifts and water jets, and explosives in salvage work.

The Wreck and Salvage Act is specific about compensation for recovered artifacts and treasure. If the Receiver of Wrecks does not release these articles to the salvor, "Then the Receiver shall pay to the finder of such wreck such compensation as may be agreed between them, or in default of such agreement, such compensation as may be determined by a sole arbitrator or arbitrators, appointed by the Governor-in-Council." In addition, the Governor-in-Council has the power to direct that the salvaged goods be returned to the salvor, in lieu of a payment that may have been awarded by the arbitrator or arbitrators.

A final provision in the act allows a list of unprotected wrecks around the island to be published periodically. These wrecks may be freely visited by anyone without a license. Some forty wreck sites are on the current list.

THE BERMUDA TREASURE WRECKS

Directly across the route of the returning armadas were the Bermudas, their three hundred low islets and banks of shoals extended for twenty miles on the Atlantic like a seine spread for catching passing galleons. And steadily they gathered in their haul, a ship or two every year, until by 1800 over three hundred victims had been enmeshed in the coral nets of Ledge Flats, North Rocks, and other outlying reefs.

These shipwrecks played a key role in the history of the islands. They provided the name Bermuda to replace "Isle of the Devils" when the *nao* of Juan de Bermúdez was stranded there in 1515. They delivered the first settlers when the Virginia-bound *Sea Venture* was wrecked off the east coast with 150 men, women and children in 1609. They helped the young colony to prosper and expand by furnishing a steady bounty of New World supplies and wealth from *pataches* and *naos* whose journeys ended abruptly on the western shoals. The early Bermudians, abetted by Governor Butler, plundered these ships and robbed their survivors so often and thoroughly that a Spanish king angrily shouted that the only reason Englishmen settled in Bermuda at all was to get in on the lucrative pastime of stealing his treasure.

There was much truth in what the king said. After the colony had been established its members developed into competent wreckers and every time a storm tossed up a broken hulk swarmed out in boats to strip it clean. Before the time of the colonists, though, Bermuda was an uninhabited coral and sand wilderness, for some reason never occupied by the Spanish as a mid-ocean refuge and provisioning base. Crews marooned there had all they could do to get away. Sometimes they

were able to recover cargo from their wrecked vessels; nearly every
island in the area has its tale of buried Spanish gold. More often the
wooden *naos*, sunk in shallow water among the reefs, disintegrated
and vanished under sand and new coral without a diver approaching
to within hundreds of miles. These early shipwrecks—those before
1640—are the ones of most interest to treasure divers. Nearly all still
hold treasure from the Indies under their sand blankets.

The *CAPITANA* (23)

The 500-ton *Capitana* of General Juan Menéndez' New Spain armada
of 1563 was separated from the other ships in a tempest and "lost in
the Bermudas." She carried about $1,500,000 in silver from Veracruz.
Although the big galleon probably smashed her bottom on a reef a
considerable distance from shore, research by Teddy Tucker confirms
that there were survivors who were picked up the following year. The
Capitana may be one of the more than 120 wrecks which have been now
located in the Bermuda area. Her remains are probably in the western
reefs, some 20 to 50 feet deep and under coral. About forty cannons,
mostly bronze, would signal her location to the searcher. Her anchors
probably lie farther out where they were broken free.

The *SAN PEDRO* (24)

When they gathered information on Spanish wrecks from documents
at Madrid and Seville our researchers were given the clues so far known
about the ship from which Teddy Tucker found his famous treasures
and asked to keep their eyes open for a possible candidate. One *nao*,
"lost at Bermuda," seemed to fit the bill. She was the *San Pedro* of unrecorded tonnage, part of a Tierra Firme armada, wrecked in this area
in 1595. Aside from the fact that the loss date and her port of loading
makes her the most likely prospect, there was an interesting notation
recorded in comments: "*The silver was not on board.*" It had evidently
been transshipped to another vessel at Havana. A painstaking research
carried out by Tucker and his many interested associates has resulted
in near-certain confirmation that this famous wreck is the *San Pedro*.

The story of the sensational salvage by Edward B. "Teddy" Tucker
and his brother-in-law Robert Canton off Bermuda in 1955 has been
featured in *Life*, *Argosy* and other magazines, and is well known. Fuller
details are given in *Dig for Pirate Treasure* by Bob Nesmith, who included an interview with Tucker. The first indication that part of an
old Spanish wreck had been found came in 1950 when Tucker and
Canton, returning one evening from sea, spotted cannons on a 30-foot-
deep sand pocket between two reefs. Over the next days they raised
some of them and other artifacts located in the area, realizing that their
salvage came from a very old ship. They reported their find to local

authorities, and finally sold the cannons to Bermuda's Monuments Trust. The wreck, referred to as "the Old Spaniard," did not seem interesting.

It was not until four years later, in 1954, that Tucker and Canton resumed their explorations there. Using an air lift and a water jet, then a wooden paddle when objects began to appear, Tucker cleared the sand pocket. Several months later his paddle had fanned up a fortune. Tucker had accomplished the first major salvage of Spanish treasure in the Western Hemisphere since the days of William Phips. Among the objects recovered were:

Two thousand silver coins, mostly Spanish with some French and English, varying in condition from sulfided biscuits to near-mint, legible markings varying in minted dates from 1495 at the earliest to 1593 at the most recent.

Six pearl-studded gold buttons, and thirteen single pearls.

One gold bar, 10½ inches in length, 36 ounces in weight, marked PINTO (probably denoting origin of the gold from the Pinto River mines in Colombia) and XXI (probably the lot or serial number). An assayer's bite had been taken from one edge.

Two roundish gold cakes, or lumps, about 3 inches in diameter. One weighed 23 ounces and was marked with lot number XXIIII and D°HERNANDZ (the assayer's name). The other weighed 19 ounces and had the lot number XX and ESPANA stamped on it.

One 11-inch, 42-ounce gold bar; another, 4 inch, 6 ounces; two gold squares, 1½ inches across, cut from bars.

The gold cakes and bars above had also been marked with the circular seal of the Royal Spanish Tax Collector meaning that the king's royal fifth had been deducted: in its center a shield showed castles (of Castile, Spain) lions (of León, Spain) and pomegranates (of the New Granada Viceroy, of which Colombia was a part). Around the shield's border ran the inscription PHILLIPVS.II.D.G.REX indicating the reign of King Philip II, 1556–98.

The *pièce de résistance* was a golden crucifix, 3 inches long and 2 inches wide, set with seven perfectly matched cabachon-cut Colombian emeralds, of Indian workmanship. Two small spikes represent the nails of the Crucifixion. It has been identified as a bishop's pectoral cross.

In addition to the above treasure, some of the eighty pieces of ordnance and artifacts salvaged were of great historical value and told a little about the ship which had carried them:

Seven muzzle-loading iron cannons weighing from 500 to 800 pounds each, 5 to 7 feet long; many cannon balls.

Four breech-loading swivel guns (*versos*) and balls.

Sixteen matchlock muskets and lead shot.

A bronze apothecary's mortar marked with the name of a famous Flemish craftsman and dated 1561.

Copper buckets, pewter plates, and pottery.

Three iron anchors 14 feet long with holes where their wooden stocks —long ago eaten away—had been.

A steel breastplate.

A lead sounding weight, a navigator's brass dividers, and other shipboard instruments.

Several bronze hand grenades.

Pieces of flint ballast.

Some wood and ballast was finally found in 1966, giving support to Tucker's theory that the galleon or *nao* had been carried by waves over the outer reef and slammed down between two ridges whose crests supported her at the bow and stern. Up-and-down pounding caused the longitudinal frames of her keel and bilge, hanging unsupported between, to split and heavy cargo and some ballast spilled out through the hole. The hull, lightened by 20 tons, was picked up and carried farther toward shore where she finally sank at a still-unknown spot.

From the salvaged artifacts the following picture can be drawn of the ship and her voyage. The ancient anchors, the seven cannons, the *versos*, the matchlock muskets and the steel breastplate were all standard fittings and cargo of a 200–400 ton *nao* of the period 1550–1600. The anchor and cannons give an indication of the ship's size. The armament conforms with Bureau of Trade orders of that period requiring 250-ton ships to carry "6 fat iron guns, 12 iron *versos*, 12 *ballestas*, 12 harquebuses or muskets . . . 12 breastplates" among other weapons. These were all sixteenth-century guns and the inclusion of shields, helmets, and breastplates in a ship's defenses was discontinued soon afterward (see Wreck Identification section). The absence of bronze guns, which were generally carried on the *Capitanas* and *Almirantas* while iron guns were placed on the cargo *naos*, indicates that this was not a galleon, but a merchant vessel.

The date of loss is after 1592, when the last legible coin was minted. Since the variety of types and dates, and two nationalities, of the money make it obviously an assortment in general circulation rather than a mint shipment, it can be assumed that this money belonged either to passengers (possibly a bishop, owner of the crucifix) or to the ship's funds. The date of loss is probably within the reign of Philip II, ending in 1598, because of his name on the tax collector's seal. This is not conclusive, though, since the gold might have been shipped years after casting and in any case about two years would have passed after the king's death before a new stamp was made and put into use at the mint. The breastplate supports an outside date of 1600, since their use was discontinued after that. The ship most probably sank, therefore, between 1592 and 1600.

The gold's origin in Colombia makes it likely that it was taken aboard at Cartagena and that the ship was of a Tierra Firme armada. A collection of Carib weapons also found could have been loaded at either Cartagena or Havana, where the Tierra Firme armadas called en route back.

When the treasure was found there were no clear-cut Bermuda laws covering the rights to such salvage. Tucker and Canton, after a year of uncertainty, decided to publicize the find in *Life*, etc. The Bermuda government reacted in a manner that would discourage any treasure finders from reporting their salvage. The door was finally opened to a barely acceptable arrangement after Ed Link and Mendel Peterson accompanied Tucker to the treasure site. A government official arrived, and in front of him Peterson offered $2000 for a gold bar. The official matched this offer, and a form of precedent was established when Tucker accepted. Under present regulations all finds must be registered with Bermuda's Receiver of Wrecks. Treasure and artifacts must be offered to the Bermuda government for first refusal, and sold at a price usually fixed by the government's own curators. That this price is not necessarily the highest is evidenced by the fact that Tucker has an offer of $50,000 for another gold bar presently on loan to the Smithsonian Institution.

The *San Pedro* treasure was found in a sand pocket nine miles from Somerset, on the North Breakers. The rest of the ship, with cargo and more treasure, was probably washed inshore.

The *SAN ANTONIO* (25)

One afternoon in 1960, while Tucker and Canton were cruising aboard their 33-foot *Brigadier* with Peter Stackpole, who had been diving with them since 1954, Teddy spotted a sand depression which aroused the sixth sense he has developed about wrecks. He stopped the boat and made a quick dive. A single cannon caught his attention immediately, and as he extended his investigation he realized that he had found a new wreck. Within a short time he had seen broken pottery, musket shot, and several coins. A piece of broken gold chain ended any doubts about working the site. Stackpole added a pair of brass navigational dividers, in perfect condition, to the salvage. The three divers penetrated the covered wreck over a period of many days. As they worked away the sand, their collection of recovered artifacts grew with the addition of bits of rope, pulley blocks, shreds of tobacco leaf, swords, pottery which included Majolica ware, and finally money and jewelry. An emerald-mounted gold ring found here is worn by Teddy Tucker's wife,

Edna. When a many-faceted clump was broken open, it yielded forty-eight silver pieces of eight minted at Potosí, in perfect condition. A probe into another part of the wreckage resulted in a flood of ink from a pocket of indigo dye. As more artifacts were retrieved from the wreck and analyzed, it was possible to make a positive identification of the ship.

She was the *San Antonio*, a 300-ton *nao* which was driven onto the rocks of Long Bar during a hurricane on September 12, 1621. Only 120 of her crew reached shore alive, bringing with them a tiny part of the ship's treasure. They were given the customary welcome by the Bermudians, who robbed and beat them for facts about the ship's cargo. The Spanish admitted that 60,000 gold crowns were on the wreck. After the storm the *San Antonio* was stripped of her anchors, four swivel guns, and all but one cannon, which Tucker found. Nearly all the gold was taken off, and probably provided the reason that Governor Butler left the island soon afterward, before his tour was ended, aboard his own ship. In a thorough dredging of the wreck, Tucker has recovered most of what the wreckers missed.

NUESTRA SEÑORA DE LA LIMPIA CONCEPCIÓN (26)

She was a small *nao*, carrying only 100 tons from Honduras, crossing the Atlantic under the command of Captain Juan Calzado in 1622. Fragmentary reports indicate that this ship was wrecked somewhere in the Bermudas with a total loss of her cargo and many people drowned. As far as is known, no salvage was carried out after the loss.

Teddy Tucker has advised that a wreck which was found in 1964 by Donald Canton could well be this ship.

The ALMIRANTA and PATACHE (27)

The combined New Spain and Tierra Firme armadas sailed from Havana on August 15, 1626, escorted by thirteen galleons under General Larraspuru. As the fleet of fifty ships approached Bermuda hurricane winds scattered them over the ocean. It was not until days later that the general was told of the damage. The New Spain *Almiranta* and a *patache* had been sunk at Bermuda. They went down with all their cargo and only three hundred survivors of their crews of nearly seven hundred. The *Almiranta* had left Veracruz with $2,000,000 in silver aboard, and the *patache* carried another $200,000. Both ships are probably deep, outside the Bermuda reefs.

The VIGA and GALGO (28)

A hurricane in 1639 wrecked two ships of the *Armada Real de la Guardia de la Carrera de las Indias* commanded by General Gerónimo Gomez de Sandoval. These were the *urca* nicknamed "*La Viga*" and the *patache* "*El Galgo*" (The Greyhound). Both vessels were salvaged to a large extent by the Bermuda wreckers, as their hulls lay in shallow water.

A major research effort was made in Madrid to find out facts about the salvage. The yellowed, handwritten pages of Navarrete's enormous work supplied a twenty-page description of the shipwrecks and partial recovery of the *Viga*'s cargo. In the *Colección* was the statement that the *Galgo* had sunk only 200 yards from the *Viga*. Despite this wealth of data, which was forwarded to Bermuda, no positive identification has yet been made of the wreckage of either ship.

The *WARWICK* (29)

Over the years, Teddy Tucker has developed a close working relationship with Mendel Peterson, under which he devotes some two months each year working in conjunction with Peterson's division at the Smithsonian Institution. In a major search for wrecks in the Bermudas, the Smithsonian contracted with Mel Fisher's Treasure Salvors, Inc., to carry out a sweep of the reefs with its proton magnetometer in 1967. The project was successful and as Mel comments, "We found Teddy enough wrecks to last him several years."

One of these was the *Warwick*, fully loaded and ready to sail for America when she sank in a gale in 1619 at anchor in Castle Harbour. Her hull, which should yield a treasury in artifacts of the early seventeenth century—and possibly money—is buried under several feet of mud. This wreck will be dredged during the calmer summer periods of the next years. Because of the muddy bottom here, visibility is unusually poor.

THE SIXTEENTH-CENTURY SPANISH WRECK (30)

Close to the *San Antonio* lies the wreckage of a ship estimated by Tucker from the nature of salvaged artifacts to be of the 1560 period. An assortment of pottery has been collected from this wreck as well as coins and a gold cross. It is possible that this ship is a *nao* which, according to Bermuda historical records, broke up on the reefs during a storm about three hundred years ago. Only seventy of her crew reached shore safely. Several sakers were salvaged, but there is no mention of treasure.

THE SEVENTEENTH-CENTURY SPANISH WRECK (31)

In 1969 Tucker discovered a wreck on the Bermuda reefs that was unusual because of its good condition. It lay 18 feet deep under a blanket of sand. After considerable dredging Tucker uncovered an 80-foot-long wooden keel flanked by the lower parts of sturdy ribs on which double planking was still in place. The ship's ballast stones were larger than usual. As he moved these rocks, Tucker retrieved a rich collection of artifacts and treasure. There were numerous short pieces of gold chain and heavy single links. The blade of a sword was encrusted with forty-five pieces of eight. These, together with other 8-, 4-, 2-, and 1-real coins found, were dated before 1639. They had all been minted at Potosí with the exception of one from Mexico City.

From the size of the keel it is apparent that this was a large ship—probably a *nao* or *urca*. Although the date and type of salvaged artifacts correspond with those of the *Viga*, Tucker states that this wreck was another ship.

THE SPANISH WRECK OF ABOUT 1700 (32)

Another unidentified wreck worked by Tucker lies on the outer edge of the northwest Bermuda reefs. Coins and other salvaged material indicate a date of about 1700.

THE "FLEMISH WRECK" (33)

This long-sought wreck, the object of searches from 1956 onward by Ed Downing and other enthusiasts, was known to have sunk on the inner reefs off Wreck Hill. It was finally discovered during the Treasure Salvors, Inc., 1967 magnetometer sweep. This is another example of the value of this electronic search aid, for, like the *Warwick*, the "Flemish wreck" was invisible to even the most experienced eye. Her remains were under 7 feet of sand.

THE "FRENCH WRECK" (34)

A French vessel whose name is not recorded is known to have sunk in 1593 off the southwest reefs. Because of the historical value of her lading, she has been the target of many search efforts.

THE VIRGINIA MERCHANT (35)

This English ship sank in 1660 on a reef off Bermuda's south coast with 173 drowned. Its wreckage, discovered by Tucker, was especially interesting to Mendel Peterson because a coating of animal hair had been used as protection against teredos. The only other known find of hair used in sheathing was made by Kip Wagner's Real Eight group.

Teddy Tucker has long deserved his position at the top of the world's treasure finders listing. He was raised in Bermuda and served in the British Navy, where he became a diver. Later he joined the Canton brothers in a salvage business which has been successful commercially —even discounting treasure finds. Much of the work is the salvage of modern wrecks, surveys for insurance companies, and similar unglamorous undertakings. Tucker's treasure finds have of course made the headlines. A number of these artifacts have been bought by the Bermuda government—for a reported tax-free $100,000—and can be seen in a

Bermuda museum. The feature attraction of this collection is the famous "bishop's cross" for which the government is believed to have paid $50,000. Photographs of Tucker's artifact and treasure finds are on pages 38–52 of Peterson's *History Under the Sea*.

The SIXTEENTH-CENTURY TREASURE OF HARRY COX (36)

"I anchored the *Shearwater* over the ballast and went down. The site was not a promising one. A few iron spikes, which turned to dust when my fingers crunched them, were found here and there among the hard granite stones, but there was no sign of a ship. I fanned little pockets of sand. Suddenly a blackened, badly corroded piece of eight rolled out of a chink in the reef. Then another, and then there was the twinkle of yellow as a couple of beautiful little gold coins spun and glided in the light reef swell. My fingers closed on a crude, double-wound gold circlet. Suddenly Bill Gillies was with me. So was Pat Maher, a pretty blonde who has dived from the *Shearwater* for three years. My movie film records us actually discovering the treasure."

Harry Cox' treasure has merited Mendel Peterson's comment: "A find of major importance." It was discovered in the afternoon of July 26, 1968, while Harry Cox was cruising along the edge of the northwest barrier reef some seven miles from shore. Bill Gillies, Cox' diving companion of five years, was scanning the reef top while in tow when he spotted a broken line of ballast stones near the reef's drop-off, 25 feet deep. Diving to examine them, he surfaced with a 5-foot-long elephant's tusk—a most curious find in the middle of the Atlantic Ocean. The *Shearwater* circled the site with all eyes searching for signs of a wreck. There were none. Cox decided to make another exploratory dive onto the ballast stones before returning home. Within an hour after uncovering the coins, he had found a magnificent golden chain with each of its double links hand-soldered. When stretched out it measures 15½ feet long. Approaching darkness stopped diving that day, but the group was on the site at seven the next morning. Within four hours nearly all the artifacts that lay in the treasure pocket were recovered. There was still no trace of a ship.

The collection of salvaged treasure was impressive. Besides the gold chain, it included a gold manicure set—possibly the only one of its kind in existence—containing four grooming tools. It was decorated with two identically matched caryatids. Because of its uniqueness, the origin has not yet been determined. There were several gold circlets and many gold rings. Seven pearls mounted on a golden wire frame formed a small cross. A large number of silver coins, in denominations from 2- to 8-reales, were collected. Some were round and bore the coat of arms of Philip II. The gold coins were significant for dating purposes.

They were rare golden Portuguese cruzados covering the period 1521–80. Gold bars were also salvaged, of two distinct types. The first appeared to be registered treasure since each ingot was stamped with markings that appear Spanish but have not been identified. The second kind, probably contraband, was a hammered gold with no marks. The single most valuable item recovered was made of base metal. It was a sixteenty-century mariners' astrolabe, which, with four others found recently in other wrecks, brings the total number of these instruments on record to twenty-four. Incongruous among such treasures was a scattering of Venetian glass trading beads.

From a study of these artifacts the "wreck" has been dated in the 1580–90 period, making it one of the oldest ever found. It could have been Spanish or Portuguese. The word "wreck" is misleading, since up to the summer of 1969 no further trace of a ship has been encountered. Were it not for the presence of ballast, it could be assumed that the recoveries were contained in a small portion of a ship's superstructure, possibly the captain's cabin, which was carried in from a ship that disintegrated in deeper water. The treasure and astrolabe could have been stored in a single wood chest. The question remains of how the ballast stones and ivory tusk were also on the site. Harry Cox is determined to solve this puzzle and to locate the wreck of a ship as well. He has purchased new equipment with which to make the search.

He is thoroughly capable of tackling this project. A Bermuda businessman today, he has been diving among the reefs since 1956 and has charted about a hundred shipwrecks off the island. Among these is another very old site which he worked in 1964. During months of hard labor he and his associates broke loose and moved over a ton of coral-cemented ballast stones and uncovered some wooden ribs. This wreck yielded several *versos* later identified by Mendel Peterson as dating back to 1560–1600. Their crude workmanship emphasized their early date, as did the quality of shot found in the wreck. The cannon balls were irregular, and one, of lead, was actually hammered into shape by hand.

Although he took up wreck diving seriously fifteen years ago, Harry Cox made his first venture into the deep at a much earlier age. "The first dives I made were in a helmet," he recalls, "with my dedicated ten-year-old brother working the pump for me overhead. While walking too deep one day, my diving career was very nearly brought to an inglorious end when the little punt capsized and I was left to contemplate the air pump as it zigzagged down to the bottom and settled at my feet. Disturbing. That was years ago. I suppose I must have been eleven or twelve at the time."

To Harry Cox, his contributions to underwater archaeology in Bermuda are particularly rewarding. He has a great pride in his island home, and for years has been dramatizing Bermuda's colorful history on his own radio and TV programs. When his boat *Shearwater* was christened by Bermuda's governor in 1960 it became the first fully-equipped diving boat for visitors to the island. Harry Cox has an especially personal association with the old wrecks he is discovering. Three ships, once owned by his family, were lost long ago on Bermuda's treacherous reefs.

CHAPTER 15

South America—East Coast

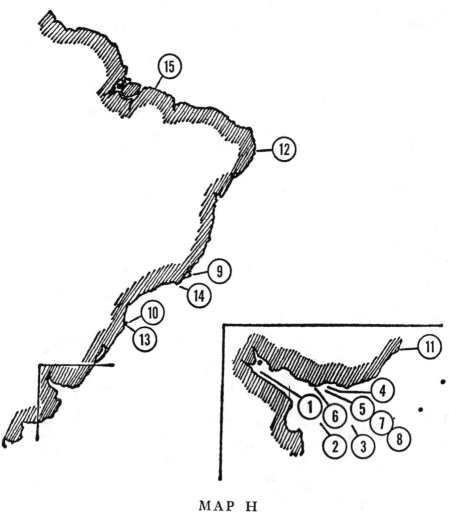

MAP H

Río De La Plata

The estuary of La Plata is the maritime gateway to Argentina on its southern border and Uruguay to the north. A shallow bay, 120 miles wide at its mouth and reaching 150 miles into South America, it was discovered in 1516 by the navigator Juan Diaz de Solís and explored by Ferdinand Magellan and Sebastian Cabot. The Spaniard Pedro de Mendoza founded Buenos Aires on its inner south bank in 1536. The whole region, being west of the demarcation line of the Treaty of Tordesillas signed in 1494 between Spain and Portugal, fell to Spain while Brazil, to the northeast, was colonized by Portugal.

It was soon apparent to the Spaniards that La Plata held no treasure empires to plunder so the territory developed slowly. Missionary-led settlers and traders drifted in and Buenos Aires gradually expanded into a city and was made the capital of the La Plata Viceroyalty in 1776. Montevideo was founded as a military post across the bay in 1717 and a port ten years later. Agriculture and cattle raising spread. Shipments began leaving for Spain: sugar cane, wheat, cotton, hides and skins, wool, tobacco, wines; then, as prospectors worked the mountains, gold and silver in moderate quantities from Argentina, and from Uruguay larger values of gold as well as amethysts, agates, and other semiprecious stones.

Buenos Aires and Montevideo became important export centers and also served as stopover ports for the frigates and warships bringing back Peru gold and silver via the Straits of Magellan. The wrecks of many vessels lie in the 10,000 square miles of La Plata bay.

The CAPITANA, ALMIRANTA, and SANTIAGO (1)

A storm in 1582 sank these three galleons off Buenos Aires. They carried cargoes of local produce and probably a small quantity of gold and silver. After settling onto the 90-foot-deep bottom, the hulls were silted over with alluvial sediment carried down by the Uruguay and Paraná rivers, and their unburied wood rotted away. The *Capitana*, *Almiranta*, and *Santiago* are not interesting to treasure divers.

The TWO NAOS (2)

The flota of Admiral Flores Valdez was crippled in the La Plata estuary in 1583 when a violent squall capsized and sank two *naos* and

damaged several others. There may have been a small value of treasure
on the lost ships.

THE GALLEON (3)
In 1679 a galleon commanded by Captain José López de Villavicencio
floundered in a storm at the mouth of La Plata bay with 160 of her
crew drowned. There is no record of treasure being aboard, except for
ship's money and plate.

The *VICTORIA* (4)
The 26-gun Spanish frigate *Victoria* was wrecked off the Isla de
Farallon on January 8, 1763. She settled in fairly shallow water and
some of her guns were raised, and most of her valuables.

The *AVENTURERO* (5)
This 20-gun barkentine was wrecked off Montevideo on the Banco
Inglés (English Shoals) in 1767 while on a voyage from Cádiz to Buenos
Aires, in convoy. Commander José de Urrutia and the crew escaped
before the ship went under. Some ship's money was lost.

The *AURORA* (6)
Ferris L. Coffman states in his book *1001 Lost, Buried or Sunken
Treasures* that this Spanish frigate sank in Montevideo Bay in 1772
while bound from Peru to Spain with a treasure consignment. He reports that dredging of the area in 1880 raised a 70-pound silver bar
from the *Aurora*.

The *CLARA* (7)
Another loss on the Banco Inglés, off Montevideo, was that of the
30-gun frigate *Clara* in 1776. The drowned numbered 120. There may
have been treasure aboard the *Clara*, particularly if she was homeward
bound from Peru.

The *ASUNCIÓN* (8)*
On May 20, 1805, the 30-gun frigate *Asunción* was dashed to pieces
against the Banco Inglés during a tempest. Commander Juan Domingo
Deslobbes and more than 300 others were drowned when powerful
waves broke up the ship and dragged her down to the 80-foot-deep
bottom. The *Asunción* was en route from Callao, Peru, to Cádiz, and
nearly certainly carried a shipment of Peru gold and silver worth somewhere between $500,000 and $2,000,000. There was no recorded salvage.

Further research should be carried out on this wreck before any attempt were made to locate her remains. If there were confirmation that
she carried treasure—as is likely, since nearly all Callao-Cádiz ships of

this period brought back silver and gold—the *Asunción* would make the most attractive target in La Plata for salvage divers. Her wreck would have to be distinguished from those of at least a dozen other ships around the Banco Inglés, and probably fairly extensive dredging would be necessary to uncover the ballast. The results would be worth it.

The Brazil Coast

Like Argentina and Uruguay, Brazil was colonized slowly since most of the Portuguese efforts were concentrated in richer territories. Rio de Janeiro was discovered on January 1, 1502—and because of this date was named "January Bay." Recife was founded in 1561 and Campos in 1634. Settlements expanded and from these and other ports were sent back shipments of sugar, hides, cotton, coffee, tobacco, grain, and manioc. Other nations encroached on the Portuguese possession: French Huguenots occupied the islands off Rio in 1555 and remained for several decades; Dutch military forces took the area around Recife in 1630, holding it against Portuguese attacks until 1654.

Then gold, silver, and precious stones were discovered, and Brazil became important. Just inland from Rio, in the Minas Gerais state, a rich gold field was developed around Ouro Preto and Belo Horizonte. From 1698 increasing quantities of precious metal were shipped from these mines which, during the period 1752–87, were among the world's largest producers. Diamonds turned up in quantity as well as silver and semiprecious stones. Portuguese and allied Spanish *naos* began setting sail from Rio de Janeiro, Recife, and Campos with million-dollar cargoes of this treasure.

The THIRTY-FIVE PORTUGUESE *NAOS* (9)

There are several written reports that a fleet of 35 Portuguese ships was wrecked off Campos in 1572. Since at that time not much precious metal and stones was being mined, they probably held little treasure between them, much of which would have been salvaged.

The *PROVEEDORA* (10)

This Spanish *nao* of Flores Valdez' armada of 1583 was wrecked as it sailed, fully loaded, from Florianópolis on Santa Catarina Island. Her cargo contained perhaps $15,000 in treasure of which most was recovered in subsequent salvage work by the Spanish.

The *SANTA MARÍA* (11)

Another Spanish merchantman, the *Santa María*, went down off the coast near Flores in 1584. There was little of interest to the treasure diver aboard.

The *PUERTO CRISTIANO* (12)

She was an armed *urca* attached to the armada of General Fadrique de Toledo which was returning from Brazil in 1625. Just off the naval base of Pernambuco (Recife) this ship ran aground and broke up on some reefs. Spanish accounts say that her people and cannons were recovered, and probably so was any treasure she may have carried.

The *GUIPÚZCOA* (13)

This 60-gun man-of-war sank off Santa Catarina Island during a storm in 1749. She carried money and quite possibly gold and diamonds, none of which was recorded as salvaged afterward.

H.M.S. *THETIS* (14)*

Often, when conversation among divers turns to sunken treasures and early salvage attempts, someone will comment something like: "But they tried to raise that stuff way back in 1830. That was before diving gear was invented. That couldn't have done anything." True, there was no modern gear available to salvors at that early date, but there was something else—a factor which in the challenge of sunken treasure hunting is often more important than the most up-to-date equipment. It is the determination of a leader, his courage and drive to persist against odds which seem impossible. Occasionally a salvage man turns up with this quality, and manages, through sheer will power and ingenious application of meager tools at his disposal, to beat the odds. Phips and Quaglia had this spirit. So did Captain Tom Dickenson of His Majesty's sloop *Lightning*.

On the night of December 6, 1830, the 46-gun frigate H.M.S. *Thetis*, homeward bound from Rio de Janeiro, smashed into the base of the cliffs at Cape Frio, Brazil. Battered by waves, she soon filled and sank, taking down a consignment of gold and silver worth $800,000 belonging to South American merchants. Survivors brought back news of the disaster to Rio.

One of the first to hear of the *Thetis'* fate was Captain Dickenson, who was in port with his sloop, the *Lightning*. While fellow officers shook their heads over the thought of retrieving the lost treasure, he put his inventive mind to work, planning its salvage. Then he applied to his superiors for permission to make the attempt. After several refusals, he was authorized to go ahead. The job would not be easy. There was no diving equipment on the *Lightning*—nor, for that matter, in all of Rio de Janeiro—so he had to make his own. He borrowed two big iron water tanks from another British ship and had them joined together into a makeshift diving bell. An air pump was constructed, and his fitters scoured the port for hose. With these tools aboard, the *Lightning* sailed north to find the sunken *Thetis*.

Late in January 1831, Dickenson began his survey of Cape Frio—a three-mile-long island, banked with cliffs, separated from the Brazil coast by a deep narrow channel. At its southern end precipitous rock dropped straight down into churning sea, forming a horseshoe-shaped cul-de-sac. It was here, in what is now called Thetis Cove, that survivors reported the ship to lie. Floating debris confirmed this, but there was no sign of the wreck itself. Boats were sent in and sounded depths averaging 60 feet. The diving bell would have to be used.

This was designed to be suspended from a short boom projecting from the *Lightning*'s gunwale, but a glance at the rough sea and rocks convinced Dickenson that he could not take his ship in. Another mounting would have to be constructed, based against the cliffs. These rose more than 100 feet, with scarcely a foothold on their surfaces. Dickenson spent several days considering the problem before him, then began the construction of a huge boom, anchored in the face of the cliff. It had to be built entirely of material available on that storm-battered, deserted jungle coast, strong enough to withstand the pressure of gales and long enough to drop the diving bell far out from shore.

During the next three weeks the top of the cliff resembled a combined shipyard and boiler factory where carpenters, blacksmiths, ropemakers, riggers, and seamen toiled at the gigantic task. Scavenging forces in boats grappled for sunken wreckage and retrieved masts and spars from the *Thetis*. The *Lightning*'s capstan, and ropes, chains and fittings were floated ashore and hauled up. Digging parties evacuated a ledge 60 feet wide and 15 feet deep at the top of the cliff's face where the boom's supporting cables would be anchored and cut a path down to the water below. Tree trunks were hewn, cut into logs, and dragged to the work base.

Yard by yard the enormous boom took form, being completed on March 7. Twenty-two lengths of wood—masts, spars, and logs—had been joined together with bolts and iron hoops into a derrick arm 158 feet long and weighing, with its diving bell, over 40 tons! Its foot was anchored in an excavated gap 30 feet above water level. Hundreds of straining men hauled at cables until the outer extremity was raised 50 feet over the sea, 150 feet from the cliff. The engineering feat had been accomplished in only two months.

On March 27 the diving bell was lowered. Soon a wooden slab floated to the surface. The boat's crew that retrieved it read a scribbled message: "*We are now over some dollars.*" The salvage had begun. For the next twelve months, despite accidents, the boom's rupture by storm waves, and other setbacks, the courageous men of the *Lightning* raised treasure. By March 1832, $600,000 in silver and gold had been recovered. The *Lightning* was relieved by H.M.S. *Algerine*, whose crew salvaged another $160,000. When the project was finally abandoned only $40,000 of the *Thetis'* wealth still remained below.

It is there today, in gold and silver coins and ingots, strewn on rocks and buried in sand, scattered about a sea bed from 50 to 80 feet deep. The *Thetis'* ballast and cannons should be easy to find, about 100 feet out from the excavations in the cliff. SCUBA divers are ideally equipped to undertake this search. Use of metal detectors would practically guarantee the salvage of a fair percentage of the $40,000 treasure.

The *MADAGASCAR* (15)

This 1200-ton English wool clipper ship sailed from Melbourne, Australia, in 1853. She carried a large number of passengers, and besides wool, a consignment of gold dust with a value of £250,000 ($1,500,000). The *Madagascar* headed eastward from Australia and literally disappeared into the blue. She was never seen again, nor were any of her complement reported to have survived.

Among different accounts of her fate is one which reported her to have sunk off the north Brazil coast a few miles from Cabo Garupí. It would be worth checking.

CHAPTER 16

The Atlantic Ocean

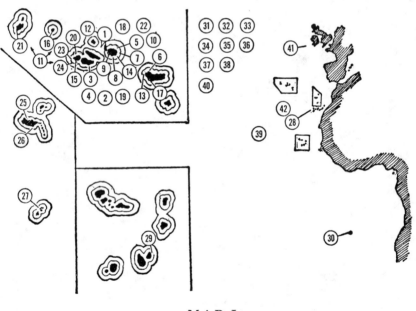

MAP I

The Azores

One of the world's richest undersea hunting grounds surrounds the Azores, a group of ten major islands and numerous smaller ones situated 1300 miles off Portugal. From Flores at their west to Santa Maria on the east they dot the Atlantic in a rough line for 350 miles. The Azores belong to Portugal, having been colonized by settlers sent there during the exploration program of Prince Henry the Navigator. They were often the point for armadas returning from the Indies to rendezvous with coast guard squadrons of galleons which escorted them through the pirate-infested waters off the Portuguese and south Spain coasts. Wrecked on the Azores shores and sunk in deep water under their cliffs lie more than forty *naos* from the New World, with $15,000,000 in treasure.

The *SANTA MARÍA De LA PIEDAD* (1)

She was the first recorded loss in the Azores area, a 120-ton caravel commanded by Sebastián de Quesada. Returning from Cuba in 1550 this ship was wrecked on the coast of Terceira Island and dropped into 100-foot depths where her cargo could not be reached. There was about $100,000 in gold, silver, and pearls aboard.

The *SAN ANTÓN* (2)

Captain Juan Basquero's *nao San Antón* was attached to the 1551 Tierra Firme armada bringing back gold from Cartagena. In the Azores region she was swamped in a storm and lost with all her cargo and many of the people that she carried. Her treasure was worth probably $150,000. It lies about 500 feet deep, somewhere among the islands.

The *CAPITANA** and *GALLEON* (3)

General Juan Tello de Guzman's armada of 1554 ran into a severe storm as it passed through the Azores. The 500-ton *Capitana* and an escort galleon, carrying between them nearly $2,000,000 in registry treasure, were wrecked against the south shore of Pico Island. No salvage of their cargoes, which included nearly a ton of gold, was attempted. This was unusual in view of the value of lost treasure and probably meant that the ships settled in water over 75 feet deep after striking rocks.

ROELES' GALLEON (4)

A galleon of General Pedro de las Roeles' 1560 armada struck a reef off one of the Azores and settled in shallow water. The comment on her loss noted that "the gold was saved, but the rest of the cargo was lost." Something like $50,000 in silver and contraband treasure might be embedded in her wreckage.

NUESTRA SEÑORA DE LA LUZ (5)

This 120-ton *nao*, under Captain Juan Garcia, carried cargo from Hispaniola and the Antilles and had set sail from Santo Domingo. She floundered near the coast of Terceira Island in 1563 during a storm. There were pearls and gold, and possibly some silver, on board. The *Nuestra Señora* settled on a bottom at least 300 feet deep and would be nearly impossible to locate.

LA CONCEPCIÓN (6)

The wreckage of this 120-ton *nao* lies under a shallow reef off São Miguel Island, probably near Point Bretanha, where she broke up in a storm of 1567. Captain Luis de Alcala and the passengers reached shore safely and "part of the cargo was saved." The remainder, which probably included about $20,000 in silver and gold, remains on ballast of this ship.

NUESTRA SEÑORA DE LA CONCEPCIÓN (7)

She was a big galleon of 600 tons and 40 cannons, *Almiranta* of the 1586 armada from the Indies. Commanded by Martín de Vittoria, *Nuestra Señora* was driven by heavy winds onto rocks near the shore of Terceira Island. She sank into shallow water and everyone on board reached safety. The following year a salvage boat was sent to the scene. Divers recovered all the guns and some of her treasure and fittings. Not all the silver was brought up, though. At least $20,000 remained in the broken hull when salvage was discontinued.

With her position pinpointed through further research this galleon's remaining treasure should not be very difficult to find and recover, as it lies against a reef, not over 50 feet deep.

The *SANTIAGO* and *NUESTRA SEÑORA DEL ROSARIO* (8)

These *naos* were attached to the Indies armada of 1588. A storm drove them both against reefs off Terceira Island, where they sank. The *Santiago*, under Captain Marcos de Escobar, carried 150 tons of cargo from Havana including perhaps $25,000 in precious metal and pearls. *Nuestra Señora del Rosario* had loaded at Santo Domingo. She was of 120 tons and commanded by Francisco Hernandez. There is no record that these ships were salvaged although they nearly certainly went down in shallow depths.

The *TRINIDAD* (9)

Rough Atlantic weather in 1589 sprang the planks of the *Trinidad* and she was leaking so badly when the armada arrived in the Azores that hope of keeping her afloat the remainder of the journey was given up. *Pataches* closed in and took off the silver and passengers while the crew tried to work the settling vessel to the harbor of Angra de Heróismo. Several miles off the south shore of Terceira the *Trinidad* gave up the fight and sank, taking with her some precious metal. Her depth is around 500 feet.

The *NAO* (10)

In 1590 an unidentified *nao* was wrecked in the Azores. Her crew, and "most of the treasure" were saved. The location of this ship was not noted.

RIVERA'S and PRADO'S ARMADAS (11)*

Fourteen galleons, *naos*, and *pataches* were swamped at sea or broken up on the Azores during the second week of September 1591. The combined Tierra Firme armada of Diego de Rivera and New Spain armada of Antonio Navarro de Prado had sailed from Havana six weeks earlier. On October 24 a hurricane dispersed the ships into two groups in mid-Atlantic, sending them scudding eastward. The weather worsened as the Azores drew near. A howling nor'wester lashed the seas into a froth and hurled the half-sunken ships against the western coasts of Flores, Fayal, São Jorge, and Terceira islands.

The 400-ton *nao San Juan Bautista* under Rodrigo Gonzales crashed onto a reef on September 5. Her crew had scarcely reached safety on Flores when the ship broke up and vanished under the white sea. *Nuestra Señora de la Peña* disappeared between the islands, with no survivors. *Santa María de Begoña* and the *Santa Catalina* were wrecked off Fayal. The 300-ton *La Salvadora* smashed against São Jorge on September 8. *El León Colorado* went down in the boiling sea. The 600-ton Tierra Firme *Almiranta*, *La Madalena*, capsized and sank off Graciosa taking down most of her people and $1,500,000 in treasure.

The scattered vessels were blown deeper into the island group, driven by seas and wind, out of control. On September 10, Captain Gaspar Nuñez and the crew found their floundering *Nuestra Señora de Juncal* in the lee of Pico Island where they managed to save themselves before the 500-ton galleon went under. Only thirty people survived the wreck of *Nuestra Señora del Rosario*, a 700-ton Tierra Firme galleon. Her captain, Pedro Rodriguez, was among those who died.

Los Tres Reyes, El Espíritu Santo and a *patache* disappeared at sea. In a final burst of fury the tempest drove two more ships to destruction on Terceira—the *Santa María del Puerto* and Captain Tomás Gallardo's New Spain *nao Nuestra Señora del Rosario*, laden with $1,000,000 in silver.

The storm subsided and the survivors, scattered throughout the islands, drifted in to the inhabited villages. Gradually the damage reports were assembled. When the final ones were in it was apparent that a third of the Tierra Firme ships had been lost, including the *Almiranta*, and several of the New Spain *naos* as well. Nearly two thousand people had died and $10,000,000 in treasure was under the sea.

A gigantic salvage force was brought together from Spain, Portugal, the Canaries, and the Azores. Throughout the calm winter shallow wrecks were stripped of cargo and guns while skin divers plunged as deep as 50 feet into the remains of others to retrieve treasure. The result was the most successful mass salvage operation carried out to that date, with three-quarters of the silver and gold recovered. The $3,000,000 that could not be reached lies in the hulls of *La Madalena, Nuestra Señora de la Peña* and several other ships which sank between the islands in depths of 100 feet or more.

The SANTA CRUZ (12)

This Portuguese carrack was sighted in July 1592 by the lookouts of a squadron under the Earl of Cumberland, lying in ambush for Indies ships at the Azores. She was on the last lap of a long run from India. The Earl's fast little vessels drove her to shelter in a cove on one of the islands where her crew took the most valuable cargo ashore and hid it. Then the captain ran the ship aground and set her afire. From captured Portuguese the English learned that a far richer ship, the *Madre de Dios*, was approaching and gave little time to the job of trying to find the *Santa Cruz*'s hidden treasures. Their decision to concentrate on the *Madre de Dios* was rewarded several days later with a $3,000,000 loot.

There are probably a few thousand dollars of gold and precious stones from India and Africa in the coral-crusted wreckage of the *Santa Cruz* but certainly not enough to warrant trying to salvage her remains.

LA MADALENA (13)*

Captain Domingo de Insaurraga's *Capitana* of the 1593 Tierra Firme armada, under General Francisco Martínez, was nicknamed "The Silver Chief"—and for good reason. As *La Madalena* approached the Azores that year there was a $2,500,000 treasure in her hold. Rounding the western end of São Miguel Island, the 800-ton galleon rammed into a reef and settled on a sea floor 40 feet deep. Salvage was started immediately. When the divers ceased work seventeen bronze cannons, eleven iron guns, a large part of the ship's fittings, and 95 per cent of the treasure had been raised.

About $100,000 still remains in the ballast of this ship and should make a relatively attractive target for treasure divers. The wreck's exact site can be tracked down with a little effort through study of salvage reports.

NUESTRA SEÑORA DE LOS REMEDIOS (14)

A $300,000 consignment of silver was lost when Captain Juan de Rexual's 600-ton *nao Nuestra Señora de los Remedios* sank off Terceira Island in 1593. The Spanish made no attempt to recover this precious cargo, which indicated that the ship went down to at least 75 feet, and probably to more than 300.

LAS CINQUE CHAGAS (15)*

Here is a wreck for treasure hunters given to wishful thinking!

Las Cinque Chagas was a 1200-ton Portuguese carrack, 150 feet long and 45 feet broad, with lofty, heavily fortified poop and forecastles. Commanded by Captain Nuno Velho Pereira, she set sail from Goa, India, in 1593 for Lisbon, laden with 1000 tons of spices, silks, gold, and jewels. The *Chagas* crossed the Indian Ocean and put in to Mozambique for the winter. When weather permitted the journey to be resumed a hundred slaves were herded aboard, and several coffers of Mozambique gold added to her other treasures. The Cape was rounded uneventfully and only the last lap of the long voyage lay ahead when the wind fell off. The *Chagas* drifted, becalmed, off Luanda for several weeks. Then an epidemic broke out. By the time it had run its course five hundred of the thousand men and women on board had died and nearly everyone else was incapacitated, lying in bunks with high fevers.

Water and food were running out when following winds set the ship on her course again. A faction of spoiled nobles among the passengers insisted that Captain Pereira put in at the Azores for supplies. At first he refused. His instructions were to return direct, for English pirates had been waylaying the India carracks off those islands. He preferred that some of those aboard die of thirst than for all to be subjected to a naval attack. Discontent spread to the crew and finally to avoid a mutiny the captain had to give in to popular feeling against his better judgment. First he extracted a promise from crew and passengers alike to fight to the death if the *Chagas* encountered pirates there. The course was changed a little to the west, and on June 13, 1594, *Las Cinque Chagas*, with only seventy of her original crew of four hundred men sound and able-bodied, was in sight of the Azores.

Captain Pereira's reluctance to stop off here was well founded. On that same morning three English warships were cruising eighteen miles south of the channel between Fayal and Pico islands, their crews waiting impatiently for a ship to plunder. They were the *Royal Exchange*, commanded by Admiral George Cave, the *Mayflower*, under Vice-Admiral William Anthony, and the *Sampson*, Captain Nicholas Downton. Accompanying them was the 24-ton pinnace *Violet*. This little squadron had been fitted out by the Earl of Cumberland, whose privateering expedition of two years earlier captured the *Madre de Dios*.

At noon a lookout shouted news of a sail to the south. All four English ships beat down against the wind while the *Chagas* plowed heavily north toward them. Captain Pereira saw only one chance for his ship and those aboard, and that was to reach safety in Angra harbor, Terceira. The *Chagas* would have to fight the English ships for a hundred miles.

It was evening before contact was made by the *Mayflower* and midnight before the other privateers came in range. With the first morning light the three warships began their bombardment of the carrack. It was the siege of a fort, carried out at sea. For six hours of hell the sides and decks of the *Chagas* exploded and splintered as iron projectiles crashed through. By noon she had been reduced to shambles, a crippled hulk. The *Royal Exchange* and *Mayflower* closed in and Englishmen swarmed aboard.

The defense of the *Chagas* by her indomitable captain and crew puts the lie to popular stories that Spanish and Portuguese would not fight. It was suicidal heroism, sustained for over thirty hours against impossible odds—glorious, tragic, and both futile and triumphant. The crew and passengers had sworn to fight to the death and they did that literally, men and women alike. The boarding attempt was repulsed, with Vice-Admiral Anthony and many of his sailors killed. The *Mayflower* fell away, to be replaced by the *Sampson* alongside. Again the defenders were attacked from ships on both flanks, and again they drove the English back. Admiral George Cave was mortally wounded and Captain Downton severely injured. Soldiers in the *Chagas'* castles repeatedly set the English ships afire by dropping incendiary projectiles on their decks, pinning down a part of their crews extinguishing flames.

Throughout the afternoon the battle continued with appalling casualties on both sides. Of her seventy able-bodied men there were less than half still alive to fight, many of these wounded, when the *Chagas* was set afire by the powder flash on one of the *Sampson's* cannon shooting point-blank into her beak. The flames spread over the carrack's prow while again and again the grimy, bloody, howling boarding parties fought across onto her waist and were pushed back. By nightfall the forecastle of the *Chagas* was an inferno and fire was spreading into her hold. Treachery by the assistant pilot and a handful of Spanish merchants —who slyly ran up a white flag of surrender—was quelled by Captain Pereira who cut down the flag and threatened to run the traitors through if they repeated the action.

The English ships fell away, their officers wary of the carrack's flames. They continued their bombardment, and still the Spanish and Portuguese refused to surrender. Throughout the night the *Chagas* burned while the *Mayflower, Royal Exchange,* and *Sampson* shot away her mast stumps and opened new gaping holes in her sides, through which red flames were visible. By morning the whole ship, from stem to stern, was a torch. People began leaping into the sea where they were shot and lanced by English sailors who were enraged at losing their prize.

The end came before noon. Settling into the sea, the *Chagas* made a final defiant gesture toward her harriers, blowing up and showering them with flaming wood and cargo. When the smoke and steam drifted away she was gone. Of the five hundred people aboard when the English attacked thirteen were alive, spared being murdered in the water by offering bribes of jewels flashed at English sailors. The beaches of Fayal were littered with drowned bodies of the others.

The last recorded position of *Las Cinque Chagas* mentioned in English and Spanish accounts examined was eighteen miles south of the channel between Pico and Fayal, on the afternoon of June 13, 1594. She was coming up from the south, and the English ships, although much faster, had many hours of maneuvering before they could reach her, so the prevailing winds that day were from the south. For about fifteen hours until late in the morning of June 14, when she was crippled, the carrack maintained a northeast course toward Terceira, and from then on until sinking she drifted for twenty hours with wind and current. The fact that many bodies washed ashore on Fayal signifies that the *Chagas* was close by, and moving in the same direction. It seems likely that she went down south of that island, not very far offshore. Unfortunately the sea floor falls off steeply here, reaching 500 feet two miles out and 2500 feet at six miles. Unless the carrack sank within a mile from Fayal she would be beyond present-day salvage range.

Her cargo was the richest ever carried up to that time on one ship from the Dutch Indies, with a high percentage of jewels and gold. After the loss the Venetian Ambassador to England admitted that it was worth 2,000,000 ducats. In 1902 Oppenheim concluded, after studying documentary evidence, that the *Chagas* carried treasure worth, in 1954 "£550,000, or some £3,500,000 now (State Paper Venetian 20th July, 1594)." He gives two authorities for these figures: Purchas, and Downton in Hakluyt's Voyages. Allowing for most of the weight to be in spices and merchandise, the treasure aboard *Las Cinque Chagas* is still one of the richest under the sea, probably about $5,000,000 in gold from the East Indies, India, and Mozambique, and rubies, diamonds, pearls, and other gems.

The *CAPITANA* (16)*

Another large fortune went down with the *Capitana* of General Francisco Martínez' 1596 armada. This galleon struck a reef off tiny São Martin Island and sank too deep for her treasure to be salvaged at that time. Her $2,000,000 gold and silver consignment should be within SCUBA range now, and careful research might turn up a closer fix on the location of the point where she struck.

The *SANTA ANA MARÍA* (17)

This 700-ton *urca* of the New Spain armada headed by General Sancho Parda Osorio was wrecked at São Miguel in 1600. The registry silver, guns, and part of the cargo were salvaged. Only a small amount of contraband money shipped in merchandise remains in shallow water where her ballast lies.

The *CAPITANA* (18)

Her cargo was also fairly completely recovered, about $2,000,000 in treasure being brought up after this *Capitana* of Juan de Salas Valdés 1608 armada sank in shallow water in the Azores.

The *NAO* (19)

An unidentified ship returning from the Indies was wrecked at the Azores in 1624. The people and some of the cargo were saved. Accounts give no further details.

The *ALMIRANTA* (20)

In 1625 the *Almiranta* of the Portuguese coast guard squadron ran aground and sank off Fayal Island. The crew reached shore safely. Divers brought up most of her guns and some money from the captain's cabin. There may have been more which could not be reached, as well as silver plate.

The GALLEON (21)

A large galleon carrying 50 cannons, of the New Spain convoy of 1727, was wrecked against Flores Island. Her "people and part of the silver were saved." This could mean either that the ship sank slowly, allowing removal of some treasure, or that part of the silver was salvaged after she sank. In either case between $100,000 and $200,000 probably remains on the wreckage, close to the Flores coast at an accessible depth today.

H.M.S. *MARLBOROUGH* (22)

British forces attacked and captured Havana in 1762, taking an enormous booty from the city. This was loaded onto their warships and transports and taken back to England. One of the men-of-war, H.M.S. *Marlborough*, was sunk in the Azores on the homeward voyage, and there was possibly some of this treasure aboard her. Gregory Robinson, well-known authority on British naval history, and eminent researcher on the subject of old ships and shipwrecks, gives this opinion:

> The value of the loot in specie, valuables & stores, was reckoned to be £3 million sterling ($20,000,000), besides the capture of 9 sail of the line. Admiral Pocock with a portion of the fleet sailed to England on 3rd November 1762. The *Marlborough*, 70 guns, lost company early in the passage and springing a leak, had to put before the wind, ditch some of her guns, and have men at the pumps continuously to keep the ship afloat. Fortunately for her on 27th November she sighted the *Antelope*, 50 guns, Captain T. Graves, homeward bound from Newfoundland. Graves took on board the *Marlborough*'s people and then sank the ship by gun fire (Laird Clowes' *The Royal Navy*, Vol. III, p. 246–50).
>
> There is no mention of salving of treasure from the *Marlborough* when the men were saved. I do not know what evidence there is of loot on board. We may be pretty certain the Admiral kept most of the gold and silver on board his flagship. I think you will agree that any diving operations should not be undertaken until there is more definite evidence of treasure . . .
>
> As a footnote you might like to know that the prize money for distribution was £736,000. Of this Pocock took £122,697-10-6; the general took a like sum. Captains, R.N. receive £1,600-10-10, petty officers £17-5-3, and every seaman and marine had £3-14-9¼. Laird Clowes in his very polite way wrote: "It was felt, and perhaps with reason, that the Administration permitted the commanding officers to appropriate far too large a share of the spoil."

The *PODEROSO* (23)

The three-year-old warship *Poderoso*, of 74 guns, was cruising in the Azores area in 1779 with other guard ships under Brigadier General Juan de Langara when a storm opened leaks in her hull. She began settling. Boats took off her crew and she went under "within sight of land." Her silver plate and probably the ship's funds were lost with her.

The *CARMEN* (24)

In the same storm a 36-gun frigate, the *Carmen*, was sunk with six drowned off Fayal Island (the *Poderoso* was probably nearby).

Her money and silver dining service would have been worth only a few thousand dollars.

Madeira Island

The GALLEGA (25)
Returning from the Indies in 1581, this Spanish *nao* was blown off course in a storm and wrecked on the north coast of Madeira Island, a Portuguese colony off Morocco. "The silver was saved" but the other cargo could not be recovered and remains with the wreckage at a shallow depth.

The SAN JOSEFE (26)
A treasure of gold and silver worth over a million dollars went down with this 600-ton galleon off Madeira in 1635. The *San Josefe* "sank with everything"' and is most likely in deep water.

The Salvage Islands

The "BIG BLACK BOX" (27)
Between Madeira and the Canary Islands off the African coast lie two groups of desolate, uninhabited rock and sand islets too small to be shown on most maps. They are the Salvage Islands, attached to Madeira and owned by Portugal. Very recently a group of Spanish and Dutch skin divers from the Canaries sailed here in a yacht to try the spear fishing. While diving off the coast of the northeast group one of them noticed odd formations on the coral, just offshore about 20 feet deep. He returned to the yacht and told his friends. They put on Aqua Lungs and went down to see what had been found.

After poking and chipping for several minutes they uncovered a cannon, of bronze. Jubilant, they chipped it free and hauled the gun on deck with a small winch. It weighed nearly half a ton, and was in perfect condition, obviously very old. Now thoroughly excited, the group returned to the bottom and soon had found two other bronze guns and an iron cannon, as well. This was big money. In Spain bronze sells for over $1000 a ton.

The search went on throughout the afternoon and about 5 P.M. one of the divers let out a bubbly squeal. He had found a coral-encrusted iron container, more than a yard square, embedded in the sea bed. What could it be? they all wondered. A treasure chest! they hoped. The gasoline-driven compressor was kept going until late that night and all the next day filling bottles while one after the other the young men dived to chip at the coral around the box. At last

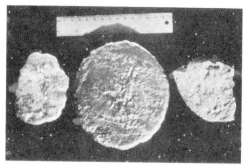

39. Large and small gold ingots and broken pieces. *Courtesy Treasure Salvors, Inc.*

40. Twenty-one carat, 85-ounce gold ingot, probably from the Lima mint, recovered from the wreck site (Florida UW 4) of the *Capitana* of the *galeones* portion of the Spanish fleet lost in 1715. *Courtesy Florida Division of Archives and History.*

41. Gold cross (10501, right), 59.3 grams, formerly pearl-studded, and gold crucifix (10500, left), 29.3 grams, recovered from (Florida UW 4) the *Capitana* of the *galeones* portion of the 1715 fleet. *Courtesy Florida Division of Archives and History.*

42. Diver with cannon ball. Ballast stone background. *Courtesy Treasure Salvors, Inc.*

43. Mr. and Mrs. Kip Wagner piecing together china from galleon wreck. *Courtesy Treasure Salvors, Inc.*

44. Gold doubloons on diver's wet suit. *Courtesy Treasure Salvors, Inc.*

45. Gold and silver coins and gold ingots just after recovery. *Courtesy Treasure Salvors, Inc.*

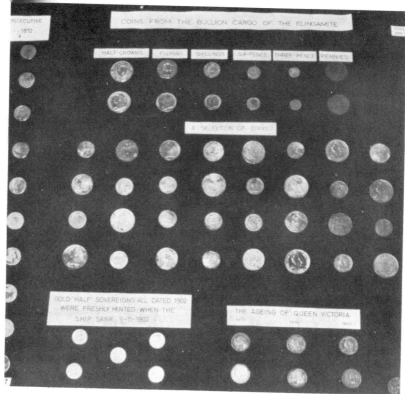

46. Coins salvaged from the *Elingamite. Photo Walt Deas.*

47. Artifacts and a clump of coins from the *Elingamite. Photo Walt Deas.*

48. Artifact display cases with underwater salvage operation on the foreground. *Courtesy of The Smithsonian Institution.*

49. Dishes to make a king's mouth water. *Courtesy Treasure Salvors, Inc.*

50. Mel Fisher, Walt Holtzworth, and Rupe Gates. *Courtesy Treasure Salvors, Inc.*

51. Mel and Dolores Fisher inspecting Spanish galleon timber and fittings uncovered from deep sand. *Courtesy Treasure Salvors, Inc.*

52. Kip Wagner and Mel Fisher with state officials. *Courtesy Treasure Salvors, Inc.*

54. Silver pieces of eight. *Courtesy Treasure Salvors, Inc.*

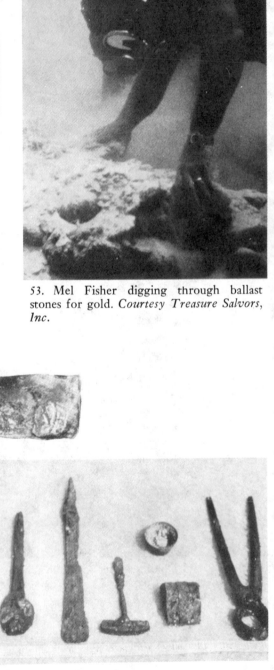

53. Mel Fisher digging through ballast stones for gold. *Courtesy Treasure Salvors, Inc.*

55. Tools from galleon wreck.

56. Two Real Eight divers with silver coins, copper disks, and lead musket balls (1715 wrecks). *Courtesy Real Eight Company, Inc.*

57. Some of the 1200 coins from the *Girona* (Robert Sténuit excavations). They are pieces of 1-, 2-, and 4-escudos of Spain and scudi and ducats of Naples. These gold coins bear the names of Jane and Charles, Charles I (of Spain, but Fifth of the Holy Empire) and Philip II. *Photo Sténuit.*

58. Royal doubloon 8-escudo was found on a 1715 wreck. *Courtesy Treasure Salvors, Inc.*

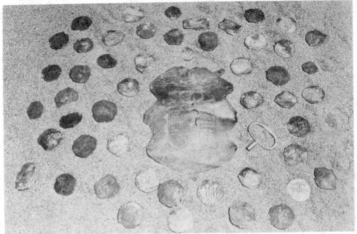

59. Spanish silver coins, brass keyhole plate and part of a brass key. All from a wooden chest containing over five hundred Spanish silver coins found at Port Royal. *Courtesy Robert Marx.*

60. Silver and pewterware from a building in Port Royal. *Courtesy Robert Marx.*

61. Carpenter's tools and brass nails and tacks found in a carpenter's shop in the sunken city. The yellow and blue rule is modern and just for scale. *Courtesy Robert Marx.*

62. Wreck of the *Yealdham. Photo by Anatole Szulga and Lee Mercer for Fathom Expeditions.*

63. Coins from Florida and Honduras. Pottery found on the *Yealdham*. *Photo by Anatole Szulga and Lee Mercer for Fathom Expeditions.*

64. Bottle was found on the *Yealdham*. *Photo by Anatole Szulga and Lee Mercer for Fathom Expeditions.*

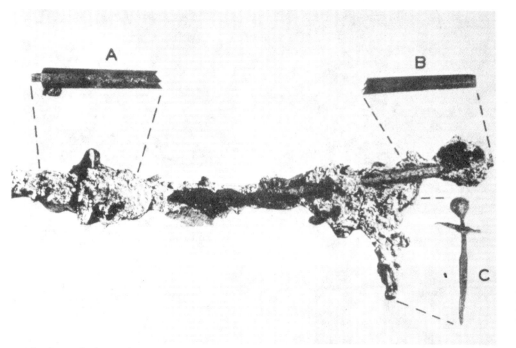

65. A typical specimen of conglomerate recovered from the "Minnie Ball" wreck. Enlargements A and B show the breech and muzzle of the arquebus which was concealed in the encrustation. Figure C shows the ancient dagger, with blood spots clearly visible, which was also within the same piece of conglomerate. *Photo by Frank F. Tenney, Jr.*

66. Gold coins found on the 1715 wrecks. *Courtesy Real Eight Company, Inc.*

67. Gold disks and coins and a silver plate. *Courtesy Real Eight Company, Inc.*

68. Golden dragon and chain sold for $50,000, and ring, cross, and coins. *Courtesy Real Eight Company, Inc.*

69. Real Eight diver underwater with a silver plate. *Courtesy Real Eight Company, Inc.*

70. Replica, one third size of original in the Real Eight Treasure Museum, of one of the 1715 ships. *Courtesy Real Eight Company, Inc.*

71. Marx and assistant lifting a piece of wood from one of the Columbus wrecks. *Courtesy Robert Marx.*

72. Treasures found on galleon *Margarita. Courtesy Treasure Salvors, Inc.*

73. Ballast stone, pig bone, and ceramic shard. Found on Columbus shipwrecks off Jamaica. *Courtesy Robert Marx.*

74. Seven-foot eighteenth-century anchor, found by Jack Haskins on Cayman. *Courtesy Jack Haskins.*

75. 1733 6-pound cannon, from *San José*, recovered by Tom Gurr. *Courtesy Jack Haskins.*

76. 1733 anchor, off the *Herrera. Courtesy Jack Haskins.*

the sides were free. They looped the steel cable around it, hooked the shackle, and hauled with the winch. The yacht's deck tilted over until the gunwale was submerged and finally the winch motor gave up. The "big box" hadn't moved.

Back they went to chipping, clearing away the coral underneath as far as they could reach. Again the winch was started and again the box refused to come up. Now they tackled the box itself. "We chipped at the sides, trying to find a lock or something we could jimmy open, but everywhere it was just smooth, rusty iron. The sides were too thick to break through."

They finally gave up, returning to their base where the cannons were sold as scrap and melted down. This was unfortunate, particularly as the divers could not describe them well enough for identification as to type, period, and nationality.

A few months later a top-secret salvage expedition slipped out of port on a larger borrowed yacht with a 3-ton winch. The box was hooked up and the winch tugged. Nothing happened. Try as they did, the treasure hunters could not move their chest. "We should have brought dynamite," one of them commented in an afterthought. "But we were sure that winch would get it up. We figure that whatever's in it is heavy, because it sure weighs more than 3 tons."

And that is the position of the "big black box" today. The owners of the yacht have left the Canaries, one of the Spaniards in the diving group was sent to the lunatic asylum for treatment of the dt's, and the project to raise it has been temporarily shelved, although it is still very much in the minds of those who saw it. Of all the mysteries of the sea this is one of the most intriguing. It seems obvious that because of its unusual weight and strength the box contains something valuable. There are undoubtedly more cannons, and probably the ballast and remains of a lost ship nearby. Once they found the chest, the divers discontinued their search for other wreckage to concentrate on getting it up. There has been frequent talk of going back with dynamite, but lack of a yacht to make the 200-mile trip and low state of finances has up to now relegated the project to "*mañana*."

In his book *Treasure Trove, Pirates' Gold*, Gordon Cooper tells of a Spanish frigate whose treasure was buried on Great Salvage Island and which conceivably might be related to the "big black box." This ship was bound from South America to Cádiz in 1804 when the crew mutinied, sailed to the Salvage Islands, killed their captain and buried him and a million-dollar treasure in a sandy beach above high water mark. Later their vessel was wrecked in the Caribbean, with only two survivors who landed at St. Thomas, in the Virgin Islands. Both died, one telling the story of the treasure to a Finnish seaman before breathing his last. The Finn passed it on to the captain of a British warship, who interested the Admiralty in undertaking the treasure hunt. H.M.S. *Prometheus* was dispatched to Great Salvage Island where her sailors dug up large tracts of beach without finding anything.

Since then at least two other expeditions have visited the Salvages to dig for treasure. The total announced recoveries to date: one copper coin, probably lost by someone in an earlier expedition. The cannons and box which were recently found might possibly have been dropped from the 1804 Spanish frigate or one of the salvaging ships. It seems more likely that they belong to a wreck nearby.

The Canary Islands (28)

The wrecks of many Spanish galleons, caravels, and *naos* lie on the reefs of Tenerife, Gran Canaria, Lanzarote, and Palma islands, but all were westbound with cargoes from Spain, and most were thoroughly salvaged by the Spanish soon after their losses.

The Cape Verde Islands

The CONCEPCIÓN (29)

In 1624 this Spanish galleon attached to the Portuguese squadron was wrecked near the Island of Maio at the south of the Cape Verde group with "the treasure and 140 lives lost." She was returning from Brazil with gold and precious stones aboard, worth probably $250,000. The *Concepción* was "shipwrecked," meaning that she probably did not sink in deep water. Yet her failure to have been salvaged by the Portuguese at that time indicated that her hull settled to below 75 feet, the outside limit of seventeenth-century skin divers. By the time diving bells were in use this wreck had been long forgotten.

St. Helena Island

The SANTIAGO (30)

Situated in the South Atlantic, on the route of the Portuguese carracks from India, St. Helena Island was a popular stopover spot for watering and replenishing supplies, and repairing damage that ships suffered while rounding the stormy Cape. Dutch pirates discovered this quickly and by the 1600s their ships were so often waiting in ambush there that the Portuguese were forced to give up this port of call. One of the last of their carracks to visit St. Helena was the *Santiago*, from Goa. Off the island she ran into three Dutchmen who sank her after a long fight. The gold and precious stones that she carried lie deep in the Atlantic nearby.

The Atlantic

Many hundreds of ships carrying treasure disappeared into the ocean vastness between the American continents and Europe, from the first Portuguese caravels bringing up African gold to the *Titanic* disaster in 1912 and more recent losses. Some of these vessels are included below because they turned up in researches on the Spanish armadas, although they will never be found.

A CARAVEL (31)
The 1554 flota from Santo Domingo, consisting of five *naos* and nine caravels, was attacked all the way from the Bahamas to the Azores by pirate ships. One caravel was captured and another sunk in deep ocean with a cargo of gold, pearls, and cochineal.

The SANTA CLARA (32)
Captain Rodrigo Alonso's 120-ton *nao* from Santo Domingo sank "with everything it carried" in mid-ocean in 1563.

The SANTA CATALINA (33)
She was the *Almiranta* of Juan Menendez' 1564 New Spain flota. East of Bermuda the galleon began leaking, and within a week she was so low that her crew, passengers, and "the gold and silver" were taken off into boats. She sank before the Azores were reached.

The TRINIDAD (34)
Part of the gold and silver was removed from this *nao*, damaged in a storm, before she went under in 1565.

LA MADALENA (35)
"Lost" in the Atlantic with her passengers and treasure in 1573.

The NAO (36)
Returning from the Indies with Lope Díaz de Armendáriz' armada in 1614, an unidentified ship disappeared with a rich cargo of silver.

The NAO (37)
A ship of the armada of General Martín de Vallecilla sank while returning from Havana in 1616.

NUESTRA SEÑORA DEL ROSARIO (38)
This 600-ton galleon commanded by Captain Francisco Rodriguez Rico left the Indies in 1623 with General Juan de Larraspuru Moran's

Tierra Firme armada. She sank during a storm, 550 people and a $2,000,000 cargo of "royal silver, treasure, and tobacco" being lost with her.

Two NAOS (39)
A storm swamped two ships of Antonio de Oquendo's 1631 armada returning from Brazil with gold and jewels. Nothing could be taken off.

The NAO (40)
In 1646 an unidentified ship from Cuba was sunk in mid-Atlantic with a large treasure on board.

The twelve TRANSPORTS (41)
A dozen English transports, returning from the looting of Havana in 1762 with some Spanish treasure on board, were sunk in a storm six hundred miles west of Land's End, England. The crews were all saved.

The CANTABRIA (42)
There was $1,000,000 in Uruguay and Argentine gold, silver, and gems on this Spanish corvette, returning alone across the Atlantic, when a storm in 1802 sank her. A boatload of survivors drifted for nearly a month, many dying of thirst, before they were picked up. They gave the position of the loss as 27° N. and 28° W. (of Cádiz).

CHAPTER 17

The Invincible Armada

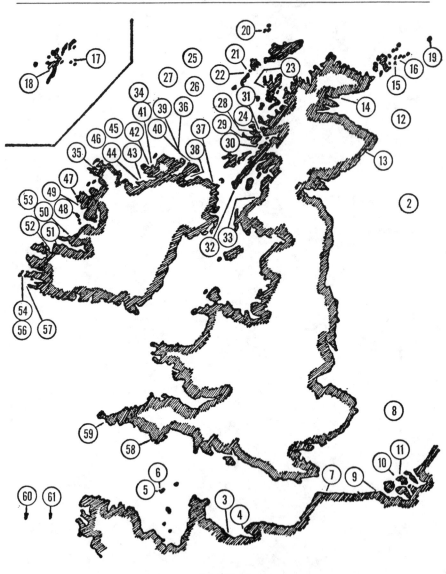

MAP J

*F*ROM THE BASQUE cliffs of northern Spain to the glacial floes of Iceland their wreckage littered the coasts of Europe. Sixty-three magnificent vessels totaling over 30,000 tons—twenty-six galleons, thirteen *urcas*, twenty *pataches* and pinnaces, a galley and three gigantic galleasses—swamped at sea and smashed to kindling on beaches, reefs, and rocky promontories. King Philip's armada may have been invincible in affairs between men and their neighbors, but in the grasp of the wild autumn tempests of 1588 it was just another toy for the elements: to be played with, broken and, finally, discarded.

The weather began its malicious work in June, while the great fleet moved up the Iberian coast from Lisbon to its staging port, La Coruña. By the time the last storm-battered stragglers had assembled here so many of them had been damaged that the commander, Don Alonso Perez de Guzman el Bueno, Duke of Medina-Sidona, wrote the king from his galleon *San Martín* begging that the whole venture be called off. Philip II impatiently ordered the duke to get started with no further delay even if it meant leaving behind twelve or fifteen unseaworthy ships. Several damaged vessels were dropped off and on July 22 the Invincible Armada of 130 ships, 2431 cannon, and 30,000 fighting men sailed north from La Coruña for its rendezvous in Flanders with the Duke of Parma's army which it was to deliver to England.

Aboard nearly every one of these warships was treasure: casks of gold sent by King Philip; Spanish, Italian, and Portuguese money brought by representatives of a dozen dukes and duchesses who were co-participating in the undertaking; glittering personal jewelry and silverware of the nobles themselves. During the months of April and May a long correspondence had taken place between the duke and king on the subject of expense and payroll money for the voyage. Again and again Medina-Sidona begged King Philip for funds, claiming that he did not have enough. King Philip, who together with his allies had already disbursed 3,000,000 gold ducats preparing the enterprise, parsimoniously suggested that another 200,000 should see the armada as far as Flanders where he would send a final 500,000 ducats with the Marquis de Santa Cruz. Repeated many-paged pleas by the duke shook another 20,000 out of the Royal Treasury but at this point King Philip stood firm. The armada sailed with approximately 220,000 golden ducats, worth some $2,500,000 on today's numismatic market. This money was divided, for precaution, into nearly a dozen consignments, each loaded on a separate vessel and controlled by a disbursing officer. Nearly every *Capitana* and *Almiranta* of the five Spanish fleets carried Royal gold.

The king's funds, however, were only a fraction of the wealth. This was no ordinary military venture which was setting off. Aboard the galleons and *naos* was the élite of Spanish Europe, the wealthiest nobles of Castile and Aragon, of León, Cataluña, Seville, Portugal, and most of Italy. Each brought with him personal gold and silver money, jeweled swords, ornaments and family treasures to give him suitable dignity when he took possession of his English estate. How many millions of dollars this treasure would represent today can only be estimated, but the total should be somewhere near $15,000,000. Most of this was stored on the major ships. Yet even some of the lowly *pataches*, commanded by aristocrats, probably carried personal fortunes of $25,000 or $50,000.

Sped on its way by following winds, the Invincible Armada lumbered up the Bay of Biscay into the English Channel, its component fleets spread out across miles of ocean. In all, it was organized into ten separate commands, subordinate to the inept authority of the Duke of Medina-Sidona who knew absolutely nothing about naval warfare. Under his direct orders was the Armada of Portugal with ten galleons and two auxiliaries. These ships mounted from twenty to fifty cannons, displaced between 350 and 1050 tons and carried crews of 350 to 500 men plus transported soldiers. Commanded by Captain-General Juan Martinez de Recalde was the Biscay Armada of ten *naos* and four *pataches*. These were slightly smaller and lighter armed, with twelve to thirty cannons. The Castile Armada totaled fourteen galleons, all of which had 24 cannons, except the *Capitana* of its competent General, Diego Flores de Valdes, which mounted 36. Two *pataches* were its auxiliaries. Another Valdes, Don Pedro, commanded the Andalucia Armada of ten big galleons and one *patache*. The Guipúzcoa Armada, under Martín de Bertendona, had ten of the largest and strongest ships with a combined displacement of 7705 tons and 280 cannons. These were the regional fleets from Spain.

Twenty-three *urcas* were assembled into the Armada of Juan Lopez de Medina. They varied in tonnage from 160 to 750 and in artillery from four guns on the smallest ships to thirty-eight on the *Capitana*. Another twenty-two *pataches* and pinnaces, called the Light Squadron, were led by Antonio Hurtado de Mendoza. Most of them were in the 75-ton class and carried less than ten guns. Two more groups— the galleys and galleasses—completed the array. There were four of each. The Portuguese galleys, under Diego Medrano, were primarily transports and carried only five cannons. They were propelled by sails and 220 galley slaves shackled to each ship. The Neapolitan galleasses, on the other hand, were the battleships of the sixteenth century—enormous floating forts, nearly 200 feet in length, with fifty cannons and towering castles fore and aft. Each of these leviathans carried a thousand soldiers in addition to three hundred oarsmen. Their commander was Hugo de Moncada.

This was the irresistible Navy which most of Europe expected would make short work of Queen Elizabeth's tiny squadrons. Its decks swarmed with Spain's most dashing cavaliers and skilled swordsmen, burning with desire to get at close quarters with the English "pirates" where they could teach the infidels how men fought. Backing them up were legions of veteran harquebus soldiers and pikemen. The armada was designed for Mediterranean-style warfare, geared to the time-honored tactics of closing and boarding. Had the English fought in the same manner the outcome would have probably been radically different.

Sir Francis Drake, Sir John Hawkins, and Sir Martin Frobisher knew Spanish fighting methods, however, and had no intention of meeting them on their own terms. Instead they used guerrilla warfare, employing to maximum advantage their assets of longer-ranged guns, faster and more maneuverable ships, and flexible tactics. When the armada reached the Channel, English ships bombarded it from beyond the Spaniards' range. They cut off stragglers, set afire and dismasted laggards in sudden thrusts, darted in and out, harassing, keeping the enemy off balance. All this while the mercurial weather bided its time. Then, at the end of July, the winds began to blow and the Channel turned white with spray. During the worst periods the English retreated to their nearby bases while the heavy galleons, struggling northward toward their destination, had to ride out the storms.

At 4 P.M. on July 31 the *Santa Catalina* was blown against the Castile Armada ship *Nuestra Señora del Rosario*, dismasting her. English ships pounced on the cripple and set her afire. According to Spanish accounts there was an explosion on board, and "two decks and the poop flew off." Then the winds subsided momentarily and other Spanish vessels were able to come alongside. The fire was put out and she was taken under tow. As the hull was leaking dangerously some of the crew and passengers transferred to other ships. Among them was Paymaster General Juan de la Huerta, who took with him his consignment of 30,000 ducats of the king's gold. This may have been loaded aboard the 60-ton Guipúzcoa *patache La Asunción* (2), which later disappeared at sea. With calmer weather the English ships renewed their attacks and later captured *Nuestra Señora del Rosario* together with another badly damaged vessel, the *San Mateo*.

The French coast claimed its casualties. On July 26 the galley

Diana put in at Bayonne in such pitiful condition that she was abandoned there. Then the 958-ton Guipúzcoa warship *San Salvador* (3), set afire by the English, broke up on rocks off the mouth of the Orne River which were later named after her. French scavengers swarmed down onto the wreckage trying to salvage treasure. Most of what she carried they got. Another ship with royal gold aboard, the *Santa Ana* (4), 768-ton *Capitana* of the Biscay Armada, fought off English attacks led by Frobisher until she grounded on the shore of Le Havre, her decks cluttered with wounded. Before she disintegrated the crewmen were able to carry ashore her treasure cargo of either 31,000 or 50,000 gold ducats. Two ships (5) (6) were reputed lost in the Channel Islands, near Guernsey.

After a week of battering by the storms the main body of the Armada put in at Calais on August 6 for shelter and repairs. The English gave them no respite. Scarcely had they anchored when Drake launched his famous fire attack to drive them back out. Seeing the flaming hulks blowing down on them, the Spanish officers tried frantically to maneuver their ships to safety in the darkness. In the confusion the *San Lorenzo* (7), *Capitana* of the giant galleasses, broke her rudder and stranded on the bar at the harbor's entrance. English ships bombarded her, then swarmed in. The Spanish crew fought bravely from the decks and castles, time and again repulsing boarding attacks, but they were finally overwhelmed. This time the English captured a treasure—22,000 gold ducats of the king's money and a fortune in Italian personal wealth, as well as small arms, 50 great guns and a supply of badly needed powder.

The weather worsened. On the first day out of Calais the 665-ton 24-gunned Biscay galleon *La María Juan* (8) sank off the coast carrying her cargo to the bottom of the Channel. A few hours later the *San Felipe* (9) was lost. This 800-ton Portuguese galleon, mounting 40 cannons, was so damaged by English attacks and storm that her commander beached the hulk off the mouth of the Schelde River, Flanders. Her crew escaped ashore, salvaging personal wealth and part of her supplies.

By now all thoughts of conquering England had long since been washed away by rain and salt water. Miserably seasick, cold and wet, the Spanish officers were totally preoccupied with keeping their ships afloat and getting back home. The bulk of the fleet was off the Flemish coast in the grip of the incessant gales which pressed it northward. Even if the commanders wanted to, this wind would prevent them from running the gauntlet back through the English Channel. Their only route to Spain was across the top of Scotland, then down the Atlantic coasts of the British Isles. On the ninth, as the armada moved outward from the Continent toward Scotland, the wind changed. Driving down suddenly from the northwest, a furious squall hurled the ships back against Zeeland, where breakers were thundering far out from shore. Every man felt that his last hour was coming, for no one could live in the violent ocean which was crashing against the approaching coast.

The 900-ton Levantine warship *La Trinidad* (*de Scala*) (10) was driven close to shore, nearly submerged under wave after wave which crossed her decks. She floundered in 30-foot depth. Her crew of 386 men drowned and her cargo was lost. Then the 2000-ton *Patrona* (11) of the Naples galleasses, galley slaves straining for their lives, was caught in gigantic breakers and dashed ashore. She grounded and broke up in 25 feet of water, where the shackled slaves drowned like trapped rats, together with the rest of the complement. Cargo and bodies were spread across the Zeeland coast. The crews on the other ships, hysterical with fright and nearly paralyzed from cold, waited for their turns. Then a miracle occurred. The wind shifted, coming up again from the southeast. The elements had not yet tired of playing with their toy.

The armada moved toward northern Scotland, its ragged ships scattered over hundreds of miles. Many were leaking badly and shipping water. Supplies were short. Entire crews were sick. One after the other the vessels succumbed to the battering waves. *La Juliana* (12), an 860-ton Levantine warship, floundered in sight of other ships which were incapable of going to her rescue. Several *pataches* and pinnaces disappeared at night. The Scottish coast came into view, bleak and unfriendly, between blinding rain squalls. Some of the captains, with their charges sinking under them, tried to take shelter in its estuaries. A 48-gunned galleon of the Portuguese Armada (13) was thrown against the rocks near Peterhead and settled on the sand bottom, decks awash. A few survivors gained the shore while the waves hammered at the wreck. Within hours it had vanished, and a treasure was swallowed by the sea. Another ship (14) crept into Dornoch Firth, trying to reach sanctuary. Just off the Doune of Criech the hull grounded on a sand bar and the ocean tore it to pieces. Floating wreckage washed ashore, but the heavy cargo dropped into the swirling sand below.

At least two ships (15) (16) went down among the rocky precipices of the Orkneys while more sank in deeper water. Another (17) jarred against the treacherous reefs of the Out Skerries, in the Shetland Islands, and was lashed into splinters there. *La Anunciada* (18), a 703-ton Levantine galleon of 24 cannon, tried to shelter in the southwest lee of the islands but grounded on Haddock Sands off Reawick.

Commanding *El Gran Grifón* (19)*, Juan Lopez de Medina navigated close to Fair Island between the Orkneys and Shetlands. He spotted an inlet at its southern point and tried to gain entry. Submerged rocks broke in the hull and the *Capitana* of the *urcas* settled to the bottom. Captain Lopez and most of the crew gained the beach safely and finally surrendered to the islanders. They were treated kindly by the native Scots, who lived in blissful ignorance of the troubles of the outside world, and settled there. This ship carried considerable money and jewels, some of which was probably salvaged. There must remain a small fortune, however, scattered among the submarine rocks and sand only 30 feet deep. The wreck's location should have been preserved in verbal traditions handed down through generations of Fair Islanders with names like Pedro MacCorkindale.

During September and October, against the northwest coasts of Scotland and Ireland, the great slaughter took place. Eight thousand men were drowned or put to the sword—if they survived their shipwrecks—by the coastal "barbarians" upon whose private wars they intruded. Over fifty ships of the armada were hurled against coasts and swamped at sea by the unchecked fury of the North Atlantic. Some of these shipwrecks were recorded. Many more vessels were last seen off shore in obvious distress and simply disappeared. One might well have been the wreck (20) near Flannon Island, off the Outer Hebrides, from which a ship's rail was raised recently by a fishing boat. Its carved designs identified it as Spanish. In the Hebrides themselves, at the end of September, two more ships (21) (22) were reported by the other galleons to have sunk "between the islets of Erth and Ila, near the Island of Faril." Another (23) was dashed to pieces at the foot of a cliff in Loch Bracadale, on the seaward coast of the Isle of Skye. Five ships were destroyed in the narrow lochs and firths separating Mull Island from the mainland. Among these is the most famous and disputed of all treasure ships, the "Tobermory Galleon" (24)*.

A great many detailed researches have been made to attempt identifying this vessel, and strong schools of opinion have developed. It has been "conclusively" proved that she is the *Duque de Florencia*, (also called the *San Francisco* and *La Regazona*). This magnificent ship was the *Capitana* of Martín de Bertendona's Levantine Armada, of 1245 tons, 30 cannon and a crew of 424 men plus soldiers, and certainly carried aboard a valuable cargo. The Glede Gun raised from this galleon in 1740, and today decorating the lawn of the Duke of Argyll's Inveraray Castle, is an archaeological treasure by itself. This masterpiece was made by Benvenuto Cellini for King Francis I of France. It was captured by Charles V of Spain, whose son Philip II later sent off the armada. Although by themselves neither this cannon nor the other artifacts and money which have been salvaged from the "Tobermory Galleon" identify her as the *Florencia*, they do prove that she was one of the important ships of the fleet—one of which money and jewels would be carried. There were ten big galleons in the Levantine Armada led by the *Florencia*. After the fiasco she was the only one of these to be officially listed as having returned to Spain. Some opinions are that this listing was deliberate camouflage.

The Tobermory Bay wreck has also been "conclusively" identified as the *San Juan Bautista*. There were two ships of this name, one of which, after a series of blood-curdling near-catastrophes along the Scottish and Irish coasts throughout September, sailed for Spain at the end of the month and arrived safely. She would have made an appetizing wreck, for she carried aboard the Treasurer of Castile. The second *San Juan Bautista* (25), also of the Castile Armada, was reported wrecked on the Irish coast. This vessel was smaller than the descriptions of the Tobermory ship, being of 650 tons and carrying 24 cannon. Moreover her shipwreck date of September 11—even taking into consideration differences of calendars—was quite different from that of the "Tobermory Galleon" which put in on September 13 and was not destroyed until several weeks later. So the *San Juan Bautista* seems eliminated. There are other candidates which could qualify: *La Lavia* (26), *Almiranta* of the Levantine Armada, was a 728-ton warship mounting 25 cannon. She was one of the great ships of the fleet, carrying royal gold and jewels, and did not return. Another possibility could be the Levantine warship *San Nicolás Prodaneli* (27) of 834 tons and 26 guns, which also vanished. Whatever ship the Tobermory Galleon may be, it seems probable that scattered in the bowels of her dispersed hull, buried under 10 to 16 feet of silt, there still remains a valuable cargo of money, gold and silver plate, and richly inlaid jewelry, as well as a wealth of historical treasures.

Ten miles past Tobermory, in the Sound of Mull, lie three other relics of the Invincible Armada. One (28) was wrecked off Lochaline, across from Mull Island. A second (29) sank at the inlet of Rudha an Ridire just beyond. The remains of a third (30) lie in Loch Don, off Lochdonhead on the easternmost point of Mull Island. Little is known of any of these although early salvage recovered guns and artifacts from their unburied remnants. More is recorded of the vessel which broke up on September 20 off Morvern, on the Scottish coast opposite the north tip of Mull. She was the *San Pedro Menor* (31), a 500-ton *urca* of Juan Lopez de Medina's armada, carrying 18 cannons. Badly disabled, this ship limped into Morvern port where the crew put ashore her guns and supplies before she sank. Treasurewise she is uninteresting.

At the southernmost tip of Kintyre peninsula, in a bay called the Mull of Kintyre, lies another unidentified ship (32) which sank there in September. A more interesting wreck can be found just eastward, across the Firth of Clyde, at the foot of Portincross Castle in West Killride. Her name is unknown, but local tradition describes her as one of the largest galleons (33) of them all. Some cannons were salvaged from this ship about one hundred years ago. One lies today in the ruins of Portincross Castle. The survivors of her crew—if there were any—may have been able to salvage something from their floundering vessel, but there should remain a valuable assortment of intrinsic and historical treasures in the silted-over wreckage.

At least twenty-three galleons and warships came to their end on the exposed coasts of Ireland and very little has been done to salvage their remnants. This area is a rich treasure-hunting field, particularly so because it is possible to identify many of these wrecks from both Spanish and Irish records, and pinpoint those which definitely sank with treasure.

Commanded by one of Spain's boldest and most capable nobles, Don Alonzo Martínez de Leiva, the 820-ton Levantine *La Rata Sancta María Encoronada* (35) was wallowing in heavy seas with a leaking hull when the west coast of Ireland was sighted. De Leiva took her into the shelter of Blacksod Bay and grounded her south of Ballycroy. After taking ashore valuables, supplies, and weapons the crew fired the hull and set up camp in an abandoned castle nearby. The local Irish chieftain, O'Neil, proved friendly and supplied food. Soon afterward *La Duquesa Santa Ana* (34), of 900 tons and 23 guns, put in for shelter. *La Rata*'s crew crowded aboard and the Andalusian *urca* set sail. Relentless southwest gales drove her northward across Donegal Bay, around the peninsula of Killybegs, and into sight of Loughros More Bay farther north. The captain took the *Santa Ana* in for shelter and dropped anchors. They failed to grip and the ship broke up against the far shore of the lough. Once again treasure, armaments, and the dwindling supply of provisions were ferried to land. A small fort was built on a slope and armed with salvaged guns—one of which, a cast-iron falcon, still lies on the hill. Scouts were sent out. One reported sails in Donegal Bay, across the peninsula they had just passed. The sick and hungry crews of the two ships staggered south for eleven miles, carrying their valuables and weapons, and sighted the towering castles of the *Girona* (36) floating off Killybegs. The Neapolitan galleass had put in with a broken rudder for repairs.

The arrivals were taken aboard the floating fortress and assisted her crew in repairing damage. A few days later the dangerously overloaded *Girona* sailed. De Leiva, in command, set a course northward, then east across the top of Ireland with the intention of reaching western Scotland, where friendly treatment could be expected from the Catholic King James II. Just beyond the massive basalt rocks of the

Giant's Causeway the jury-rigged rudder broke. As galley slaves pulled for their lives at the sweeps, gusts of north wind and cresting waves drove the 200-foot ship toward the coast. Just after midnight of October 26 "the galleass ran upon a submerged rock and went to pieces." The starboard side was splintered against the reef. The weakened hull broke, dumping cargo and ballast into the surging waves. Of 1300 men aboard, including some 50 Spanish nobles, 5 survived.

They were given sanctuary by McDonnell, Lord of Dunbuce, whose castle dominated the shore four miles westward near Portballintrae. Soon afterward three of the five remaining cannons (the others had been jettisoned) and a reported three chests of money were salvaged and taken to Dunluce. The enormous treasure lost with the *Girona* remained on the bottom until 1967 (see SALVAGE OF THE *GIRONA*).

Two inlets of the ocean penetrate North Ireland, like a finger and thumb pinching the top of the Emerald Isle. The eastern one is called Lough Foyle. Fifteen miles west is Lough Swilly. The mouth of Lough Foyle closes to a narrow gap protecting its stretches from the rough ocean, making it an ideal shelter for ships in distress. That was apparently the reasoning of her captain when he brought in *La Trinidad Valencera* (38) with her sails shredded and her hull taking water. This Levantine warship was one the largest and heaviest armed in the entire armada—1100 tons and 42 cannons. She had a crew of 360 and transported 500 soldiers. At the foot of a castle which the Spanish called "Duhort" the *Trinidad* struck a rock and sank. From indications of her size, she probably carried money and personal jewelry. During the nearly four hundred years since her loss there may well have been long-forgotten salvage work carried on over this disintegrated hull since it lies in a protected area. Two other ships (39) (40) were reported sunk off the peninsula joining the loughs of Swilly and Foyle, near Malin Head and Glergad Head, and still another (41) slightly westward at Donegal Point.

There are many reefs and rocks in the British Isles, as everywhere else, that have taken the names of ships which were wrecked on them. Others commemorate the event with a simpler connotation. An example is Spanish Rock, in Rosses Bay on the Donegal coast. The name of the galleon which sank here was known to the coast dwellers who gathered its flotsam because the crew came ashore and lived among them. Yet instead of calling the site after the ship's name, they used the simpler word "Spanish." The galleon was possibly the *San Marcos* (42) of the Portuguese Armada, a big ship of 790 tons, mounting 33 cannon, with a crew of 409. Since most of these men escaped it is likely that the valuable cargo was also saved, yet there have been several salvage attempts on this wreck. The most successful was about 1775, when it was seen in 15 feet depth and divers retrieved cannons and other artifacts. A final try was made in 1895 but by this time the ancient hulk had been buried in sand and nothing could be seen of it.

A little farther down the coast, at the entrance of Sligo Bay, is the Strand of Streedagh—a sandy beach bordered by huge boulders. Over 1500 men died here on September 9 when three ships which had anchored offshore were hurled onto the rocks by a sudden gale which dragged them from their moorings. Bodies and wreckage were piled several feet high on the sand. Two of the vessels are identified; the *San Juan de Sicilia* (43), a Levantine warship of 800 tons and 26 guns, and the *San Pedro Mayor* (44), a 581-ton *urca* of Medina's armada, with 29 cannon. The third might be either the 600-ton *Santiago* (45) or the *Falcon Blanco Mediano* (46), of 300 tons. Both *urcas* were lost in this vicinity. Clusters of human bones are still reported found on the beach and occasionally fragments from the ships wash up, while aged relics from the cargo—iron chests and cannon balls—have their traditional places in nearby homes. A massive and elaborately carved table is kept in Dromoland Castle. Any treasure that may have been carried on these ships, though, has long since been buried in thousands of cubic yards of sand by the churning waves.

Probably three ships were lost in Galway Bay. One (47) was seen off its coast for the last time. A second (48) is known to have definitely sunk in Castlefort Bay, on North Aran Island, but has never been identified. R. H. Davis refers to another (49) in his book *Deep Diving*, when he writes:

> An old English diver, employed many years ago at a salvage job on the Galway coast [met a fisherman, who] told the diver that one of the vessels of the Spanish Armada had been wrecked not far from the coast. The diver . . . made terms with the fisherman, and they were both out for many weeks dragging the spot indicated for traces of the wreck. They were at last rewarded. The diver . . . descended to what proved to be the remains of an old Spanish galleon. He came across a large number of dollars which had originally been packed in small wooden barrels; the wood, however, had rotted away and left the coins stacked in barrel shape. With the proceeds, which realized some thousands of pounds, the diver built himself a row of houses, which he called "Dollar Row."

Some twenty miles south, off the shore of Cape Clare, the *urca* *Barca de Amburg* (50) was lost. This 600-ton ship carried 23 guns and 264 men. She went down in relatively deep water and has never been located. At the mouth of the nearby Shannon River a disabled ship (51) was beached and burned, while still farther down the coast a *patache* (52) was wrecked in Tralee Bay. Two dozen survivors managed to reach shore and surrendered to the local boss, one Lady Denny. She had them run through with swords.

When the Castile galleon *San Juan Bautista* limped back to Spain her officers told a story that stunned even the most calloused listeners. During the first half of September she had crossed the top of Scotland and run down the Atlantic coast of Ireland, badly buffeted by tempests after the twelfth. On the fifteenth she took shelter in "the port of Vicey"—Blasket Sound, at the outermost tip of the long peninsula on the north of Dingle Bay—entering "through a passage fifty meters wide between the reefs." Soon afterward she was joined by one of the treasury ships, then a *patache*, which took refuge in the partial shelter of Blasket Sound. The three vessels had been locked in their haven for nearly a week when a pitiful wreck, "her sails ' own to ribbons," staggered in under a single remaining jib. She was the *Santa María de la Rosa* (54)**, once-proud *Almiranta* of the Guipúzcoa Armada, carrying nearly five hundred men. The 945-ton ship anchored not far from the *San Juan Bautista*. Don Martín de Villa Franca, her captain, was responsible not only for their safety but also for the security of a treasure consignment reported variously at from 15,000 to 50,000 gold ducats and considerable silver and jewelry. He failed in his charge.

According to the log of Marcos de Aramburu, paymaster aboard the *San Juan Bautista*, "as the tide turned, she began dragging her anchor two cable lengths from us . . . and in an instant we could see that she was going down. A most extraordinary and terrifying thing." The *Santa María de la Rosa* was swept across the bay toward a reef near its center. She struck the rocks, hung there for a short time, then broke free and settled rapidly. Within minutes she had disappeared. There was only one survivor, Giovanni de Manora, son of the ship's pilot. Clinging to a plank, he was washed ashore and taken prisoner by the local chieftain, James Trant of Dingle. Under interrogation by a Spanish-speaking translator, de Manora stated that the ship had mounted 25 bronze and iron cannons, and carried a huge amount of treasure: "Lost were 50,000 gold ducats, plus an equal value in silver, jewels and plate." Whether his tale was exaggerated or not may well be determined soon (see SALVAGE OF THE *SANTA MARÍA DE LA ROSA*). Another ship, the 530-ton Castile galleon *San Juan* (56), entered the sound in such damaged condition that she sank in a short time. Most of her crew was taken aboard the other ships. For years afterward the Blasket Islanders were said to have raised cannons, anchors, and other artifacts, as well as considerable quantities of coins, from these two Spanish wrecks.

After the storms subsided the *San Juan Bautista* and the *patache* returned safely to Spain. The other ship was not so fortunate. She was *El Gran Grin* (53)**, the 1160-ton *Almiranta* of the Biscay Armada carrying 28 guns and nearly a thousand men. Soon after leaving Blasket Sound she was sunk—reportedly off Clare Island—with half of her complement drowned. "More than 16,000 ducats in jewels and escudos" went down with the treasury ship, some of which was said to have washed up on a beach and been "robbed by the Irish." Another ship, the 26-gun Biscay *nao San Esteban* (57), may have also been wrecked nearby.

In November a hospital ship (58), which was nearly home after weathering the tempests for four months, smashed up on the southern tip of England at Bolt Head, in Devon. She carried no gold, but instead a cargo so highly prized that Queen Elizabeth sent a special delegation to collect all that had been salvaged. This was bezoar stones—the penicillin of 1588—which was believed in those days to be a panacea. The Queen was out of luck. The Devon folk wanted to keep this magic medicine for themselves. Another Spanish ship (59) was wrecked in Mounts Bay, Cornwall, early in 1589. Most opinions are that she was one of the straggling remnants of the armada which might have been returning from Iceland or Greenland.

The slaughter had still not ended. Even as they were coming home to their Spanish ports after appalling voyages with crews half dead from hunger and exposure, two more important ships went down. Off the harbor of Santander the Biscay *urca Doncella* (60) struck a rock and sank immediately. And in the entry passage to San Sebastian the *Santa Ana* (61)**, largest and heaviest-armed of all the galleons in the Invincible Armada, suddenly blew up. She was the 47-gun *Capitana* of the Guipúzcoa Armada, carrying nearly a thousand men and a large consignment of royal treasure as well as personal fortunes of a dozen wealthy nobles. The entire salvage was one incoherent burned survivor.

In addition to the exact or approximate sites of thirty-four wrecks identified above, locations of another twenty-seven unnamed wrecks have been given. There lie the remains of most of the other "lost" ships, *pataches* and pinnaces. For the record these are:

Five *urcas*, from 370 to 750 tons, carrying from 10 to 27 cannon, of Juan Lopez de Medina's armada: *Falcon Blanco Major, Ciervo Volante, Santa Barbara, Castilla Negra* and *David*. The Levantine warship *Santa María de Vison*, of 666 tons and 18 guns. Twenty-three *pataches* and pinnaces of the Light Squadron, and attached to the various armadas, from 36 to 300 tons and carrying from 2 to 12 cannon: *Nuestra Señora del Pilar* (*Capitana* of the Light Squadron), *La Caridad, El Crucifijo, Santa Catalina, San Juan, Asunción Magdalina, La Concepción* (of Cano), *La Concepción* (of Zubelzu), *Nuestra Señora de Guadalupe, María de Aquirre, Patache de Miguel Suso,*

La Concepción (of Latero), *La Concepción* (of Carasa), *San Francisco, La Concepción* (of Somanila), *La Concepción* (of Valmaseda), *San Jerónimo, Nuestra Señora de Socorro, Nuestra Señora de Castro, Nuestra Senora de Begoña, San Antonio de Padua,* and *Espíritu Santo.*

Two of the armada wrecks—the *Girona* and the *Santa María de la Rosa*—have recently become the sites of important archaeological treasure salvages. Because of widespread interest in this work and other reasons which will be apparent, the following accounts are given in some detail.

SALVAGE OF THE *GIRONA*

During the preparation of the first edition of this *Guide* in Spain ten years ago the author and Robert Sténuit spent evenings speculating about the wrecks of the Invincible Armada. Why, we wondered, with so much information about locations available, had there been no important salvages reported since the end of the last century? Why couldn't even one of the armada's 2431 cannons be found in any museum? What cargoes on the lost ships could have survived 371 years of erosion under tempestuous seas? And were the documents we had studied really factual in their references to treasure cargoes aboard? Today, thanks to Sténuit's determination to find out, we have some interesting answers.

"Since our discussions about the Armada," he recalls, "I have spent over six hundred hours in research at the Library of the British Museum and the Public Records Office, plus many more hundred hours at the Nationale in Paris, the Royale in Brussels, and the Amsterdam Naval Museum." Referring to his specific goal, he adds, "My deductions took me straight to the *Girona*."

The *Girona* rated two stars, now deleted, in the original *Guide*. The author's "first stage" research placed her wreckage among the Bunbay Rocks (now Bushfoot) off the Bush River, near Dunluce Castle. A second, unknown, wreck was described to lie in nearby "Port na Spana" under the Chimney Pot Rocks. Referring to these sites, Sténuit comments, "In fact, the two ships are the one and same *Girona*."

The account of Sténuit's salvage is the feature article in the June 1969 issue of *National Geographic Magazine*. It is told in fascinating detail in his *Treasure of the Armada*, which may well become a textbook for underwater archaeologists and treasure divers. The project, born in 1959 in Vigo, Spain, germinated during the years when Ed Link and Sténuit pioneered the "Man-in-Sea" scientific program, which proved that divers can survive at great depths for long periods of time. It came to fruition after Sténuit moved to London in 1966 to manage the British office of Ocean Systems, Inc. During free time he extended his research into the armada. As data accumulated the *Girona* stood out more and more invitingly.

In arriving at his "deductions" the Belgian archaeologist/historian analyzed many contemporary accounts. An early report stated that "the galley which departed from Killybegs, with as many Spaniards as she could carry . . . struck against the rock of Bunboyes, where both ships and men perished, save only five . . . This rock of Bunboyes is hard by Sorley Boy's house." Further digging identified Sorley Boy as Lord McDonnell, and his house as Dunluce Castle, near Portballintrae. Among other documents Sténuit found: "I hear that three fair pieces of brass [guns] which lie in view between the rocks at Bunboyes . . . will also be recovered" . . . "It is reported that there is a great store of gold and silver there" . . . "The McDonnells have planted three pieces of Ordnance, demi-cannon and culverine, which were had out of the Spanish ships" . . . "James McDonnell has helped himself to three chests of treasure which were taken to Dunluce Castle." Sténuit learned that in the years after the shipwreck McDonnell made a major enlargement and redecoration of the castle. Had the money come from salvage commissioned by the lord and carried out by "two Spaniards and a Scottish captain"?

In studying late-sixteenth-century maps, Sténuit found only two regional landmarks identified by name: Dunluce and the Boys River. Nineteenth-century maps, however, named Spaniard Rock, Spaniard Cave, Port na Spaniagh, and Lacada Point, all grouped in a small area around the point—a narrow promontory of dark rock extending 200 feet into the sea under the basalt Chimney Pot formation. Wreck hunters who faithfully followed historical research would concentrate their searches around Bunboys at the mouth of the Bush River. Sténuit selected Lacada Point, one mile away.

In June 1967 he drove up from London with his diving companion of many adventures, Marc Jasinski. From the storm-swept top of a 300-foot cliff overlooking the site the two men stared silently at pounding surf sending up geysers of spray from the point. At length Jasinski asked, "After four hundred years of this, what can be left of the wreck?"

It was June 27 before the seas calmed enough to permit launching their outboard-powered dinghy. Jasinski anchored off Port na Spaniagh. Sténuit dived, then "took a reading on the compass and set off southeast towards Lacada Point, straining to see the ocean floor through the waving seaweed. Every time I came to a cleft in the rock I stopped to move a couple of stones or beat up the sand. There was nothing. Bad weather had reduced visibility to a few yards. I was brought to a sudden halt by Lacada Point cliff and followed it northward as far as a platform ending in an enormous rock. Something white caught my eye—a pig of lead." This was a yard-long triangular ingot, narrowing at the ends. Although he had never seen one like it before, Sténuit knew he had found his wreck. During research he had read of an identical lead bar salvaged from another armada ship, a hundred years earlier.

"With some difficulty I managed to turn it over and found stamped on the upper face five Jerusalem crosses. I set off down a corridor which led me straight to a bronze cannon, half-buried in the pebbles. Its measure was my span plus one arm. The caliber was about eight centimeters. It was a demi-saker. The underwater shelf inclined sharply downward. If the ship had hit this everything must have rolled to the bottom. In a crevice further down I found a second cannon: a smaller breechloader, bearing the Spanish coat of arms in relief. Next to it were some breechblocks, two of a larger caliber than the others. They must have belonged to Sorley Boy's cannons. Nearby lay more pigs of lead, and thick plates. Shapeless masses had become fused to the rocks and filled up fissures. All around were cannon balls and rust. Between two stones lay a little copper coin."

It was July 1 before weather permitted another trip. Jasinski methodically photographed the wreckage for future reference while Sténuit extended his search. A gray flat pebble which he picked up turned out to be a sulfided 8-real piece, the cross of Jerusalem faintly visible. Another lay nearby. Mounting waves forced them back to harbor and allowed only infrequent dives during the following days. But every descent was fruitful. While Sténuit added to his collection of Spanish coins, Jasinski found an anchor off the point on July 6. It was corroded and damaged, with the arms twisted at an angle to the base of the shank. Its span was about 8 feet. Sténuit found his first underwater gold—a single link from a chain, then a part of a chain made up of six delicate figure-of-eight links. With the success of their survey established, the two Belgians returned their finds to an underwater cave and departed to prepare for the *Girona*'s salvage.

During the next months Sténuit organized the expedition. The Marseilles diving pioneer Henri Delauze contributed a truckload of equipment. Funds were made available by *National Geographic Magazine*, which had previously published articles by and about Sténuit.[1] Ocean Systems, Inc., aware of the importance of the find, granted a leave of absence. Two experienced French divers, Maurice Vidal and Louis Gorsse, and a Belgian architectural student, Francis Dumont, were added to the team. Jasinski, with a degree in chemistry, would undertake the preservation of artifacts as well as the photography.

A systematic layer-by-layer excavation of the site was unthinkable. "We were going to work in a chaotic world of cliffs, crevices and stone-filled basins," Sténuit notes. "A metal grid on the sea bed would

[1] May 1963 issue: "The Long, Deep Dive," by Lord Kilbracken; June 1964 issue: "Tomorrow on the Deep Frontier," by Edwin A. Link; April 1965 issue: "The Deepest Days," by Robert Sténuit.

have been about as useful here as on the top of Milan Cathedral. The first square wouldn't have stayed down three days, and even if it had, everything in it would have been tossed around into some other section. Every movement of the sea completely changed the layout of the bed, filling in holes and covering up cannons which it had uncovered earlier."

The expedition reached Portballintrae in April 1968. Working under gusts of sleet, the divers tied guidelines of tough half-inch nylon to cannons and rocks in an attempt to establish a rudimentary reference pattern. Each intersection of lines was numbered. Within days the surging water had snapped several lines, and nearly every work period commenced with repairs. For the next three months most of the working hours were devoted to charting the area and methodically plotting, sketching, and photographing the located artifacts *in situ* before they were moved. The wave motion was so overpowering that normal movement with flippers was impossible. Instead, the divers used the ocean's force, riding forward with each surge, then clinging to a rock or kelp stem during the backlash. The icy water attacked every part of the body, causing physical pain. Despite layers of wool underwear and sweaters covered by combinations of neoprene and dry suits, cramps and numbness were chronic. Even cellular isothermic suits failed to give sustained protection. Continuous storms limited diving to one in three days.

May 2 was one of these days, and a memorable one. The first gold coins were found. Gorsse and Vidal recovered two 4-escudos minted in Seville, along with dozens of silver and copper coins, gold buttons, and silver forks. A yellow glint caught Sténuit's eye. He picked up the golden object and recognized a fleur-de-lis on one side. He subsequently identified the find as a very rare medallion of the Order of Alcántara. The next day, surveying a blackened conglomerate of stones, cannon balls, and rusty iron which appeared to be ballast, Sténuit saw a gold chain protruding from both sides. The significance of this did not escape him. For weeks afterward every such apparently worthless mass on the bottom was carefully chipped into manageable chunks, raised on slings, and later methodically dissected. From these fused masses of stone, iron oxide, and calcium from crushed sea shells, Sténuit's team extracted a fortune in sixteenth-century coins: piasters, pieces of eight, ducats, ducatoons, and escudos. Among them were also artifacts and jewelry, including gold chains, pottery shards, lead bullets, leather straps, cartridge fragments, and silver forks and spoons.

The richest mass of this conglomeration extended into a cave whose "roof" was two 100-ton boulders held up partly by rocks and partly by the fused mass. For days the divers chipped carefully at the supports as they mined the treasure lode. As the cavern extended deeper they spent more time nervously eyeing the overhead boulders. The time finally came when consensus of opinion was that further attempts at penetration would be suicidal. In a "final" excavation Sténuit gingerly moved a few stones with the tip of his extended miner's bar to retrieve a silver candlestick he was determined to possess. A second candlestick, completing the pair, came into view and caused another "absolutely final" penetration. Then Sténuit saw a gold chain a few inches farther back. When he had finished, the cave was cleaned out. The boulders remained in place.

By mid-May warmer temperatures permitted daily immersions of four hours. With calmer water the divers even enjoyed the luxury of standing up in their dinghy while changing. At the same time the kelp grew into thick forests. When cut, the stems, as thick as an arm, floated in entangling masses. Work now moved onto a 30-foot-deep gravel-floored plateau covering some 5000 square feet in front of the cave. The pebbles and stones blanketed the underlying rock bed to depths of from 1 to 10 feet. Sector by sector, this gravel was screened and moved, and the exposed rock fissures excavated. From their deepest crevices was recovered a rich harvest of gold rings, jewels, coins, and metallic artifacts. It soon became apparent that the loose gravel contained nothing but light fragments of stone pedrero cannon balls. All the heavier objects had worked their way down to the bottom. The heaviest gold, which had penetrated faster, was unharmed; lighter silver and pewter objects, however, had moved more slowly and were nearly all bent and eroded. As nothing of interest was likely to remain in the gravel the time-consuming sifting was discontinued. A water jet connected to a pump in the dinghy was used to wash away the overburden.

The breech-loading cannon was raised with a neoprene inflatable lift bag. As it was manhandled ashore the ever-present spectators gasped in amazement. The rumor that these foreign frogmen had raised 200 tons of gold *was* true! By the time the gun was lifted onto the truck a large crowd had assembled. The news soon made the wire services and was reported in the press and on the radio. The results gave the Sténuit team some anxious moments. On May 26 a dozen divers from a Belfast club arrived, laden with salvage gear. Meeting them at the jetty, Sténuit explained that the wreck was being archaeologically surveyed and was not to be disturbed. He pointed out that his red buoy near the site served notice that he was the "salvor in possession." Undaunted, the newcomers headed for the wreck. Sténuit's team overtook them in their faster dinghy and watched carefully as they searched well away from the site. Some of the intruders finally found a guideline and followed it to the cave. Here they encountered the powerfully built Gorsse standing guard. The group departed.

The second invading team was more determined. Sténuit followed their divers underwater, unseen. When one slipped a lead fragment into his salvage bag, the Belgian tapped him on the shoulder from behind. Then Sténuit seized the bag and returned the lead to the sea floor. He was immediately surrounded by angry divers who shook him and pulled at his flippers. Surfacing, Sténuit protested. A one-sided fight was starting when the dinghy brought Gorsse and Vidal to the scene. As Gorsse plunged in, a swarm of fresh "enemies" jumped from their boat. A full-scale underwater battle was averted when the intruders withdrew to hold a conference, after which they too left. To prevent any further similar incidents Sténuit took the matter to court. A few days later the Belfast High Court officially confirmed his rights of "exclusive salvor" of the *Girona*.

If confirmation of the wreck's wide dispersal was needed, the following weeks provided this. Whenever the group searched they were rewarded. Clusters of coins and artifacts were even located under 2- to 10-ton boulders which were moved with lifting bags. Gorsse collected and assembled all the pieces of a 1½-inch gold cross of the Knights of Malta. Sténuit then found fifteen gold coins in one day, only to be outdone by Vidal, whose haul on the following day was twenty. Sténuit recognized wood protruding from a mass of bullets, bones, charcoal, and pottery fragments cemented together by the chemical action of gunpowder, lime, and sea water. After a week of careful chiseling he retrieved a musket with its lead ball still in the breech. The iron barrel was reduced to paste. Silver phials, found everywhere, were assumed to be apothecary bottles until the Belgian came upon a silver-capped quartz dauber. It fitted a phial, revealing that these dozens of little bottles were in fact perfume flasks whose owners used the contents to mask the stench of sweating galley slaves.

Some of the most precious finds were made toward the end of the summer. Vidal had already collected several delicate gold medallions decorated with a mustached Triton when Sténuit found four more of the same, still inlaid with their original lapis lazuli cameos, each with the face of a different Roman Caesar. The most valuable single item recovered was probably a 1¼-inch gold winged salamander still mounting three of the rubies that were originally inlaid along its back. A diamond-mounted gold ring was retrieved in good condition, along with dozens of gold beads, buttons, finger rings, and sections of chain. Silver was represented in crucifixes, sculptures, remnants of bowls and goblets, pieces of plates, and dining utensils. Pewter and copper medallions pathetically recalled the galley slaves who must have clutched at them as their chains dragged them under.

Navigational instruments were found, including several brass dividers and very rare sixteenth-century astrolabes. During the final diving days the second cannon was brought up. It was followed by the anchor, which, together with all the cannon balls, was to be treated to prevent deterioration. The hoard of lead ingots and sheets weighed over 1½ tons. Most of them were marked with Roman numerals or crosses. This lead was for casting into arquebus and musket balls.

The coin collection would send any numismatist into ecstasies. The gold and silver money represented mints from every corner of the sixteenth-century Spanish empire—Portugal, Naples, seven different mints in Spain, and even Mexico, which contributed well-made 4- and 8-reales. The latest coin date was 1582. The money bore the names and profile of Ferdinand and Isabella, Charles V, and Philip II, who had sent the *Girona* to her destruction.

Any lingering doubts that the wreck was that of this galleass were dispelled by a study of the salvaged cannon balls. Their sizes precisely matched the various calibers of the fifty cannons that the *Girona* was known, from historical records, to have carried. Forty-five of these guns had been jettisoned at Killybegs to lighten the ship enough for two other crews to come aboard. These, plus Sorley Boy's and Sténuit's, account for the *Girona*'s entire battery.

By the end of September 1968 Robert Sténuit's group had put in 2800 man-hours of work on their wreck. Hundreds of tons of stones had been moved under difficult and dangerous diving conditions. The reward more than justified this effort. Despite rich recoveries, however, the salvage of the *Girona* was far from completed. Sténuit's expedition returned to the diving base at Portballintrae in April 1969 to resume where they left off the previous year. Discussing his plans, he said, "I shall perhaps look for other Armada wrecks later, but before that we intend to thoroughly complete the salvage of the *Girona*. How many more diving seasons will this take? As many as necessary . . ."

SALVAGE OF THE *SANTA MARÍA DE LA ROSA*

Blasket Sound covers some four square miles off the tip of Dingle Peninsula. Partial shelter to its west is provided by a row of rocks and barren islets, of which Great Blasket, Beginish, and Young islands are the largest. The rock, sand, and shale bottom drops off in areas to below 130 feet, and the surface is broken in places by jagged reefs. The most prominent of these, near the center, is topped by Stromboli Rock. Underwater visibility is generally good, up to 30 or more yards; but icy temperatures, rough seas, and strong currents make Blasket Sound no place for beginners.

This fact was emphasized in an invitation for divers placed in *Triton* magazine in 1967 by Sidney Wignall, a Welsh businessman and underwater archaeologist, which stated: "If you like hard work, don't mind being soaked to the skin and frozen, cut and bloodied, fed up to the teeth with the word 'Armada' and tired but still determined to soldier on

with a smile, then you are probably just the chap we are looking for."
The chaps came running, including professionals and British Navy
clearance divers on leave. During the first expedition period from mid-
April to October 1968, forty-three experienced wreck salvagers participated, providing an average team strength of fifteen divers. To share in
the search for wrecks from the Invincible Armada each paid for his own
transportation and food and supplied diving gear.

Sidney Wignall had been interested in his project since 1960. Over
a period of years he undertook an extensive study of the armada,
assisted by professional researchers at the British Museum. Armed with
a portfolio of Spanish survivors' testimonies and historical data, Wignall
obtained a license from the Spanish government through its embassy
in Dublin to salvage any armada wrecks off the Kerry coast. His ten-
year contract is valid until 1977. Under its terms he posted a bond of
£1000, accepted the supervision of a custodian appointed by the
Spanish government, agreed to deposit all recovered treasure with the
National Bank of Ireland for evaluation by independent appraisers and
to pay the Spanish government 20 per cent—the royal fifth—of its
value. Salvage permit in hand, Wignall formed and financed The
Spanish Armada Salvage Association.

The divers' training got under way on April 14, under the supervision
of Diving Officer Lieutenant Commander John Grattan, O.B.E., R.N.
(presently the captain of the deep-diving research vessel H.M.S. *Re-
claim*). Equipment and Supply Officer Joe Casey was in charge of the
boats, metal detectors, underwater telephones, water jets and pumps,
and other gear. Colin Martin planned the survey and would head up the
archaeological work on recovered artifacts. Casey was thoroughly
familiar with the area. He had participated in an earlier exploratory
search with Wignall during 1963 and an expedition by the St. Helens
Underwater Group in 1967. Neither effort, nor other searches during the
interim period, had achieved success. The St. Helens Group had reported
finding a long ballast pile with cannon balls and pottery whose location
they lost afterward, but this was located by Wignall's expedition in
April 1968 and turned out to be a pile of natural stones and stacks of
iron pipes.

From research data Wignall and Casey believed that the *Santa María
de la Rosa* had sunk in the northern part of the sound. The search
started in this area, between Young and Beginish islands and the
peninsula. It was carried out by visual survey to take advantage of the
clear water and the large number of experienced eyes available. John
Gratten used the Navy bomb and mine search technique called the
"swim line," or "running jackstay," in which from six to fifteen divers,
spaced at 20-yard intervals along a nylon line, moved forward together,
keeping the line straight and taut. Each diver maintained position by

keeping an eye on the divers to both sides, while scanning the sea bed in his sector. The two end divers guided the course of each sweep from underwater compass bearings. Buoys towed by them along the surface permitted observers to chart accurately each surveyed stretch of the bottom. Depending on the number of participating divers a path from 100 to 300 yards wide could be swept. On the best single day 500,000 square feet were covered in two diving periods.

When the northern sector proved barren the search moved south across the sand bottom between Beginish and Great Blasket. Three anchors were found here. The first was very ancient, possibly of Viking origin. Of the other two, both of the armada period, one struck an immediate responsive chord. It was broken with only the lower shank and arms left. Wignall recalled a passage from Marcos de Aramburu's log which noted that when one of the *San Juan Bautista*'s anchors was raised it was found to be broken and only "the stock with half the shank" was recovered. From his ship's anchorage, the writer had witnessed the destruction of *Nuestra Señora de la Rosa*.

The swim line moved eastward into the tide-swept channel between the islands and Stromboli Reef. While combing the reef's north face the divers found their first lead to the wreck. It was a 17-foot anchor jammed into the rocks, its shank pointing southeast like a guiding arrow. The east side of Stromboli fell away steeply onto a deep and flat shingle plateau. Diving time was now limited, because simultaneous decompression of so many divers in the strong current was impractical. A short distance southeast of the reef formation two large rock piles were discovered at a depth of 115 feet. As neither revealed cannons or artifacts on their surfaces, their positions were logged for future reference, and search moved on.

The entire bottom of Blasket Sound was surveyed, with several sections covered twice. Finally the stone piles were reexamined, this time more thoroughly. One was natural rock. The other was in fact a ballast mound. It measured 80 by 35 feet, and several feet in height. Traces of corroded iron and timbers were found on the surface. The enthused divers set to work moving stones, and artifacts began to appear. All were typical of cargo carried aboard late-sixteenth-century Spanish ships. Heavy lead ingots were stamped with Spanish "stores reference" numbers; pottery fragments were of the right dating; three kinds of iron cannon balls were identified as those used by cannon, culverin, and demi-culverin which the armada galleons carried. Further substantiation was provided with the recovery of 5-inch stone pedrero balls, case shot, and lead arquebus balls. As in the case of the *Girona*, these projectiles were valuable for identification. Animal bones and the heel of a shoe were added to the artifacts. There seemed no doubt that a 1588 wreck had been located. From the distribution of ballast, artifacts, and wood beams and timbers that were uncovered, it appeared that the ship had settled on her side and that the ballast had crashed through the decks as she rolled over. By the end of the working period in 1968, several excavations in the stone revealed wood beneath.

The 1969 season resulted in deeper penetration of the ballast. Wignall's expedition includes seven permanent members and a number of visiting divers scheduled to maintain team strength at twenty. Equipment includes three 15-foot inflatable dinghies with 18-hp outboards and a 50-foot launch carrying compressors to supply one 6-inch and another 4-inch air lift, as well as a pump for a powerful water jet. A new metal detector has been put to good use. Inflatable lifting bags are being used to move ballast stones—a considerable improvement over the former bucket brigade method.

By July 1969 recoveries included quantities of iron and stone shot, a bag containing grape shot, and—from the galley section—flints for starting fires, brushwood, barrel staves, a brass balancing pan, and a 381-year-old Brazil nut. The metal detector located a large pewter plate, under which lay human arm, leg, and rib bones, a silver medallion, and the first signs of treasure: two coins. One was an unidentifiable silver piece, but the other, a Philip II double gold escudo, recalled in immediate terms those coffers of money reported aboard the *Santa María de la Rosa*. It was the find of two 8-inch pewter plates, however, that caused the real excitement. On the back of each was inscribed the word MATUTE—and in his testimony, the survivor Giovanni had stated that one of the important men aboard the *Santa María de la Rosa* was Francisco Ruiz Matute, captain of infantry in the Camp of Sicily. During the intensive search no other wreck had been found under Blasket Sound despite historical records that the less interesting *San Juan* had also sunk there. With the new evidence it seemed nearly certain that the ballast mound was that of the rich treasury ship.

As artifacts are recovered they are immediately treated for preservation in a program in which experts from University College and Trinity College in Dublin are participating. Other organizations supporting Wignall's project are the Committee for Nautical Archaeology of London, the Irish Underwater Council, and the National Maritime Institute of Ireland. Despite their endorsement, Wignall's group has encountered the usual problems with treasure-seeking scavengers. To stop unauthorized plundering legally, he obtained an interlocutory injunction from the Irish courts in June 1969.

Wignall has also extended the scope of his salvage license from the Spanish government to include other armada wrecks in Donegal Bay. He believes that one lies in Killybegs Harbor and another outside, near the *Girona*'s forty-five jettisoned cannons; a third to the east of the harbor; and three more on the shallows of Streedagh Strand. Referring to these and his future program, he says, "I now have an exclusive license for a further six Armada wrecks in the Bay of Donegal. Our plans, however, are to concentrate on the *Santa María de la Rosa.* They include metal detector and triangulation surveys and excavation by air lift and water jet. In the long term we may be working Armada wrecks on the Irish coast for the next ten years."

CHAPTER 18

Portugal and Atlantic Spain

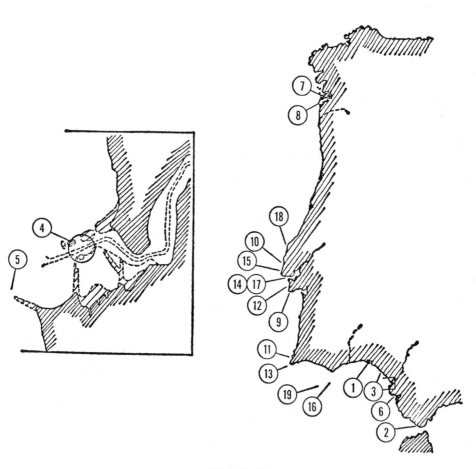

MAP K

Southwest Spain

The great majority of losses from the Spanish and Portuguese armadas were caused by uncharted reefs, or tropical hurricanes, or enemy attacks off distant shores. Yet galleons and frigates sometimes survived all the perils of long and bitter voyages, only to come to grief right at their front doors. The seas off Cádiz, Sanlúcar and Lisbon hold the bones of many homeward-bound ships, and the treasure cargoes which some of them carried.

DE LUBERZA'S GALLEON (1)

On February 16, 1544, a 300-ton galleon, cruising eastward across the Gulf of Cádiz after a rough voyage over from Havana, was caught in a gale which swept up from the south. Captain Juanes de Luberza ordered sails reefed while the helmsman tried to hold the prow two points up into the wind, but the heavily laden, clumsy ship failed to respond. As whitecaps churned the rising sea the ponderous galleon was pressed northward toward the barren Huelva coast. By midafternoon breakers came into view. Anchors were dropped but dragged without biting. The ship lurched more suddenly as it wallowed into peaking ground swells. Then it struck.

Masts splintered and went by the board, dragging down nets of tar-soaked rigging. Cannons broke loose, steam-rolling among scrambling, stumbling crewmen until they smashed through sides and leaped overboard. The keel thumped heavily on the ocean bottom, raised and slammed down by waves, rupturing and opening. The sea rushed in. Throughout the night waves pounded the dead hull. By morning there was nothing visible except a fallen forest of masts and spars and broken beams, tangled in cables, washed up against the Point Umbría beach. Scattered among the wood were cracked barrels and cases of cargo, and still bodies.

It was several weeks before the wild ocean calmed enough to permit attempts at salvage. Then small boats flocked to the scene and grapples swung below, reaching down to the wreckage of the hull. Hardy divers, holding their breaths, groped through a jumble of loose timbers undulating with the waves, tangled in ropes and seaweed. Here and there a triumphant shout signaled that a box of cargo or a cannon had been made fast and hauled up. Casks of silver and gold appeared, but very few. Then the storms returned. When the waves subsided in the spring, divers could find only a pounded mass of ribs and ballast, over which a new undersea sand hill was already forming.

Other than the contemporary comment that "many chests of gold and silver were lost" there is no record of this ship's cargo, loaded at Veracruz. There should be something like $150,000 in Mexican cobs and silver ingots buried with her ballast under sand, twenty feet deep, one hundred yards off the Point Umbría beach. During calm summer weather this would be a promising site for air lifting.

The TARIFA ARMADA (2)

A scandal that shook the sacred Bureau of Trade to its foundations followed the wrecking of General Cosme Rodriguez Farfán's Tierra Firme armada. These ships reached Spain in January 1555, but were driven by storms southeast of their destination and onto the beach of Zahara between Tarifa and Vever. Salvage work started almost immediately. When it terminated nearly a year later, 350,000 pesos in silver and gold had been recovered—three times the value of treasure officially registered aboard. Investigations followed, many petty officials and a few important ones were made scapegoats and fired or transferred . . . and then, after a suitable display of official surprise and indignation, things returned to normal and contraband shipments resumed as before.

There are undoubtedly some ingots and cobs still lying in the sand at Zahara beach and under the waves rolling in on it, but these are only for lucky finders.

The *SAN ANTONIO* (3)

In 1566 the 120-ton *nao San Antonio*, commanded by Captain Juan Arze, was wrecked twenty miles north of her destination, against the barren stretch of coast called Arenas Gordas. Most of her cargo was salvaged during the following months with the result that only a few thousand dollars' worth of precious metal lie in her buried wreckage.

The SANLÚCAR BAR WRECKS (4)*

The functionaries of the Bureau of Trade, solidly entrenched in Seville, insisted that the armadas' ships load and unload at their port up the Guadalquivir River under the Tower of Gold. At times their tight monopoly was loosened by merchant groups from other cities like Cádiz, but through much of the sixteenth century, against common sense, ships were required to make the long trip upriver before departing for the Indies and on their return. Off the mouth of the Guadalquivir they had to pass over the Sanlúcar Bar—treacherous rock and sand shoals that shifted and built up and washed away with every storm. Some years the channel here was 30 feet deep. During others it varied from 16 to 18 feet, winding like a letter S, so difficult to navigate that even the experienced Andalusian pilots lost ships that they were taking through.

When a galleon or *nao* grounded in calm weather there was seldom much danger, and she could be refloated at the next high tide. But if a southwest wind sprang up, the Sanlúcar Bar could turn into a death trap and any vessel caught there would be pounded to pieces by breakers rushing in from the Atlantic.

One of the first of many ships lost on the bar was *San Antón*, a 200-ton *nao* commanded by Benito Perez Carraso. Returning from Santo Domingo in 1566, this ship stranded and sank with a cargo which included gold.

In 1587 the 300-ton *Santa Maria Madalena*, a *nao* of the Tierra Firme armada, was wrecked here. The people and Captain Francisco Romero were taken off but all the cargo, including about $300,000 in gold and silver, went to the bottom. By the time calm weather permitted salvage operations to be undertaken most of the ship's remains were swallowed by sand and little could be recovered.

Two years later *Nuestra Señora de la Concepción*, a 120-ton *nao* from Puerto Rico under Antonio Hernandez, was broken to pieces here in a storm.

In 1612 three ships were reported "lost on Sanlúcar." Between them they must have carried several hundred thousand pesos in silver and gold.

A large treasure in Mexican silver joined the accumulations in 1642 when the New Spain *Capitana** carrying about 1,500,000 pesos was wrecked. The 600-ton vessel stranded half a mile from shore in a rising wind. The 9-foot tide ebbed, but a strong west gale drove the Atlantic up the Guadalquivir River and the returning tide came in with roaring breakers which capsized the *Capitana* and smashed her to kindling. During the ebb tide the crew members, passengers and some of the cargo were taken off but the treasurer's accounting which stated that "part of the silver" was saved indicated that some could not be salvaged. Probably $500,000 in treasure from this ship alone came to rest in the Sanlúcar sands.

In all there must be several million dollars in gold and silver, lost in the wreckage of at least a dozen returning ships, buried off the points of two sand ridges: one reaches due north for 2000 yards from Punta del Montigos on the south bank; the other extends 4000 yards southwest from Punta del Cabo on the north. A 1000-yard channel which separates their extremities would make a very attractive treasure-hunting ground.

LA CARIDAD (5)

This 350-ton *nao*, commanded by Francisco Monte, sank in 1616 off Chipiona, just south of Sanlúcar with a full cargo from Honduras. There was about $50,000 in silver aboard, none of which was recorded salvaged.

CAPITANILLA DE CARTAGENA and
URCA DE PAREDES (6)

The returning Tierra Firme armada of 1656 was rounding Cape St. Vincent when a group of sails came into view, causing General Juan de Hoyos and his officers to confer nervously. Those looked like English frigates—much faster than the sluggish galleons of the armada, whose hulls were covered with barnacles and trailed seaweed whiskers. All sails were loosed in an effort to reach the safety of Cádiz before the enemy caught up.

General de Hoyos' ships were still many miles from port when the English squadron drew alongside. The ensuing battle was lopsided. The English raiders were fighting ships, armed with larger caliber, longer ranged cannons served by experienced gunners. Except for the *Capitana*, with 30 guns, and the *Capitanilla*, with 24, the Spanish ships were merchantmen. In spite of this disparity the courageous Spanish crews fought back for six hours while they ran for shelter.

The first casualty was the *urca* of Juan de la Torre. Her mainmast was shot away and she fell behind. Enemy ships quickly closed and their crews boarded her. Not much later General de Hoyos was mortally wounded and half of his men cut down by accurate broadsides. The survivors surrendered. The remaining ships scattered, hotly pursued by the encouraged English. Two *urcas* managed to reach Cádiz safely while another two limped to shelter under the guns of Spanish-held Gibraltar. The *Capitanilla de Cartagena* and the *urca* of José de Paredes did not quite make it. With hulls shot to pieces and decks ablaze, they sank at the mouth of Cádiz Bay, off Rota. Corpses and charred wreckage drifted gently ashore onto its wide beach.

When they returned to England with their two prizes the English gleefully announced that they had found "two million pesos in gold, silver, and merchandise aboard. This was probably no exaggeration, since the armada carried a big gold shipment from Cartagena. The *Capitanilla* —probably the *Almiranta* of the armada—and Paredes' *urca* probably carried a similar cargo. Their partly buried hulls lie today in water no deeper than 150 feet somewhere off the American naval base of Rota. The *Capitanilla*, of about 500 tons, carried 24 bronze cannon. The *urca* mounted either 26 or 30, iron and bronze, of a smaller caliber. Between them they should hold nearly $1,5000,000, mostly in gold.

Northwest Spain

The VIGO GALLEONS (7)

What books, articles, and prospectuses have enthusiastically called "the richest of all sunken treasures" is supposed to lie in the mud-covered hulks of seventeen Spanish galleons scuttled in Vigo Bay during a naval battle in 1702. The gold and silver, precious stones, and pearls in their 5000-ton cargo have been valued at anywhere from $20,000,000 to $200,000,000.

Unfortunately this is not true. There are not seventeen galleons in the bay—but only bits and pieces of six.[1] And all six have been stripped, dynamited and searched over and over by the seventy-three salvage expeditions which have sent divers down into their shallow hulls. Very nearly everything of value which they contained was removed within a hundred years after their sinking. With the exception of one which fishermen call the *Tambour*, all of the Vigo Bay hulks have been completely dismantled and brought to the surface. Nothing remains except a few ballast-covered keels buried under 1 to 4 yards of fallen silt.

Lost in the mud floor of the bay are probably scattered chests of silver, loose ingots and other valuables which were blown overboard from exploding galleons before they sank, but to find these would require large-scale dredging of 100,000 square yards of the bay's southeast corner to a depth of several yards, with no assurance that the returns would cover costs. Until such a time as a selective long-ranged metal detector, capable of identifying precious metal from the litter of iron fragments there, is available, the Vigo galleons are interesting only for the archaeological objects which some of them contain. The *Tambour* and other wreck sites still hold cannons, cannon balls, pottery, and other artifacts of the late seventeenth century.

The history of the Vigo galleons is of more interest, and for a fuller account, I refer you to my book *The Treasure Divers of Vigo Bay*. But here are some highlights. Carrying the Mexican, and some of the South American and Far East treasure output of three years, General Manuel de Velasco's 1699 New Spain armada finally sailed for Cádiz in 1702. An Anglo-Dutch attack on that port caused the armada to be diverted to Vigo, where the seventeen ships anchored at the innermost reach of Vigo Bay, in San Simón lagoon. Defenses were formed to protect them in case the enemy should learn where they had hidden.

---

[1] The *Capitana* and *Almiranta* (the registry treasure had been landed ashore from both), *Nuestra Señora de las Angustias*, *Nuestra Señora de los Dolores*, *Santo Domingo*, and *Santa Margarita*.

A sharp-eared English naval chaplain overheard a conversation in which the armada's location was mentioned. Scarcely two weeks later an English and Dutch fleet of 150 ships—one of the strongest naval forces ever assembled until modern times—smashed through the Spanish and French defenses and swarmed down on the helpless galleons. Velasco's order to scuttle and burn them came too late. Eleven were seized afloat or grounded in shallow water, and the six that did sink were so shallow that skin divers could reach their charred decks. When the English and Dutch finished their plundering several weeks later they had amassed a treasure in precious metal and merchandise with a current value of nearly $50,000,000. They burned the stripped hulls of the unseaworthy galleons which they had captured and sailed for their home ports with six of the Spanish ships that were in navigable condition.

Before the attack $12,000,000 in silver pieces of eight, being the royal fifth, was put ashore. After the Anglo-Dutch force left a steady succession of salvage expeditions tackled the sunken hulls. Many raised treasure; all ripped up parts of the galleons' structures. By the time the last of these groups—the "Vigo frogman" of the Atlantic Salvage Company—arrived in 1955, there was nothing left of the ships except scattered wooden remnants and ballast stones. The treasure of the Vigo Galleons had long since vanished.

The *SANTO CRISTO DE MARACAIBO* (8)***

The Anglo-Dutch fleet left Vigo in two groups. The second, under Admiral Sir Cloudesley Shovell, sailed for England on October 26, 1702, taking three galleons manned by prize crews. Two of these, the *El Toro* and *Santísima Cruz*, arrived safely. The fate of the third is described by the reliable English naval historian Burchette:

> [Admiral Shovell] got under sail again, with design to go through the North Channel [leaving Vigo Bay], but the wind taking him short, he was obliged to stand through that which lies to the South, where the galleon, which was the *Monmouth*'s prize, struck upon a sunken rock, and immediately floundered, notwithstanding several of the frigates were on each side of her, but all the men, except two, were saved.

The *Santo Cristo de Maracaibo*, captured intact by H.M.S. *Monmouth* during the raging fury of the battle, was lost in the south channel into Vigo Bay after striking a sunken pinnacle unmarked on the English charts. The *Monmouth*'s master records the occurrence in his log with terseness typical of that time:

> . . . forenoon then a fresh gale at NE and ENE about that time our galoun being a starne struck upon a sunken rock and emedietly they fired guns for helpe they being in Distris . . .

Captain John Baker of H.M.S. *Monmouth*, accounting for the loss of his prize after he returned to England to face a court-martial (during which he was acquitted), tells something of what happened after the *Santo Cristo de Maracaibo* struck:

> Coming out of Vigo Harbour on the 26th October 1702 the Galleon struck upon a Rock and Bulged herself so that the water came up to her lower Deck and then the things following were taken out—
> 1 & 2. Two bags supposed to be Dollars weight 126 pounds Haverdupoiz taken out of the chest of Cocao in the Main Hatchway.
> 3. A bag supposed to be lumps of Silver weighing 81 lbs. taken out of a Chest of Cloaths.
> 4. A Bag supposed to be Dollars weight 64 pounds taken out of another Chest of Cloaths.
> Taken out of the Oxford's Boats commanded by Lieut. Miles and Lieut. Harper they having taken them out of the Galleon—
> 16 small parcells of Silk of severall sorts
> 4 Childrens Gownes
> 2 Mens waistcoats
> A card of Fanns
> A Bayle of Indigo
> Taken between the Decks by Wm. Fox Masters, Mate of the *Monmouth*—
> 4 Peices of Silk

Nothing more was salvaged from the "bulged" galleon before she slid under the waves, leading to the following contemporary comment:

> Their gain was much diminished by the loss which they made of the biggest of the galleons, for in going out the port of Vigo, the English pilots not being sufficiently acquainted with the coast, let it touch upon a rock belonging to the Isle of Bayona, where it broke up and sank. Outside the inner harbor in the channel going out of the Bay lies the richest of the galleons, the *Monmouth*'s prize.

These quotations are selected from scores of pages of data and opinions acquired by the Atlantic Salvage Company's researchers in England, France, Spain, and Austria during a four-year quest for the *Monmouth*'s galleon. While historical studies went on, the American and European SCUBA diver-shareholders of that company methodically examined the ocean floor of the south channel, searching 20,000 square yards during an average day when weather permitted, slowly eliminating submarine rectangles from the immense area of three square miles in which the galleon's remains must lie. The story of the first three years of this sea hunt, during which they made over three thousand dives, is told in *The Treasure Divers of Vigo Bay*. The SCUBA search was climaxed late in 1957 when a wooden pulley, identical to those found on 1700 ships, was raised from 200 feet deep. It soon crumbled to dust in the air.

By this time the depth of the search area had dropped to over 200 feet, making it impractical to continue the diving pattern. Fortunately the Atlantic Salvage Company had acquired the Dr. Furster magnetometer (described in Chapter 2). Using this "magic wand" first from a rowboat, then with a trawling rig developed after months of trial and error, the Vigo frogmen extended the area "where the galleon isn't" seaward. In July 1958, the classic treasure hunters' luck caught up with them. A local naval commander suddenly halted their work. There had been an outburst of smuggling in the Vigo region and the naval official suspected that the treasure hunt for a galleon "which everybody knows doesn't exist" was a cover for contraband activities. An investigation of the divers' activities finally exonerated them—but by that time the diving season had ended and another year had been wasted.

The magnetometer search was resumed with the first good weather in 1959. Throughout the summer the instrument's probe was trawled in parallel lines, 50 feet apart, and the swept area moved seaward. Twice the indicator needle went through its characteristic back and forth dance, and twice Robert Sténuit—the ace diver—followed the cable down through pitch-black water and looked on wreckage of fishing ships illuminated in the beam of his flashlight.

Then, in October, the needle danced again. The place was more than a mile southwest of the submarine pinnacle against which the galleon had struck—and 276 feet deep! Since the sea bed there was flat mud, the treasure hunters chartered a second boat and dragged a 400-yard-long steel cable between the two boats in a time-tried sweep. Again and again it caught but broke free. Seven small grapples were attached, three yards apart to the center of the cable. This time the sweep caught and held.

Very few SCUBA divers would have cared to undertake the job ahead —diving to near-record depth far out in an ocean where the last glow of surface light vanished halfway down. As he put on his mask, Sténuit said grimly, "This is much more than I have ever gone before. I will try to reach the bottom, but if I feel that the raptures are overcoming me I will stop." With twin double Aqua Lungs on his back, a safety rubber band holding his mouthpiece against his teeth, and flashlight in hand, the Belgian went under. He carried with him a 10-pound stone to speed his descent.

At 150 feet below he entered darkness, broken only by the yellow cone shining from his flashlight down the grapple cable. Time lost meaning as the needle on his depth gauge inched past 200 . . . 220 . . . 250 . . . Sténuit felt no raptures—he had never experienced them, even below 200 feet—but there was a strange chill in his head, as though a piece of icy lead filled the cavity behind his eyes. Then he was on the bottom, staring at the cable which lay on the mud, leading to the grapples —and treasure! Conditioned by hundreds of deep dives, he concentrated intently on his actions. Drop the stone . . . follow the cable, hand over hand . . . breathe deeply and slowly. The cold feeling in his head grew stronger . . .

The ocean around him was suffused with pale green light. He was swimming along the cable. Robert glanced at his depth gauge. It read 160 feet! He was rising to the surface! What had he done on the bottom? He could not remember. Instinct, developed through long experience, had saved his life.

Despite this experience, Robert Sténuit was determined to visit the wreck to identify it. But bad weather had set in. One more opportunity came late in November when the seas calmed moderately, and again the plucky veteran went down the grapple cable. This time he remained fully in control of his thoughts and actions while making a one-minute search on the sea floor—but during his descent the grapples had been torn free by the pressure of waves and wind on the overhead boats. Winter storms made further diving impossible.

The five-year search for the *Santo Cristo de Maracaibo* ended in 1960. Despite financing provided through a contract with Dan Stack's Treasure Hunters, Inc., funds ran out and the "Treasure Divers of Vigo Bay" disbanded. Robert Sténuit joined Ed Link and played a leading role in the "Man-in-Sea" project, then went on to salvage the *Girona*. Owen Lee became Captain Cousteau's American lecturer, and published *The Skin Diver's Bible*. Howard Williams, John Nathan, Mike Gaynor, Florent Ramaugé, and other Vigo alumni have all kept their flippers wet in various parts of the world.

Meanwhile the *Monmouth*'s galleon awaits the arrival of an expedition equipped with the more sophisticated search and salvage tools that will be needed to recover her valuable artifacts and treasure.

The Portuguese Coast

TWO *NAOS* OF DE CARVAJAL (9)
In 1556 a three-ship flota commanded by General Gonzalo de Carvajal was caught in a storm off the Portuguese coast. Two of the ships were driven ashore and wrecked: one at Guarrapatera, the other on the rocks of nearby Buarcos. Salvage operations were moderately successful ending with the recovery of most of the cargo. These wrecks are not particularly interesting to the treasure hunter, but a vacationing skin diver might come across sixteenth-century coins diving there.

The *SAN JUAN* (10)
This 250-ton *nao* of Captain Francisco Martín was wrecked on Los Cachopos fifteen miles from Lisbon while returning from Veracruz in 1564. She was a ship of that year's New Spain armada and carried silver, much of which was salvaged.

NUESTRA SEÑORA DE LA CONCEPCIÓN (11)

After a hard crossing from Santo Domingo in 1566, Francisco de Morales' 200-ton *Nuestra Señora de la Concepción* floundered off Lagos, only a hundred miles from home port. As far as is known all the cargo went down with her, about two miles off the south Portuguese coast. There was only a little treasure aboard.

The ROSARIO (12)

Early in 1589 the 400-ton galleon *Rosario* was smashed to pieces against the western shore of Cape Espichel in a tempest. Of her crew and passengers, 242 were drowned, and a treasure shipment from the Indies with a value of $500,000 was dashed into the sea. Little of this could be recovered in halfhearted salvage work which began several months later. There should be a very worth-while prize there for anyone who can find the wreckage.

The GALLEON (13)

A galleon of 300 tons was recorded as having sunk off Cape St. Vincent in 1601. She lies deep, and the nature and value of her cargo are unknown.

TWO SHIPS OF PARDA (14)*

During the period 1580–1640, with Portugal incorporated into the Spanish Empire, returning armadas frequently made landfall at Lisbon. Sometimes they replenished supplies here and sailed on down to Seville. At other times, when the Barbary pirate menace was great, cargo was unloaded in this port and sent to Seville overland or transshipped in strongly armed warships. Off the mouth of the Tagus River, which flows past Lisbon to the sea, alluvial soil and sand has formed a bar which shifts with every storm. Just as the Sanlúcar Bar imposed a steady toll on passing maritime traffic, so did that of the Tagus, straddling the passageway into Lisbon. In 1606 this toll was high.

The New Spain armada of that year had suffered a rough crossing, and General Sanchez Parda Osorio's decision to put in at Lisbon for supplies was welcomed. The ships approached the Tagus estuary at the outbreak of a storm. Two of the galleons were hurled up onto the bar. Before any rescue could be undertaken a barrier of white surf, spreading for hundreds of yards, had sealed them off from aid. They were soon battered to pieces. In the following days the familiar aftermath of shipwrecks appeared. Lage Point beaches were littered with wreckage, floating cargo and the bodies of six hundred people who had been killed.

The cannons and heavy cargo of the destroyed vessels remained on the bar with their ballast-covered hull bottoms. About $1,000,000 in precious metal should be there today, hidden under that sand and mud.

A magnetometer could find the wreck sites by detecting iron cannons and anchors. From then on large-scale dredging—and lots of luck with the weather—would be necessary to bring success.

LA ENCARNACIÓN (15)

A few hundred yards from the Sintra shore, north of Lisbon, lie the remains of Captain Pedro Reblo's 90-ton *patache Encarnación* which sank after striking a submerged rock pinnacle in 1611. A part of the merchandise and silver which she carried was reported as having been salvaged. Some is left, but only a small value of treasure.

The ISABELA (16)

Somewhere south of Cape Santa Maria is the hull of the 600-ton *Isabela,* perhaps five miles from shore at a depth of 400 feet. This galleon, part of the Duke de Veragua's armada of 1672, capsized and floundered there en route to Seville during a tempest. Her captain, Juan de Ugarte, and all four hundred aboard were drowned.

There is something like $750,000 in Colombian and Peruvian gold lying in her waterlogged beams and ribs. But this will have to wait for many years until improved detecting and deep salvage equipment will make possible her location and identification among dozens of other sunken hulls in the vicinity.

The SANTA TERESA (17)

Another victim of Lisbon's Tagus Bar was the *Santa Teresa.* Early in 1704 this Spanish merchantman, commanded by Diego de Vicuña, was taken by English warships. Coming past the Tagus Bar the galleon was wrecked with the loss of two hundred Spaniards, an English prize crew and cargo from the Indies estimated at $500,000. As in the case of the two galleons of Parda's armada, by the time salvage could be undertaken the ship's remains had already been swallowed in the sand.

The SAN PEDRO ALCÁNTARA (18)*

The story of this ship comes with superlatives. She was one of the richest-laden Spanish treasure carriers ever to cross the Atlantic; her salvage was the most successful with the greatest value of recovered cargo of any until the twentieth century. And, to keep it interesting, there is still treasure where she sank.

The *San Pedro Alcántara* belonged to the crack frigate class developed by the Spanish Navy after 1750 and was equal to or better than any ship of her type then afloat. Her specifications: 1483 tons; 123 feet in length; 23 feet 8 inches in breadth; 26 feet draft. Her armament was 68 cannons on two decks.

After long Pacific service she was ordered to transport to Spain an accumulation of valuable cargo awaiting shipment in Peru and Chile. The *San Pedro* loaded in Callao, then sailed down the coast in September 1784, to Valparaíso and Talcahuano. On her passage to Cape Horn she was becalmed and began to leak. An epidemic broke out aboard. Captain Manuel de Eguia decided not to risk rounding Cape Horn in that condition and returned to Callao for repairs. Rotted planks and ribs at the bow were replaced, then, on March 30, 1785, the *San Pedro* headed south again, laden to the limits of safety with the following cargo:

> 7,601,960 pesos in gold and silver ingots and coins
> 1,510,500 pounds of copper in 7048 slabs
> 945 boxes of cascarilla bark
> 24 cases of pine seeds
> 96 bales of cocoa
> 5 bales of vicuña wool
> 12 bales of culen
> 144 bales of balsam
> 880 bales of dried corn

No sooner had she rounded the Horn than a minor hurricane sprang her repairs and she began leaking again. Captain de Eguia headed for Rio de Janeiro and another overhaul, which took five months. The frigate finally sailed for home on November 4, reaching Ascension in December and the Azores in late January 1786. On the evening of February 2 she passed the Berlengas, ten miles off Portugal. As darkness fell lookouts were told to keep their eyes peeled for signs of the coast.

At 10:30 P.M. one of them called "Land ahead!" but he had seen the surf too late. The *San Pedro* shattered her bilge on a rock several hundred yards from shore and settled to the bottom, the top of her roundhouse barely awash. Crew and passengers scrambled up there and spent the night shivering as sheets of spray swept over them. When local fishing craft came out in the morning 147 men and five women had died.

Salvage operations were put in charge of Captain Francisco Javier Muñoz. Handicapped by continual storms, he built a camp on the deserted Cape Carvoeiro Beach while boats ventured out during breaks in the weather to grapple for the disappeared wreck. On February 16 a hook caught. Divers reported that it had snagged in a cable. The hull was located and divers brought up four chests of silver the same day. By the end of the month 586,000 pesos had been recovered. During April and May another 5,000,000 pesos came up salvaged by forty skin divers who plunged in relays. They had been drawn to the site from all parts of Europe by advertisements offering—in addition to daily wages of 8 reales—a bonus of 16 pesos for every recovered coffer of silver, and

32 for each of gold. With them arrived an assortment of inventors—experts and crackpots. A Genovese and two Maltese lugged over untried "diving machines" while Frenchmen shipped down diving bells. An Englishman offered the use of his "proven apparatus" for 10 per cent of the silver raised with it. Many of these were used.

A diversion was created by a pirate ship which appeared one morning and paralyzed work until three frigates drove it off. A sudden storm swept one of the salvage sloops, the *Vencejo*, onto the rocks causing eight of her ninety-man crew to be drowned. Despite these interruptions the operation went forward rapidly and on June 19, in what must be considered a salvage triumph, the *San Pedro*'s hull was suspended from launches and tide-lifted ashore. All the wood except that covered by heavy metal had been carried away by waves. When remaining cargo was taken out and added to previous salvage, the total came to 6,800,000 pesos in gold and silver and 5540 copper slabs.

Diving continued where the hull had been until the end of October and from March through September of the following year, when it was permanently stopped. Toward the last the divers reported that the remaining treasure was hopelessly lost in pockets of seaweed-covered sand at depths of 25 and 30 feet where they could not remain long enough, holding their breaths, to dig in. Many had been wounded by sharp spikes protruding from waterlogged beams. Of the frigate's heavy cargo 7,320,775 pesos in gold and silver, 6654 slabs of copper, the anchors, many cannon balls and 62 cannons had been salvaged in a 95 per cent efficient operation.

The remainder, 281,185 pesos in gold and silver coins, 394 copper bars weighing over 40 tons and 6 cannons, are there today, buried in sand under dense seaweed 30 feet deep, about one hundred yards off Peniche Bay. SCUBA divers on a summer vacation to this resort area could nearly certainly find some of it.

The *MERCEDES* (19)

On October 5, 1804, two squadrons, each of four frigates, met at sea twenty-seven miles SSW of Cape Santa Maria. One was English, composed of the *Indefatigable* (26 cannon of 24, 16 carronades of 42, and 12 12-inch mortars), and the *Medusa*, *Amphion*, and *Lively*, similarly armed. The other squadron was Spanish, en route to Cádiz with a treasure cargo from Peru. Commodore José Bustamante was in command of its ships *Medea* (40 cannon of 18, 8 and 6), *Fama*, *Mercedes*, and *Clara* (all mounting 34 cannon of 12, 8, and 6). The light armament of the Spaniards was due to the state of peace then existing between Spain and her neighbors, including England.

Bustamante's squadron had left Callao on April 3 and put in at

Montevideo for supplies. Its ships carried gold and silver coins, vicuña wool, hides, cascarilla bark, fruits, and ingots of silver and copper. The commodore was aboard his flagship *Medea* while his wife and children, together with seven other women, traveled as passengers on the *Mercedes*.

Bustamante and his officers were puzzled when the English squadron gave chase, for their countries were not at war. Nevertheless, for precaution, he formed his ships in a line of battle with the *Fama* foremost and the *Clara* at the rear. At 9 A.M. the English came alongside. A boat brought a message from their commodore, Sir Graham Moore, that the Spanish ships were detained "by order of His Britannic Majesty" and would be taken under escort to England. The stunned Spanish officers conferred and came to the unanimous decision to fight "against heavy odds for the honor of our country" rather than accept this humiliation. Bustamante—knowing that his family would be under fire—sent back an indignant refusal. An hour later his wife and children were dead, killed in the explosion of the *Mercedes* which was engaged by the frigate *Amphion*, whose captain's log describes the action:

> At 8:30 the *Indefatigable* made signal to prepare for battle—the ships ahead had then formed a close line of battle.
> 9:00 hove to; took our station astern of the *Indefatigable*, to windward of the Spanish ships. The *Indefatigable* sent a boat aboard the Spanish Commodore.
> 9:30 the boat returned. Observing the ship opposite was preparing to make sail, we bore up and bro^t to under her lee in order to prevent her from making her escape.
> 9:45 the *Indefatigable* fired a shot ahead of the Commodore which he instantly returned and the action then became general.
> 10:00 the ship which we engaged blew up. Made sail and engaged the Spanish Commodore: at 10:30 he struck his colors, as did also the sternmost ship. The *Indefatigable* made the *Lively's* signal to chase the headmost ship then engaged by the *Medusa*.
> At 10:45 sent Lieut. Bennett to take charge of the Spanish frigate *Clara*. Hoisted out all boats and sent them to the wreck of the Spanish ship that blew up, observing many men on the wreck.
> 12:20 the boats returned with 46 men that were saved.

When the three prizes had been taken to England such a diplomatic hullabaloo erupted that Bustamante was paid £30,000 by the British government in partial compensation for his personal fortune in gold which he also lost in the *Mercedes'* sinking. From the captured Spanish ships the English Prize Office removed 4,733,153 gold and silver pesos, 1,307,634 of which belonged to the king. Another $1,000,000 in gold and silver, including a soldiers' fund of 143,070 pesos, was estimated to have gone down with the *Mercedes*.

This will not be recovered by treasure hunters for many years, for the wreck lies about 1000 feet deep in a vaguely defined area. During the fight the engaging ships were carried SSW by the prevailing breeze. The *Mercedes* sank soon after it started, and her position is within a few miles of Lat. 36°26′ N. and Long. 8°10′ W., roughly thirty miles southwest of Cape Santa Maria.

CHAPTER 19

The British Isles

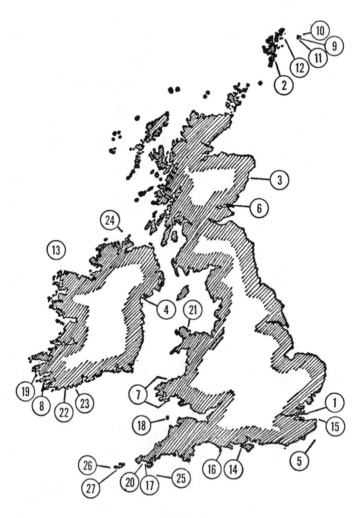

MAP L

DURING THE MIDDLE Ages there was a cry that spread terror such as no other warning could among residents of coastal and river ports of Europe. In England it was "The Danes!" In France, "The Norsemen!" In Russia, "The Varangians!" To all it meant the same thing —"The Vikings are coming!"—and the lean, shield-flanked, serpent-prowed war vessels slid in to shore, discharging hordes of yellow-bearded, horn-helmeted warriors who overwhelmed hastily assembled defenders by the sheer ferocity of their onslaught, plundered and raped . . . then disappeared over the horizon. They left their stamp on history: the tenth and eleventh centuries are still called the Viking Ages.

The *DRAKKAR* (1)
No city was immune to their raids. Even Paris, far up the Seine, was so often attacked that its importance dwindled. In 851 a fleet of Norse ships slid up the Thames and laid waste the countryside on both sides, taking booty from abandoned hamlets. On their withdrawal one of these ships, the *Drakkar* ("Serpent"), sank in the river below London. Her loot lies deeply buried under centuries of deposited silt and will probably never be found.

The *FIFA* and *HIALF* (2)
Two other Viking ships, returning from a plundering expedition to Scottish shores, were wrecked in a storm beneath the cliffs on the south side of Gulberwich Bay in the Shetland Islands. Local tradition describes them as magnificently gilded, and carrying rich ornaments. A skin-diving survey of this area might result in the recovery of some of their treasures wedged between wave-battered rocks under the cliff.

The *SANTA CATALINA* (3)
Mystery surrounds the mission of this galleon, which was wrecked about 1590 in a small bay near Collieston, Aberdeenshire, to which she gave the name St. Catherine's Dub. The man who has been trying for several years to unravel the puzzle—and, in the bargain, recover the Spaniard's treasures—is Walter C. Deas, an intrepid young skin diver from Dundee now in Australia. Since 1956, when he became interested in this wreck, Walt and his SCUBA-diving friends Alan Doyle, Roger Bruce and Geoff Wilson have been combing local history tomes and corresponding with Madrid naval experts for background information

while at every opportunity they drop under the cold and muddy waters of the Dub to search for wreckage. Describing this ship, Walt says:

"The proximity of the date of her loss to that of the Invincible Armada has led to the assumption that she is one of that scattered fleet. It has also been suggested that she was a ship sent by the King of Spain, with treasure and arms to support the rebellion of the Earls of Errol and Huntley which, after a winning start at the Battle of Glenlinet, was crushed by King James VI of Scotland in 1594 when old Slains Castle was destroyed. If this is the case, the wreck may have taken place any time between 1588 and 1594. The support was promised by the Spanish king, but never reached the Earls.

"The following attempts were made to salvage the wreck: (1) In 1840 two cannons were raised by the Collieston coastguards, but have subsequently disappeared. (2) In 1855 a much larger cannon, measuring 7′9″ and with a 4″ bore, was raised by Mr. Rust, Parish Minister of Slain, with the aid of local fishermen. It made its way to Hadds House as property of Lord Aberdeen. (3) In 1876 divers engaged by the Countess of Errol recovered two more cannon and a large anchor which the Countess presented to Queen Victoria. They remained for many years at Balmoral Castle, but were ultimately given to the United Services Museum in London. (4) In 1880 a London firm raised a further large cannon and conveyed it to London. An old rusted cannon said to be from the wreck lies beside the ruins of Slains Castle.

"We have searched eight times and found nothing so far. Have used all types of search methods. The weather has always been very bad and visibility underwater never more than six feet at the clearest. Depths range from 40 to 80 feet. Bottom is sand, fine mud with stones of all sizes."

The DUNDRUM BAY WRECK (4)

An unidentified ship, supposed to be Spanish, is reported to have sunk in 1591 near Ardglass, Ireland, in Dundrum Bay. There might have been treasure aboard.

The TWENTY SPANISH LUGGERS (5)

In 1595, during the Dutch struggle for independence from Spanish rule, King Philip sent north a fleet of twenty coastal freighters laden with supplies for Spanish forces in the Netherlands. While passing through the narrows of the English Channel between Dover and Calais they were attacked by English warships. A bloody battle took place, and the entire fleet was sunk.

The loss was a severe blow to the Spanish in Flanders. Besides badly needed arms and ammunition, these ships carried a shipment of pay money—350,000 escudos, worth today over $1,000,000. None of this is known to have ever been salvaged. Information on the battle's position can be obtained in London.

The FIRTH OF TAY TREASURES (6)

General George Monck, Duke of Albemarle, was sent by Oliver Cromwell in 1650 to subdue the rebelling Scots. As his army swept to one success after another the wealthier people in the country sent their personal fortunes for safekeeping in Dundee, which was their strongest bastion. Then, in 1651, Monck's forces broke through the Dundee defenses and captured the city and all the riches that had accumulated there. "It was the best plunder of any," commented a contemporary historian, "gotten in the wars throughout the three nations." Its estimated value: 2,500,000 Scots pounds.

Monck assembled one hundred vessels in Dundee harbor. Aboard sixty of these were loaded the boxes and barrels and bundles of loot, and the entire fleet set sail for London. They had scarcely got under way when a storm arose and "the ships were cast away within sight of the town, and all that great wealth perished. Not one particle of the immense treasure crossed the bar of the Tay."

The Firth of Tay is about two miles wide inside the bar, and its depth within SCUBA-diving range. Since the disaster many more ships have sunk there, covering the Tay River bed with a jumble of rotting hulks, many buried. Some of General Monck's transports can probably be found, but this would necessitate a long, patient elimination of other wrecks and considerable dredging. Most of the Dundee cargo was perishable. Probably something like half a million dollars of gold, silver, and jeweled ornaments have survived the mud and salt water and could be recovered.

The *SANTA CRUZ* (7)

Lieutenant Harry E. Rieseberg has written of a Spanish galleon of this name which sank off Pembroke, Wales, on January 11, 1679, with treasure. Other reports from England place the ship's location twenty-five miles farther north in Cardigan Bay, and describe her cargo as being 220 chests of gold and 2½ tons of silver worth $2,500,000.

In 1954 the members of the British Sub-Aqua Club undertook a search for the *Santa Cruz* over the sea bed not far from another treasure ship, the *Royal Charter*. They were unable to find the galleon's remains, but have not given up.

The *INFANTA* (8)

Lieutenant Rieseberg has reported this Spanish galleon as having been wrecked in Bantry Bay in 1683 with a cargo of 1100 silver bars worth about $300,000.

The Out Skerries are a cluster of bleak, rocky islets jutting out of a perennially stormy ocean some ten miles east of the main Shetland group. They lie off Holland, on the route taken by the Dutch East Indiamen during periods of warfare when the English Channel was not a safe thoroughfare. During the seventeenth and early eighteenth centuries at least four of these great carracks, outward bound with money for the purchase of spices and silks, were wrecked there.

The CARMELAN (9)**

In December 1664, en route from Texel to Batavia, this 300-ton galleon was hurled by wind and waves against the shore of Mioness, one of the southernmost of the Out Skerry group. Her prow slammed into submerged rocks at the base of a cliff—which is still known—and the force of the impact snapped off her foremast and sent her to the bottom. Within hours her wave-battered hull had been broken to pieces. Of the 263 men aboard, only three managed to reach shore alive.

The *Carmelan* reportedly had aboard one of the largest money shipments ever sent: 3,000,000 Dutch gilders. There were also hundreds of barrels of spirits. The money was dashed onto the rocks below, but not all of the Dutch gin. For weeks afterward there was scarcely a sober man in the Out Skerries.

A tempest in 1900 stirred up the lost treasure, dropping a few coins upon the nearby tidal rocks. Two brothers, walking along the shore a week later, came upon some of these. They were of silver and copper, and bore the date 1662. Other dribbles of the sunken hoard have been picked up now and then after other storms but probably never has a diving search been undertaken for the bulk of it. The reason? Probably because the existence of this wreck is not generally known. The *Carmelan* is one of the most attractive treasure ships in the British Isles. Her location can be practically pinpointed and accumulations of her $2,000,000 cargo of coins should be in plain view to divers, scattered in crevices 30 to 100 feet deep around a large area under the cliff.

The KENNERMERLANDT (10)

Some fifty years after the *Carmelan*'s loss another East Indiaman piled up on the Out Skerries. She was the *Kennermerlandt*, carrying general cargo and 120,000 gilders. Three chests containing thirty-two bags of gold and silver coins were recovered from the wreck by salvaging members of the Bruce family which owned the islands then. The remainder—some $50,000 worth—lies under the sea around the ballast and cannons.

DE LIEFDE (11)

Coins from the *Carmelan* weren't the only money found by those brothers after the storm of 1900. Only a few hundred yards farther down the shore they made a second haul: seven gold ducats, all dated 1711 and bearing the Latin inscription *Harmony Augments Small Enterprises*. These coins were a part of the shipment worth 227,000 gilders lost in October 1711, when *De Liefde* was shattered against the Mioness reefs only a few ship's lengths from the spot where the *Carmelan* broke up. Every person aboard died.

The Bruce family men had by then come to look on the arrival of Dutch money ships as a part of their regular income, and were ready for *De Liefde*. When the seas calmed they systematically went through her wreckage and collected about 200,000 gilders. The latest announced recovery from this treasure was made in 1957 when, in an unusual twist, deep sea diver Walter Pottinger found a single gold coin washed up on rocks while walking along the coast of Housay. Probably not more than $10,000 of *De Liefde*'s gold remains under the sea now, but a determined attempt started recently to recover this. The De Liefde Expedition team made a contract with the Dutch government under which their recoveries which are released by the local Receiver of Wrecks are shared. Using air lifts and inflatable lifting bags to move boulders covering the crevices in the kelp-covered rock bottom, the SCUBA divers have salvaged a reported 170 knife handles, spoons, pins, and buttons, many cannon balls and bar shot in good condition, and a small number of silver coins. The fourteen-man group is working under the usual extremely difficult conditions for this kind of salvage, and yet is making every effort to conduct its work in a planned archaeological manner to avoid destroying artifacts.

The "SILVER SHIP" (12)

An unidentified Dutch ship safely passed the dangerous Out Skerries early in the eighteenth century only to break up against the Shetland Islands themselves, on a reef near Heilinabretta, Fetlar. During the years immediately following her loss great quantities of silver coins were washed up on the Heilinabretta shores and a cannon was raised from the ship's wreckage and placed at the head of the dock at Urie. Money is still occasionally thrown up here during storms. It would be hard to find a more intriguing location for a skin-diving search. A fortune might still be there.

H.M.S. *TEMPLE* (13)

In 1762 a strong British naval force captured Havana and ransacked the city for a booty of about $2,000,000 in money and church and household treasure. A part of this was being transported back to England the following year aboard the warship *Temple*, which had participated in the action, when she was wrecked off the Irish coast. Her Captain

Collingwood and the crew got to safety but the ship and all her cargo
went to the bottom. Some of the guns and treasure were recovered afterward. Something like $25,000 in precious metal probably remains in the
wreckage (see Chapter 16).

FIVE BRITISH FRIGATES

In the July 1958 issue of *The Wide World* magazine Lieutenant
Rieseberg lists five treasure-carrying English frigates as having gone
down in British waters between 1799 and 1809. These are: the
GUERNSEY LILY (14), sunk off the entrance of Solent, Yarmouth
Roads, on December 11, 1799; the *HINDOSTAN* (15), lost in 1803
on Margate Spite, off Culvers, Kent; the *EARL OF ABERGAVENNY*
(16), which floundered two miles off Portland Bill, Dorset, on February 16, 1805; the *SUSAN AND REBECCA* (17), sunk in Gunwallow
Cove, Cornwall, in 1807; and the *JENNY* (18), carrying gold and ivory
when she met her end on the rocks of Lundy Island in 1809. More
information about these ships, their cargoes and the circumstances of
their losses can be obtained by an examination of records of the courts-
martial of their surviving captains and officers.

A PORTUGUESE GALLEON (19)

An unidentified Portuguese ship carrying "treasure" has been said to
have been sunk in Bollinskelligs Bay, County Kerry, in 1806. Nothing
concrete has yet turned up to support this.

H.M.S. *ANSON* (20)

An English skin diver reported four years ago that he had found the
remains of this British frigate off the Cornwall coast. He had counted
about twenty cannons, he said, in the wreckage. The evidence which he
brought up, a bronze bar weighing 30 pounds, was sufficient impetus
to cause nearby Porth Leven fishermen to talk about organizing an expedition for salvaging the gold bullion which many people believed
aboard when she sank.

The *Anson* was wrecked in Mounts Bay on December 29, 1807. In
official documents there is no mention of treasure, but she could have
still been carrying booty from two successful actions in which she had
recently been engaged. On August 23 of the previous year she and
another frigate, H.M.S. *Arethusa*, had captured the Spanish frigate *Pomona*, sailing from Veracruz to Havana "with specie and merchandise."
The Spaniard managed to reach shallow water under the protection of a
fort but struck her colors after thirty-five minutes. "The money belonging to the King of Spain had been landed at the castle by the Governor
of Havana and the Spanish admiral had only quitted her ten minutes

before the action commenced. There was, however, a considerable quantity of plate and merchandise still aboard which fell to the captors." About four months later, on New Year's Day, the *Anson* and three other frigates captured Curacao from the Dutch.

The *Anson* took aboard loot from both the *Pomona* and Curacao. Although it is unlikely that she would have carried it for so many months without delivering it to a British warehouse, stranger things happened in those days and perhaps there is gold bullion, after all, in her wreckage.

The *ROYAL CHARTER* (21)

She was an English steamer of 2756 tons returning from Melbourne, Australia, with a cargo of wool and $1,750,000 in gold bars and sovereigns. On the night of October 26, 1859, a terrible storm drove her aground off Anglesey, Wales. The waves that tore her to pieces were so powerful that they drove one of her gold ingots through an iron plate of the ship. Over five hundred aboard drowned or were beaten to death.

As soon as the ocean calmed salvage operations began, and continued until all but some $50,000 of the gold had been recovered. What remains are mostly loose sovereigns which were flung across a quarter-mile stretch of the coast. The ship has disintegrated entirely, and the only possibility of finding some of the remaining gold coins would be through a long and systematic search of rock crevices. Metal detectors might be useful over sand pockets but would turn up more false alarms in shreds of iron than money. This is not a particularly interesting wreck for treasure hunters.

The *CRESCENT CITY* (22)

This English steamship went down in 1869 off Galley Head, County Cork. Lieutenant Rieseberg reports that she carried "200,000 in gold specie, of which $55,000 has been salvaged."

The *LUSITANIA* (23)

On May 7, 1915, the explosion of a German torpedo in this English steamship was "a shot heard around the world." The indiscriminate loss of 1198 lives, including 124 Americans, paved the way for the United States' entry into World War I. Wartime secrecy cloaked the nature of the *Lusitania*'s cargo. It has been frequently rumored that a shipment of gold bullion, worth between $100,000 and $500,000 was aboard.

An echo-sounding run has located and identified her hull through its "silhouette" on the graph paper. The *Lusitania* lies at a depth of 310 feet about eleven miles off the old Head of Kinsale, southern Ireland. A salvage expedition was contemplated in 1936 but did not get beyond the planning stage. Unless confirmation can be obtained that this famous ship did carry an important quantity of gold, as rumored, she will not be disturbed for many years.

The S.S. *LAURENTIC* (24)

In January 1917, the 15,000-ton White Star liner *Laurentic* struck a mine off Lough Swilly, North Ireland, and sank onto a bottom 130 feet deep. In her second-class baggage room was the most valuable treasure ever lost to the sea[1]: 3211 ingots of gold worth $25,000,000. The account of its salvage—the most successful of all time—lasting from 1917 through 1924 is told in detail in Sir Robert Davis' *Deep Diving*. For sheer immensity of effort there has been nothing like it in the annals of treasure diving. When the search for the last stubborn ingots, which had vanished deep into silt under the outer bilge, was finally called off, 3186 of them had been brought up and only 25, worth $200,000, remained. The salvage score: better than 99 per cent successful!

The *Laurentic* no longer exists as a ship. Dynamite and the wild ocean in that exposed region have flattened her warped decks as though a giant sledge hammer had pounded the hull from the side. It is sunk deep into the mud of the sea bed. Unless the whole jumble is cut up and raised the unsalvaged gold will remain beneath it forever.

The *FLYING ENTERPRISE* (25)

The account of Captain Henrik Kurt Carlsen's heroic refusal to abandon his ship during the fifteen days that the Isbrandtsen 11,000-ton C1-B passenger-freighter wallowed with an incredible list off Ireland was headline news at the end of 1951. When the *Flying Enterprise* capsized and sank there was—unknown to the skipper—an important amount of British and American currency and stock certificates in her mailbags, being shipped secretly by Swiss interests to America.

Two years later the SORIMA's deep sea divers spent a month in the Atlantic off Falmouth working in the ship's hull 240 feet below. Quaglia's competent Italians raised about $100,000 in paper money. The exact quantity and nature of the remaining currency and certificates are known only to a handful of businessmen, but there might still be a fortune in waterlogged, but not necessarily ruined, paper in the *Flying Enterprise*'s number three hold.

H.M.S. *ASSOCIATION* (26)

When Admiral Sir Cloudesley Shovell's crew finished the looting of a French ship after the siege of Toulon in 1707, the lading of his flagship *Association* was richer by a considerable treasure in gold and silver money, plate, jewelry—and two handsome brass cannons. One of

---

[1] Unless that aboard the *Admiral Nakhimoff* can be confirmed.

these was destined to contribute to the discovery of treasure 265 years later. Its name, Le Duc de Beaufort, is inscribed on elaborate scrolls over crossed anchors forward of the breach. It was for the duke, who commanded King Louis XIV's navy, that the 16-pounder was cast in Le Havre about 1652. An elegant crown and coat of arms circled by fleurs-de-lis decorate the upper first reinforce of the 6½-foot barrel in low relief. Just ahead stand two exquisitely sculptured dolphins. As metal its 3 tons would bring about $1500. As a collector's treasure, Le Duc was sold at auction at Sotheby's in July 1969 for nearly $7000.

In July 1967, when this gun was turned over to the Receiver of Wrecks at St. Mary's in the Scilly Isles, an authority at the Tower of London called it "a find of international importance." It was important to the diving team who had carried out its difficult and dangerous salvage. It was also important encouragement to others who were searching for treasure rumored to lie in the long-lost wreckage of H.M.S. *Association.*

Admiral Shovell's 96-gun ship of the line sailed home from Gibraltar with his squadron in October 1707. Bad weather dogged the fleet all the way, preventing accurate navigation. At noon on the twenty-second, Shovell called a meeting of his ships' masters, who were also the navigation officers. From dead reckoning estimates they fixed their position as off Ushant, and the admiral gave orders to proceed on a northeasterly course to make the Channel. The position estimate was wrong. The error cost 1500 lives.

In the darkness that night, with a gale blowing, lookouts shouted warnings of breakers ahead. Signal guns were fired. The ships broke formation in frantic attempts to escape the deadly reefs of the Scilly Isles. Sixteen vessels succeeded, but the *Association,* the 70-gun *Eagle,* the 50-gun *Romney,* and a fire ship, *Firebrand,* were driven onto the rocks, where they broke up. There were only twenty-three survivors, all from the fire ship. Admiral Shovell's body was found near the Gilstone Ledges at the southeast tip of St. Mary's in a bay called Port Hellick.

The records of a salvage attempt by the Herbert Expedition in 1710 report the *Association*'s wreckage to have been found on a ledge four fathoms deep. Seven bronze cannons and a few iron ones were recovered before heavy seas caused the work to be called off. Shovell's flagship was forgotten. Then, over two and a half centuries later, it was brought into prominence by divers of the British Naval Air Command Sub Aqua Club.

Every summer since 1960 this experienced and active diving group, known as the N.A.C.S.A.C., goes on expeditions. The site selected in 1964 was St. Mary's. Rough seas, strong currents, and a 50° water temperature here tend to put divers into good shape. During routine work a cannon was spotted about 50 feet deep, and someone recalled the loss of the *Association* in the area. The group returned the next year but did little diving due to exceptionally rough weather. One of the members, Expedition Officer Lieutenant Terry Montgomery, had become interested. Together with the club's diving officer, Dick Larn, he dug into records at the National Maritime Museum, the Public Records Office, and the Guildhall Library. They learned that the *Association*, 1459 tons, was built at Portsmouth in 1696 and had measurements of 165 feet length, 45 feet width, and 18 feet draft. While studying a faded 1792 chart Montgomery spotted a notation that made him wonder. It read "The Shovel" and indicated the Outer Gilstone Rocks.

Intrigued by this clue, the N.A.C.S.A.C. scheduled training work there, and arrived on July 1, 1967. Their diving boat was the auxiliary minesweeper *Puttenham*, carrying outboard-powered dinghies called "geminis" for ferrying divers into the dangerous shoals. Wet suits and Aqua Lungs were used. In the group were six officers and eleven ratings who were qualified divers, and support crews. Lieutenant Commander Jack Gayton was in command. The medical officer was Squadron Leader David Denison. I am indebted to "Chippy" Pearce, equipment specialist and highly qualified diver, for this account of their work.

On July 4 Gayton and "Bomber" Brown found and marked six large iron cannons in a gully. As other divers followed, twenty more cannons were spotted on the jagged, irregular rocky floor 45 to 90 feet deep. Most of them lay within an area of roughly 150 by 50 yards. A bar anchor measuring 19½ feet long and 12 feet across the flukes lay just northeast of the site, 90 feet deep. At the opposite end was a smaller anchor. While examining one of the cannons Dick Voisey spotted a yellow glint. He picked up a gold coin, later identified as a Portuguese 4000 reis and dated 1704—just three years before the *Association*'s loss.

The following day Le Duc de Beaufort was found. On the bottom of the gully 55 feet deep, this gun had a cleaner look than the others. Knife cuts into the barrel exposed bright yellow metal. The decision was made to raise it. As the *Puttenham* could not safely approach the area, plans were made to float the gun, then tow it to the diving boat. Eight oil drums, filled with water, were taken down and fastened to the barrel with strops prepared by Jack Ivals. As compressed air from the tanks displaced the water, the drums rose over the gun, but did not provide enough lift. The *Puttenham* was ransacked for every canvas bag aboard. One by one they were tied to the barrel and inflated. The Rube Goldberg cluster of drums and bags lifted Le Duc gently from the bottom. As three geminis towed the floating contraption toward the *Puttenham* a rope fouled in a propeller. Before it could be cleared the bags had spilled their air and the prize settled onto a ledge 30 feet deep. Only 25 yards away the bottom dropped off to thirty fathoms. Strong winds and seas halted further work that day. A helicopter arrived July 10 bringing aircraft lifting bags and a cargo net. The following is extracted from Chippy Pearce's diving log:

> July 10, '67. Gilstone Ledge. Started again to recover cannon. I was put in charge of lifting operations . . . 1610: Bob Hale and Dzus Hollomby first down fixing the lifting pendant and strops, then 7 oil drums filling them with air from sets we lowered to them . . . 1730: Roy Graham and Keith Warner second divers, down to continue fixing and inflating lifting bags . . . 1735: I joined them as we were having trouble with the ropes . . . 1800: One of the bags fixed by ropes parted and shot to the surface and the cannon dropped into a gully 9 feet deeper causing a little confusion on the surface. [author's note: The "confusion" was the swamping of a dinghy when first the lifting bag came up underneath it and then the cannon, attached to the dinghy, pulled it under water!] Bob and I deflated the bag, then Keith and I took it down, fixing it to the wire with a shackle, then inflating the bag once more. We had to free the cannon from the gully this time and then she came up to the surface. Towed the cannon away from the rocks, then R.N.X. *Puttenham* passed her towing rope, then her lifting wire, and having gotten the cannon in position on the stern I dived with Brian Lewis to remove all the drums, etc. . . . 1900: Operation completed.

Photos of the bronze gun made the wire services, along with exaggerated tales of treasure trove. In fact, one more coin, a 1696 five-shilling piece, was recovered two days later. Four brass pulleys and several cannon balls, all marked with the broad arrow, left no doubt that the wreckage was English. Musket balls, lead pistol shot, two sounding leads, and two small brass cannons were also recovered. One was a 3-foot-4-inch breechloader decorated with three fleurs-de-lis. Two more bronze cannons were located under four heavy iron guns which had become encrusted to rock, but were not raised. On July 14 the diving boat returned to her base in Penzance. Total diving time logged was over 120 hours.

The N.A.C.S.A.C. was not the only group interested in the *Association*. In August 1966 Mr. Roland Morris, a former diver, had obtained salvage rights on the four 1707 wrecks from the Ministry of Defence. The terms require that all recoveries be turned over to the Receiver of Wrecks, who supervises their sale. Mr. Morris and his divers, Douglas Rowe and Geoffrey Upton, receive 50 per cent of the proceeds. Another group, the *Regency* team, was also taking part. The N.A.C.S.A.C., unable to obtain these terms, was promised a "donation" if they salvaged anything of value from a Royal Navy ship.

They returned on August 21 aboard the minesweeper *Shipham* and logged over eighty-eight diving hours in five days. The large bow anchor was moved to St. Mary's Roads. A lead inkwell was salvaged, with two pieces of bugles and a suspiciously human-looking bone. The salvage that made headlines, however, was quite different. While probing under rocks and cannons Hollomby found a gold wedding ring inscribed "God above increase our love." Then nine gold coins were retrieved —five English dated 1669 to 1701 and four Portuguese from 1687 to 1706. Another forty-four silver cobs and fifty-two round coins were also collected from the rocky bottom.

The N.A.C.S.A.C. had aroused so much interest that it was permitted a third expedition that year, arriving on September 9 aboard the mine-sweeper *Odiham*. Again they found treasure. One hundred more silver coins and four of gold, all dated prior to 1707, were delivered to the Receiver of Wrecks, with a brass candlestick holder and a silver spoon. On its handle was a family crest which, despite corrosion, re-sembled that of Flag Captain Loader of H.M.S. *Association*.

The Morris group had meanwhile been working for about a month, during which they brought up three bronze cannons, including those under the iron guns. To free them they used plastic charges. Ensuing complaints about the damage caused by these explosions resulted in the prohibition of further use of explosives. Mr. Morris had more than cannons to show, however. On September 21, just five days after the N.A.C.S.A.C. pulled out, his divers recovered about 1500 gold and silver coins. While he displayed them to the press, one of the divers announced that, only a few hundred yards from the N.A.C.S.A.C. diving area, he had found "a carpet of silver and gold right across the seabed—thousands and thousands of them; guineas, crowns, and pieces of eight!" The treasure hoard was said to be in a cave. To reach it the divers had to force their way through a narrow crevice. The location? "Well," said Mr. Morris in an *Illustrated London News* quotation, "we haven't exactly signposted it!" He estimated that the complete recovery would take several years.

In 1968 four N.A.C.S.A.C. members returned during leave. When they completed their dives, they turned over to the Receiver of Wrecks two more gold Portuguese coins, forty silver pieces of eight, and a wedding ring inscribed "Not the value but my love." Newspaper ac-counts of recent work have been more colorful. One begins with: "A skeleton with five silver coins clutched in its hand may be the clue . . ."

To what? Probably a modest fortune. The salvage so far reported represents far less than a ship of the *Association*'s stature would nor-mally have carried. As far as is known her silver plate and probably the paymaster's funds have yet to be located—to say nothing of the loot from the French prize. Although records make no mention of bullion aboard, an admiral's ship of the line often carried consignments of money for banks in that period. There should be many coins in the nearby wrecks of the warships *Romney* and *Eagle* as well. Silver coins and Spanish cobs of the 1700 period can be very valuable, and the gold coins could easily bring $100 each on today's numismatic market. While statements of "millions of dollars' worth" are wishful thinking, Shovell's ships could yield as much as $200,000.

The *HOLLANDIA* (27)

The wire services in late 1971 carried the news item that the wreck of the Dutch East Indiaman *Hollandia* had been found off the Scilly Isles, southwest of England. The discoverer, London lawyer Rex Cowan, was reported to have said that this was "one of the richest treasure ship wrecks yet found around the British isles." She sank in 1743 carrying a reported treasure in gold and silver bullion worth millions.

The news item stated that the find climaxed a three-year search by Mr. Cowan and his team of four skin divers, who had found "a considerable number of highly valuable coins."

For descriptions of other wrecks off the British Isles, see Chapter 17.

CHAPTER 20

Western Continental Europe

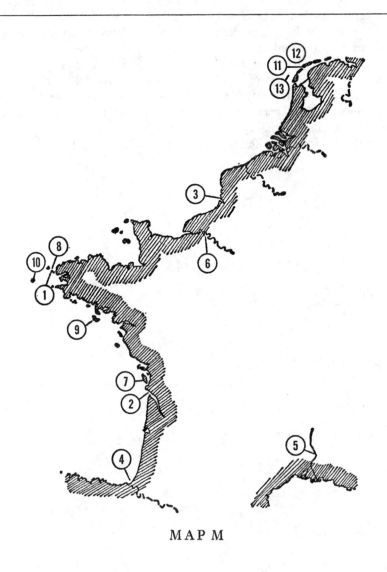

MAP M

The French Coast

The CÁDIZ (1)

Some years ago a hard hat English diver named Pearce discovered the remains of this galleon, of which little is known, at a depth of one hundred feet between the islands of Ushant and Molens. From the wreckage he retrieved a knife, set with diamonds and other jewels, which was appraised at about $40,000.[1]

The ALMIRANTA (2)

In 1593 the *Almiranta* of Pedro de Zubiaurre's armada, carrying several chests of money, sank off the mouth of the Gironde River. No recorded salvage was carried out over the wreck, now buried.

The ST. QUENTIN "GALLEON" (3)

A French *radiésthétiste*—or diviner—is convinced that about twenty feet below a vineyard near the beach at St. Quentin en Tourmont is a Spanish galleon "loaded with gold." Recent test drillings made there were reported to have struck pieces of deeply buried wood that could be the hull of this ship.

The 1627 DISASTER (4)

General Fadrique de Toledo's armada of 1626, returning from the Indies, sailed to La Coruña in northwest Spain instead of Cádiz to evade an enemy ambush. After passing the winter there at anchor, with their cargo untouched, two of these ships set off in January 1627, for Cádiz, convoyed by five war galleons of the Portugal coast guard armada under General Manuel de Meneses. Their voyage abruptly changed direction. Scarcely had the seven *naos* and galleons put out into the Bay of Biscay than a violent gale swept in from the west. The Spaniards were driven four hundred miles eastward across the top of Spain to the border of France. Here, with wind screaming through rigging and shredded sails, they were thrown against the beach at St. Jean de Luz. The warship *San Cristóbal* was the first to go—dashed to pieces with three survivors. The *Almiranta* was next, followed by the treasure *naos San Juan* and *San José*, another galleon and finally de Meneses' *Capitana*. Only one warship, the *Santiago*, weathered the storm. More

---

[1] From *Deep Diving*, by Robert Davis.

than two thousand men lost their lives and for weeks afterward, along the beach, "one sees quantities of rare and exquisite merchandise."

The contemporary comment that "much treasure was lost" indicates that salvage efforts over the broken hulls did not recover all the cargo from de Toledo's two *naos*. By now the planking and ribs of all six of these wrecks have been broken up into little pieces by waves and devoured by borers. Their ballast mounds and keels should still be fairly intact, under several feet of sand and about 15 feet of water, some 100 yards off the beach. Scattered around the remnants of the *San Juan* and *San José* could be as much as $750,000 in precious metal. These wrecks are not attractive as salvage prospects owing to the dispersal of their cargoes.

The FRENCH PRIVATEER (5)

Somewhere up the Rhone River, sunk deep under the silt bottom, are the remains of a French privateer which was reported to have carried captured treasure.

The *QUINTANADOINE* (ex-*TÉLÉMAQUE*) (6)*

On New Year's Night 1790, while nobles and clergymen were running from France with the flames of revolution licking at their heels, two little ships put out into the Seine River from Rouen, an important city downstream from Paris near the English Channel. One was a schooner; the other a brick, the former *Télémaque*, recently rebuilt and named the *Quintanadoine*. Scarcely had these ships vanished into the winter night when revolutionary authorities sent out urgent orders for their seizure. Rumors had already spread that they carried aboard a rich cargo: millions in royal jewels and specie belonging to King Louis XVI, his queen and his nobles, and the silver treasure of the Abbeys of Jumiège and St. George, near Rouen. Stevedores had reported loading aboard under the cover of darkness several large wooden cases, hurriedly banded with iron hoops, containing heavy metal.

The schooner was captured a few miles downstream and yielded boxes of silverware belonging to the Royal Family. The *Quintanadoine*, however, evaded pursuit and seemed well on her way to safety when on January 3 she suddenly grounded while attempting to cross the treacherous sand bars four hundred feet off the quai of Quilleboeuf, a fishing village near the mouth of the Seine. Battered by waves and a fierce current, she sank and was sucked into the shifting sands.

A naval engineer and three hundred men were sent from Cherbourg to salvage her. They worked for three months, then gave up, reporting that the wreck was covered over. Private salvage companies appeared on the site during the following years. One after the other they quit in failure. In 1837 one M. Magny obtained a salvage concession from the Administrative Council of the Navy, awarding him 80 per cent of his recoveries. He spent 65,000 francs before giving up the attempt. Four years later Mr. David, a former associate of Magny, was able to move the wreck a few yards downstream. His method was the same as that used by his predecessors: he cradled the hull with chains which were drawn up tight around 600-ton lighters anchored overhead at low tide. The incoming tide of the Atlantic, which reached far up the river, raised the lighters and—it was hoped—the sunken hull as well. Unfortunately the weight on the chains was unevenly distributed and they parted one after the other as the strain increased.

In June 1842, three Englishmen by the names of Taylor, Deane, and Edwards formed a company and distributed a prospectus evaluating the wreck's treasure at 80,000,000 francs. This figure was only an unsubstantiated guess, but it drew in 200,000 francs with which they made an ingenious attempt. They proposed to raise the ship like an elevator. Enormous wood piles were solidly anchored. Then a horizontal wood and iron platform was constructed on top of the ship, fitting in place between the surrounding piles. The platform was attached firmly to the hull underneath, and chains from its corners were run up around lighters used as pontoons. With rising tide, the lighters and platform— and the ship beneath—came up a few feet. At high water the platform was secured to the piles so that it would not fall back with the ebb. The process was repeated, with another few feet gained, at the next rise in tide, and so on throughout several weeks. As winter approached the wreck hung suspended well above the sand bottom. Then came December, with storms and the fear of ice flows, and the *Quintanadoine* was returned to her resting place on the river bed. Money ran out. Mr. Taylor went to London, declaring that he would resume the salvage attempt the following March with new Siebe diving suits from England.

He continued, working through the next summer. Then, on September 30, 1843, the notary of Quilleboeuf who had formed the company published this notice in local newspapers: "The shareholders of the salvage enterprise of the *Télémaque* are informed that salvage work has completely stopped. The salvaged material . . . consists of 52 pieces of the ship's wood. A quantity of hogsheads were loaded aboard but only traces of these were found showing that they had contained tallow and oil. Until September 23 the ship was still filled with sand, but after openings were made to allow the current to flow through the hull, the big tides of the end of September cleaned it out. Meticulous searches were then possible with the result that we learned with certainty that opinions stating that the *Télémaque* contained treasures were chimerical."

Editors of an English newspaper jumped on this announcement (and a simultaneous report to shareholders by Deane and Edwards confirming the failure), knocking themselves out with humor. "We have the means of knowing that the result of the salvage has been as follows: A bit of binnacle; half a yard of yardarm; a quarter of the quarter-deck; a shivered timber; a main brace and a pair of leather braces; a part of a cat-head and an old mousetrap."

But starry-eyed treasure hunters have little faith in reports of past failures. In 1902 the French engineer Berliet began planning another foray on the wreck. Not until 1939 could he bring his dream to realization. Then divers under his directions returned to the site and presently brought to the surface, for the first time, real treasure. Thirty massive silver chandeliers, identified as those from the Abbey of Jumiège, a gold chain and pendant of an Episcopal bishop and several gold Louis d'or coins were put ashore, together with tons of tallow. Part of the ship, still wrapped in the chains of the last expedition, was refloated. The hull was reported to be empty. World War II halted any further work.

In November 1957 the Belgian diver-author Robert Sténuit ran into the chief diver of the 1939–40 salvage company who told him that only the bow half of the ship had been raised during their work. From it had come the salvaged cargo and chandeliers. The broken-away stern, he explained, lay a few hundred yards upstream, intact, and never salvaged. Only he could return to its precise location. The other divers who worked with him were killed in the war. If Robert would finance the undertaking . . .

Last year another Belgian, a diving companion of Robert's visited the area and became friendly with the priest of Tancarville across the Seine River from Quilleboeuf. Together they examined the old parish record books in which were registered land transfers of past centuries. Studying the yellow pages, they noted with interest that a number of poor families living along the waterfront had suddenly begun buying farms in 1790 and 1791. They acquired so much property that their descendants today are still the largest landowners in the region. Very probably some unofficial and successful salvage took place immediately after the shipwreck.

If the assurance of Robert's diver acquaintance is to be believed there might well be coffers of royal gold and jewels still awaiting salvage in the *Quintanadoine*'s untouched stern. The scoffed-at tales of silver chandeliers were proven true by Berliet's work, and reports of royal treasure having been loaded aboard came from the same sources.

LE JEUNE HENRI (7)

This French frigate sank off Oléron Island in the winter of 1820. At the time there were rumors that she carried silver bullion.

The *DRUMMOND CASTLE* (8)

During the decades since her sinking in 1897 off Molène Island, tales of fabulous treasure shipment on this English steamer have grown steadily, reaching the figures of "millions of dollars of gold and jewels." The *Drummond Castle* lies not far from the *Egypt* and in only half the depth. Were it substantiated that such a valuable cargo was on the ship it is more than likely that the SORIMA, whose divers worked five years over the *Egypt* and also on the *Elizabethville* down the coast, would have dropped off at the *Drummond Castle* to take the easy pickings (for them) from her comparatively shallow depth. They didn't.

The *ELIZABETHVILLE* (9)

She was a Belgian steamship, en route back home from the Congo in 1917 with a cargo of ivory and a packet containing 13,000 carats of uncut diamonds valued at over $500,000. While passing to the west of Belle Island the *Elizabethville* was torpedoed and sank to a muddy sea floor 200 feet deep. The hope of recovering her diamonds drew repeated queries from interested firms, but it was not until 1928 that the bold Italian deep sea salvor Quaglia (see Chapter 28) actually made the attempt. During that summer his "iron men" and powerful grabs dropped down from the *Artiglio* into the Belgian ship's hold, ripping loose dynamited steel plates, cutting away the upper structure. Then, in a moment of triumph, the ship's safe—reported to contain the diamonds—was brought up, dripping, and deposited on the *Artiglio*'s deck. Swarthy seamen clustered around it while it was opened, then their faces fell in puzzled disappointment. No diamonds.

What had happened to the precious stones? The probable answer is supplied by Mr. Galeazzo Manzi-Fe, the late Quaglia's successor as president of CITOM-SORIMA: "The French company with whom we made the salvage agreement had taken for granted that the parcel of diamonds would have been stored in the purser's safe—which, when salved by us, was found empty. Our later inquiries revealed that on the last voyage the purser had fallen ill and his understudy, not having the safe's key, had apparently stored the parcel in a leather bag in the ship's mail room through which we had blown our way to the safe. The recovery of eight tons of ivory elephant tusks from the wreck compensated us for a small part of the outlay, if not the discomfiture."

The *EGYPT* (10)

For a full account of the remarkable salvage operations conducted on this wreck, see Chapter 28.

The North Sea

LA LUTINE (11)***

In the Underwriting Room at Lloyd's of London, suspended under a dome, is her bell which tolls whenever a ship goes down at sea or an overdue vessel reaches port. And on the board table in the Committee Room which is constructed of wood from her salvaged rudder, a silver plaque reads:

> H.B.M. Ship *La Lutine*
> 32-Gun Frigate
> Commanded by Captain Lancelot Skynner, R.N.
> Sailed from Yarmouth Roads
> On the morning of the 9th of October, 1799 with a large
> amount of specie on board,
> And was wrecked off the Island of Vlieland the same night,
> When all on board were lost except one man.

La Lutine was battered to pieces by storm waves after stranding on a treacherous sand bar off the entrance to Vlie Stroom near Terschelling Island. This captured French frigate had been sent on a mission to deliver two consignments of money. The first, £140,000 in coins, was destined for British troops then garrisoning occupied Texel Island off the Dutch coast. The second, insured for £900,000 by Lloyd's and another £160,000 by German insurance companies, consisted of a thousand gold bars and five hundred bars of silver for merchants in Hamburg. England was then at war with France and Holland, and the friendly German businessmen were in need of financial aid.

In sheer weight *La Lutine's* treasure came to about 5 tons of gold ingots, weighing from 7 to 12 pounds apiece, 14 tons of 61½-pound silver bars, and some 3 tons of gold and silver coins. Total: 22 tons of silver and gold, worth today about $8,500,000 as bullion.

The full account of the ten major salvage attempts made so far to recover this treasure is told in Bob Nesmith's book *Dig for Pirate Treasure*. The first, ending in 1801, brought up 58 gold bars, 35 silver ones, and 42,405 French, Spanish, and English coins. Their total value then was $280,000. The next, made twenty years later, was a failure. In 1860, when the third group gave up, they had raised 41 gold and 61 silver bars, plus some coins. This salvage was liquidated for $225,000. The fourth attempt ended in 1893 with only a scattering of coins recovered. A suction dredge was used in 1894 and again in 1911 with the result that a few more coins, ballast iron, cannon balls, and two 3½-ton anchors were removed from the wreck.

During the 1800s the *Lutine* had been covered and uncovered by shifting sands with each storm. Sometimes there was 40 feet of water over her wreckage; in 1900 the depth was only 5 feet. This same shifting of the bottom broke up her remnants, carrying pieces of ship and treasure scores of yards in all directions from the original burial spot. In 1924 a grab with a depth limit of 36 feet was used, but could not reach the ship at all. The eighth attempt in 1929 employed dredges and a "Radio Metal and Mineral Finding Machine." It ended in failure. Then, in 1934, a permanent steel tower supporting a form of air lock caisson was erected over *La Lutine*'s grave and its dredging apparatus was worked for two years together with other conventional shell dredges. During this time a great deal of ship's timber was raised, but there were few coins and no ingots.

The final attempt so far took place during the summer of 1938 when the 4200-ton tin dredge *Karamata*, en route to Indonesia, was diverted here for three months to burrow down into the sand. Its 400 hp bucket chain could scoop up hundreds of tons of silt per hour from a depth of nearly 100 feet. If ever a salvage instrument was suitable for the job, this was it. The *Karamata*'s giant buckets quickly ate a hole in the sand bank and brought up a substantial part of the wreckage there. Together with three large and one small cannon, a thousand cannon balls, tons of copper, iron, lead, timbers, and artifacts from the ship, it salvaged one more gold bar weighing 7 pounds 10 ounces, 123 silver coins and 10 copper coins. Unfortunately this did not begin to pay for the high cost of the dredge and in September the work was discontinued.

Over 137 years of intermittent salvage endeavors a total of about $600,000 worth of the treasure was raised against a much greater outlay. The bulk of the gold and silver, worth about $8,000,000, is still down there dispersed in an area of some 250,000 cubic yards of sand from 30 to 60 feet beneath the water's surface. The obstacles guarding it are stormy weather, swift currents, a perpetually moving mass of sand which fills up submarine excavations nearly as fast as they can be dredged and—most formidable of all—a past record of just two modest successes. Only a strongly financed venture, able to maintain heavy dredging equipment on the site for years, can hope to recover *La Lutine*'s enormous prize.

The *TUBANTHIA* (12)

For a $6,000,000 German gold shipment to be hidden in Dutch cheeses is unusual enough. Add to this the fact that the Germans sank this—their own gold—and you have an all-time classic snafu. If strong and repeated reports can be believed, this is exactly what happened on the night of March 10, 1916, when a German sub torpedoed the 14,000-ton Dutch liner *Tubanthia*, en route to Buenos Aires. Within two and a half hours after the explosion the Dutch cheeses were on the bottom.

Six years later, in 1922, divers located the *Tubantia* twenty miles off the West Frisian Islands, 160 feet deep. The hull was badly broken, one side settled into the mud. As far as was reported the search then undertaken recovered neither cheeses nor gold. There have been several other attempts since then, all fruitless.

The *RENATE LEONHARDT* (13)

Again the treasure is German gold shipped during the First World War and again the source of information is undocumented but persistent. The *Renate Leonhardt* was a German steamer of 11,126 gross tons which left Hamburg in 1917 with nine other ships for an unknown destination. Off the Dutch coast the convoy was attacked by a British destroyer. During the shelling the *Leonhardt* was so badly damaged that her captain ran her aground in fear that she was sinking. The next morning the hull floated off on a high tide, seemingly seaworthy, so the captain brought her to Rotterdam for repairs. Later he set out again, but repairs gave way and the German ship sank twelve miles off Texel Island in a depth of 65 feet.

She would have probably been forgotten like so many other wartime casualties had it not been for the fact that cocoa butter flotsam was washed up on a Holland beach the afternoon of 1936 when H. Piet Visser was taking a walk there. The Dutch engineer was curious and made inquiries. Presently he was told that the cocoa butter was part of the *Renate Leonhardt*'s cargo which included as well a rumored $2,000,000 shipment of gold and precious stones. From that day on the destinies of the ship and Mr. Visser have been closely entwined.

He spent years tracking down information about the ship and her cargo. His most encouraging lead was supplied by a sailor who had served aboard the *Leonhardt* up to the moment that he deserted in Rotterdam. The German affirmed that his ship carried gold. Mr. Visser hired divers who located the hull, but warned that it was so deeply buried in mud that only the masts emerged. A Dutch bank agreed to finance the salvage. It was just getting started in 1939 when war broke out.

By 1950 Mr. Visser was back at the attack. This time a German insurance company was willing to provide capital. The Dutch engineer, who had been carefully studying the problem of overcoming the mud over the hull, believed he had the solution in a colossal floating air lock caisson, 85 feet tall, which he constructed. When last heard of Mr. Visser was ready to tackle the *Renate Leonhardt*'s treasure.

For descriptions of other wrecks off the Continental coast, see Chapter 17.

CHAPTER 21

The Mediterranean

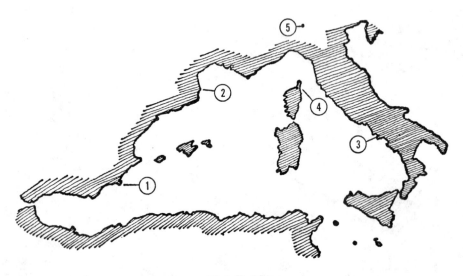

MAP N

CONCENTRATIONS of sunken treasure are found, logically, along waterways where valuable cargoes moved for long periods of time, particularly during the earlier days of sailing ships when the art of seamanship and the science of navigation were in their infancy. Add to such a shipping route the hazards of hidden reefs, regional tempests or hostile naval actions and you have all the conditions for a sea bed paved with gold. Examples: the old and new Bahamas channels.

Although the Mediterranean has been used thousands of years longer than any other western waterway by countless sailing ships which were harried by storms, shoals, and enemy vessels, it lacks the fundamental ingredient to qualify as a treasure hunters' Golconda. Nowhere along its perimeter is a major source of precious metal. And by 1870—when the Suez Canal opened its traverse to Far Eastern gems and African and Australian gold—ships were strong, reefs had been charted, navigation was well developed, and steam and radio communication were at hand.

The *ESPÍRITU SANTO* (1)

In 1563 Captain Gaspar González' 120-ton *nao Espíritu Santo*, returning to Spain from Santo Domingo with a cargo of island products including some pearls and gold, sank in a storm off Cape Palos near Cartagena. The entire crew and lading were lost.

The CAPE DE CREUX GALLEONS (2)

A few years after the destruction of the Invincible Armada, when Spanish-Portuguese naval power was still dominant in the Atlantic, two galleons crept up the Mediterranean on the last lap of a nervous voyage. They had come from Dutch and French Huguenot colonies in Brazil which the Spanish and Portuguese were trying to wipe out. The Dutch ship carried in her cargo a quantity of uncut emeralds; the Frenchman, tons of silver ingots and coins.

A blast of the mistral screamed down onto these ships as they rounded the protection of Cape de Creux, in northeast Spain. Before they reached Porto de la Selva, the violent gale capsized both and sent them to the bottom off Portaló Isle. Debris and bodies were dashed up against its shore. When the wind slacked, boatloads of Catalan fishermen, who had witnessed the disaster, swarmed to the area. The hulls were located with grapples at a depth of about 130 feet. More boats arrived, and bits of loose cargo were caught and raised. Word spread up the coast, and French fishermen appeared. As the C.R.I.S. diver-historian Roberto Díaz reports, "Documents of those times tell of offshore battles between groups of French and Spanish fishermen for control of the waters over the wrecks because some of them, using hooks and other tools, were able on various occasions to pull up sacks containing silver money."

Díaz and his companions have been gathering information about these treasure ships through researches in local archives. They have a pretty good idea where they lie now. The Spanish menfish, who have already made so many noteworthy contributions to submarine archaeology by their numerous discoveries off that coast, plan to try their hand at diving for treasure.

The *ALMIRANTA* (3)**

A bloody revolution against Spanish dominion swept through Naples in 1647, obliging Spain to send an armada there to support her hard-pressed land forces. The *Almiranta* of this squadron, a war galleon of some 450 tons, was assigned a station in Naples Bay where she rode at anchor a thousand yards from shore. Aside from her military function she was used as a floating treasury. Nearly all the Spanish wealth from shore was stored aboard for safekeeping until things quieted down.

On May 12 of that year there were slightly more than 300,000 gold ducats in her strong room. Just after midnight, with no warning whatsoever, the *Almiranta* blew up in a single terrible blast. Flames roared over her hold for a few minutes. Then she sank. Four hundred men died in the explosion. A lengthy, baffled inquiry followed the disaster with a verdict of "Cause unknown." It may have been an accident; some thought that Italian patriots had somehow gotten aboard and set it off. One thing was certain, however: in the broken hull of the *Almiranta*, then too deep to salvage, was nearly the entire wealth of Spanish Naples.

This warship is one of the most interesting sunken treasure sites in the Mediterranean. Her approximate location is known; the depth should not be excessive for today's SCUBA divers; the overhead water is warm and crystal-clear; and the treasure is just a shade over $1,000,000 in non-eroding, shiny gold coins—worth many times more on the numismatic market.

"ROMMEL'S TREASURE" (4)

An interesting accumulation of war booty may lie under the Mediterra-nean off the eastern coast of Corsica. And just as stimulating is the mystery which surrounds it. "Rommel's treasure" is generally accepted as the loot of the Afrika Korps—precious metal, jewels, and art treasures captured in 1941 and 1942 from Bizerte, Tripoli, Bengasi, and Tobruk by the "Desert Fox" on his sweep along the coast. The most reliable account—which nevertheless has many variations—is that on the night of September 18, 1943, these treasures, packed in six big iron cases, were dumped from a German boat in the Gulf of Bastia to keep them from falling into the hands of the Allies. Only one survivor, a Nazi soldier, is supposed to know exactly where they lie. The value of their contents is estimated at $5,000,000.

Many attempts—some secret, other publicized—have been made to find this loot. Italians, Germans, French, and Americans, and combinations of all four, have anchored off the Corsica coast, legally and illegally. They have made diving searches with hard hat gear and Aqua Lungs, they have used metal detectors and magnetometers, they have come with secret and exclusive information and have followed the directions of mystic diviners. But as far as is known no one has yet found these six heavy boxes, partly buried in the sand about 180 feet deep several miles off the Bastia shore.

Somewhere in Europe may be the clues to this hoard of riches, and with even the most general directions to orient it, a magnetometer search across this smooth bottom should make contact with the iron boxes. During the next few years, if it has not already been clandestinely salvaged, "Rommel's treasure" may well be brought to light.

"MUSSOLINI'S TREASURE" (5)

A million-dollar collection of Benito Mussolini's jewels, packed in two suitcases, is reported to lie on the bottom of Lake Como, Italy, not far from shore. This is the admission made in 1957 by Otto Kisnat, formerly captain in the German Army and Mussolini's bodyguard, who told Como police that he had thrown them in during the last chaotic days of 1945 when Italian partisans captured Mussolini there and murdered him. There has been no report of the jewels' recovery.

CHAPTER 22

Southeast Africa and
the Indian Ocean

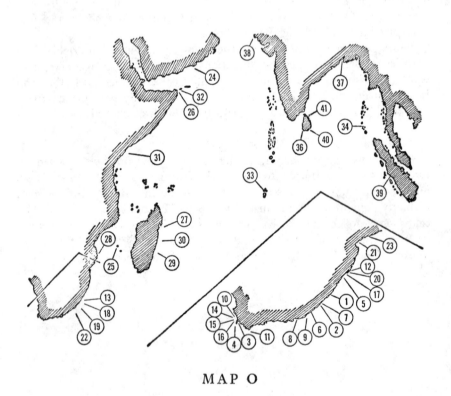

MAP O

O_F ALL THE transocean treasure-shipping waterways, the "Spice Route," joining Europe with India and southeast Asia, was notable for its superlatives. It was the longest voyage—12,000 miles to India and 16,000 miles to the Far East; it was in use for the most years—over three and a half centuries, from 1502 until the opening of the Suez Canal in 1869; it was traversed by vessels of more nations—Portugal, Spain, Holland, England, and France; and it was, by far, the most dangerous, claiming during some periods more than half of the ships that tried to navigate it.

The "Spice Route" extended for 7000 miles down the coast of West Africa, around the storm-racked Cape of Good Hope, 5000 miles across the monsoon-swept Indian Ocean to India, then past the reefs of the Andaman and Nicobar islands through the Straits of Malacca to Indonesia, China, and the Philippines. The outward crossing took eight months if conditions were favorable; the return voyage as long as twenty months for the ships that survived it. It was so hazardous that when a Portuguese carrack arrived safely to Lisbon it was a national event. Periods of years passed during which not a single ship made it back. The broken hulks of at least a hundred Portuguese *naos* and fifty Dutch and English East Indiamen lie strewn along this most hazardous of all shipping lanes.

The risks were great, but the profits even greater. The bulk of the cargoes was perishable and of no interest to treasure hunters: on eastbound vessels were European ironware, glassware, textiles; on return voyages African slaves, Persian rugs and ornaments, cotton, pepper, ginger, cinnamon, and other spices from India and Ceylon, cloves, black and red pepper, camphor, ginger, herbs, and precious woods from the Spice Islands of Sumatra, Java, Borneo, the Celebes, and Moluccas, as well as Chinese silks, brocades, and tapestries. But there was also treasure, often in great quantities, aboard the merchantmen: nearly every ship bound for the Orient carried silver "silk money" to which gold from Mozambique and Persia, picked up during trading, was sometimes added. And many returning ships were floating King Solomon's mines—their lazarettes stacked with coffers of rubies, emeralds, sapphires and star sapphires, jade, amber, and diamonds from the mines at Mogok in Burma and from Cambodia, Malaya, and Siam; rubies and sapphires from India and Ceylon; turquoise, lapis lazuli and other semiprecious gems from the treasure city of Hormuz under Persia; and gold taken aboard at Manila, Malacca, Colombo, Indian ports, Hormuz and Mozambique.

Eastbound, these trading ships could carry from $200,000 to $2,000,000 in silver, and frequently gold; returning, they held anywhere from $500,000 to $5,000,000 in gems and gold.

The "Spice Route" was opened as the result of a storm which blew a flotilla of caravels commanded by Bartholomeu Dias under South Africa into the Indian Ocean in 1488. This passing of the Cape was not entirely accidental. Since the middle 1300s, when they discovered the Canary Islands, Portuguese navigators had been probing down the long West African coastline. Impetus was given to the exploratory program in the 1440s by Prince Henry the Navigator. Caravels constructed under his farsighted directives reached Sierra Leone and brought back ivory and gold from the Gold Coast. After the voyage of Díaz, Vasco da Gama sailed to Mozambique and India in 1502, returning with samples of Middle Eastern treasures. Two years later Pedro Alvares Cabral made an epic voyage, discovering Brazil and Madagascar, then planting the first Portuguese base in India at Cochin. This foothold was expanded during the next fifty years. During frequent battles the "Portuguese Cortés," Alfonso de Albuquerque, and other bold leaders, backed by commercial and missionary interests, established Portuguese suzerainty and bases spread across ten thousand miles from Sofala and Mombassa in West Africa, Hormuz in Persia, Diu, Goa, Calicut, Colombo in India and Ceylon, to Malacca in Malaya, Macao in South China and numerous posts in present-day Indonesia.

This Portuguese empire stood until the early 1600s when the Dutch, cut off from their share of trade with Portugal by that country's absorption into Spain, struck out on their own (see Chapter 23). In a series of sweeping attacks the Dutch East India Company's aggressive forces captured the Moluccas and most of Indonesia in the 1620s, Hormuz in 1623, Cochin in 1635, then Colombo, Malacca and the other Middle and Far East outposts, leaving only Macao, Goa, Mozambique and a few other scattered fragments of the empire in Portuguese hands. In 1651 they established a colony at the Cape of Good Hope from which base their warships practically cut off Portuguese and Spanish commerce with the Far East around South Africa.

As the Dutch replaced the Portuguese, they were in turn pushed out by the English. During the fifty years from 1750 to 1800 Robert Clive and other soldiers in the service of the British East India Company drove them from India. Early in the 1800s Malacca was taken, followed by Cape Town in 1814 and the whole Cape of Good Hope in 1841. Now it was the British East India Company which dominated the "Spice Route" commerce, and British ships that brought back the Middle East treasure while the Dutch maintained their authority in

Indonesia, all that remained to them of the empire which they had wrested from Portugal.

The first Portuguese ships were their caravels, the largest reaching 200 tons. As freight tonnages increased these were replaced by larger *naos* and carracks which could stow 400 tons by 1550, 1000 tons by 1560, and 1300 tons in the 1600s. They were built of Leiria pine in Portugal and of teakwood when constructed in Goa and Cochin. The history of the Portuguese trading ships is the story of shipwrecks and disasters, largely due to the greed of Portuguese viceroys and merchants. Regulations to promote safer voyages, limiting tonnage and cargo of these *Casa de India naos,* were flouted by the very authorities who should have enforced them. As a result the ships were hurriedly and poorly built, criminally overloaded with scarcely any attempt to maintain stability through intelligent stowage of heavy cargo, overcrowded with passengers, insufficiently provisioned and nearly always leaking badly. Carracks were permitted to leave port with such a list through poor stowage that sometimes "the side of the ship served as the keel." They even capsized in port. The *Cirne* set sail with schools of fish splashing in her half-flooded hold. Badly needed water and food, and spare sails, were taken off to make room for a few extra tons of pepper to be crammed in. A classic Dutch comment to the officers of a captured Portuguese *nao,* as they wondered how the ship managed to remain afloat, was: "Tell us, you Portuguese, has there ever been such a barbarous and greedy nation in the world, who would try to round the Cape of Good Hope, buried to the bottom of the sea with cargo, putting your lives in such probable danger and losing them, and only because of your greed? It is not to be marveled that you lose so many ships, and so many lives!"[1]

The South Africa Coast

The *SÃO JOÃO* (1)*

One of the most famous of the Portuguese shipwrecks was that of the 500-ton carrack *São João,* carrying five hundred Portuguese and slaves back to Europe in 1552. This vessel sailed from Cochin, India, on February 3, in the usual badly overloaded condition. On the crossing of the Indian Ocean monsoon waves strained the hull constantly, causing it to leak so badly that attempts to round the Cape of Good Hope were abandoned. At the end of June the *São João,* in desperate condition, grounded against the coast of southeast Africa. The ship's officers and a military hero, Manuel da Sousa, with his wife and children, were put ashore in a boat. Before the others could be taken off, the carrack disappeared under the pounding of waves which reduced

[1] *Shipwreck and Empire,* by James Duffy, Harvard University Press, 1955.

the ship into splinters "no bigger than a man's arm." Fifty Portuguese
and over one hundred slaves were drowned. Those who swam ashore
brought the number of survivors to 320. Gold and jewels with a value
of probably $750,000 settled into the sandy bottom around the ship's
remains.

The Portuguese who had reached safety and their slaves, led by
da Sousa, embarked on a 1200-mile trek north toward the nearest colony
at Mozambique. The former hero soon lost control of himself and went
to pieces as hunger, injuries, and disease decimated the survivors. His
bastard son died and when Kaffir natives swarmed onto the stragglers
he turned over to them the party's weapons in return for a promise to
guide them to safety. The Kaffirs promptly attacked, taking everything else that had been salvaged and even the clothes off the survivors'
backs. Da Sousa's wife, still proud in her starved condition, refused to
let herself be seen naked. In an incident celebrated in Portuguese
literature Dona Leonor buried herself in the sand of the beach to hide
her unclothed body. There she died of hunger while da Sousa wandered
off into the jungle, insane, never to be seen again. Of the 320 who
reached shore alive 8 Portuguese and 16 slaves survived the terrible
march to Mozambique.

The São João was one of the first of a steady succession of Portuguese, Dutch, and English ships to be wrecked against the 500-mile
stretch of southeast African shoreline from Cape St. Lucia to Algoa
Bay—one of the world's richest treasure-hunting areas. Probably $30,000,-
000 in gold and gems lie off these shores, buried in sand at depths
from 20 to 40 feet, around the shattered remnants of wooden vessels.
This is a wild and rough coast, with its contours changing so often,
as waves pile up beaches, then pull them away and jungle vegetation
spreads and dies, that descriptions of wreck sites are nearly valueless
fifty years later. A survey to find sheltered harbors was made by
Manuel Mesquita Perestrelo in 1575–76 after the Portuguese king became
alarmed at the number of ships lost here. Perestrelo described the coast
northward of Point St. Lucia as sandy beaches and dunes, between St.
Lucia and Fishery Point 110 miles to southwest as rocky with cliffs
dropping into the sea, and south from there as again sandy. The reports
in this survey have been used many times since by treasure hunters in
attempts to place wrecks by topographical descriptions of survivors.

This coast was inhabited by Kaffir Negroes, frequently mistreated
by arrogant Portuguese survivors with the result that they became
hostile toward whites who were cast up on their lands. It was these
natives that attacked the São João's survivors. Those that reached
Mozambique safely stated that their ship had struck the coast at 31°
south latitude, placing its remnants in the thirty-five-mile sector from

Umzinto to Port Shepstone, at a depth of about 25 feet, 50 to 100 yards offshore. The *São João* and her treasure have never been salvaged.

The *SÃO BENTO* (2)*
Of the five *naos* in the 1553 fleet sailing from Lisbon, the *São Bento* was the only one to reach India. Her luck deserted her on the voyage back. It was another of five returning ships that became the sole survivor. On the round trip in 1553–54, eight of nine vessels were lost.

The *São Bento*, carrying 480 Portuguese and slaves and about $1,000,000 in gold and gems, set sail from Cochin with four companion carracks on February 1, 1554. She was separated from the others during storms and broke up against the southeast African coast at the latitude 32⅓° several months later. Again many of the people were drowned and most of the remainder died during a brutal trek north, others becoming slaves of the African natives.

The gold, rubies, sapphires, and other treasure aboard the *São Bento* settled in shallow water around the wreckage and lie off the shore near Port St. Johns, most likely buried.

A PORTUGUESE CARRACK (3)
In the middle 1580s a Portuguese carrack, sailing eastward from Lisbon, floundered in False Bay during a storm with the loss of most of her crew and passengers as well as about $250,000 in silver.

The *BOA VIAGEM* (4)
There were two feet of water in the hold of this 800-ton *nao* when she sailed from Cochin in 1588, yet her officers, placing the profits of the voyage above their lives, swore that she was seaworthy. During the crossing of the Indian Ocean the hull settled as more water seeped in until finally the pepper and other cargo was flooded. Cases of spices swelled and burst, their contents clogging the pumps and pressing against the side of the hold. As the *Boa Viagem* rounded the Cape of Good Hope this internal expansion was too much for the straining timbers and the hull broke open. Within minutes the *nao* had sunk beneath an ocean littered for hundreds of yards with floating merchandise.

The remains of the *Boa Viagem* lie in fairly deep water off the tip of the Cape, with gold and jewels worth $1,000,000.

The *SANTO ALBERTO* (5)
The *Santo Alberto* set out from Cochin on January 31, 1593, as usual carrying half again as much cargo as was safe. After a stormy crossing her captain, Nuno Velho Pereira, had to ground the sinking

ship on a beach of Natal. Nearly all aboard reached shore safely and were led by Captain Pereira to Mozambique. The orderly removal of passengers and crew permitted most of the ship's treasure to be salvaged before she broke up, and probably only $100,000 in gold remains in the wreckage off the Natal coast.

The SÃO JOÃO BAPTISTA (6)

Two Dutch ships attacked the São João Baptista, five months out of Goa, in July 1622. For nearly three weeks the running sea battle was fought, the only respites being when storms drove the ships apart. Eventually the Portuguese nao escaped from the pirates but was in such bad condition that her captain, Pedro de Moraes, ran the hulk onto a sandy stretch of beach at 33° on the southeast African coast, not far from the East London of today. The evacuation of the wreck was carried out smoothly, despite rough weather, and most of the passengers and treasure reached shore safely. A camp was established there with a small chapel decorated with gold and silks. After a period of indecision de Moraes set out with the 450 Portuguese and slaves for the north. With them went $500,000 in jewels. Less than 30 reached Mozambique.

The lower hull and ballast of the São João Baptista, with a small amount of treasure that was not salvaged, is buried in sand near the shore.

NOSSA SENHORA DE BELÉM (7)

This 1000-ton nao was grounded about 1630 at 32° latitude, near today's Port St. Johns, on the point of floundering from leaks. Some cargo was taken off by the crew and little treasure remains in the wreckage.

The SACRAMENTO (8)*

On February 20, 1647, the two carracks Nossa Senhora de Atalaya and Sacramento sailed from Goa for Europe. Four months later the Sacramento broke up near Algoa Bay. Only seventy-two of her four hundred people reached shore, taking with them several small packages of jewels which hostile natives soon stole. About $1,000,000 in treasure lies in the ship's wreckage only 30 feet deep in Algoa Bay, but probably buried under sand.

NOSSA SENHORA DE ATALAYA (9)*

Four days after the Sacramento was wrecked her sister ship, long since separated, crashed against the coast between Port Alfred and East London and sank with only a handful of survivors getting off. A great fortune in jewels was lost with her, and several cases of gold. This is spread over her buried and disintegrated wreckage about one hundred yards from shore.

The *HAARLEM* (10)

The Dutch East Indiamen contrasted sharply with the Portuguese carracks. Instead of being clumsy, stubby, and top-heavy they had long keels and low poops and prows. Their cargo loads were limited to about 500 tons, carefully stowed, and safety precautions were carefully enforced. Outward bound from Holland they carried gold and silver money; returning, these carracks brought spices, gold, tin, and precious stones.

The *Haarlem* encountered violent storms as she rounded the Cape in 1647 and on March 25 was driven ashore in Table Bay and smashed to bits there by enormous waves. She was returning from Batavia with several hundred tons of tin, and a reported $500,000 in gold and gems aboard. It is unlikely that any of this was saved.

During the past few years two men have been making preparations to salvage treasure wrecks along the coast of southeast Africa. One is Tromp van Diggelen, a Cape Town businessman who recently obtained salvage rights to certain ships in this sector. The other is his associate, Commander Peter Keeble, R.N., O.B.E., a much-decorated former Royal Navy salvage officer. On their agenda are such ships as the *Grosvenor* and several Dutch East Indiamen including the *Haarlem*. Reports say that Commander Keeble believes he has located this ship's wreckage, buried in a sand bottom 20 feet deep, off Woodstock Beach. He and Mr. van Diggelen have high hopes for success in their projects and there is every reason that these expectations will be borne out. With a few exceptions, the southeast Africa treasure wrecks are virgin fields, never having been the objects of salvage attempts.

A SIAMESE VESSEL (11)

There are reports that a Siamese ship, carrying their ambassador to Spain and a small fortune in gems and silks, sank off Cape Agulhas during a storm in 1687. This vessel lies probably too deep to salvage.

The DUTCH CARRACK (12)

An unidentified Dutchman was wrecked against Cape St. Lucia in 1693, according to several published accounts. The direction of the voyage is not known, but there would have been precious metal aboard regardless of her destination.

The *DAGERAAD* (13)

In his book *1001 Lost, Buried or Sunken Treasures*, Ferris L. Coffman tells of a Dutch galleon *Dageraad* having sunk off Robbin Island, South Africa, in 1694.

The *MERESTYN* (14)

This Dutch carrack, loaded with Indonesian spices, tin and gold, was reported sunk in Table Bay about 1702.

The DUTCH FLEET (15)

Upwards of thirty Dutch carracks and frigates were wrecked and swamped at their anchorages in Table Bay by a sudden storm about 1715. Probably some treasure was lost in the disaster.

The *MIDDLEBERG* (16)

The British East India Company was a privately owned military, administrative, and trading corporation. Queen Elizabeth incorporated it by royal charter dated December 31, 1600. From then until 1858 it enjoyed near-complete control of immense Indian and other Eastern holdings, with only a few short intervals when the government took over its functions. The East India Company maintained large fleets of armed merchantmen to carry its textiles and other exports and bring back Indian merchandise and treasure. The *Middleberg*, reported to have sunk in Table Bay as she rounded the Cape in 1781, was one of these ships. There was money and possibly Indian gems aboard.

The *GROSVENOR* (17)***

This British East Indiaman has gone down in treasure-hunting history as one of the all-time classics, attacked periodically over nearly two hundred years by a succession of salvage syndicates. The *Grosvenor* was a three-masted square-rigged frigate of 729 tons lading, 120 feet long, and mounting 26 guns. She was built in England in 1770 and in October of that year began the first voyage to India. Her final one was in 1782. Early that year, commanded by Captain John Coxon, she set out for England in a convoy under Admiral Edward Hughes. The British ships were attacked off Ceylon by a French fleet. The battle was a draw and the English withdrew to Trincomalee in Ceylon.

The *Grosvenor* did not resume her voyage until June 13, a time of the year dangerously late to take advantage of the monsoon winds. She sailed alone, with the confidence that she could outrun larger enemy warships and outgun Arabian-based pirate vessels which infested the Indian Ocean. On board were about 120 English men and women, 29 lascars, general cargo, and accumulated company and personal consignments of gold and gems that came to one of the richest treasure shipments ever to leave India.

The passage was unusually rough and the mainmast was soon sprung. Late in July, as the African coast drew near, favorable monsoon winds gave way to storms, then a blast from the west. The rudder was damaged as Captain Coxon had his ship tack toward the Cape. Overcast skies had prevented a celestial fix from being taken for a week when, on the evening of August 3, Coxon cheerfully informed his passengers that the *Grosvenor*, by his dead reckoning calculations, was still a hundred leagues from the coast. The frigate had to be lain to under a foresail and mizzen-staysail that night.

Just before dawn of August 4, lookout John Hynes gave a sudden start, then bellowed down to his mate on watch, Thomas Lewis. "Ahoy!" he called. "Land ahead there . . . and breakers!" Lewis dashed to the captain's cabin with the news. Waking Coxon, he panted, "Sir! We're close inshore!"

The ship's master hurried on deck. After a glance at the ghostly gray surf breaking just off the bow he ordered: "Wear ship!" Slowly the *Grosvenor*'s stem swung around. There was a bump, then a jarring crash. Pressed on by fitful winds that now blew from the stern, the frigate slid up onto a reef where her keel began pounding under the rise and fall of 15-foot waves. Masts were chopped away to lighten the ship, but it was too late. With the first glow of dawn ominous cracks were heard from below. The *Grosvenor* was breaking in two.

Boats were launched and just as promptly capsized in the surf. Then lascar swimmers were sent ashore with lines. A group of Kaffirs who had assembled there, surprisingly friendly, helped haul a cable across the 300 yards of foaming water separating the vessel from shore. As preparations were under way to abandon ship the seas themselves did the job. A series of splintering noises came from below, then the crowded bow broke free and was hurled nearly to shore by waves, carrying 142 people to safety. The treasure-laden stern filled quickly and settled on the 30-foot-deep bottom under the weather side of the reef where waves soon broke up the housing and buried the lower hull under sand.

The *Grosvenor*'s crew members and passengers knew that they were on a rocky, rough coast, in Kaffir country, but beyond that had no idea in what part of South Africa they had been shipwrecked. Captain Coxon proved an inept leader, making most of the mistakes during the following weeks that the worst of the Portuguese commanders had made centuries before. His betrayal of a promise to the natives lost their friendship and eventually led to attacks, later reported in a London newspaper, the *Morning Chronicle and London Advertiser:*

> . . . the Ship was driven ashore near the river St. Christopher, on the African coast . . . four of the crew arrived at Moselle Bay and gave an account . . . that the Caffres had come down on the people, carried off the female passengers, and killed several of the men who had attempted to protect them.

This was the fate of one party into which the dissent-ridden marchers had split up after the first weeks. Most of the *Grosvenor*'s people

died or were made slaves; a handful survived and from their accounts
the officers of the East India Company and Lloyd's tried to fix the
position of the wreck. Sir Alexander Dalrymple, famous English hydrog-
rapher, finished a long report in August 1783, which was submitted
to the board of directors of the East India Company. He concluded
that the *Grosvenor* lay seven hundred miles northeast of Cape Town,
just south of Point St. Lucia in latitude 28°30′ S. Despite nationwide
interest in the treasure ship then, the Napoleonic Wars had precedence
and nothing was done to attempt her salvage until 1840.

Over a dozen attempts have been started to recover the *Grosvenor*'s
treasure. The first was in 1840 when the British Admiralty sent a
salvage ship under Captain Bowden to investigate the site. A short search
located the wreck, which was still visible then, partly covered with
sand. Divers tried again and again to enter the remains of the hold
but were checkmated each time by the heavy surf. A few years later
the British Governor of Natal, Sir Theophilus Shepstone, sent a shore
survey party to the site, but nothing else was attempted. Cecil Rhodes
was interested. A local man, William Carter, recovered timbers from
the wreck in the 1870s and joined a company headed by Captain
Sidney Turner which, in 1892, recovered about eight hundred gold
star pagodas—small Indian coins about the size of a shirt button—
picked up from rocks and sand along the shore. Four years later an
expedition under Alexander Lindsay and Baron de Malmaison blew
up sections of the bottom under the reef and recovered several cannons,
cannon balls, wood, and about four hundred star pagodas so eroded
by moving sand that their value was substantially diminished.

The Cape Town dredge *Duiker* was the spearhead of an assault
launched in 1907 by The Grosvenor Treasure Recovery Company of
Johannesburg, directed by Harry S. Lyons. Carrying a large crew and
two experienced divers, Jacobson and Abrams, the ship anchored off
the wreck site on March 14. A week later the *Duiker* very nearly
joined the *Grosvenor* on the bottom when waves drove her on the
rocks. With the aid of a tug she just managed to reach Durban, with
4 feet of water in the hold. She was back in April and the two divers
began their undersea reconnaissance. After five more days the expedition was suddenly terminated. Jacobson's lines had been severed on sharp
rocks and he was dead. Recoveries included several star pagodas, Venetian
gold ducats, silver and copper coins, porcelains, and diverse artifacts.

The Webster Syndicate was the next to try, in 1921, with the
amazing plan of burrowing out to the wreck under the ocean bottom
from shore! Work was directed by the mining engineer C. D. Chapman and Mr. Dickenson. A numerous crew of laborers, a steam engine
and tons of mining equipment were hauled to the wilderness camp
from Empageni and a village called Lusikisiki, twenty-five miles away.

And incredible as it seems, an undersea tunnel was dug, reaching 416 feet out under the raging surf by 1922. Just short of 700 feet, as the excavation crept under the wreck, the roof collapsed. The human moles miraculously escaped. Three years later the project was resumed by a Durban man who tried first to pump out the Webster tunnel, then started another of his own. His funds ran out and an American sportsman, Mr. Pitcairn, took over the project. At 240 feet from shore the second tunnel was halted for lack of further capital.

At the end of World War II a new suggestion was put forward to outmaneuver the obstacle of perpetual heavy surf. This time it was to be a mole reaching out from shore, the end of which would overhang the wreck site. Again lack of funds ended the attempt. Today Commander Peter Keeble is making preparations for a back-to-normal attack with divers. His survey ship *Steenbok* visited the area a few years ago and divers relocated the *Grosvenor*'s wooden wreckage, by good fortune uncovered at that time, and raised timbers, cannons, cannon balls, and anchors by which they identified the frigate. Meanwhile other skin divers have been reported to have recovered four cannons from a wreck in this vicinity—perhaps the same ship.

The *Grosvenor*'s site is by no means secret. A sign reading TO GROSVENOR WRECK stands by a roadside not far away and the shore adjacent to her sea grave is littered with rusty equipment and fallen huts of previous expeditions. Only one barrier stands between her treasure and salvage men—the same that has existed for all these years. That is the powerful, relentless surf, crashing in against those reefs month after month with scarcely a respite. For a salvage attempt on the *Grosvenor* to be successful considerable capital would be needed: enough to maintain a salvage ship on the site for long periods of time with divers descending whenever ocean conditions permitted; or sufficient to sink a cement-filled hulk beyond the wreck as a breakwater, to provide a sheltered lee where work could be carried out.

Is the *Grosvenor*'s treasure worth it? Her cargo is described only by secondhand reports. There was talk of a manifest in the early 1800s, but this seems to have disappeared. Insurance records at Lloyd's were destroyed in the burning of the Royal Exchange in 1838. English newspaper reports of 1782 state that she carried treasure "reckoned upwards of £300,000" ($1,600,000).[2] In addition there are stories of diamonds and rubies worth millions belonging to a passenger, a Mr. Hosea, and to others. A generally accepted breakdown of the *Grosvenor*'s cargo, probably from an account of the late 1780s, includes 720 gold ingots worth $2,100,000, nineteen chests of diamonds, emeralds, rubies, sapphires, and other gems valued at $2,600,000, star pagodas worth

---

[2] A letter from the Governor of Madras to the company referred to 162,378 gold pagodas and diamonds worth 24,334 pagodas—worth in total about $500,000.

$3,400,000, and other gold, silver and copper coins valued at $200,000.
This totals $8,300,000. Somewhere along the line reports of a jewel-
crusted gold "peacock throne of India," by itself worth $10,000,000,
were added. There is no doubt that an immense value of treasure lies
there, 25 feet deep in the shifting sand. It seems likely that this exceeds
$2,000,000 in value, placing the *Grosvenor* well up on the list of attrac-
tive targets for treasure divers.

The *WILHELM DE ZWEITE* (18)

There are reports of a Dutch East Indiaman, carrying tin and
gold, having been wrecked on the Pondoland coast in 1815. She may
have been the *Wilhelm de Zweite*, lost about this time.

The *STAR OF AFRICA* (19)

This English merchantman, bound from India to England with a
cargo of cotton and reported gold and gems, sank off Cape Province
in the late 1870s. She is believed to lie near Simon's Bay.

The *DOROTEA* (20)*

> ". . . .There is something in a treasure that fastens upon a man's mind.
> He will pray and Blaspheme and still persevere, and will curse the day
> he heard of it, and will let his last hour come upon him unawares, still
> believing that he missed it only a foot. He will see it every time he closes
> his eyes. He will never forget it until he is dead. There is no way of
> getting away from a treasure . . . once it fastens itself upon our mind."
> —Joseph Conrad

How many reasonably normal men, plodding their way through
life in a carefree manner, have suddenly found themselves enmeshed
in the spider web of a treasure hunt! One little fling after lost gold
—deceptively innocuous as the first puff on an opium pipe—and they're
up to the neck in the fascinating quicksand of the *hunt*. Men have
spent their fortunes in treasure quests; they have let their lives become
enslaved; they have died in their efforts.

Scarcely fifty years have passed since "Kruger's Gold" went to the
ocean bottom off southeast Africa. Already its hypnotic lure has enslaved one lifespan, cost a fortune, and drawn six men to horrible deaths.

The richest mines in the world are in South Africa, yielding one-
third of the world's gold and over a half of its diamonds. Gold was
discovered in 1884 at Witwatersrand, near Pretoria in the Transvaal
lands of the Dutch-ancestored Boers. By 1889 shafts sunk to nearly
600 feet there reached a reef of ore the equal of which had never
been encountered. Diamonds were found in 1871 at Kimberley, in
the Orange Free State, bringing in hordes of English, among other
prospectors. Friction between the Boers, who owned these newly coveted

territories, and the English, was one of the reasons for the Boer Wars which erupted with the Jameson Raid in 1895. After early defeats the British landed heavy reinforcements and by 1899 began to press back the outnumbered Boers.

In the fall of 1898, as British forces neared the boundaries of Transvaal and the Orange Free State, the great Boer leader Paul Kruger had brought to his home in Pretoria a large part of his people's fortunes for shipment abroad to safety. Many tons of gold and packages of rough diamonds were assembled and sent secretly to the port of Lourenço Marques in southern Mozambique. Here they were stowed aboard three ships, entrusted to patriotic crews, who were to deliver their cargo to foreign banks.

One of these ships was the barkentine *Dorotea*, badly in need of repairs before embarking on a long voyage. She was headed south to Durban for an overhaul but never reached her destination. Off the Zululand coast a storm sprung her masts and carried off the rigging. With the hull half-flooded the crew panicked and abandoned their cargo in two lifeboats. The *Dorotea* was driven shoreward, stern-first, and thrown onto the reefs off Cape St. Lucia. Here she hung, brutally pounded by heavy surf, until at last her hull broke in two. The bow went down on the weather side of the reef; the stern under its protected lee.

News of the *Dorotea*'s fate reached Durban, together with tales of the treasure aboard. One of the men who listened was a young South African named Hall. With scarcely a thought to the consequences, he decided to take that little treasure-hunting fling. With two friends Hall set out on foot to survey the site of the wreck. The many-month trip through jungles, across miasmic swamps and crocodile-inhabited rivers is an epic by itself. When at last the three adventurers reached Cape St. Lucia, though, they decided the trek was worth it. Not 200 yards offshore they saw wreckage over the water. The sea was unusually calm. There were no sharks in sight so Hall, a good swimmer, stripped and swam out to the wreck. When he returned he reported to his companions that the stern was about 20 feet deep, inside the reef. He could not find the deeper bow, beyond.

From that day on Hall's life was one long, futile quest. "Kruger's Gold" had fastened itself upon his mind. His first attempt to salvage the treasure took place the following spring, when accompanied by six friends he retraced the long overland journey with hopes to retrieve the ship's cargo from the shore. He had not counted on the suspicions of English police. Also aware of the *Dorotea*'s gold, they sent detachments who followed the treasure hunters, hounding them to such an extent that at length they abandoned the attempt.

Learning from experience, Hall made the next voyage by sea on a small ship carrying two divers among the crew. Battling rough weather most of the way, they finally reached Cape St. Lucia only to be cut off from shore by a barrier of enormous waves crashing against the coast. After appraising their chances they anchored the ship safely offshore and went in aboard a smaller diving launch, hoping to be able to reach the wreck. Near the reefs the craft was abruptly capsized by a breaker. Six of its occupants were drowned or killed by sharks. Hall and two others reached shore alive.

This experience might have discouraged others, but not Hall. Within months he had organized another expedition. Seven men, two of whom were divers, lugged a boat and equipment overland to the now-familiar coast. The ocean was reasonably calm and the boat was launched. Following several days of search the divers located both halves of the *Dorotea*, but reported that they had filled with sand. The slow, methodical job of excavation by hand was begun and carried on for several weeks. Then the lull ended. After waiting at the shore base for a month, barred from the ocean by white combers lashing the reefs, the members of Hall's fourth attempt gave up.

But the man with the treasure fastened upon his mind would not quit. Within a year he had assembled seven more soldiers of fortune, and again they carried a boat and equipment across those miles of coastal jungle. There was only one diver with them, and he was inexperienced. After looking at the wreckage he became afraid and would not continue. Neither persuasion nor threats could change his mind. Another attempt had ended in failure. This broke Hall's indomitable spirit. Penniless and discouraged, he was forced to give up.

As far as is known, there have been no other efforts to recover "Kruger's Gold" from Cape St. Lucia. There are several versions of what lies there, ranging from 2 to over 5 tons of gold. Any diamonds would have certainly been taken off by the crew. The gold was reported embedded in a thick floor of cement poured over the ship's ballast. If this is true the treasure should be easily recoverable since waves would not have dispersed it. The cement block was probably in the stern half of the brig and now lies buried in sand under the sheltered lee of the reef, about 150 yards from shore at a depth of no more than 20 feet. If the story of "Kruger's Gold" checks out through careful research, this treasure, between $2,500,000 and $6,500,000 in value, should be a natural for SCUBA divers with a strong boat, air lifts, and time to wait out periods of rough weather. The somewhat protected site of the *Dorotea*'s stern does not make rough ocean quite the barrier that it is for the *Grosvenor*.

KRUGER'S LUGGER (21)

Two other ships set sail from Lourenço Marques with the *Dorotea*. The fate of one, its crew and its treasure sounds like a Dashiell

Hammett story ending with the death of seven men after they had stolen the gold entrusted to them and buried it somewhere along the banks of the Crocodile River. The third ship, carrying about $4,000,000 in gold and diamonds, reportedly sank in a storm less than a day after leaving port somewhere in Delagoa Bay. The depth here exceeds 1000 feet and the ship's position is no longer remembered.

The UNIDENTIFIED EAST INDIAMAN (22)
There are reports that a Dutch or English ship sank off Jutten Island in Saldanha Bay. Gold and silver are rumored to be in her cargo.

East Africa and Madagascar

The GARÇA (23)
Two of the four Portuguese *naos* departing from Cochin in January 1559 were leaking so badly that instead of rounding the Cape they put in to Mozambique for repairs. In November of the same year the *Garça* and *Aguia* set out again, their burden increased by several chests of African gold and slaves. Off Cape Correntes, in latitude 25° S., pumps on the *Garça* could no longer keep up with the leaks and the ship floundered, taking down 1000 tons of cargo and one ape. Over the selfish protests of most of his passengers Captain Barreto of the accompanying *Aguia* had rescued the people.

The *Garça* lies deep, probably at over 500 feet, off Vila de João Belo, Mozambique. Most of the gems which she carried must have been taken off, but there should be half a million dollars of gold in her hull.

The CORPO SANTO (24)
This *nao* sank about 1584 off the coast of Arabia in deep water, with treasure aboard.

The SANTIAGO (25)*
The wrecking of the *Santiago* brings forth starkly the inhuman selfishness of the nobles and officers aboard the Portuguese Indiamen. This 800-ton *nao* sailed from Lisbon on April 1, 1585, bound for India. On the voyage down Africa there was a scare when an English sloop drew near but what frightened the people aboard more was a fish—evidently a whale shark—that followed them for several weeks and was interpreted as an evil omen. In July the Cape of Good Hope was rounded without damage and in August the *Santiago* was becalmed off Natal. Short provisions decided Captain de Mendonca against making the Indian Ocean crossing direct and he steered the ship north

toward the Mozambique Channel with the intention of replenishing supplies at Mozambique.

On the night of August 19 the *Santiago* ran aground on the reefs of the treacherous Bassas da India. She slipped off and once again waves pounded her stem on the rocks, and still again. The bottom of her hull was shorn off with the two lower decks. The two upper decks had slid forward and were planted solidly on the reef. There she sat, full of water, her crew and screaming passengers scrambling over the housing.

With the coming of dawn it was seen that the ship was on the south edge of a coral atoll some forty miles in circumference. About ten miles to the north were several high rocks but otherwise the entire reef was submerged. The *Santiago* had broken into three parts, settled on the multihued reef surface 6 to 10 feet deep at high tide. There was only one undamaged lifeboat, soon lowered and occupied by the captain, mate, twenty-one of the crew and two rich passengers. With assurances to the others that they were going to make a reconnaissance trip to the rocks this group left over four hundred stranded on the ship and departed for Africa.

The ensuing chaos on the slowly disintegrating ship resulted in only one damaged boat being repaired—and immediately taken away by nobles and priests with a few of the crew to row them. Over four hundred died when the *Santiago* was finally shattered and could no longer hold her passengers above water. Her wreckage, overgrown with coral, should be easy to find with a magnetometer on the south edge of the Bassas da India atoll halfway between Sofala, Mozambique, and Cape St. Vincent, Madagascar. There was a silver cargo of perhaps $300,000 aboard in addition to considerable gold and jewelry of wealthy passengers. All of this, except a small part taken by those who went in the boats, is there today.

The MADRE DE DEUS (26)

Bound from Lisbon to Goa in 1594, the ornate *Madre de Deus* was wrecked at the tip of Cape Guardafui in Somaliland. She was built of teakwood and carried five hundred people and about $500,000 in precious metal and jewelry, scarcely any of which was saved. Half her crew members and passengers drowned when the *nao* broke up at a depth of about 25 feet, while most of those who swam ashore died in the coastal desert.

The FLOR DA ROSA (27)

This *nao* was wrecked on the shore of Madagascar Island about 1600 with the loss of all her cargo and most of the people aboard.

The *SÃO LOURENÇO* (28)

Nearly all the 678 passengers and crew escaped to safety ashore, taking much of their personal valuables with them, when the 1000-ton *São Lourenço* was beached in a sinking condition near Mozambique after striking a reef in the channel. She had left Lisbon in April 1649, destined for India. There is some silver money in the ship's wreckage, in shallow water near the coast.

LA GLOIRE (29)

In the early 1760s the French frigate *La Gloire* was reported wrecked on the east coast of Madagascar Island with a shipment of gold and silver valued at over $100,000 being lost.

The *WINTERTON* (30)*

She was one of the largest and "best-appointed" of the British East India Company frigates, bound from India to England in 1792 under command of Captain Dundas. After crossing the Indian Ocean the *Winterton* was caught in a storm and dashed against the coast of Madagascar on a rocky shoal six miles off the Bay of San Augustine. There was a quantity of gold and jewels estimated at over $800,000 aboard this ship. None of it was recorded as being saved.

The frigate's wreckage, partly hidden under coral, lies no deeper than 30 feet and the wreck site can be found by a magnetometer survey for her 26 cannons and anchors. The *Winterton's* treasure would make an interesting treasure-hunting target.

The *QUEEN OF THE THAMES* (31)

This British merchantman was reported wrecked about 1867 on a sand bar about fifteen miles east of Cape Struyo—probably on the East Africa coast, but not indicated on general charts. She could have carried a cargo of gold dust and nuggets.

The *GEORGES PHILIPPAR* (32)

In 1932 the French steamship *Georges Philippar* was reported to have sunk in the Arabian Sea near Cape Guardafui, carrying a cargo from the Far East including "treasure" from the Celebes.

The Indian Ocean

The *CONCEIÇÃO* (33)

With over five hundred aboard and about $600,000 in gold and silver, the *nao Conceição* sailed from Lisbon in 1555 bound for Goa. After a long voyage across the Indian Ocean the ship was coming north when she ran aground on the Pedro de Baños (Peros Banhos) reefs about 1100 miles south-southwest of India. Within a short time the *nao* broke up. Her captain, Francisco Nombre, and a group of ranking officers appropriated the longboat, loaded it with provisions, jewels and several chests of the king's money, and informed 350 men and women who had gone ashore on the rocks that they planned to make a survey voyage. Instead they abandoned their passengers and sailed north to India, telling a sad tale of their own hardship when they arrived. Of the marooned people over two hundred died of hunger and exposure while about fifty built boats from the *Conceição's* wreckage and eventually reached safety.

The wreck of this ship has been completely destroyed during the four hundred years since she sank, but anchors, cannons, and iron artifacts should still be on the shallow rocky sea floor where she broke up. There is also a small quantity of silver probably there. The Peros Banhos Reefs, named after a Portuguese navigator who discovered them, are situated in the position 6° S. and 72° E., far from the main shipping lanes.

The PORTUGUESE *NAO* (34)

In 1583 a Portuguese ship, bound from Malacca, Malaya, to Goa, India, was wrecked on a shoal off the Nicobar Islands. Fifty were drowned. Three hundred survivors grouped on shore, and a party set off in the only undamaged boat to seek help. When a ship returned from Malacca a few weeks later none of those left behind could be found; cannibals from the Andaman and Nicobar group had carried them off. Some gold and jewels were lost in the wreckage of this vessel.

The *CABALAVA* (35)*

She was a 1200-ton frigate of the British East India Company, under Captain James Dalrymple, en route to China in 1818 with a cargo of iron, lead, muslin, paper, watches, perfume, and some $400,000 in Spanish silver pesos. On July 7 the *Cabalava* was driven against the sharp points of Cargados Garrados Reef in the Indian Ocean where she broke up and sank about 45 feet deep.

As far as is recorded there has never been an attempt to salvage the silver lost with this ship, in a remote sector of ocean. For skin divers on a cruise through these waters a visit to the *Cabalava's* wreck site would probably result in some exciting shark encounters and perhaps treasure. The site of this vessel might still be identifiable visually; otherwise a magnetometer survey should make contact with her anchors and carronades.

The *MALABAR* (36)
The walled town of Galle, near the mouth of the Gin Ganga River on the southwest coast of Ceylon, was the island's main seaport in the eighteenth century. A storm in 1860 sank the P & O steamer *Malabar*, carrying $450,000 in silver, off the fort. At least half—and more likely nearly all—of this was salvaged soon afterward.

The *THUNDERER* (37)
There have been published reports that a British steamship carrying several hundred thousand dollars' worth of gold and silver sank downstream from Calcutta in the Hooghly River on November 1, 1867. Much of the cargo was probably salvaged.

SUNKEN CONTRABAND GOLD (38)
During the past year Pakistani authorities have disclosed the existence of an amazing new gimmick in smuggling: the transfer of gold and precious stones under the ocean. Because gold is worth nearly three times more in Pakistan than abroad, a flood of this precious metal has been entering the country despite efforts of the customs to check it. Foreign boats drop it at predetermined rendezvous points in the sea, about ten miles off Karachi, and later it is recovered by divers operating out of the city.

By using the smugglers' own methods, Pakistani police have recently been beating the smugglers at their game, however. Frogmen teamed up with the customs have discovered and salvaged some million dollars of gold and diamonds. During a single week in November 1958 three separate hauls netted 197 gold bars, 2399 gold sovereigns, and hundreds of uncut stones worth $400,000. Rarely has treasure diving been so successful!

The GREAT BASSES REEF SILVER WRECK (40)*
The history of this important find may read like the movie review of a detective mystery thriller: It names the cast, describes the scene and enough of the plot to stimulate interest—and stops right there.

The cast is rich with diving celebrities. Arthur C. Clarke, famous author of space travel and undersea adventures and producer (with Stanley Kubrick) of the Cinerama film *2001: A Space Odyssey*, has colorfully described his role in the book *The Treasure of the Great Reef*. Mike Wilson, Clarke's partner in Clarke-Wilson Associates, has filmed many undersea documentaries on the Great Barrier Reef and the waters around Ceylon (*The Reefs of Taprobane*, etc.). Rodney Jonklaas, the third of these diving veterans living in Ceylon, is an ichthyologist whose company, Seadive Ceylon, exports tropical fish to

all parts of the world. Two American boys introduce the story: Bobby
Kriegel (age fourteen) and Mike Smith (age thirteen). Both are strong
and competent divers. The role of scientific detective is played by
Peter Throckmorton, international authority on submarine archaeology
whose excavations off the Turkish coast of a 1300 B.C. Bronze Age
wreck near Gelidonya and a Byzantine period ship off Bodrum[3] are
described in his book *The Lost Ships*. Guest stars include Hans and Lotte
Haas, who dropped in aboard their three-master *Xarifa* and were among
the first to see the treasure. The suspense element is provided by a treasure
ship who identity and history still remain a mystery.

Just off southeast Ceylon two sandstone-and-coral reefs stretch in an
east-west direction roughly parallel to the coast, from three to nine
miles offshore. The one to the east is Little Basses. On the west lies
the Great Basses Ridge. Together they form a death trap for ships
nearly forty miles long. Over the centuries countless vessels, driven by
monsoon winds and waves, have piled up on their sharp points. Among
these wrecks are certainly Portuguese carracks and Dutch and British
East Indiamen. The lighthouse near the eastern end of the sixteen-
mile-long Great Basses Reef began flashing its red warning in 1873.
When weather permits, its four-man crew is supplied by the relief boat
Pharos, based at Kirinda on the Ceylon coast. The boat's crew is adept
at maneuvering close enough to the wave-swept rock base of the lighthouse for supplies to be delivered via a primitive breeches buoy.

During the monsoon season it is unthinkable to dive among the
Great Basses. Even in the "calm" period—a few weeks in March and
April—10-foot waves breaking over the outer rocks and a strong current
test the mettle of veterans. Although the deeper water is clear, foam
and bubbles reduce visibility around the upper reef to nearly zero.
This was discovered by Mike Wilson and Rodney Jonklaas when they
explored the Great Basses in 1958 on a shark expedition. They returned
the following year with Arthur Clarke, who was introduced to the
reef's large population of groupers. It was these groupers, and an
abundance of sharks, which caused Wilson to select the Great Basses
as the location for a movie about two boys under the sea which led to
surprising developments.

In March 1961 Wilson and these two boys—Kriegel and Smith—
arrived at the Great Basses aboard a surfboat towed by the *Pharos*.
The trio made the cliff-hanging ascent to the lighthouse aboard the
breeches buoy, carrying light diving and photographic equipment. Their
temporary home was now in the 100-foot-tall concrete structure. Filming was going well and the boys had become quite friendly with their co-

[3] See *National Geographic Magazine*, May 1960 issue: "Thirty-three Centuries
Under the Sea," and May 1962 issue: "Oldest Known Shipwreck."

stars, three tame groupers named Ali Baba, Aladdin, and Sinbad, when murky water forced a temporary halt. While passing the time snorkeling on March 22, Wilson and the boys chased a school of porpoises for some 1000 feet westward along the protected inner reef. At length they paused over a shallow ledge. Wilson and Kriegel spotted a small cannon there, which Wilson recognized as a 2½-foot brass signal gun. It weighed 30 pounds. Reasoning that it might have been swept over the reef top from the ocean side, he crossed the main rock spine through a deep crevice, followed by the boys. On the other side lay another practically identical gun. As they had no equipment and were an hour's swim from the lighthouse, the three adventurers returned for a hurried lunch.

Early that afternoon they swam back towing a large inner tube. The cannons were fastened to it and the ocean face of the reef was explored. It dropped sharply from its high point of 1 yard under the surface onto a valley 25–35 feet deep and 25–40 feet across. On the far side of this gully was an outer reef, jutting up to within 9 feet of the surface, against which the main force of the waves was shattered. Despite unusually calm conditions, powerful wave surges swept the divers back and forth between the two reefs as they surveyed the little valley. Its bottom was sand and small stones with upcroppings of coral.

A new bronze cannon lying there, nearly 5 feet long, drew immediate attention. The next find was a stack of anchors, overgrown with coral. Another camouflaged pile turned out to be iron cannons. Kriegel was probing in the sand near one when he saw a coin. He pointed it out to Wilson, who let out a bubbly exclamation: "Silver!" Within moments all three divers were sifting the sand. Dozens of other coins were found, some fairly clean and others heavily sulfided. What had seemed to be small chunks of stone and coral turned out to be encrusted clumps of coins. These were put into collecting bags. By the time the group set off they had amassed a sizable collection of silver. After the long swim back to base, Wilson and the boys hauled their loot up onto the barnacle-studded rocks during incoming surges of the sea. The lighthouse keepers were asleep, and they were able to hide the salvage unnoticed.

Early the next morning the trio brought back their inner tube, chisels and crowbars. By noon their collecting bags were full and included several silver clumps chipped loose from rock and coral. The afternoon was spent in the lighthouse, out of sight of the keepers, cleaning coral and sulfide from the coins. The big treasure recovery was made the next day. Four large clumps of silver money, each weighing between 25 and 30 pounds, were lifted from the bottom. Several hundred more loose coins filled the sacks. When the large masses were examined later they were found to be cylindrical in shape with rounded ends, suggesting that they had been packed in bags about 1½ feet long. The coins under the sulfided outer layer were in mint condition.

That was the boys' last visit to their treasure wreck. The water had cleared, and the final days were spent filming the finale of the movie. The silver, stashed away in bags to prevent detection by the lighthouse crew, was loaded with the two signal guns and equipment aboard the *Pharos*. Soon afterward the treasure was displayed in Colombo before the boys' astonished parents and Arthur Clarke, who had been awaiting the group's return.

To dissolve the remaining coral from the coins Clarke and Wilson soaked several dozen of the best in battery acid. Their markings were clearly revealed—and provided the first clues to the wreck's identity. Every one of the coins was identical, and decorated in Persian script. Inquiries revealed them to be rupees, minted at Surat, northwest India, in the Muslim year 1113. After initial confusion owing to differences between the Muslim and Christian calendars, the mint date was established as 1702. At that time these coins were common currency in much of southern Asia. The four large clumps provided further information. Each had contained about a thousand coins when packed, indicating that they were part of a consignment of money. Therefore in 1702, or shortly afterward, the wrecked ship probably loaded this silver in northwest India and sailed south, around the tip of the country, toward an unknown destination to the east. Ceylon was then under Dutch rule, and the money could have been consigned to merchants or East India Company officials at Trincomalee just up the coast. Clarke learned that there was a severe shortage of silver in that city during 1706 which might have been caused by the non-delivery of this shipment. At the same time he found out that in 1703 a Dutch East Indiaman had carried nearly 500,000 silver rupees from Surat to Batavia. The ship could have been headed there. Or, since the English were in control of much of India, the vessel could have been British.

The signal guns were searched for clues, but any identifying marks had been scoured away during centuries of erosion by sand and waves. A faint trace of engraved lines remained on one gun, but neither Mendel Peterson nor experts at London's National Maritime Museum could make an identification from photographs. It was possible that these guns were of oriental manufacture. In appreciation of Peterson's assistance, one large clump of coins was donated to the Smithsonian Institution, where it lies on display. Clarke learned that the individual coins have a market value of about $1 each.

For months afterward, while trying to identify the wreck, Clarke also made efforts to determine its legal status. He encountered so many confusing and contradictory regulations and precedents that it became apparent no clear-cut decision was likely to be obtained. Readers interested in exploring the wilder shores of marine salvage law, as it applies to Ceylon, will find rich pickings in Chapter 8 of Clarke's book *The Treasure of the Great Reef*. The recoveries were declared to the Ceylon customs authorities, who generously allowed the salvors to retain them. Quasi-legal rights to the site were obtained from Ceylon's able and co-operative archaeological commissioner, who in 1963 awarded the group permission to "excavate for antiquities" on the Great Basses.

Wilson, Clarke, and their associate Rodney Jonklaas had no intention of abandoning the wreck. In only a few hours, with practically no equipment, two boys and a man had raised 200 pounds of silver while literally only scratching at the surface of that sand and stone valley. If the wreck had carried the same quantity of rupees as the 1703 ship to Batavia, there were nearly 5 tons of silver still buried there. During 1962 Wilson supervised the building of a 28-foot work boat. Its name, *Ran Muthu,* translated appropriately into "Pearls and Gold." By early 1963 the craft had been fitted with twin diesels which occasionally ran. Other equipment included a Cornelius compressor, SCUBA gear, and two collapsible outboard-powered dinghies. A competent crew was signed on. After some difficulties with the engines the treasure expedition reached Kirinda in spring 1963, where they established base in a storage shed.

Peter Throckmorton, who had flown from Greece to join the group, brought his expertise on underwater wreck excavation techniques. He was a welcome addition to the *Ran Muthu*'s complement when she set off on the fifteen-mile trip to survey the reef. After anchoring on the protected inner side of the Great Basses the divers discovered a new wreck right underneath their boat. The size of the ballast pile and distribution of artifacts indicated a large ship, probably lifted right over the reef by monsoon waves. The site was littered with rusted mortar projectiles, corroded artifacts, and thousands of glass bottles. Some were brandy containers still containing a brownish liquid, but the main cargo was green glass bottles of soda water. Wilson discovered the British broad arrow mark on an artifact. As the wreck, about a hundred years old, did not look interesting, the group headed for the reef.

Wilson located the crevice passage to the other side under a seething mass of foam. Bracing himself against the barnacle-covered rocks, he plunged through. Throckmorton followed. Jonklaas was deep inside the passage, blinded by bubbles, when his SCUBA regulator malfunctioned and water poured into his mouthpiece. Disciplined by years of dangerous work, he turned and swam back under the surf. After a desperately long time he finally reached water where he could surface and breathe. It had been close. Although Jonklaas changed his regulator and returned to the reef, he could not find the passage and the two others made the visit without him.

With an archaeologist's approach, Throckmorton closely examined the wreckage and its distribution. He concluded that the ship was probably sailing northward when she struck the outer reef and bilged herself on one of the higher points. Wind and waves pushed her across the rocks and she settled onto the narrow valley between the reefs with her bow toward the east. Smaller objects from the superstructure, like the two signal guns, were swept onto the main inner ridge. The wooden hull and perishable material disintegrated rapidly under pounding waves. As the decks and hull collapsed, the ballast and more durable artifacts dropped through to the bottom of the valley. Turbulent water churned the ship's remnants into the pebble-and-sand bottom and deep into crevices.

The guns, anchors, and heavy cargo such as silver had probably settled under their respective sites on the ship. They were spread along the valley for 150 feet, indicating this as the vessel's approximate length. There were five main groupings of visible artifacts. At the extreme east, where the bow had been, lay four piled-up anchors and four cannons. The anchors were so thoroughly corroded that the upper three had collapsed the bottom one. Taking measurements was difficult, but Throckmorton estimated the shanks at 13 feet in length and the spread between the splayed flukes at 12 feet. Through the encrustation there were signs of square holes in the upper shanks where wooden stocks had been. The four guns, from what measurements were possible through their corrosion and coral, seemed to be 8-foot carronades. Another three of these lay in the next grouping a few yards west. The third site, near the center of the wreckage, contained at least thirteen more carronades as well as a single 10½-foot iron cannon.

It was the westernmost distribution area that most interested Throckmorton. It measured some 20 by 10 feet, with the big brass cannon imbedded in its center. Here were the artifacts from the ship's stern, including material from the captain's cabin, the treasure lazarette, and the gun room. The whole bottom was a scrambled mass of ballast, decomposed iron and rust, cannon balls and hollow carronade shot, hand grenades still containing powder and wood plugs, grenade fragments, pieces of flintlock pistols and muskets, lead musket balls, shards of rough clay and fine bone pottery, wood fragments and bits of glass, other recognizable and unidentifiable artifacts—and silver in broken pieces, coins, and clumps. Most of this had solidified into a hard mass formed by chemical reactions of pitch and gunpowder combined with sulfides and oxides of copper, silver and iron, calcium and sea water. The concretion was further cemented by coral. Throckmorton chose this site for his excavations.

He tagged the brass gun and prominent objects and drove in a few pitons to establish reference points. Then he chipped into the mass to free selected artifacts such as ballast stones of a reddish slate, hard wood pistol stocks, cannon balls and grenades, pottery fragments, green glass beads and a glass bottle neck, fragments of cloth, bits of wood, a bronze pestle, and other objects whose origin might be traced for clues. The wood chips and fragile artifacts were sealed in plastic sacks for preservation. Aided by Wilson and Jonklaas, he chipped loose entire chunks of concretion from which other objects were extracted when they were broken up later. Holes in these masses where iron nails had once been were measured. Throughout this work each section of the bottom was photographed by Wilson and Jonklaas with the artifacts *in situ* and again while they were being excavated. While the other two divers shared Throckmorton's interest in archaeology, they did not overlook any silver that turned up. Their collection of rupees grew apace with Throckmorton's artifacts.

After Jonklaas' near-fatal experience with the inner reef passage, the *Ran Muthu* was anchored well off the reef's seaward side. The divers were tended by an alert sailor on one of the dinghies. He kept it just outside the line where ocean swells peaked before breaking, giving the divers assurance that someone up there was watching over them—even at a distance of 100 feet. Arthur Clarke was still recuperating from a serious illness, but occasionally snorkeled around the dinghy.

On April 14, an unusually calm day, he was able to swim above the wreck site and watch his friends from 10 yards overhead. Wilson and Jonklaas were cracking the bottom with hammer and chisel while Throckmorton, using a measuring line with a small grapple at one end, was attempting to mark off exact distances between tagged landmarks. All three clung to heavy objects as they worked, but were swept loose when unusually strong waves surged over the valley. At these times Clarke could hear their Aqua Lungs clang against rocks. Toward noon he returned to the *Ran Muthu*. Wilson had made another determined search for silver clumps that day but had recovered only coins and artifacts—some as far as 100 feet from the main wreck site. He and Jonklaas surfaced with their air exhausted and took a dinghy to the lighthouse, where Jonklaas went ashore. Throckmorton, wearing a double Lung, worked on until early afternoon. When he returned to the boat he announced to Clarke, almost casually, "I've found the mother lode. There's at least a ton there." Switching to a fresh tank he headed back to the site.

Presently Wilson returned from the lighthouse. Hearing the news, he flung on an Aqua Lung and raced to the reef. Four 30-pound "bags" of rupees were slung under a Port-A-Lift which Throckmorton had brought. Filled to capacity with air bled from Aqua Lungs, it could barely support the silver load. The two divers maneuvered it alongside the dinghy and shepherded their treasure carefully to the *Ran Muthu*, where several men got it aboard. These clumps of coins were longer and narrower than those raised in 1961, but had originally contained the same number (a thousand) of rupees.

Throckmorton and Wilson returned to the bronze cannon where Throckmorton had been chipping when he found the silver. The gun was still solidly imbedded. Underneath its barrel were many more coins. By late afternoon part of the gun had been freed. Chipping continued the next day, and with Jonklaas' contribution to the effort, an excavation was made under the barrel. The divers brought down an automobile jack. While Throckmorton hammered it into the cavity, Wilson worked at the lever. Tons of pressure forced the gun loose. Both dinghies were maneuvered overhead and ropes were lowered and tied to the gun. The Port-A-Lift was attached and filled with air. While Jonklaas and Throckmorton hauled from above, Wilson manhandled the heavy brass through crevices in the outer reef. After many hours of heroic efforts the gun was hoisted aboard the *Ran Muthu*.

As coral was carefully chipped from its surface with small hammers, the divers watched anxiously for the expected message to appear. For hours they saw only clean brass. Then, on the breech, four numbers were uncovered. They read: 2 3 23 8. There was no other identification. The gun measured just over 4 feet 7 inches. The muzzle diameter of 2 inches indicated a one-pounder. A wood tampon with a hempstring pullcord still plugged the barrel. The touchhole, when cleaned, was found full of gunpowder. In reply to an inquiry about the significance of the numbers, Mendel Peterson explained that this was the English system of indicating a cannon's weight. The first three numbers were, respectively, hundredweights (in England, 112 pounds), quarter-hundredweights (28 pounds), and odd pounds. By this count the gun weighed 331 pounds, one less than shown on the scales in Colombo, where it was later weighed. The final digit was probably the gun's serial number.

During the final working days several more silver clumps were recovered with hundreds of rupees and a large assortment of relics from the ship. Among these was an 18-inch copper serving plate cemented to cannon balls and coins. Wilson climaxed his salvage with two more big "bags" of coins on his last dive. When monsoon seas had sealed off the site for that year, the group left with the largest haul of treasure from the Indian Ocean in recent times. Eight "bags" weighing from 20 to 30 pounds each, dozens of smaller clusters, and hundreds of loose coins made a total of over 10,000 rupees. The artifacts were also valuable. Following detailed instructions from Peterson they were treated for preservation. With the co-operation of the archaeological commissioner in Ceylon and the director of the Colombo Museum, a permanent museum exhibit of the treasure, cannons, and artifacts was prepared.

Nearly the entire salvage had been made in an area of 3 square yards, by three people, in a very short time. There were countless more square yards of the valley floor still untouched. To preserve the valuables remaining there from looting, arrangements were made to safeguard the site.

The artifacts collected by Throckmorton yielded further information, but not enough to identify the wreck. Cloth samples were identified as coir, a coconut fiber from which the treasure sacks were made. Other fiber material was bamboo. Both kinds of cloth would be used to pack a shipment from India. The wood samples, upon examination by the Forest Products Laboratory of the U. S. Department of Agriculture, were identified as teak (the brass cannon tampon, a musket stock, a grenade stopper, etc.); walnut (a pistol butt); and the red pine group (part of what could be a chest). All the wood seemed to be of either European or Asiatic origin. The ship itself mounted probably 22 or 24 carronades, plus the brass gun, the iron long gun, and the signal guns. Throckmorton determined that such armament might correspond with a Dutch *fluyt* of that period. The ship was probably iron-fastened, since the fossil holes in the concreted masses were those of square iron nails 2 centimeters in size and round iron nails 4 centimeters in diameter.

Somewhere in that mass of concretion from the wreck is a ship's bell, or an engraved plate, or any number of other artifacts that could reveal the ship's identity. Until further excavations are made, however, the Great Basses Silver wreck will remain a mystery—and the amount of silver treasure still lying on that reef the subject of wistful speculation. Commenting on future plans, Mike Wilson says, "We plan to go back and do a proper job after we have more information on the wreck. Research is going on in The Hague and we feel that we will get her identity from Indonesia. She was probably Dutch."

The INDUS (41)
In his *The Treasure of the Great Reef* Arthur Clarke tells of the loss of this 3462-ton P & O ship on Mullaitivu Shoal fifty miles north of Trincomalee. Although she was salvaged, there is a possibility that a priceless collection of second century B.C. statues from the stupa of Bharut in India was overlooked by the divers.

The Sumatra Coast

The SÃO PAULO (39)

In April 1560 the *nao São Paulo* left Lisbon from India with about 450 aboard and $500,000 in silver, gold, and jewels. She was becalmed in the Atlantic for several weeks, resulting in a decision to take on supplies at Brazil before continuing the voyage under the Cape. On October 2 the ship sailed from Baía, Brazil, rounded Africa and crossed the Indian Ocean, but due to what must have been incredible incompetence on the part of the pilot completely missed the Indian continent. On January 22, 1561, the *São Paulo* was wrecked against the coast of Sumatra, 1500 miles beyond, at the equator line near the village of Sasak.

Most of the valuables were taken off the ship before she broke up, yet in the confusion of abandoning her probably $150,000 in money and jewels were left behind. There has probably never been an effort to salvage this *nao*'s wreckage.

CHAPTER 23

The South Pacific

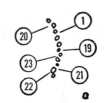

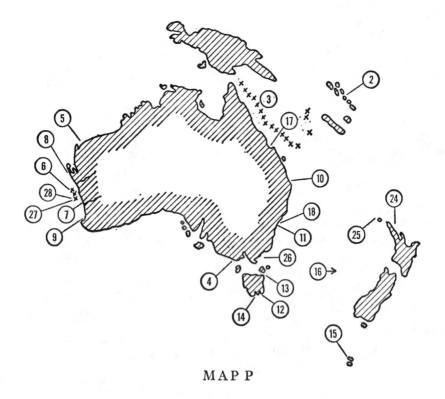

MAP P

*E*UROPEAN CONQUEST of the Pacific began in the first half of the sixteenth century, with Spanish and Portuguese navigators attacking its eight-thousand-mile width from east and west, feeling their way over its vast watery stretches, exploring and charting as they progressed. Magellan set off the Spanish entry by crossing from Chile to the Philippines in 1521 and discovering the Moluccas and Marianas (which he named the Ladrones—or "Robber Islands"). He was followed by other exploratory armadas of two and three little caravels which probed boldly westward from Acapulco and other Pacific ports on the American continents. By the middle of the century the Marshalls, Carolines, and Melanesia had been roughly charted, followed by the New Hebrides and other archipelagoes.

The Portuguese, meanwhile, were moving eastward from their India colonies. In 1511 they established a base at Malacca in Malaya. From here their caravels and *naos* pressed into the "Spice Islands," establishing military and trading posts throughout Indonesia and even as far north as Macao in South China by 1557. Inevitably the two forces, approaching from east and west, met. Both nations were bound by the Treaty of Tordesillas which split the world into Spanish and Portuguese spheres of influence with the dividing parallel running through eastern Brazil. The agreement said nothing about the other side of the globe, however, and a ticklish situation was avoided over the Moluccas when Spain ceded these islands to Portugal in 1529 for 350,000 gold ducats. This temporarily stabilized the "ownership" of the Pacific. The western fringe belonged to the Portuguese and just about everything else, including the Philippines, to the Spanish.

Then a new force entered the picture. Following the successful voyages of Houtman in 1595 and van Neck's fleet in 1599, the United East India Company was formed by the Dutch in 1602 with the frank objective of taking over the Indies spice trade. Previously Dutch merchants had enjoyed a lucrative middleman role as European distributors of Portuguese imports from the Far East: Sumatra pepper and ginger, cinnamon from Ceylon, Borneo camphor, cloves from the Moluccas, and Chinese silks. When Portugal was incorporated into the Spanish empire in 1580 these trading privileges were abruptly terminated. The Hollanders, to keep in business, launched a military-economic attack on Portuguese and British possessions that gained control of key regions from Africa to the South Pacific. In 1619 Batavia, Java, was the headquarters of the Dutch East India Company's commercial empire. Throughout the seventeenth century this company dominated south-west Pacific commerce, with its aggressive trading fleet of 150 ships protected by ten or more warships and an army of ten thousand mercenary soldiers. Incredible as it seems, the entire enterprise was a private company.

The discovery and charting of Australia developed slowly. Although back in 1426 the captain of a Chinese junk made a map of the north coast that ended up in a Peking museum, Europeans did not discover the continent until much later. In 1605 a flotilla of three Spanish ships[1] en route from Callao to the Marquesas went off course and after many adventures reached the edge of "a large mass of land" which was named Australia del Espíritu Santo in honor of King Philip's Austrian origin. The next year Captain Willem Jansz' yacht *Duyfken* charted the west coast of Cape York and the Spanish navigator Torres gave his name to Torres Strait while charting southern New Guinea, although he did not find Australia. The first European to set foot on the continent was Dirk Hartog, of the Dutch ship *Eendracht*, who gave his name to an island off the west coast which the Dutch subsequently called Een-dracht's Land. It was the English who first showed any interest in the new continent. Captain James Cook, who eight years later found the Sandwich (Hawaiian) Islands, explored the east and northeast coasts in 1770 and claimed the continent for Britain. In 1829 Australia was officially declared a British possession. A few years later New Zealand, which the Dutch navigator Abel Tasman had discovered in 1642, was taken under the same administration.

At first the English shared the earlier Spanish and Dutch lack of enthusiasm about the Australian territory. Its barren, distant stretches were a convenient place to send convicts to get them out of the way, and that was about all. Then gold was discovered on the same barren plains. Suddenly Australia became important. Shipping increased and cargoes of dust and nuggets began leaving Melbourne and Perth. Some of these Australian gold shipments met with disaster and ended on the bottom of the sea. Together with chests of silver pesos lying on the wrecks of westward-crossing Manila galleons they became the most valuable sunken treasures in the South Pacific.

Pacific Island Treasures

The SANTA MARGARITA (1)

Most of the sites shown in the Mariana Islands refer to descriptions of lost Manila galleons in that chapter. One more Spanish ship, the

[1] The *San Pedro y San Pablo, Capitana,* of 155 tons; the *San Pedro,* of 120 tons; and the *Tres Reyes,* a *patache.*

Santa Margarita, may also hold a small quantity of silver money. She was the *Capitana* of a trading-exploring venture into the Pacific, commanded by Pedro de Acuña. While crossing the Marianas chain in 1552 this caravel sank off one of the islands with the loss of most of her crew and all the cargo.

The *SANTA ISABEL* (2)

This 200-ton *nao,* commanded by Alvaro de Mendaña, was reconnoitering the islands of the New Hebrides in 1595 when a tropical storm sent her to the bottom. Among the 182 who lost their lives was Admiral Lope de Vega. There was a "considerable sum of coined money" aboard, none of which was salvaged.

The GREAT BARRIER REEF TREASURES (3)

Lyle Davis, one of the contingent of enthusiastic Aussie SCUBA divers from Brisbane, has made frequent visits to the Great Barrier Reef—a 1200-mile-long labyrinth of coral islets and shoals, as wide as 150 miles in places, that twists and turns off the northeast Australian coast. "We have explored quite a few wrecks on the reef," he states, "but the closest I have got to treasure is finding many barrels of what at first appeared to be gunpowder from a Spanish galleon but which eventually turned out to be cement. Most of the wrecks on the Barrier Reef are so overgrown with coral that it is only possible to find them by judging the general outline first, then breaking the coral to see what is underneath.

"Many tales are told of old coins being found in coral broken by anchors, etc., but localities are so roughly given that it is almost impossible to check them." Two of these tales, which might be considered, stem from the pearling activities of the Jardines of Somerset. In 1902 one of the luggers owned by Frank Jardine was caught in a blow while working off the Barrier east of Cape York. Her captain ran for shelter, entering a small basin in a section of the reef known as Boat Reef. Here, protected by a natural breakwater, they rode out the storm. When things had quieted down it was discovered that the pearler was trapped and the only way to get out was to deepen the channel through which they had entered. Divers went to work. While hacking below they found a chest which was embedded in the coral. It was brought up and discovered to be full of Spanish silver coins dated from 1880 to 1883, and a few more of gold. They were distributed to the lugger crew as a bonus, and melted down into a silver dinner set for the Jardine home. Divers from another Jardine lugger were working on the edge of the Great Barrier Reef farther north when "in a cleft of coral they stumbled on a heap of silver dollars weighing about 150 pounds. At the same site the divers also found three Spanish cannons." It seems from these accounts that nearly certainly one or more Spanish ships—probably westward-bound Manila galleons carrying Mexican silver—were wrecked on the reefs. A search through the old records of the Jardine enterprise at Somerset could yield exact locations.

Possibly the above salvages are related to legends of shipwrecks in the Torres Strait. One tells of a ship sinking near Mer Island about 1840, from which a raft came ashore carrying white men and an iron-bound chest which they buried. Islanders killed and ate the survivors. Years later an old hourglass and a silver coin were found on the Mer Island beach, while gold and silver coins, the latest dated 1833, were unearthed at nearby Dowar Island. Another tale tells of a shipwreck near Stephen Island, from which the survivors were all eaten except for the captain's wife, who wore a great deal of jewelry. The islanders draped the precious gems over their stone idol. There is a report that in 1934 a trochus shell fisherman found this idol with a gold ring and several rubies nearby.

Through the centuries the Great Barrier Reef has claimed countless ships, including over three hundred whose losses were documented. Descriptions of other recent salvages by SCUBA divers, including the recovery of cannons from Captain James Cook's *Endeavour*, are found in the "Submarine Archaeology" chapters.

Australia—Eastern Coast

The "MAHOGANY SHIP" (4)

In 1836 a whale boat carrying three sealers capsized at the mouth of the Hopkins River about one hundred miles from Melbourne. On their trek to civilization, about six miles northwest of the present city of Warrnambool, the two survivors found the half-buried remains of a ship in the sand dunes above high water mark. Their descriptions caused it to be referred to thereafter as "The Mahogany Ship" or "The Spanish Wreck." The oldest members of the local Yangery tribe, when questioned about the ship, said that it had been there as long as they could remember. Over the following years shifting sand gradually covered the bleached and weather-worn wooden ribs. By 1880 there was nothing left that could be seen.

Early estimates of the size varied from 50 to 200 tons, and the ship-wreck date could be placed at about 1750. The wood was described as mahogany, which could have been the Philippine *luán* from which many Pacific galleons were built. The only artifacts ever found from the ship were a bronze bolt and some rotted cording which are now in the Warrnambool museum. Deeply buried in the sand around her rotted timbers might be more—perhaps, even, chests of Mexican silver pesos.

The LONG ISLAND WRECK (17)

Grounded remnants of another vessel, called the "Long Island wreck," could offer interesting prospects. Her wooden hull lies off the beach at Long Island, Queensland, and was visible at low tide until a few years ago. There are many stories about this ship. One reports the finding of gold and silver coins in 1890 along the facing beach and in shallow tidal water, together with silverware and Chinese pottery of the 1740–1860 period. Another tells of six 30-pound cannon balls located on a nearby hill. The well-known ex-Dundee diver Walter Deas, who is carrying out research on Australian wrecks, is interested in this lost ship.

The *PRINCEZA* (10)

Norm McLennan reported finding in 1957 what he thinks is the wreckage of this 141-ton sloop which sank near the northern tip of Moreton Island, near Brisbane, on March 15, 1863. Local opinion is that she carried U.S. gold money with a value of several hundred thousand dollars. None of this has been reported salvaged.

The *DUNCAN DUNBAR* (11)

There were rumors about that the *Duncan Dunbar* had aboard a consignment of money when she sank off Sydney in 1857. Her hull was located in 1955 and searched by divers recently, and anchors and other artifacts have been salvaged. No silver or gold coins were encountered.

The *CATTERTHUN* (18)

Fifty-five people were drowned when this 2179-ton steamer struck Seal Rocks, between Port Stephens and Newcastle, in August 1895. The following year two helmet divers, Briggs and May, were reported to have salvaged $16,000 of the $20,000 in gold aboard. There may remain a few thousand dollars scattered in the wreck.

The *FAVORITE* (26)

Another unsolved mystery of the sea is the disappearance of the 96-ton schooner *Favorite*, which sailed from Melbourne on May 9, 1852, for Sydney. Besides general cargo she carried about 2000 ounces of gold dust worth over $70,000. She was last seen off Cape Howe by crews of two passing ships, who reported that she showed signs of storm damage. The only clue to her fate turned up the next year when settlers at Tarwin Beach found wreckage at "Ten Mile" with the name *Favorite* marked on it.

Western Australia

The WESTERN AUSTRALIAN MUSEUM and the MUSEUM AMENDMENT ACT (1964)

In Western Australia, as in other regions off whose shores lie historically valuable wrecks, the growing popularity of SCUBA diving in the 1950s led to the discovery and working of sites by competent and enthusiastic divers. Unfortunately few were experienced in underwater archaeology. The results, and subsequent action taken, are told by Dr. Colin Jack-Hinton, formerly of the Western Australian Museum:

> Skin divers, untrained as archaeologists, looked to the sites as objects for salvage and have brought up material indiscriminately. The expeditions mounted with official approval were simply enthusiastic salvage operations which, although they attempted some survey and brought to the surface objects of considerable interest, were not archaeologically supervised. They had the effect of disturbing the sites, leading in some cases to material being recovered which subsequently deteriorated and wasted for want of proper laboratory treatment.

> On November 30, 1964, a Museum Amendment Act was introduced with penal provisions to protect historic wrecks: it provides that a person discovering an underwater shipwreck should not interfere with it and should report the matter to the State Museum Board. The State Museum will investigate the wreck and determine its historic interest and value. There is provision for the wreck to be vested as Crown property in the Museum Board and scheduled accordingly: its preservation and excavation become the responsibility of the Museum.

> The wrecks which had already been located were scheduled in the Act: the *Batavia, Gilt Dragon, Zuytdorp, Zeewyck* and the unidentified Cottesloe wreck—all with the cautionary addition "known as"—and the as yet unlocated *Tryall*. Provision exists for a reward of up to a $2,000 to be paid to the finder of a wreck after the Act was introduced, and for the refund of legitimate expenses. No compensation is payable, however, in respect of the wrecks scheduled in the Act. In future, the finder of an unscheduled wreck which contains bullion will be paid the current mineral market value of the bullion, or the bullion may be turned over to him. Persons who removed or obtained material from scheduled wrecks before the introduction of the Act must inform the Museum, which may then examine the material over a period of thirty days, or longer if the Board and the person are agreeable, and photograph, copy and record it. The property is then returned to the owner, unless some other agreement is reached. The Museum may permit him in writing to sell, destroy or dispose of it, but he must not do so without permission. Material brought off the scheduled wrecks after the introduction of the Act is regarded as Crown property illegally seized, and provision exists for the punishment of offenders.

> Skin divers are extremely interested in wreck exploration, and their interest must be recognized and used . . . Strict legislation must exist

to control the inveterate treasure hunters . . . but, more importantly, divers must be educated by archaeologists to recognize the damage they can do and also the useful work they can perform under supervision. Their co-operation and understanding must be wooed and won, not forced by legalism . . . They clearly have some right to participate in work on "their" wrecks. Certainly, in Western Australia an obligation towards skin divers is felt.

At the end of 1964 the Western Australian Museum was entrusted with the sweeping responsibility of developing a complete underwater archaeology program. Neither experienced staff nor equipment was on hand. However, the officer taking charge, Colin Jack-Hinton,[2] M.A., Ph.D., was already an authority on marine history and had just completed a tour of Europe where he conferred with leading marine archaeologists. On December 19, 1966, Dr. Jack-Hinton was appointed Senior Curator in Charge of the Division of Human Studies, whose Department of Maritime and Colonial History and Historical Technology was also charged with underwater archaeology. Two museum assistants were added to the department in February 1967: Mr. E. J. Car, experienced in restoration techniques, started the Preservation Laboratory and Workshop for treating salvaged artifacts; ex-Petty Officer Clearance Diver H. E. Bingham, B.E.M., became field assistant and diver. He was sent on a three-month visit to Holland where he studied marine archaeology and Dutch colonial naval architecture. Dr. Jack-Hinton later attended the Third Conference of Underwater Archaeologists in Florida.

A Historic Wreck Advisory Committee was set up. Members include Miss M. Lukis; Dr. G. C. Bolton, Professor of History at the University of Western Australia; Mr. Harold Roberts, State Archivist; and Mr. Hugh Edwards, who contributed so importantly to the location and salvage of the *Batavia* and other wrecks. During 1966 and 1967 Edwards gathered material and prepared a comprehensive study of the historical wreck sites off the coast. Dr. R. E. Playford, B.Sc. (Hons.), Ph.D., was appointed Honorary Associate. For specific survey and salvage jobs a number of experienced men were brought in under contract, including ex-Naval Clearance divers W. Beckhouse and R. Beveridge, and John Cowen and George Brenzi. Salvage equipment was acquired, together with the 24-foot launch *Balamara*.

Despite these optimistic plans for organized archaeological salvage and preservation of the Dutch wrecks, results to date have been disappointing. Due to difficulties with financing, and keeping adequate skilled staffers to oversee the museum's heavy responsibilities, one project after another was postponed. In late 1971 only limited work was being undertaken, on the *Batavia*, under the supervision of a capable

---

[2] Dr. Jack-Hinton later left the museum to assume another post.

English expert Mr. Jerome Green. Hopefully new financing will provide the museum's management with means to strengthen the staff and go ahead with the commendable program.

The Western Australia Wrecks

The TRYAL (5)

The distinction of being the first master to have his charge wrecked in Western Australian waters went to John Brookes, whose English ship *Tryal* struck a reef fourteen miles off the Monte Bello Islands in 1622. The weather was calm late in the evening when the ship grounded, but turned bad soon afterward. Before dawn, with the ship breaking up, two boats set off from the site with the captain and nearly fifty of the crew. Ninety-six others were left behind to die. The two boats sailed to Batavia, where they reported the disaster.

For years, Western Australian divers tried to locate the wreck, which was believed to have aboard 500 gold sovereigns and a consignment of jewels. On May 3, 1969, after a planned search, a team which included Eric Christiansen, Alan Robinson, Naom Haimson, and David Nelley succeeded. Over the centuries the fierce tides and marine worms had obliterated the hull, and all that remained were anchors, guns, a brass pulley wheel and some lead. Of the treasure there was not a sign.

The Western Australian Museum sent expeditions to the site in 1969 but bad weather prevented divers from accomplishing anything. An expedition arriving in 1971 found that the wreck site had been blasted by divers looking for treasure.

It is largely the bones of Dutch East Indiamen that litter the reefs off Australia's western shores. For the first years after the consolidation of Dutch power in the East Indies, their lumbering, shallow-bottomed Indiamen followed the traditional route eastward, hugging the east African coast north to the equator, then striking across the Indian Ocean just above this latitude, passing Sumatra. Then in 1611 Hendrick Brouwer, one of the captains with a venturesome streak in his blood, liked the feel of the wind after rounding the Cape of Good Hope and headed east along the "Roaring Forties" in the southern latitude. He cut the passage time to Batavia by half. After studying his report the directors of the East India Company presently authorized other ships to use the new route.

It was all too easy for captains to sail too far east before striking north. Such an error in navigation caused Hartog unwittingly to discover Western Australia in 1616. Another Dutch captain, Houtman, of the ship *Dordrecht,* nearly met disaster on the deadly Abrolhos

Reefs (and later gave his name to a stretch of them now called Houtman's Rocks). The name Abrolhos itself, also given to other reefs in other parts of the world, deserves a word of explanation. According to Hugh Edwards, "Abrolhos was a corruption of the old Portuguese lookout's cry *Abn vossos olhos*—meaning 'Open your eyes!' The Houtmans and many other Dutch seamen had served under the Portuguese during their seafaring careers."

In 1627, after a governor-general-designate of the East Indies was nearly wrecked on the Abrolhos, Dutch captains were ordered to make landfall farther north at 27° south latitude near Shark Bay, where high red cliffs of the Australian coast would give them a longitude bearing for Java. Even with this order many skippers clung to the lower latitudes with their favorable westerlies as long as they dared, to make a faster passage. And during the seventeenth and eighteenth centuries the Dutch ships, and English vessels as well, were wrecked one after the other along the barren West Australian shore. The East Indiamen were richly laden with merchandise and money for delivery to Batavia. Besides coffers of gold and silver coins for payrolls and trading, they carried personal jewelry of wealthy passengers, and silverware, wines, laces, and other valuable cargoes.

The deadly Abrolhos claimed their share of these ships. Their chains of coral reef and barren islets stretch for some fifty miles along the coast near Geraldton, reaching out thirty and forty miles into the ocean. Dutch East Indiamen destroyed here include the *Batavia* and *Zeewyck*, and probably also the *Aagtekerke*, which disappeared between the Cape of Good Hope and Batavia. In more recent years the Abrolhos have wrecked the *Ocean Queen, Cochituate, Hadda, Marten, Ben Ledi, Mary, Eveline* and *Windsor.*

The *BATAVIA* (6)

This 300-ton *retour-schip*, Francisco Pelsaert commanding, was flagship of a Dutch East India Company convoy that left Texel, Holland, in October 1628. She carried treasure amounting to some 250,000 guilders in rix-dollars. Over three hundred passengers were squeezed aboard, and among these was a piratical supercargo named Jerome Cornelis.

From the start the voyage seemed jinxed. After rounding the stormy Cape, the *Batavia* was separated from the other ships of the convoy. An atmosphere of tension grew during the long crossing of the Indian Ocean, and mutiny, instigated by Cornelis, was constantly on the point of breaking out.

The trip ended suddenly on June 4, 1629, when the Indiaman smashed into the reefs of the Abrolhos just before dawn. She settled to the bottom with her deck awash. The crew and passengers were able to reach a nearby island, where jewels and some of the treasure, and provisions, were taken ashore. Awnings made from canvas sails were set up to protect the women and children from the hot sun, and the men searched their islet for water.

When none was found, Commander Pelsaert and a few of the crew took a boat and combed the neighboring islands, again unsuccessfully. Then they set off for the Australian mainland, some forty miles away, hoping to establish a base near fresh water and a supply of food. Along the shore there was only barren wasteland. As nothing could be gained by returning to the wreck site, Pelsaert navigated the boat on an epic voyage that finally landed the men, half dead from starvation and exposure, at Batavia on July 7. The frigate *Sardam* was made ready within a week and dispatched to rescue the *Batavia*'s marooned survivors and the treasure.

When Captain Pelsaert failed to return, Jerome Cornelis made his move. Leading some thirty of the worst elements in the crew he divided the other people among the islands and sent gangs to murder them secretly. By the end of a month they had killed 125 men, women, and children. Only seven of the youngest women were spared. Some of the men were able to escape to a large island five miles distant where they were soon joined by a few loyal soldiers and built a small coral fort. Cornelis and his mutineers attacked twice, but were driven off. Then they returned to their island and settled down to an orgy of drinking wine salvaged from the wreck and fighting over the women.

The rescue ship *Sardam* arrived on September 16—104 days after the shipwreck. After a short battle the mutineers were captured. Cornelis, with seven others, was hanged. The survivors, and ten chests of treasure salvaged from the ship by Indian divers, were taken back to Batavia, where testimonies were put on paper and filed in the archives.

Western Australian interest in the *Batavia* developed in 1955, when Henrietta Drake-Brockman suggested that the wreck's location might be at Noon Reef in the Wallabi Group of the Abrolhos. In 1963 an expedition headed by Max Cramer made a thorough survey of the area which was climaxed with the salvage of a small brass cannon from Morning Reef, off Beacon Island. Marks on the gun identified it as Dutch East India Company property. Soon afterward a major salvage operation was carried out, organized by author-diver Hugh Edwards and Cramer, in which a Royal Australian Naval unit commanded by Lieutenant H. Donohue and civilian divers participated. Mr. C. Halls, of the Western Australian Museum, was invited as an observer. The recoveries confirmed that the wreckage was nearly certainly that of the *Batavia*. Among artifacts recovered from the reef were four bronze cannons—the oldest dated 1602 and cast in Rotterdam—a number of coins dated 1575–1624, pottery, cannon balls, powder canisters, and tableware. Of particular significance was the find of several rare navigational instruments including an astrolabe, dividers, and a set square. Beacon Island itself yielded relics from the camp, including a sword-chopped skull and skeleton. As a result of his experience, Hugh Edwards published the exciting book *Islands of Angry Ghosts*, which more than lives up to the title.

Some of the *Batavia*'s artifacts are on view in the Fremantle Maritime Museum in Western Australia, together with other material from Dutch wrecks. Included are one of the bronze cannon, coins, pottery, and armaments.

The ZEEWYCK (27)

Nearly a hundred years after the *Batavia* tragedy another Dutch Indiaman went down on the Abrolhos. She was the *Zeewyck*, wrecked on a reef in 1727. Her crew was able to salvage a great deal of her cargo including ten chests of silver worth 315,836 guilders on to a nearby island. They built a large sloop from the ship's wood and sailed safely to Batavia, taking the treasure with them.

In 1840 Darwin's famous H.M.S. *Beagle* was making a survey of the Southern Abrolhos group when her crew found a brass gun, clay pipes, glass bottles, and other relics on an island there. They named it Gun Island. The small cannon was given to the collection at the Tower of London (it was recently loaned to the Western Australian Museum). More bottles and pipes were found on Gun Island in the 1880s by laborers excavating guano, as well as tobacco boxes and a few coins. In more recent years cannons from a portion of the wreck washed over the reef were seen just off the island in shallow water by crayfishermen. Two of these were raised in 1952 by salvors working from H.M.A.S. *Mildura*. Hugh Edwards and a group of SCUBA divers made a search of the surrounding reefs in the summer of 1963–64, finding many more artifacts, and returned in 1967–68 and discovered the main wreck lying behind the Half-Moon Reef. With Max Cramer and Geraldton divers he found ivory tusks, wine bottles, bronze cannon breechblocks, four anchors, seventeen guns, and many artifacts from the wreck. In appreciation, the Western Australian Museum paid Edwards a $2000 reward. The full and exciting story of the *Zeewyck*'s location and salvage is told in Hugh Edwards' new book, *The Wreck on the Half-Moon Reef*.

The COTTESLOE WRECK (28)

For years there was speculation that the wreck of another Dutch East Indiaman lay in shallow water off Cottesloe Beach. Several old cannons had been recovered, and tentatively identified as Dutch. Three

Indiamen known to have been lost after rounding the Cape were considered likely candidates: the *Aagtekerke*, lost in 1726, the *Fortuyn*, in 1724, and the *Ridderschap van Holland*, in 1694.

Hugh Edwards has cleared up the mystery of this wreck. It is the remains of an 1839 vessel which had picked up some old Spanish cannons in Manila for ballast! The *Fortuyn* was lost in mid-ocean, he advises, while the *Holland* was wrecked on Madagascar.

The VERGULDE DRAEK (GILT DRAGON) (7)

One of the most famous of all Western Australian wrecks was a 160-foot Indiaman which left Texel in October 1655, with 250 people aboard. She carried a treasure of 78,600 guilders, mostly in pieces of eight, stored in eight chests. En route, the *Gilt Dragon* put in at Africa and loaded a consignment of ivory tusks. Then she struck out for Batavia. On April 28, 1656, at four in the morning, the East Indiaman shattered her bow against a submerged reef three miles off the coast. Wind and waves battered the wooden hull along the rock ledge for several hundred yards. As she heeled over, cannons and heavy cargo broke loose, smashing through the sides into the waves. The *Gilt Dragon* finally settled on the outer reef, only 15 feet deep.

Of the 193 people who had lived through the long voyage, only 75 reached the Australian coast. Captain Pieter Aberts sent off seven of the best seamen aboard the only seaworthy craft, a 19-foot skiff. They landed at Batavia on June 7 after a voyage in the tradition of Captain Bligh. Rescue expeditions found timbers on the shore, but could not locate the wreck. One group came upon an abandoned camp on the shore, just north of the Moore River, indicating that the marooned survivors were either killed or assimilated into aborigine tribes.

The search for the ship's lost treasure, whose approximate site is shown on Dutch documents, went on for years. Then in 1931 a boy stumbled upon some seventeenth-century coins and the skeleton of a man north of the mouth of the Moore River. The coins were dated 1618 through 1645. Nearby were some brass hinges and part of a chest. A broken ship's mast was reported seen on rocks north of the Moore River. In 1957 Alan Robinson and Bruce Phillips made headlines with their announcement that they had located the *Gilt Dragon*. Robinson was quoted as describing the wreck to be about 150 feet long, covered with sea growths, with "fourteen cannons pointing skyward." His statement was promptly rebutted by the salvage veteran Captain A. G. Jacob, who claimed that the site was probably the *Redomtoara*, whose cargo he had raised. Although they returned to the site several times, Robinson and Phillips could not find the wreck again.

On Easter Day 1963 Robinson was spearfishing with John Cowen, Jim Henderson, and Henderson's two sons, some three and a half miles off the coast, about eight miles south of Ledge Point. One of the boys, Graeme, surfaced with a pink brick in his hand and drew attention to the wreckage 15 feet deep. The divers retrieved several more bricks—identified as ballast—and a 4-foot elephant tusk. Dr. Philip Playford, a noted amateur historian, was consulted and gave his opinion that the artifacts and location pointed strongly to the *Gilt Dragon*.

A salvage operation got under way in which divers Hugh Edwards, George Brenzi, Mauri Hammond, and Denis Bennets joined the original group. A survey showed that the ship had broken into several parts. A large quantity of artifacts was salvaged, including more ballast bricks and elephant tusks, cannon balls, domestic utensils, bellarmine jugs, and two cannons. As the lime crustation was chipped from one gun, the letters V O C A—insignia of the Amsterdam chapter of the Dutch East India Company—appeared. The drinking mugs were decorated with a bearded face which research identified as that of an unpopular seventeenth-century Dutch churchman whose caricature was incorporated into such mugs as an insult. Several bronze candlesticks and a chemist's mortar inscribed "Love Conquers All" in Latin were also of interest.

When a crumpled lead sheet was unfolded the first piece of treasure fell onto the deck. It was a sulfided piece of eight. Brenzi, who had raised it, led the others to a stretch of sand on whose surface lay other coins, mostly Spanish 8-reales, which were collected and cleaned. When 1654 was found to be the latest identifiable date, it seemed certain that the *Gilt Dragon*, which had sailed the following year, had been located. Alan Robinson later recovered a reported eight to sixteen thousand pieces of eight.

When the government passed legislation to control the wrecks in the Museum Amendment Act (1964), the *Gilt Dragon* site was put under the jurisdiction of the Western Australian Museum. In 1966 John Cowen and George Brenzi, assisted by Kevin Morgan, made a survey, a chart, and a model of the wreckage for the museum. A museum field base was established on Ledge Point to keep watch on the wreck site. In November 1968 excavation and preservation of some of the wreckage was under way, and the *Gilt Dragon*'s historical treasures were being added to the museum's Dutch wrecks section, then in Perth. Dr. Jack-Hinton, in his article "Archaeology Under the Sea", gives this description of the site:

> The *Gilt Dragon* site . . . is a craggy undulating mass of what appears at first to be nothing but reef formation with considerable variation in depth, valleys, pockets and holes, arches and grottoes. Although a certain amount of material lies around in an immediately moveable form, with varying amounts of encrustation or conglomeration, the greater part of the wreck must lie . . . within a thick encrustation of marine growth. It has, in fact, been worked out that in parts the encrustation may be four feet thick, and it is fairly solid.

As the smaller objects are salvaged, the problem of recovering the main body of the wreck will be further examined. At present, according to Dr. Jack-Hinton, "the only solution appears to lie in cutting the reef formation into reasonably workable sections, and lifting and transferring it to the shore, laboratory and workshop." In this operation cutting plastic explosives (but not shattering gelignite) would be used.

A collection of salvaged Spanish cobs is on display at the museum. Work on the site is expected to continue very slowly until the priority salvage of the *Batavia* is completed.

The *ZUYTDORP* (8)

Only a few feet underwater, on a flat reef riddled with knife-edged blowholes at the base of a 200-foot-high overhanging rock cliff, and pounded nearly every day of the year by tremendous breakers, lies the *Zuytdorp's* wreckage. It has been widely dispersed during over two and a half centuries of battering by the seas, and swirling sand hides the ship's remnants, which are already camouflaged by marine growths. A more dangerous diving site would be hard to find, and the problems of salvage are bewildering. Yet many of Western Australia's tough SCUBA veterans have ventured into this maelstrom—and with good reason: Somewhere in the *Zuytdorp's* wreckage probably lies a treasure of 250,000 guilders worth of pieces of eight, ducatoons, and other coins.

The famous Dutch East Indiaman was wrecked forty miles north of the Murchison River in 1712. Despite the surf, some survivors reached the top of the cliff, where broken glass navigation instruments, clay pipes, and the remnants of old water casks were seen in 1927 by a stockman named Tom Pepper. Climbing down to the base of the cliff he found several coins and a carved wooden sternpost. Further searches along the spray-drenched sand and rocks yielded more money and ship's artifacts. A geologist, Dr. Philip Playford, surveyed the foot of the cliff in 1955 during a newspaper-sponsored project and tentatively identified the wreck from its coins and artifacts, including navigational instruments. More relics were recovered in 1958.

The first salvage attempt was made between February and May 1964 by a group of Geraldton divers. The team included Max and Graeme Cramer, Tom Brady, Neil McLaughlan, Gordon Hancock, and Eric Barker. During four diving periods they brought up three small brass cannons, artifacts, and coins. The guns were put on public display in Geraldton, and the group claimed salvage rights to the wreck in letters addressed to the Western Australian Museum and Captain R. R. Elliott, Receiver of Wrecks in Western Australia. In both applications Tom Pepper was named joint discoverer.

In May 1968 the museum gave Alan Robinson permission to survey the wreck. His team of experienced divers included Naom Haimson, Bill Johnston, Clive Daw, Joe Varris, Bill Noonan, Ned Harold, Leith Goodall, and Robinson himself. Among them were engineers, photographers, and a doctor.

Ingenious salvage methods were planned. Transportation to and from the ocean was to be via a 400-yard "flying fox" connected to a cliff top and a strongly-moored buoy beyond the heavy surf. A steel mesh was to be suspended in front of the cliff to cushion the impact when divers were swept in by waves. These devices were never successfully constructed, and finally the salvors resigned themselves to entry from the shore, timing their dives with the giant surges of foaming water. Within a short time Haimson was hospitalized with an injured back, Varris had his face badly cut, and several of the others were injured.

In spite of this Robinson's team went ahead with the job. According to reports, nineteen cannons and many artifacts were found, and when one cannon was chipped clean, the date 1710 appeared. Dutch coins dated 1711 were found in a crevice on the cliff 4 feet above sea level, attesting to the violence of the surf. Injuries continued to reduce the diving force, however, and the expedition was disbanded.

Several days later Robinson returned to the wreck site and found what he described as "a reef of solid silver." Others divers who have been there since report seeing this, as well, and describe it as a bank of impacted silver coins fully 10 feet long and 2 feet high. Because of the surf it is possible to retrieve only a handful at a time.

West Australian divers have worked out what they consider a practical plan to salvage this rich lode, but their suggestion was not accepted by museum authorities. There is no current program to recover the wreck's silver and archaeological treasure because of the heavy seas, and the *Zuytdorp* continues to be "off limits."

The *LANCIER* (9)

This English bark crushed into Stragglers Rocks, near Fremantle, in 1839 and sank soon afterward. In addition to general cargo, she carried an iron chest containing seven thousand gold sovereigns with a current value of over $45,000. This chest was reported to have fallen into the sea while being lowered into a small boat. SCUBA divers believe they have located the *Lancier*, but despite searches in the ballast, the lost treasure chest has not been found.

The Tasmanian Wrecks

Under the southeast corner of Australia, separated by the hundred-mile-wide Bass Strait, is an island whose shores are literally ringed with sunken ships dating from 1800. In the foreword of his book

Wrecks in Tasmanian Waters, Captain Harry O'May, Council Chairman of the Shiplovers' Society of Tasmania, explains part of the reason why:

> The Island lies in the track of the "Roaring Forties" with thousands of miles of unbroken sea rolling in from Argentina. Hazards were created by the smaller islands which cluster around our Tasmanian shores and by the rocks and reefs of the Furneaux Group. An additional danger for small sailing ships lurked in the strong tide that set through Banks Strait . . .

The *HOPE* (12)

It was more probably the liquor on the pilot's breath that sent the *Hope* crashing onto a sandy beach between Betsy Island and the Iron Pot just before dawn on April 29, 1827. Panic followed as her crew tried to reach safety through heavy surf. In the consternation no one seemed to remember that down below was a coffer of pay money for troops stationed in Hobart Town. By the time someone got around to looking for it, the treasure chest had vanished. It was under the guard of an ensign and two soldiers who were immediately suspected of having hidden it somewhere—either in the dunes ashore or on the 7-foot-deep sand bottom where the doomed ship was grounded. Whatever the fate of the chest, it could not be found and the soldiers never had a chance to return to the site.

During the years since the *Hope*'s loss there have been several secretive and unsuccessful searches made for this stolen loot, the latest by an engineer with a metal detector with which he combed Hope Beach. Whether buried in sand dunes or sunk offshore in seven feet of water the mysterious chest should still be there.

The *PORTLAND* (13)

This bark was wrecked in 1833 on the north coast of Tasmania, east of Hebe Reef. There was money aboard: One man drowned from the weight of the fifty sovereigns he tried to take ashore and "boxes of silver plate were buried in a bluff near the mouth of the Piper River and never located again." Probably more was lost in the wreck itself.

This would be an interesting spot for a diving search combined with a metal detector survey of the shore for the lost silver.

The *ENCHANTRESS* (14)

This 376-ton bark broke her stem against submarine rocks about six miles off Bruni Island off Hobart on the night of July 17, 1835. Within twenty minutes she sank with the loss of twenty-four lives. A month later the schooner *Eliza* was sent out and a cursory search could find no trace of her, although her hull probably lies in shallow water. In a subsequent report was the comment that "the cargo of the *Enchantress* was exceedingly valuable," with no further details given as to its nature.

The very active Tasmanian SCUBA diving fraternity intend to try to find out. Dr. Eric Canning of Hobart, commenting on their plans, says: "It is by no means impossible that some of her passengers carried their worldly wealth in gold with them. We intend running over the area where we think she may lay with an echo sounder, and are hopeful that the bottom will be sand. We will dive on and investigate any objects which show on the tracing." Besides O'May and Canning, the strong Tasmanian contingent includes T. E. Davis, Don Reid, Mervin Morley, and Peter Brothers among others. This is the group that has located and thoroughly searched such wrecks as the *Catherine Sharer* in the past years (see Chapter 3).

Lost Australian Gold Shipments

In 1851 gold was discovered at Ballarat, near Melbourne, and the wool clippers to England began carrying increasingly large cargoes of precious metal. These sleek, fast ships, after picking up their loads at Perth and Melbourne, swept off eastward on the route of the Dutchmen to the Straits of Magellan. Despite great improvements in ships and navigation some of them, too, failed to arrive at their destinations.

The *GENERAL GRANT* (15)**

She was a beautiful clipper of 1103 tons, built and owned in Boston. On May 4, 1866, the *General Grant* set out from Melbourne for London carrying a cargo of the season's wool clip, hides and skins, nine tons of zinc spelter and, in her strong room, two boxes containing 2576 ounces of gold. The whole amount was insured for £165,000. On board were sixty-one passengers, including a number of successful prospectors bringing home fortunes in dust and nuggets in their personal chests. Captain Laughlin set her course eastward through Bass Straits and she vanished into the deep blue—literally.

It was one and a half years before the story of her incredible fate unfolded, told by the handful of survivors brought back to New Zealand. These accounts have been carefully studied by Captain O'May, who integrated them into his other researches on this ship. Since he knows more of her history than anyone else, he should tell it in is own words.

> Nine days after she cleared Melbourne, on the evening of May 13th, land was sighted and later passed in the east. It was one of the Auckland Islands. They lie down south of New Zealand—a group of wild, precipitous, desolate and windswept islands discovered in 1806 by the

whaler *Ocean.* They were the home of the fur seal until after 1830, when the ruthless slaughter almost wiped out these beautiful animals. They lie on the route of the wool clippers.

The night was dark. Later another island was sighted dead ahead. The wind died and the *General Grant* lost steerage way. Then it was discovered that the set of the sea was driving her in, but nothing could be done. There was no use giving her the anchors . . . no soundings. The jib boom struck the sheer cliff about midnight and carried away. She swung around broadside on and started to drift sternfirst along the base of the cliff, the backlash keeping her off. About half a mile along the spanker boom struck and carried away. Then she lost her rudder and continued the drift.

It was hoped that with the help of her backwash she would drift clear, but luck was dead against her. A huge cavern—some accounts give it as 250 yards deep—opened in the cliff. She lost the help of the backwash and drifted in. Her topmasts struck the overhead opening and carried away. She continued her inward drift, her masts raking the roof of the cave, dislodging tons of rock. The booming roar of the sea mingling with the shrieks of disturbed sea birds was deafening. Then the mainmast wedged into the overhead roof and pressed down, its heel breaking through. She settled onto the cave floor, thirty-five feet deep, with waves crossing her main deck.

Dawn broke, which enabled three men on the small boat to get clear with a kedge anchor and a light line. The kedge was dropped at the entrance and a larger boat hauled clear on the line. A second boat got away. The longboat swamped. Only three of her complement managed to reach the boats outside the breakers. The boats hung around until they were satisfied that not another soul was left—only 15 of the 83 got away. The survivors included the Mate Bart Brown, nine of the crew and five passengers, one of them a woman, Mary Ann Jewell.

They reluctantly rowed away and attempted to land on a small island, but the small boat swamped. Its occupants managed to reach the rocks but could not climb the cliff. The larger boat secured and bailed out the smaller boat and rescued its crew at daylight, but they had lost much of their scanty provisions. After two days of battering they reached a sheltered bay on one of the larger islands known to the sealers as Saraha's Bosom. They were wet, cold and hungry but by good fortune one of the passengers had one match only which enabled them to kindle a fire. They put two hour watches on it and never allowed it to go out. Next morning they explored the island and discovered a dilapidated sealer's hut and killed a seal for food.

Lookouts were posted, but day after day passed without sign of sail. Seals provided food and clothing. Small boats about three feet in length were carved, with masts to which were fastened pieces of tin for sails. A message was carved on their decks. Many of these were sent off but none picked up. Inflated seal bladders attached to buoyant pieces of wood also were sent away. The Mate then decided to try to reach New Zealand in the small boat. She was decked with seal skins and provisioned with smoked seal meat and bird eggs and water in seal bladders. The Mate and three A.B. pushed off on January 22, 1867, with no compass. They were never heard of again.

Finally in October of that year a sail was sighted. They lit huge fires to attract attention with no result. The same thing happened again on

November 19th. Then, on November 21st, a sail was sighted close in. The boat was manned and proceeded to intercept her. She was the brig *Amherst* who took them off.

The first to try to retrieve the *General Grant*'s gold was one of her passengers, James Teer, who chartered the iron paddle tug *Southland* in 1863. The cave was located but the sea would not let up. The crew became discontented and the expedition quit.

The next was Captain Wallace with the 51-ton schooner *Daphne*. She anchored in Port Ross, fifteen miles from the wreck. Wallace and a crew of five left in a well-equipped whale boat to investigate. After five weeks, with nothing heard from Wallace, the three remaining on the *Daphne* got up anchor and sailed for New Zealand. Not a thing was done to ascertain the fate of Wallace and his men until a public meeting was called which brought pressure to bear, with the result that the *Daphne* was sent back with two boat crews of marines to search the islands. Her captain was surprised to find H.M.S. *Blanch* at anchor in Ross. This second warship had been sent to investigate a report that fires had been seen on the island, and had steamed around it but saw no signs of life. The sea was too rough to lower a boat so both ships made another circle of its shore, which was scanned with glasses. Again nothing was sighted, and the ships left.

In 1874 two more treasure hunters, Taylor and Stephens, sailed on the chartered 130-ton schooner *Flora*, with no success.

In 1877 another of the survivors, Mr. Drew, chartered the S.S. *Gazelle* of 47 tons to make a try with no success.

An American, Captain Sonerson, formed a syndicate with a $100,000 capital in 1911 to have a go. This was an elaborate expedition, well-equipped—including a bullock team to convey their gear from the lee side of the island to the location of the cave on the weather side. The chartered steamer *Wairoa* was about to ease off when the sheriff boarded her and placed a detaining plaster on her mast for a debt of £400. Two years later Captain Sonerson made another attempt. Luck was again dead against him. He lost his vessel before he left the American coast. In 1915 Captain Catlong made a preliminary visit in the cutter *Enterprise* to locate the cave. She sailed again in 1916 with the latest diving gear. Like others before him, Catlong was held up for weeks by weather but he hung on. He got a slant of calm weather which allowed him to explore the cavern which he estimated ran in approximately 600 feet with a height of 60 feet. He spent two days exploring the cavern and was convinced that there was no sign of a wreck in there.

A tenacious treasure hunter is Bill Havens of Sydney, who received a permit from the New Zealand government to try for the gold. He went to England in 1954 and purchased a small vessel which he renamed *Absit Omen* (let no evil befall). However the black wind of misfortune struck him when *Absit Omen* decided to pile up on an uncharted reef in the Red Sea. However Bill was not disheartened. He returned to England and purchased another little craft which he named the *Goldseeker*. The black wind of misfortune was still sleeping with one eye open and coped him in the Timor Sea, again wrecking his chance . . .

Of all the salvage tries Captain Catlong's was the only one to even enter the cave unless Captain Wallace made it before perishing. From the tone of Catlong's report it would seem that his exploration was limited to above the water, for under such rough conditions a thorough underwater search could not have been made in such a short time.

An underwater search was made, however, in the spring of 1969, by Kelvin Tarlton and the salvors of the *Elingamite*'s money. Their report is just as puzzling as it is disappointing. "We have searched the cave very thoroughly and all the surrounding area within a half-mile," writes Tarlton, "plus every other cave to the north and south, and did not find a single nail or other trace of the *General Grant*. We went on our 90-foot steel twin motor boat the *Hamutana*. The weather was bad but not unworkable with aqualung gear. The bottom of the cave is loose rock, but I am sure that if that is where the *Grant* went we would have found some trace—unless she drifted out in one piece again. We found a 150-pound anchor outside and to one side of the cave which we think was probably from a previous salvage attempt. Anyway, we had no joy."

The Elingamite Syndicate's divers are pros, and would not have missed any artifacts from the clipper ship if they were visible. Question: What happened to the ship and gold?

The *MARLBOROUGH* (16)

This wool clipper sailed in 1890 from her last port of call in New Zealand with about $200,000 in gold aboard, headed for England. Like the *Madagascar* she disappeared without a trace. There have been repeated rumors during the years since then that her wreckage has been found off the tip of South America, and even that she has been sighted icebound near the South Pole like a "ghost" ship, the *Starry Crown*.

Wrecks Off New Zealand

The *NIAGARA* (24)

For a full account of her salvage, see the "Denting the Depth Barrier" chapter.

S.S. *ELINGAMITE* (25)

The loss of this 2585-ton steamship followed a pattern all too familiar in the early 1900s before navigation equipment became well developed. En route from Sydney to Auckland, she was proceeding at half speed through heavy fog on the morning of November 9, 1902. Lookouts peered ahead for signs of danger as the ship approached the north tip of New Zealand. Their warning shouts were still echoing from the cliffs as the *Elingamite* plowed headlong into the sheer rock facing of West King Island of the Three Kings group. Twenty minutes later she settled on the ocean floor under the cliff 150 feet deep.

Her 194 passengers and crew had managed to launch six lifeboats and two rafts. Three boats and one raft, buffeted by rip tides at the convergence of two strong currents here, reached a cliff several miles away where passengers scrambled up to precarious safety. Another boat carrying fifty-two people arrived the next day at Houhora. Five rescue vessels picked up the survivors from shore and from a raft on which sixteen had drifted for five days. Only eight, crazed with thirst and sunburn, were still alive. The last boat, with forty-five aboard, disappeared.

The *Elingamite* sank with a consignment of £17,320 in English money: six thousand golden half sovereigns packed in four wooden boxes, and another forty-eight boxes containing silver half crowns, shillings, and florins. Six salvage attempts were made to recover this treasure. Three were moderately successful, netting about £4000 at the cost of three divers, E. G. Harper, H. Clarke, and Percy Leigh, who died of the bends between 1908 and 1911. The *Elingamite* was considered too dangerous for further salvage, and abandoned.

In December 1965 a group of New Zealand SCUBA divers visited the Three Kings group to take photographs and prepare a story for *Dive South Pacific.* Among them were underwater photographer Kelvin Tarlton and the editor, Wade Doak, of this popular magazine. As the expedition prepared to return, Tarlton and Doak persuaded the others to take the boat to the site of the *Elingamite*'s wreck, where they made a quick dive. As Kelvin Tarlton recalls, "I recognized the area from a photo I had seen of an earlier—and ill-fated—salvage attempt working over the ship. We found the wreck on our first dive. The ship was completely broken up and lay scattered over several acres of rock and sand bottom. We had to return to New Zealand because of worsening weather and then wait twelve months, because only over the Christmas period can you be reasonably sure of workable conditions at the exposed site."

During these long months, Tarlton and Doak made a thorough research into the *Elingamite*'s history. They learned that coins with a face value of over £13,000, which lay in the wreckage, belonged to the Northern Assurance Company. An agreement was made under which the owners would be paid the metallic value of any recovered coins, less expenses. On December 25, 1966, in the middle of the New Zealand summer, Tarlton and Doak finally returned with equipment sufficient for several days' diving aboard their boat. They studied and mapped the conglomeration of rusted and shattered iron battered into the sea bed. Twisted pipes, broken porcelain, copper and lead fittings, and old bottles lay everywhere. Although underwater visibility was a good 100 feet, diving was dangerous. Strong currents and rip tides, combined with rough seas, made it difficult to maintain decompression depth. Kelvin Tarlton remarks, "The swell was so fierce that at times we were getting swept 30 feet in each direction at 150 feet. The surface was a seething mass of foam and spray. Several times we were swept away by currents." It was not until the last day that Wade Doak found money—a crevice full of silver coins. With air running low and a decompression stop ahead, he could only scoop up a handful. The money was later valued at £15.

No time was lost in organizing a regular salvage expedition. Its members were Tarlton, Doak, John Gallagher, Jeff Pearch, and John Pettit. They were all aboard the dive boat *Lady Gwen* when she anchored over the site on January 8, 1967. Besides fifty-five fully-charged air tanks and storage cylinders, equipment included two air lifts, since reconnaissance had indicated that the coins probably lay buried under overburden in rock crevices and pleats in the rusted iron sheeting. Early recoveries were limited to scattered coins, all silver. Then excitement broke out when John Pettit climbed aboard with his salvage bag bulging. A hundred silver coins, and one gold half sovereign, spilled out. He had located the crevice where Doak had found his silver.

Diving in relays, the team members worked to the maximum their decompression times would allow. Gradually loot piled up. Doak completed the dredging of the crevice and found many silver coins and one more half sovereign with the emblem of St. George and the Dragon as he reached bedrock. The others were bringing up gold and silver money, as well as artifacts, from the wreckage. By the time the *Lady Gwen* set off for the mainland eleven golden half sovereigns, all dated 1902, and several hundred silver coins had been salvaged.

Tarlton, Doak, Pettit, and Gallagher formed the Elingamite Syndicate and returned during the summer of 1967–68. "This time we took explosives," said Tarlton, "and started working on a seam of coins that had been solidified by marine growth and corrosion into a solid reef of money. We hoped that the seam would continue, but after a short distance it thinned and faded out. We had still done quite well—one lump of coins which broke off in one piece weighed 120 pounds! The bulk of the money seemed to be buried under vast quantities of rock and wreckage. Many coins were also scattered loose in the stones of the bottom. We brought up good quantities of money with every dive until the project became uneconomical. We made up to three descents per day apiece, working between 120 and 150 feet. Using our automatic decompression meters, we logged up to twelve hours bottom time without mishap. We returned to New Zealand with another eight thousand coins valued on the souvenir market at about $15,000." After settling with the Northern Assurance Company, the Elingamite Syndicate made up parcels of three different coins, with a leaflet, which are being marketed to collectors at $10 per set. They can be ordered c/o Box 20, Whangarei, New Zealand.

Another salvage attempt was made in January 1969, during which a few more coins were recovered. The ship's bronze propeller was raised and sold for a price sufficient to cover expenses. According to Tarlton, about two-thirds of the *Elingamite*'s money still remains under the wreckage, but a large expedition with heavy equipment will be needed to recover it. The numismatic value of the unsalvaged money could run as high as $100,000. Wade Doak has announced that the syndicate has purchased the wreck. "We have salvaged twelve thousand coins to date," he says. "One and a half tons of silver is estimated to remain in the wreck."

The full story of the salvage is told in Doak's new book, *The Elingamite and Her Treasure*, published in 1969 by Hodder & Stoughton. Treasure and artifacts from the ship are on display at The New Zealand Maritime Museum in Whangarei, of which Tarlton is director.

CHAPTER 24

The Manila Galleons

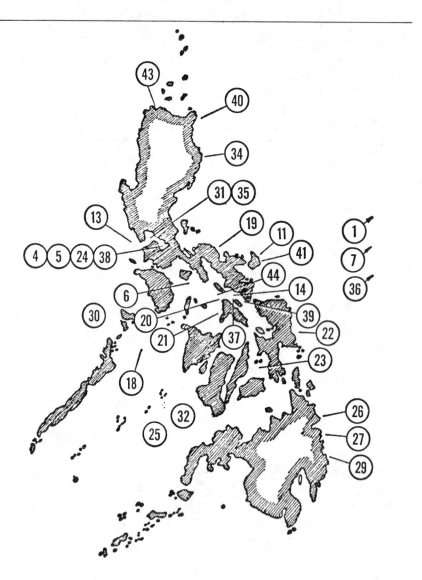

MAP Q

AN OLD WRECK discovered in the Caribbean region is always a gamble. There may be Indies treasure or not, depending on the ship's original lading and the success of earlier salvage attempts. If a diver wants to assure himself of an absolute 100 per cent certainty of a rich salvage, however, there is a way of doing so: find a Manila galleon. Their distintegrating hulls lie spread across the Pacific from California to the China coast. And every one comes with a double-your-money-back guarantee. Shipwreck for shipwreck, with very few exceptions among the *Capitanas*, *Almirantas* and Peru gold transports, none of the Spanish galleons could approach these Pacific giants for volume and richness of cargo. Just as important, the Manila galleons are new, untapped treasure trove. Although most lie off accessible shores within skin-diving depth not one has been salvaged in recent years. In the following pages the approximate sites of most of these lost ships are given for the first time. A little further research can pinpoint many of their positions with considerable accuracy. Their cargoes varied with the direction of their voyage. Whether in golden ornaments, silver dollars or Ming and Ching porcelains, however, they are rich. Almost every Manila galleon stowed durable cargo worth from $500,000 to $3,000,000 in present-day values—guaranteed.

Forty-three years after Magellan's great navigator Juan Sebastián Elcano reported the existence of the "Spice Islands" King Philip II sent a small armada from Chile to explore them. In November 1564 four ships[1] left Natividad and set out toward the west. They passed the "Islas de los Reyes, Caroles, Matalotes, Arricifes, Marianas" and after a fifty-seven-day voyage their crews finally

> . . . saw many islands among which was a larger one and there we went. We met on the coast people who were whiter than our Indians, the women whiter than the men. They were wearing clothes of woven palm and hats of color. Their teeth were red and pierced with holes, and in the holes they wore gold nails. Among them came a person of quality dressed all in silks, carrying a cutlass whose hilt and decorations were of gold and precious stones. We asked them for provisions and gave them trinkets in barter; but they asked for iron . . . and paid with powdered gold.

The Spanish flotilla sounded its way through the Philippine archipelago and anchored in Manila Bay, where the crew established a beachhead which they named San Miguel. From here they set out to take possession

---

[1] The *San Pedro* (500 tons), *San Pablo* (300), *San Juan* (80), and *San Lucas* (40).

of the islands. King Philip had made a wise choice in his first administrator, Miguel López de Legazpe, who became known as "The Pacifier." Had another Cortés or Pizarro made the first contact, the islands' small population of 667,000 would have probably been wiped out and Manila would have never grown into the prosperous trade center known far and wide as "The Pearl of the Orient." As it was, de Legazpe and his missionary counterpart Fray Andres de Urdenata established a humanitarian administration. Under their guidance Cavite soon became the western hub of a vast trading organization with China, Japan, Siam, Indonesia, and India, linked to the East by the Manila galleons.

During the first decade these transports made their American base at Callao, Peru. From here the voyage across was easy, since favoring winds and currents carried them to Manila in two months. The return trip bucked the same elements, however, and often took a full year during which casualties through thirst and disease were appalling. The Pacific pilots soon learned, as their predecessors in the Atlantic had years before, that eastward crossings were more successful in the north latitudes. By 1565 the galleons' route went northeast from Manila and followed the Japan current over the Hawaiian Islands down the Pacific coast of America. The American anchorage was changed to Acapulco. This was a sensible move, for Acapulco lay about halfway between the northern latitude of the return voyage and the equatorial latitude of the westward crossing, and moreover was easy to supply across Mexico. By 1570 it had been developed into a major port with a shipyard and foundry.

There were attempts during these early years to establish a direct Manila-Spain shipping link. Despite its length and dangers, galleons made the voyage under the Cape of Good Hope until 1602, when hostile Dutch colonies along this waterway cut it off. Manila became a dependency of the Viceroyalty of Mexico and all communication and trade with the Far East outpost was carried on the Manila galleons.

The Philippines at first proved disappointing as a country to be exploited. There was little natural wealth except for the gold which was panned in Luzon rivers. For this reason the Manila colony had to be subsidized by the Spanish king. Since Philip was much happier when money was moving his way the islands came close to being abandoned on more than one occasion. When trade got rolling, however, and gold production reached 5,000,000 pesos yearly, the king recouped his investment (by 1690 royal income came to a yearly 400,000 pesos) and he was much happier about the Far East adventure.

Other Spanish interests weren't. In Seville and Cádiz strong anti-Philippine lobbies sprang up and badgered Philip to suppress the Far East commerce. Merchants and manufacturers in Spain and the Americas were being pressed to the wall by a flood of China silks and Indian cotton fabrics which competed with their products. Silver from Mexico was being diverted to China. Even wine exporters from Jerez complained that Filipinos had taught Mexicans to make palm brandy causing greatly reduced exports from Spain. In the face of these protests the king and his successors took the middle road, allowing the trade to continue on a restricted basis. Attempts were made to control it through limitations on cargo shipments. A number of edicts appeared to this effect. The first, in 1593, fixed the number of Pacific ships at six small transports, based three in Manila and three in Acapulco. Every year two from each port would cross the ocean while the third stood by in reserve. The galleons from Acapulco to Manila could carry 300 tons of cargo each; returning, they were limited to 200, with 100 set aside for water and provisions. The maximum value of cargo to the Philippines was first set at 500,000 pesos, then 600,000, while competing cargo from the Far East was limited to a yearly 250,000 pesos.

These restrictions were never enforced and soon relaxed. In the 1600s and 1700s the Manila galleons were the largest ships which Spain had—seagoing monsters of 1200 and even 2000 tons, carrying 40 to 60 cannons and over a thousand people. One, two, and even three sailed from Acapulco in March, reaching Manila in June. After a month there the same ships returned, leaving in July and usually reaching Mexico by January. The round trip took a year. Limits on cargo values were scoffed at. These ships were so heavily laden that at least one sank from overloading as it was leaving port. Both going and coming the yearly cargoes totaled thousands of tons. And ton for ton, few cargoes ever had so much value.

The galleons to Acapulco carried exports from all over the Far East, brought to Manila on Spanish and Chinese trading ships. China products included rich silks and brocades, silk stockings—of which as many as 50,000 pairs a year were sent to Mexico and Peru—tea, gold and porcelain art treasures, carved wood furniture and fruits. The Japanese shipped lacquerware, porcelains and cutlery. Borneo and the South Seas islands supplied cocoa, sago, ceramics, pearls and semiprecious stones. From Siam and Burma came spices, ivory, gold, jade, and amber. India sent gold, ivory and precious stones, calicoes and chintz, perfumes, and musk. And from the Philippines themselves were shipped pearls and precious ornaments made by Chinese goldsmiths in Manila, and gold bullion.

The galleons returning from Acapulco carried goods for barter: wines, dyestuffs, millinery, finished merchandise, and silver—barrels and coffers of silver pesos, millions every year, fresh from the mints of Mexico and Peru. The self-sufficient Chinese of the Ching Dynasty scorned the products of Europe and it was not until years later that the wily English traders found another economic equalizer, opium; so Chinese products were paid for in coin. So many millions of silver dollars went into that nation that as late as 1930 its monetary standard was based on the Mexican peso, called the "Dollar Mex." Consequently the galleons from Acapulco all carried anywhere from 500,000 to 3,000,000 silver pieces of eight, referred to throughout the Orient as "silk money."

Most of the Manila galleons were built at Cavite and in Albay Province in a shipyard at Palantiau, where nearby was a plentiful supply of the best lumber: Philippine mahogany called *luán*, and *molave*. The products of this yard were among the strongest wooden ships ever constructed, with sides of *lanang* wood, nearly impenetrable to cannon shot. Crews and officers were mostly Filipinos, who, unlike the native Americans, were excellent seamen. On the other hand, the captains were invariably figureheads. The governor-general who made appointments to this post, which paid the unusually high salary of 40,000 pesos per year, often gave it to a friend "whom he wished to make happy." Since the voyages were long and dangerous a large part of the success of the Pacific ships was due to the plucky, capable little Filipinos who stood at their helms. But even plucky seamen and strong ships gave no assurance against loss.

In 1576 the *San Juanillo* (1), commanded by Juan de Ribera, sailed from Manila for Acapulco with a cargo of about $750,000 in oriental products, including at least $150,000 in gold. This 300-ton galleon headed east into the San Bernardino Strait and was never heard of again.

In 1583 Captain Alonso Sánchez' trading ship (R-12)[2] was returning from Amoy to Manila, loaded with silks, spices, and gold, when it was wrecked off the southwest coast of Formosa. There is no record of salvage. Four years later, in 1587, another China trader was lost. This was the *patache San Martín* (R-13) broken up on the coast near Canton. Aboard was a fortune in silver money.

Not all losses were from shipwreck. Ever since Sir Francis Drake's devastating run up the Pacific coast of South America other English corsaires had been striving to duplicate his success. And, in 1587, the first of several did. After a moderately profitable ravaging of the Peru coast Thomas Cavendish decided to try intercepting a Manila galleon. He cruised west to the Moluccas then headed north to California where he knew these ships made landfall. He was in luck. On July 2 of that year the *Santa Ana* had left Cavite with a full load of China treasures. For four and a half months this ship butted across the North Pacific, reaching the California coast on November 14 only to find an English warship waiting there. The *Santa Ana*'s crew fought desperately and bravely for five hours against the heavier-armed attacker. When

2 See Map R.

they finally surrendered the decks were cluttered with their dead and wounded and the ship so badly damaged that Cavendish burned it after stripping the cargo. He wasn't too disappointed about losing the prize, for the booty which he had taken off was "more than 700,000 pesos in gold, a big quantity of pearls, 1,500,000 pesos in brocades and other Chinese silks" as well as nearly 600 pounds of musk.

In 1589 two partly loaded Spanish ships (4) (5) sank in Cavite port. Little is recorded of their cargo or whether it was salvaged. The following year the *San Felipe* (6), *Almiranta* of an armada from Acapulco, was wrecked on a reef of Marinduque Island in the Philippines near shore. Her crew got to safety and her cargo, which included over $500,000 in silver, was partly saved. There should still be pesos scattered over the bottom in this area.

Manila, whose economy depended entirely on the success of the galleons' crossings, suffered a depression in 1596 when two big ships were lost. The *Santa Catalina* (7), from Acapulco, disappeared somewhere in the South Pacific. Her wreck will probably never be found, nor the million silver pesos lying over it. And shortly after leaving Manila, headed the other way, the *San Felipe* (R-14) was damaged in a storm. With his ship leaking badly, Captain Matias de Landecho decided to head for the nearest port. This was Tosa, Japan. Diplomatic relations were just being established with Nagasaki at that time, but the local official was not aware of the fact. Tosa natives treated the *San Felipe*'s crew like enemy invaders, killing some of them. After plundering the cargo worth $1,500,000 they left the hulk to sink.

The south China coast claimed two more ships in 1598 when the *Capitana* (R-15) and *Almiranta* (R-16) of Luis Pérez das Mariñas' trading armada were lost off Canton. Aboard both ships were small fortunes.

If 1596 was a depression year in Manila, 1600 was sheer disaster. Two of the Pacific ships, with a combined cargo worth $3,000,000, were lost. The galleon *San Jerónimo* (11)* under Captain Fernando de Castro, had battled storms for four months all the way from Mexico to the edge of the Philippines. Late in June, with Luzon almost in sight, the ship was dashed against the reefs of Catanduanes where it broke up. Captain de Castro and nearly the whole crew were wiped out while 1,500,000 pesos in minted silver sank onto the rocky shoal. This treasure should be there today. Only a month later a second ship was lost. She was the *Santa Margarita* (P-19).[8] After leaving Manila this galleon was blown and battered about the Pacific for eight months by storms, and finally tossed against Carpana Island of the Marianas. There were only fifty survivors, some of whom were killed by the natives, who plundered the sinking hulk of much of her $1,500,000 treasure.

[8] See Map P.

While tempests took their toll, another menace entered the Pacific. Four years earlier, in 1596, the Dutch navigator Cornelis de Houtman had cruised through the "Spice Islands" with a fleet to establish trading relations in that area. Other Dutch warships appeared with more aggressive commanders. Then in early 1600 Admiral Oliver van Noort raided the Peru coast, inflicting damage on Spanish shipping and capturing the *Buen Jesus* (see Chapter 12). Furious over having lost her cargo of gold the Hollander struck out for the Philippines with a squadron led by his flagship *Hope*, arriving late in the year. Off Cavite he surprised the *patache San Antonio* (13). The Spanish put up a brave battle against the superior enemy ships, fighting to the end. When the little *patache* sank most of her crew were wounded or dead. Aboard was probably a small quantity of gold and silver. Van Noort's attack marked the entry of the Dutch in the Far East. During the next decades their powerful fleets of as many as eighty ships drove the Portuguese from their colonies and wedged the Dutch East India Company firmly into Java, Sumatra, the Celebes, Borneo, the Moluccas, Bengal, and Ceylon. The Spanish sent a fleet to Manila in 1601 to protect their own interests and many battles took place over the next years.

The galleon *Santo Tomás* (14) from Acapulco was wrecked on the Catanduanes in 1601. Her crew got ashore with most of the cargo, and very little silver was lost. In 1603 another ship from Acapulco, the *Santa Margarita* (P-20), sank in the Marianas. About 1,500,000 pesos lie in her wreckage today. Later in the same year the *San Antonio* (R-17), *Almiranta* of the Manila to Acapulco flota, floundered at sea off eastern Japan with a valuable lading of gold. All aboard were lost. Still another westbound ship was wrecked during this period. She was the galleon *Concepción* (P-21), returning to Acapulco along the equator with a million-dollar treasure cargo when a storm broke her up on a reef off Guam.

After this period of calamities all went well until 1608. Then the *San Francisco* (R-18)*, carrying the Governor of the Philippines and an unusually rich gold consignment, was wrecked off eastern Kyushu. Most of those aboard escaped, but $2,000,000 in treasure went to the bottom.

Growing pressure from Dutch fleets based in Indonesia was forcing Spain to maintain increasingly large naval forces in the Far East to defend her possessions as well as those of allied Portugal. In 1613 a squadron (18) commanded by Admiral Heredia headed south from Cavite to reinforce Spanish and Portuguese under attack in the Moluccas. As it passed through the Mindoro Canal a typhoon came up. All six war galleons were wrecked or sunk in the passage. Not much later the *Buen Jesús* (19) from Acapulco had to be burned by her crew off eastern Luzon to prevent her silver from being captured. Most of the cargo was destroyed and the pieces of eight sent to the bottom.

The Dutch had learned that returning galleons crossed the Philippine archipelago through the San Bernardino Strait, coming up under the south coast of Luzon. In 1620 a squadron of seven warships under Joris de Spielbergen was stationed here in ambush. It did not have long to wait. The two galleons *Jesús María* (20) and *Santa Ana* (21) entered the trap unsuspecting. When they saw the sails of Spielbergen's ships they believed them to be that of an escort fleet and it was only when they had closed to short range that their officers realized the mistake. A violent battle was fought all day, during which the greatly out-numbered Spaniards held off the Dutch until their ships were battered wreckage and their casualties enormous. Even when the *Jesús María* began to settle into the sea her 460-man crew refused to strike their flag. Late in the afternoon this *Almiranta*, with scarcely any gunners left alive to serve her 24 cannons, sank under the San Bernardino Strait. The *Santa Ana* fought on alone for several hours, until evening, when her exhausted, decimated crew could no longer continue. As dusk fell Captain Pedro Alvarez Piger surrendered. But the galleon was already damaged beyond survival. During the night it sank, taking down cargo, crew, and the Dutch prize crew stationed aboard. About 2,000,000 silver pesos were lost in these two ships.

At the same place, later in the same year, a Dutch squadron indirectly caused the loss of two more ships from Acapulco. The *San Nicolas* (22) and a *patache* (23) entered the strait and ran right into the waiting enemy. Again their captains believed these ships to be friendly until too late to avoid contact. The running battle down the Samar coast lasted all day and the Spanish were still fighting back strongly when under cover of night they broke away and escaped. The *San Nicolas'* captain anchored her in the nearby Bay of Borongán to repair damage. A wind came up. Her mooring ropes parted and she drifted onto rocks near the shore. Her crew got off safely and the silver was carried ashore. A few days later the *patache* was wrecked at Palapag but her crew and cargo were salvaged.

The galleon *Madalena* (24) sank in Cavite harbor in 1631 during a storm. Some cargo and fourteen people were lost. On November 29, 1637, the *Capitana de España* (25), a junk—built on the lines of the Chinese ships and used for interisland trading—was wrecked in the Philippines. Two of her crew were drowned and possibly some gold lost. Then in 1639 came another major loss of the Manila galleon fleet. The *San Ambrosio* (26)* and another ship (27)* from Acapulco were smashed against the coast of Cagayan during a typhoon. One hundred and fifty were drowned and over 2,000,000 silver pesos scattered on the rocks below.

In a move to solidify their position against the Dutch encroachments and to further trade with China and Japan the Spanish established an advance base in Formosa. It was founded in 1626 on Santiago Bay at the north tip of the island and was named Puerto de los Españoles. Here was stationed a garrison to check Dutch advances on Formosa from the nearby Pescadores. In 1639 a Spanish junk (R-19) was en route to this port, carrying silver money for trade and the garrison's payroll, when it floundered in the ocean off the west coast. The silver was too deep to be salvaged.

In 1646 the *San Luis* (29), arriving from Acapulco under the command of General Fernando Lopez Perona, stranded on reefs off the Cagayan coast. Her crew, silver and other cargo were all saved. The *San Francisco Javier* (30), with General Lorenzo de Ugalde aboard, was shipwrecked in the Philippines in 1653 and the *San Diego* (31) sank in Manila Bay in 1654 with no casualties or loss of cargo. Not so lucky were the seamen aboard the warship *Victoria* (32) which floundered in 1660 en route from Manila to Zamboanga with many of her crew drowned.

In 1690 *Nuestra Señora del Pilar* (P-22)** was passing the south tip of Guam on her way from Acapulco to Manila with 1,5000,000 silver pieces of eight in her hold when she struck a coral reef off Cocos Island and filled. The 1000-ton galleon soon settled to the bottom, where her cargo remains today. The *Santo Cristo de Burgos* (34) caught fire east of Luzon in 1693 shortly after leaving Manila with a $1,000,000 treasure of Far East exports. Before any of this could be salvaged the flaming ship settled into the sea. Her gold, pearls, ivory, and gems went down with her. The following year the *San José* (35) was dashed to pieces on Lubang Island off Manila Bay during a typhoon. She carried a full cargo and crew of four hundred men, all of whom drowned. Her hull lies in shallow water. Somewhere in the ballast should be a fortune in precious metal.

In 1705 the *San Francisco Javier* (36) loosed sail and slipped out of Cavite for America, carrying the usual export cargo. She was never heard of again. Over the next few years a widespread revolt in the Philippines failed to affect the galleon trade which continued with no incidents. Relations with Siam grew closer when a Spanish ambassador was received by its king and an exchange of gifts followed. The result was a surge of trade with that rich part of Asia bringing an influx of gold, gems, and ivory for the galleons leaving Manila. Much of this was lost in 1726 when the *Santo Cristo de Burgos* (37) grounded near the shore of Ticao Island in the Philippines a few days after leaving Manila Bay. Although the crew and passengers were saved, the cargo and ship were destroyed by fire. Another interesting treasure, unless shallow water permitted its recovery, lies in the *Santa María Madalena*

(38)*. This large galleon was crammed with cargo until the waterline reached a dangerous level, and still more merchandise was stowed in her upper hold. When she finally set sail in 1734 from Cavite, heading for the outlet to Manila Bay, she capsized and sank a few hundred yards from her anchorage.

Any doubts over the astonishing wealth carried in these Manila galleons can be referred to the salvage from a *patache* (39) which broke up on the reefs of Calantas in the Philippines in 1735. Though scarcely one-fifth the tonnage of the huge galleons, this little ship yielded 1,518,000 pesos—768,000 official and 750,000 private—to salvors before work was finally discontinued, with still more silver below. The 200-ton ship must have been ballasted with coins, for she carried nearly 50 tons of them!

Since Cavendish's capture of the *Santa Ana* in 1587 the English sea raiders had not bothered Manila or her galleon trade. During the eighteenth century they more than made up for this oversight. In 1709 Captain Rogers of the *Duke* took the *Encarnacion* off Mexico. In 1742 Admiral George Anson led a British squadron on a plundering expedition to Santa Catarina Island, off Brazil, then to the Rio Plata, where he took several Spanish ships with some treasure. Rounding the tip of South America he attacked Paita, Peru, capturing there booty estimated at £30,000. His ships had been reduced by now to the *Centurion* and *Gloucester*, which was in such bad condition that he transferred all the loot into the *Centurion*. Then he crossed the Pacific to capture a Manila galleon. He missed the one for which he was searching and went to Macao for careening and supplies. From here Anson headed to the good hunting grounds on the eastern entrance to San Bernardino Strait. The *Nuestra Señora de Covadonga*, fresh from Acapulco, sailed into his arms on June 30, 1743. There was a two-hour battle and the prize was his: "more than 1,5000,000 pesos in silver" plus personal treasures and other cargo. The Spanish ship was sold in Macao and Admiral Anson returned to England in triumph.

The next major galleon loss was due to the bullheadedness of an incompetent captain. In 1750 the *Pilar* (40) started leaking before she had cleared Corregidor in Manila Bay. Passengers and crew begged Captain Ignacio Martinez to return and he was reported to have roared in reply: "To Acapulco or purgatory!" He certainly didn't reach Acapulco. Drowned bodies and debris from the ship drifted in onto the eastern coast of Luzon, indicating that the galleon sank near there. The Catanduanes, off San Bernardino Strait, claimed another ship in 1756. As she reached the Philippines from Acapulco the *Capitana* (41) of Pedro Vertiz sank off this island. All the silver and all but a handful of survivors were lost. This galleon carried probably 2,000,000 silver pesos, but lies in deep water.

The British returned in 1762 and set the whole Spanish Philippine establishment on its ear. A strong force under Admiral Cornish and General Draper captured Manila and Cavite, taking 546,000 silver pesos in loot among other treasures. This done, the men-of-war *Argo* and *Panther* sailed southeast to the hunting ground to seize the expected galleon from Acapulco. They never did intercept it. Instead they captured the *Santísima Trinidad*, which had left Manila several months earlier but had to turn back after a siege of storms. Unaware that the British had occupied Manila this ship was totally unprepared when the English put a shot across her bow. The captain refused to surrender. Instead he and his sailors put up a determined but hopeless fight with the ship's pitifully small armament of five 8-pounders. When they finally gave up it was for the sake of the women among the eight hundred passengers and crew. The *Santissima Trinidad* made a rich prize. The gold, silks, porcelains, and other Far East treasures came to a value of 3,000,000 pesos, half of it registered and the rest contraband. The 2000-ton prize was taken to England where it was sold. Two years later the British withdrew from the Philippines under the terms of the Treaty of Paris.

The Manila galleons resumed their yearly crossings, now under convoy of warships and frigates. This move was effective, for from then onward not one of these vessels was lost through enemy attacks. Shipwrecks continued just the same. On October 29, 1775, the frigate *Nuestra Señora de la Concepción* (P-23) grounded on a reef in the Marianas en route to the Philippines. Her silver was taken off before the ship broke up. Two more ships were lost in 1797. During the night of April 24 the frigate *María* (43) sank in a typhoon off Cape Bojeador with the death of Commander Fernando Quintano, 13 officers and 322 men. There was little of intrinsic value aboard. In October the *San Andrés* (44), commanded by Manuel Lecoraz, was wrecked on the Naranjos shoals near Ticao after leaving Manila for Mexico. The people aboard this galleon were saved, but a part of her valuable cargo could not be taken off in time.

New regulations came into effect. In 1766 King Charles III of Spain allowed direct Manila-Spain sailings once a year. Then in 1786 control of the Manila-Acapulco trade was transferred to the *Compañia de Filipinas*, created for this purpose, which supervised the galleons until 1815 when it was disbanded. Taking the new route authorized to Europe, the transports sailed west across the south China coast, passing near Macao. In 1798 English warships tried to intercept two galleons carrying 4,000,000 pesos in exports here. This time they were unsuccessful and the ships got through.

The *urca Ferroleña* (R-20)** belonging to the *Compañia de Filipinas*, was on her way westward from Manila to Cádiz in 1802 when she struck the Cauchi Reefs one hundred miles up the coast from Hong Kong. Powerful waves smashed her to pieces as the crew tried to swim ashore. One hundred and fifty men managed to scramble up onto the rocks, some badly wounded, while twenty-nine were drowned. Local Chinese villagers pounced on the survivors, robbing them. The Spanish commander Joaquin Zarauz called for help on the "grand Santuc" of Canton, and he responded with clothes, food, and an armed guard to protect the shipwrecked Spaniards until they were picked up later by the English ship *Caromandel*. There was no recorded salvage of the *Ferroleña's* cargo, which makes those Cauchi Reefs a very interesting spot. Some "850,000 pesos in silver and gold" are waiting there for someone who can get a salvage permission from Mao Tse-tung.

A number of other galleon wrecks along the Oregon and California coasts are described in Chapter 26. There were no other important losses in the western Pacific after 1802, although the big ships continued crossing to Mexico and Spain until 1815, when the last of the Manila galleons dropped her anchor. From here on the Philippine commerce was opened to private companies, with the official yearly export limit ludicrously raised to 750,000 pesos. Acapulco lost its monopoly when other American ports—San Blas, Guayaquil, and Callao—were permitted to take part in this trade. In 1837 Manila was thrown open to foreign companies. Silver pesos from Mexico and Peru continued to be imported even after the revolt of Spain's American colonies, until 1898, when a revolution and Admiral George Dewey finally marked the end of Spanish dominion in the Philippines which de Legazpe, "The Pacifier," had established nearly two and a half centuries before.

Visitors to Manila should visit the Museum of the Marine Science and Archaeological Foundation in the Walled City. Here are displayed many recoveries by the active Philippine diving group headed by Pedro "Pete" Lopez, Dr. Gil Ramas, and Lee Del Pan. With Felix Ramos, Tim Sevilla, Serafín Barcelona, and members of the Philippine Sport Divers Association, they have been salvaging wrecks around Luzon. The "BUHATAN WRECK" has produced most of the museum's artifacts, including two of the five anchors. These have 12-foot shanks, iron stocks, and chains which date them after 1820. Other salvage from this site include large black and white ballast rocks, well-preserved wood planking, copper sheathing with square 1-inch copper nails, bronze butterfly hinges, and pottery. Pieces of an iron nameplate, with parts from both ends missing, form the lettering TAUNTO and IVERPOOL, giving a good lead to the name of a Liverpool-registered ship.

The wreck was located by Lopez in May 1967, 100 yards off Nabasagan (meaning "wreck") Point, Barrio Buhatan, Albay. The bow was wedged in coral 40 feet deep while the rest of the ship, estimated 150 feet long, was dispersed over 150 yards to a depth of 90 feet, and largely buried. Air-lifting the overburden exposed a metal keel, ribs, and the rudder assembly. A surprising find at the site was a small anchor of obviously older construction. When the shank was cleaned of coral the date 1649 appeared. The group's researchers feel that this may have come from a second wreck, and suggest as candidates the *SAN ANTO-NIO DE PADUA,* lost in 1679, or *NUESTRA SEÑORA DE LA GUÍA,* which vanished in 1741. A short iron carronade was found in the Sula Channel about one and a half miles east of the Buhatan site.

Lopez' group has recently located two other wrecks with the earmarks of Manila galleons. A 9-foot anchor with spade flukes has been raised from one, fairly deep off Calintaan Island, Bical, which is rumored to have yielded silver coins. The other ship lies under 170 feet of water and is just being investigated.

CHAPTER 25

Asia

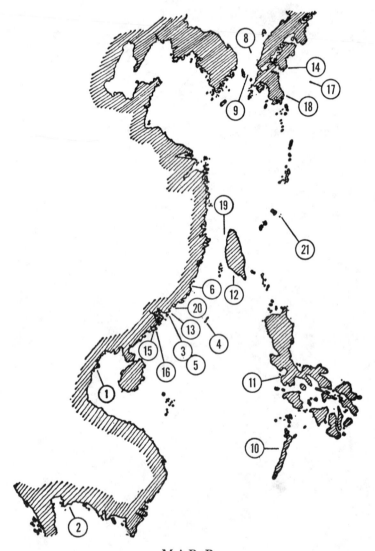

MAP R

The Vietnam Coast

NUESTRA SEÑORA DE LORETO (1)

This was the *Capitana* of an armada commanded by General Francisco de Echeveste which was convoying several merchantmen to Siam in 1719. Somewhere along the coast of Tonkin she struck a reef and sank. The crew was rescued by boats from the other ships but several chests of money were lost.

The Siam Coast

The PORTUGUESE *NAO* (2)

In 1623 a trading vessel of the Portuguese East Indies fleet, under Captain Fernando da Silva, broke up "off the Siamese coast" while bound for Macao. No lives were lost, but a valuable cargo and some gold went to the bottom.

The China Coast

There have been written reports that the following ships were lost off the south China coast with varying quantities of treasure aboard: The American clipper ship *PHANTOM* (3), described as having gone down off Hong Kong in 1862; the German squarerigger *GEORGE SAND* (4), wrecked on Praetus Shoals in 1863; the *NINA* (5), an English steamer lost off Hong Kong in 1873; the *JAPAN* (6), an American steamship wrecked near Swatow in 1875.

The Japan Coast

KUBLAI KHAN'S WAR JUNKS (8)

After defeating the last remnants of China's Sung Dynasty in 1279 Kublai Khan set his eyes on the conquest of Japan and south Asia. In 1274 a war fleet of nearly a hundred junks which he had constructed, carrying soldiers, colonists and some treasure, set off across the Sea of Japan. As they neared the west coast of Honshu a typhoon came up from the south, scattering the fleet and swamping at least a dozen of its junks. This disastrous beginning to his ambitions caused the Mongol to postpone his plans for Japan until they were forgotten, while the Japanese priests attached a religious connotation to the storm, calling it a *kamakaze*—or holy wind—a name that became all too familiar nearly seven hundred years later. In the wreckage of the sunken junks is believed to be some jeweled gold and silver ornaments, and money.

The *ADMIRAL NAKHIMOFF***(?) (9)

The richest of all sunken treasures may well be sealed in the steel hull of a cruiser more than 300 feet beneath the Straits of Korea between Kyushu and Tsushima Island. There is no concrete documentary proof available to support this belief, but enough circumstantial evidence has been assembled to convince some Americans and Japanese to invest in a salvage project.

The *Admiral Nakhimoff* was a light battlecruiser launched in 1887, 333 feet long, displacing 7782 tons, and armored with steel plating from 3 to 10 inches in thickness. After twelve years of service she was overhauled and given new engines and guns, resulting in a new displacement of 8000 tons and a speed of 18 knots. During 1899–1904 she saw service with the Russian Far East fleet, then was ordered to the Libau naval base on the Baltic Sea. On October 15, 1904, with the outbreak of the Russo-Japanese War, she was sent back to the Pacific with a squadron of battleships and other cruisers to reinforce the Czar Nicholas II's Far East position. When the *Admiral Nakhimoff* left European waters she was believed to have carried on board over $50,000,000 in British gold sovereigns. Facts and opinions supporting this were assembled and included in a prospectus issued in 1955 by the Pacific Far East Salvage Company, Inc., which was formed with the primary objective of recovering this treasure. Some quotations from this prospectus are:

> 1. In a report in *The World Almanac for 1950* (on page 287), published by the New York-World-Telegram, the following appears:
>
> "1905—May 28. Russian battle crusier, Admiral Nachimov [Nakhimoff], sank in fight with Japan's fleet in Bay of Tsushima; loss of life unknown. The vessel carried $53,000,000 in gold."
>
> 4. Sidney Tyler stated in his book (*The Japan Russia War*) on page 554, that as a result of the naval battle off Tsushima in May of 1905 "Russia suffered a loss of seventy-five million dollars in gold."
>
> 5. Charles A'Court Repington was the author of *The War in the Far East*. On page 615 of that work he confirms that on May 13, 1904, a Russian loan of 800,000,000 francs (£32,000,000) was issued by the Banque de Paris group . . .
>
> Offered data from Mr. Tanaka Chikashi (former businessman now living in Osaka):
>
> 1. During the Russo-Japanese War, it was reported in the Japanese Army Intelligence Bureau that a Russian ship had sailed from Libau

loaded with gold coins valued at 20,000,000 pounds Sterling. (The late General Fukada, Masataro of the Japanese Army Intelligence Bureau, furnished this information.)

2. When the "Adm. Nakhimoff" sailed eastward from Europe, she took the long way, around the Cape of Good Hope, with the other battle-ships, though her draught was very light. At the battle of Tsushima Straits, although she was one of the best-equipped cruisers of those times, with a speed of 18 knots, she ran away, avoiding engagement in battle. It can be assumed from her strange actions, that she had an important mission.

3. On the morning of May 28, 1905, the "Adm. Nakhimoff" suffered two torpedo hits in the bow, and at 9:30 A.M., sank. Most of the crew had been rescued, but the navigation officer and a brave garrison of men refused to let the boarding party of Japanese officers . . . enter the third deck and stood guard with bayonets at ready.

4. Ninety-nine of the "Adm. Nakhimoff's" crew members landed at Mogi seashore on Tsushima Island. All of them were in possession of English gold currency. The total amount was recorded at 238,000 yen . . . Mr. Takarabe, the head-man of the village, treated them kindly, so they thanked him profusely, and the officers and sailors advised him to retrieve the gold coins some day, explaining through an interpreter, that the "Adm. Nakhimoff" had carried a huge cargo of gold coins.

5. Returning to Russia, Captain Ruitoff of the "Adm. Nakhimoff" offered a memorial to the Throne of Russia. The following sentence was found in his memorial. "I sank the things, which I was bringing to you, with the "Adm. Nakhimoff" in 50 fathoms of sea, and they can never be utilized by the enemy."

6. On two different dates telegrams of similar content were sent to the Japanese Government by Hayashi Gonsuke, Minister Plenipotentiary to France (Oct. 25, 1904). They contained the following information: "When the Baltic Fleet sailed eastward, it was decided that the funds for the restoration of the Russian Far East Fleet would be carried with it. The Russian Government floated loans at Berlin and Paris. At Paris she gathered 700,000,000 francs and at Berlin she gathered 800,000,000 marks. This money was exchanged for British gold coins which have already been loaded aboard ship."

In its descriptions of salvage progress to date, the prospectus states:

Mr. Akiyuki Suzuki, President of the Shintiki Deep Diving Research Institute of Japan, has been conducting salvage operations on the Admiral Nakhimoff since 1938 and has developed a method for salvage . . . at depths below 300 feet. His operations were disrupted in 1944 by the war and he commenced operations again in August 1953 . . .

Effective diving operations commenced during the summer of 1954, and have been concentrated in cutting away the third deck in the after part of the vessel, the first and second decks having been cut away during previous years operations . . . The vessel lies just over 300 feet below the surface at an angle of about 50 degrees to starboard on a generally even longitudinal keel, in open water where fast currents are wont to run . . .

While the two upper decks were of lighter construction made of iron and easier to cut, the third deck is of semi-armoured steel which is very

difficult to cut particularly at these depths. Mr. Suzuki's divers, with
the exception of two helmet divers, are skin divers who wear a mask
with a simple air supply. They remain on the bottom for a maximum of
about four minutes. Most of the demolition is done by planting fairly
small charges of explosives, the size of which has been increased during
the year at the recommendation of the company's observers. Because
of the condition of the vessel the use of large charges of explosives is
precluded. Qualified American divers engaged by the company . . . to
observe and report were impressed with the work being done by the
Japanese divers and with the efforts being made . . .

During the 1954 saeson . . . a passage had been blasted up to about
four feet from the base of the after gun turret . . . It is hoped that the
treasure is located in the magazine situated below the after turret.

The purpose of this prospectus was to raise additional capital besides
the $100,000 which was then being expended in the work. In this
connection it states:

> While the Company would like to conduct the operation with more
> elaborate and efficient equipment including most modern underwater
> cutting gear, the divers with pressure suits experienced in the operation
> of such gear and at such depths, the cost of obtaining such equipment
> and employing such personnel . . . would be prohibitive.

The task of salvaging the *Admiral Nakhimoff*'s gold is staggering.
In addition to the problems of bad weather during most of the year,
strong currents, and the great depth—the only known case where
helmet divers are being used at 300 feet in a treasure salvage—there is
another wicked factor lurking in the vicinity: the cruiser's ammunition,
which could be exploded sympathetically if some of it has remained
intact despite water under great pressure seeping into the cartridges.

The Philippine Coast

The *ANTELOPE* (10)

She was a packet boat of the British East India Company, returning
from Macao with a valuable cargo of silks, and possibly gold and
silver payments for opium. Somewhere off the western shores of Pala-
wan Island the *Antelope* was wrecked with the loss of all her cargo,
valued at over $100,000. None was known to have been salvaged.

The TREASURE OF CORREGIDOR (11)*

One of the last accomplishments of our American forces holding
out on Corregidor in the spring of 1942 was to save the Philippine
national treasury from the Japanese invaders. Right after Pearl Harbor,
before Manila fell, all of the movable wealth from its banks was sent
to the temporary security of subterranean vaults cut deep under this

island fortress in Manila Bay. Early in February the treasury's gold—6½ tons of ingots—was removed from the vaults and shipped to America aboard the submarine U.S.S. *Trout*. Then as conditions worsened hundreds of millions of pesos in paper currency were burned. The great bulk of the national treasure was in silver pesos, however, which could be neither shipped out from the isolated "rock" or burned. To prevent the enemy from capturing this Major General George F. Moore, Harbor Commander, decided to dump it in the deepest part of the bay to which his boats had access. The site selected was south of Corregidor, about halfway to Caballo Island, where the bottom fell away to 110 feet.

During the last week of April 1942, the minelayer *Harrison* made six trips to this point under cover of darkness, in greatest secrecy, during which her crew jettisoned 2632 heavy wood boxes. Each contained 6000 silver pesos nearly as large as a dollar and worth $0.61. When the *Harrison*'s mission was completed 325 tons of silver—15,792,-000 pesos worth $9,633,000—lay under Manila Bay in a place known exactly to only three officers.

Despite all precautions the Japanese managed to learn the location of the dumping ground and were soon hard at work trying to salvage the silver. For divers they used Filipinos and American prisoners of war, who, while giving the outward appearance of co-operating in the task, were really doing everything possible to sabotage it. So effective was their hindrance that by the end of 1942, when the Japanese gave up the attempt, only 2,240,000 pesos had been recovered.

Soon after V-J Day a mysterious group of Americans made an attempt to steal the sunken treasure, working illegally from a small boat. While no one except themselves knows how much they took, the best estimate is less than 500,000 pesos. U. S. Army and Navy crews were assigned to recover the silver in June 1945. During this year and 1946 divers operating from the *Teak* and her replacement the *Elder* raised 5,383,173 pesos. Throughout their work they noticed evidence of the terrible tension under which the *Harrison*'s crew carried out the jettisoning. On their nightly dashes through Japanese-controlled waters the sailors had begun dumping cases long before they reached their marks with the result that instead of being assembled in one spot, the silver was distributed along trails leading from near Corregidor to the general dumping area which itself covered some 250,000 square yards. With boxes scattered over such a widespread zone, most of the divers' time was spent searching. Luckily submarine visibility was excellent, and usually not too long after one pile of boxes was salvaged another came into view. Many were broken open with their contents spilling out and buried in the mud, often stuck together in blackened lumps of coins. To facilitate gathering these up, an air lift was tried, but it was not powerful enough to raise metal disks 100 feet to the surface, so the divers resumed their laborious work of filling buckets by hand.

In 1946 the Philippine government acquired jurisdiction over the sunken pesos. From that year on the salvage was undertaken by a number of private companies under contracts whereby they received from 10 to 35 per cent of their recoveries. Three of these were American groups, all successful, who raised between them over 4,000,000 pesos. In all 6,492,707 coins were turned in by the private salvors by the end of 1956.

Of the original 15,792,000 pesos jettisoned under Manila Bay, 2,240,000 were taken by the Japanese, less than 500,000 by the American salvage pirates, 5,383,173 by Army-Navy divers and 6,492,707 by private companies, for a total of less than 14,615,880 recovered. At least 1,176,000 pesos are still under the bay in the general area between Corregidor and Caballo islands. These coins are blackened by chemical action, but retain their value of $0.61 each. Many are still packed in their rotted boxes, having never been discovered; others are scattered about areas where salvage has been made, many buried in mud which varies in consistency from soft silt to hard clay. The general area of the main dumping ground has been searched so frequently that most of the unsalvaged money should be in deposits as much as half a mile distant, easily visible upon the mud surface.

At least $717,000 in pesos remain unsalvaged. Under favorable terms they should make good hunting for SCUBA divers covering the bottom in a search pattern, using submarine metal detectors over areas where broken boxes lie. Aided by the good visibility, a team of five divers should be able to cover a square mile of bottom in a few months with individual dives limited to one hour per day, including decompression time. The profit from such an operation could reach $100,000.

The Ryukyu Islands

The MIYAKO ISLAND WRECK (21)

Miyako Islanders of the Yaeyama group near Okinawa have records of a large foreign ship which sank near their shore about two hundred years ago. Two local divers are now searching for this wreck. A silver candelabrum and a large flag, believed salvaged from this likely Manila galleon, are on nearby Ishigaki Island in the Miyara Dunchi Palace. The wood of part of the structure itself is said to have come from the sinking ship.

CHAPTER 26

North America—West Coast

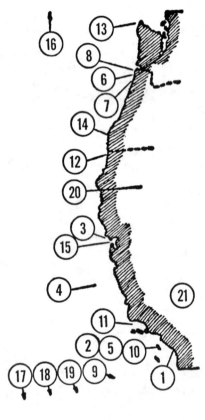

MAP S

The *TRINIDAD* (1)*

It could only be appropriate that the first western ship to visit "The Golden State," California, carried treasure. That is exactly what happened. At the end of August 1540, a tiny unmanned caravel was torn loose from her mooring off San Luis Rey by a gale and blown down the California coast to her destruction somewhere off Point La Jolla. The last three men to leave her had sailed away several days earlier in a longboat, headed for Mexico. They reached Acapulco safely where one of them, Pablo Salvador Hernandez, penned an account of the caravel's voyage up to the time he saw her last. This found its way to the Archives of Seville where it lay, forgotten, for four centuries. Then in 1951 an American historian, Dr. J. J. Markey, unearthed its yellow pages, translated them, and fitted Pablo's report into the amazing pattern of other records patiently tracked down in archives at Madrid, Vienna, and Mexico City in an immense research program by the San Luis Rey Historical Society lasting twenty years and costing $150,000. The result was a correction in early American history—and a saga of plunder, bloodshed, treachery, and treasure lost to the sea. . . .

The infamous conquistador Hernán Cortés, subduer of Mexico, was in trouble. He had plundered the land of all its Aztec wealth and his shipments of gold and jewels to the Spanish King were dwindling. The king, and his new Mexican Viceroy, ambitious and jealous Antonio de Mendoza, suspected that Cortés was still capturing treasures and holding out on their delivery. To redeem his falling prestige Cortés was desperately searching for more cities to conquer, when, in 1536, the answer to his hopes turned up in the form of a ragged straggler from the north. His name was Cabeza de Vaca—"Cowhead"—and he told a tale which only a man who had himself looked upon Aztec loot would believe.

Cabeza le Vaca had been shipwrecked on the west Florida coast in 1528, and had spent the six interim years wandering through the continent trying to find his way back to Mexican civilization. Somewhere in the area of the present Texas, he said, Indians had told him of incredibly rich cities to the north, called the Seven Cities of Cibola, whose streets were paved with gold. Cortés began preparations to lead his little band of four hundred avaricious soldiers of fortune to conquer them when orders from Mendoza—who had also heard the story—halted him. The Viceroy had selected his favorite, Francisco Coronado, to do the job. Embittered Cortés chafed at the bit while Coronado, then De Soto, led expeditions to futile searches for the treasure cities. Then, in 1539 at his base in western Mexico, he could restrain himself no longer. He decided to flaunt the Viceroy's ban and capture the "Seven Pearls." Where others had failed by land he would succeed by sea. Somewhere up the unexplored western coast of America, he felt sure, was a navigable waterway along which small ships could travel inland. He had three suitable ones at Acapulco: the *Santo Tomás,* the *Santa Agueda,* and the *Trinidad.* Early in 1539 he sent them north under the command of his trusted lieutenant, Francisco de Ulloa.

Those were days of the really big double-cross on the road to wealth and power. No sooner had the small squadron got under way than Ulloa put into effect plans to take the expected loot for himself. Off the Mexican coastal city of Caliacan he scuttled the *Santo Tomás* which carried a crew loyal only to Cortés. The two remaining ships sailed on, charting Lower California and its gulf, which they named the Sea of Cortés, and determining for the first time that the land was a peninsula and not, as previously thought, an island. When they reached the island of Cedros, Ulloa packed the remaining pro-Cortés men from both ships into the *Santa Agueda* and sent them back to Acapulco. With twenty-four hard-bitten followers loyal to him, he continued north in the 35-ton *Trinidad.*

Aboard the caravel was a fortune in gold and silver. Nearly all Ulloa's followers were riffraff of the nobilities of Spain, Portugal, and Italy, driven permanently from Europe years before because of troubles with the Church, or gambling, or angry husbands and fathers. When they had set off for the New World they took all the money they possessed since they had no hope of ever returning. During years of looting Mexico they had added to this wealth treasures sacked from the Indians. Each soldier of fortune had acquired one or more native mistresses who followed her man westward carrying his loot. All of this was aboard when the Trinidad set out from Acapulco.

Ulloa put in at the mouth of the San Luis Rey River on June 30, 1540, hoping that he had found the inland passage. Unsatisfied, he continued north up the coast as far as Santa Barbara looking for a better river, then returned to his first landfall and anchored. On August 21, all but three of the *Trinidad's* crew went ashore, taking some of their wealth, and marched inland. They established camp near a group of native Indian settlements where the Spaniards tried to learn about the Seven Cities. The Indians were peaceful, but incredibly dirty. Their bodies crawled with vermin and they lived in filth. Within three days Ulloa's party had contracted a deadly form of dysentery which so debilitated them that they were soon scarcely able to even crawl. By the end of a week they realized that the sickness came from the natives' filth and set off for the safety of their ship. They were too weak to carry the treasure they had brought, so they buried it near the Indian settlements. A six-day storm pinned them down in caves and when they finally reached the beach the *Trinidad* was gone. During the interim since the three caretakers had abandoned her she had been wrecked. With nothing better to do, Ulloa's party returned to their camp. Here they died, one by one, burying each other among the rocks of an abandoned native fort.

Pablo Salvador's account described the death throes of the shore party, and the approximate location where Ulloa and his followers, and that part of the treasure which they had carried ashore, were buried. By meticulously tracking its clues Dr. Markey and his associates have recently unearthed the skulls and bones of Ulloa and his men, and a cache of European money. Referring to it, Dr. Markey says, "We have recovered 2000 coins of a vintage extending from 1500 back to Roman coins pressed out 2000 years ago. These have been identified by experts. This collection which we have has been estimated as being worth a quarter of a million dollars. The bulk of the treasure brought up the coast by Ulloa may be worth anywhere from four to six million dollars . . ."

It should lie in the wreckage of the *Trinidad*, for which the San Luis Rey Historical Society has been searching with the aid of 150 volunteer skin divers. As to why Dr. Markey believes that the ship drifted south, he explains, "During the month of September on three successive years we floated rafts ballasted with concrete and iron from the point where the ship was anchored, permitting them to drift freely. All three, weighing about 35 tons each—the same as the *Trinidad*—drifted south and floundered near Point La Jolla." It is here, at a depth of 40 feet and 200 feet from shore, that a capable and attractive young oceanographer was reported a few years ago to have found eight Roman coins similar to those unearthed ashore. Using powered sea scooters, she methodically explores a grid search pattern on the sea bed. Both she and Dr. Markey are confident that one of these days she will put skeptics to shame by finding the remains of the *Trinidad*.

The *SANTA MARTA* (2)

In 1582 one of the earliest Manila galleons, after a rough four-month crossing of the Pacific, ran aground on Santa Catalina Island. Before she broke up her crew and passengers escaped ashore. Some of her cargo was also saved, while the remainder, probably two hundred tons of Far East treasures, went down with her shattered hull. There is no record of it being recovered although it is quite possible that since the location was known to survivors a Spanish salvage expedition was

sent from Acapulco the following year. What remains could be worth
anywhere from a few thousand dollars to half a million.

The SAN AGUSTÍN (3)*

Returning from Manila in 1599, en route to Acapulco, Captain Sebastián Carmenon anchored his galleon *San Agustín* off an interesting
part of the California coast. The year before he had received the new
orders from the *Casa de Contratación* requiring captains and navigators
of the Manila ships to chart the areas through which they sailed, and
here, reaching far inland, was a huge bay that might connect with
a navigable river. To find out he ordered most of the ship's crew ashore
to build a shallow-draft boat suitable for exploring its inlets and streams.
Only a skeleton crew was left aboard when the sou'wester struck.
The *San Agustín* was caught in the grip of rising wind and waves
and dragged anchor. Before any of the shore complement could attempt
returning to the ship it smashed onto reefs off Point Reyes and sank.
Most of those caught on board and all of her cargo were lost.

Captain Carmenon and the shore crew completed their boat in which
they returned to Acapulco with news of the galleon's fate and the
impressive new waterway which they named San Francisco Bay to
commemorate the saint's day on which it was discovered. Their
report interested the authorities there, and at the end of the year
a mapping expedition was authorized to return to the site to try to
salvage some of *San Agustín*'s valuable Manila cargo and to accurately
chart the area. The new bay seemed just what was wanted for a port
north of Acapulco. During 1602 the exploratory flotilla of two caravels,
the *San Diego* and *Santo Tomás*, a frigate *Los Tres Reyes* and a launch
for river navigation mapped the coast from Cape San Lucas to Cape
Blanco. It anchored off another natural harbor and founded a colony
which was named after the *San Diego* in December. Then it headed
north to San Francisco. Here another colony was put ashore. The
wreckage of the galleon *San Agustín* was sighted underwater and some
salvage was carried out, but by then two years of storms had dispersed
the galleon's hull and most of her treasure was unrecoverable with
available diving equipment. It lies today around a reef off Point Reyes,
just north of San Francisco Bay—about a half million dollars of worked
gold and silver, gems, ivory, porcelains, and precious woods.

The CAPITANA (4)

This Spanish galleon is suspected to have sunk somewhere along
the California coast, for her captain, General Juan de Velasco, was
headed there when last seen. The *Capitana* had been voyaging in the
South Seas on a trading and exploratory mission. There was probably

valuable cargo and silver money aboard when she disappeared with all hands in 1600.

The *NUESTRA SEÑORA DE AYUDA* (5)

Returning from Manila with a rich cargo, this 230-ton galleon struck a rock west of Santa Catalina Island and sank in 1641. Some of her crew made their way ashore to safety but the Far East treasure and merchandise which she carried was not recovered. It is there somewhere, strewn over patches of stone ballast on a shallow reef. Its nonperishable portion is worth about $500,000.

The NEHALEM WRECK (6)

Years ago beachcombers of the Oregon coast came across unusual chunks of stuff partly buried in sand about 200 yards from the mouth of the Nehalem River. On examination it was found to be beeswax in pieces weighing from 10 to 200 pounds. Some carried the inscription "J.H.S." on one side, recognized as the abbreviation for "Jesus Hominum Salvador"—an indication that it was the property of the Roman Catholic Church. One of these chunks, now in the Pioneer Museum at Tillamook, carries the date 1679. The explanation as to how the wax got there was provided in 1900 when an Astoria resident found ship's wood buried in the sand. Recently after storms changed the shape of Nehalem spit new wreckage, identified as teakwood, was uncovered. It is known that Philippine beeswax was sent to Mexico on Manila galleons for making tapers, and that teak was used in the construction of these ships. Possibly one broke up off the coast, blown north of her course by a storm, and the light wax and wood drifted ashore.

The TREASURE COVE WRECK (7)

An old Oregon legend tells of a mysterious "treasure chest" carried ashore in a boat hundreds of years ago from an anchored Spanish galleon, and buried in the southwest slope of Mount Neah-Kah-Nie. There are variations of this tale, one being that the unknown ship sank. A few years ago there was a report that a wreck had been located in deep water off the foot of the mountain. Who knows? There may be some truth to that old legend.

The CLATSOP BEACH WRECK (8)

When early explorers reached the mouth of the Columbia River they were surprised to find the Clatsop Indians wearing ornaments made from Chinese coins. Some members of the tribe were seen to have fair hair. When the Indians were questioned, they told of stories that a ship was wrecked against the Clatsop coast years earlier. There were five survivors who lived with the tribe for several years, then walked away up the river. A few years ago some of the Chinese coins were reported to have been examined and found to be dated from 1614 to 1796. If this is true, the combination of oriental money and fair-haired descendants point only to a Manila galleon. Although research has not identified a loss in the immediate post-1796 period, a wreck may lie off the coast.

The CORTEZ BANK GALLEON (9)

There are several published accounts that a Spanish galleon, carrying some gold, sank at the outer point of Cortez Bank in 1717. This ship was reported to have struck a 15-foot-deep shoal now called Bishop Rock—after the clipper *Bishop*, which went down there in 1855.

The *SAN SEBASTIÁN* (10)*

She was possibly a Manila galleon, heading down toward Acapulco through the outer Santa Barbara Channel on January 7, 1754, when the English pirate George Compton attacked. Her captain tried to escape the shots of the closing enemy ship but only succeeded in running the *San Sebastián* aground on a rock fang a short distance from Santa Catalina Island. The galleon sank quickly. Twenty-one of her crew and passengers were all that were able to reach shore, where they were killed in various unpleasant ways by the cutthroats. The broken ship lies off the west shore of Catalina in about 170 feet of water, undoubtedly buried deep under shifting sands. On her ballast should be a valuable cargo from the Orient.

The *YANKEE BLADE* (11)**

During the twenty years between 1849 and 1869 an estimated $300,000,000 in California gold was sent east overland or by sea. A tiny fraction of this lies in the Pacific Ocean off Southern California in the wreckage of the American steamer *Yankee Blade*. Under command of Captain Harry Randell, this paddle wheeler set off from San Francisco at 4 P.M. on September 30, 1854. She carried eight hundred passengers and a cargo of gold specie shipped by Page, Bacon & Company worth $153,000 at that date, and insured. No sooner had the ship reached open ocean than she entered a dense fog. Twenty-four hours later, still advancing rapidly with her paddles turning at thirteen revolutions, the *Yankee Blade* struck violently and slid forward along a sharp rock which opened a seam in her bottom a foot wide and 30 feet long. She started to fill immediately. Captain Randell soon saw that she was doomed. He and the purser set about saving the passengers and their valuables.

During the night the sea rose. The stern broke and settled and the foremast crashed down through the keel. The passengers, many drunk, spent the night on the half-sunken ship. The next day they were picked up by a passing steamer, the *Goliath*, and delivered to San Diego. Two days later the *Yankee Blade* had disappeared beneath the sea. Within a week the only recorded salvage attempt got under way, with the diver-equipped tug *Carolina* steaming to the site. Efforts to raise the gold were not successful.

It remains there still, increased in value through depreciation of the dollar to approximately $275,000 all neatly packed in a heavy steel vault at a relatively shallow depth on the north side of the Point Arguello Reef, one and a half miles from shore. Bill Wood was quoted in a newspaper story as having found the wreck in 1948, but no salvage was attempted. More recently a syndicate composed of Lawrence Thomas, Ernest Porter, and Dean Tyler, working from their salvage boat *Hornet*, was reported to have located the *Yankee Blade* and to be making plans to recover her long-sought treasure cargo.

The BROTHER JONATHAN (12)*

This 220-foot, 1359-ton wooden steamer, owned by the California Steam Navigation Company, sailed from San Francisco headed north for Victoria in July 1865. Captain Samuel de Wolfe protested that the ship was overloaded, but the company agent overruled the objection. Two days out, on July 28, the side-wheeler was forced by strong gales onto Northwest Seal Rock, a part of St. George's Reef off Crescent City. She hung onto the rocks, battered by waves, until the heel of her foremast broke through the bottom. She went down immediately with 166 people drowned. In her safe was about $250,000 in gold and paper money—a payroll for U. S. Army troops—and possibly another consignment of gold for Canada.

This ship, with her location so well known, has been the target of several treasure hunts. Because of the deep water surrounding St. George's Reef no report of success appeared until April 1969, when Crescent City SCUBA diver Donald N. Short announced that he had found the wreck two years earlier with metal-detecting equipment. He described the ship as split into two parts and nearly entirely buried under sand, about one and a half miles offshore, at a depth exceeding 75 feet. With a two-year lease on the site, Short said that he had interested financiers in the salvage.

The PACIFIC (13)

To treasure hunters this is not an interesting wreck, because of her depth and the uncertainty of her position. The *Pacific* was an 875-ton American paddle wheeler with three masts. She collided on the night of November 4, 1875, with the *Orpheus* and sank immediately somewhere off Cape Flattery. Of the 277 people aboard, 2 survived while many of the remainder were washed up along the Washington coast for weeks afterward. In her strongbox was $79,220—most in paper currency, some in gold coin. Her general cargo included 280 tons of coal, 2000 sacks of oats, 261 hides, and 2 cases of opium.

The *SUNSHINE* (14)

The loss of this American schooner led to tales that her precious cargo —one keg of gold—was buried near the Oregon port of Coos Bay. In fact, the *Sunshine* did carry a keg of gold coins, but this probably fell out into the Pacific, a few miles offshore, when she capsized in a sudden gale. Her hull drifted in against North Beach Peninsula minus much of its cargo.

The *H. J. CORCORAN* (15)

On February 14, 1912, two iron steamships collided in San Francisco Bay and sank. One was the *H. J. Corcoran,* carrying a full cargo of sugar and gold bullion variously estimated as being worth from $96,000 to half a million. The most reliable reports state that there was gold aboard, but not in excess of $30,000. Records of salvage attempts, beginning in May 1913, were not studied. There is a good chance that both ships were raised.

The *ISLANDER* (16)

During the years 1897 to 1904 nearly $100,000,000 in Yukon gold was shipped out of Alaska down the West Coast. When the English steamship *Islander* left Juneau in August 1901, an estimated $3,000,000 in nuggets and dust was aboard. Her captain conned his ship carefully through the narrow fjord-like passage toward the sea, but he was scarcely an hour out of port when she struck either ice or a submerged rock and sank in deep water in Steven's Passage, Alaska.

Salvage groups came and went during the next decades, their divers descending to great depths in freezing water in attempts to regain the lost treasure. A web of conflicting tales surrounds these efforts and it is difficult to separate fact from fantasy. In 1928 several hundred cases of Scotch whiskey, which the ship was bringing from the British Isles, were apparently recovered, as well as some of the belongings of returning miners who drowned. Three years later a Portland, Oregon, company made an unsuccessful try, and the following year, in 1932, another salvage organization is reported to have raised the entire ship from 365 feet below and lifted her to shallow water! Divers in hard hat gear were then said to have searched the wreck thoroughly and recovered more whiskey and a camera that still worked, but no gold. This gave rise to a theory in the ship's raising she spilled out most of her cargo.

It is hard to believe that the *Islander* was ever raised at all, and still more incredible that precious gold would have been stored on a comparatively modern steamer in a place where it could have "spilled out." Before anyone tries to crack this tough nut it would be advisable to make a very careful study of what actually was done in those salvage attempts.

The *GOLDEN GATE* (17)
This American ship can hardly be called an attractive target. The *Golden Gate* was rumored to be carrying a shipment of California gold valued at several hundred thousand dollars when she caught fire off the Mexican coast. Her captain ran her aground near Manzanillo and the passengers and crew escaped. There were salvage attempts immediately, of course, and most of her unburned cargo was saved. There was no mention of precious metal in the recovery which only confirms that probably the only gold in this one was in her name.

The *GOLDEN CITY* (18)
She was another American vessel said to be down to her Plimsoll mark under the weight of California gold in her strongroom. Somewhere west of Lower California she sank to the bottom.
Same comment.

The *COLUMBIA* (19)
This modern American steamship sank in a depth of 60 feet off Point Tasco, Mexico, in September 1931, with an announced $200,000 in gold aboard. Not much later divers working for the salvage firm, Merritt-Chapman & Scott Corp., entered the hull and removed $190,000. When they left they said that the ship was already broken open by waves when they reached her, and that they had to search all over the wreckage for the contents of the strongroom.

The *WINFIELD SCOTT* (21)
Some two hundred passengers from San Francisco were aboard this side-wheeler when she sailed for Panama in 1852. On the night of December 2, maneuvering through fog, she sank after striking a rock near Anacapa Island just east of Santa Cruz. No major gold consignment was known to have been loaded aboard, but there was yellow metal in the passengers' lost baggage. This was confirmed in 1965 by Glenn E. Miller, whose boat *Emerald* took a party of divers to the site. One of them, Ed Larralade, told Miller of a wreck he had just seen on the bottom when he returned from a dive. It was unusual because of a large spoked wheel standing upright, amid wreckage, on the rock and sand bottom. An article in *The Skin Diver* describes how the salvage came about.
Miller began his research on the unknown wreck at the Santa Barbara

County Historical Society, where he learned the ship's name and history. Then he teamed up with an old friend, Jim Gurdy, who was in town with a 6-inch gold dredge with which he had been working river gold. The two men visited Anacapa Island aboard the *Emerald* and Miller went down and worked the sand pockets around the wreckage. A second wheel was discovered on the far side of the rock which the *Winfield Scott* had struck. The sea floor was strewn with parts of machinery, brass, iron and lead fittings and pipes, a champagne bottle, and even a spittoon. The powerful dredge sucked overburden from one depression after another in the vicinity of the wreckage. On the bottom of these potholes were metal artifacts. Picking up a shiny yellow shapeless mass, Miller realized that it was a gold nugget, with veins of quartz. He soon found another. When the dredge's riffle box was emptied on deck later, several more small nuggets were found among the contents. Miller's venture into deep sea river gold dredging—probably the first such endeavor in history—was successful. There are probably more nuggets and pockets of gold dust still lying in crevices around the wreck.

RIVER GOLD (20)

What started some twenty-five years ago as a weekend sport has become a full-time business for hundreds of underwater gold miners from California Mother Lode country to the Yukon. For a detailed article on underwater placer gold, with maps, see pages 80–91 of *Treasure . . . How and Where to Find It* by Nesmith and Potter.

The *YUKON* (22)

This 5746-ton steamship left Seward, Alaska, in February 1946 with 497 passengers and 350 pounds of gold in 25-pound bars stored in the mail room. Just forty miles south, in the snowstorm, she ran aground against the rock coast of Cape Fairfield. Tremendous waves battered the steel hull but the following day all but three of those aboard reached safety. Within a few months the violent seas had started breaking up the hull, which gradually vanished into the ocean. Salvage attempts were started in 1946 by George Giardina, a local helmet diver, and again in 1955. In each case the seas were too rough. In the early 1960s two SCUBA veterans, Dick Anderson and Bill Hogan, were flown to the site by a pilot. They were joined by Giardina. Wearing their SCUBA gear, Anderson and Hogan launched a rubber raft and were able to get out far enough to make several dives. The water temperature was just over freezing and visibility varied from 2 to 10 feet.

They found the ship completely disintegrated after twenty years of hammering by waves. Parts of the twisted wreckage covered the rock and sand bottom from an inshore depth of 20 feet to a 60-foot-deep ledge farther out, where an undersea cliff fell away into deeper water.

Hanging out over this ledge were huge propellers on the ends of their massive shafts. From here, inshore to two big rusted boilers on the rocky underwater beach, the floor was a mass of twisted steel plates and girders, copper tubes from the condensers, and brass, copper, iron, and lead fittings and ship's parts of all types. Anderson recovered a brass key with the mark "Stateroom ✕ 19" still legible.

During five days' diving many artifacts were raised from the wreckage. Although every crevice was carefully searched for the golden ingots, not one was found. A single silver dollar, chipped loose from its encrustation of sand, was the total treasure find. Somewhere in that labyrinth of jagged metal and rock, blasted continuously by turbulent seas, lie those fourteen gold ingots worth about $14,000.

CHAPTER 27

North America—East Coast

The Canadian Coast

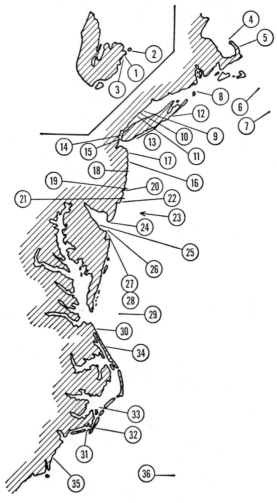

MAP T. North America—East Coast.

LE CHAMEAU (1)

In the stormy pre-dawn darkness of August 26, 1725, after a six-week crossing of the Atlantic, this 600-ton French transport was dashed to pieces on a reef near the coast of Cape Breton. All 316 of her crew and passengers were drowned. Lost in the shattered wreckage was a payroll for French troops in Canada with a value of 82,010 livres in gold and silver coins of King Louis XV's treasury.

Until only a few years ago the value of Le Chameau's treasure was doubted by skeptics. Then, in a blaze of publicity in April 1966, news of one of the great treasure finds of recent time focused the attention of numismatists, underwater archaeologists, and treasure hunters alike on Louisbourg—and the team of three determined and capable young salvage men who had converted the skeptics into believers.

The account of the location and salvage of Le Chameau's treasure is detailed in Canada's Treasure Hunt, by Alex Storm as told to Brian Shaw, published in 1967. This should be required reading for anyone considering the salvage of a wooden wreck in shallow water. For the following pages I am indebted to this book and supplementary information supplied by Alex Storm.

When he immigrated to Canada in 1959, Storm was fully qualified to be a treasure diver. His background was salted with diving adventures throughout the world, including the discovery of an ancient wreck off Ceylon in 1956. It was inevitable. that once he heard the tale of Le Chameau, after settling in Louisbourg in 1960, Storm would be drawn to the wreck.

While questioning Cape Breton fishermen for local information, he undertook a research into documented history. Before long he had two important pieces of information: confirmation of the ship's treasure cargo from the Musée de la Marine in Paris; and the fact that a reef top situated some 4200 feet off the southeast tip of Cape Breton was named Chameau Rock. Accounts of salvage attempts revealed that only one, carried out a year after the disaster, had been at all successful. Using primitive diving equipment its crew had located most of the ship's wreckage and light cargo; but only about 6000 livres of the treasure were recovered—most of which was picked up along the coast. Le Chameau was then forgotten until the early 1900s when several attempts were made with no recorded success. Even allowing for another 6000 livres in unrecorded recoveries, there still remained 70,000 livres more in coins somewhere under the sea.

By May 1961 Alex Storm had acquired an Aqua Lung and equipment. Test dives made it obvious that salvage would not be easy. The water temperature was close to freezing; visibility, occasionally good, could close to a few feet; currents were strong; the weather was chronically stormy and frequent fogs made navigation through reefs hazardous.

But the elements were friendly on July 15, 1961, when Storm visited Chameau Rock aboard a trawler skippered by Manuel Sequeira. While searching the shallow reef top through a water glass, Sequeira sighted several cannons. Storm dived and confirmed that they were iron, and very old. Four days later he salvaged one 8-pounder, along with two brass cannon breeches and scattered cannon balls. The cannon's low trunnions dated them as older than 1760. Heavy oxidation had obliterated any markings. Storm made a diving reconnaissance down the reef. At 45 feet he found a mound of encrusted cannon balls in which a small metallic object caught his attention. He pried it loose from the rust. After cleaning it on deck, Alex Storm looked at his first piece of *Le Chameau*'s treasure—a 1724 Louis XV silver livre, in good condition. The iron had protected it.

Storm was able to make only five more dives that year. He salvaged cannons, silver spoons, bronze sword hilts, shards of pottery and glass, cannon balls (some still attached to patches of their burlap bags in good condition), lead musket balls, and partridge shot, but no more coins.

It was not until 1965 that the next phase of salvage got under way. During the interval Storm extended his researches. From the director of the Musée de la Marine he received the plans of the ship and its statistics: length, 133 feet; breadth, 32; draft, 16; armament, 20 eight-pounders, 22 six-pounders, and 6 four-pounders. From sketchy histories and his own observations Storm concluded that *Le Chameau* had struck the eastern side of the rock, splitting her bow. The Chameau Rock cannons had gone overboard with the impact. Battered along the reef by waves, the damaged hull had broken into sections. From the first salvage report Storm reconstructed the ship's disintegration and accounted for the final grounding against the shore of every piece of the hull except the lower after section of the hold. Heavily laden with ballast, cannons and shot, and treasure, this had sunk before reaching the coast. Storm calculated the direction of its drift as west-northwest.

To obtain legal rights to the treasure he applied for a salvage license under Nova Scotia's Treasure Trove Act. On February 1, 1965, Alex Storm was granted a three-year permit "to search for treasure trove over a certain area of land underwater off the Island of Cape Breton and to recover and to retain any treasure trove found therein by him upon payment to the Provincial Secretary of a royalty thereon at a rate of ten percent of the value thereof."

Two friends, Harvey MacLeod and Dave MacEachern, had joined the venture. Together they converted an old lobster boat, the *Marilyn B II*, into a cantankerous but serviceable salvage craft. Work started in June 1965. To ensure that no part of the sea floor was overlooked in visual search, a long grid pattern was laid down over the rocks and sand patches from 30 to 70 feet deep. Each square was outlined with ropes, anchored by numbered cement-filled beer bottles as reference points. As the three partners were employed during the week, diving was generally restricted to weekends, and many of these were lost due to stormy weather.

By the end of June a pattern of wreckage, supporting Storm's reasoning, had been charted. Crumpled lead sheathing on the reef, in strips about 8 inches wide and ⅛ inch thick, with square nail holes along the edges, confirmed that an old wooden hull had scraped there. A large 2-ton eighteenth-century anchor, with flukes over 2 feet wide, was found. Its square shank, 13 feet long and ½ foot thick, pointed west-northwest—the direction the ship's rope had pulled it before parting. Cannons and other artifacts located during dives formed a trail across the ocean floor. Some 700 feet from the rock another 2-ton anchor was discovered with its shank pointed in the same direction as the first.

After only eleven diving days, on September 18, forty-four plain cast-iron cannons had been located. They were of three different sizes, confirming the statistics supplied by the French museum. An enormous variety of solid cannon balls were found, with small musket shot, brass artifacts, two more large anchors and one smaller anchor of about a ton, and more crumpled lead sheathing on a rock upcropping. Storm spotted a black stone alien to the sea bed—the first of the ballast which was identified as dark basalt. Much of this was salvaged. Then, about 2000 feet west-northwest of Chameau Rock, the trail ended.

To pick it up again the two divers, Storm and MacEachern, took turns on an underwater platform towed behind the boat. Sixty feet deep and some distance away two new cannons were spotted, then a third and two square sounding leads weighing over 50 pounds each. Storm probed into the rocky crevices in this area. Under a 16-inch-long signal gun he struck pay dirt—the first of many rich pockets of coins that would be discovered. Storm scooped up handfuls of silver livres, then a silver spoon, and finally a pocket watch. Bursting with excitement, he surfaced to announce the news. The coins were silver and the ancient pocket watch, after cleaning and opening, revealed the marks HANET LONDON. Moments later Storm and MacEachern were back on the bottom swimming over clusters of heavy artifacts. They had found the grave of *Le Chameau*'s treasure. Their canvas bags filled rapidly.

Three days passed before the salvage could be resumed. Then some five hundred silver coins were collected, varying in condition from fairly clean to corroded clumps. The glint of gold sent both divers scrambling into a crevice. After they surfaced with their bags crammed to capacity MacLeod sang the "Goldfinger" theme as ten yellow louis d'or were counted. Inventory was taken that night at Storm's home. Besides the ten gold coins, they had recovered in just two days 1068 silver livres, of which 510 were in fair condition, plus eight clumps of silver coins cemented with coralline.

The team was able to make only eight more diving sallies that year. Every trip produced a harvest of gold and silver coins from rock crevices and sand patches in the treasure field spread across an area of about 80 feet. Again and again the divers surfaced to hand up to MacLeod their heavy bags. During evenings the coins were cleaned and carefully entered into a salvage record ledger. Also entered were descriptions of valuable artifacts: silver candle snuffers, spoons, knives and forks, copper sword hand guards, broken pewter plates, shards of seventeenth- and eighteenth-century pottery and stoneware, pieces of glass in a variety of green and blue colors from ancient bottles. There was jewelry too: an emerald mounted on gold, and a golden ornament inlaid with white, green, and red enamel.

By the middle of October the treasure pocket was nearly exhausted. Coin recoveries now came from deep crevices, often under several inches of gravel and sea shells. The final dive was made on the eighteenth, when Storm and MacEachern raised three hundred gold, silver, and copper coins, twenty-five silver spoons, and a broken shoe buckle. Then they hauled up the rope grid and other clues to the location and closed business for the year.

During the whole operation the three men and their wives had kept the news secret. Now Storm was ready for the next stage. An experienced Canadian numismatist, Jack Stephens, arrived from nearby Sydney to appraise the coins. Many were French of the Louis XV era, with dates up to 1725. Then the gold and silver went into a bank vault. Conforming to his contract terms, Storm notified the provincial secretary of the salvage. Other appraisers arrived. The valuation of the coins reached a figure of $700,000! As news of the treasure find exploded through the press and TV, Storm and his friends found themselves international celebrities. The door to the sale of the treasure was just opening when it suddenly slammed shut.

A writ claiming part of the money was issued on April 7, 1966, in the Supreme Court of Nova Scotia by a group of men with whom Storm had signed a partnership agreement in 1961. Although they had played no part in the salvage, these men succeeded in blocking any sale until the outcome of litigation. A series of legal battles lasted until December 5, 1967, when a fifty-one page decision was finally handed down by the Supreme Court. Thunderstruck, Storm, MacEachern, and MacLeod listened to a verdict awarding 25 per cent of their treasure to the claimants. They appealed, and another long period of frustrated waiting began. Hearings were held in 1968. The case finally closed in December, with their appeal approved.

What remains unsalvaged, and where is it? Comments Alex Storm: "The recoverable coins have pretty well been salvaged. I would not doubt that perhaps a few still remain, but are nearly impossible to find. Financially it would not be worthwhile exploring for them."

H.M.S. *FEVERSHAM* (2)

Long before *Le Chameau*'s final artifact had been raised, Alex Storm, MacLeod, and their new SCUBA-diving associate Adrian Richards had begun a thorough historical research covering the many other wrecks off the Nova Scotia coast. One looked particularly promising. She was H.M.S. *Feversham*, wrecked on the rocks of Scatari Island with all hands lost during a storm in September 1711. The 36-gun man-of-war was part of a large British task force sent to America earlier that year to support an assault on Quebec. When the fleet was badly damaged she sailed with several ships into the St. Lawrence, putting in at Gaspé. En route out into the Atlantic, the *Feversham* ran into a violent gale off Cape Breton which swept her and three accompanying transports to destruction.

For 257 years heavy seas broke over the warship's shallow wreckage. Very little remained by September 1968 when Storm, MacLeod, and Richards set out to find her artifacts. They had done their homework well, and years of practical experience paid off. While MacLeod took shore bearings from the deck, Storm and Richards searched the ocean floor with practiced eyes. Within weeks they had found wreckage on the rock and gravel bottom only 35 feet deep. Three sizes of plain iron cannon, all badly corroded, were found. The rusted cannon balls were all solid, varying in size. There were many large musket balls, but the muskets themselves had corroded so badly that only a few brass parts remained. Two 4000-pound anchors lay nearby.

Then, according to Storm, "All of a sudden we found pieces of eight —the nicest I have ever seen. Very ancient coins, all between 1616 right up to 1704. Dutch, New England, British, Spanish, French, and West Indian. A real tutti-frutti, this!" The great variety and age of the salvaged money make its value nearly impossible to estimate accurately, although the eventual figure will be substantial. The group's agent, numismatist Jack Stephens, has stated that "There are coins of great rarity" in the find. Among the most valuable are Massachusetts pine-tree shillings and several Dutch coins used in their colony of New Amsterdam.

The salvaged early-eighteenth-century artifacts are just as exciting to archaeologists. They include sword hilts, navigational dividers, candle snuffers, and two interesting-sounding weights. The first resembled a carpenter's plumb bob and weighed only 2 pounds. The other, 15 pounds and round, had the letter F cut into the lead.

With two valuable salvages under his belt, Alex Storm is already making plans for the future. Although he does not go into specifics he hints of two more "ancient wrecks—good prospects." There should be little doubt that he will find them.

H.M.S. *TILBURY* (3)

During the bitter fighting for Nova Scotia between French and British forces in 1758, an English frigate was swept against a reef near Louisbourg and sank off that coast. The *Tilbury* was payship for Admiral Edward Boscawen's squadron. Her loss was forgotten until 1939, when reports that fishermen had dragged up a few gold sovereigns from the strait between Baleine and Scatari Island brought a stampede of treasure hunters to the scene. No treasure was salvaged, and the searchers gradually lost interest. Could this ship be one of the two "good prospects" to which Alex Storm refers above?

The American East Coast (excluding Florida)

The *PORTLAND* (4)

This coastal steamer sank off the tip of Cape Cod on November 26, 1898, with 176 people drowned. In addition to about $18,000 in money and valuables believed in the safe, she may have carried a valuable cargo of tin. The *Portland* was found by a diver in the 1930s who described the wreck as 60 feet deep and so badly filled with sand that he was unable to penetrate the hull.

The *WHIDAH* (5)

A few years ago Bob Nesmith was shown a coin picked up by a young man on a Cape Cod beach. The veteran numismatist identified it as a Peruvian piece of eight dated in the 1660s. "It's an authentic pirate souvenir," he told the finder. "I have no doubt that it came from the wreck of the pirate ship *Whidah*."

Fragmentary records indicate that the *Whidah* was a galley engaging in Africa-Caribbean trade when she was captured by Captain Bellamy near Martinique. The prize was richly laden with ivory and gold as well as other merchandise. Bellamy transferred his guns, crew, and his own accumulated loot to the larger *Whidah*, disposed of his other vessel, and sailed north to fence his cargo with friendly New England merchants. On the way he passed and captured another ship, the brig *Mary Ann*, near Nantucket. The prize crew put aboard discovered barrels of rum and wine and promptly went to work on them.

Approaching Cape Cod on April 26, 1717, the two ships ran into rough and foggy weather. The drunken crew on the *Mary Ann* allowed her to pile up on the coast near East Orleans. The *Whidah* struggled against onshore winds for another few miles, then struck a sand bar off North Eastham. All but 2 of the 146 pirates drowned. When the seas calmed, experienced Cape Cod wreckers swarmed over both the swamped hulks. By the time an agent from the governor arrived to take delivery of salvaged cargo it had disappeared.

Testimony by surviving pirates from both ships indicated that about $100,000 in gold and silver money was stored belowdecks on the *Whidah*. None of this was known to have been recovered by the wreckers. Most of these coins are dispersed under a blanket of sand some 20 feet deep off the beach. Nearly every storm stirs up money, and gold or silver souvenirs of the ship reach the beach. There have been attempts to salvage the *Whidah*—in the early days be refloating her hull and more recently by dredging away the covering sand—but none were successful. If an intact lower hull could be encountered by probing, an all-out dredging attack during the comparative calm of summer might uncover some treasure. Fast work with a powerful blaster would be necessary, for one siege of rough weather could fill in the dredging of months.

The *REPUBLIC* (6)

The iron hull of this White Star liner lies some twenty-five miles east of Nantucket Island. When it sank there on January 23, 1909, a rumor spread that $3,000,000 in gold, shipped from the West Coast, was locked in the *Republic*'s safe. This tale needs careful evaluation before any treasure-hunting attempt is started. It is interesting to note that all but six of the *Republic*'s passengers were saved by emergency calls sent out by the ship's wireless operator, Jack Binns—the first time radio was used in a rescue at sea.

The *ANDREA DORIA* (7)

Ever since her loss on July 26, 1956, this famous ship has been in the news. The first publicity was given to daring dives on her hull by Peter Gimble, *Life's* Ken MacLeish (see page 30), and others. Lately news stories have emphasized projects to salvage the ship and/or the contents of her vault. Suggested methods run the gamut from the conventional to the absurd. The gashed hull of this steel giant has settled deep into the sea bed more than 220 feet below the surface, from which tremendous additional lift would be required to free it from suction. More workable would be the separation and raising of the more valuable sections of the metal structure. Arrangements with the underwriters who paid millions of dollars in claims would be a prerequisite.

A salvage project is planned by Norman Scott's Expeditions Unlimited, Inc., possibly in association with New York financier Alan Krasberg. The company would "send divers into the vessel in pressurized underwater living quarters. From this habitat they will penetrate the *Doria* in the area that contains the ship's safe and her safety deposit vaults." These are similar to those in a bank, requiring two keys—one held by the purser and the other by the passenger. In the panic following the collision the passengers were more interested in saving their lives than in standing in line outside the strongroom while deposit boxes were opened one by one. A large value in jewelry and money remains in the *Andrea Doria*'s vault.

The *U-853* (8)

On May 5, 1945, the collier *Black Point* was sunk by a German submarine between Montauk Point and Block Island. Within two hours the *Moberly*, *Atherton*, and *Amick* arrived. Depth charges and hedgehog attacks brought up oil slicks and debris. The assaults stopped the following day, when the captain's cap and chart table floated to the surface. Divers later identified the sub as the *U-853*, type IXC, 231 feet long. She lay in 125 feet of water, east of Block Island.

A tale went the rounds that $500,000 in jewels and U.S. currency had been smuggled aboard by Captain Helmut Sommer in 88-mm. shell cases, sealed with wax. In 1953 two helmet divers from the chartered *Maureen* were reported to have salvaged the propeller. More recently SCUBA divers have recovered items from inside the hull. Burton Mason, Dave Trisko, and others brought up life jackets, a yellow raft, helmets, weapons, and even a German body. Of money and jewels there has been no trace.

The *DEFENCE* (9)

She was a Connecticut privateer of the Revolutionary War days, doing what she could to make the coast off the thirteen colonies inhospitable for English merchant ships when she was wrecked in Long Island Sound. It has been widely accepted that cargo and money from at least two prizes were aboard the *Defence* on March 10, 1779, when she struck Bartlett Reef (then called Goshen Reef) off Waterford.

Research has been carried out by several people in the area interested in the wreck. Mr. W. D. Wedgwood of Litchfield found a letter from the privateer's captain, Sam Smedley, in which he stated that he swam ashore. The obvious conclusion is that the ship went down quickly. However, more recent investigations by Mr. Ramon Eaton of Hamden,

Connecticut, have indicated that the *Defence* remained afloat some thirty hours before settling on the 35-foot-deep reef. Eaton believes that "there was nary a dime aboard."

With or without treasure, the wreckage of the American privateer should make interesting salvage because of its historical significance.

The *SAN JOSÉ* (10)

Ray Wagner of New York became interested in marine salvage in 1952 when he was scarcely twenty. After diving adventures in the Caribbean, he teamed up with Howell Brose to form the Wagner-Brose Marine Expedition Company. These men have worked several wrecks around Long Island. One in which Wagner is particularly interested is the Spanish frigate *San José*, which he believes broke up on a reef off New London Harbor with several chests of coins.

The *LEXINGTON* (11)

This side-wheeler is another of Wagner's pet projects. He learned that some $60,000 in specie was stored in an express car on deck when she burned and sank on January 13, 1840, off Bridgeport. As he describes the salvage attempt, he and his fellow SCUBA divers Cliff Hayes, Mike Krosted, Lon Adler, and Howell Brose located the charred wreckage and found the express car. This was hoisted aboard the salvage boat *Mela II*, where it was found to be empty except for broken containers. Wagner's theory is that the silver lies scattered on the bottom of Long Island Sound near the wreck.

The SHINNECOCK "MONEY SHIP" (12)

In November 1816 residents of Southampton, L.I., noticed a ship with unusual rigging offshore. It seemed to be abandoned, with the wheel lashed down. By the following afternoon it had moved west to Shinnecock, where it struck a sand bar. The masts broke and the hull settled with a list. A boatload of men who boarded the next day found the ship in perfect order, with clothes, food, and an armory of muskets, pistols, and cutlasses all in place. Not a person was aboard. Two curious men, Green and Jagger, made a visit to the ship and found a silver dollar on the deck. That night they returned, and during a careful search noticed that the board ceiling of the captain's cabin was sagging. When they pried this loose, a cascade of dollars knocked out their lantern. The two men returned frequently during the next days for loads of money. How much they got was never discovered. Storms broke up the hull soon afterward.

And then money began appearing on the Shinnecock beach. One man found sixty of these "beach dollars," as they were called. Hundreds more, bearing dates about 1800, were picked up as far away as East

Hampton. The mystery of the abandoned ship was solved when it became known that her crew of seventeen had headed ashore earlier in boats. Heavy surf had capsized these, and the few who staggered onto the beach were murdered by a group of wreckers. The "beach dollars" may have come from the capsized boats, or the wrecked ship, or both. There should be many more buried under sand off the beach. The full account of this treasure saga can be found in old issues of the *Long Island Forum*.

The GREENPORT WRECK (13)

A gold bar, coins, and charred wood were reported to have been dredged off Greenport, L.I., in 1894. This would be an interesting lead for those given to historical research, as there are tales that a ship burned off the coast here about 1750.

The *ROMA'S* GOLD BOX (14)

Just off a New York City pier lies a little 200-pound wooden case containing about $100,000 in gold ingots. It was dropped into the river from a sling while being loaded aboard the Italian liner *Roma* in 1928. Immediate diving attempts to recover this package were unsuccessful. By now it must lie at least 10 feet below the mud, which has been churned by countless ships' propeller washes, along with tons of rusted iron and junk.

The STORY'S FLAT SILVER INGOTS[1] (15)*

On September 27, 1903, a string of canal boats passed through Staten Sound on their way to Perth Amboy. The flat deck of the last barge was stacked with 7678 ingots weighing about 100 pounds each, being delivered to the American Smelting and Refining Company after a journey from Mexico. They were an alloy of 75 per cent silver and 25 per cent lead. During the night, the barge rolled on its side somewhere between Elizabethport and Perth Amboy. All but two hundred of the ingots plunged into the water. With their weight removed, the barge righted itself. Although the sound had attracted attention, the barge and tow-boat crews misunderstood each other as to what had happened, and the string of boats proceeded on its way.

There was hell to pay the next morning when representatives of the insurance company learned that no one had taken bearings of the spot where the ingots were lost. The Baxter Wrecking Company was brought in to attempt their salvage. After nine days of futile dragging and grappling along the many-mile path, metal was contacted on the floor of Story's Flat. Three divers found ingots strewn over an acre of the mud bottom. A heavy grab from a salvage barge began raising ingots,

---

[1] This account is condensed from a chapter in Dave Horner's book *Shipwrecks, Skin Divers, and Sunken Gold.*

a dozen at a time, in great gobs of mud. In five days, 2938 had been recovered. Salvage was then turned over to divers, since it was apparent that the grab was forcing many of the silver pigs deep into the mud bottom. Within a week another 3000 or so were raised. The salvage master announced that 80 per cent of the lost cargo had been recovered, and operations stopped.

There should be about 1400 100-pound ingots still lost under the mud of Story's Flat, with the exact location available from salvage records. As far as is known these remain the property of the underwriters, the British and Foreign Marine Insurance Co., Ltd. (whose name may now be changed). With a salvage contract and the bearings of the site, SCUBA divers equipped with metal detectors could do well here. There are about 75 pounds of silver in each of those pigs.

The *LIVE OAK* (16)

New Jersey's veteran wreck explorer Gene Khordahl has supplied the following information about one of the many sunken ships that he knows off the coast: "The *Live Oak,* a sloop bound from Santo Domingo to New York, was broken to pieces against Squan Beach on October 20, 1769. Her Captain Foy and the owner, Jacobus van Zant, both testified that $20,000 in specie was lost with her. Since then her wreckage has been covered and uncovered by the shifting sands, but the money is still there, somewhere under the beach or just off it in shallow water."

The HIGHLANDS BEACH GOLD COINS (17)

In his well-researched book *Shipwrecks, Skin Divers, and Sunken Gold* Dave Horner describes a find of money that could indicate a treasure wreck off the New Jersey coast. The first six of these Portuguese gold coins were picked up on a private beach near Highlands, in 1948, by a lobsterman. News spread, and before the property owner could bring in police to stop the scramble, several hundred people had found at least twenty-eight more gold johannes on the waterfront. Comments Horner, "It is likely that the owner carefully searches this area each time a good nor'easter blows up."

The *DELAWARE* (18)

This 1646-ton Clyde Line wooden steamship was under tow after a bad fire when she sank suddenly on July 9, 1893, about two miles off Bay Head, New Jersey. In 1949 Bud Sharp and Bill Conway found the wreck 68 feet deep and recovered several artifacts including dinner plates. The *Delaware* has since been visited by many divers, none of whom have come across any sign of the $250,000 in gold bullion that she was rumored to have been carrying.

The LONG BEACH ISLAND COINS (19)

Frequently after storms coins have been found on the shore of Long Beach Island, New Jersey. These range from corroded silver pieces of eight to gold doubloons, and could have their source in a number of wrecks off this area which are identified in Walter and Richard Krotee's authoritative *Shipwrecks off the New Jersey Coast.*

The *BETSY* (20)

About 1778 this brig broke up on a beach that then existed just north of Little Egg Inlet. Artifacts found recently in this area could have been aboard the *Betsy*. It is known that she carried silver plate and valuables.

The *ELLIS* (21)

En route from England to New York, the schooner *Ellis* was wrecked on the southern end of Brigantine Shoals in 1775. Much of her cargo, largely tea, was washed ashore. In addition to this the ship carried a large amount of silver plate, probably worth $100,000, of which no salvage is recorded.

The *FAME* (22)

This American privateer carried booty from several rich prizes when she capsized and sank off Great Egg Harbor Inlet during a gale on February 22, 1781. Twenty of her crew were killed and the prize cargo, including money, went to the bottom. There is no record of salvage.

The *JUNO* (23)

This 34-gun Spanish frigate carried "a large quantity" of silver ingots and money from Veracruz as she sailed up the New Bahamas Channel in 1802. At the upper end of the passage, strong following winds drove her farther north and heavy seas caused her hull to leak. Other scattered ships of the armada caught sight of her intermittently until October 27, when the *Juno* was last seen wallowing low in the water off Delaware Bay. During that night she sank with 425 people drowned. Her hull lies probably just east of Cape May, at a depth that could be anywhere from 20 to 200 feet. Gold coins have been picked up along the coast here. While their dates are not on record, they could have washed in from this wreck.

The *BETHANY* (24)

After a long voyage from Hongkong, the brig *Bethany* was wrecked just off Two Mile Beach near Cape May on March 9, 1877. Her cargo from the Orient was estimated at $600,000 worth of china and other merchandise. There was probably also gold aboard. If any of the Chinese porcelain could be recovered in good condition, it would bring a high price on today's market.

The DELAWARE CHANNEL SILVER BULLION (25)

Silver ingots found off the shore near Milford suggest that a treasure ship—possibly one of the pirate vessels that used this bay until the early 1700s—may have been wrecked here.

H.M.S. *DE BRAAK* (26)**

The sloop-of-war *de Braak* had a varied and violent history. Built by the Dutch in 1787, she was captured by French naval forces, and several years later, by the British. On June 3, 1797, she was formally placed under the command of Captain James Drew and dispatched to the Caribbean to harass Spanish shipping. The sloop mounted 16 bronze carronades and carried 86 men. For such a relatively small ship she did a big job during her few remaining months afloat. From July 1797 when the *de Braak* became separated from her squadron, until May of the following year, she played the lone wolf in the Caribbean and Bahamas, capturing at least three Spanish *pataches* and *naos* including the *San Francisco Javier*. All of her prizes carried precious metal.

Bullion and valuable merchandise accumulated on board together with a growing company of shackled prisoners. In May 1798 Captain Drew decided to return to England. His ship was overladen and needed an overhaul. On May 25 he put into Delaware Bay for supplies before setting out across the Atlantic. As he was preparing to drop anchor one mile east of the tip of Cape Henlopen, a sudden squall struck. The sloop, with her stability reduced by 70 tons of copper which had been loaded above the metacenter, capsized and sank. Captain Drew, thirty-eight of the crew, and an estimated two hundred trapped prisoners were drowned. A few days later a Halifax newspaper described the loss:

> H.M.S. *Braak*, we are informed, was capsized off the Cape of Dela-ware, returning from a successful cruise on the Spanish main: she had on board . . . an immense amount of treasure consisting of gold and silver bars and precious stones, and also eighty thousand pounds in English gold taken on board at Jamaica for transportation to England.

The total value of her treasure was calculated at between five and ten million dollars. This was sufficient to bring salvage boats swarming. The *de Braak* was easily located since she had righted herself on the way down and the upper tips of her masts protruded over the water. Yet for some reason every salvage attempt was unsuccessful. The first was made by H.M.S. *Assistance* that summer. Her diving bell went down repeatedly over the *de Braak* while divers tried vainly to reach precious cargo. After two months, work was called off. The next summer an all-out effort was made by a team working from the frigate *Resolute* which had brought the stripped and lightened hull of another ship in tow. Loops of chain from the second ship's hull were passed under the bow and stern overhang of the *de Braak* and brought up tight at low water. This effort to tide-lift the sunken hull failed. Because of the wreck's weight, the strongest chains parted with the rising tide. Reluctantly, the British gave up.

Private groups tried time and again over the next century while the *de Braak*'s stout oak and teakwood hull gradually fell apart and was consumed by sea life. The weighted hull sank into the mud bottom until all but a few stumps and ribs had been swallowed. A major attempt in 1880–82 by the International Submarine Company could do no more than report the ship's location after examination of teakwood raised by grappling. Six years later the S.S. *Tamasse* was sent by a syndicate with divers under the direction of Captain Jeff Townsend. They found a chain identified as probably one of those used from the *Resolute*. It ran down into the mud bottom where no trace of a wreck was visible, and could not be pulled free. In the early 1900s one of the *de Braak*'s cannons may have been raised, complete with its teakwood truck carriage. In 1930 the Baltimore Derrick & Salvage Corporation reported finding the wreck amid a graveyard of other sunken hulks. Loss of a ship through fire and other difficulties caused their work to be suspended.

Despite subsequent unsuccessful attempts, interest in this ship is by no means dead. In 1967 the D. & D. Salvage Company of Delaware, Lou DeCerchio, and "The Treasure Divers of Delaware Bay" entered the picture. Mr. M. S. Busa, president of D. & D., announced the previous year that the wreck had been definitely located. The *de Braak* contains a valuable, unperishable cargo. Her approximate location is known, and the sea bed is only 90 feet deep. The obstacles are mud and a tremendous current. These can be overcome with the new generation of underwater salvage equipment now available to a moderately capitalized salvage company.

The *THREE BROTHERS* (27)*

There was "coin and specie" aplenty aboard this English sailing vessel when she crossed the Atlantic about 1775. She was wrecked just off the Delaware coast, probably against a bar near the old Indian River Inlet. Nearby is "Coin Beach," which has fully earned its name. For years copper and gold coins have been found along its shore. Many of these are now on display at the Zwaanendale Museum in Lewes. It is a good bet that one gold coin, a beautiful King George III rose guinea dated 1775, came from the wreckage of the *Three Brothers*.

The *FAITHFUL STEWARD* (28)

Beachcombers working "Coin Beach" often find copper coins on the surface of the sand. The gold ones are usually located with metal detectors, 6 to 8 inches deep. Those that may not have washed ashore from the *Three Brothers* may have come from the *Faithful Steward,* which was wrecked in nearly the same spot on September 2, 1785. There is little doubt that she carried money, but accounts that this reached a figure of $500,000 in gold should be viewed skeptically.

The *MÉRIDA* (29)

This "treasure ship" has cost investors millions of dollars and has been the subject of more fanciful tales, costly salvage expeditions, and headaches for authorities than any other Atlantic coast wreck. Bound from Veracruz to New York, this coastal liner collided with the freighter *Admiral Farragut* just after midnight, May 12, 1911, about sixty-five miles off the Virginia Capes. The wreck is shown on charts at 37° 23′30″ N. latitude and 74°42′00″ W. longitude. The *Mérida* did not sink until 5:30 A.M., and the passengers and crew were all transferred to the other ship. Many were refugees from Mexico, where Porfirio Díaz was planning to abdicate. They told stories about treasure that were embellished with repetition until it was practically accepted that each *émigré* on board had lost a personal fortune, and that $5,000,000 in gold and silver, as well as the crown jewels of Maximilian, went down with the ship. Promoters flourished on stock sales to ever-green investors, and between 1916 and 1933 probably thirty salvage companies set out to retrieve the fabulous treasures.

The *Mérida* was located in 1925 when diver Fred Nielson brought up her nameplate. It was not until 1933 that Captain H. L. Bowden of the Sub Aqua Salvage Corporation managed to salvage the locked purser's safe, after a mutiny and amid a storm of lawsuits by competing treasure hunters. There were so many claims that Charles B. Driscoll suggested that Bowden call all the claimants together and throw the safe back onto the wreck site before their eyes. When it was finally opened before witnesses the contents were found to be a waiter's badge No. 13, a Mexican copper coin, and a counterfeit American half dollar. Then someone remembered that during the five hours between the *Mérida*'s ramming and sinking the purser had saved the valuables.

Insurance payments were made for a total of $176,000 in lost personal belongings, $26,730 for copper ingots, $240,197 for silver matte, and about $130,000 for hides, rum, and merchandise. The Mexican government claimed nothing. The *Mérida* would be in the "Ghost Galleons" section of this book except for one thing: There *was* treasure aboard. In two salvage expeditions in the 1930s, three silver bars were brought up. Their value was $22.50; the cost of the recoveries: over $100,000.

And what about the crown jewels of Maximilian? They were right where they should be, in Mexico's National Museum.

The SANDBRIDGE and CEDAR ISLAND COINS (30)

The possibility that eighteenth-century ships were wrecked off Virginia is suggested by finds of coins of that period. On the shore of Sandbridge, south of Virginia Beach, a 1786 gold doubloon and other money was picked up years ago. The north end of Cedar Island has yielded English, Spanish, and Portuguese coins to beachcombers.

The outer banks of North Carolina have earned their reputation as the "Graveyard of the Atlantic." In his book of that title, David Stick has compiled the histories of six hundred ships lost here from 1526 to 1945. The following offer interesting prospects. Four were wrecked during August 1750, when a hurricane swept up the Atlantic coast and caught the New Spain armada of General Juan Manuel de Bonilla off Cape Hatteras.

EL SALVADOR (31)

This *nao* was the first to go. As her captain tried to bring her into shelter through the Topsail Inlet passage west of Cape Lookout, she grounded and was pounded to bits in the heavy sea. There were few survivors and all the guns and heavy cargo—including a silver shipment worth about $200,000—were lost.

NUESTRA SEÑORA DE LA SOLEDAD (32)

Another part of the armada's silver went to the bottom of Drum Inlet off Atlantic Beach when *Nuestra Señora de la Soledad* broke up under the furious battering of hurricane waves. Most of her cargo and nearly all the people were never seen again.

NUESTRA SEÑORA DE GUADALUPE (33)

This was General de Bonilla's *Capitana*, carrying probably $1,000,000 in silver. His crew managed to bring the galleon to safety in the shelter of Ocracoke Inlet, where she weathered the storm, barely remaining afloat. As soon as was possible heavy cargo was transferred to other boats but some of the silver was still probably on board, stored in chests of merchandise, when the *Guadalupe* settled with her upper deck awash. What remained in the galleon was largely recovered.

LA GALGA (or LA GASCA) (34)

This frigate was carried clear up to Virginia and dashed aground at Currituck Inlet. Wreckage was scattered along the offshore sand bar, where wreckers found a bonanza. Some of the silver was lost in the sand around the wrecked hull, 15 feet below the surface. Governor Johnson sent a ship to impound what had been salvaged. By the time the official delegates arrived, most of it had disappeared.

The *FANNY AND JENNY* (35)

This side-wheeler, running the blockade from Nassau to Wilmington, was attacked on February 10, 1864, by U.S.S. *Florida*. Her captain grounded the ship near Masonboro Inlet, where she burned. SCUBA divers searching the shallow wreck have not yet found a gold sword presented to General Robert E. Lee which was aboard.

The *CENTRAL AMERICA* (36)**

Thanks to research by Dave Horner (*Shipwrecks, Skin Divers, and Sunken Gold*), this wreck has been upgraded to two stars. During the Gold Rush she was put on the New York-Panama run to carry cargo transshipped at the Isthmus. The value of the gold aboard on return trips is attested to by a manifested $1,951,721 in June 1856. The 2141-ton *Central America* was en route from Panama in 1857 when she began shipping water in a heavy storm. Throughout September 11 the crew and passengers worked at the pumps, but by the twelfth the engines failed. That evening the passing ship *El Dorado* determined her position as 31°25′ N. latitude and 77°10′ W. longitude. Soon afterward the *Central America* sank, with 423 drowned. The few survivors were picked up by the *Ellen*.

Lost with the *Central America* was a cargo of California gold worth at least $1,000,000. Horner, in his research, has determined that five consignments for Wells Fargo and other companies were insured in England for $750,000, while probably another $500,000 was covered by American underwriters. In addition he estimates that the passengers had about $250,000.

It is likely that the *Central America* settled on the sea floor 170–200 feet deep about 250 miles southeast of Cape Hatteras. Soon after the loss, various of the underwriters began negotiations with salvage companies, which were not concluded. During recent years there has been publicity about salvage attempts, including one whose personnel were to use the latest electronic detection equipment to locate the wreck. This task is formidable—as is the prospect of salvaging the ship at such a depth in a strong current. Advances being made in search and salvage technology should place the *Central America*'s gold within reach of one of the "new generation" salvage groups within the next decade.

CHAPTER 28

The Great Lakes

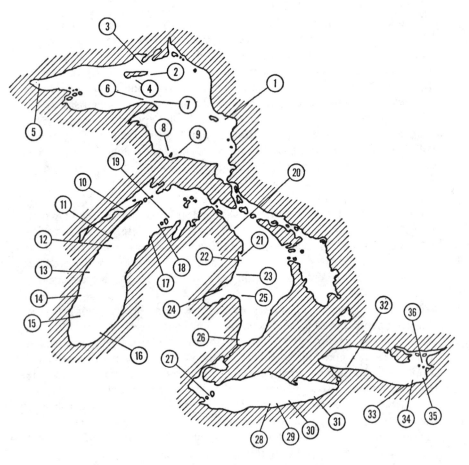

THE GREAT LAKES.

To DESCRIBE all the known information about wrecks in these five bodies of water would take volumes. About 15,500 ship losses have been recorded. Considerable data is available about thousands of these, many of which are visited frequently by SCUBA divers. The Great Lakes, like the Mediterranean, have never been natural passageways for gold and silver shipments. Most of the cargoes crossing their waters have been coal, iron ore, lumber, wheat, salt, farming tools, and general merchandise. Because of this, the definition of "treasure" in this section is extended to include other ladings shipped on the lakes whose salvage can be counted on to produce good profits: copper, lead, steel, iron, and valuable ore concentrates. A ton of copper ingots is worth about $1000; lead, at least $250; steel rails and even pig iron are easy to recover and have a good market. Other valuable, and unusual, cargoes lost under the lakes include aged whiskey, often still intact in barrels and bottles, and vintage automobiles from Detroit whose immersion in fresh water has not seriously damaged them. There is real treasure, too, in the hulls of passenger ships which floundered suddenly in storms, sometimes with no survivors. Their safes and passengers' cabins contain jewelry, and coins whose age and good condition gives them a real numismatic value.

Probably the most comprehensive collection of facts about promising wrecks in the lakes can be found in the archives of Walter and Teddy Remick, whose Great Lakes Research service at 6103 Dennison Avenue, Cleveland, has assisted many divers with facts about cargoes, locations, and earlier salvage work. Their fees are reasonable. Comments Teddy: "Few people realize the potential for salvage here in the lakes. The loot runs from hard cash to copper ingots. A good salvage tug with the right gear and men, and accurate data to work from, could go through these lakes like Jesse James through a train. The last really serious wreck-hunting expedition was made by Captain Chapman of Buffalo, in 1844. He found and passed up a wreck, then several years later divers recovered $235,000 from the same ship!" Another good source of information is The Association, P. O. Box 412, Oscoda, Michigan, whose president, Gene Ballinger, has accumulated a large reference library. In addition, articles on Great Lakes wrecks and salvage appear frequently in *Skin Diver* magazine. Many good books have been published on Great Lakes wrecks. Some of the most factual are listed in the Bibliography.

The thirty-six sites that follow have been well researched by the Remicks and others, and should produce good returns on investments for anyone who salvages their cargoes. Values given for each are estimated very conservatively.

LAKE SUPERIOR: Largest of the lakes with 31,800 square miles of surface, it is also the deepest, with areas dropping below 1000 feet.
(1) *GUNILDA:* Luxury yacht, sank 1911 off Rossport, about 200 feet deep; jewelry and money; at least $15,000.
(2) *ALGOMA:* Steamer, sank 1885 against south shore of Isle Royale; 200 tons steel rails, partly salvaged 1903; about $12,000 left.
(3) *MAGGIE McRAE:* Schooner, sank 1888 off south tip of Thunder Bay; about 300 tons copper ore; $15,000.
(4) *KAMLOOPS:* Steamer, sank 1927 about 500 yards off Isle Royale; whiskey and machinery; $10,000.
(5) *BENJAMIN NOBLE:* Steamer, sank 1914 off base of Knife Island in shallow water; steel rails, possibly some salvaged; $20,000.
(6) *MANISTEE:* Steamer, sank 1863 off Eagle Harbor; 100 tons copper ingots; at least $80,000.
(7) *SUNBEAM:* Steamer, sank 1863 two miles east of Copper Harbor; gold and silver money reported in safe; if true, at least $15,000.
(8) *SUPERIOR:* Steamer, sank 1856 off Grand Island; whiskey, plus gold reported in safe; $10,000–$30,000.
(9) *SMITH MORE:* Steamer, sank 1889 about five miles east of Grand Island; 150 barrels silver ore, 350 kegs whiskey; $20,000–$40,000.

LAKE MICHIGAN: Third largest of the Great Lakes with 22,400 square miles of surface, and depths of nearly 1000 feet in spots.
(10) *LAKELAND:* Steamer, sank 1924 in Sturgeon Bay; cargo of vintage automobiles; $25,000–$50,000.
(11) *VERNON:* Luxury steamer, sank 1887 three miles off Two Rivers; personal jewelry and money; $20,000 minimum.
(12) *HUMKO:* Yacht, sank 1956 off Twin Rivers Point; hull and fittings valued at $237,000; at least $10,000.
(13) *TOLEDO:* Passenger steamer, sank 1856 half mile off Point Washington; personal jewelry and money; $10,000.
(14) *SEABIRD:* Side-wheel steamer, sank 1886 about seven miles off Waukegan; passengers' valuables and money; $10,000.
(15) *WISCONSIN:* Steamer, sank 1929 six miles off Kenosha; vintage automobiles, etc.; $50,000. This ship has been located.
(16) *CHICORA:* Steamer, sank 1895 probably about seven miles southwest of St. Joseph; whiskey, passengers' valuables, money in safe; $25,000.
(17) *BLACK HAWK:* Brig, sank 1862 half mile off Point Betsy near Frankfort; stained glass and reported $4000 in coins; $10,000.

(18) *ELLEN SPRY:* Schooner, sank 1886 just south of South Manitou Island; 150 tons pig iron; $7500.

(19) *WESTMORELAND:* Steamer, sank 1865 off North Manitou Island; money and passengers' valuables; $10,000.

Other well-known wrecks under salvage include the *PRINZ WILLEM V, MEEKS,* and *NIAGARA,* from whose wreckage Great Lakes pro Pat Delaney has raised many artifacts. (See *Skin Diver,* March 1967). An intriguing article in the March 1969 issue of *Skin Diver* magazine by Bill Barada discusses a possible treasure of five chests of gold near Poverty Island, just north of Washington Island, for which the veteran Great Lakes salvage expert Art Reetz and others have searched.

LAKE HURON: Including Georgian Bay, the second largest of the Great Lakes with 23,000 square miles of surface, and depths of 750 feet. Good underwater visibility.

(20) *ANN SMITH:* Steamer, sank 1889 two miles off Rogers City; pig iron; $5000–$10,000.

(21) *PEWABIC:* Steamer, sank 1865 off Thunder Bay; 200 tons copper of which 70 salvaged in two jobs; 130 tons copper remain, worth $110,000. Great Lakes Research has exact location.

(22) *VENUS:* Schooner, sank 1887 about one mile off south end of Thunder Bay; 200 tons pig iron; $10,000.

(23) *WATER WITCH:* Steamer, sank 1863 probably within two miles of Oscoda; passengers' valuables, money; $10,000.

(24) *R. G. COBURN:* Steamer, sank 1871 three miles off north shore entrance of Saginaw Bay; copper ingots, thirty barrels silver ore; reported gold and silver money in safe; $30,000–$50,000.

(25) *KEYSTONE STATE:* Steamer, sank 1861 about three miles northeast of Point Austin; reported $3000 in gold in safe; $10,000.

(26) *NORTHERNER:* Steamer, sank 1856 about four miles off Gratiot Light; safe containing $25,000 in silver probably in wreck, some cargo washed ashore; $40,000.

Although no wrecks have been included here in the Mackinaw Straits joining Lakes Huron and Michigan because of their questionable salvage value, many sunken ships clutter this narrow waterway. For general descriptions and a good map, see William Brown's article in the September 1967 issue of *Skin Diver* magazine.

LAKE ERIE: Although only 9910 square miles in area and very shallow (maximum depth: 200 feet), this lake holds the most valuable cargoes of any. Ships plying between New York, Pennsylvania, Ohio, Michigan, and Canada crossed this body of water years before the other lakes were used.

(27) *GRAY GHOST:* Rumrunner, sank 1931 in area known as Middle Ground north of Kelleys Island; $30,000 worth of "top shelf Canadian whiskey"; $10,000–$50,000, depending on cargo condition; never located.

(28) *MARQUETTE AND BESSEMER NO. 2:* Car ferry, sank 1909 probably about seven miles northeast of Conneaut; thirty-seven railroad cars containing steel, castings, and a reported $50,000 in coins in safe; $20,000 minimum. This should be an ideal target for a magnetometer search.

(29) *CHESAPEAKE:* Steamer, sank 1847 about three miles north-northeast of Conneaut; $8000 in gold and silver in safe, plus passengers' valuables; $10,000–$30,000.

(30) *"SPANISH COIN WRECK":* Probably ancient wooden craft, sank after 1698 about ten miles northeast of Erie; silver Spanish cobs minted in 1698, and wood, were sucked up from "an obstacle" in shallow water a few years ago by a sand dredge; value unknown, but intriguing possibilities of an archaeologically valuable discovery.

(31) *DEAN RICHMOND:* Steamer, sank 1893 a few miles northeast of Dunkirk; 200 tons lead, about 100 tons zinc spelter, 40 tons copper ore, 500 sheets copper, reported $141,000 gold and silver bullion in strong room; $80,000–$200,000. This famous lost ship is probably the most promising of those in the Great Lakes.

Two other tantalizing Lake Erie prospects for treasure divers are being investigated by Great Lakes Research. One is an English trading ship reported lost in the late eighteenth century en route from Erie to Detroit with $50,000 in gold and silver in her strongbox. The second, which may not exist at all, could lie close to shore off Wheatley, Ontario, where "really old" pieces of eight are said to have been found on a beach after storms during the past few years. It is known that the payrolls for "Roger's Rangers," which could have been delivered by ship, consisted of these old Spanish coins—and more than one treasure ship has been located because of coins on a beach.

Other Erie wrecks offering fair salvage returns, some of which are now being worked, are described by Charles Handy and W. E. McBride in the March and April 1968 issues of *Skin Diver* magazine. Among these are the *ST. LOUIS, F. H. PRINCE, UNCLE SAM, ADVENTURE, ATLANTIC* (a safe containing $36,000 was salvaged soon after she sank), *ANTHONY WAYNE, C. P. GRIFFITH* (divers salvaged her engines after she burned and broke in half), *W. C. Richardson* (practically demolished by salvage work), and *AMARETTA MOSHER.*

LAKE ONTARIO: the smallest (7600 square miles) and second shallowest of the Great Lakes, Ontario has many wrecks at snorkeling depth.

(32) *DELAWARE:* Schooner, sank 1887 one mile north of Port Dalhousie; pig iron; $5000.

(33) *ATLAS:* Schooner, sank two miles northwest of Oswego; pig iron; $5000.

(34) *LADY WASHINGTON:* Sloop, sank about five miles west of Oswego; valuable old chinaware; $5000–$10,000.

(35) *BLACK DUCK:* Sloop, sank 1872 near the shore of Mexico Bay; whiskey in barrels; $5000 or more, depending on condition

(36) *J. S. BROOKS:* Steamer, sank 1856 off Sackets Harbor; steel billets and reported $4000 in coins in safe; $5000–$10,000.

Like Lake Erie, Lake Ontario is rich in historically valuable wrecks, including many carrying military supplies during the War of 1812, the Patriots' War, and other periods of fighting between the British, French, and Americans. Archaeological work on sunken ships is being carried out today by groups of SCUBA divers operating independently or under sponsorship of historical societies, museums, and universities. Salvage work done on the U. S Navy frigate *JEFFERSON* by a SCUBA group under Jackson Jenks is an example. Another well-known wreck, the paddle wheel *COMET*, was located in 1967 by Jim McCrady, Robert McCaldon, and other divers 170 feet deep near Wolfe Island. They have recovered a collection of artifacts dating to the time of her loss in 1861. Charles Handy and Don Ward have accumulated a historically valuable assortment of War of 1812 muskets, cannon balls up to twenty-four-pounders, artifacts, and even coins from several supply ships that they are salvaging.

Several wrecks on popular Great Lakes "treasure lists" have been omitted from this section. The *BRUNO*, thought to have carried valuable cargo, was found to have had only iron ore aboard by the Great Lakes Research; the *ERIE* was raised in two sections. One, towed to Buffalo, yielded over $200,000; the other was worthless. The *CLARION* did not carry a reported $130,000 in gold or a cargo of locomotives; the *GLENORA* did not sink; and what is believed to be the remains of de la Salle's ship *GRIFFIN*, sunk in 1679 with $12,000 in gold reported aboard, was recently discovered in Georgian Bay, stripped of cargo and cannons, and apparently abandoned by her crew.

CHAPTER 29

Denting the Depth Barrier

DENTING THE DEPTH BARRIER

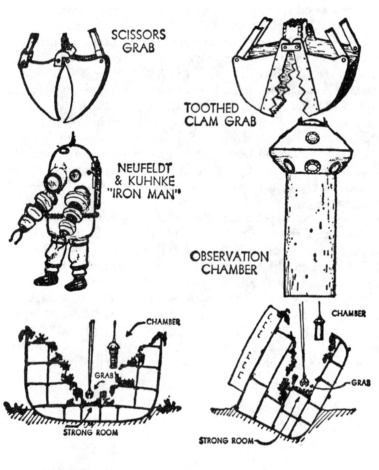

SCISSORS GRAB

TOOTHED CLAM GRAB

NEUFELDT & KUHNKE "IRON MAN"

OBSERVATION CHAMBER

CHAMBER

GRAB

STRONG ROOM

EGYPT

CHAMBER

GRAB

STRONG ROOM

NIAGARA

M ORE THAN any other cargo, sunken treasure has inspired salvage men to their greatest feats. This is not necessarily because treasure salvage is more profitable—dozens of million-dollar shiploads of commercial cargo, like the 8000 tons of tin, copper, and lead, worth $7,000,000 in the *Príncipe de Asturias* off Brazil—still remain uncovered after decades. It is more likely because the lure of sunken treasure is selective. Its goading challenge seems especially to strike imaginative men—men who are impulsive, resourceful, willing to experiment. Where conservative salvors with their proven tried-and-true methods are held at bay by previously unbeaten obstacles, bright-eyed treasure hunters, bursting with iconoclastic new ideas, come rushing in. They try metal locating devices, dig tunnels out to offshore reefs, send down miniature submarines—anything and everything is thrown into the fight. Only one in twenty may have the resources and tenacity to push through to success, but when he does the results are sensational.

Two of the richest gold shipments ever lost to the ocean went down within the past forty years. In each case recovery was considered unfeasible—if not impossible—by old line salvage directors, yet others with revolutionary thoughts came forward willing to try something new. Their resounding successes established mileposts in salvage history and the methods which they had the courage to use, then considered radical, earned respectability through their efforts. The stories of the *Egypt* and *Niagara* run nearly parallel in many respects, yet diverge widely in the personalities of the principals and the role which Lady Luck played in their work. Neither could have been brought to a successful conclusion had it not been for the experiments of a hundred other imaginative men who for two centuries beforehand had been laboriously bringing about the development of submarine armor.

The nemesis of all diving operations is pressure. Its physiological effect on the human body fixes the maximum depth at which a diver can effectively work. For practical purposes this is 200 feet—and despite all of man's progress in the fields of biology this limit still stands. Back in the eighteenth and nineteenth centuries, when rivers and bays were cluttered with the corpses of audacious inventors who were drowned or squeezed to death in embryonic diving bells and flexible suits, a parallel development was taking form in another approach to conquer the ocean depths: with body armor. It was not difficult to visualize that if some way could be devised to hold back the water pressure from a diver his range would be practically unlimited.

A long succession of designs, some ingenious and others comically naïve, were hammered together and put to the test. Wooden tubs collapsed around their occupants; unprotected arms and legs protruding from head and torso shielding were squashed back inside; when metal plating was extended to cover the limbs its joints leaked and tightened under pressure; lead breathing tubes to the surface were too limiting in mobility; wheels below the feet—and even headlights—were tried and found to be impractical. One after the other unsatisfactory designs were discarded, and through a survival of the fittest several basic requirements for a workable armored diving suit came to be recognized. The armor must enclose the entire body; the air supply must be self-contained; the most promising flexible joint was the ball and socket.

From 1900 to 1920 no less than seventeen different models, nearly all incorporating these features, were developed by American, German, Italian, Australian, English, French, and Mexican inventors. Among them appeared suits that for the first time really worked. Perhaps the best of these was a German design, constructed by the Hamburg firm of Neufeldt & Kuhnke. It went through several stages of improvement and by 1920 had evolved into a colossal monster standing 8 feet tall, a yard in diameter and weighing nearly half a ton. Ball and socket joints along the arms and legs gave the limbs some flexibility. The enclosed diver breathed through a regenerative system fed from a six-hour supply of oxygen carried in bottles behind the suit. He could see forward through a quartz glass face plate and to the sides and above through peepholes. A ballast chamber was built in the steel frame around his hips allowing him to adjust his buoyancy like a miniature submarine. Pincers protruded from the ends of the arms. The whole contraption was suspended on cable from a ship's derrick.

Despite its successful testing as deep as 700 feet, however, none but an experimentally-minded salvor would consider using it. There were too many things that went wrong. The diver inside had practically no mobility. The joints stiffened under pressure and in great depths it required a man's strongest exertions to move them. By trimming the ballast tank the occupant could attain a slight negative buoyancy on the bottom, but only under optimum underwater conditions could he push forward to where he wanted to go. The slightest current spun him around facing downstream, since his forward-reaching arms acted as fins. A one-knot flow swept "the iron man" off the bottom, tethered to its overhead derrick, and carried it downstream toward the surface. And God help the occupant if his cable became entangled in overhead wreckage. The unwieldy claws might not be able to free him even if he were able to float up to the right place facing the right direction.

He would have to unhook the cable, which could be released from within, blow his ballast tank and hope for the best.

The armored diver had one remarkable advantage, though. He could enter great depths, far below the limits of a helmet diver, and if current and visibility permitted could telephone up reports of what he saw. And this capacity is what brought "the iron man" to the attention of a dynamic, fat little Italian with revolutionary ideas and tenacious conviction that they were right. His name: Giovanni Quaglia.

Already successful in shipping enterprises, Quaglia had decided after World War I to go into salvage, specializing in recoveries from wrecks too deep to interest ordinary salvage men. This was in character. Quaglia took pride in tackling jobs too tough for others—and pulling them through. He was an ebullient, self-confident fellow with a colorful personality, nervous and impatient, irrepressibly optimistic, generous and beloved by his employees. His recently formed company, the Società Ricuperi Maritimi, was then nearly unknown. Within a few years it would be world famous as the SORIMA. When Quaglia learned of the qualifications of the Neufeldt & Kuhnke armored diving suit he came to an agreement with the manufacturers whereby his divers would use it, serving as guinea pigs for its testing. Following their recommendations it went through several improvements.

SORIMA's new methods gained international respect during an operation over the freighter *Washington* sunk off the Italian coast. The wreck lay 300 feet deep. For four years Quaglia's personnel brought up its cargo, learning through trial and error how to best employ "the iron man" in co-ordination with grabs suspended from their salvage ships. The armored diver was too clumsy usually to carry out physical work, so he was dangled with his feet on the deck, or his pincers clinging to a solid anchorage. From this submarine vantage point he directed the placing of tubes of explosives on the ship's deck or against its bulkheads. When these were blasted loose and the water had cleared, grabs were lowered. The submarine observer telephoned a rapid series of directions until their gripping teeth were maneuvered into place onto steel plates or uncovered cargo and clamped shut. Then powerful winches, capable of raising 15 tons, hauled them up, sometimes ripping metal which had not been completely severed by the charges. Quaglia's method was revolutionary, but so effective that when his company finished with the *Washington*, 7000 tons of her cargo, including seven locomotives, had been salvaged.

He went on to other successes, which in 1927 led him out to the Atlantic coast of France where the *Elizabethville* was sunk 200 feet deep (see Chapter 20.) After this, SORIMA's schooling was complete. The doughty Italian salvors were ready for anything, the tougher the better, and Quaglia had just the job in mind. Only a hundred miles

away—and 200 feet deeper—a gold and silver cargo worth nearly
$6,000,000 lay awaiting them.

S.S. *EGYPT*

On the evening of May 20, 1922, the 7941 ton "P & O" liner *Egypt*
was rammed by the freighter *Seine* while creeping southward through
a fog en route from London to Bombay. During the twenty minutes
that she remained afloat the radio operator signaled her position to be
48°10′ N, 5°30′ W, placing the sinking ship some twenty-five miles
southwest of Ushant Island off the tip of Brittany. News of this
disaster reached Lloyd's underwriters the following morning, sending
them hurrying to their charts. Heads shook in resignation. The *Egypt*,
and £1,054,000[1] in gold and silver destined for Indian banks in her
strong room, were 400 feet under the Atlantic. The underwriting syndicates paid the claim and accepted a total loss.

All except two of them, members of the Salvage Association, and
an engineer named Peter Sandburg. This trio of forward-looking Englishmen knew of developments in submarine observation chambers and
felt that there might be a chance for recovery if the *Egypt* could be
found. They commissioned a Swedish Captain Hedback to search for
the wreck in the chartered *Fridthjof*. For eight weeks Hedback dragged
the ocean floor. Then his sweep caught in an obstacle in the right
place. Soundings showed that it was a wreck. Several astronomical
bearings were taken to fix the spot, and the English group began a
long quest for satisfactory equipment. It was not for three years, in
1926, that German divers using the "iron man" were dropped. They
could not find the wreck, despite bearings, and the project was abandoned.

For seven years after she sank the *Egypt* lay invitingly on her sea
bed before a man came forward with sufficient perseverance to tackle
the obstacles guarding her treasure. Then, in the spring of 1929, Quaglia's
little salvage fleet set out from Brest to find her. The SORIMA was
well equipped for the task. Its larger salvage ship, the converted 300-
ton trawler *Artiglio*, bristled with masts and booms for her armored
diving suits and grabs, and powerful steam winches cluttered the deck.
The smaller auxiliary vessel *Rostro* carried similar equipment. The ships
were manned by thirty-five swarthy Italian salvage men who worked
together in confident teamwork that only years of successful co-operation
can develop. Among them were some of the best divers in the world.
There was nothing lacking in the forces with which Quaglia launched
his attack on the *Egypt*'s gold.

The task which faced him lay in two stages. The first was to locate
the correct ship in a graveyard of wrecks. Early researches had produced four clues to the *Egypt*'s position: the not very reliable bearings

[1] Insured value, 1922.

given in her SOS; a radio fix taken on this broadcast by shore stations; Captain Hedback's submarine obstacle; and the position of floating debris spotted after the sinking, which had already drifted for half a day. All possibilities were considered, with the result that a hypothetical rectangle enclosing forty square miles was laid out on the surface of the ocean, out of sight of land. Somewhere in its wide stretches, nine miles from corner to opposite corner, must be the *Egypt*.

The spring weather was stormy, but finally broke for two days. The first was spent in a futile attempt to investigate Hedback's submarine obstacle. The *Artiglio* and *Rostro* found the marks with no trouble, but a strong current frustrated efforts to lower the armored suits onto the site. With this, one of those frequent machinations of bad luck which beset treasure divers—for Hedback's wreck was the *Egypt*—the project was inexplicably abandoned. On the second day Hedback's obstacle was forgotten in concerted efforts to get the buoys placed before a threatening storm broke. Since there were no shore reference points in sight artificial ones had to be made. By nightfall rows of iron drums bobbed over the ocean, their chains held to the bottom by 4-ton anchors.

The sweeping search began when the weather cleared. It was made with a steel cable nearly a mile long joined to the sterns of the two ships. Flanking each other, a quarter of a mile apart, they advanced cautiously with the cable dragging across the ocean floor between and behind them. From the first this method was unsatisfactory. Again and again the sweep snagged on rocks. Usually it slipped free, but days were wasted on unproductive surveys by the armored divers and the frequent snagging frayed and broke the cable. A modification was introduced. The cable was strung tightly from anchors suspended below each ship, high enough off the bottom to keep free of rocks—in theory. In practice it sagged and still caught. Finally floats were attached to it at regular intervals. Now the sweep worked. The cable, suspended at a uniform height, would catch only tall protrusions like a wreck. The evolution in its design had taken place over many months. Every improvement was preceded by mistakes and work stopped frequently to repair the broken cable. By the end of the summer the *Egypt* had still not been found. Storms and fog had held them to less than one working day out of three.

The winter passed, and once again the SORIMA fleet set out. The sweeping search was varied with intriguing attempts to locate the wreck by a Capuchin monk with a divining rod and an Englishman named Brooks with a metal-detecting electric galvanometer, but neither system worked. Hostile weather continued to rob the Italians of time, and as the second summer drew to a close Quaglia became a very worried man. His entire fortune and nearly every cent he had been able to borrow were spent, and for practical purposes he was no further along than when he started. His reputation was suffering: people were calling him a failure. And more ominous, there was a growing suspicion in Brest, the French naval base where SORIMA had its shore headquarters, that his men were Italian spies.

But the search area was nearly covered. Cruising back and forth over its buoyed limitations, the *Artiglio* and *Rostro* steadily approached the position of Hedback's obstacle. They would have reached it in another week when the mercurial ocean, so long their violent enemy, suddenly gave them a helping push. During a gale it dragged off one of the marker buoys. The *Artiglio* went to retrieve it. When the winches were started to raise its chain the buoy's anchor would not come free. It was finally broken loose and brought up, carrying with it, entangled in the chain, a broken-off ship's davit. Dragged by the force of the storm, the anchor had become fouled in the *Egypt*.

The grabs were dropped. Over the next days they brought up in their teeth a 6-ton winch, parts of the superstructure, and finally the captain's safe. The "iron men" were sent down and their observers reported that the *Egypt* sat upright. With rekindled enthusiasm the SORIMA crews worked whenever weather conditions permitted right through to December. When Quaglia left on a fund-raising campaign at the end of the year he was armed with concrete accomplishments with which to back his desperate fight for credit.

He had arranged winter work for his company: leveling a sunken munitions ship which lay in shallow water in nearby St. Nazaire. This was a routine demolition job, easy if the ship's cargo could be induced to blow up with starter explosions, bothersome if the ship had to be razed. Quaglia's exuberant superintendent, Gianni, was entrusted with the job. He made several unsuccessful tries to set off the cargo, each time with the *Artiglio* at a respectful distance, then evidently became convinced that the waterlogged artillery shells would not explode and tried a larger charge from only 300 yards away. This time he succeeded. The tidal wave which swamped the *Artiglio* left only seven of the crew alive.

Months passed before Quaglia recovered from the shock. Then, with characteristic determination, he briskly set out once more to challenge the bad luck which so persistently dogged him. Another ship was found, outfitted and renamed *Artiglio*. New crewmen were signed on, and the attack on the *Egypt* was resumed.

Her upright position was the worst possible for the salvors. Their equipment—the grabs and armored observers—could be moved only in vertical lines. With the strong room situated on the *Egypt*'s lowest level just forward of the bridge, four overhead decks and countless crisscrossing bulkheads as well as part of the superstructure had to be cut away to give access to the treasure. Quaglia and his engineers calculated that a hole as wide as the ship was needed at the top. As the excavation was blasted down lower into the steel honeycomb of interlocking decks and bulkheads it would be narrowed in diameter until it measured 10 by 20 feet at the ceiling of the strong room. This aperture should give the smaller grabs sufficient mobility to pluck ingots out of its every corner.

Calm weather was essential for this work. Every motion of the ship was duplicated by the armored suit and the grabs, and the slightest rocking, nearly unnoticed on deck, transposed itself into violent up and down banging against the wreck below. If the wind swung the ship from her position she had to be warped back into place. The current was an exasperating time killer. When it flowed with any strength the observer was swept off with it, facing the wrong way. To partially overcome this vulnerability "the iron man" was presently replaced by an observation chamber with portholes on all sides. Now the observer, even if he were carried off a few yards, could still look back and see what was going on.

During 1931 the English Channel was battered by one storm after another, the weather being so consistently bad that by the end of the summer the SORIMA group had enjoyed only thirty days of working weather. When they could, the Italians labored like demons, averaging ten dives daily. In this short time they carved down through the *Egypt* to the ceiling of her strong room. When winter drove their ships back to port, the treasure—if there had been any visibility on the dark bottom —would have nearly been in sight.

The blasting and ripping was resumed early in June. New spirit swept through the crews as reports came up that the hole in the treasure room ceiling was getting larger. On June 7 it was wide enough to permit entry to the smallest scissors grab. The first loads of salvage were guns, silk, and books. Then came silverware and valueless banknotes. Weeks went by with not a glimmer of gold but growing worries were put to rest when the *Egypt's* captain communicated that he had covered the metal with other merchandise. Then on June 22, when Quaglia sifted through the grab's droppings, he gave a happy shout. In his hand was a gold sovereign.

For the next three days gold ingots and coins thumped and tinkled onto the deck with monotonous regularity, each trip of the grab bringing up nearly $50,000. Then, with nearly $1,000,000 in gold aboard, Quaglia could restrain himself no longer. After all these years of humiliation he had to enjoy his triumph. The *Artiglio* set off for England and an English equivalent of a ticker-tape reception. Quaglia was suddenly an international hero.

Work was resumed soon afterward, and carried on through the summers of 1933, 1934, and 1935. Toward the end, as the main stacks of bullion and coins were exhausted, less and less was recovered daily. Quaglia kept at it, though, until nearly the last dregs were sucked up—literally. When the scissors grab no longer seized loose coins it was replaced with a vacuum grab,[2] into whose large chamber hundreds of sovereigns, and even ingots, were sucked in at a crack.

The salvage was so thorough that when SORIMA finally terminated operations, over 95 per cent of the *Egypt's* treasure had been raised. Quaglia's company, under its "no cure no pay" contract giving it half of the value of the salvage, received nearly $3,000,000. Of the 1089 gold bars, 1229 silver ingots, and tons of gold and silver coins which went down with the *Egypt*, only seven gold and a dozen silver bars and about 10,000 gold sovereigns—worth about $250,000—remained.

This treasure is still there, buried under the litter of iron rust and silt which has filled the strong room. It is likely to remain in the *Egypt* for many more years. The SORIMA continued its work as long as it was profitable with their salvage methods. Until a better system is devised to work at 400 feet any attempt to recover the balance is likely to result in a loss.

S.S. *NIAGARA*

Had it not been for the fact that Fascist Italy was on the other side in World War II, Quaglia might have again had the opportunity to demonstrate his capabilities over another deep gold cargo, worth nearly twice as much as that of the *Egypt*, sunk at the opposite end of the world. But then, had the war not started, the *Niagara's* treasure would have never existed, nor been sunk. One of the first victims of the Nazi minelayers, whose operations reached all the way to South Pacific waters, was the Royal Mail ship *Niagara*. A few hours out of Whangarei harbor, New Zealand, just before dawn on June 19, 1940, this 13,415-ton liner shuddered as a submarine explosion banged against her hull. Nine minutes later a fix was taken, showing her position to be thirty miles east of the uppermost peninsula of North Island. For another ninety minutes the *Niagara* drifted with a two-knot current as crew and passengers took to the boats. Then she sank in deep water.

Five decks below her bridge, in the strong room, were 590 gold ingots. Each weighed 31½ pounds and was worth $17,800. In all, 9 tons of gold with a value of $10,250,000 went down with the ship. It was uninsured, being sent to Canada in payment of badly needed armaments, but despite its importance to Britain's war effort, neither Admiralty salvage forces, which were just being organized, nor Australian naval authorities, would undertake its recovery. The reasons were obvious.

---

[2] Described in Davis' book, *Deep Diving*.

The *Niagara's* position was only approximately known; her probable depth was too great; and there was no deep salvage equipment available in the area.

Private enterprise came forward to tackle the job. Approached by naval officers, two Australian captains—J. P. Williams, and soon afterward, J. W. Herd—decided to make the attempt. They were joined by chief diver John "Johnno" Johnstone and his brother William. Since nearly every floating craft in the area had already been commandeered, this optimistic group had a long search before finding their salvage ship. This was the 190-ton *Claymore*, an old hulk discovered beached near Auckland awaiting dismantling for scrap. Johnstone learned that her engines could still turn over after a fashion, and after a few months of repairing and oiling their parts, cleaning off debris and patching rusted-through plates, the junked *Claymore* was once again navigable.

As in the case of the *Egypt*, the project ahead was divided into two distinct phases: the search for the wreck and penetration to its strong room. No noteworthy technological advance in either, except for the development of the echo-sounder, had been made since Quaglia's breakthrough a few years before, so the Aussies decided to exploit the pioneering of their enterprising Italian forerunners. Their search would be made with a sweep, and salvage would be carried out with grabs directed by an observer. When Williams learned that there was no submarine observation chamber available he commissioned an engineer, David Isaacs, to build one. The finished product was a 3-ton cylinder standing 9½ feet tall with two rings of portholes opening outward and downward from its flaring top. It was tested to withstand a pressure of 400 pounds per square inch—twice that existing at the *Niagara's* estimated depth. A regenerative breathing system was installed within. Below the ballast tank hung 500 pounds of weights which could be jettisoned if necessary.

More to learn about the depth and conditions of the ocean floor than with hopes of locating the wreck, an echo-sounding reconnaissance of the area was made from a chartered launch. The findings were strongly encouraging. The bottom was level flat mud, unbroken by the rock protrusions that had so impeded the SORIMA search. The results were also disturbing. Little blurbs, floating just under the keel, had been recorded on the echo-sounder's tape. They would be working in a mine field, in continual danger.

On December 9, 1941, the *Claymore* set out on her mission. It was calculated that the *Niagara* lay somewhere within the area of sixteen square miles downcurrent from the position of her last fix taken ninety minutes before she sank. Buoys were dropped at the corners of this square, four miles apart, and sweeping got under way with navigation facilitated by bearings on the nearby Chicken Island. Steaming side by side the *Claymore* and the chartered auxiliary ship *Betsy* trawled behind them an inch-thick cable. Paravanes at its flanks stretched it out so that a lane 500 feet wide was swept between the vessels. Work went smoothly with none of the troubles which had so hindered the SORIMA.

A week after they started, the sweep caught an obstacle. Rough weather interfered with attempts to lower the observation chamber, and it was not until after Christmas that Johnstone could investigate what had been snagged. On the bottom he saw a dark object resembling a big stone. The chamber was briefly entangled in a mysterious wire coming up, then freed itself. When the anchor was raised the mystery of the dark object and the wire was alarmingly solved. A horned mine bobbed on the surface just off their bow, its mooring tangled in the anchor chain. Gingerly the chain was paid out as the *Claymore* backed away. The crew attached a buoy to a link and slipped the mooring.

The following day a minesweeper accompanied the *Claymore* to the site. John Johnstone went down in a suit to hook the mine to a cable from the sweeper. Before he realized it the *Claymore*'s anchor chain had again become entangled with the mine's mooring cable and his own lifeline was snagged among its 5-inch horns. He was drifting under the ship. Suddenly the mine's cable gave way and the deadly egg carried him up against the *Claymore*'s hull. For nerveracking minutes he strained to hold its horns from the ship's bottom as the minesweeper pulled it away. Then he untangled himself and returned aboard. Seven hours after the unwelcome intruder had attached itself to the ship it was harmlessly exploded by gunfire. The Australian group had been luckier than Quaglia's.

On January 31, 1942, less than two months after the search started, the *Niagara* was located 438 feet deep. She was lying on her starboard side, 70° off vertical. Since salvage with the grab could be made only by up and down movements, the gold would have to be approached through the port side. A dummy model of the ship was built and studied. The strongroom was located between C and D deck, underneath the bridge. Besides the steel side of the ship, B and C decks would have to be broken through to reach it. A hole 60 by 30 feet was necessary to allow sufficient mobility for the grab.

Five months were spent blasting this hole, a few feet at a time. Each placing of explosives involved an irritating period of telephoned directions from the observation chamber to the overhead *Claymore*, which was moved by tightening and slacking her mooring cables until the weighted explosive charge hanging in the water below her was lowered to the right plate or beam of the wreck. After each blast, the grab bit on the ruptured plates and pulled them away. Rough weather compounded the difficulties. At last, however, a path was cleared and the observation chamber was lowered into the ship to within a dozen feet of the gold, separated only by a final bulkhead. Now the ticklish work began. One mistake and the treasure, stored in a 9 by 8 foot cabin, could be blasted through the opposite bulkhead and scattered deeper in the hold.

On October 13 the grab hung over the *Claymore*'s deck, dripping. A shout went up: "It's a bloody box o'gold!" Moments later the delirious crew members were fondling two gleaming yellow ingots. From then on it was downhill coasting. Despite periods of days at a time when nothing but rubble was brought out of the treasure room, the boxes of ingots came up. The climax took place on November 11, when in twenty-eight round trips the clam salvaged 92 bars, worth $1,700,000. Work was abandoned at the end of 1942 with 555 ingots recovered from the greatest depth at which treasure salvage has ever been made.

The Australian undertaking recovered $9,400,000 in gold—second only to the salvage from the *Laurentic* in value. Thirty-five ingots, worth $625,000, lie in the ruptured strong room or in the cabins and passages below if the lower bulkhead has finally given away. As in the case of the *Egypt*, this treasure will probably stay there until better salvage methods are developed. And chief diver "Johnno" Johnstone is still in the Pacific, pursuing his favorite vocation—this time in the salvage of more prosaic scrap from American and Japanese ships sunk during World War II. As one of the principals in the enterprise, he writes: "I've given over the diving, and am content to look on. But I've lost no interest in salvage work . . ." As a man who played a major role in raising nearly $10,000,000 in treasure from the sea, how could he?

Although the achievements of salvaging the *Niagara* and *Egypt* were magnificent, they circumvented the two basic obstacles preventing man from working in the great depths: nitrogen narcosis, and long decompression times. Experiments to eliminate narcosis or "rapture" have been going on for years. Since 1921 the U. S. Navy has been testing various mixtures of gases, and its Experimental Diving Unit long ago proved that guinea pigs breathing oxygen/helium could survive short exposures to great pressures. But the replacement of nitrogen with helium alone was not sufficient, since the normal 21 per cent oxygen content of air becomes toxic under pressure. It was found that with increasing depth—and pressure—the proportion of oxygen must be reduced until at 200 feet it is only 3 per cent versus 97 per cent helium. In his spectacular "bounce" dive to 1000 feet in 1962, Hannes Keller applied the accumulated knowledge in this field.

The challenge of overcoming wasted decompression time has been attacked with success by several groups, among which Edwin Link's and Captain Cousteau's were the forerunners. In 1962 these two dynamic pioneers, working in collaboration, achieved the first breakthrough by applying the premise that decompression time for a certain depth did not vary much after the diver had been exposed to the pressure at that depth long enough for his body to become saturated with dissolved "air." In effect, there would be little additional decompression time needed at, say, 200 feet after one or two weeks as compared with a few hours. The solution was to keep the diver under pressure, working, for longer periods of time and have him decompress less frequently. To accomplish this, a "home" under the sea where the diver could live in comfort while he was not working would be necessary.

Cousteau's "home," named Diogenes, was anchored 33 feet deep off Marseilles. Two of his expert divers, Falco and Wesley, lived in it for a week. At the same time the famous Link/Sténuit experiment took place off Villefranche. An aluminum cylinder designed and constructed by Link was the "home" for Sténuit. A little over 1 yard in diameter and 11 feet long, it was a combined house, observation chamber, submarine elevator, and decompression chamber, suspended from Link's ultramodern oceanographic research ship Sea Diver. Based in the Link cylinder, Sténuit established the world record dive during which he spent over twenty-four hours at 200 feet. Two years later the Sea Diver anchored over a 432-foot-deep ocean bottom in the Bahamas and a new Link-invented "home" was lowered into the depths. This was his SPID (submersible portable inflatable dwelling), a blimplike rubber undersea base for two people. Sténuit and his companion Jon Lindbergh were lowered to the site in Link's submersible decompression chamber (SDC) during the morning of June 30, 1964, and swam to the SPID. For two days and two nights they lived and worked at over 400 feet, adding an important new page to the "Man-in-Sea" project.

By 1969 three major programs had proved conclusively that man can live and work in the cold blackness of the depths. Cousteau's CONSHELF II project, following his first, took place in the Red Sea in 1963, and CONSHELF III maintained six divers at depths from 325 to 430 feet under the Mediterranean in 1965. The U. S. Navy SEALAB experiments began in 1964, when four "aquanauts" spent eleven days off Bermuda at depths of about 200 feet. SEALAB II placed more divers at 205 feet off La Jolla, California, and SEALAB III and subsequent experiments will maintain larger groups at depths that will increase progressively to 600 and more feet. As with the space program, new equipment is being developed to assist the human body to withstand the unfamiliar environment, particularly the cold, which is augmented by the use of heat-draining helium. The problem of vocal communication, where the new breathing mixture under pressure causes a "Donald

Duck" effect, is also being solved through electronic means.[3] Within a decade it seems likely that man will be able to live and work at depths of 1000 feet on the continental shelves, and entire new industries such as mining and fish ranching will be established there.

Penetration of the very great depths is also well under way with the development of a whole family of deep research vehicles following Cousteau's Diving Saucer. The *Aluminaut, Alvin, Deep Diver, Deep Quest, Trieste II, Pisces,* and *Dolphin* are only a few of the many vehicles in operation and on the drawing board.

[3] New York's Integrated Electronics Corporation is reported to have developed an electronic system that shifts voice frequencies making sounds into understandable words. The device is marketed by the Aquasonics Engineering Company, San Diego, California.

Bibliography

GENERAL REFERENCE WORKS

César Fernández Duro	*Armada Española* (vols. I–IX)
César Fernández Duro	*La Marina de Castilla desde su Origen*
César Fernández Duro	*Naufragios de la Armada Española*
J. March y Labores	*Historia de la Marina Reál Española*
F. de Castro y Bravo	*Las Naos Españolas en la Carrera de las Indias*
M. Ortiz de la Vega	*Las Glorias Españolas*
Navarette	*Colección* (folios)
H. and P. Chaunu	*Seville et l'Atlantique* (vols. I–VII)
A. Thomazi	*Les Flottes de l'Or*
Thomas Lediard	*The Naval History of England*
Laird Clowes	*The Royal Navy*
John Campbell	*Lives of British Admirals*
Oppenheim	*Naval Tracts of Sir William Monson*
—	*Admiralty List of Lost H.M. Ships*
C. de la Roncière	*Histoire de la Marine Française*
	The Mariners' Mirror, published by the Society for Nautical Research, England
	The Belgian Shiplover, published by The Belgian Nautical Research Association
	Publications of The Hakluyt Society (Hakluyt's Voyages), London
	The Encyclopaedia Britannica
Robert Marx	*The Treasure Fleets of the Spanish Main*
—	*They Dared the Deep*
H. I. Chapelle	*The History of American Sailing Ships*
Arthur C. Clarke	*The Challenge of the Sea*
Owen Lee	*The Skin Diver's Bible*
Robert M. Fleming	*A Primer of Shipwreck Research and Records for Skin Divers*

BOOKS DESCRIBING SUNKEN TREASURES (GENERAL)

César Fernández Duro	*Armada Española* (lists of lost ships)
César Fernández Duro	*Naufragios de la Armada Española*
R. I. Nesmith	*Dig for Pirate Treasure*
P. de Latil & J. Rivoire	*Tésors Engloutis*
C. B. Driscoll	*Doubloons*
—	*Shipwrecks and Disasters at Sea*

Nora B. Stirling   *Treasure under the Sea*
Sir Robert H. Davis   *Deep Diving and Submarine Operations*
Gregory Robinson   *Ships That Made History*
W. and R. Chambers   *Shipwrecks and Tales of the Sea*
—   *Shipwrecks and Adventures at Sea*
—   *Notable Shipwrecks*
Philip Gosse   *The History of Piracy*
Lt. H. E. Rieseberg   *I Dive for Treasure*
F. L. Coffman   *1001 Lost, Buried or Sunken Treasures*
Gordon Cooper   *Treasure Trove, Pirates' Gold*
John D. Craig   *Danger Is My Business*
R. I. Nesmith and J. S. Potter *Treasure . . . How and Where to Find It*
Dave Horner   *Shipwrecks, Skin Divers, and Sunken Gold*
Robert Marx   *Always Another Adventure*
Hans Roden   *Treasure Seekers*
Brad Steiger   *Treasure Hunting*
James Burney   *History of the Buccaneers of America*
Esquemeling   *The Buccaneers of America*

HISTORICAL BACKGROUND

Victor Gebhardt   *Historia General de España y Sus Indias*
Modesto Lafuente   *Historia General de España*
C. H. Harding   *Trade and Navigation Between Spain and
                               the Indies*
M. Ortiz de la Vega   *Historia General de Peru*
Barnabé Cobo   *Historia del Nuevo Mundo*
Victor W. von Hagen   *Realm of the Incas*
W. H. Prescott   *Conquest of Peru*
Carl F. Lummis   *Los Exploradores Españoles del Siglo XVI*
A. F. Bandelier   *The Gilded Man, El Dorado*
W. H. Prescott   *History of the Reign of Philip II, King of
                               Spain*
S. Francisco Trigoso   *Ensaio Sobre os Descubrimentos e Comér-
                               cio dos Portugueses*
Sir E. Cotton   *East Indiamen*

THE MANILA GALLEONS

William L. Schurz   *The Manila Galleon*
César Fernández Duro   *Armada Española* (vols. III–IX)
R. I. Nesmith   *Cross Roads of South American Trade with
                               the Orient*
R. I. Nesmith   *The Treasure Drake Missed in 1585*
                               (article)
Gilbert S. Perez   *Manila Galleons and Mexican Pieces of
                               Eight* (Philippine Social Sciences and
                               Humanities Review)

PORTUGUESE SHIPWRECKS

James Duffy	*Shipwreck & Empire*
D. António Pérez	*Viagems e Naufrágios Célebres*
António Sergio	*Historia Tragico-Marítima*
B. Gomez de Brito	*Historia Tragico-Marítima*

INVINCIBLE ARMADA

César Fernández Duro	*La Armada Invencible* (vols. I and II)
G. R. Hale	*The Story of the Great Armada*
Robert Sténuit	*National Geographic Magazine*, June 1969
Sidney Wignall	*Treasure of the Armada* (to be published)

BOOKS DESCRIBING TREASURE WRECKS IN SPECIFIC AREAS

H. A. Chilvers	*The Seven Lost Trails of Africa*
F. R. Goldsmith	*Treasure Lies Buried Here* (Australia)
Harry O'May	*Wrecks in Tasmanian Waters*
David Stick	*Graveyard of the Atlantic* (Cape Hatteras)
E. R. Snow	*Great Storms and Famous Shipwrecks of the New England Coast*
James A. Gibbs, Jr.	*Shipwrecks of the Pacific Coast* (U.S. West Coast)
Marion Link	*Sea Diver* (Caribbean, Florida Keys, Silver Bank)
Dee Woods	*Blaze of Gold* (Padre Island, Texas)
F. Vidal Gormaz	*Algunos Naufragios en las Costas Chilenas* (Chile)
Walter and Richard Krotee	*Shipwrecks off the New Jersey Coast*
William Nelson	*The New Jersey Coast*
John T. Cunningham	*The New Jersey Shore*
J. M. Erving, Jr.	*Skin Diving Guide of the East and Northeast*
Clay Blair, Jr.	*Diving for Pleasure and Treasure*
A. L. Lonsdale and H. R. Kaplan	*A Guide to Sunken Ships in American Waters*
Teddy Tucker	*Treasure Diving with Teddy Tucker*
Capt. D. T. Bowen	*Shipwrecks of the Lakes* (the Great Lakes)
	Memories of the Lakes
	Lore of the Lakes
Walter Deas and C. Lawler	*Beneath Australian Seas*
Richard Larn and Clive Carter	*Cornish Shipwrecks: the South Coast*
James A. Gibbs, Jr.	*Pacific Graveyard*
Dave Horner	*The Blockade-Runners*
Robert Marx	*Shipwrecks in Florida Waters*
	Shipwrecks of the Virgin Islands
Martin Meylach	*Diving to a Flash of Gold* (Florida)

REFERENCES DESCRIBING SPECIFIC TREASURE WRECKS

H. Magen   *Les Galions de Vigo* (Vigo Bay)
A. Rodríguez Elías   *La Escuadra de Plata* (Vigo Bay)
Carlos Iberti   *Tre Miliardi Nella Baia di Vigo* (Vigo
                                  Bay)
Robert Sténuit   *Les Épaves de l'Or* (Vigo Bay)
J. S. Potter, Jr.   *The Treasure Divers of Vigo Bay*
David Scott   *The Egypt's Gold* (S.S. *Egypt*)
David Scott   *Seventy Fathoms Deep* (S.S. *Egypt*)
J. R. W. Taylor   *Spoils from the Sea* (S.S. *Niagara*)
Sir Alexander Dalrymple   *An Account of the Loss of the Grosvenor
                                  Indiaman*
P. R. Kirby   *A Source Book on the Wreck of the Gros-
                                  venor East Indiaman, 1783*
                                  New Light on the Wreck of the Grosvenor
                                  El Farol magazine, Sept./Oct. 1957 (San
                                  Pedro Alcántara)
                                  Caza y Pesca magazine, Feb./Mar. 1956
                                  (San Pedro Alcántara)
Hugh Edwards   *Islands of Angry Ghosts* (the *Batavia*)
Hugh Edwards   *The Wreck on the Half-Moon Reef*
Alex Storm (told to Brian   *Canada's Treasure Hunt* (*Le Chameau*)
Shaw)
Arthur C. Clarke   *The Treasure of the Great Reef* (the Great
                                  Basses)
Peter Throckmorton   *The Great Basses Reef Wreck*
Lt. R. H. Graham   *Royal Naval Diving Magazine* (H.M.S.
                                  Association)
Jack Slack   *Finders, Losers* (the Lucayan treasure)
Kip Wagner   *Pieces of Eight* (the 1715 armada)
Wade Doak   *The Elingamite and Her Treasure*

SALVAGE

Sir Robert H. Davis   *Deep Diving and Submarine Operations*
David Masters   *Epics of Salvage*
Francisco Gorostidi   *Salvamento de Naufragios*
                                  The Illustrated London News, July 21,
                                  1956
Elgin Ciampi   *The Skin Diver*
Edward M. Brady   *Marine Salvage Operations*
Carl J. Clausen   "The Proton Magnetometer: Its use in
                                  Plotting the Distribution of the Ferrous
                                  Components of a Shipwreck Site as an
                                  Aid to Archaeological Interpretation."
                                  Florida Anthropologist, Vol. XIX, No.
                                  2, Gainesville.

MONEYS AND TREASURE

R. I. Nesmith	*Dig for Pirate Treasure* (section on numismatics)
Gilbert S. Perez	*The Dos Mundos Pillar Dollars*
	The Lost Treasure of King Philip IV, booklet issued by The Development Board, Nassau, the Bahamas
	Pamphlets I–XV, issued by the Exposición Iberoamericana de Numismática y Medallística (1958)

WRECK IDENTIFICATION

de Artíñano y de Galdácano	*La Arquitectura Naval Española*
Charnock	*History of Marine Architecture*
Fineham	*History of Naval Architecture*
Chapman	*Architectura Navalis*
Falconer	*Marine Dictionary*
Sir Robert H. Davis	*Deep Diving and Submarine Operations*
A. Jal	*Glossaire Nautique*
Faulkner	*Evolution of Naval Armament*
John Müller	*A Treatise of Artillery*
Albert Manucy	*Artillery Through the Ages*
R. de Salas	*Memorial Histórico de la Artillería Española*
	Cannon by José Solano, issued by the Hispanic Society of America
	Catálogo General, Museum of Artillery, Madrid
Mendel Peterson	*History Under the Sea*

SUBMARINE ARCHAEOLOGY

Prof. Fernand Benoit	*Fouilles Sous-marines en Ligurie et en Provence*
James Dugan	*Man Under the Sea*
Philippe Diolé	*Promenades d'Archéologie Sous-Marine*
Philippe Diolé	*The Undersea Adventure*
Philippe Diolé	*Les Portes de la Mer*
Antoni Ribera	*The Menfish*
Philippe Tailliez	*To Hidden Depths*
Capt. J. Y. Cousteau	*The Silent World*
Marion Link	*Sea Diver*
Sir Robert H. Davis	*Deep Diving and Submarine Operations*
R. I. Nesmith	*Dig for Pirate Treasure*
S. E. Morison	*Admiral of the Ocean Seas*
Mendel Peterson	*History Under the Sea* (Smithsonian Institution)

Hanns-Wolf Rackl	*Diving into the Past: Archaeology Under Water*
John M. Goggin	*Underwater Archaeology*
Frederic Dumas	*Deep Water Archaeology*
Honor Frost	*Under the Mediterranean*
Dr. George F. Bass	*Archaeology Under Water*
—	*The Cape Gelidonya Wreck*
—	*Diving into the Past*
Joan du Plat Taylor	*Marine Archaeology*
Robert Marx	*Pirate Port* (Port Royal)
E. J. Ryan and G. F. Bass	*Underwater Surveying and Dredging*
Peter Throckmorton	*The Lost Ships*
Pablo Bush Romero	*Under the Waters of Mexico*
Dr. S. F. Borhegyi	*Report on the 1958 Summer Activities in Guatemala*
Elgin Ciampi	*The Skin Diver*
Eduardo Admetlla	*Guía Submarina de la Costa Brava*
Michael Buckmaster	*Two Articles on the Sea Venture, Sunk at Bermuda*
J. and B. Crile	*Treasure Diving Holidays*
	Bulletin Officiel de Club Alpin Sous-Marin ＃8 (1956)
	The Swedish Man o'War Vasa, Her Disaster in 1628 (a report)
	The Illustrated London News, July 12, 1958 and other issues
Carl J. Clausen	"A 1715 Spanish Treasure Ship." *Contributions of the Florida State Museum*, Social Science Series, No. 12, Gainesville

SALVAGE LAW

Charles W. and Jacquelin Jensen	*Modern Laws Relating to Treasure Trove*
Martin J. Norris	*Law of Salvage*
Gilmore and Black	The *Laws of Admiralty*

OTHER VALUABLE REFERENCE SOURCES

Documents of the Archivo de las Indias, Seville, Spain
Documents of the Archivos General, Simancas, Spain
Documents of the British Museum Reading Room, London
Colonial State Papers, British Museum, London
Documents at the Museo Naval, Madrid, Spain
Documents at the Musée de la Marine, Paris
Documents at La Bibliothèque Nationale, Paris
Documents of Le Service Historique de la Marine, Paris
Documents at the Public Records Office, London

Documents at the Netherlands Royal Archives, The Hague
Documents at the National Archives, Washington, D.C.
Publications by the Florida Board of Archives and History, Tallahassee
Documents at the Archivos Generales de la Nación, Mexico City
Documents at the Arquivo Nacional, Lisbon
Documents at the Library of Congress, Washington, D.C.
Documents at the Steamship Historical Society of America, Staten Island, N.Y.
Documents at the Biblioteca Nacional, Madrid
Documents at the Royal Institute for the Tropics, Amsterdam
Material available at various marine museums (see Museums section)

MUSEUMS

(outside U.S.A.)

Museo Naval, Madrid (Spain)
Museo Marítimo, Barcelona (Spain)
Museu de Marinha, Lisbon (Portugal)
Musée de la Marine, Paris (France)
Musée Royale, Brussels (Belgium)
Nederlandisch Historisch Scheepvart Museum, Amsterdam (Holland)
The British Museum, London (England)
The National Maritime Museum, Greenwich (England)
State Historical Maritime Museum, Stockholm (Sweden)
Norsk Sjofartsmuseum, Oslo (Norway)
The Western Australian Museum, Perth (Australia)
The Colombo Museum (Ceylon)
Museum of the Marine Science and Archaeological Foundation, Manila (the Philippines)
Institute of Jamaica, Kingston (Jamaica)
Bodrum Archaeological Museum, Bodrum (Turkey)
The C.E.D.A.M. Underwater Archaeological Museum, Mexico City (Mexico)
The Fremantle Maritime Museum, Western Australia

(in the U.S.A.)

The Smithsonian Institution, Washington, D.C.
The Peabody Marine Museum, Salem, Mass.
The Mariners Museum, Philadelphia, Pa.
Ocean City Museum, Ocean City, N.J.
The Mystic Museum, Mystic, Conn.
The McKee Fortress of Sunken Treasure, Treasure Harbor, Plantation Key, Fla.
Museum of Sunken Treasure, on A1A just north of Cocoa Beach, Fla.
The *Golden Doubloon* Spanish galleon replica, at the foot of S.E. 17th Street, Fort Lauderdale, Fla.
Mariners Museum, Newport News, Va.
San Francisco Maritime Museum, San Francisco, Cal.

MAGAZINES

Skin Diver magazine (issues 1955–59)
l'Adventure Sous-Marine (issues 1955–59)
National Geographic Magazine (various issues)
Life magazine (various issues)
Sports Illustrated magazine (various issues)
The Saturday Evening Post
True magazine
Triton (various issues)
Dive South Pacific (various issues)
The Gold Bug Newsletter (every issue)
Underwater World (various issues)
Fin Diver (all issues)

ABBREVIATIONS USED

In Vessels' names:

N.S.	—	Nuestra Señora
S.C.	—	Santo Cristo
Sto.	—	Santo
Sta.	—	Santa
Cap.	—	Capitana
Alm.	—	Almiranta

In Nationalities:

Sp.	—	Spanish
Po.	—	Portuguese
Eng.	—	English
Br.	—	British
Fr.	—	French
Du.	—	Dutch
Ger.	—	German
Ru.	—	Russian
Ch.	—	Chinese
Jap.	—	Japanese
No.	—	Norse
U.S.	—	American
Sc.	—	Scotch
Bel.	—	Belgian
Ind.	—	American Indian

In Vessels's Names:

G.	—	Galleon
N.	—	Nao

Car.	—	Carrack
P.	—	Patache (packet boat)
E.I.	—	East Indiaman
Sch.	—	Schooner
Bark	—	Barkentine
Brig	—	Brigantine
Lug.	—	Lugger
Br.	—	Brick
Sl.	—	Sloop
Vik.	—	Viking
Ga.	—	Galley
Ju.	—	Junk
C.	—	Caravel
Ur.	—	Urca
F.	—	Frigate
Nav.	—	Navio (warship)
Cor.	—	Corvette
Cr.	—	Cruiser
Sh.	—	Sailing ship (clipper)
Tr.	—	Transport
S.S.	—	Steamship
Sub.	—	Submarine

Symbols:

{ — ships lost in same
 action or storm
? — name unknown

INDEX OF SUNKEN TREASURES BY YEAR

YEAR OF LOSS	NUMBER (if over one)	NAME (if on ship) or description		NATION- ALITY	CLASS	LOCATION (off shore of)	PAGE
850?		Fifa		No.	Vik.	Shetland Is., G.B.	355
850?		Hialf		No.	Vik.	Shetland Is., G.B.	355
851		Drakkar		No.	Vik.	Thames R., Eng.	355
1274	100	Kublai Khan's Fleet		Ch.	Ju.	Sea of Japan	451
1501	2	?		Sp.	C.	Hispaniola	134
		El Dorado		Sp.	C.	Hispaniola	134
	27	?		Sp.	C.	Hispaniola	134
1504		Cap.		Sp.	C.	Cartagena, Col.	180
1504	4	?		Sp.	C.	Gulf of Urabá	180
1527		La Nicolasa		Sp.	C.	Yucatán	167
1532		Lake Orcus' Gold Chain		—	—	Lake Orcus, Peru	190
1533		Inca Gold Sun Mirror		—	—	Lake Titicaca, Peru	191
1540		Trinidad	*	Sp.	C.	California	459
1544		?		Sp.	G.	SW Spain	339
1544		Sta. María de la Isla		Sp.	C.	Cuba	147
1545		?		Sp.	N.	Veracruz, Mex.	158
1550		Visitación		Sp.	N.	Florida Keys	215
1550		?	*	Sp.	N.	Puerto Rico	138
1550		Sta. María de la Piedad		Sp.	N.	Azores	299
1551		San Miguel		Sp.	N.	Hispaniola	136
1551		San Antón		Sp.	N.	Azores	299
1551		San Nicolás		Sp.	N.	Florida	207
1552		Sta. Margarita		Sp.	C.	Marianas, Pacific	415
1552		São João	*	Po.	N.	SE Africa	385
1552		Cap.	*	Sp.	G.	Gulf of Mexico	161
1553	16	?	*	Sp.	N.	Hispaniola	135
1553		?		Sp.	N.	Padre Is., Texas	162
1554		Cap.	*	Sp.	G.	Azores	299
1554		?		Sp.	G.	Azores	299
1554	3–4	?		Sp.	N.	E Florida	207
1554		?		Sp.	C.	Atlantic	311
1554		São Bento	*	Po.	Car.	SE Africa	387
1555	5	?		Sp.	N.	Tarifa, SE Spain	340
1555		Sta. María del Camino		Sp.	N.	Bahamas	261
1555		?		Sp.	N.	Veracruz, Mex.	160
1555		Conceiçao		Po.	Car.	Pedro de Baños, Indian Ocean	399
1556	2	?		Sp.	N.	Hispaniola	136
1556	2	?		Sp.	N.	Portugal	347

YEAR OF LOSS	NUMBER (if over one)	NAME (if on ship) or description	NATION-ALITY	CLASS	LOCATION (off shore of)	PAGE
1559		Garça	Po.	Car.	Mozambique	397
1559	6	?	Sp.	N.	E Florida	205
1560		?	Sp.	G.	Azores	300
1560?		Pedro Serrano	Sp.	N.	W Caribbean	181
1561		?	Sp.	C.	Venezuela	139
1561		São Paulo	Po.	Car.	W Sumatra	410
1562		N.S. de Atocha	Sp.	N.	Tortuga Is., Carib.	217
1563		N.S. de la Luz	Sp.	N.	Azores	300
1563		Cap.	Sp.	G.	Bermuda	280
1563		Santa Clara	Sp.	N.	Atlantic	311
1563		Espíritu Santo	Sp.	N.	E Spain	379
1563	5	various **	Sp.	N.	Jardine Reef, Cuba	147
1563	7	?	Sp.	N.	E Panama	186
1563		San Cristóbal	Sp.	N.	Bahamas	262
1564		San Juan	Sp.	N.	Portugal	347
1564		Santa Catalina	Sp.	N.	Atlantic	311
1564		Sta. María de Begoña *	Sp.	N.	Is. of Pines, Cuba	148
1564		Sta. Clara	Sp.	N.	Is. of Pines, Cuba	148
1564		Sta. María de Guadalupe	Sp.	N.	Gulf of Mexico	198
1565		Trinidad	Sp.	N.	Atlantic	311
1565		Sta. Lucia	Sp.	N.	Cuba	148
1565	2	?	Sp.	N.	Cuba	148
1566		San Antonio	Sp.	N.	SW Spain	340
1566		San Antón	Sp.	N.	Sanlúcar, SW Spain	341
1566		N.S. de la Concepción	Sp.	N.	Portugal	348
1567		La Concepción	Sp.	N.	Azores	300
1567		?	Sp.	N.	E Florida	263
1567		?	Sp.	Ur.	N Cuba	149
1567	5	? *	Sp.	N.	Dominica, B.W.I.	137
1568	2	Vizcayo "El Mulato"	Sp.	N.	Florida	207
1572		San Felipe	Sp.	N.	W. Caribbean	182
1572	5	?	Sp.	N.	Tobago, N Venez.	137
1572	2	?	Sp.	P.	E Florida	206
1572	35	?	Po.	N.	E Brazil	293
1573		La Madalena	Sp.	N.	Atlantic	311
1576		San Juanillo	Sp.	N.	Pacific	440
1578		silver	Sp.	—	Peru	192
1578		silver	Sp.	—	La Plata Is., Ecuador	193
1579		Alm.	Sp.	G.	Yucatán, Mex.	169
1581		Gallega	Sp.	G.	Madeira Is., Atlantic	308
1581	2	?	Sp.	N.	Gulf of Mexico	170
1582		Sta. Marta	Sp.	G.	Catalina Is., Calif.	461

YEAR OF LOSS	NUMBER (if over one)	NAME (if on ship) or description	NATION-ALITY	CLASS	LOCATION (off shore of)	PAGE
1595		San Crucifijo de Burgos	Sp.	N.	Gulf of Mexico	165
1595		Sta. Isabel	Sp.	N.	New Hebrides, Pacific	415
1595	20	?	Sp.	Lug.	English Channel	356
1596		Cap. *	Sp.	G.	Azores	306
1596		Sta. Catalina	Sp.	G.	S. Pacific	441
1596		?	Sp.	N.	Chile	194
1596		San Felipe	Sp.	G.	Japan	441
1596?		?	Fr.	N.	NE Spain	379
1596?		?	Du.	N.	NE Spain	379
1598		Cap.	Sp.	G.	SE China	441
1598		Alm.	Sp.	G.	SE China	441
1599		San Agustín *	Sp.	G.	California	462
1599		? (pirate)	?	?	Inagua Is., Bahamas	262
1600		San Jerónimo *	Sp.	G.	Philippines	441
1600		Stan Antonio	Sp.	P.	Philippines	442
1600		Sta. Margarita *	Sp.	G.	Marianas	441
1600		Sta. Ana María	Sp.	N.	Azores	306
1600		San Juan Bautista	Sp.	N.	Chile	194
1600		Gold from Buen Jesús	Sp.	—	Chile	194
1600		Cap.	Sp.	G.	California	462
1600		Flor da Rosa	Po.	Car.	Madagascar, Indian Ocean	398
1601	14	various	Sp.	var.	Veracruz, Mex.	158
1601		Buen Barco	Sp.	N.	Chile	195
1601		?	Sp.	G.	Portugal	348
1601		Santo Tomás	Sp.	G.	Philippines	442
1603		Cap.	Sp.	G.	Guadalupe, B.W.I.	137
1603	2	?	Sp.	N.	Guadalupe, B.W.I.	137
1603		?	Sp.	N.	Hispaniola	136
1603		San Antonio	Sp.	G.	E Japan	442
1603		Sta. Margarita	Sp.	G.	Marianas, Pac.	442
1603?		Concepción	Sp.	G.	Guam, Pac.	442
1604?		Santiago	Po.	Car.	St. Helena Is., Atlantic	310
1605		Alm.	Sp.	G.	Hispaniola	136
1605	4	?	Sp.	N.	Margarita Is., Venezuela	139
1605		?	Sp.	G.	Dominica, B.W.I.	137
1605	4	various *	Sp.	N.	Serranilla Bank, Carib.	182
1606	4	various	Sp.	N.	Florida Straits, Bahamas	263
1606	2	various *	Sp.	N.	Portugal	348
1608		Cap.	Sp.	G.	Azores	306
1608		San Francisco *	Sp.	G.	E Japan	442
1610		Cap.	Sp.	G.	Bonaire Is., Caribbean	140
1610		?	Sp.	P.	Bonaire Is., Caribbean	140

YEAR OF LOSS	NUMBER (if over one)	NAME (if on ship) or description	NATION-ALITY	CLASS	LOCATION (off shore of)	PAGE
1635		San Josefe	Sp.	N.	Madeira Is., Atlantic	308
1637		Capitana de España	Sp.	Ju.	Philippines	443
1638	3	?	Sp.	N.	N Cuba	151
1639		{ Viga	Sp.	Ur.	Bermuda	284
1639		{ Galgo	Sp.	P.	Bermuda	284
1639		?	Sp.	Ju.	Formosa	443
1639		San Ambrosio *	Sp.	G.	Philippines	443
1639		? *	Sp.	G.	Philippines	443
1639		N.S. de Ayuda	Sp.	G.	California	463
1641		N.S. de la Concepción	Sp.	G.	Bahamas	264
1641		{ ?	Sp.	N.	Bahamas	264
1641	3	{ various	Sp.	var.	N Cuba	151
1641	5	{ various	Sp.	N.	Florida	207
1641	5	Cap. *	Sp.	G.	Sanlúcar, SW Spain	341
1642						
1643		Cap. (doubtful)	Sp.	G.	Bahamas	267
1643		?	Sp.	N.	Bahamas	268
1646		?	Sp.	N.	Atlantic	312
1646		San Luis	Sp.	G.	Philippines	444
1647		{ Cap.	Sp.	G.	Cuba	151
1647		{ ?	Sp.	P.	Cuba	151
1647		Alm. **	Sp.	G.	Naples, Italy	380
1647		Santiago	Sp.	N.	Campeche, Mexico	168
1647		San Nicolás	Sp.	N.	Chile	195
1647		Sacramento *	Po.	Car.	SE Africa	388
1647		Nossa Senhora de Atalaya *	Po.	Car.	SE Africa	388
1647		Haarlem	Du.	Car.	SE Africa	389
1647	2	?	Sp.	G.	Chile	195
1649		São Lourenço	Po.	Car.	Mozambique	399
1650		Sto. Tomás de Villanueva	Sp.	N.	Chile-Peru	196
1651		San José *	Sp.	G.	Chile	196
1651	60	various	Sc.	var.	Scotland	357
1653		San Francis Javier	Sp.	G.	Philippines	444
1654		San Diego	Sp.	G.	Philippines	444
1654		Cap. ***	Sp.	G.	Ecuador	196
1656		{ Urca de Paredes	Sp.	Ur.	SW Spain	342
1656		{ Capitanilla de Cartagena *	Sp.	G.	SW Spain	342
1656		Vergulde Draek	Du.	Car.	W Australia	424
1656		N.S. de los Maravillas ***	Sp.	G.	Florida Keys	219
1658		Santiago	Sp.	N.	Venezuela	140
1658		San Martis	Sp.	N.	Venezuela	140
1660		Santiago	Sp.	N.	Caribbean	183
1660		Victoria	Sp.	N.	Philippines	444
1660		Virginia Merchant	Br.	Tr.	Bermuda	286
1664		Carmelan **	Du.	Car.	Shetland Is., G.B.	358
1668		Cap.	Sp.	G.	Venezuela	140

YEAR OF LOSS	NUMBER (if over one)	NAME (if on ship) or description	NATION- ALITY	CLASS	LOCATION (off shore of)	PAGE
1711		Alm.	Sp.	G.	Cuba	152
1711	3	?	Sp.	N.	Cuba	152
1711		Feversham	Br.	Fr.	E Canada	475
1712		Zuytdorp	Du.	Car.	W Australia	426
1714?		Kennermerlandt	Du.	Car.	Shetland Is., G.B.	358
1715	30	?	Du.	var.	S Africa	390
1715	10	various **	Sp.	var.	E Florida	209
1717		Whidah (pirate)	?	—	Cape Cod, Mass.	477
1717		?	Sp.	G.	California	463
1719		N.S. de Loreto	Sp.	N.	Vietnam	451
1719		Cap.	Sp.	G.	Campeche, Mex.	168
1719		Alm.	Sp.	G.	Campeche, Mex.	168
1719		S.C. de Maracaibo	Sp.	N.		
1720		?	Sp.	N.	Florida Keys	231
1720		San Luis	Sp.	Nav.	Bahamas	275
1720		San Andrés	Sp.	F.	Bahamas	275
1720		Carlos V	Sp.	Nav.	Puerto Rico	138
1721		Speedwell (pirate)	Eng.	—	Juan Fernandez Is., Pacific	198
1724		Guadalupe	Sp.	G.	Hispaniola	136
1724		Tolosa	Sp.	G.	Hispaniola	136
1724		Fortuyn	Du.	Car.	Indian Ocean	424
1725		Cambi	Sp.	G.	Gulf of Mexico	168
1725		Le Chameau	Fr.	F.	E Canada	471
1726		S.C. de Burgos	Sp.	G.	Philippines	444
1726		San Bartolomé	Sp.	N.	Veracruz, Mex.	158
1726		Aagtekerke	Du.	Car.	Indian Ocean	424
1727		Rubí Primero	Sp.	Nav.	Cuba	152
1727		?	Sp.	G.	Azores	306
1727		Constante	Sp.	Nav.	Gulf of Mexico	165
1727		Zeewyck	Du.	Car.	W Australia	423
1730		Genovés	Sp.	F.	Caribbean	185
1730		N.S. de Lorento Y San Francisco Xavier	Sp.	G.	Anageda Is.	139
1731		?	Sp.	G.	Anageda Is.	139
1732		Concepción	Sp.	F.	Veracruz, Mex.	159
1733	16	various *	Sp.	var.	Florida Keys	220
1733	2	various	Sp.	N.	N Cuba	155
1734		Sta. María Madalena *	Sp.	G.	Philippines	444
1735		?	Sp.	P.	Philippines	445
1736		La Rosa	Sp.	Nav.	Veracruz, Mex.	159
1738		Sto. Cayetano	Sp.	F.	Florida	212
1738		La Victoria *	Sp.	Nav.	Virgin Is., Caribbean	138
1739		Incendio	Sp.	Nav.	Veracruz, Mex.	159
1739		Lanfranco	Sp.	Nav.	Veracruz, Mex.	159
1740		Andalucia	Sp.	Nav.	Old Bahamas Channel	275

YEAR OF LOSS	NUMBER (if over one)	NAME (if on ship) or description	NATION- ALITY	CLASS	LOCATION (off shore of)	PAGE
1741		Invencible	Sp.	Nav.	Cuba	153
1742		Zuytdorp	Du.	E.I.	W Australia	426
1742		San Ignacio	Sp.	N.	Virgin Is., Caribbean	138
1743		Hollandia	Du.	E.I.	Scillies, G.B.	367
1744		H.M.S. Looe	Br.	F.	Florida Keys	232
1745		?	Sp.	Ur.	Jardine Reef, Cuba	153
1746		S.C. de León	Sp.	N.	Peru	198
1749		Guipúzcoa	Sp.	Nav.	Brazil	294
1750	4	various	Sp.	N.	Cape Hatteras, N.C.	486
1750		Pilar	Sp.	G.	Philippines	445
1750		?	Sp.	Sl.	Anegada Is.	139
1754		San Sebastián	Sp.	G.	California	464
1756		Cap.	Sp.	G.	Philippines	445
1758		H.M.S. Tilbury	Br.	F.	E Canada	476
1762		Encarnación	Sp.	F.	Chile	198
1762		San Juan Evangelista	Sp.	F.	Chile	198
1762		San Judas Tadeo	Sp.	F.	Chile	198
1762		H.M.S. Marlborough	Br.	Nav.	Azores	307
1762		H.M.S. Temple	Br.	Nav.	W Ireland	359
1762	12	various	Br.	Tr.	Atlantic	312
1763		La Gloire	Fr.	F.	Madagascar, Indian Ocean	399
1763		Victoria	Sp.	F.	Rio de la Plata	292
1766	3-5	?	Sp.	G.	Gulf of Mexico	174
1767		Aventurero	Sp.	Bar.	Rio de la Plata	292
1768	70	various	Sp	var.	Havana, Cuba	153
1769		N.S. de la Ermita	Sp.	N.	Chile	199
1769		Live Oak	?	Sl.	E America	481
1770		Oriflama	Sp.	G.	Chile	199
1771	5	various	Sp.	var.	Veracruz, Mex.	159
1772		Aurora	Sp.	G.	Rio de la Plata	292
1775		N.S. de la Concepción	Sp.	G.	Marianas, Pacific	446
1775		Three Brothers	Br.	Sh.	Delaware	484
1775		Ellis	Br.	Sch.	E America	482
1776		Clara	Sp.	F.	Rio de la Plata	292
1778?		Betsy	Br.	Brig.	E America	482
1779		Defence ✶	U.S.	F.	Connecticut	478
1779		Poderoso	Sp.	Nav.	Azores	307
1779		Carmen	Sp.	Nav.	Azores	307
1780		?	Sp.	F.	Cuba	153
1780		Sta. Marta	Sp.	F.	Campeche, Mexico	169
1781		Middleberg	Eng.	E.I.	S Africa	390
1782		Grosvenor ✶✶✶	Eng.	E.I.	SE Africa	390
1783		Dragón II	Sp.	Nav.	Campeche, Mexico	169
1784		Cazador	Sp.	Nav.	Gulf of Mexico	165
1784		San Francisco de Paula	Sp.	Nav.	Venezuela	141

YEAR OF LOSS	NUMBER (if over one)	NAME (if on ship) or description	NATION-ALITY	CLASS	LOCATION (off shore of)	PAGE
1785		Faithful Steward	Eng.	Sh.	Delaware	485
1786		Transito	Sp.	F.	Chile	199
1786		San Rafael	Sp.	Nav.	Chile	199
1786		San Pedro Alcántara *	Sp.	F.	Portugal	349
1788		Infanta *	Sp.	Bar.	Bahamas	275
1788		N.S. de la Balbanera *	Sp.	F.	Chile	199
1790		Brillante	Sp.	Nav.	Cartagena, Colombia	186
1790		Quintanadoine (Télémaque) *	Fr.	Br.	France	370
1791		Diana	Sp.	F.	Bahamas	275
1792		Winterton *	Br.	F.	Madagascar, Indian Ocean	399
1794		⎰ Flor	Sp.	Ga.	Havana, Cuba	154
1794	78	⎱ various	Sp.	var.	Havana, Cuba	154
1794	5	various *	Sp.	N.	Cuba	154
1797		María	Sp.	F.	Philippines	446
1797		San Andrés	Sp.	G.	Philippines	446
1797		Palas	Sp.	F.	Cuba	154
1798		H.M.S. de Braak **	Br.	Sl.	Delaware	483
1799		H.M.S. Leviathan	Br.	Nav.	Gulf of Honduras	170
1799		La Lutine ***	Br.	F.	Holland	374
1799		H.M.S. Guernsey Lily	Br.	F.	England	360
1800		Sta. Leocadia **	Sp.	F.	Ecuador	199
1800		Yealdham	Br.		Gulf of Mexico	175
1802		Juno	Sp.	F.	New Jersey	482
1802		Cantabria	Sp.	Cor.	Atlantic	312
1802		Ferroleña **	Sp.	Ur.	SE China	446
1803?		San Carlos II	Sp.	Sch.	Is. of Aves, Caribbean	144
1803		H.M.S. Hindostan	Br.	F.	England	360
1804		Postillón	Sp.	Brig.	Old Bahamas Channel	276
1804		Mercedes	Sp.	F.	SW Spain	351
1805		H.M.S. Earl of Abergavenny	Br.	F.	England	360
1805		Asunción *	Sp.	F.	Rio de la Plata	292
1806		?	Po.	N.	Ireland	360
1807		H.M.S. Anson	Br.	F.	England	360
1807		H.M.S. Susan and Rebecca	Br.	F.	England	360
1808		Ardilla	Sp.	F.	Gulf of Mexico	166
1809		H.M.S. Jenny	Br.	F.	England	360
1810		Volador	Sp.	Bark	Veracruz, Mex.	159
1811		Araucana	Sp.	Sch.	E Florida	276
1811		Tigre III	Sp.	Br.	Veracruz, Mex.	159
1815		Volador II	Sp.	Sch.	Florida	205
1815		San Pedro Alcántara **	Sp.	Nav.	Coche Is., Venezuela	141

YEAR OF LOSS	NUMBER (if over one)	NAME (if on ship) or description	NATION-ALITY	CLASS	LOCATION (off shore of)	PAGE
1815		Wilhelm de Zweite	Du.	E.I.	SE Africa	394
1816		Galga	Sp.	Sch.	Bahamas	276
1818		Cabalava *	Br.	E.I.	Cargados Garrados, Indian Ocean	400
1818		Ifigenia	Sp.	F.	Campeche, Mexico	169
1820		?	U.S.	Sch.	Florida	206
1820		Le Jeune Henri	Fr.	F.	France	372
1821		Almirante	Sp.	Bark	Bahamas	276
1822		Ligera	Sp.	F.	Cuba	155
1824		Mágica	Sp.	Bark	Bahamas	276
1827		Hope	Br.	Sch.	SE Australia	428
1830		H.M.S. Thetis *	Br.	F.	E Brazil	294
1833		Portland	Br.	Sh.	SE Australia	428
1835		Enchantress	Br.	Sh.	SE Australia	428
1839		Lancier	Br.	Sh.	Australia	427
1840		Lexington	U.S.	S.S.	Off Connecticut	479
1846	200	various	var.	var.	Havana, Cuba	155
1850		Anthony Wayne	U.S.	Sh.	Great Lakes	492
1850?		Antelope	Br.	P.	Philippines	454
1852		Favorite	Br.	Sch.	Australia	417
1852		Winfield Scott	U.S.	S.S.	California	467
1853		Madagascar	Br.	Sh.	N Brazil	296
1854		Yankee Blade **	U.S.	Sh.	California	464
1857		Central America	U.S.	Sh.	Cape Hatteras, N.C.	487
1857		Duncan Dunbar	Br.	Sh.	SW Australia	417
1859		Royal Charter	Br.	Sh.	Wales	361
1860		Malabar	Br.	Sh.	Ceylon Indian Ocean	401
1860?		Golden Gate	U.S.	Sh.	W Mexico	467
1860?		Golden City	U.S.	Sh.	Lower California	467
1862		Phantom	U.S.	Sh.	SE China	451
1863		George Sand	U.S.	Sh.	SE China	451
1863		Princeza	Br.	Sh.	E Australia	417
1864		Fanny and Jenny	Br.	Sh.	Cape Hatteras, N.C.	487
1865		Brother Jonathan *	U.S.	Sh.	California	465
1865		Westmoreland	U.S.	Sh.	Great Lakes	491
1866		General Grant **	Br.	Sh.	Auckland Is., South Pacific	429
1867		Queen of the Thames	Br.	Sh.	E Africa	399
1867		Thunderer	Br.	Sh.	India	401
1869		Crescent City	Br.	Sh.	Ireland	361
1871		R. G. Coburn	U.S.	Sh.	Great Lakes	491
1873		Paisano	U.S.	S.S.	Padre Island, Gulf of Mexico	166
1873		Nina	Br.	S.S.	SE China	451
1875		Pacific	U.S.	S.S.	California	465

YEAR OF LOSS	NUMBER (*if over one*)	NAME (*if on ship*) or description	NATION- ALITY	CLASS	LOCATION (*off shore of*)	PAGE
1875		Japan	Br.	S.S.	SE China	451
1875		various	U.S.	S.S.	Galveston, Tex.	167
1877		Bethany	?	Brig.	Cape May	482
1878		Star of Africa	Br.	Sh.	SE Africa	394
1890		Marlborough	Br.	Sh.	SE Pacific	432
1893		Dean Richmond	U.S.	Sh.	Great Lakes	491
1893		Delaware	?	S.S.	New Jersey	481
1895		Catterthun	Br.	T.	Australia	417
1897		Drummond Castle	Br.	S.S.	France	373
1898		Dorotea *	Boer	Sh.	SE Africa	395
1898		"Kruger's Lugger"	Boer	Lug.	SE Africa	396
1898		Portland	U.S.	S.S.	Cape Cod, Mass.	476
1901		Islander	Br.	S.S.	S Alaska	466
1902		Elingamite	Br.	S.S.	New Zealand	432
1905		Admiral Nakhimoff * * ?	Ru.	Cr.	Str. of Tsushima, Japan	452
1909		Republic	U.S.	S.S.	Rhode Island	477
1911		Mérida	U.S.	S.S.	Virginia	485
1912		H. J. Corcoran	U.S.	S.S.	California	466
1915		Lusitania	Br.	S.S.	Ireland	361
1916		Tubanthia	Du.	S.S.	Holland	375
1917		Elizabethville	Bel.	S.S.	France	373
1917		Laurentic	Br.	S.S.	N Ireland	362
1917		Renate Leonhardt	Du.	S.S.	Holland	376
1922		Egypt	Br.	S.S.	English Channel	498
1931		Columbia	U.S.	S.S.	W Mexico	467
1932		Georges Philippar	Fr.	S.S.	Arabia	399
1940		Niagara	Br.	S.S.	New Zealand	432
1942		Treasure of Corregidor *	—	—	Philippines	454
1943		"Rommel's Treasure"	—	—	Mediterranean	380
1945		U-853	Ger.	Sub.	Rhode Island	478
1945		"Mussolini's Treasure"	—	—	Lake Como, Italy	381
1946		Yukon	U.S.	S.S.	Alaska	468
1951		Flying Enterprise	U.S.	S.S.	SW England	362
1956		Andrea Doria	It.	S.S.	E America	477

INDEX OF SUNKEN WRECKS, BY NAME

Those in italics are in the treasure chapters.
Those in normal type are of archaeological interest.

GENERAL INDEX (WRECKS BY NAME)

Treasure sites are shown in capital letters.
(For wrecks, see Index of Sunken Wrecks.)

McNickle, Andrew J. S., 274
Mablethorpe, port of, 107
Madagascar, 384, 397–99
Madeira Island, 308
Madre de Dios, 20, 302, 304
Magellan, Ferdinand, 5, 10, 239, 291, 413
Magen, H., 512
Magnetic Anomaly Detector (MAD), 32
Magnetometer sweep, 286
Magnetometers, x, 31–37, 113, 125–26,
    148, 163, 164, 197, 218, 252, 258, 271,
    345–46, 349, 400; buying or renting,
    33, 34; compared to supersensitive
    compass, 32; development of, 32; Dis-
    coverer series, 33; flux gate, 33; "sea"
    recoveries, 33–37; types of, 33–34
Magny, M., 370–71
Mahdia, 105–6
Maher, Pat, 287
MAHOGANY SHIP, 416–17
"Major Dashiell's $23,000 Payroll," 208–9
Majorca Sharks, 105
Malacca, 400
Malmaison, Baron de, 392
Malta, siege of (1565), 99
Malta, treasure of, 50
Mámora, port of, 108
Man Under the Sea (Dugan), 513
Man-under-Sea programs, 28
Manganese, undersea mining for, 41–42
Manieri, Ray, 228
Manifests, ships', 25
Manila Galleon, The (Schurz), 510
Manila galleons, xix, xx, 60, 64, 157, 244,
    414, 416, 436–48; armaments, 439;
    cargo worth, 437; overseas treasure
    movements, xxii–xxiii; treasure loca-
    tions, 436–48
*Manila Galleons and Mexican Pieces of
    Eight* (Perez), 510
Manini, Domingo, 116
Manora, Giovanni de, 325
Manrique, General Antonio, 170
Mansfield (diver), 49
Mansvelt (pirate), 21
Manucy, Albert, 513
Manzi-Fe, Galeazzo, xii, 373
Mao Tse-tung, 447
Maps, explanation of, 130
Maqueda, Duke of, 108
Marathon Salvage Company, 228
Maravedi (coin), 65
March y Labores, J., 509
Marcos Sestios' galley, 92, 100, 124
Marden, Luis, 117, 124, 242
Mardorf, William, 118
Margarita Island, 6, 116, 133, 139–40, 141,
    157

Marianas Islands, xx, xxiv, 128, 413, 414–
    15, 441
Marilyn B ll, 473
Marina de Castilla Desde su Origin, La,
    xxiv, 509
Marinduque Island, 441
Marine Archaeological Research Corpo-
    ration, Ltd., 182, 218
Marine Archaeology (Taylor), 514
Marine Dictionary (Falconer), 513
Marine Salvage Operations (Brady), 512
Marine Science and Archaeological
    Foundation, 447
Mariners' Mirror, The (Science for
    Nautical Research), 509
Mariners Museum (Newport News), 515
Mariners Museum (Philadelphia), 515
Marine-Tech Salvage Company, Inc., xv,
    225, 226, 227
Maritime history books, 27
Markey, Dr. J. J., 459, 461
Marshall Islands, 413
Martín, Captain Alonso, 261–62
Martin, Colin, 334
Martín, Captain Francisco, 347
Martín, Captain Vincente, 147
Martin County Historical Society, 203
Martínez, General Francisco, 302–3, 306
Martínez de Leiva, Don Alonzo, 322–23
Martínez de Recalde, Captain-General
    Juan, 316
Marx, Robert, xii, xiv, xxv, 27, 91, 113–16,
    117, 193, 207, 235, 254–55, 258, 509, 510,
    511, 514
Mary, 85
Mason, Burton, 478
Masonboro Inlet, 487
Massachusetts Institute of Technology
    (MIT), 119
Masters, David, 512
Masters, William Fox, 345
"Matamoras Wrecks," 166–67
Matanceros Point, 115
Matanilla Shoal, 220
Matanzas Bay, 20, 127, 211, 276
MATANZAS BAY DISASTER, 149–50
Matchblock musket, 69
Matheson, Hugh, 222
Matute, Francisco Ruiz, 336
Maureen, 478
Maximilian, Emperor, 166, 485, 486
MAXIMILIAN'S TREASURE, 166
Maxwell, E. Lewis, xii
May (diver), 417
Maya Indians, 92, 115, 116–17, 157, 167,
    168
Mayflower, H.M.S., 304, 305
Mayol, Jacques, 270